KT-227-335

CONTENTS

second edition

international business

JOHN J.
UNIVERSITY OF WISCONSIN, MADISON

KENNETH L. WILD
UNIVERSITY OF LONDON, ENGLAND

J. JERRY C.Y. HAN
UNIVERSITY OF HONG KONG

PRENTICE HALL
UPPER SADDLE RIVER, NEW JERSEY 07458

Library of Congress Cataloging-in-Publication Data
Wild, John J.
  International business / John J. Wild, Kenneth L. Wild,
Jerry C.Y. Han – 2nd ed.
    p. cm.
  Includes bibliograhical references and index.
  ISBN 0-13-0-035311-6
   1. International business enterprises – Management.
   2. International trade. I. Wild, Kenneth L. II. Han, Jerry C.Y.
III. Title.
HD62.4.W586 2003
658'.049—dc21   2002070361
                                    CIP

Acquisitions Editor: Jennifer Glennon
Editor-in-Chief: Jeff Shelstad
Assistant Editor: Melanie Olsen
Senior Marketing Manager: Shannon Moore
Media Project Manager: Michele Faranda
Editorial Assistant: Kevin Glynn
Managing Editor (Production): Judy Leale
Production Editor: Marcela Maslanczuk
Permissions Coordinator: Suzanne Grappi
Associate Director, Manufacturing: Vincent Scelta
Production Manager: Arnold Vila
Art Director: Janet Slowik
Interior Design: Lee Goldstein/Janet Slowik
Cover Design: Janet Slowik
Cover Illustration/Photo: KAN Photography, Inc.
Photo Researcher: Teri Stratford
Manager, Print Production: Christy Mahon
Composition: Ashley Scattergood, Suzanne Duda
Printer/Binder: R.R. Donnelley & Sons - Willard

Credits and acknowledgments borrowed from other sources and reproduced,
with permission, in this textbook appear on pages 494–504.

Pearson Education LTD.
Pearson Education Australia PTY, Limited
Pearson Education Singapore, Pte. Ltd.
Pearson Education North Asia Ltd.
Pearson Education, Canada, Ltd.
Pearson Educación de Mexico, S.A. de C.V.
Pearson Education–Japan
Pearson Education Malaysia, Pte. Ltd

10 9 8 7 6 5 4 3 2
ISBN 0-13-035311-6

BRIEF CONTENTS

second edition

international business

PREFACE

Welcome to the second edition of International Business. *This book resulted from extensive market research with instructors and students at a wide range of institutions. We are delighted with the success of the first edition in that an overwhelming majority agrees with a fresh approach to international business. This book forges a new path for international business, one that responds to the requests and needs of both instructors and students. A main goal in this second edition is to continue the progress made in the first—developing the most **progressive, accessible, current, and customer-driven textbook on the market**.*

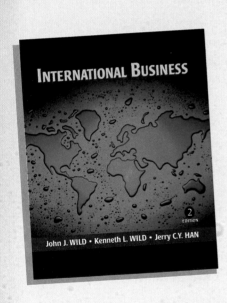

We know that international business is rich in people, culture, geography, politics, economics, and other human and environmental factors. This book draws upon this richness to present international business as it genuinely is—as a dynamic, culturally rich subject. This book goes beyond a "U.S.-centric" outlook and takes an inclusive view of international business by addressing its cultural aspects early and often. While it is appropriate for use in the introductory course at either the undergraduate or graduate level, International Business *is written to give the instructor maximum flexibility in fitting different teaching styles and incorporating outside readings and cases—thereby increasing its scope and breadth as desired.*

WILD • WILD • HAN

www.prenhall.com/wild

How Students Will Benefit from *International Business*

This book's approach to international business benefits students in several ways.

CULTURE EARLY AND OFTEN Culture is an inescapable element of all international business activities. This book presents culture early (Chapter 2) and integrates it throughout every chapter of the book. This is partly accomplished by starting each chapter with a culture-rich opening company profile. Reading the opening company profiles in Chapters 1, 2, and 3 will wash away any doubt about this. We also integrate culture within each chapter by including lively examples that show how differences in culture affect international business activities.

INTEGRATIVE International business is much more than a simple collection of separate business functions and environmental forces. Rather, it is an integrated whole consisting of national environments, the international environment, and business activities all interacting with one another. The model in the figure on page **xx** of this preface is unique to this book and lays the foundation for an integrated approach to international business. Feedback on the first edition tells us that students benefit by studying international business in this way—as it is in the real world. We first present the major components of national business environments and the international business environment. We then show how these environments interact with international business management, making international business different from purely domestic business.

INCLUSIVE Appreciating the dynamic nature of the global marketplace requires an unbiased approach to international business. Feedback from the first edition shows that this is the only international business book written from a truly global perspective. This goal was achieved by members of an author team having collective expertise in three major economic regions of the world—Asia, Europe, and North America. This book

---

PART TWO   NATIONAL BUSINESS ENVIRONMENTS

2 culture in business

LEARNING OBJECTIVES

After studying this chapter, you should be able to

1 Describe *culture,* and explain the significance of both national culture and *subcultures.*

2 Identify the *components of culture,* and describe their impact on business activities around the world.

3 Describe *cultural change,* and explain how companies and culture affect one another.

4 Explain how the *physical environment* and *technology* influence culture.

5 Describe the two main *frameworks* used to classify cultures and explain their practical use.

BEACONS

A Look Back
CHAPTER 1 introduced us to international business and the impact of globalization. We learned why companies "go international" and about the many external and internal forces with which companies must deal when doing business internationally.

A Look at This Chapter
This chapter introduces the important role of culture in international business. We explore the main elements of culture and show how they affect business policies and practices. We learn different methods of classifying cultures and how these methods can be applied to business.

A Look Ahead
CHAPTER 3 describes the political and legal systems of nations. We learn how these systems differ from one country to another and how they influence international business operations. We also show how managers can reduce the effects of political risk.

also is written from a non-provincial viewpoint: Rather than "take sides" in key debates, it presents the viewpoints of each group or culture involved (see Chapter 2).

ACCESSIBLE A successful book for the first course in international business must be accessible to all students. In this book, conceptual material and specialized business activities are described in concrete, straightforward terms and appropriately illustrated (see Chapters 5, 9, and 10).

Our goal—presenting complex material in an accessible manner—is reflected throughout the book. We are convinced that students who use a more readable international business book will master such material more readily.

TOPICAL This book strives to capture the contemporary, topical aspects of international business. Topical coverage is developed to foster enthusiasm and to motivate students to go beyond the classroom to see how concepts relate to the real world. Many fun and interesting examples allow students to reflect upon the experiences of real companies— to see both what worked and what didn't. Finally, this book's comprehensive Companion Website contains updates of important events

that keep the book continuously up-to-date. To visit our Website, go to (**www.prenhall.com/wild**).

INNOVATIVE FEATURES: THE PEDAGOGY OF INTERNATIONAL BUSINESS
We firmly believe that students are motivated to learn when a book demonstrates how important concepts are applied. To emphasize the practical side of international business, we have integrated the following innovative features into this book.

www.prenhall.com/wild

ENTREPRENEURIAL FOCUS Each chapter contains an *Entrepreneurial Focus* box to underscore the various ways in which chapter topics affect entrepreneurs and small businesses. Entrepreneurial and small business issues are also woven into the content of each chapter and illustrated with current, colorful examples. These examples, both in the text and in feature boxes, highlight the activities of entrepreneurs and small businesses from countries all around the world.

ENTREPRENEURIAL FOCUS

Give Your Web Site a Local Feel

When going global with an Internet presence, the more a company localizes, the better. Web surfers want an online experience corresponding to their cultural context offline. Here are some pointers for companies when first launching an online presence. Do the international Web sites you visit follow these rules?

➡ **Choose Colors Carefully** A black-and-white Web site is fine for many countries, but in Asia visitors may think you are inviting them to a funeral. In Japan and across Europe, Web sites in pastel color schemes often work best.

➡ **Select Numbers with Care** Many Chinese-speaking cultures consider the number four unlucky while eight and nine symbolize prosperity. Be careful that your Web site address and phone numbers do not send the wrong signal.

➡ **Watch the Clock** If marketing to countries that use the 24-hour clock, adjust times stated on the site so it reads, "Call between 9:00 and 17:00," instead of, "Call between 9 A.M. and 5 P.M."

➡ **Mind Your Tongue** English in Britain is different from that in the United States, Spanish in Spain is different from that in Mexico, and French in France is different from that in Quebec. Avoid slang to lessen the impact of such differences, or go further and offer different site versions for each language.

➡ **Wave the Flag Cautiously** Be careful using national flags as symbols for buttons to click to see different language versions of your site. British visitors to your site may be put off if you use a U.S. flag to signify the English version of the site—likewise for the diverse Spanish- and Chinese-speaking populations.

➡ **Do the Math** Provide conversions into local currencies for buyer convenience. For online ordering, be sure your site calculates accurately any shipping costs, tax rates, tariffs, and so on. Also allow enough blanks on the order form to accommodate longer international addresses.

➡ **Get Feedback** Finally, talk with customers or prospective customers to know what they want to do or buy on your Web site. Then test the Web site to ensure it functions properly.

GLOBAL MANAGER

Each chapter features a *Global Manager* box that shows how key issues actually affect the daily duties of managers working for large international businesses. This feature expands on issues discussed in the text and delves into those that pose special problems for international managers. In Chapter 16, for instance, we show how managers cope with the effects of culture shock when relocating to unfamiliar cultures. Again, this feature drives home some relevant, down-to-earth lessons learned by veterans of international business management.

GLOBAL MANAGER

A Globetrotter's Guide to Manners

Good manners are obviously essential when doing business in the home market and the same holds true internationally. Here are just a few things managers should be aware of when meeting colleagues from other cultures. Can you think of any others that you would add to this list?

➡ **Don't Rush Familiarity** Avoid the temptation to get too familiar too quickly. Use titles such as "doctor" and "mister." Switch to a first-name basis only when invited to do so and do not shorten people's names from, say, Catherine to Cathy.

➡ **Adapt to Personal Space** What is considered appropriate distance between people is cultural. Middle Eastern and Latin American nations close the gap significantly. Expect more touching in Latin America, where the man-to-man embrace occurs regularly.

➡ **Respect Religious Values** Be cautious so that your manners do not offend people. Former Secretary of State Madeline Albright briefly acquired the nickname of "the kissing ambassador" because she apparently kissed the Israeli and Palestinian leaders of these profoundly religious nations.

➡ **Maintain Good Posture** Do not slouch, or "spread out" by hanging your arms over the backs of chairs. But don't be too stiff either. Look people in the eye lest they deem you untrustworthy but don't stare too intently.

➡ **Give and Receive Business Cards Respectfully** In Asia, business cards are considered an extension of a person. Cards in Japan are typically exchanged after a bow, with two hands and the wording facing the recipient. Leave the card on the table for the entire meeting—don't quickly stuff it in your wallet or toss it into your briefcase.

➡ **Use Comedy Sparingly** Finally, use humor cautiously because it often does not translate well. Avoid jokes that rely on wordplay and puns or events in your country of which local people might have no knowledge.

WORLD BUSINESS SURVEY

Each chapter contains a *World Business Survey* to highlight the attitudes of consumers, workers, managers, and policymakers toward important chapter topics. Underscored in these surveys is the importance of culture in forming people's attitudes. This feature is designed to help students recognize the important role of people from other cultures in international business.

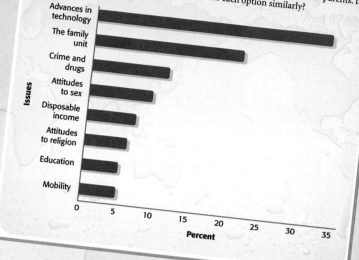

FULL-COLOR WORLD ATLAS

Our experiences and those of many international business instructors tell us that far too many students are inadequately prepared in geography for their first course in international business. In response, this book includes, as a primer and reference, a full-color world atlas as an appendix to Chapter 1. Students are able to test their knowledge of the global landscape by completing 20 questions accompanying the atlas, which is also broken out into several detailed maps for closer study. Important issues regarding world geography and their impact on international business are also integrated throughout the book and its assignment materials.

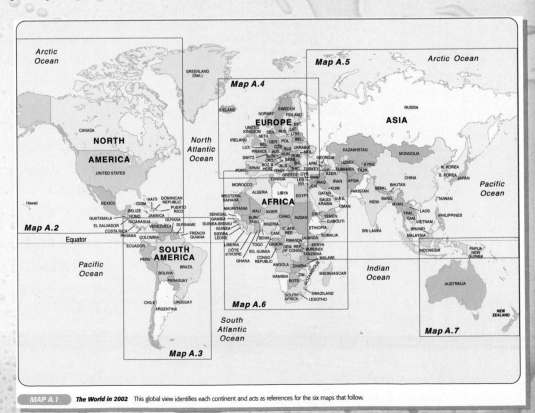

MAP A.1   **The World in 2002**   This global view identifies each continent and acts as references for the six maps that follow.

D'oh! "The Simpsons" Goes Global

SPRINGFIELD, U.S.A.—What people are yellow, have three fingers and a thumb on each hand, and are loved around the world? They're everybody's favorite dysfunctional family, the Simpsons (www.thesimpsons.com). This animated TV comedy, about the everyday events in the lives of Homer, Marge, Bart, Lisa, and Maggie, is a huge success in over 60 countries.

The show wonderfully illustrates the globalization of markets. Apart from sometimes being translated into other languages, the show is exactly the same in each market. When the show opens with Bart scribbling his punishment on the blackboard, "Funny noises are not funny," kids around the world get it. The show's content also has a global flavor. Bart had to appear in court in Australia and spent a semester abroad in France where he brought down an illegal winery. Around the world, the likenesses of the Simpsons family members grace stickers, key chains, backpacks, T-shirts, and small figurines.

"The Simpsons" also illustrates the globalization of production. Film Roman (www.filmroman.com) produces the show but provides key poses and step-by-step frame directions to AKOM Production Company (www.akomkorea.com) in Seoul, South Korea, which fills in the remaining poses and links them into an animated whole. But there are bumps along the way. In a middle-of-the-night phone call, animation director Mark Kirkland was explaining to the Koreans how to draw a shooting gun. "They don't allow guns in Korea; it's against the law," says Kirkland. "So they were calling me: 'How does a gun work?' " Kirkland and others put up with cultural differences and phone calls at odd hours to tap into the cheaper yet highly qualified pool of South Korean animators. As you read this chapter, think about how globalization is affecting the marketing and production of goods and services around the world.[1]

BEACONS

Students learn better when they are provided with a "roadmap" to show them how chapters and topics relate to one another. Therefore, this book contains *Beacons* at the start of each chapter to reinforce the interrelatedness of topics across chapters. Appropriately titled "A Look Back," "A Look at This Chapter," and "A Look Ahead," these signposts provide a structure for students as they read through the book.

LEARNING OBJECTIVES WITH CORRESPONDING SUMMARIES

Learning objectives are designed to focus on the main lessons students should take away from their study of chapter material. Each chapter also includes summaries that correspond *exactly* to the chapter's learning objectives.

CHAPTER-OPENING VIGNETTES

Opening company profiles launch each chapter with brief but highly informative introductions to the chapter's materials. These vignettes are designed to pique students' interest in chapter material— not bog them down in fine details to be discussed within the chapter. We find students are motivated to turn the page and read on when given short, interesting, relevant introductions to the material that they are about to study.

TOOLS FOR ACTIVE LEARNING

Feedback on the first edition shows that this book has more— and more useful—end-of-chapter assignment material than any other international business book. Well-planned assignment materials span the full range of complexity to test students' knowledge and ability to apply key principles, including:

➡ *Questions for Review* help students check to see that they have retained each chapter's key terms and important concepts.
➡ *Questions for Discussion* raise important issues currently confronting entrepreneurs, international managers, policymakers, and others. They can be used as the basis for in-class discussion, as in-class team assignments, or as homework assignments.
➡ *In Practice* exercises ask students to consider actual scenarios taken from the international business press.
➡ *Projects* take students beyond the text, engaging them in in-class debates or presentations, library or Web-based research, and interviews with local managers. One on-going project is the *Investment Opportunity Notebook*. This exercise asks students to apply what they've learned in each chapter to a particular investment opportunity in a particular country. Students gradually develop a report on a potential opportunity as they proceed through the course.
➡ *Business Cases* let students analyze the responses of real-world companies to the issues, problems, and opportunities discussed in each chapter.
➡ *A Question of Ethics* exercises allow students to consider the ethical dimensions of important managerial decisions.

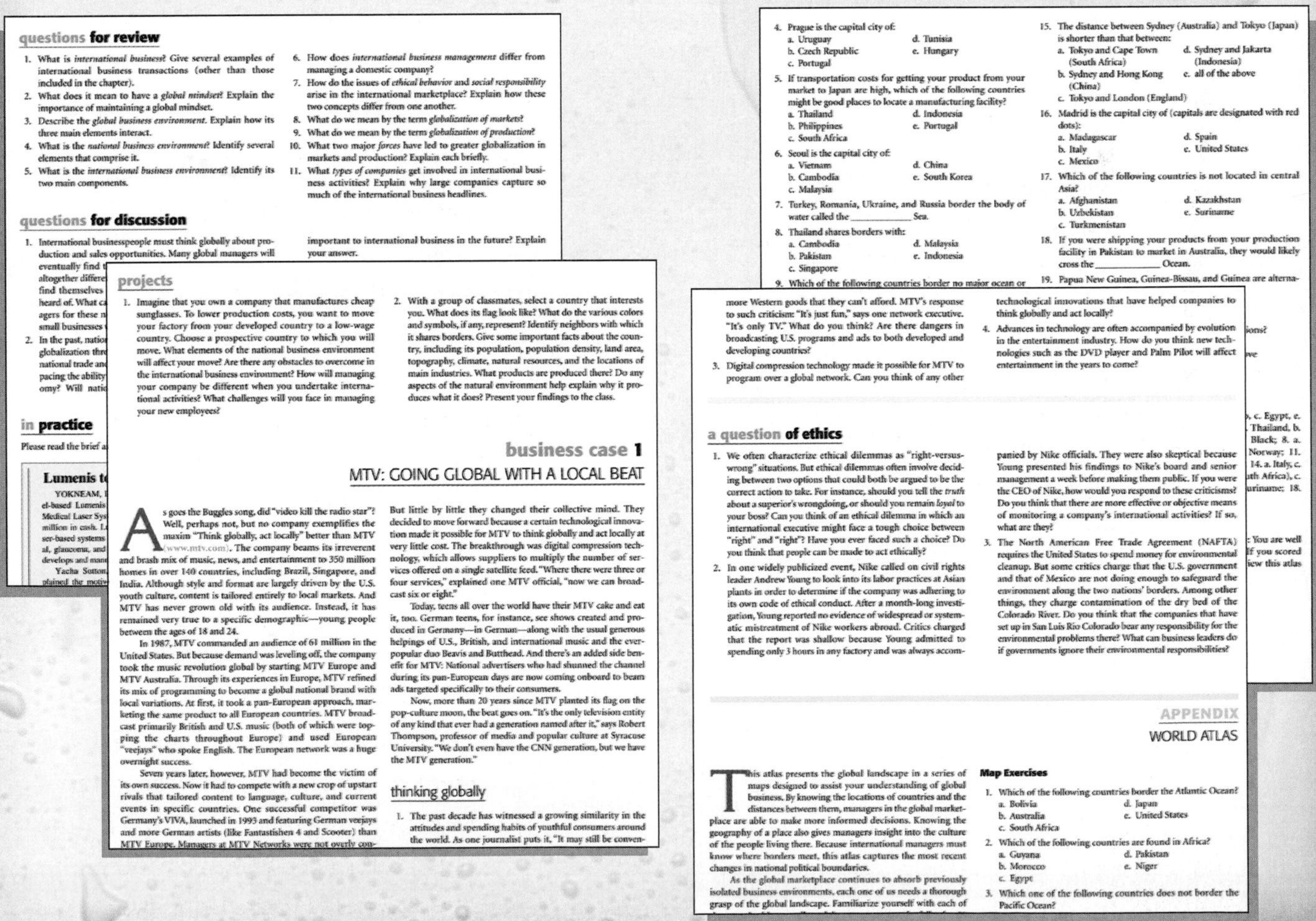

questions for review

1. What is *international business*? Give several examples of international business transactions (other than those included in the chapter).
2. What does it mean to have a *global mindset*? Explain the importance of maintaining a global mindset.
3. Describe the *global business environment*. Explain how its three main elements interact.
4. What is the *national business environment*? Identify several elements that comprise it.
5. What is the *international business environment*? Identify its two main components.
6. How does *international business management* differ from managing a domestic company?
7. How do the issues of *ethical behavior* and *social responsibility* arise in the international marketplace? Explain how these two concepts differ from one another.
8. What do we mean by the term *globalization of markets*?
9. What do we mean by the term *globalization of production*?
10. What two major forces have led to greater globalization in markets and production? Explain each briefly.
11. What *types of companies* get involved in international business activities? Why do large companies capture so much of the international business headlines?

questions for discussion

1. International businesspeople must think globally about production and sales opportunities. Many global managers will eventually find that ... altogether different ... find themselves ... heard of. What ca... agers for these ... small businesses ...
2. In the past, natio... globalization thr... national trade and ... pacing the ability ... omy? Will natio...

important to international business in the future? Explain your answer.

projects

1. Imagine that you own a company that manufactures cheap sunglasses. To lower production costs, you want to move your factory from your developed country to a low-wage country. Choose a prospective country to which you will move. What elements of the national business environment will affect your move? Are there any obstacles to overcome in the international business environment? How will managing your company be different when you undertake international activities? What challenges will you face in managing your new employees?

2. With a group of classmates, select a country that interests you. What does its flag look like? What do the various colors and symbols, if any, represent? Identify neighbors with which it shares borders. Give some important facts about the country, including its population, population density, land area, topography, climate, natural resources, and the locations of main industries. What products are produced there? Do any aspects of the natural environment help explain why it produces what it does? Present your findings to the class.

in practice

Please read the brief...

Lumenis to...
YOKNEAM, ...
el-based Lumenis ...
Medical Laser Sys...
million in cash. L...
ser-based systems ...
al, glaucoma, and ...
develop and manu...
Yacha Sutton...
plained the motive...

business case 1
MTV: GOING GLOBAL WITH A LOCAL BEAT

As goes the Buggles song, did "video kill the radio star"? Well, perhaps not, but no company exemplifies the maxim "Think globally, act locally" better than MTV (www.mtv.com). The company beams its irreverent and brash mix of music, news, and entertainment to 350 million homes in over 140 countries, including Brazil, Singapore, and India. Although style and format are largely driven by the U.S. youth culture, content is tailored entirely to local markets. And MTV has never grown old with its audience. Instead, it has remained very true to a specific demographic—young people between the ages of 18 and 24.

In 1987, MTV commanded an audience of 61 million in the United States. But because demand was leveling off, the company took the music revolution global by starting MTV Europe and MTV Australia. Through its experiences in Europe, MTV refined its mix of programming to become a global national brand with local variations. At first, it took a pan-European approach, marketing the same product to all European countries. MTV broadcast primarily British and U.S. music (both of which were topping the charts throughout Europe) and used European "veejays" who spoke English. The European network was a huge overnight success.

Seven years later, however, MTV had become the victim of its own success. Now it had to compete with a new crop of upstart rivals that tailored content to language, culture, and current events in specific countries. One successful competitor was Germany's VIVA, launched in 1993 and featuring German veejays and more German artists (like Fantastishen 4 and Scooter) than MTV Europe. Managers at MTV Networks were not overly con-

But little by little they changed their collective mind. They decided to move forward because a certain technological innovation made it possible for MTV to think globally and act locally at very little cost. The breakthrough was digital compression technology, which allows suppliers to multiply the number of services offered on a single satellite feed. "Where there were three or four services," explained one MTV official, "now we can broadcast six or eight."

Today, teens all over the world have their MTV cake and eat it, too. German teens, for instance, see shows created and produced in Germany—in German—along with the usual generous helpings of U.S., British, and international music and the ever-popular duo Beavis and Butthead. And there's an added side benefit for MTV: National advertisers who had shunned the channel during its pan-European days are now coming onboard to beam ads targeted specifically to their consumers.

Now, more than 20 years since MTV planted its flag on the pop-culture moon, the beat goes on. "It's the only television entity of any kind that ever had a generation named after it," says Robert Thompson, professor of media and popular culture at Syracuse University. "We don't even have the CNN generation, but we have the MTV generation."

thinking globally

1. The past decade has witnessed a growing similarity in the attitudes and spending habits of youthful consumers around the world. As one journalist puts it, "It may still be conven-

4. Prague is the capital city of:
   a. Uruguay   d. Tunisia
   b. Czech Republic e. Hungary
   c. Portugal
5. If transportation costs for getting your product from your market to Japan are high, which of the following countries might be good places to locate a manufacturing facility?
   a. Thailand   d. Indonesia
   b. Philippines   e. Portugal
   c. South Africa
6. Seoul is the capital city of:
   a. Vietnam   d. China
   b. Cambodia   e. South Korea
   c. Malaysia
7. Turkey, Romania, Ukraine, and Russia border the body of water called the _____ Sea.
8. Thailand shares borders with:
   a. Cambodia   d. Malaysia
   b. Pakistan   e. Indonesia
   c. Singapore
9. Which of the following countries border no major ocean or

15. The distance between Sydney (Australia) and Tokyo (Japan) is shorter than that between:
    a. Tokyo and Cape Town   d. Sydney and Jakarta
       (South Africa)   (Indonesia)
    b. Sydney and Hong Kong e. all of the above
       (China)
    c. Tokyo and London (England)
16. Madrid is the capital city of (capitals are designated with red dots):
    a. Madagascar   d. Spain
    b. Italy   e. United States
    c. Mexico
17. Which of the following countries is not located in central Asia?
    a. Afghanistan   d. Kazakhstan
    b. Uzbekistan   e. Suriname
    c. Turkmenistan
18. If you were shipping your products from your production facility in Pakistan to market in Australia, they would likely cross the _____ Ocean.
19. Papua New Guinea, Guinea-Bissau, and Guinea are alterna-

more Western goods that they can't afford. MTV's response to such criticism: "It's just fun," says one network executive. "It's only TV." What do you think? Are there dangers in broadcasting U.S. programs and ads to both developed and developing countries?
3. Digital compression technology made it possible for MTV to program over a global network. Can you think of any other

technological innovations that have helped companies to think globally and act locally?
4. Advances in technology are often accompanied by evolution in the entertainment industry. How do you think new technologies such as the DVD player and Palm Pilot will affect entertainment in the years to come?

a question of ethics

1. We often characterize ethical dilemmas as "right-versus-wrong" situations. But ethical dilemmas often involve deciding between two options that could both be argued to be the correct action to take. For instance, should you tell the *truth* about a superior's wrongdoing, or should you remain *loyal* to your boss? Can you think of an ethical dilemma in which an international executive might face a tough choice between "right" and "right"? Have you ever faced such a choice? Do you think that people can be made to act ethically?
2. In one widely publicized event, Nike called on civil rights leader Andrew Young to look into its labor practices at Asian plants in order to determine if the company was adhering to its own code of ethical conduct. After a month-long investigation, Young reported no evidence of widespread or systematic mistreatment of Nike workers abroad. Critics charged that the report was shallow because Young admitted to spending only 3 hours in any factory and was always accom-

panied by Nike officials. They were also skeptical because Young presented his findings to Nike's board and senior management a week before making them public. If you were about the CEO of Nike, how would you respond to these criticisms? Do you think that there are more effective or objective means of monitoring a company's international activities? If so, what are they?
3. The North American Free Trade Agreement (NAFTA) requires the United States to spend money for environmental cleanup. But some critics charge that the U.S. government and that of Mexico are not doing enough to safeguard the environment along the two nations' borders. Among other things, they charge contamination of the dry bed of the Colorado River. Do you think that the companies that have set up in San Luis Rio Colorado bear any responsibility for the environmental problems there? What can business leaders do if governments ignore their environmental responsibilities?

... c. Egypt, e. ... Thailand, b. ... Black; 8. a. ... Norway; 11. ... 14. a. Italy, c. ... th Africa), c. ... uriname; 18.

... : You are well ... . If you scored ... view this atlas

APPENDIX
WORLD ATLAS

This atlas presents the global landscape in a series of maps designed to assist your understanding of global business. By knowing the locations of countries and the distances between them, managers in the global marketplace are able to make wiser business decisions. Knowing the geography of a place also gives managers insight into the culture of the people living there. Because international managers must know where borders meet, this atlas captures the most recent changes in national political boundaries.

As the global marketplace continues to absorb previously isolated business environments, each one of us needs a thorough grasp of the global landscape. Familiarize yourself with each of

Map Exercises
1. Which of the following countries border the Atlantic Ocean?
   a. Bolivia   d. Japan
   b. Australia   e. United States
   c. South Africa
2. Which of the following countries are found in Africa?
   a. Guyana   d. Pakistan
   b. Morocco   e. Niger
   c. Egypt
3. Which one of the following countries does not border the Pacific Ocean?

SPECIAL FEATURES OF INTERNATIONAL BUSINESS

Dynamic Art and Maps Program

This text contains a variety of colorful maps that not only convey and reinforce the knowledge of where important places are located, but which supplement concepts and data with visual learning aids. A map index assists instructors and students in quickly locating every map in the book. Highly colorful charts and figures help students grasp important information. Numerous color photos are strategically placed to add value to the text and provide students with a look at life and work around the world; informative, detailed captions tie photos to in-text material. We underscore important terms by boldfacing them in the text, defining them in the margin, and collecting them in a comprehensive glossary at the end of the book.

FIGURE 2.5

Power Distance and Uncertainty Avoidance

Small 4 — 1

- Singapore
- Jamaica
- Denmark
- Sweden
- Hong Kong
- Ireland — Great Britain
- Malaysia
- India
- New Zealand — United States
- Canada — South Africa — Indonesia — Philippines
- Norway — Australia
- Netherlands — East Africa
- West Africa

Uncertainty Avoidance

- Finland — Iran
- Switzerland — Thailand — Ecuador
- Pakistan — Arab Countries
- Austria — Germany — Taiwan
- Italy
- Israel — Colombia — Brazil — Venezuela
- Argentina — Spain — Chile — Turkey — Mexico
- Costa Rica — France — Yugoslavia — Panama
- South Korea — Peru
- Japan — Salvador
- Belgium — Guatemala
- Uruguay
- Portugal
- Greece

Large
Small — Power Distance — Large

MAP 3.1

Political and Civil Liberties Around The World

This map illustrates the level of political rights and civil liberties of the people of each nation and territory. It does not rate national governments, but represent the rights and liberties of individuals. As defined by *Freedom House*, political rights refer to people's ability to vote and run for public office and, as elected officials, to vote on public policies. Civil liberties include people's freedom to develop views, institutions, and personal autonomy apart from the state.

In all, 87 countries (45 percent of the world population) are listed as being *free*, 57 countries (30 percent of the world population) as *partly free*, and 48 countries (25 percent of the world population) as *not free*.

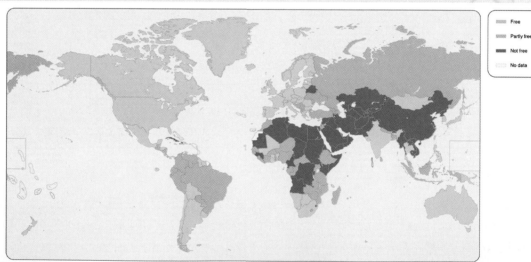

- Free
- Partly free
- Not free
- No data

International companies engage in development assistance as a way to insulate themselves from potentially adverse political changes. Here, a child in the African nation of Chad uses a water pump built by ExxonMobil—a large investor in the country. But the company has come under fire from critics who claim the firm lags behind the efforts of industry rivals. What more do you think ExxonMobil could do to help the local people?

WHAT'S NEW IN THE SECOND EDITION?

The success of the first edition of *International Business* was due to its culture-rich, integrative approach and its innovative features. This edition builds on those strengths and improves upon them in several ways. First, every *chapter-opening company profile* is new. Because of highly positive feedback on our chapter-opening company profiles in the first edition, we continue this approach but bring fresh culture-rich company profiles to our readers (see Chapters 1, 2, and 3). Second, every *chapter-closing case* is either new or updated. Third, all maps, figures, and tables reflect the most recently available data at the time of publication. Fourth, because of the positive response to the *Investment Opportunity Notebook* included in the first edition's Instructor's Resource Manual, it has been revised and expanded to include greater detail. Fifth, we have included a completely new set of *video cases* that emphasize the cultural aspects of international business.

In addition to these changes, here are some specific examples of improvements to the book:

Chapter 2: Culture in Business

Responding to users' requests, we expanded and updated our discussion of culture. We did this by adding more and fresher examples to keep the presentation of culture's influence as current as possible. We also include extensive examples to show the application of the Hofstede and Kluckhohn-Strodtbeck frameworks for classifying cultures.

Chapter 4: Economic Systems and Development

We further streamlined the presentation of the different types of economic systems and economic development. In the second edition, we responded to your feedback and focus on certain country examples within the coverage of different systems. For example, when discussing central planning we include a special section on China's experience over the years and how it is adapting to market forces today.

Chapter 8: Regional Economic Integration

Based on feedback, we updated and streamlined our discussion of the major efforts toward regional economic integration around the world. The new presentation of the European Union (EU), for example, reflects less on the past events surrounding integration and more on key issues currently facing the EU such as future enlargement. For instance, we discuss the all-important Copenhagen Criteria that central and eastern European nations must satisfy before they will be considered for EU membership.

Chapter 10: International Monetary System

Feedback from the first edition tells us that instructors and readers want less discussion of the historical development of the international monetary system. Accordingly, we lessened the historical emphasis and focus on the present structure of the system. We also cover recent crises such as those in Russia and Argentina and the debate they are causing over the current system.

Chapter 11: Planning and Organizing International Operations

This chapter now appears before the chapter on analyzing international opportunities. We responded to your preference and moved the strategic and organizational coverage prior to market research activities. In this way, students get an appreciation for the larger issues international businesses face before getting into the details.

Chapters 14, 15, and 16

Although presentation of this material has been reorganized based on user feedback, it retains its tightly integrated flow. Accordingly, marketing issues are now separated from the coverage of other topics and reside in Chapter 14, Developing and Marketing Products. The popular section on acquiring physical resources now lies at the start of Chapter 15, Launching and Managing Production. After presenting important international production issues, Chapter 15 closes with a brief discussion of how companies finance their operations. As requested, Chapter 16, Hiring and Managing Employees, is now a stand-alone chapter but retains its integrated, sequential emphasis.

THE PLAN OF INTERNATIONAL BUSINESS This book's coverage of international business follows the model shown in the figure below. Part One of this book discusses how the world's national economies are increasingly intertwined. We learn that as *globalization* penetrates further into national business environments, managers everywhere must take a global perspective on business activities.

In Part Two, we explore *national business environments*, showing how people's attitudes, values, beliefs, and institutions differ from one culture to another. We also explain how companies modify business practices and strategies when operating under different political, legal, and economic systems.

We discuss the major components of the *international business environment* in Parts Three and Four. We learn why trade and investment flow across borders and why governments try to encourage or discourage them. We explore the process of regional economic integration sweeping the global economy and outline its implications for international companies. We also explain how global financial markets and the global monetary system function and show how they affect international business activities.

• **Outer Ring:** International Business Environment • **Middle Ring:** National Business Environments
• **Core:** International Business Management

In Part Five, we describe the ways in which *international business management* differs from management in a purely domestic firm. We begin by explaining the strategies and structures that companies use for their international operations. We then show how companies analyze markets or production sites and why they select different entry modes. We wrap up our study of international business by learning how companies manage their marketing activities, their production efforts, and their human resources.

SUPPLEMENTS PACKAGE

This text is supported with a comprehensive supplement package that includes the following:

For the Professor

➡ *Instructor's Resource Manual.* The *Instructor's Resource Manual* is designed to guide instructors through the text. It includes *chapter summaries*, *lecture outlines*, *critical thinking exercises*, *additional student projects*, a guide to the integration of *technology resources*, and guidance answers to all end-of-chapter assignment material.

➡ *Companion Website* is the most advanced text-specific site on the web. Resources are updated every two weeks by professors from around the world. Features of interest to instructors include *bimonthly news articles* made relevant to the text with accompanying *discussion questions* and *group exercises*. There is also online delivery of *PowerPoint slides* and additional instructor's material. *Sample syllabi* and *teaching suggestions* are posted on a faculty community chat room (see www.prenhall.com/wild).

➡ *Instructor's Resource CD-rom.* The Instructor's Resource CD-rom includes the computerized Test Item File, PowerPoint Electronic Transparencies, and the Instructor's Manual. The set of PowerPoint slides contains figures from the text, and is designed to aid the educator in supplementing in-class lectures. The Windows-based Prentice Hall *Test Manager 4.0* is a comprehensive suite of tools for testing and assessment, and contains a wide variety of questions, including true/false, multiple-choice, fill-in-the-blank, short-answer/essay, and situation-based questions. The *Test Manager* makes it easy for instructors to create and distribute tests either by printing and distributing them or by delivering them online over a Local Area Network (LAN) server.

➡ *AcrossFrontiers™ cases*—including:
- International Business Today—Case Study: China
- Culture in Business—Case Study: Latin America
- Foreign Direct Investement—Case Study: Hong Kong

For the Student

➡ *Companion Website.* In addition to *bimonthly news articles* relevant to the text, the Website features *Internet resources* for in-depth research on selected topics, *online testing with immediate grading and feedback*, and additional resources for *improving study and writing skills*. Check out: www.prenhall.com/wild

www.prenhall.com/wild

➡ *Financial Times student subscription only $10.00* when professors adopt a FT/Wild/Wild/Han text value-pack. Participating professors will qualify for **a complimentary one-year personal subscription to the** *Financial Times* (Value: $298 at regular subscription rates).

ACKNOWLEDGMENTS

We are grateful for the encouragement, suggestions, and counsel provided by many instructors, professionals, and students in preparing the second edition of *International Business.* We especially thank those individuals who provided valuable comments and suggestions to improve this and the previous edition:

Wendell Armstrong	Central Virginia Community College
Constance Bates	Florida International University
Marca Marie Bear	University of Tampa
Tope A. Bello	East Carolina University
Derrick Chong	University of London, England
Randy Cray	University of Wisconsin at Stevens Point
Desislava Dikova	University of Groningen, The Netherlands
John W. Eichenseher	University of Wisconsin at Madison
Herbert B. Epstein	University of Texas at Tyler
Blair Farr	Jarvis Christian College
Carolina Gomez	University of Houston
James Gunn	Berkeley College
James Halteman	Wheaton College
Alan Hamlin	Southern Utah University

Charles Harvey	University of the West of England
James S. Lawson Jr.	Mississippi State University
Ian Lee	Carleton University
Carol Lopilato	California State University at Dominguez Hills
Donna Weaver McCloskey	Widener University
John L. Moore	Oregon Institute of Technology
Rod Oglesby	Southwest Baptist University
Susan Peterson	Scottsdale Community College
Janis Petronis	Tarleton State University
Abe Qastin	Lakeland College
C. Richard Scott	Metropolitan State College of Denver
Coral R. Snodgrass	Canisius College
William A. Stoever	Seton Hall University
Kenneth R. Tillery	Middle Tennessee State University
Paula Weber	St. Cloud State University
David C. Wyld	Southeastern Louisiana University

It takes a dedicated group of individuals to take a textbook from first draft to final manuscript. We would like to thank our partners at Prentice Hall for their tireless efforts in bringing the second edition of this book to fruition. Special thanks on this project go to Executive Editor, David Shafer and Senior Managing Editor, Jennifer Glennon; Production Editor, Marcela Maslanczuk and Managing Editor for Production, Judy Leale; Editor in Chief, Jeff Shelstad; New Media Project Manager, Michele Faranda; Director of Marketing, Leslie Cavaliere and Senior Marketing Manager, Shannon Moore; Assistant Editor, Melanie Olsen; Editorial Assistant, Kevin Glynn; Designer, Janet Slowik; Permissions Coordinator, Suzanne Grappi; Photo Researcher, Teri Stratford; Multimedia Project Manager, Christy Mahon; and Formatters, Ashley Scattergood and Suzanne Duda.

A Final Word

In sum, we believe that international business is a rich and dynamic subject. As instructors, one of our challenges is to instill in our students a passion for international business. Another is to give our students every advantage possible in the global marketplace. As authors, our primary mission in writing *International Business* is to equip today's student with the passion, skills, and knowledge necessary to compete in this marketplace. We trust that you share our mission. It is also our view that quality instructional materials, particularly this textbook, will greatly assist us in achieving our shared mission.

John J. Wild
Kenneth L. Wild
Jerry C.Y. Han

As a team, John Wild, Kenneth Wild, and Jerry Han provide a blend of skills uniquely suited to writing an international business textbook. They combine award-winning teaching and research with a global view of business gained through years of living and working in cultures around the world. Together, they make the topic of international business practical, accessible, and enjoyable.

John J. Wild is the Robert and Monica Beyer Professor of Business at the University of Wisconsin at Madison. Professor Wild previously held appointments at the University of Manchester in England and Michigan State University. He received his Ph.D., M.S., and B.B.A. degrees from the University of Wisconsin at Madison.

Teaching business courses at both the undergraduate and graduate levels, Professor Wild has received several teaching honors, including the Mabel W. Chipman Excellence in Teaching Award and the Beta Alpha Psi Excellence in Teaching Award. He is a prior recipient of national research fellowships from KPMG Peat Marwick and the Ernst and Young Foundation. He is also a frequent speaker at universities and at national and international conferences.

The author of more than 50 publications, in addition to three best-selling textbooks, Professor Wild conducts research on a wide range of topics, including corporate governance, capital markets, and financial analysis and forecasting. He is an active member of several national and international organizations, including the Academy of International Business, and has served as Associate Editor or editorial board member for several respected journals.

Kenneth L. Wild is affiliated with the University of London, England. He previously taught at Pennsylvania State University. He received his Ph.D. from the University of Manchester (UMIST) in England and his B.S. and M.S. degrees from the University of Wisconsin. Dr. Wild also undertook postgraduate work at École des Affairs Internationale in Marseilles, France.

Having taught students of international business, marketing, and management at both the undergraduate and graduate levels, Dr. Wild is a dedicated contributor to international business education. An active member of several national and international organizations, including the Academy of International Business, he has spoken at major universities and at national and international conferences in Austria, Britain, Kuwait, Portugal, and the United States.

Dr. Wild's research, on a range of international business topics including market entry modes, country risk, and international expansion strategies, have taken him to countries spanning the globe. Additionally, he serves as an Associate Editor of the *Middle East Business Review*.

Jerry C.Y. Han is the Pong Ding Yuen Professor at the University of Hong Kong School of Business. He also holds appointments at several Chinese Universities, including Beijing University and Renmin University. Professor Han previously held appointments at the University of Buffalo, Hong Kong University of Science and Technology (HKUST), Michigan State University, and National Chung Hsing University. He received his Bachelors degree from National Chung Hsing University, Masters degree from National Chengchi University, and Ph.D. from the University of Buffalo.

Teaching at both the undergraduate and graduate levels, Professor Han is a highly recognized teacher, known for his commitment and creativity in business education. He is a prior recipient of research fellowships from the government of Hong Kong, HKUST, Price Waterhouse, and National Chengchi University. Dr. Han is actively involved in several national and international organizations, including previously serving as President of the North American Chinese Association.

The author of more than 40 publications on various business topics, including international regulatory and disclosure issues, Professor Han serves on the editorial boards of several prestigious journals. He consults with international companies and government agencies, and also teaches business courses for international companies in a number of industries.

SPECIAL FEATURES

Global Manager These boxes show how key issues affect the daily duties of managers working in the international business arena.

World Business Survey These boxes highlight the attitudes of consumers, workers, managers, and policymakers toward important chapter topics.

Entrepreneurial Focus These boxes underscore the various ways in which chapter topics affect entrepreneurs and small businesses around the world.

international business

1

international business today

BEACONS

A Look at This Chapter

This chapter defines the scope of international business and introduces us to some of its most important topics today. We begin by explaining why future managers should have a global mindset within the context of the global business environment. This is followed by a description of globalization, the forces behind its growth, and the backlash against it. We close by identifying the key players in international business today.

A Look Ahead

Part II, encompassing **CHAPTERS 2, 3,** and **4,** introduces us to different national business environments. **CHAPTER 2** describes important cultural differences among nations. **CHAPTER 3** examines different political and legal systems. **CHAPTER 4** presents the world's various economic systems and issues surrounding economic development.

D'oh! *The Simpsons* Goes Global

SPRINGFIELD, U.S.A.—What people are yellow, have three fingers and a thumb on each hand, and are loved around the world? They're everybody's favorite dysfunctional family, the Simpsons (**www.thesimpsons.com**). This animated TV comedy, about the everyday events in the lives of Homer, Marge, Bart, Lisa, and Maggie, is a huge success in over 60 countries.

The show wonderfully illustrates the globalization of markets. Apart from sometimes being translated into other languages, the show is exactly the same in each market. When the show opens with Bart scribbling his punishment on the blackboard, "Funny noises are not funny," kids around the world get it. The show's content also has a global flavor. Bart had to appear in court in Australia and spent a semester abroad in France where he brought down an illegal winery. Around the world, the likenesses of the Simpsons family members grace stickers, key chains, backpacks, T-shirts, and small figurines.

The Simpsons also illustrates the globalization of production. Film Roman (**www.filmroman.com**) produces the show but provides key poses and step-by-step frame directions to AKOM Production Company (**www.akomkorea.com**) in Seoul, South Korea, which fills in the remaining poses and links them into an animated whole. But there are bumps along the way. In a middle-of-the-night phone call, animation director Mark Kirkland was explaining to the Koreans how to draw a shooting gun. "They don't allow guns in Korea; it's against the law," says Kirkland. "So they were calling me: 'How does a gun work?' " Kirkland and others put up with cultural differences and phone calls at odd hours to tap into the cheaper yet highly qualified pool of South Korean animators. As you read this chapter, think about how globalization is affecting the marketing and production of goods and services around the world.[1]

international business
Sum of all business transactions that cross the borders of two or more nations.

imports
All goods and services brought into a country that were purchased from organizations located in other countries.

As this chapter's opening profile of Film Roman and *The Simpsons* demonstrates, each of us experiences the result of dozens of international transactions every day. Your radio–alarm clock was probably made in China. The news broadcast buzzing in your ears comes from Britain's BBC radio (**www.bbc.com**). You slip into a Gap T-shirt (**www.gap.com**) made in Egypt, Levi's (**www.levistrauss.com**) made in Bangladesh, and Nikes (**www.nike.com**) assembled in Vietnam from components made in several other countries. You get into your Toyota (**www.toyota.com**), which was made in Kentucky, and pop in a Dutch-made CD of music performed by a Swedish band. At the local Starbucks (**www.starbucks.com**), you charge up with coffee brewed from a blend of beans harvested in Colombia and Indonesia. A quick glance at the "Made in" tags on your jacket, backpack, watch, wallet, or other items with you right now will demonstrate the pervasiveness of international business transactions.

International business is the sum of all business transactions that cross the borders of two or more nations. You don't even have to set foot out of a small town to find evidence of international business. No matter where you live, you'll be surrounded by **imports**—all

MAP 1.1

International Trade Volume

the goods and services brought into a country that were purchased from organizations located in other countries. Your counterparts around the world will undoubtedly spend some part of their day using your nation's **exports**—all the goods and services sent from one country to other nations. An astonishing amount of export and import activity occurs daily. Map 1.1 shows the total value of goods and services, including both imports and exports, now crossing each nation's borders. The annual total value is a staggering $13,776,300,000,000 (nearly $13.8 trillion). That is more than 65 times the annual revenue of the world's largest company, ExxonMobil (www.exxonmobil.com), and almost as much as the combined annual revenues of the *Fortune* Global 500 (the 500 largest companies in the world).

But companies don't just sell their products to customers in other countries. They also cross borders to get products made in the first place. This is particularly true in the information age. Say you're an IBM (www.ibm.com) computer programmer based in Seattle. You may never leave the state of Washington, but you'll be working with colleagues in places such as central Europe and India. Consider the following actual example:

exports
All goods and services sent from one country to other nations.

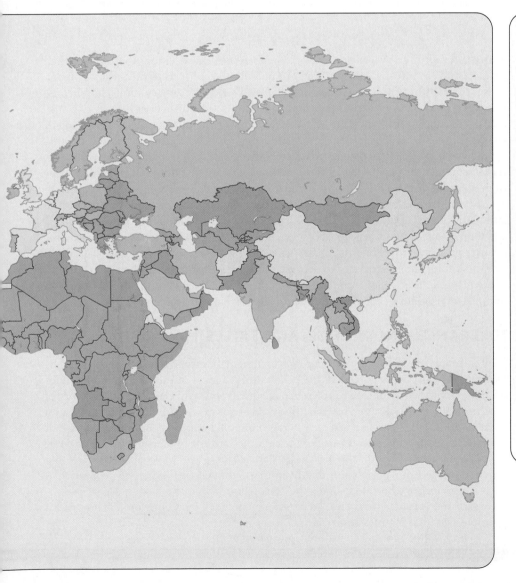

TRADE VOLUME
(millions of U.S. dollars)

$220,000 and up

40,000–219,999

10,000–39,999

0–9,999

No data

Top Sixteen

United States	2,512,232
Germany	1,266,670
Japan	1,042,749
United Kingdom	803,047
France	746,223
Canada	600,486
Italy	586,662
China	540,398
Netherlands	513,928
Hong Kong, China	484,881
Belgium-Luxembourg	457,436
South Korea	395,332
Mexico	379,411
Spain	351,122
Taipei, Chinese	334,270
Singapore	320,305

A team of computer programmers at Beijing's Tsinghua University (www.tsinghua.edu.cn) writes software using Java technology for IBM. At the end of each day, they send their work over the Internet to an IBM facility in Seattle. There, programmers build on it before zapping it 5,000 miles to the Institute of Computer Science in Belarus and the Software House Group in Latvia. From there, the work goes to India's Tata Group (www.tata.com), which passes the software back to Tsinghua by the next morning. The process repeats itself until the project is done.[2]

IBM's vice president for Internet technology calls this global relay race "Java around the Clock," and it is fast becoming the way things are done.

We begin this chapter by explaining the importance of future managers developing and maintaining a global mindset. We then describe the global business environment and its three main components: national business environments, the international business environment, and international business management. We then discuss the increasingly powerful influence of globalization on markets and production and look at the forces behind its growth. We close with a brief look at the key players in international business. The world atlas at the end of the chapter provides a reference for our discussion in this chapter and as we proceed throughout the remainder of the book.

A GLOBAL MINDSET

A provincial attitude toward international business can cause nations to barricade their markets and cut off one another from the potential benefits of trade and investment. This is exactly what happened following the First World War when nations discouraged imports and built trade barriers to protect their domestic industries. This way of thinking was an important contributing factor to the worldwide Great Depression in the 1930s.

To avoid the potential dangers associated with this way of thinking, future managers should consider the perspective of those with whom they do business. Companies today want their managers to think from a broader perspective that is unhindered by the blinders of nationalism. Enormous rewards await those who can break out of the cultural boundaries placed upon them by years of living and working within their native countries, and think about business in a global context. Future managers also will need to master the nuances of managing an internationally active business as opposed to a domestic one. In essence, if future managers want to become more valuable players on their global teams, they will benefit from a *global mindset*—a mental attitude characterized by tolerance and a minimal level of knowledge about international business management.

TOLERANCE, KNOWLEDGE, AND SKILLS

First and foremost, a global mindset requires a mental attitude that is characterized by *tolerance*—a sensitive awareness of the beliefs and practices of other peoples that differ from or conflict with one's own. Tolerance means accepting the cultural peculiarities of another group of people as being equally as valid as your own, and not looking down on them as being "inferior." The first step in developing tolerance toward other cultures is to understand their histories. Consider the cautious attitude of Japanese businesspeople when doing business with non-Japanese. This cultural trait can be traced back to a largely homogeneous population that lived in a tightly closed society for centuries. A U.S. sales manager who understands the reasons for his Japanese counterpart's seemingly excessive wariness would not be personally offended by it but would realize that it is simply a cultural manifestation.

Second, a global mindset requires *international business knowledge and skills*. The type of knowledge and skills required can include the ability to design effective promotional strategies abroad, manage an international sales force, manage risk in international financial markets, and communicate effectively across cultures. For instance, senior international marketing managers play a critical role in a firm's market selection, entry, and penetration decisions, which in turn influence firm performance. Those with greater knowledge and skills in both international marketing and business are more aware of opportunities and threats in the business environment and more capable of managing across borders.[3]

The importance of hiring managers with a global mindset is causing some internationally active companies to apply personality-testing techniques to measure the global aptitude of potential new managers. One test that attempts to capture a person's aptitude of doing business globally is the Global Mentality Test developed by the Intercultural Business Center (www.ib-c.com). The test evaluates an individual's (1) openness and flexibility in mindset, (2) understanding of global principles and terminology, and (3) strategic implementation abilities. It also identifies areas in which improvement and/or additional training is needed and generates a list of recommended training programs.[4]

MAINTAINING A GLOBAL MINDSET

Developing a global mindset is not a one-time event, but is a continual process. Maintaining a global mindset means keeping up on social, cultural, political, and economic *events and trends*. Consider the continual march toward market-based economics by formerly communist nations. As these countries recreate their economies away from extreme socialist ideals, certain aspects of their cultures are taking on more individualist characteristics. For instance, unlike their parents, young people in Eastern Europe are not guaranteed jobs with their governments or in state-owned firms upon graduation. Instead, the collapse of communism has meant that it is their individual responsibility (with some basic assistance) to find work after graduation. In some nations, including Bulgaria, Macedonia, and Romania, young people cannot find work. Yet many are taking it upon themselves to find work abroad in the West—often accepting jobs far below their qualifications. These social, political, and economic changes are profoundly affecting international business. Apart from the obvious shifts in demographics, they are affecting people's attitudes toward, for example, private business, risk-taking, financial markets, product marketing, and human resource management. The up-to-date manager will be better able to exploit the opportunities that such trends present.

Maintaining a global mindset also means not allowing oneself to fall into the trap of *stereotyping* groups of people as a result of current events. Consider the terrorist attacks on the United States in September 2001, which literally altered the course of world history. Following the attacks, Samuel Huntington's "Clash of Civilizations" thesis reignited debate about the potential for a post–cold war era dominated by conflict along the fault lines between civilizations (the highest cultural groupings of people). One conclusion that the author arrived at is that the West's relations with Islam will be characterized by significant conflict in the future. He foretells a scenario in which increasing modernization of non-Western cultures could potentially cause the expansion of fundamentalist Islam.[5] Two polls conducted nearly six months after the attacks showed just how different were the views of U.S. citizens and those of nine Muslim nations. The polls were virtual mirrors of one another: Most U.S. citizens surveyed said they believe Muslims don't respect Western values, and residents of such countries said the United States does not respect Islamic culture.[6] But the manager with a global mindset will not allow herself to fall into the trap of stereotyping an entire group of people. Instead, she will strive for greater knowledge, understanding, and tolerance of differences between her own culture and that of other people.

THE GLOBAL BUSINESS ENVIRONMENT

Today, international business is more influenced by global events and forces than perhaps at any time in the past. Therefore, it helps if we view international business not as a collection of distinct forces, environments, and business functions, but as it is in the real world—occurring within an integrated, global environment. Figure 1.1 identifies the three elements that make up the global business environment:

1. Many *national business environments*
2. The *international business environment*
3. *International business management*

In order for international managers to be successful in their jobs they need to understand how the global business environment functions. Although the world is becoming increasingly integrated, *national business environments* remain important. Each nation has a distinct culture and systems of politics, law, and economics that define business activity within its borders. Yet, no nation is entirely immune to events in the *international business environment* as evidenced by the long-term trend toward more porous national economic borders. Both of these business environments (national and international) define the context of *international business management*. Companies operating across borders must play by the rules in their home market as well as those in the countries in which they do business. But they also help shape those environments by actively participating in both arenas.

NATIONAL BUSINESS ENVIRONMENTS

Although cross-border business activity is stitching the world's economies closer together, many differences among countries remain. In fact, when a company begins analyzing a nation's potential as a host for international business activity, it first examines the overall business climate. This means addressing some important questions related to a nation's culture and systems of politics, law, and economics. Answers to those questions—plus statistical data on items such as income level and labor costs—allow businesses to evaluate the attractiveness of a particular location as a place for doing business.

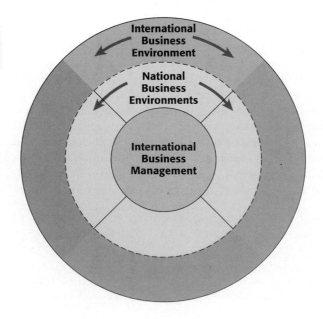

The Importance of Culture   All business activity revolves around people, whether they are individual consumers, entrepreneurs, the owners of a small or medium-size company, or the employees of a huge global firm. When buyers and sellers from around the world come together to conduct business, they bring with them different backgrounds, expectations, and ways of communicating—in other words, culture. Among other things, culture reflects many aspects of a people's way of life, including values, manners, social structure, religion, and ways of communicating.

Because culture is so deeply ingrained in people, a deep understanding of it can help businesses to be more effective at marketing, for example. Campbell Soup Co. (www.campbellsoup.com) entered the Japanese market 40 years ago but never seemed to win consumers over. Several years ago, the company realized that its Campbell Soup Kids (a hit with U.S. consumers since 1904) just wasn't arousing the interest of Japanese soup lovers. It replaced the Kids' well-known slogan, "M'm M'm Good," with a talking can called "Mr. Campbell" who teases consumers with the advertising tagline: "Have a date with me tonight." Today, Campbell is successfully selling eight varieties of soups in Japan, including mushroom with seafood.[7] Because culture plays such a fundamental role in international business, we devote all of Chapter 2 to its discussion and return repeatedly to it throughout the remainder of the book.

The Roles of Politics, Law, and Economics   Similar to dealing with cultural forces, doing business in other countries involves navigating tricky political and legal issues. Understanding the nature of politics and laws in other nations can lessen the risks of conducting business there and help companies to manage the associated risks. For instance, bookseller Barnes and Noble (www.bn.com) stopped selling the English-language version of *Mein Kampf* to Germans through its online bookstore when the German government complained. It did so even though selling only the German-language version of the book there is illegal. A statement by Barnes and Noble read, "Our policy with regard to censorship remains unchanged. But as responsible corporate citizens, we respect the laws of the countries where we do business."[8]

Economic systems also differ from one country to another and include economic forces such as tax and interest rates, productivity levels, and the quality of telecommunications networks, roads, and airports. Furthermore, economic development and the implementation of market-based economic reforms are dramatically affecting business in many nations. We discuss the pivotal roles of political, legal, and economic forces in Chapters 3 and 4.

INTERNATIONAL BUSINESS ENVIRONMENT

Managers of international companies must be concerned with external forces in each national business environment in which their company operates. It is in the international business environment that the actions of consumers, workers, companies, financial institutions, and governments from different countries converge. And it is the international business environment that links the world's national business environments and becomes the conduit through which events in one country can influence events in others. We can think of the international business environment as comprising two main components: (1) International trade and investment, and (2) the international financial system.

The Dynamics of Trade and Investment   Today, people around the world are accustomed to purchasing goods and services from companies in other countries. As a matter of fact, trade allows a nation's people to obtain goods that they cannot produce or that they cannot produce efficiently. Trade and investment can free a nation's entrepreneurial spirit and bring economic development. Yet, despite the theoretical benefits of trade and investment, nations do not simply throw open their doors and force their domestic businesses to sink or swim. Governments become involved in international business to accomplish social, economic, and military goals by regulating international flows of products, labor, information, and capital.

Even nations that are the world's most ardent supporters of free trade can find it difficult to submit entirely to its unbridled force. United States President George W. Bush ruffled the feathers of governments around the world when he announced in March 2002 that his administration would slap tariffs of up to 30 percent on steel imports to the U.S. for several years. The stated aim was to protect the U.S. steel industry and the jobs it supports until the industry has time to restructure itself. The U.S. steel industry had been suffering under an onslaught of steel imports from many nations, including Brazil, the European Union, Japan, and South Korea.[9]

Similar to trade, navigating the choppy waters of cross-border investment also can be a tricky endeavor. In early 2002 it was confirmed that India would allow foreign investors to hold up to 49 percent of the equity of private banks, up from 20 percent previously. But there's a catch: Foreign investors' voting rights would continue to be capped at 10 percent of total voting shares. So, the money of foreigners in the banking sector is welcome, but they had better not be too concerned about how their investment is managed. Policies such as this are behind India's rank of 126th out of 150 nations in its ratio of foreign direct investment to total investment.[10]

Groups of countries are creating regional trade agreements to dismantle trade and investment barriers that threaten the potential gains from trade. Eastman Kodak (**www.kodak.com**) estimates that it could save $25 million annually on import duties under a free trade agreement between Central, North, and South America. Christopher Padilla, director for international trade relations, says "If you've got tariff-free trade, you can use your factories in new and different ways." Kodak would also save money by supplying the entire region from just a few plants, rather than plants in each nation.[11] We cover the international trade and investment environment in Chapters 5 through 8.

The International Financial System   Well-functioning financial markets are an essential element of the international business environment. The international capital market mainly helps companies to raise capital and invest excess cash in financial markets. The foreign exchange market supplies companies with the currencies of other countries in order to pay for needed imports, among other things. Many of a company's financial decisions are heavily influenced by currency exchange rate changes. For instance, exchange rates influence production and marketing decisions because they affect demand for a company's products in the global marketplace. When a country's currency is weak (valued low relative to other currencies), the price of its exports on world markets declines and the price of imports increases. That is why a weak currency can make a country's exports more appealing on world markets.

Because the international financial system is highly efficient, economic shocks can be remarkably swift and severe. Argentina was the star of Latin America in the 1990s, yet the country defaulted on its $155 billion of public debt in early 2002, the largest default by any country ever. The Argentine peso, which had been fixed to the dollar, quickly lost two-thirds of its value when it was allowed to float freely on currency markets. In 2002, Argentina's economy was expected to shrink anywhere from 5 to 10 percent while unemployment hovered around 25 percent. The government, strapped for cash, seized the savings accounts of its citizens and restricted how much they could withdraw at a time. When street protesters turned violent they beat up several politicians and attacked dozens of banks. Michael Smith, manager of HSBC's Argentine subsidiary (**www.hsbc.com.ar**), summed up people's feelings of distrust when he said, "We're somewhat less popular than serial killers."[12] We discuss how all aspects of the international financial system affect international business in Chapters 9 and 10.

INTERNATIONAL BUSINESS MANAGEMENT

Our understanding of national and international business environments provides a solid foundation for our study of international business management. When a business ventures into international business, forces and elements at work in the national and international environments present it with many challenges. All aspects of managing a business are affected, including strategy, marketing, production, and human resource management.

Globalization's Impact on Management   Globalization is having a profound impact on the strategies of international businesses. Today, because of technological advances in communication and transportation, many of the largest companies can realistically consider nearly every location on earth as either a potential market or a site for business operations. In addition, managers often find themselves simultaneously screening and analyzing locations as potential markets *and* as potential sites for operations. When Mercedes (**www.mercedes.com**) introduced the M-class sport utility vehicle to the U.S. market, executives also decided to build the vehicle there. Thus the company was obliged not merely to estimate the size of the potential market for the vehicle, but to decide at the same time on a suitable production site.

Globalization is also affecting marketing strategies. Some companies can take advantage of globalization's effects and create a single product that is marketed identically around the world. Red Bull (**www.redbull.com**) markets an identical energy drink in the same manner in over 45 countries around the world, for example. Others realize that differences in national business environments are too great to ignore—they create new products, modify promotional campaigns, or adjust their marketing strategies in some other way.

Managing Employees Globally   The most important resource of any successful business is likely to be the people who comprise it, and this is no less true for an international company. Yet, human resource management in an international setting differs considerably from that in a domestic one. Every aspect of a company's human resource policies needs to be examined to see whether it is appropriate for the local market. Some of those policies are recruiting and hiring practices, training and development programs, methods and levels of compensation, and labor–management relations.

Especially complicated are the unique circumstances surrounding those employees sent from the home country to work abroad in local markets—called *expatriates*. In the past, many companies would simply boost the salaries of their expatriates to compensate for all the complications that arise when relocating. Some of those include auto and home sales and purchases, language training, confusion over where and how much taxes to pay, and adjusting to an unfamiliar culture. But it can cost a company three times more to send an employee on an international assignment than to keep him or her on home-country status. Because the cost of failure is simply too high, companies today are getting more involved in helping their employees prepare for their international assignments and settle in once they arrive.[13] For some insight into traits that can help managers and their companies succeed in the international marketplace, see the Global Manager titled "The Keys to Success." We address all the issues important to managing an international business in Chapters 11 through 16.

ETHICS AND SOCIAL RESPONSIBILITY

As we said earlier, when companies venture into the global business environment, managers are exposed to different cultures. This means that they are exposed to different conceptions of ethical behavior, and different guidelines for socially responsible behavior. Confronting unfamiliar practices presents companies with both tremendous opportunities and potential pitfalls. Child labor, human rights, the environment, and plant closings are at the heart of many debates on the actions of international companies. Today, managers must monitor their own behavior, that of all the firm's employees, and even the behavior of those with whom the firm does business abroad.

ethical behavior
Personal behavior that is in accordance with rules or standards for right conduct or morality.

Ethical Behavior Ethical behavior is personal behavior that is in accordance with rules or standards for right conduct or morality. Ethical dilemmas are not legal questions. When a law exists to guide a manager toward a legally correct action, the legally correct path must necessarily be followed. In ethical dilemmas there are no right or wrong decisions, but there are alternatives, each of which may be equally valid, depending on one's perspective.

Ethical questions often arise when managers attempt to either abide by local management practices or import practices from their home country. One viewpoint believes that home-country policies should be implemented wherever a company operates. Another viewpoint agrees with the old saying "When in Rome, do as the Romans do." However, this philosophy often runs into trouble when large international companies from developed nations do business in developing nations. Consider one case publicized by human rights and labor groups investigating charges of worker abuse at the factory of one of Nike's Vietnamese suppliers. Twelve of 56 female employees reportedly fainted when a supervisor forced them to run around the factory as punishment for not wearing regulation shoes. Nike confirmed the report and, in suspending the supervisor, took steps to implement practices more in keeping with the company's home-country ethics.[14]

On November 8, 2001, Enron acknowledged in a federal filing that it had overstated earnings by nearly $600 million since 1997. The company said that about two-thirds of that was because two partnerships had improperly been treated as separate entities. The disclosure sent a signal that Enron hadn't been forthcoming about its true financial condition and sent investors fleeing in droves.[15] The company's stock price, which hit a high of $90 in August 2000, was trading at $1.01 per share within a month of the disclosure—when Enron sought bankruptcy-law protection. Although Enron executives earned millions over the years in salaries and bonuses, the company's rank and file saw their retirement savings disappear along with the firm's demise. Enron's failure sent a shock wave around the world, as investors feared the effect that "Enronitis" would have on their markets. Banks across Europe would never see the roughly $2 billion that they had lent to Enron and its subsidiaries. At its peak, Enron accounted for about 20 percent of the total volume traded on European energy exchanges and its collapse threw energy trading markets into chaos. The futures of people at energy operations in which Enron had a stake in Brazil, England, Germany, India, and other markets were suddenly uncertain.[16] U.S. Congress opened hearings into the Enron debacle and the possibility of criminal charges against senior executives was real. The U.S. Justice Department filed a criminal indictment against the firm's auditor, Arthur Andersen, on obstruction of justice charges for the shredding of important documents related to its work for Enron. Around the world, governments, accounting standards boards, and other regulators and interest groups called for higher accounting standards and more transparent financial reporting by companies.

Social Responsibility   In addition to individual managers behaving ethically, corporations are expected to exercise **social responsibility**—the practice of going beyond legal obligations to actively balance commitments to investors, customers, other companies, and communities. In recent years governments, labor unions, consumer groups, and human rights activists have combined to force apparel companies from developed nations to implement codes of conduct and monitoring principles in their international production activities. Pertinent issues include trade initiatives with developing nations (a government issue), the relocation of home-country factories to locations abroad (a labor issue), and the treatment of workers by local contractors abroad (a human rights issue).

Today, companies often don't wait for governments to pressure them before undertaking policy changes. Most business leaders realize that the future of their companies rests on healthy workforces and environments worldwide. Levi-Strauss (**www.levistrauss.com**)

social responsibility
Practice of companies going beyond legal obligations to actively balance commitments to investors, customers, other companies, and communities.

A fresh coat of bright yellow paint is applied to the ends of these logs as they sit on the banks of the Madeira River deep in Brazil's Amazon forest. The logs belong to Gethal Amazonas, the first tropical plywood maker in the world to be certified by the Forest Stewardship Council (FSC). The goal of the FSC—a nonprofit initiative between environmentalists, logging companies, and wood merchants and retailers—is to convert the world's timber companies to sustainable forest management.

is a pioneer in using a set of practical codes both to control working conditions at contractors' facilities and to assess countries as potential locations for doing business. A global staff then monitors working conditions in the factories of Levi's contractors abroad. The company does business only with partners that meet its so-called "Terms of Engagement," which involve meeting demands on matters of ethical standards, legal requirements, environmental requirements, employment standards, and community involvement.[17]

Another company that is working hard to operate in a socially responsible manner is Starbucks (www.starbucks.com). The company tries to help ease the plight of citizens in poor coffee-producing countries. Starbucks does this by building schools, health clinics, and coffee-processing facilities to improve the well-being of families in coffee-farming communities. Also, the company sells what it calls "fair trade coffee." "Fair trade" products are those that involve companies working with suppliers in more equitable, meaningful, and sustainable ways. For Starbucks, this is coffee bearing the "fair trade" logo, which indicates its certification by TransFair USA (www.transfairusa.org), a nonprofit organization that provides independent certification of fair trade products. In part, the alliance between Starbucks and TransFair USA is designed to ensure that coffee farmers earn a fair price for their coffee crop and to help coffee growers farm in environmentally friendly ways.[18]

GLOBALIZATION

globalization
Trend toward greater interdependence among national institutions and economies.

Although national governments still retain ultimate control over the products, people, and capital crossing their borders, the global economy is becoming increasingly intertwined. **Globalization** is the trend toward greater interdependence among national institutions and economies. It is a trend that is characterized by "denationalization" in which national boundaries are becoming less relevant. It is not the same as *internationalization*, which refers to cooperation between national actors.[19] The increased interdependence that globalization causes means an increasingly freer flow of goods, services, money, and people across national borders. We saw the power of globalization to expand the global flow of products and services in our chapter-opening company profile of Film Roman (www.filmroman.com) and the Simpsons. Let's now take a look at two areas in which globalization is having profound effects: Globalization of markets and globalization of production.

GLOBALIZATION OF MARKETS

Globalization of markets refers to convergence in buyer preferences in markets around the world. This trend is occurring in many product categories, including consumer goods, industrial products, and business services. Clothing retailer L.L.Bean (www.llbean.com), shoe producer Nike (www.nike.com), and electronics maker Sony (www.sony.com) are just a few companies that sell so-called *global products*—products marketed in all countries essentially without any changes. Global products and global competition characterize many industries and markets, including semiconductors (Intel, Philips), aircraft (Airbus, Boeing), construction equipment (Komatsu, Mitsubishi), autos (Mercedes, Volkswagen), financial services (Citicorp, HSBC), air travel (KLM, Singapore Airlines), accounting services (Ernst & Young, KPMG), consumer goods (Procter & Gamble, Unilever), and fast food (KFC, McDonald's).

The globalization of markets is important to international business because it offers companies several important advantages. First, companies that sell global products can reduce costs by *standardizing* various aspects of their marketing activities. A company selling a global consumer good, such as shampoo, can make an identical shampoo for the global market, and then simply design different product packaging to account for the language spoken in each market. Further cost savings could be achieved by creating an advertisement that has the same visual component for all markets but has its narration dubbed into local languages for television and translated for print ads.

Second, a company that sells a global product can explore opportunities abroad when the home market becomes saturated. Consider the current strategy of McDonald's (www.mcdonalds.com). Although there is one McDonald's outlet for every 29,000 people in the United States, there is only 1 for every 40 million people in China.[20] Not surprisingly, McDonald's is expanding aggressively in China (indeed, all across Asia), where the long-term growth potential is enormous. Seeking sales growth abroad can be absolutely essential for companies who sell global products with limited home markets. Duncan MacGillivray of Adelaide, Australia, developed Two Dogs alcoholic lemonade (www.twodogs.com) by using surplus lemons from his friend's orchard, adding sugar, and fermenting the mix with yeast. After quickly reaching its potential in Australia, Two Dogs expanded worldwide. It was an immediate hit in Asia because lemons are a popular source of vitamin C to fight the common cold there. Today, Two Dogs is produced on three continents and sells millions of cases worldwide each year.[21]

Third, a company selling a seasonal global product (such as suntan and sunblock lotions) can use international sales to level off its income stream. By supplementing domestic sales with international sales, the company can reduce or eliminate wide variations in sales between seasons and steady its cash flow.

Although global products offer advantages, companies must constantly monitor their markets to ensure that they are not overlooking the needs of buyers. The benefit of serving those needs with an adapted product may outweigh the benefit of standardization. For instance, consumer products such as soft drinks and fast food are clearly global products that continue to penetrate markets around the world. But sometimes these products need small modifications made to them so that they better suit local tastes. In southern Japan, for example, Coca-Cola (www.cocacola.com) sweetens its traditional formula to compete with sweeter-tasting Pepsi (www.pepsi.com). In India, where cows are sacred and the consumption of beef taboo, McDonald's (www.mcdonalds.com) markets the "Maharaja Mac"—two all-mutton patties on a sesame-seed bun with all the usual toppings.

The globalization of markets and production is having a profound impact on worldwide flows of trade and investment. The port of Shanghai, China, shown here, is experiencing double-digit growth annually in its exports. The reason? To take advantage of low-cost labor in China, multinational companies continue to move their production activities there. They then export the goods—everything from stuffed animals to computer components—to markets worldwide.

GLOBALIZATION OF PRODUCTION

Today, many production activities are also becoming global. *Globalization of production* refers to the dispersal of production activities to locations around the world that are low-cost or high-quality producers of a particular good.

Like globalization of markets, the globalization of production also offers companies several advantages. First, companies can take advantage of globalization of production to access low-cost labor—a very common way for many types of firms to reduce production costs. But labor unions in industrialized nations commonly complain that this practice is causing a "race to the bottom" in terms of employee wages and benefits. Whether or not this in fact the case, low wages are not all that attracts companies to a particular location. Low wages must be accompanied by adequate worker skills that are appropriate to the task. If low-cost labor were the only reason a nation attracted international companies, businesses would be stampeding into all sorts of less developed nations across the globe. In order to attract investment a location must offer low-cost, adequately skilled workers in an environment with acceptable levels of social, political, and economic stability.

Although services typically must be produced where they are consumed, some services can be performed at remote locations where labor costs are lower. This is precisely why many European companies are moving their call centers to Ireland and even to far-away places such as India. According to management consultants, Accenture (www.accenture.com), the U.K. insurance industry is shedding costs by moving customer service call centers abroad. "It will only be a few years before U.K. insurance and pension customers will, as a matter of course, have almost all their business dealt with abroad," said Accenture insurance partner Steve Lanthrope. As compared to the United Kingdom, a similar call center facility in India could present cost savings between 40 and 60 percent for a company.[22]

Second, companies will produce abroad to take advantage of technical know-how. Over the years, India has become a major source of quality information technology (IT) services for companies around the world. A group of former Microsoft employees led by 36-year-old Swain Porter is taking advantage of the know-how of Indian software engineers. Porter and his colleagues are enduring cobra snakes, constant power outages, and the twin seasonal dangers of torrential rains and temperatures soaring over 100 degrees to create their dream: A self-sustaining software producing community in southern India, near the tech city of Hyderabad. Their company, Catalytic Software (www.catalyticsoftware.com), is already producing high-quality, just-in-time software using the excellent programming talent in India. In the process, they are helping make "Made in India" a coveted label for software.[23]

Third, globalization of production allows companies to access resources that are unavailable or more costly at home. The quest for natural resources draws many companies into international markets. Japan, for example, is a small, densely populated island nation with very few natural resources of its own—especially forests. But Japan's largest paper company, Nippon Seishi, does more than simply import wood pulp. The company owns huge forests and corresponding processing facilities in Australia, Canada, and the United States. This gives the firm not only access to a much-needed resource, but control over earlier stages in the papermaking process. As a result, the company is guaranteed a steady flow of its key ingredient (wood pulp) that is less subject to the uncertainties (swings in prices and supply) associated with buying pulp on the open market. Likewise, to access cheaper energy resources used in manufacturing a variety of Japanese firms, for example, are relocating production to China, Mexico, and Vietnam where energy costs are lower.

Two main forces underlie the globalization of markets and production: *falling barriers to trade and investment* and *technological innovation*. Let's take a look at each of these factors in greater detail.

FALLING BARRIERS TO TRADE AND INVESTMENT

In 1947, 23 nations made history when they created the *General Agreement on Tariffs and Trade (GATT)*—a treaty designed to promote free trade by reducing both tariffs (taxes on traded goods) and nontariff barriers such as quotas (restrictions on the volume of goods allowed into a country). The treaty was quite successful in its early years—in 1988 world merchandise trade was 20 times larger than in 1947 and average tariffs dropped from 40 percent to 5 percent. Further progress was made with a 1994 revision of the treaty. Average tariffs on merchandise trade were to be reduced further still and subsidies (price supports) for agricultural products were to be reduced significantly. *Intellectual property rights* were clearly defined, giving protection to copyrights (including computer programs, databases, sound records, and films), trademarks and service marks, and patents (including trade secrets and know-how). But perhaps the greatest accomplishment was the creation of the *World Trade Organization (WTO)*—an international organization with the power to enforce the rules of international trade; a power that the 1947 GATT lacked. As of early 2002 the WTO recognized 144 members and over 30 "observer" members.

The three main goals of the WTO (www.wto.org) are to help the free flow of trade, to help negotiate further opening of markets, and to settle trade disputes between its members. The various WTO agreements are essentially contracts between member nations that commit them to maintaining fair and open trade policies. Offenders must realign their trade policies according to WTO guidelines or suffer financial penalties and perhaps trade sanctions. Because of its ability to penalize offending member nations, the WTO's dispute settlement system is the spine of the global trading system.

A new round of negotiations to lower trade barriers further still was agreed to at the WTO meeting in Doha, Qatar, in late 2001. The new round of negotiations could bring particular benefits for developing nations. Agricultural subsidies in the world's rich countries are worth $1 billion per day—more than six times the value of their combined aid budgets. Poor countries should also obtain greater access to rich countries' textile markets and other markets that are labor intensive. The potential benefits are enormous considering that over 70 percent of poor nations' exports are agriculture and textiles. The Doha round also will prompt poor nations to reduce tariffs among themselves. Finally, poor nations are to receive help from rich nations in integrating themselves into the global trading system.[24]

In addition to the WTO, smaller groups of nations are integrating their economies as never before. For example, the *North American Free Trade Agreement (NAFTA)* groups three nations (Canada, Mexico, and the United States) into a free-trade bloc. The even more ambitious *European Union (EU)* combines 15 countries. The *Asia Pacific Economic Cooperation (APEC)* consists of 18 nations committed to creating a free-trade zone around the Pacific. All these agreements aim to lower trade barriers. As a result of such initiatives, growth in international trade now outpaces growth in worldwide production.

TECHNOLOGICAL INNOVATION

While falling barriers to trade and investment encourage globalization, technological innovations are accelerating the process. In fact, technology is making it possible for many products to be made practically anywhere it is cheapest to do so. Specifically, significant advancements in information technology and transportation methods are making it easier, faster, and less costly to move data, goods, equipment, and people around the world.

Business activities, such as managing employees and scheduling production in several locations, are more difficult and costly when conducted across borders and time zones. But the use of technology can speed up the flow of information, making coordination and control easier and cheaper. With electronic mail (e-mail) managers can stay in contact with international operations and respond quickly to important matters. Videoconferencing allows managers to meet while still in different branch offices and engineers to view models of new products from remote locations. In fact, about 70 percent of a company's videoconferencing is done within the company and 30 percent is for external communications.[25] The main reasons for videoconferencing's rapid growth (around 20 to 25 percent per year) is lower-cost bandwidth used to transmit information, lower-cost equipment, and decreased travel among some businesspeople for cost and safety reasons. This quick pace of growth is causing companies like V-Span (www.vspan.com), which rents videoconferencing facilities and assistance by the hour, to sprout up. By using rented facilities a manufacturer in Denver can hold a 2-hour conference with branch managers in six other nations for about $2,700. Comparing this figure to the travel, lodging, and feeding cost of having these employees from abroad in Denver for a single day, V-Span senior marketing manager Josh Cartagenova calls videoconferencing "Quite affordable."[26]

Companies also use the Internet and World Wide Web to quickly and cheaply call on managers in remote locations to check up on production runs, revise sales strategies, and check on distribution bottlenecks. Private networks of internal company Web sites and other information sources (called *intranets*) allow employees to access their company's information from distant locations using personal computers. For instance, a particularly effective marketing tool on Volvo Car Corporation's (www.volvocars.com) intranet is a quarter-by-quarter database of marketing and sales information. The cycle begins when headquarters submits its corporate-wide marketing planning information. In this way, the database acts as a communication tool between headquarters and the national markets because subsidiaries are alerted to the corporate activities that are

Thirty-seven years after its introduction, videoconferencing is finally gaining popularity and helping shrink the world. Imagine that you're in your office at 7 A.M. in New York having a virtual face-to-face meeting with colleagues in London, where it is Noon, and Tokyo, where it is 9 P.M. At the same time, you all are logged onto your firm's Web site reviewing recent sales charts and discussing future strategies. What other ways do you think companies can benefit from videoconferencing?

planned. Marketing managers at the company's subsidiaries around the world then select those items from this menu that apply to their particular markets. After the marketing plan of each market is developed, it is uploaded to the database—allowing each marketing manager to examine the marketing plan of every other market and adapt any relevant aspects to their own plan. In this way, the system acts as a tool for the sharing of best practices and gives managers the ability to develop the most appropriate marketing plan for their market.[27]

Also, today *extranets* give distributors and suppliers access to a company's database so that they can place orders or restock inventories electronically and automatically. All these new technologies permit managers to respond to both internal and external conditions more quickly, and more appropriately, than ever before.

Computer technologies are also increasing the competitiveness of small companies by reducing the costs of reaching an international customer base. In fact, small companies were among the first to use the Web as a global marketing tool. "I think we're fairly typical," says Jim Macintyre of Tropical Jim's Remake Shop (**www.ve.net/remakers**), a Web designer located in Caracas, Venezuela. "Our firm was in the red until we started selling to the American market. Now 90 percent of our customers are Americans." For Jonathan Strum, a Tropical Jim's customer based in Los Angeles, the Web makes Caracas seem as though he is next door. "Not long ago," he admits, "I would have thought depending on a firm in Caracas for the services we need for our business was outlandish. Now I am importing all my graphic design and most of my programming from overseas."[28]

Some companies realize the value of the Internet in cutting postproduction costs. It is estimated that an average of 60 percent of a product's cost results from *activities occurring after the production process*.[29] Using the World Wide Web to bypass intermediaries like wholesalers and retailers, companies can enter global markets, cut postproduction costs, and pass savings on to customers. This strategy is best suited to firms that offer products such as music, books, computer software, and travel services. Yet, many Internet startups forgot a fundamental rule of running a business—attracting paying customers. Companies without partners in cyberspace were disappointed with traffic in their online stores. Online intermediaries (called portals), such as America Online (AOL) (**www.aol.com**), Yahoo (**www.yahoo.com**), and Excite (**www.excite.com**), funnel Web surfers to Web sites for a fee. But generating traffic in an online store can be difficult without a partner. As one expert noted, "Launching an e-commerce site without a portal partner is like opening a retail store in the desert. Sure, it's cheap, but does anybody stop there?"[30]

Like advancements in technology, advances in transportation methods are helping to globalize both markets and production activities. Advancements in the shipping industry are facilitating globalization by making shipping more efficient and dependable. In today's global marketplace retailers around the world rely on imports to stock their storerooms with autos and bicycles, and their shelves with mobile phones, backpacks, and clothing. In the past, a cargo ship would sit in port up to 10 days while it was unloaded one pallet at a time. But today, cargo is loaded onto a ship in 20- and 40-foot containers that are quickly unloaded onto railcars or truck chassis at its destination. As a result, it is commonplace today for a 700-foot cargo ship to be unloaded in just 15 hours. Also, technological advancements such as computerized charts that pinpoint a ship's movements on the high seas using Global Positioning System (GPS) satellites makes them easier and safer to operate.[31]

THE BACKLASH AGAINST GLOBALIZATION

In thinking about globalization, it might be helpful to take a brief look at the past. Globalization is not such a new phenomenon as one may think. In fact, although foreign assets accounted for 20 percent of the collective gross domestic products of the world before 1914, they only regained those levels in 1985 and just recently reached a peak of 57 percent. Some believe that this early era of globalization, characterized by fierce competition in trade and unfettered immigration, stoked nationalist sentiments and aggravated tensions between countries leading up to World War I. Then a backlash to globalization in the early 1900s led to high tariffs and barriers to trade and immigration—important contributors to the Great Depression. Today, researchers are examining this earlier era of globalization and asking whether there are parallels to the current one and if there are inherent limits to globalization.[32]

But today's backlash feels different. It all began in Seattle, Washington, in December 1999 at a ministerial meeting of the World Trade Organization. A protest staged by a 40,000-strong crowd of anti-globalization activists deteriorated into window smashing and looting of local businesses. Then in February 2000, the annual World Economic Forum in Davos, Switzerland, saw protestors trash a McDonald's restaurant. In September 2000, demonstrations against the IMF–World Bank annual meeting in Prague turned violent and left the city's streets littered with stones and broken glass. Other cities had similar experiences that year when hosting the meetings of supranational organizations including the World Economic Forum, European Union, and Summit of the Americas. Then, in June 2001, a European Union summit in Gothenburg, Sweden, ended with three people shot—the first occasion in modern times that live ammunition was used against anti-globalization protestors in the Western world. The low point came in July 2001 in Genoa, Italy, where 200,000 protestors converged on the G8 summit. Two days of rioting left one protestor shot dead by police and an estimated $45 million in property damage. The 23-year-old man was the first to die in violence linked to the anti-globalization movement.

What do these protestors want? The complaints range from the reasonable—simply a greater say in organizations such as the World Trade Organization—to the radical—the destruction of capitalism itself. The breadth of gripes about globalization is apparent in a statement by consumer advocate Ralph Nader. "The essence of globalization is a subordination of human rights, of labor rights, consumer, environmental rights, democracy rights, to the imperatives of global trade and investment," lamented Nader.[33]

Here, Italian police guard a McDonald's restaurant in Genoa, Italy, against attack by demonstrators. McDonald's is a favorite target in the anti-globalization debate because of its visibility—it serves 45 million people a day at 28,000 restaurants in 120 countries. Among the arguments of the protestors is that McDonald's promotes the homogenization of cultures. Do you agree or disagree with the "McTrashers" on this point, and why?

Many protestors complain that the world is not sharing equitably the fruits of globalization. In this area, it appears that the anti-globalization protestors (the violent and the peaceful) have achieved results in that they have prompted a dialogue on the merits and demerits of globalization. "What is happening now is a recognition that the global marketplace, left to itself, is not going to automatically produce wealth and prosperity in less-developed countries unless there is rule-making and new structures that reduce the potential for destructiveness," says Clyde V. Prestowitz, Jr., president of the Economic Strategy Institute. The protests against globalization was one factor behind the enhanced power of poor nations at the launch of a new round of trade talks in late 2001. The United States and other rich nations were forced to acknowledge the problems faced by the world's poorest economies. Among other things, the guidelines for the new round of talks give poor countries the right to license less expensive, generic versions of brand-name drugs in emergencies—thus weakening patent protection for multinational drug companies. The Doha guidelines also recognize that less-developed nations face problems when trading with developed ones and therefore deserve special treatment.[34]

A concern of other anti-globalization protestors is the fear that globalization is homogenizing the world and destroying the rich diversity of cultures it contains. They say that in some drab, new world we all will be wearing the same clothes bought at the same brand-name shops, eating the same foods at the same brand-name restaurants, and watching the same movies made by the same production companies. But others counter that globalization allows us all to profit from our differing circumstances and skills.[35] Trade allows a country to specialize in producing those goods and services in which it is most efficient. It can then trade those products to other nations in exchange for goods and services it desires but does not produce. In this way, France will still be France, with the world's finest wines, South Africa will always produce much of the world's diamonds, and the Germans and Japanese will continue to design high-quality automobiles. Then other nations can trade their goods and services with these countries and thereby enjoy the wines, diamonds, and autos that they do not, or cannot, produce.

Evidence also suggests that the influence of developing nations' music, art, and literature has grown (not shrunk) throughout the last century, with artists from Picasso to the Beatles drawing on African cultures. In fact, developing countries' share of world exports of cultural goods rose from 12 percent to 30 percent over a recent twenty-year period.[36] See the World Business Survey titled "The Global Market for Culture" for more evidence on trade flows in cultural goods.

Although companies of all types and sizes and in all sorts of industries become involved in international business, they vary in the extent to which they get involved. While a small shop owner might only import supplies from abroad, a large company may have dozens of factories located around the world. And while large companies from the most developed nations used to dominate international business, firms from other nations such as China, Indonesia, Brazil, and Mexico are accounting for a larger share of international business activity. And largely due to advances in technology, small and medium-size companies are accounting for a greater portion of international business.

KEY PLAYERS IN INTERNATIONAL BUSINESS

MULTINATIONAL CORPORATIONS

A **multinational corporation (MNC)** is a business that has direct investments (in the form of marketing or manufacturing subsidiaries) abroad in multiple countries. Multinational corporations vary widely in size, ranging from the security firm Pinkerton (www.pinkertons.com), with about $900 million in annual revenue, to Mitsubishi Corporation (www.mitsubishi.co.jp), with revenues of about $130 billion.

multinational corporation (MNC)
Business that has direct investments abroad in multiple countries.

The Global Market for Culture

Trade statistics confirm the multidirectional flow of cultural exports, which according to UNESCO includes printed matter, music, visual arts, cinema and photography, radio and television, and games and sporting goods. The figures below show the countries running trade surpluses and deficits in the export of culture.

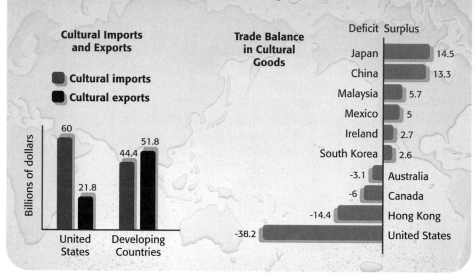

Why do business headlines focus so sharply on large international companies? First of all, their economic and political muscle makes them highly visible in the eyes of the media. Large companies generate significant jobs, investment, and tax revenue for the regions and nations they enter. Likewise, they can leave many hundreds, perhaps thousands of people out of work when they decide to close or scale back operations. It is because of their large economic impact that the business media focuses so strongly on multinationals.

Second, their dealings typically involve huge sums of money. It is common for the income and dealings of large companies, such as mergers and acquisitions, to be valued in the billions of dollars. Consider the merger between the two global petroleum companies, Exxon and Mobil. The deal created a merged company that had assets worth nearly $150 billion. In fact, international mergers are becoming more common and more valuable. In 2000 alone, the world's largest firms were involved in $1.1 *trillion* worth of cross-border mergers and acquisitions, nearly 50 percent higher than a year earlier.[37] But as the chairman of the Federal Trade Commission points out, "More and more deals . . . should be judged on a global-market scale. . . . Mergers go through now that would have been challenged just 10 years ago because competition now comes from all corners of the world."[38] Figure 1.2 highlights the rapid growth in mergers and acquisitions since 1995 and the large annual increase in value. It also shows that developing nations are accounting for a greater portion of the value of these deals.

Profiling the Largest Multinationals
We can see the enormous economic clout of multinational corporations when we compare the revenues of the world's largest companies to the value of goods and services generated by various countries. Figure 1.3 shows how the revenues of the top 10 multinationals of the *Fortune* Global 500 compare with a ranking of nations in terms of their national output. Our measure of national output is **gross domestic product (GDP)**—the total market value of all goods and ser-

> **gross domestic product (GDP)**
>
> *Value of all goods and services produced by a country's domestic economy over a one-year period.*

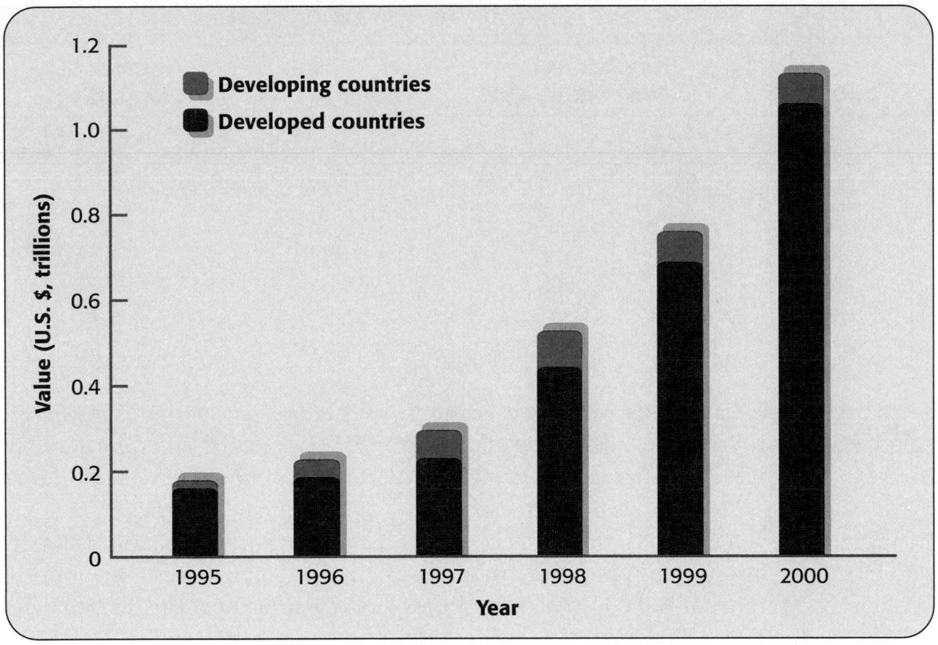

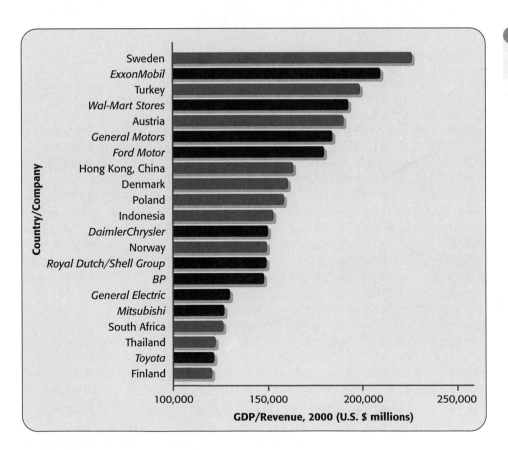

FIGURE 1.2

Cross-Border Mergers and Acquisitions

Developing countries
Developed countries

Value (U.S. $, trillions)

1995 1996 1997 1998 1999 2000

Year

FIGURE 1.3

Comparing the Global 500 with Selected Countries

Sweden
ExxonMobil
Turkey
Wal-Mart Stores
Austria
General Motors
Ford Motor
Hong Kong, China
Denmark
Poland
Indonesia
DaimlerChrysler
Norway
Royal Dutch/Shell Group
BP
General Electric
Mitsubishi
South Africa
Thailand
Toyota
Finland

Country/Company

100,000   150,000   200,000   250,000

GDP/Revenue, 2000 (U.S. $ millions)

TABLE 1.1 *Distribution of the Global 500*

Country	Number of Companies	Country	Number of Companies
United States	185	China	12
Japan	104	South Korea	11
France	37	Switzerland	11
Germany	34	Netherlands	9
Britain	33	All others	49
Canada	15		

vices produced by a country's domestic economy over a one-year period. This means that if ExxonMobil were a country, it would weigh in as a rich nation and rank ahead of Turkey. Even the 500th largest firm in the world, Sodexho Alliance of France (www.sodexho.com), has revenues larger than the GDPs of many countries.[39]

Some companies even have more employees than many of the smallest countries and island nations. China National Petroleum has 1,292,558 employees—the most of any company in the Global 500. Wal-Mart Stores (www.walmart.com) is second, with 1,244,000 employees. Finally, all types of industries are represented in the Global 500, ranging from food and beverages to mining and crude oil production.[40] Table 1.1 shows the international distribution of the Global 500.

ENTREPRENEURS AND SMALL BUSINESSES

Small companies are becoming increasingly active in international trade and investment. As a result, companies are exporting earlier and growing faster often with help from technology. Whereas traditional distribution channels often gave only large companies access to distant markets, electronic distribution is a cheap and effective alternative for many small businesses. Some small companies reside exclusively in cyberspace, reaching out to customers around the world solely through the World Wide Web. For instance, Alessandro Naldi's *Weekend a Firenze* (Weekend in Florence) Web site (www.waf.it/mall) offers global villagers more authentic Florentine products than they'll find in the scores of overpriced tourist shops crowded into downtown Florence. A Florentine himself, Naldi established his site to sell high-quality, authentic Italian merchandise made only in the many small factories of Tuscany. Currently, Weekend a Firenze averages 20,000 visitors each month, with 40 percent of its "guests" coming from Japan, 30 percent from the United States, and the remainder from Greece, Australia, Canada, Mexico, Saudi Arabia, and Italy.[41]

Unfortunately, many small businesses that are capable of exporting have not yet begun to do so. By some estimates, only 10 percent of companies in the United States with fewer than 100 employees export; the numbers are twice as high for companies of all sizes. Although there are certain real obstacles to exporting for small businesses—lack of investment capital, for example—some common myths create artificial obstacles. To explore some of these myths and the facts that dispute them, see the Entrepreneurial Focus titled "Untapped Potential: Four Myths That Keep Small Businesses from Export Success."

A FINAL WORD

The main theme of this chapter is that the world's national economies are becoming increasingly intertwined through the process of globalization. Cultural, political, legal, and economic events in one nation are increasingly impacting the lives of people in

ENTREPRENEURIAL FOCUS

Untapped Potential: Four Myths That Keep Small Businesses from Export Success

Myth 1: Only large companies can export successfully. Fact: Exporting increases sales and profitability for small firms and can make both manufacturers and distributors less dependent on the health of the domestic economy. It can also help businesses to avoid seasonal fluctuations in sales. Selling abroad also gives small businesses the advantage of competing with companies from other countries *before* they enter the domestic market.

Myth 2: Small businesses have no place to turn for export advice. Fact: Whether a company is just starting out or is already exporting profitably, the federal government has an assistance program to meet its needs. The U.S. Department of Commerce's Trade Information Center (**www.trade.gov/td/tic**) is a comprehensive resource for information on all federal export-assistance programs. Firms can get advice from international trade specialists on how to locate and use federal, state, local, and private-sector programs. They also receive free information on sources of market research, trade leads, financing, and trade events.

Myth 3: The licensing requirements needed for exporting are not worth the effort. Fact: "Most products," according to international trade specialist Linda Jones, "don't need export licenses. Exporters simply write 'NLR' for 'no license required' on their Shipper's Export Declaration. There is no onerous paperwork involved." A license is needed only when exporting certain restricted commodities (such as high-technology or defense-related goods) or when shipping to a country currently under U.S. trade embargo or other restriction. To find out about license requirements, companies can visit the Commerce Department's Bureau of Export Administration Web site at (**www.bxa.doc.gov**).

Myth 4: There is no export financing available for small businesses. Fact: The Small Business Administration (**www.sba.gov**) and the Export-Import Bank (**www.exim.gov**) work together in lending money to small businesses. Whereas the SBA is responsible for loan requests below $750,000, the Ex-Im Bank handles transactions over $750,000. The Overseas Private Investment Corporation (**www.opic.gov**) and the Trade and Development Agency (**www.tda.gov**) also help small and medium-size firms obtain financing for international projects.

---

other countries. As globalization penetrates further into national business environments, astute managers will try to take advantage of the opportunities it presents. By the same token, as globalization knits the world more tightly together, managers everywhere can benefit from a global mindset. Whether you work for a global firm in a large cosmopolitan city or for a small business in a rural town, the information in this book will help you to be a valuable employee, an effective manager, or a successful entrepreneur.

This chapter has simply introduced you to the study of international business—we hope you enjoy the rest of your journey. In Part II, we explore *national business environments*, showing how people's attitudes, values, beliefs, and institutions differ from one culture to another. We also explain how companies modify business practices and strategies when operating under different political, legal, and economic systems. We discuss the major components of the *international business environment* in Parts III and IV. We learn why trade and investment flow across borders and why governments try to encourage or discourage their movement. We also explore the process of regional economic integration sweeping the global economy and outline its implications for international companies. Finally, we explain how global financial markets and the global monetary system function and show how they influence companies' international business activities. In Part V, we describe the ways in which *international business management* differs from managing a purely domestic firm. We explain how a company plans and organizes itself for international operations, and how it decides on which markets to enter. We explore why different companies choose to enter markets in different ways, and how they market and produce their products. We close with a look at the importance of human resource management in an international setting.

There is a variety of additional material available on the Companion Website that accompanies this textbook. You can access this information by visiting the Website at (www.prenhall.com/wild).

summary

1 **Explain why it is important for future managers to have a *global mindset*.** A *global mindset* is a mental attitude characterized by tolerance and a minimal level of knowledge about international business management. Adopting a global mindset means breaking out of the boundaries placed on us by years of living within our respective cultures. *Tolerance* is a sensitive awareness of the beliefs and practices of other peoples that differ from or conflict with one's own. It means accepting the cultural peculiarities of another group of people as being equally as valid as your own. *International business knowledge and skills* required could include the ability to design effective promotional strategies abroad or manage an international sales force, for examples. A global mindset will increase the effectiveness of future managers.

2 **Describe the *global business environment* and identify its three main elements.** It is helpful to view international business as occurring within an integrated, *global business environment*. Three elements comprise the global business environment: (1) Separate *national business environments*, which include elements related to culture and systems of politics, law, and economics. (2) The *international business environment*, which is where the actions of consumers, workers, companies, financial institutions, and governments from different nations converge. Its two main components are international trade and investment activity, and the international financial system. (3) *International business management* differs from management of a domestic firm in nearly all respects. When a firm ventures into international business, environmental forces present it with many challenges and opportunities. Ethical dilemmas and the need to act in a socially responsible manner can present special challenges for an international company.

3 **Describe the process of *globalization* and how it affects *markets* and *production*.** The trend toward greater interdependence among national institutions and economies is called *globalization*. It is marked by "denationalization" in which national borders are becoming somewhat less relevant. It is affecting *markets* in several ways. Companies that sell global products can standardize aspects of their marketing activities to reduce costs. They are also able to explore international markets for their products when the home market becomes saturated. Finally, makers of seasonal products can rely on global markets to level their sales and income streams. Globalization also affects *production*. Firms take advantage of the globalization of production by accessing low-cost labor to make their goods more price-competitive. They can also benefit by gaining access to technical know-how or natural resources that are either nonexistent or too expensive at home.

4 **Identify the *two forces* causing globalization to expand.** The first main force behind increasing globalization is *falling barriers to trade and investment*. The world has made great strides in reducing trade barriers through institutions such as the *General Agreement on Tariffs and Trade* and the *World Trade Organization*—an international organization with the power to enforce the rules of international trade. Smaller groups of nations are also banding together in regional trade agreements to reduce trade barriers. *Technological innovation* is also a main force behind globalization. Companies are more able than ever to monitor their global business activities with the use of e-mail, videoconferencing, intranets, and extranets. These devices increase the speed with which companies can manage their far-flung activities. Innovations in transportation technologies are also making the shipment of goods between nations more efficient and dependable.

5 **Identify the *types of companies* that participate in international business.** Almost any company can participate in international business. Thanks to the Internet and other technologies that permit them to surmount such obstacles as prohibitively high advertising and distribution costs, many small businesses have become increasingly active in international trade and investment. However, large *multinational corporations (MNCs)* conduct most international business transactions. Multinationals dominate the international business news for two reasons: (1) They are highly visible because of their economic and political muscle and (2) their mergers and acquisitions are often valued in the billions of dollars.

questions for review

1. What is *international business*? Give several examples of international business transactions (other than those included in the chapter).
2. What does it mean to have a *global mindset*? Explain the importance of maintaining a global mindset.
3. Describe the *global business environment*. Explain how its three main elements interact.
4. What is the *national business environment*? Identify several elements that comprise it.
5. What is the *international business environment*? Identify its two main components.
6. How does *international business management* differ from managing a domestic company?
7. How do the issues of *ethical behavior* and *social responsibility* arise in the international marketplace? Explain how these two concepts differ from one another.
8. What do we mean by the term *globalization of markets*?
9. What do we mean by the term *globalization of production*?
10. What two major *forces* have led to greater globalization in markets and production? Explain each briefly.
11. What *types of companies* get involved in international business activities? Explain why large companies capture so much of the international business headlines.

questions for discussion

1. International businesspeople must think globally about production and sales opportunities. Many global managers will eventually find themselves living and working in cultures altogether different from their own. Many entrepreneurs will find themselves booking flights to places they had never heard of. What can companies do now to prepare their managers for these new markets? What can entrepreneurs and small businesses with limited resources do?
2. In the past, national governments greatly affected the pace of globalization through agreements to lower barriers to international trade and investment. Is the pace of change now outpacing the ability of governments to manage the global economy? Will national governments become more or less important to international business in the future? Explain your answer.
3. Information and communication technologies are developing at a faster rate than ever before. How have these technologies affected globalization? Give specific examples. Do you think globalization will continue until we all live in one "global village"? Why or why not?
4. Consider the following statement: "Globalization and the resulting increase in competition harm people as international companies play one government against another to get the best deal possible. Meanwhile, governments continually ask for greater concessions from their citizens, demanding that they work harder and longer for less pay." Do you agree? Why or why not?

in practice

Please read the brief article below and answer the questions that follow.

Lumenis to Acquire HGM

YOKNEAM, Israel—In a press release Thursday, Israel-based Lumenis Ltd. announced the purchase of HGM Medical Laser Systems Inc. of Salt Lake City, Utah for $9.7 million in cash. Lumenis manufactures pulsed light and laser-based systems for use in treatments such as hair removal, glaucoma, and removal of age spots and tattoos. HGM develops and manufactures medical laser devices.

Yacha Sutton, CEO and President of Lumenis, explained the motive for the purchase. "The acquisition of HGM is a good technology fit with Lumenis. HGM has developed specialized technologies to reduce the cost of manufacturing certain parts and accessories which can be integrated into high-end existing product lines and can provide the basis for future development."

Lumenis said that the transaction is part of the company's strategy to grow through both organic development and strategic acquisitions. The company also said that it already has integration teams reviewing product, distribution, and manufacturing rationalization.

1. In this chapter we discussed reasons why companies go international. What do you think are the main reasons for Lumenis' purchase decision? Identify as many potential reasons as you can.
2. Go to the Web site of Lumenis (**www.lumenis.com**) and locate information about the company's activities. In what locations around the world does it have production facilities? Where are its main markets? Based on the information contained on the Web site, report on one aspect of the company's activities that interests you.
3. Referring to the world atlas in the appendix to this chapter, locate Lumenis' home country. What is the nation's capital? What countries border the nation?
4. What variables in Israel's national business environment do you think might impact Lumenis' activities? What variables in the international business environment? How do you think all these variables affect the management of Lumenis or any other Israel-based company?

projects

1. Imagine that you own a company that manufactures cheap sunglasses. To lower production costs, you want to move your factory from your developed country to a low-wage country. Choose a prospective country to which you will move. What elements of the national business environment will affect your move? Are there any obstacles to overcome in the international business environment? How will managing your company be different when you undertake international activities? What challenges will you face in managing your new employees?

2. With a group of classmates, select a country that interests you. What does its flag look like? What do the various colors and symbols, if any, represent? Identify neighbors with which it shares borders. Give some important facts about the country, including its population, population density, land area, topography, climate, natural resources, and the locations of main industries. What products are produced there? Do any aspects of the natural environment help explain why it produces what it does? Present your findings to the class.

business case 1
MTV: GOING GLOBAL WITH A LOCAL BEAT

As goes the Buggles song, did "video kill the radio star"? Well, perhaps not, but no company exemplifies the maxim "Think globally, act locally" better than MTV (www.mtv.com). The company beams its irreverent and brash mix of music, news, and entertainment to 350 million homes in over 140 countries, including Brazil, Singapore, and India. Although style and format are largely driven by the U.S. youth culture, content is tailored entirely to local markets. And MTV has never grown old with its audience. Instead, it has remained very true to a specific demographic—young people between the ages of 18 and 24.

In 1987, MTV commanded an audience of 61 million in the United States. But because demand was leveling off, the company took the music revolution global by starting MTV Europe and MTV Australia. Through its experiences in Europe, MTV refined its mix of programming to become a global national brand with local variations. At first, it took a pan-European approach, marketing the same product to all European countries. MTV broadcast primarily British and U.S. music (both of which were topping the charts throughout Europe) and used European "veejays" who spoke English. The European network was a huge overnight success.

Seven years later, however, MTV had become the victim of its own success. Now it had to compete with a new crop of upstart rivals that tailored content to language, culture, and current events in specific countries. One successful competitor was Germany's VIVA, launched in 1993 and featuring German veejays and more German artists (like Fantastishen 4 and Scooter) than MTV Europe. Managers at MTV Networks were not overly concerned because MTV was still extremely popular. But they did realize they were losing their edge (and some customers) to the new national networks. What should the company do? Split up MTV Europe into MTV Germany and MTV Spain or continue doing business as it always had?

Because they had spent almost two decades building a global brand identity, MTV executives initially rejected that idea. But little by little they changed their collective mind. They decided to move forward because a certain technological innovation made it possible for MTV to think globally and act locally at very little cost. The breakthrough was digital compression technology, which allows suppliers to multiply the number of services offered on a single satellite feed. "Where there were three or four services," explained one MTV official, "now we can broadcast six or eight."

Today, teens all over the world have their MTV cake and eat it, too. German teens, for instance, see shows created and produced in Germany—in German—along with the usual generous helpings of U.S., British, and international music and the ever-popular duo Beavis and Butthead. And there's an added side benefit for MTV: National advertisers who had shunned the channel during its pan-European days are now coming onboard to beam ads targeted specifically to their consumers.

Now, more than 20 years since MTV planted its flag on the pop-culture moon, the beat goes on. "It's the only television entity of any kind that ever had a generation named after it," says Robert Thompson, professor of media and popular culture at Syracuse University. "We don't even have the CNN generation, but we have the MTV generation."

thinking globally

1. The past decade has witnessed a growing similarity in the attitudes and spending habits of youthful consumers around the world. As one journalist puts it, "It may still be conventional wisdom to 'think globally and act locally,' but in the youth market, it is increasingly a case of one size fits all." Do you agree or disagree? Why or why not?

2. Some people are concerned that teens exposed to large doses of U.S. youth culture on MTV networks will begin to identify less and less with their own societies. Others worry that teenage consumers in developing countries want more and more Western goods that they can't afford. MTV's response

to such criticism: "It's just fun," says one network executive. "It's only TV." What do you think? Are there dangers in broadcasting U.S. programs and ads to both developed and developing countries?

3. Digital compression technology made it possible for MTV to program over a global network. Can you think of any other technological innovations that have helped companies to think globally and act locally?

4. Advances in technology are often accompanied by evolution in the entertainment industry. How do you think new technologies such as the DVD player and Palm Pilot will affect entertainment in the years to come?

a question of ethics

1. We often characterize ethical dilemmas as "right-versus-wrong" situations. But ethical dilemmas often involve deciding between two options that could both be argued to be the correct action to take. For instance, should you tell the *truth* about a superior's wrongdoing, or should you remain *loyal* to your boss? Can you think of an ethical dilemma in which an international executive might face a tough choice between "right" and "right"? Have you ever faced such a choice? Do you think that people can be made to act ethically?

2. In one widely publicized event, Nike called on civil rights leader Andrew Young to look into its labor practices at Asian plants in order to determine if the company was adhering to its own code of ethical conduct. After a month-long investigation, Young reported no evidence of widespread or systematic mistreatment of Nike workers abroad. Critics charged that the report was shallow because Young admitted to spending only 3 hours in any factory and was always accompanied by Nike officials. They were also skeptical because Young presented his findings to Nike's board and senior management a week before making them public. If you were the CEO of Nike, how would you respond to these criticisms? Do you think that there are more effective or objective means of monitoring a company's international activities? If so, what are they?

3. The North American Free Trade Agreement (NAFTA) requires the United States to spend money for environmental cleanup. But some critics charge that the U.S. government and that of Mexico are not doing enough to safeguard the environment along the two nations' borders. Among other things, they charge contamination of the dry bed of the Colorado River. Do you think that the companies that have set up in San Luis Rio Colorado bear any responsibility for the environmental problems there? What can business leaders do if governments ignore their environmental responsibilities?

APPENDIX
WORLD ATLAS

This atlas presents the global landscape in a series of maps designed to assist your understanding of global business. By knowing the locations of countries and the distances between them, managers in the global marketplace are able to make more informed decisions. Knowing the geography of a place also gives managers insight into the culture of the people living there. Because international managers must know where borders meet, this atlas captures the most recent changes in national political boundaries.

As the global marketplace continues to absorb previously isolated business environments, each one of us needs a thorough grasp of the global landscape. Familiarize yourself with each of the maps in this appendix and then try to answer the following 20 questions. We urge you to return to this atlas frequently in order to refresh your memory of the global landscape and especially when you encounter the name of an unfamiliar city or country.

Map Exercises

1. Which of the following countries border the Atlantic Ocean?
   a. Bolivia   d. Japan
   b. Australia   e. United States
   c. South Africa

2. Which of the following countries are found in Africa?
   a. Guyana   d. Pakistan
   b. Morocco   e. Niger
   c. Egypt

3. Which one of the following countries does *not* border the Pacific Ocean?
   a. Australia   d. Mexico
   b. Venezuela   e. Peru
   c. Japan

4. Prague is the capital city of:
   a. Uruguay
   b. Czech Republic
   c. Portugal
   d. Tunisia
   e. Hungary

5. If transportation costs for getting your product from your market to Japan are high, which of the following countries might be good places to locate a manufacturing facility?
   a. Thailand
   b. Philippines
   c. South Africa
   d. Indonesia
   e. Portugal

6. Seoul is the capital city of:
   a. Vietnam
   b. Cambodia
   c. Malaysia
   d. China
   e. South Korea

7. Turkey, Romania, Ukraine, and Russia border the body of water called the _____ Sea.

8. Thailand shares borders with:
   a. Cambodia
   b. Pakistan
   c. Singapore
   d. Malaysia
   e. Indonesia

9. Which of the following countries border no major ocean or sea?
   a. Austria
   b. Paraguay
   c. Switzerland
   d. Niger
   e. all of the above

10. Oslo is the capital city of:
    a. Germany
    b. Canada
    c. Brazil
    d. Australia
    e. Norway

11. Chile is located in:
    a. Africa
    b. Asia
    c. the Northern Hemisphere
    d. South America
    e. Central Europe

12. Saudi Arabia shares borders with:
    a. Jordan
    b. Kuwait
    c. Iraq
    d. United Arab Emirates
    e. all of the above

13. The body of water located between Sweden and Estonia is the _____ Sea.

14. Which of the following countries are located on the Mediterranean Sea?
    a. Italy
    b. Croatia
    c. Turkey
    d. France
    e. Portugal

15. The distance between Sydney (Australia) and Tokyo (Japan) is shorter than that between:
    a. Tokyo and Cape Town (South Africa)
    b. Sydney and Hong Kong (China)
    c. Tokyo and London (England)
    d. Sydney and Jakarta (Indonesia)
    e. all of the above

16. Madrid is the capital city of (capitals are designated with red dots):
    a. Madagascar
    b. Italy
    c. Mexico
    d. Spain
    e. United States

17. Which of the following countries is *not* located in central Asia?
    a. Afghanistan
    b. Uzbekistan
    c. Turkmenistan
    d. Kazakhstan
    e. Suriname

18. If you were shipping your products from your production facility in Pakistan to market in Australia, they would likely cross the _____ Ocean.

19. Papua New Guinea, Guinea-Bissau, and Guinea are alternative names for the same country.
    a. true
    b. false

20. Which of the following countries are island nations?
    a. New Zealand
    b. Madagascar
    c. Japan
    d. Australia
    e. all of the above

Answers

1. c. South Africa, e. United States; 2. b. Morocco, c. Egypt, e. Niger; 3. b. Venezuela; 4. b. Czech Republic; 5. a. Thailand, b. Philippines, d. Indonesia; 6. e. South Korea; 7. Black; 8. a. Cambodia, d. Malaysia; 9. e. all of the above; 10. e. Norway; 11. d. South America; 12. e. all of the above; 13. Baltic; 14. a. Italy, c. Turkey, d. France; 15. a. Tokyo and Cape Town (South Africa), c. Tokyo and London (England); 16. d. Spain; 17. e. Suriname; 18. Indian; 19. b. false; 20. e. all of the above.

Self-Assessment

If you scored 15 correct answers or more, well done: You are well prepared for your international business journey. If you scored fewer than 8 correct answers, you may wish to review this atlas before moving on to Chapter 2.

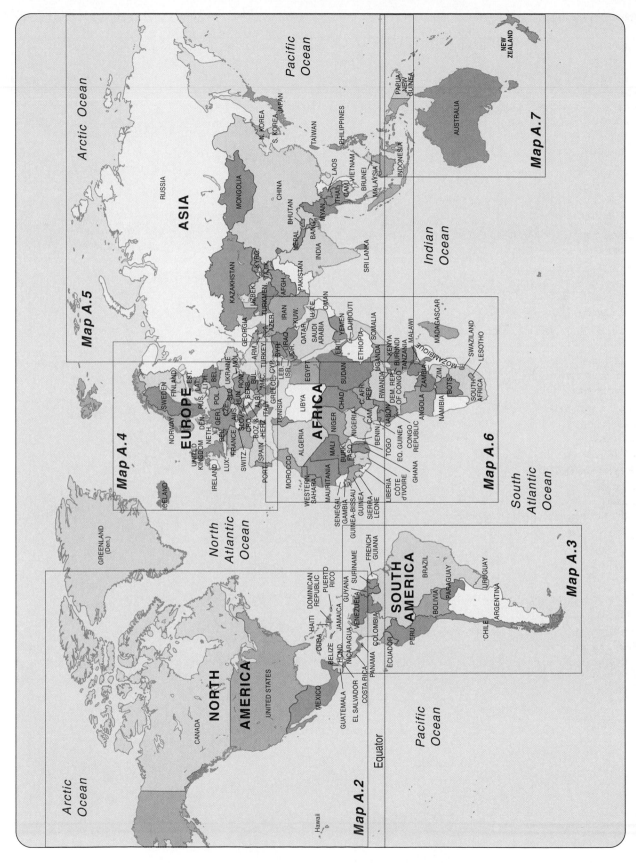

MAP A.1 **The World in 2002** This global view identifies each continent and acts as references for the six maps that follow.

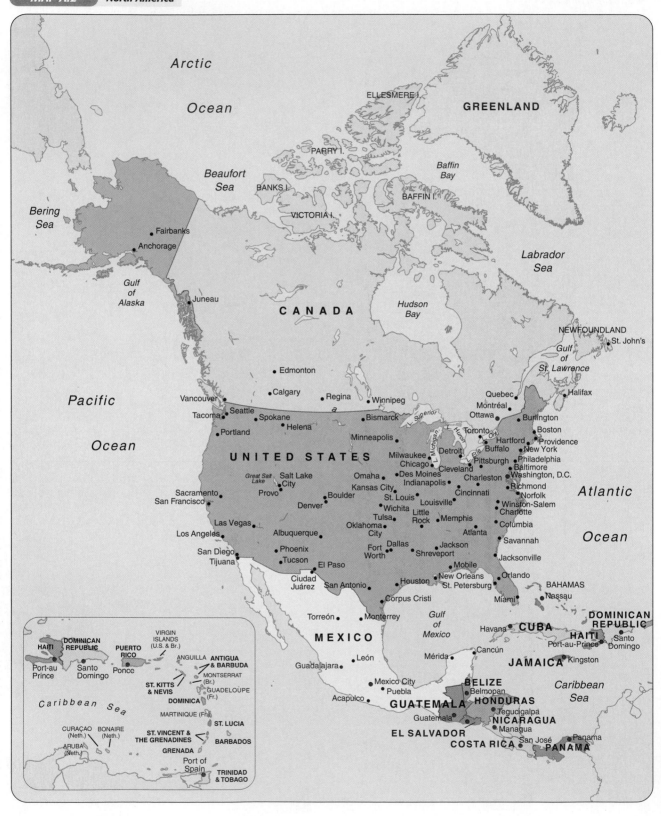

Arctic

Ocean

ELLESMERE I.

GREENLAND

PARRY I.

Baffin Bay

Beaufort Sea

BANKS I.

BAFFIN I.

VICTORIA I.

Bering Sea

• Fairbanks
• Anchorage

Labrador Sea

Gulf of Alaska

• Juneau

C A N A D A

Hudson Bay

NEWFOUNDLAND
• St. John's

Gulf of St. Lawrence

• Edmonton

Pacific

• Calgary

• Regina

• Winnipeg

Quebec •
Montréal •
Ottawa •

• Halifax

Vancouver •
Tacoma •
Seattle •
• Spokane
• Helena

• Bismarck

L. Superior

Toronto •
Buffalo •
Burlington •
Boston •
Hartford • Providence •

Ocean

Portland •

Minneapolis •

L. Michigan
L. Huron
Detroit •
L. Erie •
Pittsburgh •

New York •
Philadelphia •
Baltimore •
Washington, D.C.

U N I T E D   S T A T E S

Milwaukee •
Chicago •

Cleveland •

Great Salt Lake
Salt Lake • City
• Provo

Omaha •
Des Moines •
Indianapolis •
Cincinnati •

Charleston •

Richmond •
Norfolk •

Atlantic

Sacramento •
San Francisco •

Kansas City •
St. Louis •

Louisville •

Winston-Salem •
Charlotte •

Boulder •
Denver •

Wichita •
Little
Rock •
Memphis •

Columbia •

Ocean

Las Vegas •

Tulsa •

Oklahoma City •

Atlanta •

Savannah •

Los Angeles •

Albuquerque •

Dallas •
Fort Worth •
Jackson •
Shreveport •

Jacksonville •

San Diego •
Tijuana •

• Phoenix
• Tucson

El Paso •

Mobile •

Orlando •

Ciudad Juárez •

San Antonio •

New Orleans •
Houston •
St. Petersburg •

BAHAMAS
• Nassau

Corpus Cristi •

Miami •

Torreón •

Monterrey •

Gulf of Mexico

DOMINICAN
REPUBLIC

Havana •
CUBA

MEXICO

• León

Cancún •

Mérida •

Guadalajara •

Acapulco •

Mexico City •
• Puebla

GUATEMALA

Guatemala •

BELIZE
Belmopan •
HONDURAS
Tegucigalpa •
NICARAGUA
Managua •

Port-au-Prince •
HAITI
• Santo Domingo

JAMAICA • Kingston

Caribbean Sea

EL SALVADOR

San José •
COSTA RICA

• Panama
PANAMA

Inset (Caribbean):

HAITI
DOMINICAN REPUBLIC
Port-au-Prince
Santo Domingo

PUERTO RICO
Ponce

VIRGIN ISLANDS (U.S. & Br.)

ANGUILLA
ANTIGUA & BARBUDA

MONTSERRAT (Br.)

ST. KITTS & NEVIS

GUADELOÙPE (Fr.)

DOMINICA

MARTINIQUE (Fr.)

ST. LUCIA

CURAÇAO (Neth.)   BONAIRE (Neth.)

ST. VINCENT & THE GRENADINES

BARBADOS

ARUBA (Neth.)

GRENADA

Caribbean   Sea

Port of Spain

TRINIDAD & TOBAGO

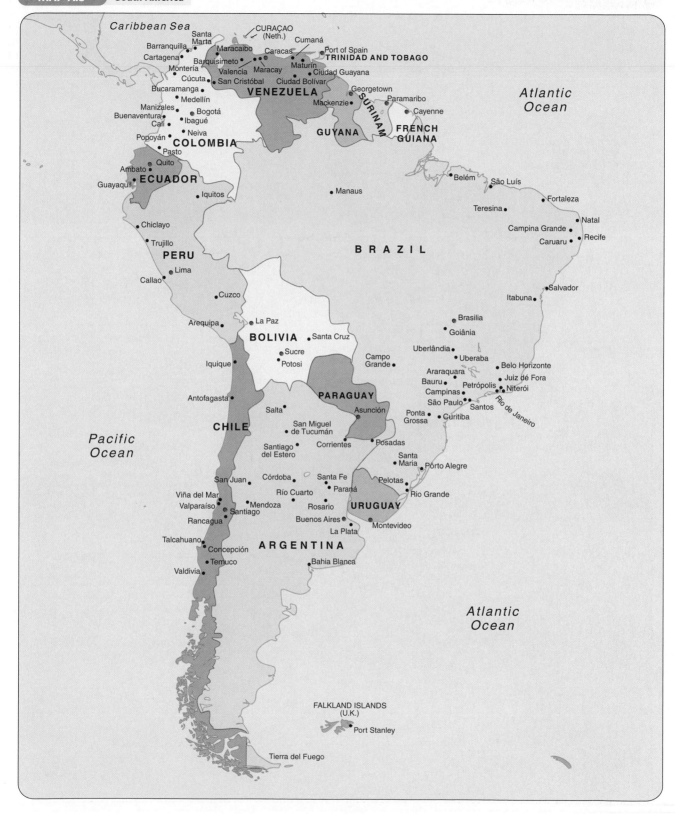

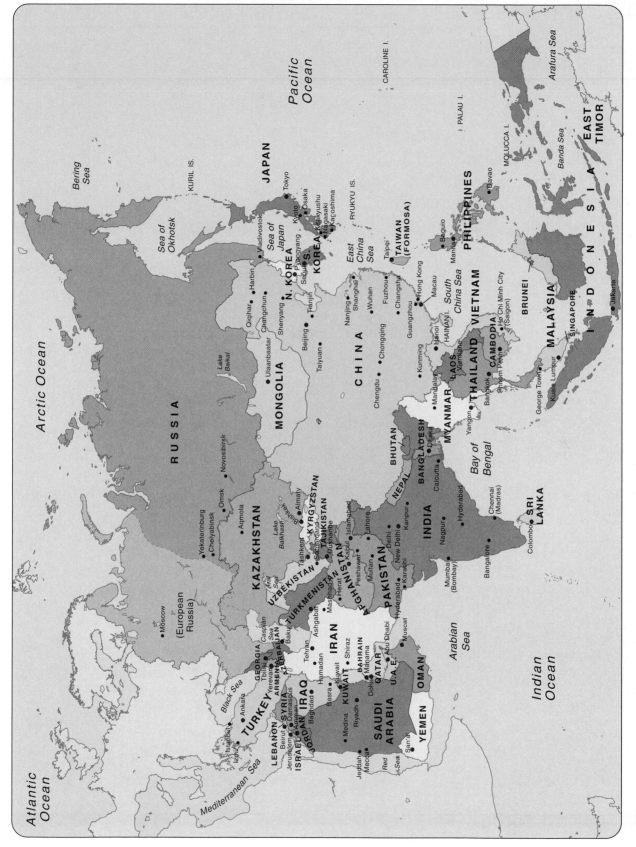

Atlantic Ocean

Arctic Ocean

Bering Sea

Pacific Ocean

CAROLINE I.

PALAU I.

Arafura Sea

EAST TIMOR

Banda Sea

MOLUCCA I.

KURIL IS.

Sea of Okhotsk

JAPAN

•Tokyo

•Vladivostok

Sea of Japan

•Kyoto

•Osaka

•Kitakyushu

•Nagasaki

•Kacoshima

RYUKYU IS.

Baguio•

PHILIPPINES

•Davao

•Manila

•Harbin

•Qiqihar

•Changchun

•Shenyang

N. KOREA

•Pyongyang

KOREA

S. KOREA

•Seoul

East China Sea

TAIWAN (FORMOSA)

•Taipei

•Beijing

•Tianjin

•Nanjing

•Shanghai

•Wuhan

•Fuzhou

Macau

Hong Kong

South China Sea

HAINAN I.

BRUNEI

•Ulaanbaatar

MONGOLIA

Lake Baikal

•Taiyuan

C H I N A

•Chengdu

•Chongqing

•Changsha

•Guangzhou

•Kunming

VIETNAM

•Hanoi

LAOS

•Mandalay

MYANMAR

•Vientiane

THAILAND

•Bangkok

CAMBODIA

•Phnom Penh

Ho Chi Minh City (Saigon)

MALAYSIA

•George Town

•Kuala Lumpur

SINGAPORE

•Jakarta

I N D O N E S I A

•Novosibirsk

R U S S I A

(European Russia)

•Moscow

•Yekaterinburg

•Chelyabinsk

•Omsk

•Aqmola

KAZAKHSTAN

Aral Sea

Lake Balkhash

•Almaty

Bishkek

KYRGYZSTAN

•Tashkent

UZBEKISTAN

•Samarqand

TAJIKISTAN

•Dushanbe

TURKMENISTAN

•Ashgabat

•Herat

AFGHANISTAN

•Kabul

•Mashhad

•Peshawar

PAKISTAN

•Islamabad

•Lahore

•Multan

•Hyderabad

•Karachi

BHUTAN

NEPAL

BANGLADESH

•Calcutta

•Dhaka

I N D I A

•Delhi

•Kanpur

New Delhi•

•Nagpur

•Hyderabad

•Mumbai (Bombay)

•Chennai (Madras)

•Bangalore

SRI LANKA

•Colombo

Bay of Bengal

Arabian Sea

Indian Ocean

Caspian Sea

•Baku

GEORGIA

•Tbilisi

ARMENIA

•Yerevan

AZERBAIJAN

•Tehran

IRAN

•Hamadan

•Shiraz

Black Sea

TURKEY

•Ankara

•Istanbul

•Izmir

Mediterranean Sea

SYRIA

LEBANON

•Beirut

•Damascus

ISRAEL

•Jerusalem

•Amman

JORDAN

IRAQ

•Baghdad

•Basra

KUWAIT

•Kuwait

BAHRAIN

•Manama

QATAR

•Doha

U.A.E.

•Abu Dhabi

OMAN

•Muscat

SAUDI ARABIA

•Riyadh

•Medina

•Mecca

•Jeddah

YEMEN

•Sana

Red Sea

MAP A.5 Asia

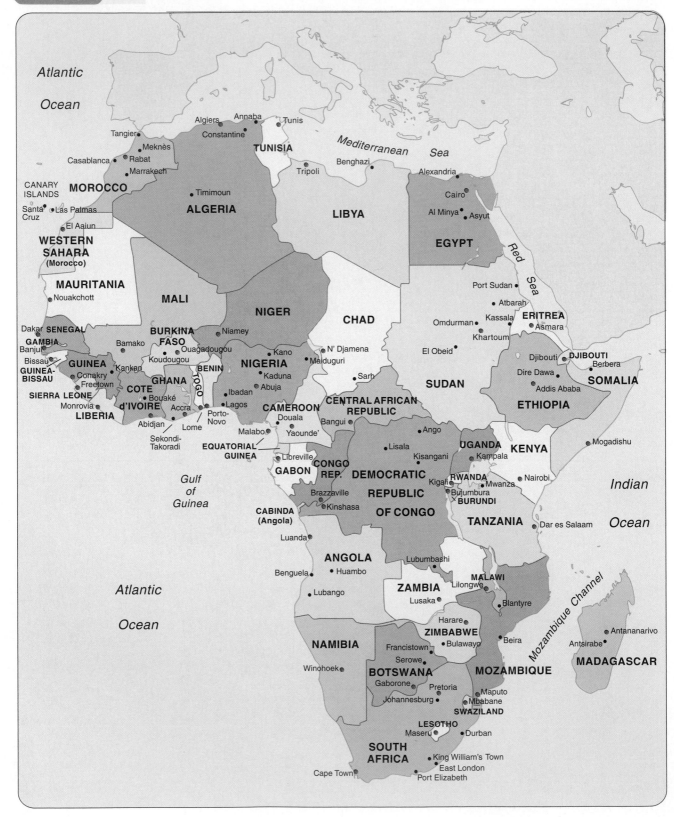

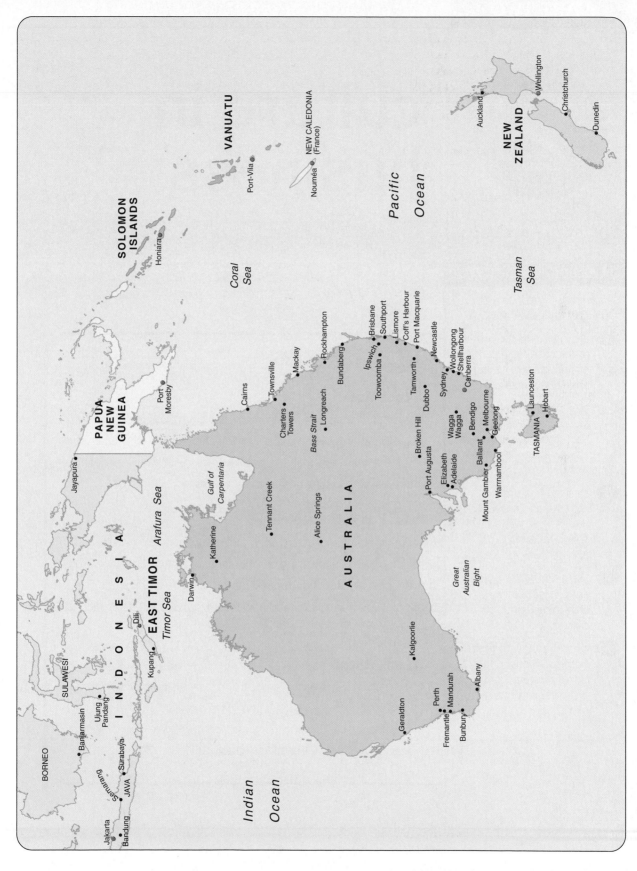

MAP A.7   *Oceania*

2 culture in business

After studying this chapter, you should be able to

1 Describe *culture,* and explain the significance of both national culture and *subcultures.*

2 Identify the *components of culture,* and describe their impact on business activities around the world.

3 Describe *cultural change,* and explain how companies and culture affect one another.

4 Explain how the *physical environment* and *technology* influence culture.

5 Describe the two main *frameworks* used to classify cultures and explain their practical use.

BEACONS

A Look Back
CHAPTER 1 introduced us to international business and the impact of globalization. We learned why companies "go international" and about the many external and internal forces with which companies must deal when doing business internationally.

A Look at This Chapter
This chapter introduces the important role of culture in international business. We explore the main elements of culture and show how they affect business policies and practices. We learn different methods of classifying cultures and how these methods can be applied to business.

A Look Ahead
CHAPTER 3 describes the political and legal systems of nations. We learn how these systems differ from one country to another and how they influence international business operations. We also show how managers can reduce the effects of political risk.

Hold the Pork, Please!

BONN, Germany—"Kids and grownups love it so, the happy world of Haribo!" So goes the phrase that drives sales of the Gummi Bear candies made by Germany-based Haribo AG (**www.haribo.com**). This little candy, with names such as Gold Bears and Horror Mix and available in 46 shapes including Coke bottles and glowworms, is enjoyed worldwide. Haribo supplies 83 countries from its 17 factories at home and abroad, producing 70 million gummi bears a day.

But despite its success, Haribo was not meeting the needs of a globally dispersed subculture potentially worth $2 billion annually. The culprit: the pork-based substance that gives the candy its sticky, rubbery feel made the candy off-limits to Muslims and Jews who adhere to a strict religious diet. So the company set out on a 4-year mission to create a candy free of the pork-based gelatin so that it conformed to Islamic and Judaic dietary restrictions.

"The first time we made it, we got a marmalade you could spread on bread," reported Neville Finlay, the British exporter who ships the new product under his own brand. "And at the other extreme was something you could fill a swimming pool with and drive a truck across," he added. Haribo found success eventually with a bacteria-based compound already common in salad dressings and sauces. But then a local supplier committed a language blunder—a common occurrence in international business. The printing on the first packages of candies destined for Hebrew communities was backward—Hebrew is read right to left, not left to right, like English.

Today, production is going smoothly. Haribo even has a Jewish rabbi (for *kosher* candies) or a Muslim cleric (for *halal* candies) inspect ingredients and oversee production to ensure that it adheres to religious customs. In this chapter you will learn how important culture is in interna-

tional business and how companies can avoid making cultural snafus. As you read through this chapter, think of the cultural differences you've experienced while traveling abroad or when you've met someone from another culture.[1]

This chapter is the first of three that discuss aspects of a nation's business environment (culture, politics, law, and economics) that affect international business activities. We begin our study of international business by examining the business environment because of its strong influence on the way business is conducted in different countries. In fact, many successes in international business can be traced directly to a deep understanding of some aspect of a people's cultural, political, legal, or economic environments.

The first step in the process of analyzing a nation's potential as a host for international business activity is to assess its overall business climate. This means addressing some important questions, such as the following. What language(s) do the people speak? What is the climate like? Are the local people open to new ideas and new ways of doing business? Do government officials and the people want our business? Is the political situation stable enough so that our assets and employees are not placed at unacceptable levels of risk? Answers to these kinds of questions—plus statistical data on items such as income level and labor costs—allow businesses to evaluate the attractiveness of a particular location as a place for doing business.

Cultural understanding is crucial when a company does business in another country. All business activity revolves around people, whether they are individual consumers, entrepreneurs, or the employees of a huge global firm. When buyers and sellers from around the world come together to conduct business, they bring with them different backgrounds, expectations, and ways of communicating—in other words, culture.

This chapter describes *culture* in the context of international business. We explore the ways in which social institutions, religion, language, and other elements of culture affect international business activities. We learn how each nation's culture affects such things as its business practices and international competitiveness.

WHAT IS CULTURE?

culture
Set of values, beliefs, rules, and institutions held by a specific group of people.

When traveling in other countries, we often perceive differences in the way people live and work. In the United States dinner is commonly eaten around 6:00 P.M.; in Spain it's not served until 8:00 or 9:00 P.M. In the United States people shop in large supermarkets once a week; Italians shop in smaller local grocery stores every day. Essentially, we are experiencing differences in **culture**—the set of values, beliefs, rules, and institutions held by a specific group of people.[2] Culture is a highly complex portrait of a people. It includes everything from high tea in England, to the tropical climate of Barbados, to Mardi Gras in Brazil, to segregation of the sexes in Saudi Arabian schools. As you will see later in this chapter, the main components of any culture include its *aesthetics*, *values* and *attitudes*, *manners* and *customs*, *social structure*, *religion*, *personal communication*, *education*, and *physical* and *material environments*.

ethnocentricity
Belief that one's own ethnic group or culture is superior to that of others.

Accommodating Culture: Avoiding Ethnocentricity   **Ethnocentricity** is the belief that one's own ethnic group or culture is superior to that of others. It causes people to *view other cultures in terms of their own*, causing them to overlook important human and environmental differences among cultures.

International business projects can be undermined by ethnocentricity when a firm's employees are insensitive to cultural nuances. The archives of business contain stories of many international projects that failed because companies tried to change something at a factory or office that was fundamental to a culture, and therefore was resisted by local government, labor, or the general public.

Today globalization demands that businesspeople approach other cultures far differently than they did in the past. In particular, new technologies and their applications allow many suppliers and buyers to treat the world as a single, interconnected, global marketplace. Because globalization is bringing people face to face with each other more and more often, companies need employees who are not blinded by ethnocentricity.

Understanding Culture: Developing Cultural Literacy   Globalization demands that people directly involved in international business exhibit a certain degree of **cultural literacy**—detailed knowledge about a culture that enables a person to function effectively within it. Cultural literacy improves the ability to manage employees, market products, and conduct negotiations in other countries. Global brand names like GAP (www.gap.com) and Starbucks (www.starbucks.com) provide a competitive advantage, but cultural differences continue to force modifications to some aspect of the business to suit local markets. Because culture dictates that many products incorporate local tastes and preferences, cultural literacy brings us closer to customer needs and desires and improves our competitiveness. In Chapter 16 you will learn about the different types of cultural training used to develop cultural literacy.

> *cultural literacy*
> *Detailed knowledge about a culture that enables a person to function effectively within it.*

NATIONAL CULTURE AND SUBCULTURES

Whether rightly or wrongly, we tend to invoke the concept of the *nation-state* when speaking of culture. In other words, we usually refer to British and Indonesian cultures as if all Britons and all Indonesians were culturally identical. Why? Because we have been conditioned to think in terms of *national culture*. But this is at best a generalization. For example, in Great Britain campaigns for Scottish and Welsh independence continue to gain momentum. In remote parts of Indonesia, people build homes in the treetops even as other parts of the nation pursue ambitious economic development programs. Let's now take a closer look at national cultures and the diversity that lies within them.

National Culture   Nation-states *support* and *promote* the concept of a national culture by building museums and monuments to preserve the legacies of important events and people. In so doing, they affirm the importance of national culture to their citizens and organizations. Nation-states also intervene in business to help *preserve* their national cultures. Most nations, for example, regulate culturally sensitive sectors of the economy, such as filmmaking and broadcasting. France continues to voice fears that its language is being tainted with English and its media with U.S. programming. To stem the English invasion, French laws limit the use of English in product packaging and storefront signs. At peak listening times, at least 40 percent of all radio station programming must be reserved for French artists. Similar laws apply to television broadcasting.[3] The French government even fined the local branch of a U.S. university for failing to provide a French translation on its English-language site on the World Wide Web.

Cities, too, get involved in enhancing national cultural attractions, often for economic reasons. Lifestyle enhancements to a city can help it attract companies who benefit by having an easier task retaining top employees. The Guggenheim museum in Bilbao, Spain (www.guggenheim-bilbao.es), designed by Frank Gehry, has revived that old Basque industrial city. Hong Kong's government is enhancing cultural attractions to lure businesses that may locate elsewhere in the region, such as Singapore and Shanghai, China.[4]

Many companies take advantage of the public relations value of supporting national culture. Today, some of India's most precious historical monuments and sites are crumbling due to neglect and the corrosive effect of pollutants. Such sites include the

Today, the government of India is facing financial difficulties in properly maintaining India's historic monuments, like the Taj Mahal shown here. So private companies in India are restoring these sites to their original splendor and performing routine maintenance. In return, these companies hope to build goodwill with consumers that will translate into greater sales. Do you know of companies that sponsor the upkeep of historic sites or public places in your city?

tomb of Mughal Emperor Humayun and the Taj Mahal itself. Although the government budgets $30 million per year to maintain its monuments, proper upkeep requires 10 times that amount. That is why companies are actively assisting the government in privatizing the maintenance of India's roughly 5,000 sites. The government is released from the financial burden of upkeep, while companies earn goodwill among tourists and the general public.[5]

Subcultures   A group of people who share a unique way of life within a larger, dominant culture is called a **subculture**. A subculture can differ from the dominant culture in language, race, lifestyle, values, attitudes, or other characteristics.

Although subcultures exist in all nations, they are often glossed over by our *impressions* of cultures. But companies must nevertheless be mindful of subcultures when formulating business strategies. For example, the customary portrait of Chinese culture often ignores the fact that the total population of China is comprised of more than 50 distinct ethnic groups. Decisions regarding product design, packaging, and advertising must consider each group's distinct culture. Marketing directed at Tibetans must respect their unique history and ethnic pride. Tibetans would certainly resent any campaign referring to them as Chinese. Marketing campaigns in China must also acknowledge that Chinese dialects in the Shanghai and Canton regions differ from those in the country's interior and that not everyone is fluent in the official Mandarin dialect.

A multitude of subcultures also exist within the United States. The most recent U.S. Census revealed that of slightly more than 280 million U.S. residents, nearly 80 million are black, Hispanic, and Asian. Because these groups represent an estimated $1 trillion in spending power, marketers are keenly interested in their tastes, preferences, and buying habits. One company that's had success with Hispanics, for example, is Mott's, Inc. (**www.motts.com**). The company's Mott's Juice, Hawaiian Punch, and Clamato brands have been popular with Hispanic consumers—despite a lack of detailed data on Hispanic purchasing habits. One technique Mott's used to reach Hispanics was to beef up marketing in those cities in which Latin American bands such as Banda El Recodo and Los Tucanes were touring.[6]

Political boundaries do not always correspond to cultural boundaries—subcultures sometimes exist across national borders. People who live in different nations but who share the same subculture can have more in common with one another than with their

subculture
Group of people who share a unique way of life within a larger, dominant culture.

fellow nationals. Arab culture, for instance, extends from northwest Africa to the Middle East, with pockets of Arabs in many European countries and the United States. Because Arabs share a common language and tend to share purchasing behaviors related to Islamic religious beliefs, marketing to Arab subcultures can sometimes be accomplished with a single marketing campaign. The company profile at the start of this chapter showed us how Haribo (www.haribo.com) worked to make its product acceptable to Muslim (and Jewish) consumers worldwide.

Firms must also take special care when marketing medicines, dangerous chemicals, and other products requiring detailed instructions. If a product's labels and warnings cannot be read and understood by all subcultures, it might inflict physical harm rather than satisfy a need.

COMPONENTS OF CULTURE

Both the actions of nation-states and the presence of subcultures help define the culture of a group of people. But a people's culture also includes what they consider beautiful and tasteful, their underlying beliefs, their traditional habits, and the ways in which they relate to one another and their surroundings. Let's now take a detailed look at each main component of culture: *aesthetics*, *values* and *attitudes*, *manners* and *customs*, *social structure*, *religion*, *personal communication*, *education*, and *physical* and *material environments*.

AESTHETICS

What a culture considers to be in "good taste" in the arts (including music, painting, dance, drama, and architecture), the imagery evoked by certain expressions, and even the symbolism of certain colors is called **aesthetics**.

Aesthetics are important when a firm considers doing business in another culture. The selection of appropriate colors for advertising, product packaging, and even work uniforms can enhance chances of success. For instance, green is a favorable color in Islam and adorns the national flags of most Islamic nations, including Jordan, Pakistan, and Saudi Arabia. That is why product packaging is often green in these countries—companies want to take advantage of the emotional attachment to the color. Across much of Asia, on the other hand, green is associated with sickness. In Europe, Mexico, and the United States, the color of death and mourning is black; in Japan and most of Asia, it's white.

Shoe manufacturer Nike (www.nike.com) recently experienced firsthand the importance of imagery and symbolism in international marketing. The company emblazoned a new line of shoes with the word "Air" written to resemble flames or heat rising off blacktop. The shoes had names including *Air Bakin'*, *Air Melt*, *Air Grill*, and *Air B-Que*. But what Nike did not realize was that the squiggly lines of the logo resembled Arabic script for "Allah," the Arabic name for God. Under threat of a worldwide boycott by Muslims who considered it a sacrilege, Nike recalled the shoes and agreed to build several playgrounds in Muslim communities as part of its apology.

The importance of aesthetics is just as great when going international using the Internet. A company called Web of Culture (www.webofculture.com) based in Burlingame, California, is helping companies cross the cultural divide on the Web. The company is dedicated to educating corporations on how to globalize their Internet presence. The company provides professional guidance on how to adapt Web sites to account for cultural preferences such as color scheme, imagery, and slogans.[7] For information on how small companies can tailor a Web site to suit local aesthetics and other cultural variables, see the Entrepreneurial Focus titled, "Give Your Web Site a Local Feel."

Finally, music is also deeply embedded in culture and should be considered when developing promotions. It can be used in clever and creative ways or in ways that are

aesthetics
What a culture considers to be in "good taste" in the arts, the imagery evoked by certain expressions, and the symbolism of certain colors.

Give Your Web Site a Local Feel

When going global with an Internet presence, the more a company localizes, the better. Web surfers want an online experience corresponding to their cultural context offline. Here are some pointers for companies when first launching an online presence. Do the international Web sites you visit follow these rules?

➡ **Choose Colors Carefully.** A black-and-white Web site is fine for many countries, but in Asia visitors may think you are inviting them to a funeral. In Japan and across Europe, Web sites in pastel color schemes often work best.

➡ **Select Numbers with Care.** Many Chinese-speaking cultures consider the number four unlucky while eight and nine symbolize prosperity. Be careful that your Web site address and phone numbers do not send the wrong signal.

➡ **Watch the Clock.** If marketing to countries that use the 24-hour clock, adjust times stated on the site so it reads, "Call between 9:00 and 17:00," instead of, "Call between 9 A.M. and 5 P.M."

➡ **Mind Your Tongue.** English in Britain is different from that in the United States, Spanish in Spain is dif-

ferent from that in Mexico, and French in France is different from that in Quebec. Avoid slang to lessen the impact of such differences, or go further and offer different site versions for each language.

➡ **Wave the Flag Cautiously.** Be careful using national flags as symbols for buttons to click to see different language versions of your site. British visitors to your site may be put off if you use a U.S. flag to signify the English version of the site—likewise for the diverse Spanish- and Chinese-speaking populations.

➡ **Do the Math.** Provide conversions into local currencies for buyer convenience. For online ordering, be sure your site calculates accurately any shipping costs, tax rates, tariffs, and so on. Also allow enough blanks on the order form to accommodate longer international addresses.

➡ **Get Feedback.** Finally, talk with customers or prospective customers to know what they want to do or buy on your Web site. Then test the Web site to ensure it functions properly.

offensive to the local population. The architecture of buildings and other structures should also be researched to avoid making cultural blunders attributable to the symbolism of certain shapes and forms.

VALUES AND ATTITUDES

values
Ideas, beliefs, and customs to which people are emotionally attached.

Ideas, beliefs, and customs to which people are emotionally attached are **values**. Values include things like honesty, marital faithfulness, freedom, and responsibility.

Values are important to business because they affect a people's work ethic and desire for material possessions. Whereas certain cultures (say, in Singapore) value hard work and material success, others (in Greece, for instance) value leisure and a modest lifestyle. The United Kingdom and United States value individual freedom, whereas Japan and South Korea value group consensus. Because values are so important to both individuals and groups, the influx of values from other cultures can be fiercely resisted. Muslims believe drugs, alcohol, and certain kinds of music and literature will undermine important values. Nations under Islamic law (including Iran and Saudi Arabia) exact severe penalties for the possession of items such as drugs and alcohol.

attitudes
Positive or negative evaluations, feelings, and tendencies that individuals harbor toward objects or concepts.

Attitudes are positive or negative evaluations, feelings, and tendencies that individuals harbor toward objects or concepts. Attitudes reflect underlying values. For instance, a Westerner would be expressing an attitude if he or she were to say, "I do not like the Japanese purification ritual because it involves being naked in a communal bath." The

Westerner quoted here, for instance, might hold conservative beliefs regarding exposure of the body.

Like values, attitudes are learned from role models, including parents, teachers, and religious leaders. Like values, they also differ from one country to another because they are formed within a cultural context. But although values generally concern only important matters, people hold attitudes toward both important and unimportant aspects of life. And whereas values are quite rigid over time, attitudes are more flexible. Young people across Europe are experiencing an unprecedented degree of cultural, political, and economic change as the European Union continues to develop. The World Business Survey titled "Generation Gap" details what young Europeans view as the most significant differences between their generation and that of their parents.

Cultural knowledge can tell a company whether promotions must be adapted to local attitudes in order to maximize the effectiveness of its promotional efforts. For instance, it is often believed that people around the world respond similarly toward technological products. So advertising agency Euro RSCG Worldwide (www.eurorscg.com) conducted a survey of consumer attitudes toward technology and their purchasing habits using technological products. Among other things, the survey revealed that consumers in the United Kingdom were far more likely to purchase online than Italian and German consumers. It also found that Web sites were useful in Finland as a source of information on technological products but considered not at all useful by

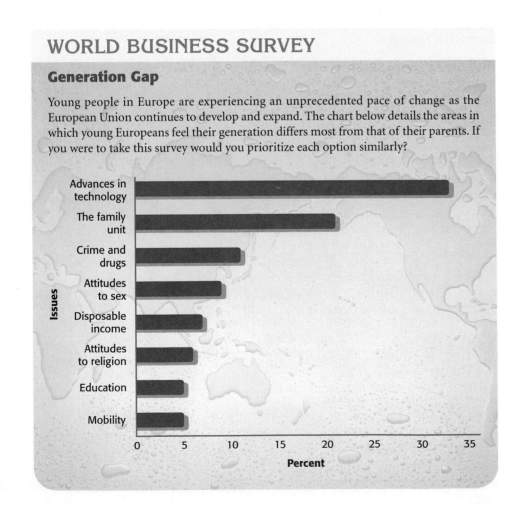

WORLD BUSINESS SURVEY

Generation Gap

Young people in Europe are experiencing an unprecedented pace of change as the European Union continues to develop and expand. The chart below details the areas in which young Europeans feel their generation differs most from that of their parents. If you were to take this survey would you prioritize each option similarly?

Italians. Ira Matathia, global director of business development for RSCG, said, "Marketers will have to forfeit the notion of global marketing and look to each country's highly individualized adaptation of technology for clues as to how to build and satisfy consumer desire."[8]

Let's now look at how people's attitudes differ regarding three important aspects of life that directly affect business activities—attitudes toward time, work and achievement, and cultural change.

Attitudes Toward Time   People in many Latin American and Mediterranean cultures are casual about time. They maintain flexible schedules and would rather enjoy their time than sacrifice it to unbending efficiency. Businesspeople, for example, often arrive after the scheduled meeting time and prefer to spend time building personal trust before discussing business. Not surprisingly, it usually takes longer to conduct business in these parts of the world than in the United States or northern Europe.

In contrast, people in Japan and the United States typically arrive promptly for meetings, keep tight schedules, and work long hours.[9] The emphasis on using time efficiently reflects the underlying value of hard work in both these countries. However, Japanese and Americans sometimes differ in how they use their work time. Americans, for example, strive toward workplace efficiency and sometimes leave early if the day's tasks are done. This attitude reflects the value that Americans place on producing individual results. In Japan, it is important to look busy in the eyes of others even when business is slow. Japanese workers want to demonstrate their dedication to superiors and co-workers—an attitude grounded in values such as the concern for group cohesion, loyalty, and harmony.

Attitudes Toward Work   Whereas some cultures display a strong work ethic, others stress a more balanced pace in juggling work and leisure. People in southern France like to say, "We work to live, while people in the United States live to work." Work, they say, is for them a means to an end. In the United States, they charge, it is an end in itself. Not surprisingly, the lifestyle in southern France is slower-paced. People tend to concentrate on earning enough money to enjoy a relaxed, quality lifestyle. Businesses practically close down during August, when many workers take month-long paid holidays, usually outside the country. This attitude is unheard of in many Asian countries, including Japan.

People tend to start their own businesses when capital is available for new business start-ups and when the cultural stigma of entrepreneurial failure is low. In both the United Kingdom and France, start-ups are considered quite risky, and capital for entrepreneurial ventures is relatively scarce. This remains true despite limited progress during the dot-com boom when many Internet companies obtained funding.[10] Moreover, if at some point an entrepreneur's venture in one of those countries goes bust, he or she can find it very hard to obtain financing for future projects because of the stigma of failure. The opposite attitude tends to prevail in the United States. Reference to prior bankruptcy in a business plan is sometimes considered valuable learning experience (assuming, of course, that some lessons were learned). As long as U.S. bankers or venture capitalists see promising business plans, they are generally willing to loan money.[11] Today, many European nations are trying to foster an entrepreneurial spirit like that in the United States in order to achieve the level of job growth that occurred in the United States over the past several decades.

However, the cause of national differences in work attitudes do involve factors in addition to culture. The perceived opportunity for financial reward is no doubt a strong element in attitudes toward work. A recent study reported that both U.S. and German employees work longer hours when there is a greater likelihood that good performance will lead to a promotion and increased pay. However, it appears that this is relatively less true in Germany, where wages are less variable, and job security and jobless benefits (such as free national health care) are greater.[12] These other aspects of German society (resulting from tradeoffs made in German politics and economics) likely affect work attitudes there. You will read more about the complexity of national politics and economics in Chapters 3 and 4.

Attitudes Toward Cultural Change   A **cultural trait** is anything that represents a culture's way of life, including gestures, material objects, traditions, and concepts. Such traits include bowing to show respect in Japan (gesture), a Buddhist temple in Thailand (material object), relaxing in a tearoom in Kuwait (tradition), and practicing democracy in the United States (concept). Let's look more closely at how cultures change over time and the roles that international companies play in cultural change.

Cultural Diffusion   The process whereby cultural traits spread from one culture to another is called **cultural diffusion**. As new traits are accepted and absorbed into a culture, *cultural change* occurs naturally and, as a rule, gradually. Globalization and technological advances are increasing the pace of both cultural diffusion and cultural change. Satellite television, videoconferencing, and the Internet are increasing the frequency of international contact and exposing people of different nations to new ideas and practices.

When Companies Change Culture: Charges of Cultural Imperialism   International companies are often agents of cultural change. As trade and investment barriers fall, for example, U.S. consumer-goods and entertainment companies are moving into untapped markets. Critics in some of these markets charge that in exporting the products of such firms, the United States is practicing **cultural imperialism**—the replacement of one culture's traditions, folk heroes, and artifacts with substitutes from another. That is why products from the Walt Disney Company (**www.disney.com**) and its Disneyland Paris theme park met opposition from some French, who saw them as harmful to local culture. McDonald's (**www.mcdonalds.com**) is also a frequent target of criticism by anti-globalization protesters. Some consumers across Asia and Europe resent Ronald McDonald and Mickey Mouse because they so quickly dominate their domestic markets. Politicians in Russia have decried the so-called Snickerization of their culture—a snide term that refers to the popularity of the candy bar made by Snickers

cultural trait
Anything that represents a culture's way of life, including gestures, material objects, traditions, and concepts.

cultural diffusion
Process whereby cultural traits spread from one culture to another.

cultural imperialism
Replacement of one culture's traditions, folk heroes, and artifacts with substitutes from another.

Global companies such as McDonald's, with 28,000 restaurants in 120 countries, must be wary of being charged with *cultural imperialism*. For example, it has been reported that the average Japanese child thinks that McDonald's was invented in Japan and exported to the United States. And Chinese children, like the one shown here, consider "Uncle" McDonald "funny, gentle, kind, and understanding." Do you think this form of cultural change is harmful over the long term?

(www.snickers.com). And when the Miss World Pageant was held in India, conservative groups criticized Western corporate sponsors for spreading the message of consumerism and portraying women as sex objects.

Because of the potential charge of cultural imperialism, companies must be sensitive to the needs and desires of people in every culture in which they do business. They must focus not only on meeting people's product needs, but on how their activities and products affect people's traditional ways and habits. When resistance to cultural change peaks, the result is often laws designed to preserve culture. In such cases, rather than view their effects on culture as the inevitable consequence of doing business, companies can take several steps to soften those effects.

For instance, policies and practices that are at odds with deeply held beliefs must be introduced gradually. Managers should consult highly respected individuals in the local culture about such activities (in many developing countries elders play a leading role). There are, of course, volatile times in every society, and trying to inject new values or attitudes into an already unstable environment is not advisable. Launching new investment projects or implementing unfamiliar management methods are best reserved for times when a culture is experiencing relative stability. In any case, managers should always make clear to workers the benefits of any proposed changes.

When Cultures Change Companies Culture often forces companies to adjust their business policies and practices. Managers from the United States, for instance, often encounter cultural differences that force changes in how they motivate Mexican employees. Although it's a time-consuming practice, they sometimes use *situational management*—a system in which a supervisor walks an employee through every step of an assignment or task and monitors the results at each stage. This technique helps employees fully understand the scope of their jobs and clarifies the boundaries of their responsibilities.

Other types of changes might also be needed to suit local culture. Because Vietnam has a traditionally agriculture-based economy, people's concept of time revolves around the seasons. The local "timepiece" is the monsoon, not the clock. Consequently, managers must modify their approach and take a more patient, long-term view of business. Companies entering Vietnam also must often modify employee evaluation and reward systems. Individual criticism must be delivered privately to save employees from "losing face" among coworkers. Individual praise for good performance can be delivered either in private or in public. But because the Vietnamese place great value on group harmony, an individual can be embarrassed if singled out publicly as being superior to the rest of the work unit.

Is a Global Culture Emerging? What does the rapid pace of cultural change around the world mean for international business? Are we witnessing the emergence of a new, truly global culture in which all people share similar lifestyles, values, and attitudes? The rapid pace of cultural diffusion and increased human interaction across national borders are causing cultures to converge to some extent. And it might even be true that people in different cultures are developing similar perspectives on the world and beginning to think along similar lines.

But it seems that just as often as we see signs of an emerging global culture, we discover some new habit unique to one culture. When that happens, we are reminded of the roles of history and tradition in defining culture. Whereas cultural convergence is certainly taking place in some market segments for some products (say the teenage market for pop music), it seems likely that a broader global culture will take a very long time to develop, if ever. Yes, values and attitudes are under continually greater pressure as globalization continues. But because they are so deeply ingrained in culture, their transformation will continue to be gradual rather than abrupt.

MANNERS AND CUSTOMS

When doing business in another culture, it is important to understand a people's manners and customs. At a minimum, understanding manners and customs helps managers to avoid making embarrassing mistakes or offending people. In-depth knowledge, meanwhile, improves the ability to negotiate in other cultures, market products effectively, and manage international operations. Let's explore some important differences in manners and customs around the world.

Manners Appropriate ways of behaving, speaking, and dressing in a culture are called **manners**. In Arab cultures from the Middle East to northwest Africa, one does not extend a hand to greet an older person unless the elder first offers the greeting. In going first, a younger person would be displaying bad manners. Moreover, because Arab culture considers the left hand the "toilet hand," using it to pour tea or serve a meal is considered very bad manners.

Conducting business during meals is common practice in the United States. In Mexico, however, it is poor manners to bring up business at mealtime unless the host does so first. Business discussions typically begin when coffee and brandy arrive. Likewise, toasts in the United States tend to be casual and sprinkled with lighthearted humor. In Mexico, where a toast should be philosophical and full of passion, a lighthearted toast would be offensive. See the Global Manager titled, "A Globetrotter's Guide to Manners" for some additional pointers on the proper manners when abroad on business.

Customs When habits or ways of behaving in specific circumstances are passed down through generations, they become **customs**. Customs differ from manners in that

manners
Appropriate ways of behaving, speaking, and dressing in a culture.

customs
Habits or ways of behaving in specific circumstances that are passed down through generations in a culture.

GLOBAL MANAGER

A Globetrotter's Guide to Manners

Good manners are obviously essential when doing business in the home market and the same holds true internationally. Here are just a few things managers should be aware of when meeting colleagues from other cultures. Can you think of any others that you would add to this list?

➡ **Don't Rush Familiarity.** Avoid the temptation to get too familiar too quickly. Use titles such as "doctor" and "mister." Switch to a first-name basis only when invited to do so and do not shorten people's names from, say, Catherine to Cathy.

➡ **Adapt to Personal Space.** What is considered appropriate distance between people is cultural. Middle Eastern and Latin American nations close the gap significantly. Expect more touching in Latin America, where the man-to-man embrace occurs regularly.

➡ **Respect Religious Values.** Be cautious so that your manners do not offend people. Former Secretary of State Madeline Albright briefly acquired the nickname of "the kissing ambassador" because she apparently

kissed the Israeli and Palestinian leaders of these profoundly religious nations.

➡ **Maintain Good Posture.** Do not slouch, or "spread out" by hanging your arms over the backs of chairs. But don't be too stiff either. Look people in the eye lest they deem you untrustworthy but don't stare too intently.

➡ **Give and Receive Business Cards Respectfully.** In Asia, business cards are considered an extension of a person. Cards in Japan are typically exchanged after a bow, with two hands and the wording facing the recipient. Leave the card on the table for the entire meeting—don't quickly stuff it in your wallet or toss it into your briefcase.

➡ **Use Comedy Sparingly.** Finally, use humor cautiously because it often does not translate well. Avoid jokes that rely on wordplay and puns or events in your country of which local people might have no knowledge.

they define appropriate habits or behaviors in specific situations. Sharing food gifts during the Islamic holy month of Ramadan is a custom, as is the Japanese tradition of throwing special parties for young women and men who turn age 20. Let's now define two types of customs and see how instances of each vary around the world.

folk custom
Behavior, often dating back several generations, that is practiced within a homogeneous group of people.

popular custom
Behavior shared by a heterogeneous group or by several groups.

Folk and Popular Customs   A **folk custom** is behavior, often dating back several generations, that is practiced within a homogeneous group of people. The wearing of turbans by Muslims in southern Asia and the art of belly dancing in Turkey are both folk customs. A **popular custom** is behavior shared by a heterogeneous group or by several groups. Popular customs can exist either in just one culture or in two or more cultures at the same time. Wearing blue jeans and playing golf are both popular customs across the globe. Many folk customs that have spread by cultural diffusion to other regions have developed into popular customs.

We can distinguish between folk and popular food. Popular Western-style fast food, for instance, is rapidly replacing folk food around the world. In many Asian countries, widespread acceptance of "burgers 'n' fries" (born in the United States), and "fish 'n' chips" (born in Britain) is actually altering deep-seated dietary traditions, especially among young people. They are even becoming part of home-cooked meals in Japan and South Korea.

The Business of Gift Giving   Although giving token gifts to business and government associates is customary in many countries, the proper type of gift varies. A knife, for example, should not be offered to associates in Russia, France, or Germany where it signals the severing of a relationship. In Japan, gifts must be wrapped in such a delicate way that it is wise to ask someone trained in the practice to do the honors. It is also Japanese custom not to open a gift in front of the gift giver. Tradition dictates that the giver protest that the gift is something small and unworthy of the recipient. In turn, the recipient waits until later to open the gift. This tradition does not endorse trivial gifts but is simply a custom.

On the other hand, large gifts to business associates sometimes raise suspicion. Cultures differ in their legal and ethical rules against giving or accepting bribes. The U.S. Foreign Corrupt Practices Act, which prohibits companies from giving large gifts to government officials to win business favors, applies to U.S. firms operating at home *and* abroad. In many cultures, however, bribery is woven into a social fabric that has worn well for centuries. In Germany, bribe payments may even qualify for tax deductions. However, gift giving remains controversial. Although governments around the world are adopting stricter measures to control bribery, in some cultures large gifts continue to be an effective means of obtaining contracts, entering markets, and securing protection from competitors.

SOCIAL STRUCTURE

social structure
A culture's fundamental organization, including its groups and institutions, its system of social positions and their relationships, and the process by which its resources are distributed.

Social structure embodies a culture's fundamental organization, including its groups and institutions, its system of social positions and their relationships, and the process by which its resources are distributed. Social structure affects business decisions, including production-site selection, advertising methods, and ultimately the costs of doing business in a country. Three important elements of social structure that differ across cultures are *social group associations*, *social status*, and *social mobility*.

social group
Collection of two or more people who identify and interact with one another.

Social Group Associations   People in all cultures associate themselves with a variety of **social groups**—collections of two or more people who identify and interact with one another. Social groups contribute to each individual's identity and self-image. Two groups that play especially important roles in affecting business activity everywhere are family and gender.*

Family   Here are two different types of family groups:

- The *nuclear family* consists of a person's immediate relatives, including parents, brothers, and sisters. This concept of family prevails in Australia, Canada, the United States, and much of Europe.
- The concept of the *extended family* broadens the nuclear family to include grandparents, aunts and uncles, cousins, and relatives through marriage. It is more important as a social group in much of Asia, the Middle East, North Africa, and Latin America.

Extended families can present some interesting situations for businesspeople unfamiliar with the concept. In some cultures, owners and managers in extended families obtain supplies and materials from another company in which someone in the family works before looking elsewhere. Gaining entry into such family arrangements can be difficult because quality and price are not sufficient motives to ignore family ties.

In extended-family cultures, managers and other employees often try to find jobs for relatives inside their own companies. This practice (called nepotism) can present a challenge to the human resource operations of a Western company, which typically must establish explicit policies on the practice.

Gender   Let's first define *gender*. Gender refers to socially learned traits associated with, and expected of, men or women. It refers to such socially learned behaviors and attitudes as styles of dress and activity preferences. It is not the same thing as sex, which refers to the biological fact that a person is either male or female.

Although many countries have made great strides toward gender equality in the workplace, others have not. For instance, countries operating under Islamic law sometimes segregate women and men in schools, universities, and social activities, and restrict women to certain professions. Sometimes women are allowed teaching careers, but only in all-female classrooms. At other times they can be physicians, but for female patients only.

In Spain, as in many countries, women have traditionally been denied equal opportunity in the workplace. Although the overall unemployment rate is 14 percent in Spain, the rate for women is 20 percent, more than double that for men and the highest rate in the European Union. It is also true that Spanish women earn 30 percent to 40 percent less than men in the same occupation. One prominent reason for this situation is the shortage of low-cost day care for children. Many times, salaries are so low and the cost of child care so high that it simply makes more sense for mothers to stay home with their children. Another reason is that caring for children and performing household duties are considered women's work in Spain, rather than the responsibility of the entire family.[13]

A similar situation exists in Japan, where men traditionally hold nearly all positions of responsibility. Women generally serve as office clerks and administrative assistants until their mid- to late twenties, when they are expected to marry and stay at home tending to family needs. Although this is still largely true today, progress is being made in expanding the role of women in Japan's business community. Although women own nearly a quarter of all businesses in Japan, many of these are very small and do not carry a great deal of economic clout. Although greater gender equality prevails in Australia, Canada, Germany, and the United States, women in these countries still tend to earn less money than men in similar positions.

---

*We put these two "groups" together for the sake of convenience. Strictly speaking, a gender is not a group. Sociologists regard it as a category—people who share some status. A key to group membership is mutual interaction. Individuals in categories know that they are not alone in holding a particular status, but the vast majority remain strangers to one another.

Social Status   Another important aspect of social structure is the way a culture divides its population according to *status*—that is, according to positions within the structure. Although some cultures have only a few categories, others have many. The process of ranking people into social layers or classes is called **social stratification**.

> **social stratification**
> Process of ranking people into social layers or classes.

Three factors that normally determine social status are family heritage, income, and occupation. In most industrialized countries royalty, government officials, and top business leaders occupy the highest social layer. Scientists, medical doctors, and others with a university education occupy the middle rung. Below are those with vocational training or a secondary-school education, who dominate the manual and clerical occupations. Although rankings are fairly stable, they can and do change over time. For example, because Confucianism (a major Chinese religion) stresses a life of learning, for centuries Chinese culture frowned on businesspeople. In modern China, however, those who have obtained wealth and power through business are now considered important role models for young people.

Social Mobility   Moving to a higher social class is easy in some cultures and difficult or impossible in others. **Social mobility** is the ease with which individuals can move up or down a culture's "social ladder." For much of the world's population today, one of two systems regulates social mobility: a *caste system* or a *class system*.

> **social mobility**
> Ease with which individuals can move up or down a culture's "social ladder."

Caste Systems   A **caste system** is a system of social stratification in which people are born into a social ranking, or *caste*, with no opportunity for social mobility. India is the classic example of a caste culture. Little social interaction occurs between castes, and marrying out of one's caste is taboo. Opportunities for work and advancement are defined within the system, and certain occupations are reserved for the members of each caste. Because personal clashes would be inevitable, a member of one caste cannot supervise someone of a higher caste. The caste system forces Western companies to make some hard ethical decisions when entering the Indian marketplace. They must decide whether to adapt to local human resource policies or import their own because they think of them as "more developed."

> **caste system**
> System of social stratification in which people are born into a social ranking, or caste, with no opportunity for social mobility.

Although the Indian constitution *officially* bans discrimination by caste, its influence persists. But change is taking place rapidly in many urban areas in India. As globalization introduces new values the social system will undoubtedly adapt.

Class Systems   A **class system** is a system of social stratification in which personal ability and actions decide social status and mobility. It is the most common form of social stratification in the world today. But class systems vary in the amount of mobility they allow. Highly class-conscious cultures offer less mobility and, not surprisingly, experience greater class conflict. Across Western Europe, for instance, wealthy families have retained power for generations by restricting social mobility. As a result, they must sometimes deal with class conflict in the form of labor–management disputes that can increase the cost of doing business there. Strikes (and sometimes even property damage) occur when European companies announce plant closings or layoffs.

> **class system**
> System of social stratification in which personal ability and actions decide social status and mobility.

Conversely, lower levels of class consciousness encourage mobility and lessen conflict. Most U.S. citizens, for instance, share the belief that hard work can improve one's living standards and social status. They attribute higher status to greater income or wealth, but often with little regard for family background. Material well-being is important primarily because it affirms or improves status. A more cooperative atmosphere in the workplace tends to prevail when people feel that a higher social standing is within their reach.

RELIGION

Human values often originate from religious beliefs. Different religions take different views of work, savings, and material goods. Understanding why they do so may help us to understand why companies from certain cultures are more competitive in the global marketplace than companies from other cultures. It also may help us understand why some countries develop more slowly than others. Knowing how religion affects business practices is especially important in countries with religious governments.

Map 2.1 shows where the world's major religions are practiced. In the following sections, we explore several of these religions—Christianity, Islam, Hinduism, Buddhism, Confucianism, Judaism, and Shinto—to examine their potential effects, both positive and negative, on international business activity.

Christianity Christianity was born in Palestine around 2,000 years ago among Jews who believed that God sent Jesus of Nazareth to be their savior. Although Christianity boasts more than 300 denominations, most Christians belong to the Roman Catholic, Protestant, or Eastern Orthodox churches. With over 1.7 billion followers, Christianity is the world's single largest religion. The Roman Catholic faith asks its followers to refrain from placing material possessions above God and others. Protestants believe that salvation comes from faith in God and that hard work gives glory to God—a tenet known widely as the "Protestant work ethic." Many historians believe this conviction to be a main factor in the development of capitalism and free enterprise in nineteenth-century Europe.

Christian organizations sometimes get involved in social causes that affect business policy. For example, some conservative Christian groups have boycotted the Walt Disney Company (www.disney.com), charging that in portraying young people as rejecting parental guidance, Disney films impede the moral development of young viewers worldwide.

The Church itself became involved in some highly publicized controversies lately. Ireland-based Ryanair (www.ryanair.com), Europe's leading low-fare airline, ruffled the feathers of the Roman Catholic Church with a recent ad campaign. The ad depicted the pope (the head of the Church) claiming that the fourth secret of Fatima was Ryanair's low fares. The Church sent out a worldwide press release accusing the airline of blaspheming the pope. But much to the Church's dismay, the press release generated an enormous amount of free publicity for the company.[14]

Several years earlier, the French Bishops' Conference sued Volkswagen-France (www.volkswagen.fr). They felt that a billboard ad insulted Christians by parodying the famous image of Leonardo Da Vinci's *The Last Supper*. The conference explained that it was reacting to increasing use of sacred things in advertising throughout Europe. "Advertising experts," said a conference spokesman, "have told us that ads aim for the sacred in order to shock because using sex does not work anymore." Volkswagen halted the $16 million ad campaign in response to the Church's complaint.[15]

Islam With 925 million adherents, Islam is the world's second-largest religion. The prophet Muhammad founded Islam around the year 600 A.D. in Mecca, the holy city of Islam located in Saudi Arabia. Islam thrives in northwestern Africa, the Middle East, Central Asia, Pakistan, and some Southeast Asian nations, including Indonesia. Muslim concentrations are also found in most U.S. and European cities. The word *Islam* means "submission to Allah," and *Muslim* means "one who submits to Allah." Two important religious rites include observance of the holy season of Ramadan and making the pilgrimage (the *Hajj*) to Mecca at least once in one's lifetime.

Religion strongly affects the kinds of goods and services acceptable to Muslim consumers. Islam, for example, prohibits the consumption of alcohol and pork. Popular alcohol substitutes are soda pop, coffee, and tea. Substitutes for pork include lamb, beef, and poultry (all of which must be slaughtered in a prescribed way so as to meet *halal* requirements). As we saw in this chapter's opening company profile, German candy maker Haribo (www.haribo.com) produces a pork-free gummi bear that satis-

MAP 2.1

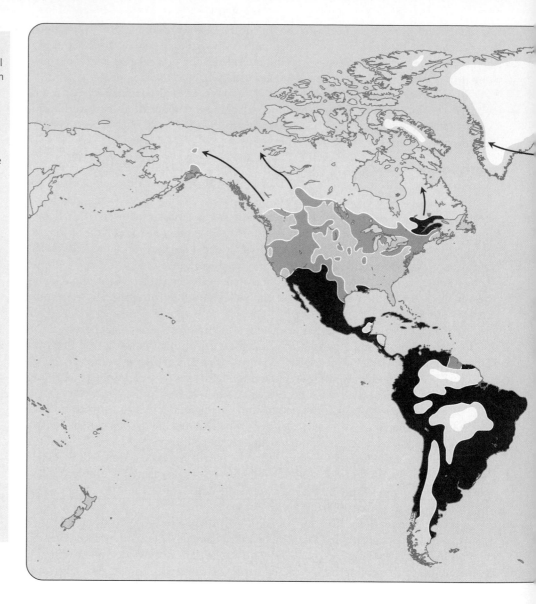

Major Religions of The World
Religion is not confined to national political boundaries but can exist in different regions of the world simultaneously. Different religions can also dominate different regions in a single nation. This map shows where the world's major religions are prominent. The map shows several religions in addition to those discussed in this chapter including: **Taoism**, which began in the 100s B.C. in China. Taoists pray to a mixture of deceased humans who displayed extraordinary powers during their lives, and nonhuman spirits embodying various elements of Tao; **Sikhism**, dating back to 1469, teaches breaking the continuous cycle of reincarnation by waking early, cleansing, meditating, and devoting all activities to God; **Animism**, describes all religions involving honoring the souls of deceased humans and worshiping spirits in nature; **Lamaist Buddhism** is a Buddhist sect that emphasizes meditation and has as its spiritual leader, the Dalai Lama; and **Southern Buddhism**, the Buddhist sect that is older than Lamaism and stresses following the teachings of Buddha.

fies *halal* requirements. Because hot coffee and tea often play ceremonial roles in Muslim nations, the markets for them are quite large. And because usury (charging interest for money lent) violates the laws of Islam, credit card companies collect management fees rather than interest, and each cardholder's credit line is limited to an amount held on deposit.

Nations governed by Islamic law (see Chapter 3) sometimes segregate the sexes at certain activities and in locations such as schools. In Saudi Arabia, women cannot drive cars. In orthodox Islamic nations, men cannot conduct market research surveys with women at home unless they are family members. Women visiting Islamic cultures need to be especially sensitive to Islamic beliefs and customs. In Iran, for instance, the Ministry of Islamic Guidance and Culture posts a reminder to visiting female journalists: "The body is a tool for the spirit and the spirit is a divine song. The holy tool should not be used for sexual intentions." Although the issue of *hejab* (Islamic dress) is hotly debated, both Iranian and non-Iranian women are officially expected to wear body-concealing garments and scarves over their hair (which is considered enticing).[16]

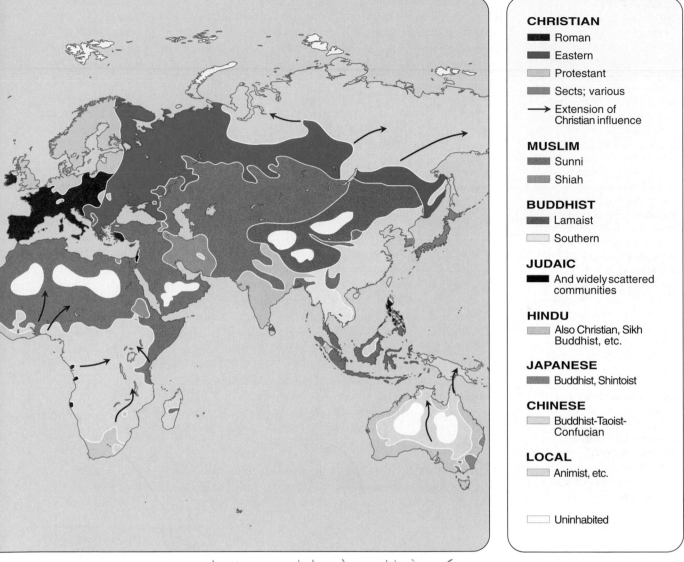

CHRISTIAN
- Roman
- Eastern
- Protestant
- Sects; various
- → Extension of Christian influence

MUSLIM
- Sunni
- Shiah

BUDDHIST
- Lamaist
- Southern

JUDAIC
- And widely scattered communities

HINDU
- Also Christian, Sikh Buddhist, etc.

JAPANESE
- Buddhist, Shintoist

CHINESE
- Buddhist-Taoist-Confucian

LOCAL
- Animist, etc.

- Uninhabited

~ one of the oldest religions

Hinduism   Hinduism was formed around 4,000 years ago in present-day India, where over 90 percent of its nearly 690 million adherents live. It is also the majority religion of Nepal and a secondary religion in Bangladesh, Bhutan, and Sri Lanka. Considered by some to be a way of life rather than a religion, Hinduism recalls no founder and recognizes no central authority or spiritual leader. Integral to the Hindu faith is the caste system described earlier.

Hindus believe in reincarnation—the rebirth of the human soul at the time of death. For many Hindus the highest goal of life is *moksha*—escaping from the cycle of reincarnation and entering a state of eternal happiness called *nirvana*. Strict Hindus do not eat or willfully harm any living creature because it may be a reincarnated human soul. Because Hindus consider cows sacred animals they do not eat beef. However, consuming milk is considered a means of religious purification. Firms like McDonald's (www.mcdonalds.com) must work closely with government and religious officials in India to respect Hindu beliefs. In many regions, McDonald's has removed all beef products from its menu and prepares vegetable and fish products in separate kitchen areas.

And for those Indians who do eat meat (but not cows because of their sacred status) the company sells the Maharaja Mac, made of lamb, in place of the Big Mac.[17]

In India, there have been attacks on Western consumer-goods companies in the name of preserving Indian culture and Hindu beliefs. Some companies such as Pepsi-Cola (www.pepsi.com) have been vandalized, and local officials even shut down a KFC restaurant (www.kfc.com) for a time. Although it currently operates in India, Coca-Cola (www.cocacola.com) once left the market completely rather than succumb to demands that it reveal its secret formula to authorities. India's investment environment has improved greatly in recent years. Yet labor–management relations sometimes deteriorate to such a degree that strikes cut deeply into productivity.

Buddhism   Buddhism was founded about 2,600 years ago in India by a Hindu prince named Siddhartha Gautama. Today, Buddhism has approximately 311 million followers, mostly in Asian nations such as China, Tibet, Korea, Japan, Vietnam, and Thailand. There also are small numbers of Buddhists in Europe and North and South America. Although founded in India, Buddhism has relatively few adherents there, and unlike Hinduism, it rejects the sort of caste system that dominates Indian society. But like Hinduism, Buddhism promotes a life centered on spiritual rather than worldly matters. Buddhists seek *nirvana* (escape from reincarnation) through charity, modesty, compassion for others, restraint from violence, and general self-control.

Although monks at many temples are devoted to lives of solitary meditation and discipline, many other Buddhist priests are dedicated to lessening the burden of human suffering. They finance schools and hospitals across Asia and are active in worldwide peace movements. In Tibet, where most people still acknowledge the exiled Dalai Lama as the spiritual and political head of the Buddhist culture, the Chinese Communist government suppresses allegiance to any outside authority. In the United States, a coalition of religious groups, human rights advocates, and supporters of the Dalai Lama continue to press the U.S. Congress to apply economic sanctions against countries that, like China, are judged to practice religious persecution.

Confucianism   An exiled politician and philosopher named Kung-fu-dz (pronounced *Confucius* in English) began teaching his ideas in China nearly 2,500 years ago.

Buddhism instructs its followers to live a life characterized by simplicity and one void of materialistic ambitions. It also says that one source of human suffering is sense pleasure. But as countries across Asia continue to modernize, the products of Western multinationals are streaming in. Here a young Buddhist passes in front of an advertisement for Heineken beer. Do you think modernization has to mean "westernization?"

Today, China is home to most of Confucianism's 150 million followers. Confucian thought is also ingrained in the cultures of Japan, South Korea, and nations with large numbers of ethnic Chinese, including Singapore.

South Korean business practice reflects Confucian thought in its rigid organizational structure and unswerving reverence for authority. Whereas Korean employees do not question strict chains of command, non-Korean managers and workers often feel differently. Efforts to apply Korean-style management in overseas subsidiaries have caused some high-profile disputes with U.S. executives and even physical confrontations with factory workers in Vietnam.

Some observers contend that the Confucian work ethic and educational commitment helped spur east Asia's phenomenal economic growth. But others respond that the link between culture and economic growth is weak. They argue that economic, historical, and international factors are at least as important as culture. They say Chinese leaders distrusted Confucianism for centuries because they believed that it stunted economic growth. Likewise, many Chinese despised merchants and traders because their main objective (earning money) violated Confucian beliefs. As a result, many Chinese businesspeople moved to Indonesia, Malaysia, Singapore, and Thailand, where they launched successful businesses. Today, these countries (along with Taiwan) are financing much of China's economic growth.

Judaism   More than 3,000 years old, Judaism was the first religion to preach belief in a single God. Nowadays, Judaism has roughly 18 million followers worldwide. In Israel, Orthodox (or "fully observant") Jews make up 12 percent of the population and constitute an increasingly important economic segment. In Jerusalem, there is even a modeling agency that specializes in casting Orthodox Jews in ads aimed both inside and outside the Orthodox community. Models include scholars and even one rabbi. In keeping with Orthodox principles, women model only modest clothing and never appear in ads alongside men.[18]

Employers and human resource managers must be aware of important days in the Jewish faith. Because the Sabbath lasts from sundown on Friday to sundown on Saturday, work schedules might need adjustment. Devout Jews want to be home before sundown on Fridays. On the Sabbath itself, they do not work, travel, or carry money. Several other important observances are Rosh Ha-Shanah (the 2-day Jewish New Year, in September or October), Yom Kippur (the Day of Atonement, 10 days after New Year), Passover (which celebrates the Exodus from Egypt, in March or April each year), and Hanukkah (which celebrates an ancient victory over the Syrians, usually in December).

Marketers must take into account foods that are banned among strict Jews. Pork and shellfish (such as lobster and crab) are prohibited. Meat is stored and served separately from milk. Other meats must be slaughtered according to a practice called *shehitah*. Meals prepared according to Jewish dietary traditions are called *kosher*. Most airlines offer *kosher* meals and, as we saw earlier, German candy maker Haribo (**www.haribo.com**) makes a special *kosher* gummi bear.

Shinto   Shinto (meaning "way of the gods") arose as the native religion of the Japanese. But today Shinto can claim only about 3.5 million strict adherents in Japan. Because modern Shinto preaches patriotism, it is sometimes said that Japan's real religion is nationalism. Shinto teaches sincere and ethical behavior, loyalty and respect toward others, and enjoyment of life.

Shinto beliefs are reflected in the workplace through the traditional practice of lifetime employment (although this is waning today) and through the traditional trust extended between firms and customers. Japanese competitiveness in world markets has benefited from loyal workforces, low employee turnover, and good labor–management cooperation. The success of Japanese companies since the Second World War gave rise to the concept of a Shinto work ethic, certain aspects of which have been emulated by Western managers.

PERSONAL COMMUNICATION

communication
System of conveying thoughts, feelings, knowledge, and information through speech, actions, and writing.

People in every culture have a **communication** system to convey thoughts, feelings, knowledge, and information through speech, actions, and writing. Understanding a culture's spoken language gives us great insight into why people think and act the way that they do. Understanding a culture's body language helps us avoid sending unintended or embarrassing messages. Let's now examine each of these forms of communication more closely.

Spoken Language   Spoken language is the part of a culture's communication system that is embodied in its spoken and written vocabulary. It is the most obvious difference we notice when traveling in another country. We overhear and engage in a number of conversations, and must read many signs and documents to find our way. Because understanding a people's language is the key to understanding their culture, it is essential for success in international business.

Linguistically different segments of a population are often culturally, socially, and politically distinct. For instance, Malaysia's population is comprised of Malay (60 percent), Chinese (30 percent), and Indian (10 percent). Although Malay is the official national language, each ethnic group speaks its own language and continues its traditions. The United Kingdom includes England, Northern Ireland, Scotland, and Wales—each of which has its own language and traditions. Ireland's native language, one dialect of Gaelic, is staging a comeback on Irish television and in Gaelic-language schools. Scotland's native language is another dialect of Gaelic.

The importance of understanding the local language in business is becoming increasingly apparent on the Internet. By 2005 it is estimated that between 70 percent and 75 percent of the 1 billion Internet users will be nonnative English speakers. But English is the language of nearly 70 percent of all Web pages on the Internet (Table 2.1). That is why software solutions providers are assisting companies from English-speaking countries in adapting their Web sites for global e-business. As these software companies are telling their clients, "The 'e' in e-business doesn't stand for English." Web surfers from cultures across the globe bring their own specific tastes, preferences, and buying habits online with them. The company that can provide its customer in Mexico City, Paris, or Tokyo with a quality buying experience in his or her native language will have an edge on the competition.[19]

Language proficiency is also critical in production facilities where nonnative managers are supervising local employees. In the wake of the North American Free Trade Agreement U.S. corporations continue to expand operations in Mexico. Because Mexican factory workers generally appear relaxed and untroubled at work, one U.S. manager was confused when his workers went on strike at his seemingly happy plant. The problem lay in different cultural perspectives. Mexican workers tend not to take the initiative in matters of problem solving and workplace complaints. In this case, they

TABLE 2.1 *Languages of the Web*			
Language	**Portion of All Web Pages (%)**	**Language**	**Portion of All Web Pages (%)**
English	68.4	Russian	1.9
Japanese	5.9	Italian	1.6
German	5.8	Portuguese	1.4
Chinese	3.9	Korean	1.3
French	3.0	Czech	0.3
Spanish	2.4	Polish	0.3

concluded that the plant manager knew but did not care about their complaints because he did not trouble to question employees about working conditions.

Language Blunders   There are many stories of companies making terrible language blunders in their international business dealings. Chevrolet (www.chevrolet.com) made perhaps the most well-known blunder when it first launched its Chevrolet Nova in Spanish-speaking markets. The company failed to notice beforehand that "No va" means "No go" in Spanish. In Sweden, Kellogg (www.kellogg.com) had to rename its Bran Buds cereal because the Swedish translation came out roughly as "burned farmer." San Francisco–based start-up Evite (www.evite.com) allows visitors to its Web site to send e-mail invitations to special events. But the company's name presents a problem internationally. In the Romance languages, such as French and Spanish, variations of the verb *evite* (*eviter* and *evitar*) mean "to shun or to avoid." Apparently "Avoid My Party" couldn't get European partygoers excited. CEO Josh Silverman concedes, "It's a terrific brand in English, but we're going to have to rebrand for the Romance languages."[20]

But such blunders are not the exclusive domain of humans. The use of machine translation—computer software used to translate one language into another—is booming along with the explosion in the number of nonnative English speakers using the Internet. Nowhere is this technology hotter than in Asia, although its results are often less than perfect. Singapore-based EWGate (www.ewgate.com) allows its users to search the Internet in English and Asian languages, translate Web pages, and compose e-mail in one language and send it in another. Its product EWSurf attempted a translation and came up with this meaning in Chinese: "The Chinese Communist Party is debating whether to deny its ban in join the Party is allowed soldier enterprise owners on." The original English sentence: "The Chinese Communist Party is debating whether to drop its ban on private-enterprise owners being allowed to join the party."[21] Various other machine translators turned the French version of "I don't care" ("*Je m'en fou*") into "I myself in crazy," "I of insane," and "Me me in madman."[22] See Figure 2.1 for additional language blunders companies have made in international business.

Lingua Franca   A **lingua franca** is a third or "link" language that is understood by two parties who speak different native languages. Although only 5 percent of the world population speaks English as a first language, it is the most common *lingua franca* in international business, followed closely by French and Spanish. A recent survey in the

lingua franca
Third or "link" language that is understood by two parties who speak different native languages.

FIGURE 2.1

What Did You Say?

Advertising slogans and company documents must be translated carefully so that messages are received precisely as intended. Some humorous (but sometimes expensive) translation blunders include the following:

Braniff Airlines' English-language slogan "Fly in Leather" was translated into "Fly Naked" in Spanish.

A sign for non-Japanese-speaking guests in a Tokyo hotel read, "You are respectfully requested to take advantage of the chambermaids."

An English sign in a Moscow hotel read, "If this is your first visit to the USSR, you are welcome to it."

A Japanese knife manufacturer labeled its exports to the United States with "Caution: Blade extremely sharp! Keep out of children."

European Union confirmed the widespread use of English as a *lingua franca* among different nationalities of Europeans. Seventy percent of those surveyed agreed that "everyone should speak English," although almost as many said their own language needs to be protected.[23] Even the Cantonese dialect of Chinese spoken in Hong Kong and the Mandarin dialect spoken in Taiwan and on the Chinese mainland are so different that a *lingua franca* is often preferred. And although India's official language is Hindi, its *lingua franca* among the multitude of dialects is English because it was once a British colony. Yet many young people speak what is referred to as "Hinglish"—a combination of Hindi, Tamil, and English words alternated within a single sentence.

Because they operate in many nations, each with its own language, multinational corporations sometimes choose a *lingua franca* for official internal communications. Philips (**www.philips.com**) (a Dutch electronics firm), Asea Brown Boveri (**www.abb.com**) (a Swiss industrial giant), and Alcatel (**www.alcatel.com**) (a French telecommunications firm) all use English for internal correspondence. Japan-based Sony and Matsushita also use English abroad, even in some non-English-speaking countries.

Body Language Body language communicates through unspoken cues, including hand gestures, facial expressions, physical greetings, eye contact, and the manipulation of personal space. Like spoken language, body language communicates both information and feelings and differs greatly from one culture to another. Italians, French, Arabs, and Venezuelans, for example, animate conversations with lively hand gestures and other body motions. Japanese and Koreans, although more reserved, communicate just as much information through their own body languages; a look of the eye can carry as much or more meaning as two flailing arms.

Most body language is subtle and takes time to recognize and interpret. For example, navigating the all-important handshake in international business can be tricky. In the United States it is a firm grip and several pumps of the arm. But in the Middle East and Latin America a softer clasp of the hand with little or no arm pump is the custom. And in

body language
Language communicated through unspoken cues, including hand gestures, facial expressions, physical greetings, eye contact, and the manipulation of personal space.

some countries, like Japan, people do not shake hands at all, but bow to one another. Bows of respect carry different meanings, usually depending on the recipient. Associates of equal standing bow about 15 degrees toward one another. But proper respect for an elder requires a bow of about 30 degrees. Bows of remorse or apology should be about 45 degrees.

Proximity is an extremely important element of body language to consider when meeting someone from another culture. If you stand or sit too close to your counterpart (from their perspective), you may invade their personal space and risk appearing aggressive. If you remain too far away, you risk appearing untrustworthy. For North Americans, a distance of about 19 inches is about right between two speakers. For Western Europeans, 14 to 16 inches seems appropriate, but someone from the United Kingdom might prefer about 24 inches. Korean and Chinese are likely to be comfortable about 36 inches apart, while people from Middle Eastern cultures will close the distance to about 8 to 12 inches.[24]

Physical gestures often cause the most misunderstanding between people of different cultures because they can convey very different meanings. The thumbs-up sign is vulgar in Italy and Greece but means "all right" or even "great" in the United States. Figure 2.2 demonstrates how the meaning of other gestures varies across cultures.

EDUCATION

Education is crucial for passing on traditions, customs, and values. Each culture educates its young people through schooling, parenting, religious teachings, and group memberships. Families and other groups provide informal instruction about customs and how to socialize with others. In most cultures, intellectual skills such as reading and mathematics are taught in formal educational settings.

Education Level Data provided by governments on the education level of their people must be taken with a grain of salt. Because many nations rely on literacy tests of their own design, they often provide little basis for comparison across countries. Some administer standardized tests, whereas others require only a signature as proof of literacy. But because few other options exist, searching for either an untapped market or a new factory site forces managers to rely on such undependable benchmarks. Moreover,

FIGURE 2.2

Some Regional Differences in the Meaning of Gestures

Although Western Europe may be moving toward economic unity, its tapestry of cultures remains diverse. Gestures, for example, continue to reflect centuries of cultural differences. As in the United States, the thumb-and-index circle means "okay" in most of Europe; in Germany, it's an indelicate reference to the receiver's anatomy. In most of Great Britain— England and Scotland—the finger tapping the nose means, "You and I are in on the secret"; in nearby Wales, however, it means, "You're very nosy." If you tap your temple just about anywhere in Western Europe, you're suggesting that someone is "crazy"; in Holland, however, you'll be congratulating someone for being clever.

TABLE 2.2	Illiteracy Rates of Selected Countries		
Country	Adult Illiteracy Rate (Percent of People 15 and Above)	Country	Adult Illiteracy Rate (Percent of People 15 and Above)
Niger	84	Brazil	15
Cambodia	60	Indonesia	13
Pakistan	54	Zimbabwe	11
Morocco	51	Jordan	10
Haiti	50	Mexico	9
Egypt	45	Singapore	8
India	43	Venezuela	7
Nigeria	36	Philippines	5
Guatemala	31	Thailand	5
Nicaragua	31	Chile	4
Saudi Arabia	23	Argentina	3
China	16	Hungary	1

as you can see from Table 2.2, some countries have further to go in increasing national literacy rates. Nations with excellent programs for basic education often attract relatively high-wage industries. Those nations that invest in worker training are usually repaid in productivity increases and rising incomes. It is an undisputed fact that whereas nations with skilled, well-educated workforces attract all sorts of high-paying jobs, countries with poorly educated populations attract the lowest-paying manufacturing jobs. By investing in education, a country can attract (and even create) the kind of high-wage industries that are often called "brainpower" industries.[25]

Newly industrialized economies in Asia owe much of their rapid economic development to solid education systems. Hong Kong, South Korea, Singapore, and Taiwan focus on rigorous mathematical training in primary and secondary schooling. University education concentrates on the hard sciences and aims to train engineers, scientists, and managers.

The "Brain Drain" Phenomenon   Just as a country's quality of education affects its economic development, the level and pace of economic development affects its education system. **Brain drain** is the departure of highly educated people from one profession, geographic region, or nation to another.

Political unrest and economic hardship is causing many Indonesians to flee their homeland for the shores of other nations, particularly Hong Kong, Singapore, and the United States. Most of the brain drain occurring there is among Western-educated professionals in finance and technology (exactly the people Indonesia needs to retain to get it on the road to recovery). In the first five months of 2001, Indonesian applications for non-immigrant visas to the United States were up 50 percent over the previous year—more than 700 people a day. Others have stayed closer to home, going to work in Singapore and commuting home on weekends to see their families.[26]

But one country's brain drain is another's brain gain. Australia reportedly experienced a net gain of more than 155,000 skilled workers over a recent 5-year period. According to the Immigration Minister, Australia gained 40,000 managers and administrators, 57,000 professionals, and 21,000 tradespeople, among others. Many of these gains were made in the all-important information technology sector.[27]

Many countries in Eastern Europe experienced high levels of brain drain during their transition to market economies. Economists, engineers, scientists, and researchers in all fields fled westward to escape poverty. But as these nations continue their long march away

brain drain
Departure of highly educated people from one profession, geographic region, or nation to another.

from communism, some are luring professionals back to their homelands—a process known as *reverse brain drain*. In Serbia, economic and legal reforms aimed at remaking the country in the likeness of the Irish Republic (with its young, vibrant, high-tech economy) are helping to reverse a devastating, decade-long brain drain.[28] Similarly, the ascendancy of Simeon Coburgotski (King Simeon II) to the position of Prime Minister of Bulgaria is expected to cause a certain amount of reverse brain drain in that nation.[29]

PHYSICAL AND MATERIAL ENVIRONMENTS

The physical environment and material surroundings of a culture heavily influence its development and pace of change. In this section, we first look at how physical environment and culture are related and then explore the effect of material culture on business.

Physical Environment   Although the physical environment affects a people's culture, it does not directly determine it. Let's take a brief look at two aspects of the physical environment that heavily influence a people's culture: topography and climate.

Topography   All the physical features that characterize the surface of a geographic region constitute its **topography**. Some surface features such as navigable rivers and flat plains facilitate travel and contact with others. In contrast, treacherous mountain ranges and large bodies of water can discourage contact and cultural change. Cultures isolated by impassable mountains or large bodies of water will be less exposed to the cultural traits of other peoples. That is why cultural change tends to occur more slowly in isolated cultures than in cultures not isolated in such a manner.

Topography can have an impact on consumers' product needs. For example, there is little market for Honda scooters (**www.honda.com**) in most mountainous regions because their engines are too small. These are better markets for the company's more rugged, maneuverable motorcycles with larger engines. Thinner air at higher elevations might also entail modifications in carburetor design for gasoline-powered vehicles.

Topography and Communication   Topography can have a profound impact on personal communication in a culture. For instance, mountain ranges and the formidable Gobi Desert consume two thirds of China's land surface. Groups living in the valleys of these mountain ranges continue to hold on to their own ways of life and speak their own languages. Although the Mandarin dialect was decreed the national language many years ago, the mountains, desert, and great land area of China still impair personal communication and, therefore, the proliferation of Mandarin.

Climate   The weather conditions of a geographic region are called its **climate**. Climate affects where people settle and helps direct systems of distribution. In Australia, for example, intensely hot and dry conditions in two large deserts, combined with jungle conditions in the northeast, have pushed settlement to coastal areas. As a result—and because water transport is less costly than land transport—coastal waters are still used to distribute products between distant cities.

Climate, Lifestyle, and Work   Climate plays a large role in lifestyle and work habits. The heat of the summer sun grows intense in the early afternoon hours in the countries of southern Europe, northern Africa, and the Middle East. For this reason, people often take afternoon breaks of 1 or 2 hours in July and August. People use this time to perform errands, such as shopping, or even take short naps before returning to work until about 7 or 8 P.M. Companies doing business in these regions must adapt to this local tradition. Production schedules, for instance, must be adjusted to allow for hours during which machines stand idle. Shipping and receiving schedules must also reflect afternoon downtime and accommodate shipments made later in the day.

topography
All the physical features that characterize the surface of a geographic region.

climate
Weather conditions of a geographic region.

Climate and Customs   Climate also has an impact on customs such as clothing and food. For instance, people in many tropical areas wear little clothing and wear it loosely because of the warm, humid climate. In the desert areas of the Middle East and North Africa, people also wear loose clothing, but they wear long robes to protect themselves from intense sunshine and blowing sand.

A culture's food customs are perhaps more influenced by the physical environment than by any other aspect of culture. But here, too, a people's beliefs can have a major impact on diet. Pigs, for example, are a good source of protein in many parts of the world, including China, Europe, and the Pacific Islands. In the Middle East, however, both Judaism and Islam regard pigs as unclean and prohibit their consumption. The taboo probably originated in environmental factors: Pigs were expensive to feed and produced no materials for clothing. However, because some people were still tempted to squander resources by raising pigs, the prohibition became cultural and was incorporated into both Judaic and Islamic religious texts.[30]

material culture
All the technology employed in a culture to manufacture goods and provide services.

Material Culture   All the technology employed in a culture to manufacture goods and provide services is called its **material culture**. Material culture is often used to measure the technological advancement of a nation's markets or industries. Generally, a firm enters a new market under one of two conditions: (1) Demand for its products has developed, or (2) the market is capable of supporting its production operations. For example, companies are not flocking to the Southeast Asian nation of Myanmar (Burma) because the nation does not fulfill either condition. The primary reason is that a wide range of political and social problems under a repressive military government have stalled economic development there.

Changes in material culture often cause change in other aspects of a people's culture. Eastern Europe is having a difficult time keeping up with the industrialized nations when it comes to Internet access (Figure 2.3). One reason is clearly the language gap, as few Web sites are in an Eastern European language. But another reason is the technolog-

FIGURE 2.3   *Eastern Europe and the Internet*

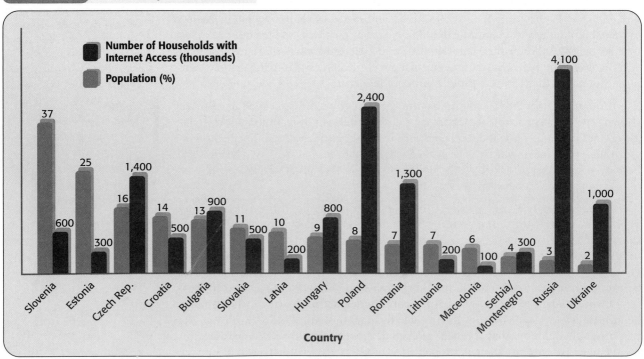

ical gap due to underdeveloped telecommunications systems.[31] But as countries in Eastern Europe continue to upgrade their material cultures through economic development programs, people's greater access to information on the Internet will surely affect their cultures.

Uneven Material Culture   Material culture often displays uneven development across a nation's geography, markets, and industries. For example, much of China's recent economic progress is occurring in coastal cities such as Shanghai. Shanghai has long played an important role in China's international trade because of its strategic location and superb harbor on the East China Sea. Although it is home to only 1 percent of the total population, Shanghai accounts for about 5 percent of China's total output—including about 12 percent of both its industrial production and its financial-services output.

Likewise, Bangkok, the capital city of Thailand, houses only 10 percent of the nation's population but accounts for about 40 percent of its economic output. Meanwhile, the northern parts of the country remain rural, consisting mostly of farms, forests, and mountains.

CLASSIFYING CULTURES

Throughout this chapter, you've seen how cultures can differ greatly from one another. People living in broadly different cultures tend to respond differently in similar business situations. There are two widely accepted ways to classify cultures based on differences in characteristics such as values, attitudes, social structure, and so on. Let's now take a detailed look at each of these tools: the Kluckhohn-Strodtbeck and Hofstede frameworks.

KLUCKHOHN–STRODTBECK FRAMEWORK

The **Kluckhohn–Strodtbeck framework** compares cultures along six dimensions. It studies a given culture by asking each of the following questions:[32]

1. Do people believe that their environment controls them, that they control the environment, or that they are part of nature?
2. Do people focus on past events, on the present, or on the future implications of their actions?
3. Are people easily controlled and not to be trusted, or can they be trusted to act freely and responsibly?
4. Do people desire accomplishments in life, carefree lives, or spiritual and contemplative lives?
5. Do people believe that individuals or groups are responsible for each person's welfare?
6. Do people prefer to conduct most activities in private or in public?

> *Kluckhohn–Strodtbeck framework*
> Framework for studying cultural differences along six dimensions, such as focus on past or future events and belief in individual or group responsibility for personal well-being.

Case: Dimensions of Japanese Culture   By providing answers to each of these six questions, we can briefly apply the Kluckhohn–Strodtbeck framework to Japanese culture:

1. *Japanese believe in a delicate balance between people and environment that must be maintained.* Suppose an undetected flaw in a company's product harms customers using it. In many countries, a high-stakes class-action lawsuit would be filed against the manufacturer on behalf of the victims' families. This scenario is rarely played out in Japan. Japanese culture does not feel that individuals can possibly control every situation but that accidents happen. Japanese victims would receive heartfelt apologies, a promise it won't happen again, and a relatively small damage award.

2. *Japanese culture emphasizes the future.* Because Japanese culture emphasizes strong ties between people and groups, including companies, forming long-term relationships with people is essential when doing business there. Throughout the business relationship, Japanese companies remain in close, continuous contact with buyers to ensure that their needs are being met. This relationship also forms the basis of a communication channel by which suppliers learn about the types of products and services buyers would like to see in the future.

3. *Japanese culture treats people as quite trustworthy.* Business dealings among Japanese companies are based heavily on trust. Once entered into, an agreement to conduct business is difficult to break unless there are extreme uncontrollable factors at work. This is due to the fear of "losing face" if one cannot keep a business commitment. In addition to business applications, society at large reflects the Japanese concern for trustworthiness. Crime rates are quite low and the streets of Japan's largest cities are very safe to walk at night.

4. *Japanese are accomplishment-oriented—not necessarily for themselves, but for their employers and work units.* Japanese children learn the importance of groups early by contributing to the upkeep of their schools. They share such duties as mopping floors, washing windows, cleaning chalkboards, and arranging desks and chairs. They carry such habits learned in school into the adult workplace, where management and labor tend to work together toward company goals—Japanese managers make decisions only after considering input from subordinates. Also, materials buyers, engineers, designers, factory floor supervisors, and marketers cooperate closely throughout each stage of a product's development.

5. *Japanese culture emphasizes individual responsibility to the group and group responsibility to the individual.* This trait has long been a hallmark of Japanese corporations. Traditionally, subordinates promise hard work and loyalty, and top managers provide job security. But a decade of stagnation for the Japanese economy is threatening this tradition. To remain competitive internationally, Japanese companies have eliminated jobs and moved production to low-wage nations like China and Vietnam. As the tradition of job security falls by the wayside, more and more Japanese workers now consider working for non-Japanese companies, whereas others are finding work as temporary employees.[33] But although this trait is diminishing in the business world, it remains a prominent feature in other aspects of Japanese society, especially the family.

6. *The culture of Japan tends to be public.* You will often find top Japanese managers located in the center of a large, open-space office surrounded by the desks of many employees. By comparison, Western executives are often secluded in walled offices located on the perimeter of workspaces in their home countries. This characteristic reaches deep into Japanese society—consider, for example, Japan's continued fondness for public baths.

HOFSTEDE FRAMEWORK

The **Hofstede framework** grew from a study of more than 110,000 people working in IBM subsidiaries (**www.ibm.com**) in 40 countries.[34] From the study's results, Dutch psychologist Geert Hofstede developed four dimensions for examining cultures.[35] Let's now examine each of these in detail.

1. *Individualism versus collectivism.* This dimension identifies the extent to which a culture emphasizes the individual versus the group. Individualist cultures (those scoring high on this dimension) value hard work and promote entrepreneurial risk-taking, thereby fostering invention and innovation. Although people are given

freedom to focus on personal goals, they are held responsible for their actions. That is why responsibility for poor business decisions is placed squarely on the shoulders of the individual in charge. At the same time, higher individualism may be responsible for higher rates of employee turnover.

On the contrary, people in collectivist cultures (those scoring low on this dimension) feel a strong association to groups, including family and work units. The goal of maintaining group harmony is probably most evident in the family structure. People in collectivist cultures tend to work toward collective rather than personal goals and are responsible to the group for their actions. In turn, the group shares responsibility for the well-being of each of its members. Thus, in collectivist cultures success or failure tends to be shared among the work unit, rather than any particular individual receiving all the praise or blame. All social, political, economic, and legal institutions reflect the group's critical role.

2. *Power distance.* This dimension conveys the degree to which a culture accepts social inequality among its people. A culture with large power distance tends to be characterized by much inequality between superiors and subordinates. Organizations tend also to be more hierarchical, with power deriving from prestige, force, and inheritance. This is why executives and upper management in cultures with large power distance often enjoy special recognition and privileges. On the other hand, cultures with small power distance display a greater degree of equality, with prestige and rewards more equally shared between superiors and subordinates. Power in these cultures (relative to cultures with large power distance) is seen to derive more from hard work and entrepreneurial drive and is therefore often considered more legitimate.

Figure 2.4 shows how the Hofstede study ranked selected countries according to these first two dimensions: power distance and the individualism versus col-

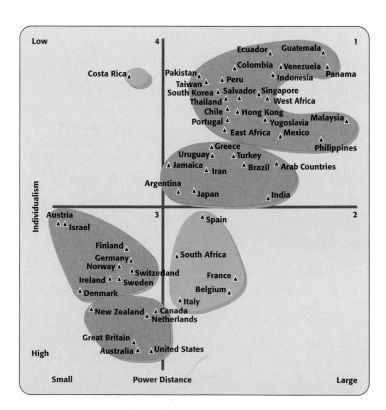

FIGURE 2.4

Power Distance and Individualism versus Collectivism

lectivism. What is striking about this figure is the tight grouping of nations within the five clusters (plus Costa Rica). You can see the concentration of mostly African, Asian, Central and South American, and Middle Eastern nations in Quadrant 1 (cultures with relatively larger power distance and lower individualism). In contrast, Quadrants 3 and 2 comprise mostly the cultures of Australia and the nations of North America and Western Europe. These nations had the highest individualism scores and many had relatively smaller power distance scores.

3. *Uncertainty avoidance.* This dimension identifies the extent to which a culture avoids uncertainty and ambiguity. A culture with large uncertainty avoidance values security and places its faith in strong systems of rules and procedures in society. It is perhaps not surprising then that cultures with large uncertainty avoidance normally have lower employee turnover, more formal rules for regulating employee behavior, and more difficulty implementing change. Cultures scoring low on uncertainty avoidance tend to be more open to change and new ideas. This helps explain why individuals in this type of culture tend to be entrepreneurial and organizations tend to welcome the best business practices from other cultures. However, because people tend to be less fearful of change, these cultures can also suffer from higher levels of employee turnover.

Figure 2.5 plots countries according to the second and third dimensions: power distance and uncertainty avoidance. Although the lines of demarcation are somewhat less obvious in this figure, patterns do emerge among the six clusters (plus Jamaica). Quadrant 4 contains nations characterized by small uncertainty avoidance and small power distance, including Australia, Canada, Jamaica, the United States, and many Western European nations. Meanwhile, Quadrant 2 contains many Asian, Central American, South American, and Middle Eastern nations—nations having large power distance and large uncertainty avoidance indexes.

FIGURE 2.5

Power Distance and Uncertainty Avoidance

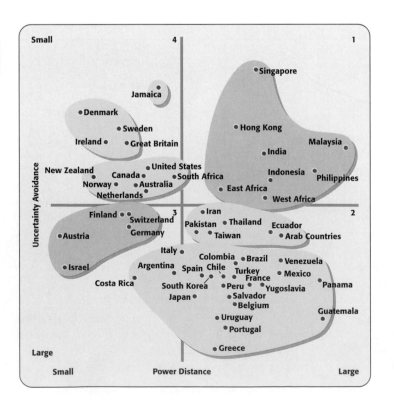

Locate your country in Figures 2.4 and 2.5. In your personal experience, do you agree with the placement of your nation in these figures? Do you believe managers in your country display the types of behaviors depicted in each of the described dimensions?

4. *Achievement versus nurturing.* Finally, this dimension captures the extent to which a culture emphasizes personal achievement and materialism versus relationships and quality of life. Cultures scoring high on this index tend to be characterized more by personal assertiveness and the accumulation of wealth, typically translating into an entrepreneurial drive. Cultures scoring low on this dimension generally have more relaxed lifestyles, wherein people are more concerned about caring for others as opposed to material gain.

Bottom Line: The dimensions described in the Kluckhohn–Strodtbeck and Hofstede frameworks are important for companies engaged in international business. As stated at the outset of our discussion of classifying cultures, people living in broadly different cultures tend to respond differently in similar business situations. This is why companies that send personnel abroad to unfamiliar cultures must be concerned with cultural differences. An interesting story comes to us from Japan. A Norwegian manager working in Japan for a European car manufacturer, but whose colleagues were mostly Japanese, soon became frustrated with the time needed to make decisions and take action. The main cause for his frustration lay in the fact that the uncertainty avoidance index for Japan is much larger than that in his native Norway (see Figure 2.5). In Japan, the greater aversion to uncertainty led to a greater number of meetings and consultations than would be needed in the home market. The frustrated manager eventually left Japan to return to Europe. The importance of culture for human resource management issues are discussed much further in Chapter 16.

Similarly, a company exploring international markets for its products must consider the local culture. We see the significance of power distance if we consider the export of luxury items. A nation with large power distance accepts greater inequality among its people and tends to have a wealthy upper class that can afford luxury goods. Thus, companies marketing products such as expensive jewelry, high-priced autos, and even yachts could find wealthy market segments within relatively poor nations. The role of culture in marketing is discussed at greater length in Chapter 14.

A FINAL WORD

This chapter discussed many of the cultural differences among nations that affect international business. We saw how problems can erupt from cultural misunderstandings and learned how companies can improve their performance with cultural literacy. Being culturally literate can mean the difference between returning home with a signed contract or returning empty-handed. As globalization propels more and more companies into the international business arena, localizing business policies and practices can help managers succeed. Moreover, understanding a people's values, beliefs, rules, and institutions makes managers more effective marketers, negotiators, and production managers. In the next two chapters we survey differences between nations' political, legal, and economic systems.

There is a variety of additional material available on the Companion Website that accompanies this book. You can access this information by visiting the Website at (**www.prenhall.com/wild**).

summary

1 **Describe** *culture*, **and explain the significance of both national culture and** *subcultures*. Culture is the set of values, beliefs, rules, and institutions held by a specific group of people. Successfully dealing with members of other cultures means avoiding *ethnocentricity* (the tendency to view one's own culture as superior to others) and developing *cultural literacy* (gaining the detailed knowledge necessary to function effectively in another culture).

We are conditioned to think in terms of national culture—that is, to equate a nation-state and its people with a single culture. Nations affirm the importance of "national culture" by building museums and monuments to preserve national legacies. Nations also intervene in business to help protect the national culture from the unwanted influence of other cultures. Most nations are also home to numerous *subcultures*—groups of people who share a unique way of life within a larger, dominant culture. Subcultures contribute greatly to national culture and must be considered in marketing and production decisions.

2 **Identify the** *components of culture*, **and describe their impact on business activities around the world.** Culture includes a people's beliefs and traditional habits and the ways in which they relate to one another. These factors fall into one or more of the eight major components of culture: (1) aesthetics; (2) values and attitudes; (3) manners and customs; (4) social structure; (5) religion; (6) personal communication; (7) education; and (8) physical and material environments.

Each of these components affects business activity. *Aesthetics*, for instance, determines which colors and symbols will be effective (or offensive) in advertising. *Values* influence a people's *attitudes* toward time, work and achievement, and cultural change. Knowledge of *manners* and *customs* is necessary for negotiating with people of other cultures, marketing products to them, and managing operations in their country. *Social structure* affects business decisions ranging from production-site selection to advertising methods to the costs of doing business in a country. Different *religions* take different views of work, savings, and material goods. Understanding a people's system of *personal communication* provides insight into their values and behavior. A culture's *education* level affects the quality of the workforce and standard of living. The *physical* and *material environments* influence work habits and preferences regarding products such as clothing and food.

3 **Describe** *cultural change*, **and explain how companies and culture affect one another.** *Cultural change* occurs when a people integrate into their culture the gestures, material objects, traditions, or concepts of another culture through the process of *cultural diffusion*. Globalization and technology are increasing the pace of cultural change around the world. Companies can influence culture when they import business practices or products into the host country. In order to avoid charges of *cultural imperialism*, they should import new products, policies, and practices during times of stability. Cultures also affect management styles, work scheduling, and reward systems. Adapting to local cultures around the world means heeding the maxim "Think globally, act locally."

4 **Explain how the** *physical environment* **and** *technology* **influence culture.** A people's *physical environment* includes *topography* and *climate* and the ways (good and bad) in which they relate to their surroundings. Cultures isolated by topographical barriers, such as mountains or seas, normally change relatively slowly, and their languages are often distinct. *Climate* affects the hours of the day that people work. For example, people in hot climates normally take siestas when afternoon temperatures soar. Climate also influences customs, such as the type of clothing a people wear and the types of foods they eat.

Material culture refers to all the technology that people employ to manufacture goods and provide services. It is often used to measure the technological advancement of a nation. Businesspeople often use this measure to determine whether a market has developed adequate demand for a company's products and whether it can support production activities. Material culture tends to be uneven across most nations.

5 **Describe the two main** *frameworks* **used to classify cultures and explain their practical use.** There are two widely accepted frameworks for studying cultural differences: (1) The *Kluckhohn–Strodtbeck framework* compares cultures along six dimensions by seeking answers to certain questions, including: Do people believe that their environment controls them or vice versa? Do people focus on past events or the future?

Do they prefer to conduct activities in public or private? (2) The *Hofstede framework* develops four dimensions, such as individualism versus collectivism and equality versus inequality. Understanding a culture's orientation regarding these four dimensions helps companies see the cultural obstacles awaiting personnel being sent abroad, and increases their chances of success. It also allows companies to identify market segments for their products. These frameworks help companies to understand many aspects of a people's culture including risk-taking, innovation, job mobility, team cooperation, pay levels, and hiring practices.

questions **for review**

1. What is *culture*? Explain how *ethnocentricity* distorts one's view of other cultures.

2. What is *cultural literacy*? What factors are forcing businesspeople to understand more about other cultures?

3. How do *nation-states* and *subcultures* affect a nation's cultural image?

4. What is meant by a culture's *aesthetics*? Give several examples from several different cultures.

5. How do *values* and *attitudes* differ? Explain how cultures differ in their attitudes toward time, work, and cultural change.

6. Describe the process of *cultural diffusion*. Why should international businesses be sensitive to accusations of *cultural imperialism*?

7. How do *manners* and *customs* differ? Give examples of each from several different cultures.

8. What are *folk* and *popular customs*? Describe how a folk custom can become a popular custom.

9. To what does *social structure* refer? How do social rank and mobility affect business activities?

10. Identify the dominant religion in each of the following countries.
    a. India
    b. Ireland
    c. Mexico
    d. Russia
    e. China
    f. Brazil
    g. Thailand

11. What specific advantages do companies gain when they learn how to *communicate* in another culture?

12. Why is the *education* of a country's people important to both native and nonnative companies operating there? What is meant by *brain drain* and *reverse brain drain*?

13. How are a people's culture and *physical environment* related? How does technology affect culture?

14. Describe the dimensions of the *Kluckhohn–Strodtbeck* and *Hofstede frameworks*. Contrast two cultures by applying one of these frameworks to them.

questions **for discussion**

1. Two students are discussing the various reasons why they are *not* studying international business. "International business doesn't affect me," declares the first student. "I'm going to stay here, not work in some foreign country." "Yeah, me neither," agrees the second. "Besides, some cultures are real strange. The sooner other countries start doing business our way, the better." What counterarguments can you present to these students' perceptions?

2. In this exercise, two groups of four students each will debate the benefits and drawbacks of individualist versus collectivist cultures. After the first student from each side has spoken, the second student questions the opponent's arguments, looking for holes and inconsistencies. A third student attempts to reply to these counterarguments. Then a fourth student summarizes each side's arguments. Finally, the class votes on which team presented the more compelling case.

in practice

Read the short article below and then answer the questions that follow.

Speaking in Fewer Tongues

PAPUA NEW GUINEA—One day this year, somewhere in the world, an old man or woman will die and with them will go their language.

The vulnerability of many languages is self-evident. Only 250 or so languages are spoken by more than a million people, and something like 90 percent have fewer than 100,000 speakers. In all, it is thought that there are about 6,000 languages. Linguists estimate that by the end of the twenty-first century over half of the world's languages will have been lost. They are understandably concerned that such a valuable part of human culture should vanish without a trace.

As minority languages die out, the popularity of three languages continue to grow: Mandarin, Spanish, and English. But English, the universal language of commerce, has emerged as the second and sometimes the first language of choice of people who have little or no historic links with England.

In Papua New Guinea, many young people now communicate between themselves in *tok psin,* which literally means "talk pidgin" English.

1. In this chapter and in Chapter 1 you learned how globalization is affecting people's lives. In your opinion, what role is globalization playing in the disappearance of languages? Be specific regarding the forces or trends you believe threaten the world's linguistic diversity.

2. Do you think a nation should try to preserve endangered languages as part of its cultural heritage? If so, give several examples of how it could do this. What do you think companies could be doing to help such languages survive? Be specific.

3. Select a language that you never knew existed. A good place to begin searching is Eurolang (**www.eurolang.net**) (a European Union organization) and The Linguistic Society of America (**www.lsadc.org**). Find out all you can about the language by asking such questions as: Where is it spoken and what are its origins? Which languages are closely related to it? How many people speak it and is it in danger of dying out? What is unique regarding its syntax, grammar, etc.? Write a brief report on your findings and present it to the class.

projects

1. Select a recent business periodical or news source in print or online—say, the *Far Eastern Economic Review* (**www.feer.com**), or the *Financial Times* (**www.ft.com**)—and find an article discussing the role of culture in international business. Write a short summary detailing the cultural elements identified by the author, being sure to explain how they pertain to actual business activities in the country being discussed.

2. Select a company in your city or town that interests you and make an appointment to interview the owner or a manager. Your goal is to learn how international opportunities and competition affect the decisions of this owner/manager and his or her company. Be sure to ask for specific examples.

Write a short report of your interview and present a brief talk on your findings to the class.

3. In your library or on the Internet, locate annual reports or similar information issued by companies like IKEA (**www.ikea.com**), Lands' End (**www.landsend.com**), Nokia (**www.nokia.com**), or Yahoo! (**www.yahoo.com**)—most libraries have annual reports in either paper or electronic form. Review this information and report on the (1) main products or services the company offers, (2) extent to which the company pursues international business operations (often expressed as percentage of sales or assets), and (3) ways that the company has adapted to local cultures around the world.

business case 2
ASIAN VALUES UNDER FIRE

Many cultures in Asia are in the midst of an identity crisis. In effect, they are being torn between two worlds. Pulling in one direction is a traditional value system derived from agriculture-based communities and extended families—that is, elements of a culture in which relatives take care of one another and state-run welfare systems are unnecessary. Pulling from the opposite direction is a new set of values emerging from manufacturing- and finance-based economies—elements of a culture in which workers must often move to faraway cities to find work, sometimes leaving family members to fend for themselves.

For years, spectacular rates of economic growth in a few short decades elevated living standards in many Asian countries far beyond what was thought possible. Young people in countries like Malaysia and Thailand felt the lure of "Western" brands. Gucci handbags (www.gucci.com), Harley-Davidson motorcycles (www.h-d.com), and other global brand names became common symbols of success. Some parents even encouraged brand-consciousness among their teenage children because it signaled family-wide success. Meanwhile, polls of young people showed them holding steadfast to traditional values such as respect for family and group harmony. Youth in Hong Kong, for example, overwhelmingly continued to believe that parents should have much to say about how hard they study, about how they treat family members and elders, and about their choice of friends.

But when the currencies of Thailand, Indonesia, Malaysia, South Korea, and other nations crumbled in the late 1990s, things changed. Financial investment shifted from relatively high-cost Southeast Asian nations toward the low-cost market that China offers and toward safe havens in highly industrialized countries. These nations' economies seemed to be picking up steam 2 or 3 years after the initial crisis. But they were hampered by continued economic weakness in Japan and an economic slowdown in Europe and the United States in late 2001. Meanwhile, investment into China soared as not only Western companies, but those based in the hard-hit Asian nations themselves, moved factory work to China to slash production costs. Living standards in China rose while those of neighboring countries languished.

Some Asians in hard-hit economies blame "westernization" for a decaying value system and declining morality. Many Asians, it seems, want modernization but also want to hold on to traditional beliefs and values. Nevertheless, Western companies continue to scoop up failing enterprises from Thailand to Japan and are implementing Western business practices. Asian businesses themselves continue to introduce Western management practices.

Prior to these recent economic troubles, many respected analysts in Asia, Europe, and the United States discussed the virtues of the so-called Asian way of doing business. But continued stagnation has put an abrupt end to that discussion. Some observers say that talk of an "Asian" way of doing business was overstated and misplaced. They argue that belief in the importance of family became the practice of nepotism, belief in the importance of relationships became cronyism, belief in the building of consensus became corrupt politics, and belief in conservatism and respect for authority became rigidity and an inability to innovate. If Asian culture esteems family loyalty so highly, they ask, why was it necessary for Singapore to enact legislation *requiring* that children take care of elderly parents?

thinking globally

1. If your international firm were doing business in Asia, would you feel partly responsible for these social trends? Is there anything that your company could do to ease the tensions being experienced by these cultures? Be specific.

2. In your opinion, is globalization among the causes of the increasing incidence of divorce, crime, and drug abuse in Asia? Why or why not?

3. Broadly defined, Asia comprises over 60 percent of the world's population—a population that practices Buddhism, Confucianism, Islam, and numerous other religions. Given the fact that there are considerable cultural differences between countries such as China, India, Indonesia, Japan, and Malaysia, is it possible to carry on a valid discussion of "Asian" values? Why or why not?

4. Consider the following statement: "Economic development and capitalism require a certain style of doing business for the twenty-first century. The sooner Asian cultures adapt, the better." Do you agree or disagree? Explain.

a question **of ethics**

1. Some businesspeople and other experts argue that bribery helps cut through mounds of red tape. Do you agree? By calling for reforms in nations that condone bribery, are international agencies (strongly backed by U.S. interests) promoting a certain set of values and morals? Are they practicing *cultural imperialism*?

2. When international firms enter the Indian market, they soon learn about the various ways in which a rigid caste system can affect business activities. Should these companies adjust to local management styles and human resource practices?

Or should they import their own styles and practices because they are so-called "more developed"?

3. Companies often relocate factories from industrialized nations with high labor costs to low-wage countries such as China, India, Mexico, and the nations of Central America. Is there a reasonable response to charges that, in so doing, they frequently exploit child labor, force women to work 75-hour weeks, and destroy family units?

3

politics and law in business

LEARNING OBJECTIVES

After studying this chapter, you should be able to

1. Describe each main type of *political system*.

2. Identify the origins of *political risk* and how managers can reduce its effects.

3. List the main types of *legal systems* and explain how they differ.

4. Describe the major *legal issues* facing international companies.

5. Explain how *international relations* affect international business activities.

BEACONS

A Look Back

CHAPTER 2 explored the main elements of culture and showed how they affect business practices. We learned about different methods used to classify cultures and how these methods can be applied to business.

A Look at This Chapter

This chapter explores the roles of politics and law in international business. We begin by explaining the different types of political systems and how managers cope with political risk. We then take a look at different forms of legal systems and how they affect international business.

A Look Ahead

CHAPTER 4 discusses the world's different economic systems. We learn about economic development and explore the challenges facing countries that are transforming their economies into free-market systems.

Taming the Wild, Wild Web

BEIJING, China—No doubt, the story on the U.S. Web site of Yahoo!, Inc. (**www.yahoo.com**) and some of its other national sites was gruesome. The news was that doctors in China were harvesting organs from executed Chinese prisoners, including some not quite dead. But one place the story never ran was Yahoo's Web site in China. Yahoo decided it was better to censor itself rather than risk offending Chinese politicians. "We're not looking to put provocative information up on the site," admits Maury Zeff, regional director of production for Yahoo Asia. "It's all up to the interpretation of the government." Except for sports news and stock quotes, foreign sources of news about China are out of bounds.

But this was not the first time that Yahoo had to adapt itself to local market constraints; it had already been forced to adapt to laws in Europe. French judge Jean-Jacques Gomez ordered Yahoo to stop offering Nazi artifacts to French consumers on its auction sites because buying Nazi memorabilia is illegal there. But because identifying every French bidder on its auction sites would be impossible, Yahoo withdrew all such items and filtered its Web sites globally to comply with French law.

Across the globe, from Tokyo to Toronto, Yahoo helps people communicate, access information, and sell things on the Internet. As such, the company's managers must be conscious of political and legal differences worldwide. Yet, Yahoo's founders probably never thought they would eventually get caught up in such sensitive issues around the world. David Filo and Jerry Yang started Yahoo in a trailer on their college campus in 1994 as "Jerry's Guide to the World Wide Web." Wanting a snappier name, the pair liked the general definition of a yahoo: "rude,

unsophisticated, uncouth." Today the company has over 200 million users in 24 countries communicating in 12 languages. As you read this chapter, think about how companies adapt to local conditions around the world.[1]

Chapter 2 explained that an understanding of culture is essential to achieving success in the international marketplace. Yet it is only one element of that success. Another crucial element is political and legal savvy. As Yahoo! (www.yahoo.com) learned in our opening company profile, doing business in other countries involves tricky political and legal issues. Yahoo's travails are a striking reminder that although the Internet shrinks the distance between two points, it still matters where those two points are. The Internet community consists of more than 240 country domains, and as many sets of political and legal environments. This is why just as "bricks and mortar" companies have always adapted to local politics and law in the global marketplace, so too must Internet companies.

But Yahoo is not the first company to censor itself or adapt its policies to local laws. Rupert Murdoch's News Corp. (www.newscorp.com) removed BBC news (www.bbc.co.uk) from its Asian television broadcasts because it occasionally criticized China.[2] Barnesandnoble.com (www.bn.com) and Amazon.com (www.amazon.com) stopped selling the English-language version of *Mein Kampf* to Germans when the German government complained—although it's illegal only to sell the German-language version. A statement by Barnesandnoble.com read, "Our policy with regard to censorship remains unchanged. But as responsible corporate citizens, we respect the laws of the countries where we do business."[3]

Understanding the nature of politics and laws in other nations lessens the risks of conducting international business. In this chapter, you will learn about the basic differences between political and legal systems around the world. Also, you will see how disputes grounded in political and legal matters affect business activities and how companies can manage the associated risks.

POLITICAL SYSTEMS

> **political system**
> Structures, processes, and activities by which a nation governs itself.

A **political system** includes the structures, processes, and activities by which a nation governs itself. The Japanese system, for instance, features a prime minister who is chosen by the Japanese Diet (Parliament) to carry out the operations of the government with the help of the Cabinet ministers. The Diet consists of two houses of elected representatives who enact the nation's laws. These laws affect not only the personal lives of people living in or visiting Japan but also the activities of companies doing business there.

POLITICS AND CULTURE

Politics and *culture* are closely related. A country's political system is rooted in the history and culture of its people. Factors such as population, age and race composition, and per capita income influence a country's political system.

Consider the case of Switzerland, where the political system actively encourages all eligible members of society to vote. By means of *public referendums*, Swiss citizens vote directly on many national issues. Contrast this practice with that of most other democracies, in which representatives of the people, not the people themselves, vote on such issues. The Swiss system works because Switzerland consists of a relatively small population living in a small geographic area.

POLITICAL PARTICIPATION

Political systems can be characterized by who participates in them and *to what extent* they participate. *Participation* occurs when people voice their opinions, vote, and show general approval or disapproval of the system.

Participation can be wide or narrow. *Wide participation* occurs when people who are capable of influencing the political system make an effort to do so. For example, most adults in the United States have the right to participate in the political process. Everyone has the right to approve or disapprove of elected representatives and the government in general. *Narrow participation* occurs when few people participate. For instance, in Kuwait participation is restricted to citizens who can prove Kuwaiti ancestry at some time in the past.

But sometimes people eligible to vote don't even bother. For example, turnout in recent national elections ranged from more than 90 percent of the voting-age population in Malta to less than 35 percent in Senegal and Kazakhstan. Figure 3.1 shows voter turnout for the world's major geographic regions.[4]

POLITICAL IDEOLOGIES

We can think of the world's different political systems as falling on a continuum that is defined by three political ideologies:

➡ At one extreme is *anarchism*—the belief that only individuals and private groups should control a nation's political activities. It views public government as unnecessary and unwanted because it tramples personal liberties.

➡ At the other extreme is *totalitarianism*—the belief that every aspect of people's lives must be controlled in order for a nation's political system to be effective. Totalitarianism has no concern for individual liberties. In fact, people are often considered slaves of the

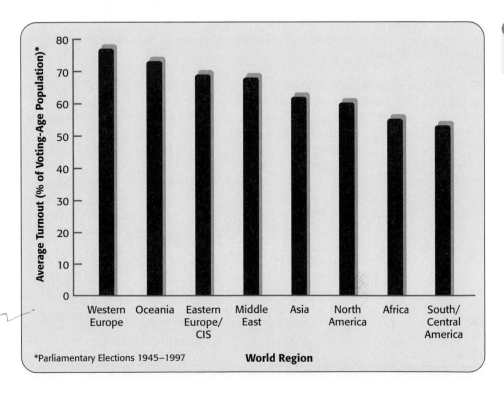

FIGURE 3.1

Voter Turnout around the World

political system. Institutions such as family, religion, business, and labor are considered subordinate to the state. Totalitarian political systems include such authoritarian regimes as communism and fascism.

➡ Between anarchism and totalitarianism lies *pluralism*—the belief that both private and public groups play important roles in a nation's political activities. Each of these groups (consisting of people with different ethnic, racial, class, and lifestyle backgrounds) serves to balance the power that can be gained by the other. Pluralistic political systems include democracies, constitutional monarchies, and some aristocracies.

Let's take a look at two prevalent types of political systems—democracy and totalitarianism—to gain a fuller understanding of the political elements that cause differences in business practices from one country to another.

Democracy   A **democracy** is a political system in which government leaders are elected directly by the wide participation of the people or by their representatives. The foundations of modern democracy go back at least as far as the ancient Greeks.

The Greeks tried to practice a *pure democracy*, one in which all citizens participate freely and actively in the political process. But a "pure" democracy is more an ideal than a workable system, for several reasons. First, some people have neither the time nor the desire to get involved in the political process. Second, as population expands and the barriers of distance and time increase, each citizen's ability to participate completely and actively is reduced. And third, because direct voting usually results in conflicting popular opinion, leaders in a pure democracy can find it difficult, if not impossible, to form cohesive policies.

Representative Democracies   For practical reasons, most nations have resorted to **representative democracies,** in which citizens nominate individuals from their groups to represent their political needs and views. These representatives then help govern the people and pass laws. Representatives performing to the people's satisfaction can be voted back into office. Meanwhile, those who fail to retain a minimum level of popular support are voted out of office.

To varying degrees, representative democracies strive to provide some or all of the following freedoms:

➡ *Freedom of expression*. A constitutional right in most democracies, freedom of expression ideally grants the right to voice opinions freely and without fear of punishment.

➡ *Periodic elections*. Each elected representative serves for a period of time, after which the people (or *electorate*) decide whether or not to retain these representatives. This is why U.S. presidential elections are held every four years, whereas those in France are held every seven years.

➡ *Full civil and property rights*. Civil rights include freedom of speech, freedom to organize political parties, and the right to a fair trial. Property rights are the privileges and responsibilities of owners of property (homes, cars, businesses, and so forth). Map 3.1 (on pages 80–81) illustrates the extent to which people of 191 nations around the world have political rights and civil liberties.

➡ *Minority rights*. In theory, democracies try to preserve peaceful coexistence among groups of people with diverse cultural, ethnic, and racial backgrounds. Ideally, the same rights and privileges are by law extended to each group, no matter how few its members.

➡ *Nonpolitical bureaucracies*. The bureaucracy is the part of government that implements the rules and laws passed by elected representatives. In *politicized bureaucracies*, bureaucrats tend to implement decisions according to their own political views rather than those of the people's representatives. This clearly contradicts the purpose of the democratic process.

democracy
Political system in which government leaders are elected directly by the wide participation of the people or by their representatives.

representative democracy
Democracy in which citizens nominate individuals from their groups to represent their political needs and views.

Despite such shared principles, countries vary greatly in the practice of representative democracy. Britain, for example, practices *parliamentary democracy*. The nation is divided into geographical districts, and people in each district vote for competing *parties* rather than individual candidates. But the party that wins the greatest number of legislative seats in an election does not automatically win the right to run the country. Rather, a party must gain an *absolute majority*—that is, the number of representatives that it gets elected must be greater than the number of representatives elected of all other parties.

If the party with the largest number of representatives lacks an absolute majority, it can join with one or more other parties to form what is called a coalition government. In a *coalition government*, the strongest political parties share power by dividing government responsibilities among themselves. Coalition governments are often formed in Italy, Israel, and the Netherlands. The large number of political parties in these countries makes it difficult for single parties to gain absolute majorities.

Nations also differ in the relative power possessed by each of its political parties. In some democratic countries, a single political party has effectively controlled the system for extended periods. In Japan, for example, the Liberal Democratic Party (which is actually conservative) has enjoyed nearly uninterrupted control of the government since the 1950s. In Mexico, the Institutional Revolutionary Party (PRI) ran the country for 71 years until Vicente Fox of the conservative National Action Party (PAN) won the presidency in 2000.

Doing Business in Democracies Democracies maintain stable business environments primarily through laws that protect individual property rights. In theory, commerce prospers when the **private sector** includes independently owned firms that exist to make profits. Bear in mind that although participative democracy, property rights, and free markets tend to encourage economic growth, they do not always do so. India, for example, is the world's largest democracy; but it experienced slow economic growth for decades. Meanwhile, some countries achieved rapid economic growth under nondemocratic political systems. The so-called four tigers of Asia—Hong Kong, Singapore, South Korea, and Taiwan—built strong market economies (despite recent economic setbacks) in the absence of truly democratic practices.

> **private sector**
> *Segment of the economic environment comprised of independently owned firms that exist to make a profit.*

Totalitarianism

In a **totalitarian system**, individuals govern without the support of the people, government maintains control over many aspects of people's lives, and leaders do not tolerate opposing viewpoints. In this sense, totalitarianism and democracy are opposites. Nazi Germany under Adolf Hitler and the former Soviet Union under Joseph Stalin are historical examples of totalitarian governments. Today, China, Iraq, Myanmar (formerly Burma), and North Korea are prominent examples of totalitarian governments.

> **totalitarian system**
> *Political system in which individuals govern without the support of the people, government maintains control over many aspects of people's lives, and leaders do not tolerate opposing viewpoints.*

Another important distinction between democratic and totalitarian governments is the concentration of power. Totalitarian leaders attempt to silence those with opposing political views. Unlike democracies, therefore, totalitarian regimes require the near-total centralization of political power. Much like the ideal of "pure democracy," a "pure" form of totalitarianism is not possible either. No totalitarian government is capable of entirely silencing all of its critics.

Totalitarian governments tend to share three features:

➡ *Imposed authority.* An individual or group forms the political system without the explicit or implicit approval of the people. Thus, a totalitarian system is marked by narrow participation. Leaders often acquire and retain power by military force or fraudulent elections. In some cases, they come to power through legitimate means but then remain in office after their terms expire.

MAP 3.1

Political and Civil Liberties around the World

This map illustrates the level of political rights and civil liberties of the people of each nation and territory. It does not rate national governments, but represents the rights and liberties of individuals. As defined by *Freedom House*, political rights refer to people's ability to vote and run for public office and, as elected officials, to vote on public policies. Civil liberties include people's freedom to develop views, institutions, and personal autonomy apart from the state.

In all, 87 countries (45 percent of the world population) are listed as being *free*, 57 countries (30 percent of the world population) as *partly free*, and 48 countries (25 percent of the world population) as *not free*.

theocracy
Political system in which a country's political leaders are religious leaders who enforce laws and regulations based on religious beliefs.

theocratic totalitarianism
Political system in which religious leaders govern without the support of the people and do not tolerate opposing viewpoints.

➡ *Lack of constitutional guarantees.* Totalitarian systems deny citizens the constitutional guarantees woven into the fabric of democratic practice. They limit, abuse, or reject outright institutions such as freedom of expression, periodically held elections, guaranteed civil and property rights, and minority rights. Also, the bureaucracy may be politicized rather than nonpolitical.

➡ *Restricted participation.* Political representation is limited either to parties that are sympathetic to the government or to those that pose no credible threat. In most cases, political opposition is completely banned, and resisters are severely punished.

Let's now take a detailed look at the two most common types of totalitarian political systems: *theocratic* and *secular*.

Theocratic Totalitarianism　When a country's religious leaders are also its political leaders, its political system is called a **theocracy**. Religious leaders enforce laws and regulations that are based on religious beliefs. A political system that is under the control of totalitarian religious leaders is called **theocratic totalitarianism**.

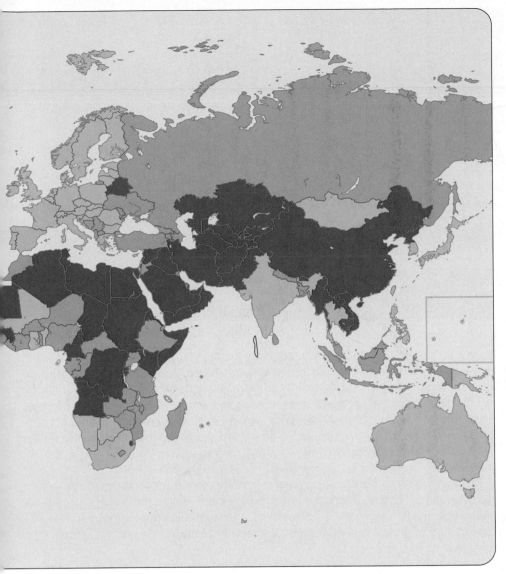

	Free
	Partly free
	Not free
	No data

Iran is a prominent example of a theocratic totalitarian state. Iran has been an Islamic state since the 1979 revolution in which the reigning monarch was overthrown. Today, many young Iranians appear disenchanted with the strict code imposed on many aspects of their public and private lives, including strict laws against products and ideas deemed too "Western." They do not question their religious beliefs but yearn for a more open society. Iranian president Muhammad Khatami pushed through some changes in government policies in recent years despite opposition from conservative religious leaders.

Secular Totalitarianism   A political system in which political leaders rely on military and bureaucratic power is called **secular totalitarianism**. It takes three forms: *communist*, *tribal*, and *right-wing*.

Communist Totalitarianism   Under *communist totalitarianism* (referred to here simply as *communism*), the government has sweeping political and economic powers. The Communist Party controls all aspects of the political system, and opposition parties

> **secular totalitarianism**
> *Political system in which leaders rely on military and bureaucratic power.*

Iran is arguably more pro-business than at any time in the more than 22 years since the revolution. Two beneficiaries of the change are entrepreneurs Abdollah Fateh, 28, and Madjid Emami, 30, who together started their Internet service provider, (**www.parsonline.com**.) The pair hope to become the Iranian, or even regional, America Online. They certainly have a following. Says a female admirer, "They are the two coolest guys in Tehran."

communism
The belief that social and economic equality can be obtained only by establishing an all-powerful Communist Party and by granting the government ownership and control over all types of economic activity.

socialism
The belief that social and economic equality is obtained through government ownership and regulation of the means of production.

capitalism
The belief that ownership of the means of production belongs in the hands of individuals and private businesses.

are given little or no voice. In general, each Party member holding office is required to support all government policies, and dissension is rarely permitted. **Communism** is the belief that social and economic equality can be obtained only by establishing an all-powerful Communist Party and by instituting **socialism**—an economic system in which the government owns and controls all types of economic activity. This includes granting the government ownership of the means of production (such as capital, land, and factories) and the power to decide what the economy will produce and the prices at which goods are sold.

However, important distinctions separate communism from socialism. Communists follow the teachings of Marx and Lenin, believe that a violent revolution is needed to seize control over resources, and wish to eliminate political opposition. Socialists believe in none of these. Thus, communists are socialists, but socialists are not necessarily communist.

Communist and socialist beliefs differ markedly from those of **capitalism**—the belief that ownership of the means of production belongs in the hands of individuals and private businesses. Capitalism is also frequently referred to as the *free market*. (The economics of communism and capitalism are covered in detail in Chapter 4.)

Communist totalitarianism and economic socialism seem to have lost the battle against capitalism. In the late 1980s, shortly after the former Soviet Union implemented its twin policies of *glasnost* (political openness) and *perestroika* (economic reform), its government began to crumble, as people complained openly about their government. Communist governments in Central and Eastern Europe soon followed suit, and today countries such as the Czech Republic, Hungary, Poland, Romania, and Ukraine have elected republican governments. As a result, there are far fewer communist nations than there were two decades ago. North Korea remains the most prominent, hard-line communist nation today.

Tribal Totalitarianism   Under *tribal totalitarianism*, one tribe (or ethnic group) imposes its will on others with whom it shares a national identity. The least understood form of totalitarianism, it characterizes the governments of several African nations, including Burundi and Rwanda. With the departure of European colonial powers, many national boundaries in Africa were created with little regard to ethnic differences among inhabitants. Thus, people of different ethnicities live within the same nation, whereas members of the same ethnicity live in different nations. Over time, certain ethnic groups gained political and military power, and animosity among the different groups often erupted in bloody conflict.

Right-Wing Totalitarianism   Under *right-wing totalitarianism*, the government endorses private ownership of property and a market-based economy but grants few (if any) political freedoms. Leaders generally strive for economic growth while opposing *left-wing* totalitarianism (communism). Argentina, Brazil, Chile, and Paraguay all had right-wing totalitarian governments in the 1980s.

Despite theoretical differences between the two ideologies, the Chinese political system is currently a mix of communist and right-wing totalitarianism. China's leaders are engineering high economic growth by implementing certain characteristics of a capitalist economy while retaining a hard line in the political sphere. The Chinese government is selling off many of its decrepit state-run factories and changing laws to further encourage the international investment needed to modernize the country's production technologies. But the government still has little patience for the dissidents who are demanding greater political freedom. And as Yahoo discovered in this chapter's opening company profile, complete freedom of the press does not exist in China.

Doing Business in Totalitarian Countries   What are the costs and benefits of doing business in a totalitarian nation? On the plus side, international companies need not be concerned with political opposition to their activities by those outside the government. On the negative side, they might need to pay bribes and kickbacks to government officials. Refusal to pay could result in loss of market access or even forfeiture of investments in the country.

In any case, doing business in a totalitarian country can be a risky proposition. Many facets of business law pertain to contractual disputes. In a country such as the United States, laws regarding the resolution of such disputes are quite specific. In totalitarian nations, the law can be either vague or nonexistent, and people in powerful government positions can interpret laws largely as they please. For instance, in China it may not matter so much what the law states as it does how individual bureaucrats interpret the law. The, at times, arbitrary nature of totalitarian governments makes it hard for companies to know how laws will be interpreted and applied to their particular business dealings.

Companies that operate in totalitarian nations are sometimes criticized for their lack of compassion for the people hurt by the oppressive political policies of their hosts. Executives must decide whether to refrain from investing in totalitarian countries—and miss potentially profitable opportunities—or invest and bear the brunt of potentially damaging publicity. The issues are complex, and the controversy remains heated.

The Bottom Line   Do democratic governments provide more "stable" national business environments than totalitarianism? This question is not easily answered. Democracies, for example, pass laws to protect individual civil liberties and property rights. But totalitarian governments could also grant such rights. What would be the difference? Whereas democracies strive to *guarantee* such rights, totalitarian governments retain the power to repeal them whenever they wish.

What about prospects for a nation's rate of economic growth—the increase in the amount of goods and services produced by a nation? We can say with certainty only that a democracy does not guarantee high rates of economic growth and that totalitarianism does not doom a nation to slow economic growth. The rate of growth is influenced by many variables other than political and civil liberty, including a country's tax system, its encouragement or discouragement of investment, the availability of capital, and the trade and investment barriers that it erects or guards against.

POLITICAL SYSTEMS IN TIMES OF CHANGE

People around the world are demanding greater participation in the political process and forcing many nations to abandon totalitarian for democratic systems. But the economic consequences of globalization are causing fundamental changes in people's values and attitudes. In Latin American nations, the selling off of state-owned companies is having a great impact on people's attitudes toward democracy. A survey done in 2001 showed a sharp decline in support for democracy across the region. At the same time, there was a modest increase in the numbers of people who favor dictatorship. The World Business Survey titled "Doubting Democrats" shows exactly how thin the support for democracy is getting across the region. But only in Paraguay do a majority say that an authoritarian government might be preferable to a democratic one.[5]

One of the most closely watched nations in terms of its political change is China. After 1949, when the communists defeated the nationalists in China's civil war, China imprisoned or exiled most of its capitalists. But in 2001 private businesspeople were allowed to join China's Communist Party for the first time ever. The move represents the leadership's struggle to maintain order in the face of increasingly rapid economic and social change. A government report issued in 2001 spoke of difficulties facing the nation, including the collapse of state-owned industry, a social safety net unable to cope with millions of unemployed, poor relations with the nation's ethnic minorities, an unjust legal system, and a restless peasantry increasingly willing to take up arms against the system.[6] Workers are also being allowed for the first time ever to elect local representatives to the official trade union. Meanwhile, without Beijing's approval, scores of townships in Sichuan, Guangdong, and Shanxi provinces are holding elections for township chiefs, who are normally chosen by Party representatives.[7]

POLITICAL RISK

political risk
Likelihood that a government or society will undergo political changes that negatively affect local business activity.

All companies doing business internationally confront **political risk**—the likelihood that a government or society will undergo political changes that negatively affect local business activity. Political risk affects different types of companies in different ways. It can threaten the market of an exporter, the production facilities of a manufacturer, or the ability of a company to pull out profits from the country in which they were earned. Map 3.2 (on pages 86–87) shows how the level of political risk varies from nation to nation.

Political risk arises from a variety of sources, including the following:

➡ Corrupt or poor political leadership
➡ Frequent changes in the form of government
➡ Political involvement of religious or military leaders
➡ An unstable political system
➡ Conflict among races, religions, or ethnic groups
➡ Poor relations with other countries

International businesses can unwittingly *increase* their own political risk by stirring up local emotions and sentiments. For example, they can add to their political risk if they harm the local society in some way or damage the natural environment and fail to provide adequate compensation. If any harm done by an international company in the local market is severe enough, it may even spur lawmakers to enact laws not in their favor. In order to reduce their companies' exposure to political risk, international managers should have a solid grasp of local values, customs, and traditions.

WORLD BUSINESS SURVEY

Doubting Democrats

Which of the following statements do you agree with most?

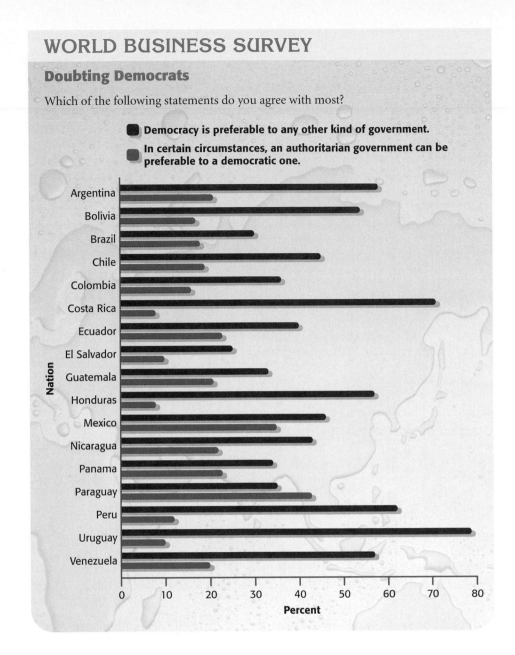

- Democracy is preferable to any other kind of government.
- In certain circumstances, an authoritarian government can be preferable to a democratic one.

TYPES OF POLITICAL RISK

Managers must be aware of how political risk can affect their companies. In a broad sense, we can categorize political risk according to the range of companies subjected to it. *Macro risk* threatens all companies regardless of industry. For example, every company doing business in Myanmar fears violence against its assets and employees, and shares an abiding concern about government corruption. Macro risk affects equally all companies in a country, both domestic and international. *Micro risk* threatens companies within a particular industry or even smaller groups. Japanese exporters of mobile phones, air conditioners, or vehicles to China were crippled by a 100 percent punitive tariff that China slapped on these goods. The move was in retaliation for Japan's temporary curbs on shiitake mushrooms, leeks, and rushes for tatami mats imported from China.[8]

MAP 3.2

Political Risk around the World

A nation's political risk is an important factor in a company's decision to do business with or in that country. This map shows how much political risk can vary from one country to another. Some of the factors included in this assessment of political risk levels include government stability, internal and external conflict, military and religion in politics, corruption, law and order, and bureaucracy quality.

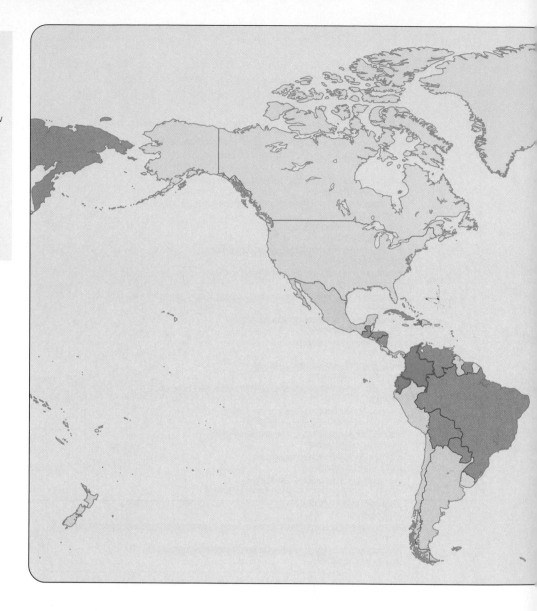

In addition to these two broad categories, we can classify political risk according to the actions that cause it to arise. Let's now examine five different events that can cause political risk:

➡ Conflict and violence
➡ Terrorism and kidnapping
➡ Property seizure
➡ Policy changes
➡ Local content requirements

Conflict and Violence   Local conflict can strongly discourage investment by international companies. Violent disturbances impair a company's ability to manufacture and distribute products, obtain materials and equipment, and recruit talented personnel. Open conflict also threatens both physical assets (including office buildings, factories, and production equipment) and the lives of employees.

LEVEL OF RISK

- Very high
- High
- Moderate
- Low
- Very low
- No data

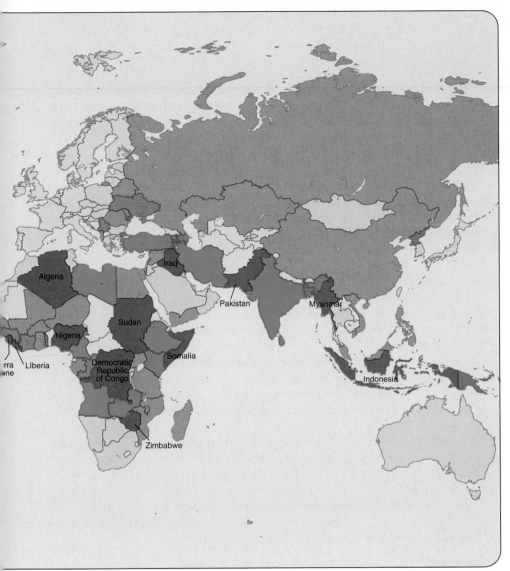

Conflict arises from several sources. First, it may result from people's resentment toward their own government. When peaceful resolution of disputes between people (or factions) and the government fails, violent attempts to change political leadership can ensue. In early 2000 ExxonMobil (**www.exxonmobil.com**) was forced to suspend production of liquid natural gas at its facility in Indonesia's Aceh province. The reason for the shutdown was that separatist rebel forces in the province were increasingly making the complex a target of their violence.[9]

Second, conflict may arise over territorial disputes between countries. For example, a dispute over the Kashmir territory between India and Pakistan has resulted in major armed conflict between the two at least several times. And a border dispute between Ecuador and Peru has caused these South American nations to go to war three times—most recently in 1995.

Finally, disputes between ethnic, racial, and religious groups may erupt in violent conflict. Indonesia comprises 13,000 islands, more than 300 ethnic groups, and some 450 languages. Former Indonesian President Suharto had a policy of relocating people from crowded, central islands to remote, less populated ones, but without regard to ethnicity and religion. But violence between these different groups displaced more than 1 million people. Today, companies doing business in Indonesia still face the risk that ethnic and religious violence will disrupt business operations.[10]

Terrorism and Kidnapping Kidnapping and other terrorist activities are means of making political statements. Small groups dissatisfied with current political or social situations can resort to terrorist tactics aimed at forcing change through fear and destruction. Such groups sometimes have silent approval from a substantial portion of the local population, but just as often do not.

The world witnessed terrorism on a scale never before seen on September 11, 2001. On that day two passenger planes were flown into the twin towers of the World Trade Center in New York City and one plane was crashed into the Pentagon in Washington, D.C. Financial and commodity markets plunged in the United States when they reopened after being closed for days. Roughly $1.4 trillion in market value was eliminated in just five days of trading.[11] But in spite of the geopolitical ramifications of those events, markets regained their lost values relatively quickly and the long-term economic impact was rather muted.

Kidnapping and the taking of hostages may be used to fund a terrorist group's activities. Executives of large international companies are prime targets because their employers have the "deep pockets" from which to pay large ransoms. Latin American countries have some of the world's highest kidnapping rates. Colombia, where some 3,000 kidnappings occur annually, has what can only be described as a thriving kidnapping industry. Annual security costs for a company with a sales office in the capital city of Bogota can be $125,000, and up to $1 million for a company with operations in rebel-controlled areas. Top executives are forced to spend about a third of their time coordinating their company's security in Colombia.[12]

When high-ranking executives are required to enter countries with high kidnapping rates they should enter unannounced, meet with only a few key people in secure locations, and leave just as quickly and quietly. Some companies even purchase kidnap, ransom, and extortion insurance, but most security experts agree that training managers and executives to avoid trouble in the first place is a far better investment. For a checklist of ways to avoid risk during overseas assignments, see the Global Manager titled "Your Global Security Checklist."

Property Seizure Governments sometimes seize the assets of companies doing business within their borders. Seizure of assets falls into one of three categories: *confiscation*, *expropriation*, or *nationalization*.

confiscation
Forced transfer of assets from a company to the government without compensation.

Confiscation The forced transfer of assets from a company to the government *without compensation* is called **confiscation**. Usually the former owners have no legal basis for requesting compensation or the return of assets. The U.S. 1996 Helms–Burton Law allows U.S. companies to sue companies from other nations that use property confiscated from U.S. companies following Cuba's communist revolution in 1959. But U.S. presidents repeatedly waive the law so that U.S. relations with other countries are not harmed.

expropriation
Forced transfer of assets from a company to the government with compensation.

Expropriation The forced transfer of assets from a company to the government *with compensation* is called **expropriation**. The government doing the expropriating normally determines compensation. There is no framework for legal appeal, and compensation is typically far below market value. Today, governments rarely resort to confiscation or expropriation because by doing so, they jeopardize future investment in their countries. Also, companies already doing business there may leave for fear of losing their valuable assets.

GLOBAL MANAGER

Your Global Security Checklist

➡ **Getting there**. Take nonstop flights when possible—takeoffs and landings are a flight's most risky moments. Move quickly from an airport's public areas and check-in to more secure areas beyond passport control. Report abandoned packages to airport security.

➡ **Getting around**. Kidnappers watch for daily routines. Vary the exit you use to leave your house, office, and hotel, and vary the time that you depart and arrive. Drive with your windows up and doors locked. Swap cars with your spouse occasionally, or take a cab one day and ride the tram/subway the next. Avoid night driving when possible. Be discreet regarding your itinerary.

➡ **Keep a low profile.** Don't draw attention by pulling out a large wad of currency or paying with large denominations. Avoid public demonstrations. Dress like the locals when possible and leave expensive jewelry at home. Avoid loud conversation and being overheard. If you rent an automobile, avoid the flashy and choose a local, common model.

➡ **Guard personal data**. Be friendly but cautious when answering questions about you, your family, and your employment. Keep answers short and vague when possible. Give out your work number only—all family members should do the same. Don't list your home or mobile phone numbers in directories. Do not carry items in your purse or wallet that contain your home address.

➡ **Use good judgment**. Be cautious if a local asks directions or the time—it could be a mugging ploy. When possible, travel with others and avoid walking alone after dark. Avoid narrow, dimly lit streets. If you get lost act as if you know where you are and ask directions from a place of business, not passersby. Beware of offers by drivers of unmarked or poorly marked cabs. Do not accept food or drinks from strangers.

➡ **Know local S.O.S. procedures**. Be familiar with the local emergency procedures before trouble strikes. Keep phone numbers of police, fire, your hotel, your nation's embassy, and a reputable taxi service in your home and with you.

Nationalization   Whereas expropriation involves one or a small number of companies in an industry, **nationalization** means government takeover of an *entire* industry. Nationalization is more common than confiscation and expropriation. Likely candidates include industries important to a nation's security and those that generate large revenues. In the 1970s Chile nationalized its vast copper industry and paid international companies a price substantially below market value. Nationalization appeals to governments for four main reasons:

1. Governments may nationalize industries when they believe that international companies are transferring profits to operations in other countries with lower tax rates. Nationalization gives the government control over the cash flow generated by the industry.
2. Governments may nationalize an industry for ideological reasons. The leading political party, for instance, might believe that the government can protect an industry with subsidies. Such was the ideology of the Labor Party that governed Britain for many years after the Second World War.
3. Nationalization is sometimes used as a political tool. Candidates may promise to save local jobs by nationalizing ailing industries.
4. Government ownership may support industries in which private companies are unwilling or unable to invest. For instance, the investment required to build public utilities and train employees is more than most private companies can afford. Governments often approach this problem by controlling utilities industries and subsidizing them with tax revenues.

The extent of nationalization varies widely from country to country. Whereas the governments of Cuba, North Korea, and Vietnam control practically every industry,

nationalization
Government takeover of an entire industry.

those of the United States and Canada own very few. Many countries, including France, Brazil, Mexico, Poland, and India, try to strike a balance between government and private ownership.

Policy Changes   Government policy changes are the result of a variety of influences, including the ideals of newly empowered political parties, political pressure from special interests, and civil or social unrest. One common policy tool restricts ownership to domestic companies or limits ownership by nondomestic firms to a minority stake. This is why PepsiCo's (**www.pepsico.com**) ownership of local companies was restricted to 49 percent when it first entered India.

Other policies relate to investments made across borders. Because a global slowdown in the tech sector in 2001 hit Taiwanese companies hard, business leaders and politicians called for a scrapping of the long-held "go slow, be patient" policy. That policy capped investments in mainland China at $50 million and banned investments in infrastructure and those that the Taiwanese government believed were too high-tech (for national security reasons). Taiwan President Chen Shui-bian responded by announcing a new policy referred to as "active opening, effective management." Although implementing the policy change would take several years, its announcement had an immediate impact on corporate strategies. The general consensus was that the change would have a serious negative impact on Hong Kong's tourism industry and its intermediary role in trade.[13]

Local Content Requirements   Laws stipulating that a specified amount of a good or service be supplied by producers in the domestic market are called **local content requirements**. These requirements can force companies to use locally available raw materials, procure parts from local suppliers, or employ a minimum number of local workers. They ensure that international companies foster local business activity and help ease regional or national unemployment. They also help governments maintain some degree of control over international companies without resorting to extreme measures such as confiscation and expropriation.

But local content requirements can jeopardize an international firm's long-term survival because they pose two potential disadvantages. Specifically, a company may be required to:

1. Hire local personnel, which might force it to take on an inadequately trained workforce or take on excess workers.
2. Obtain raw materials or parts locally, which might increase production costs or reduce quality.

> **local content requirements**
> *Laws stipulating that a specified amount of a good or service be supplied by producers in the domestic market.*

MANAGING POLITICAL RISK

Aside from monitoring and predicting potential political changes, international companies must try to manage political risks that threaten their operations and future earnings. There are four main methods of managing political risk: *avoidance*, *adaptation*, *information gathering*, and *influencing local politics*.

Avoidance   *Avoidance* simply means restraining from investing in a country: a poor choice when opportunity knocks. When risk is manageable and the local market is appealing, managers find another way to deal with political risk.

Adaptation   *Adaptation* means incorporating risk into business strategies, often with the help of local officials. Companies can incorporate risk by means of five strategies: *local equity and debt*, *localization*, *development assistance*, *partnerships*, and *insurance*.

Local Equity and Debt   *Local equity and debt* involves financing local business activities with the help of local firms, trade unions, financial institutions, and government. As partners in local business activities, these groups may help to keep political forces from interrupting operations. If they own shares in local operations (*equity*), the partners get cuts of the profits. If they loan cash (*debt*), they receive interest. The international company's risk exposure is reduced because local partners take an interest in the operation's success and because it has less of its own capital at risk.

Localization   *Localization* entails modifying operations, the product mix, or some other business element—even the company name—to suit local tastes and culture. This strategy is behind the global success of MTV (www.mtv.com). By customizing the content of certain aspects of MTV programming to regional and sometimes national tastes, the company succeeds in localizing its image. Because MTV is sensitive to local sociocultural and political issues, it is less of a target for nationalists in turbulent times.

Development Assistance   Offering local *development assistance* allows an international business to assist the host country or region in developing its distribution and communications networks and improving the quality of life for locals. Because the company and the nation become partners, they both benefit. For example, Anglo-Dutch oil company, Royal Dutch/Shell (www.shell.com), operates in many developing nations worldwide. One of the company's current development efforts is a 10-year project to improve the economic opportunities of 100 villages (120,000 people) in Kenya. It has as its goals the doubling of incomes of 60 percent of the poorest households, and increasing the average period of food security from 3 to 9 months.[14] Canon (www.canon.com), the Japanese maker of copiers and printers, goes beyond mere assistance. By practicing *kyosei* ("spirit of cooperation") the firm uses its economic influence to press local governments into making social and political reforms.

Partnerships   An increasingly popular way of managing risk, *partnerships* can be excellent for leveraging a company's expansion plans. Such partnerships can be informal arrangements but often include joint ventures, strategic alliances, and cross-holdings of

International companies engage in development assistance as a way to insulate themselves from potentially adverse political changes. Here, a child in the African nation of Chad uses a water pump built by ExxonMobil (**www.exxonmobil.com**)—a large investor in the country. But the company has come under fire from critics who claim the firm lags behind the efforts of industry rivals. What more do you think ExxonMobil could do to help the local people?

company stock (Chapter 13 discusses these types of arrangements in detail). By partnering with other international firms or local players a company can share the risk of loss, which is often particularly important in developing countries.

Insurance   Companies that enter risky national business environments routinely purchase *insurance* against the potential effects of political risk. The *Overseas Private Investment Corporation (OPIC)* (**www.opic.gov**), for example, insures internationally active U.S. companies against loss and can provide project financing. Some policies protect companies when local governments restrict the convertibility of local money into home-country currency. Others insure against losses created by violent events, including war and terrorism. Among other services, the *Foreign Credit Insurance Association (FCIA)* (**www.fcia.com**) insures companies against damages from war, revolution, and the cancellation of licenses.

Information Gathering   International firms often attempt to gather information that will help it predict and manage political risk. There are two sources of data that companies use to conduct accurate political risk forecasting:

1. *Current employees with relevant information.* Employees who have worked in a country long enough to gain insight into local culture and politics are often good sources of information. Individuals who formerly had decision-making authority while on international assignment probably had contact with local politicians and other officials. But because political power can shift rapidly and dramatically, it is important that the employee's international experience be recent.
2. *Agencies specializing in political-risk services.* These include banks, political consultants, news publications, and risk-assessment services that estimate risk using a variety of criteria and methods. Many of these agencies offer reports that detail the levels and sources of political risk for nations. Because these services can be expensive, small companies and entrepreneurs might consider the many free sources of information that are available, notably from their federal governments. Government intelligence agencies are excellent, inexpensive sources to consult.

Influencing Local Politics   Managers must cope with the rules and regulations that apply in each national business environment. Laws in many nations are susceptible to frequent change, with new laws continually being enacted and existing ones modified. To influence local politics in their favor, managers can propose changes that affect their local activities in a positive way.

Influencing local politics always involves dealing with local lawmakers and politicians, either directly or through lobbyists. **Lobbying** is the policy of hiring people to represent a company's views on political matters. Lobbyists meet with local public officials and try to influence their position on issues relevant to the company. They describe the benefits that a company brings to the local economy, natural environment, infrastructure, and workforce. Their ultimate goal is to get favorable legislation enacted and unfavorable legislation rejected.

Corruption   As we saw in Chapter 2, bribes are one method of gaining political influence. They are routinely used in some countries to get distributors and retailers to push a firm's products through distribution channels. Sometimes they mean the difference between obtaining important contracts and being completely shut out of certain markets.

In the early 1970s the president of United States–based Lockheed Corp., now Lockheed Martin (**www.lockheedmartin.com**), bribed Japanese officials in order to obtain large sales contracts. Public disclosure of the incident resulted in passage of the 1977 U.S. **Foreign Corrupt Practices Act**, which forbids U.S. companies from bribing government officials or political candidates in other nations (except when a person's life

lobbying
Policy of hiring people to represent a company's views on political matters.

Foreign Corrupt Practices Act
1977 statute forbidding U.S. companies from bribing government officials or political candidates in other nations.

TABLE 3.1	Who Do You Trust?	
The Least Corrupt . . .	**. . . and the Most Corrupt**	
1. Finland	82. Tanzania	
2. Denmark	83. Ukraine	
3. New Zealand	84. (*tie*) Azerbaijan	
4. (*tie*) Iceland	84. (*tie*) Bolivia	
4. (*tie*) Singapore	84. (*tie*) Cameroon	
6. Sweden	84. (*tie*) Kenya	
7. Canada	88. (*tie*) Indonesia	
8. Netherlands	88. (*tie*) Uganda	
9. Luxembourg	90. Nigeria	
10. Norway	91. Bangladesh	

is otherwise in danger). A bribe can constitute "anything of value"—money, gifts, and so forth—and cannot be given to any "foreign government official" empowered to make a "discretionary decision" that may be to the payer's benefit. That law also requires firms to keep accounting records that reflect their international activities and assets.

Like many cultural and political elements, the prevalence of corruption varies from one country to another. Corruption is detrimental to society and business for many reasons. Among other things, corruption leads to the misallocation of resources (not always to their most efficient uses), can hurt economic development, distorts public policy, and can damage the integrity of "the system." Table 3.1 shows the least and most corrupt countries according to recent surveys. In addition to the countries shown, the United Kingdom ranked 13, Germany ranked 20, and the United States ranked 16 (tied with Israel).

In our discussion of political systems and how companies deal with political uncertainty, we touched on several important legal issues. Although there is a good deal of overlap between a nation's political and legal systems, they are distinct. Let's now take a look at several types of legal systems and how they influence the activities of international companies.

LEGAL SYSTEMS

A country's **legal system** consists of its laws and regulations, including the processes by which its laws are enacted and enforced, and the ways in which its courts hold parties accountable for their actions. A legal system is influenced by many cultural variables, including class barriers, religious beliefs, and whether individualism or group conformity is emphasized. Many laws, rules, and regulations are used to safeguard cultural values and beliefs.

A country's legal system is also influenced by its political system. Totalitarian governments tend to favor public ownership of economic resources and enact laws limiting entrepreneurial behavior. In contrast, democracies tend to encourage entrepreneurial activity and to protect small businesses with strong property-rights laws. The rights and responsibilities of parties to business transactions also differ from one nation to another. For all these reasons, business strategies must be flexible enough to adapt to different legal systems.

Also important are political "moods," including upsurges of **nationalism**—the devotion of a people to their nation's interests and advancement. It typically involves intense national loyalty and cultural pride, and it is often associated with drives toward national independence. In India, for instance, because most business laws originated when the country was struggling for "self-sufficiency," the legal system tended to protect local businesses from international competition. In the 1960s and 1970s India national-

legal system
Set of laws and regulations, including the processes by which a country's laws are enacted and enforced and the ways in which its courts hold parties accountable for their actions.

nationalism
Devotion of a people to their nation's interests and advancement.

ized many industries and intensely scrutinized applicants wanting licenses to start new businesses. Today, however, although nationalism still runs strong in India, the government is responding to globalization by passing laws that are more pro-business.

TYPES OF LEGAL SYSTEMS

There are three main types of legal systems (called legal traditions) in use around the world: *common law*, *civil law*, and *theocratic law*. This section examines each of these legal traditions and shows how it affects international business activities.

Common Law   The practice of common law originated in England in the eleventh century and was adopted in its territories around the world. Thus, the U.S. legal system, for example, though integrating elements of civil law, is based largely on the common law tradition. A **common law** legal system reflects three factors:

➡ *Tradition*: a country's legal history
➡ *Precedent*: past cases that have come before the courts
➡ *Usage*: the ways in which laws are applied in specific situations

    Under common law, the justice system decides cases by interpreting the law on the basis of tradition, precedent, and usage. However, each law may be interpreted somewhat differently in each case to which it is applied. In turn, each new interpretation sets a *precedent* that may be followed in future cases. As new precedents arise, laws are altered to clarify vague wording or to accommodate situations not previously considered.

    Business *contracts*—legally enforceable agreements between two parties—tend to be lengthy (especially in the United States) because they must consider the many possible contingencies that can arise and the many possible interpretations of the law that may apply in case of a dispute. Companies must devote a good deal of time to devising clear contracts and commit large sums of money to acquiring legal advice. On the positive side, common law systems are flexible. Instead of applying uniformly to all situations, laws take into account particular situations and circumstances. The common law tradition is practiced in Australia, Britain, Canada, Ireland, New Zealand, the United States, and some nations in Asia and Africa.

Civil Law   The civil law tradition can be traced back to Rome in the fifth century B.C. It is the world's oldest and most common legal tradition. A **civil law** system is based on a detailed set of written rules and statutes that constitute a legal *code*. Civil law can be less adversarial than common law because there tends to be less need to interpret laws according to tradition, precedent, and usage. Because all laws are codified and concise, parties to contracts tend to be more concerned only with the explicit wording of the code. All obligations, responsibilities, and privileges follow directly from the relevant code. Therefore, less time and money are typically spent on legal matters. But civil law systems can ignore the unique circumstances of particular cases. The civil law tradition is practiced in Cuba, Puerto Rico, Quebec, all of Central and South America, most of Western Europe, and in many nations in Asia and Africa.

Theocratic Law   A legal tradition based on religious teachings is called **theocratic law**. Three prominent theocratic legal systems are Islamic, Hindu, and Jewish law. Although Hindu law was restricted by India's 1950 constitution, in which the state appropriated most legal functions, it does persist as a cultural and spiritual force. Likewise, after most Jewish communities were stripped of judicial autonomy in the eighteenth century, Jewish law lost much of its influence and today serves few legal functions—although it remains a strong religious force.

    Islamic law is the most widely practiced theocratic legal system today. Islamic law was initially a code governing moral and ethical behavior and was later extended to

---

common law
Legal system based on a country's legal history (tradition), past cases that have come before its courts (precedent), and the ways in which laws are applied in specific situations (usage).

civil law
Legal system based on a detailed set of written rules and statutes that constitute a legal code.

theocratic law
Legal system based on religious teachings.

commercial transactions.[15] It restricts the types of investments that companies can make and sets guidelines for the conduct of business. According to Islamic law, for example, banks cannot charge interest on loans or pay interest on deposits. Instead, borrowers give banks a portion of the profits they earn on their investments, and depositors receive returns based on the profitability of their banks' investments. Likewise, because the products of alcohol- and tobacco-related businesses violate Islamic belief, firms abiding by Islamic law cannot invest in such companies.

Firms operating in countries with theocratic legal systems must be extremely sensitive to local values and beliefs. They should evaluate all business activities, including hiring practices and investment policies, to ensure compliance not only with the law but also with local values and beliefs.

GLOBAL LEGAL ISSUES

In general, laws related to product quality, product liability, environmental pollution, and the treatment of employees are far tougher in European countries and the United States than they are in many countries in Africa, Asia, and Latin America. Some international companies take advantage of these differences in standards. For example, they might sell products abroad that are banned in their home countries. Thus, *legal* differences often develop into *ethical* issues for many international businesspeople. Let's now take a look at several important global legal issues facing international businesses.

STANDARDIZATION

Because of differences among legal systems, companies often hire legal experts in each country in which they operate. This can be a very costly practice. Fortunately, standardization of laws across countries is occurring in a few areas. However, *standardization* refers to uniformity in interpreting and applying laws in more than one country, not to the standardizing of entire legal systems.

Although there is no well-defined body of international law, treaties and agreements do exist in several areas, including intellectual property rights, antitrust (antimonopoly) regulation, taxation, contract arbitration, and general matters of trade. In addition, several international organizations promote the standardization process. Among others, the *United Nations (UN)* (**www.un.org**), the *Organization for Economic Cooperation and Development (OECD)* (**www.oecd.org**), and the *International Institute for the Unification of Private Law* (**www.unidroit.org**) in Rome work to standardize rules of conduct in international business. In order to remove legal barriers for companies operating in Western Europe, the European Union is also standardizing some areas of its nations' legal systems. Although, as Yahoo discovered in this chapter's opening company profile, further progress is needed on some areas of law across the European Union.

INTELLECTUAL PROPERTY

Property that results from people's intellectual talent and abilities is **intellectual property**. It includes graphic designs, novels, computer software, machine-tool designs, and secret formulas, such as that for making Coca-Cola (**www.cocacola.com**). Technically, it results in *industrial property* (in the form of either a *patent* or a *trademark*) or *copyright* and confers a limited monopoly on its holder.

Many legal systems protect **property rights**—the legal rights to resources and any income they generate. Like other types of property, intellectual property can be traded, sold, and licensed in return for fees and/or royalty payments. Intellectual property laws are designed to compensate people whose rights are infringed.

intellectual property
Property that results from people's intellectual talent and abilities.

property rights
Legal rights to resources and any income they generate.

But nations vary widely in their intellectual property laws. Business Software Alliance (BSA) (www.bsa.org), the trade body for business software makers, issues an annual study of software piracy rates around the globe. Whereas illegal copies of business software recently made up just 24 percent of the U.S. domestic market (the lowest in the world), pirated software made up a whopping 97 percent of the Vietnamese market. Running a close second was China (94 percent). Worldwide, business software piracy averaged 37 percent in 2000 and cost business software makers nearly $12 billion.[16] Figure 3.2 shows piracy rates for some nations included in the BSA study.

As such figures suggest, the laws in some countries are soft in comparison with those in places such as Canada, Japan, the United States, and across much of Western Europe. European and U.S. software companies continue to lobby their governments to pressure other nations into adopting stronger laws. So far, their efforts have had mixed results. In Ireland recently, BSA implemented a program in which about $5,800 are awarded to members of the public who provide information to BSA regarding the illegal use of business software. The program is getting results. In 2001 BSA took legal action against seven Irish companies on behalf of Adobe (www.adobe.com), Microsoft (www.microsoft.com), and others.[17]

But when there is software piracy, there is often music piracy as well. According to Le Hong Thanh, director of Saigon Audio Company in Vietnam, up to 95 percent of all compact discs sold in Ho Chi Minh City are pirated. "Our CDs are released in the morning; they already have pirated copies in the afternoon," he lamented. The problem is rooted in the fact that fakes can cost nearly 20 percent less.[18] Industry officials say the problem is ubiquitous because of technological advances—a fake CD can be made in less than 4 seconds for under a dollar.[19]

Intellectual property can be broadly classified as either *industrial property* or *copyrights*. Let's explore the main issues associated with each category.

industrial property
Patents and trademarks.

Industrial Property   **Industrial property** includes patents and trademarks—often a firm's most valuable assets. Laws protecting industrial property are designed to reward

FIGURE 3.2

Business Software Piracy

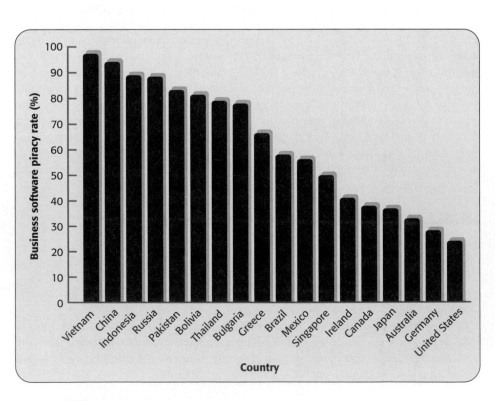

inventive and creative activity. The purpose of the U.S. Federal Patent Statute is to provide an incentive for inventors to pursue inventions and make them available to consumers. Likewise, trademark law creates incentives for manufacturers to invest in developing new products and also allows consumers to be sure that they are always getting the same product from the same producer. Industrial property is protected internationally under the *Paris Convention for the Protection of Industrial Property* (**www.wipo.int**), to which nearly 100 countries are signatories.

Patents   A **patent** is a right granted to the inventor of a product or process that excludes others from making, using, or selling the invention. Current U.S. patent law went into effect on June 8, 1995, and is in line with the systems of most developed nations. Its provisions are those of the **World Trade Organization (WTO)** (**www.wto.org**), the international organization that regulates trade between nations. The WTO typically grants patents for a period of 20 years. The 20-year term begins when a patent application is *filed* with a country's patent office, not when it is finally *granted*. Patents can be sought for any invention that is new, useful, and not obvious to any individual of ordinary skill in the relevant technical field.

> **patent**
> *Property right granted to the inventor of a product or process that excludes others from making, using, or selling the invention.*

> **World Trade Organization (WTO)**
> *International organization that regulates trade between nations.*

One field in which patents are drawing special attention is biotechnology. In fact, by mid-2001 there were 506,794 gene sequences included in patents on life and 9,364 patents related to the human body. Some question whether a gene sequence is an invention or in fact a discovery.[20] But these patents often include the method used to discover the gene sequences. The argument for awarding patents in such areas is to protect companies' research and development efforts in creating new treatments for all sorts of illnesses.

Trademarks   **Trademarks** are words or symbols that distinguish a product and its manufacturer. The Nike (**www.nike.com**) "swoosh" is a trademark, as is the name "Sony" (**www.sony.com**). Consumers benefit from trademarks because they know what to expect when they buy a particular brand. In other words, you would not expect a canned soft drink labeled "Coca-Cola" to taste like one labeled "Sprite."

> **trademark**
> *Property right in the form of words or symbols that distinguish a product and its manufacturer.*

Trademark protection typically lasts indefinitely, provided the word or symbol continues to be distinctive. Ironically, this stipulation presents a problem for companies such as Coca-Cola and Xerox, whose trademarks "Coke" and "Xerox" (**www.xerox.com**) have evolved into generic terms for all products in their respective categories.

Designers who own trademarks, such as Chanel (**www.chanel.com**), Christian Dior (**www.christiandior.com**), and Gucci (**www.gucci.com**), have long been plagued by shoddily made counterfeit handbags, shoes, shirts, and other products. But recently, pirated products of equal or nearly equal quality are turning up, especially in Italy. Most Italian makers of luxury goods—notably leather and jewelry—outsource production to small manufacturers across the country. Therefore, it is not hard for these same artisans to counterfeit extra copies of a high-quality product. Bootleg copies of a Prada (**www.prada.com**) backpack that costs $500 in New York can be bought for less than $100 in Rome. Jewelry shops in Milan can buy fake Bulgari (**www.bulgari.com**) and Rolex (**www.rolex.com**) watches for $300 and sell them retail for $2,500.

Like trademark laws themselves, enforcement policies differ by country. The maximum penalty for a trademark violation in Italy is 3 years in prison and a $4,000 fine; in Germany, it is 5 years and an unlimited fine. But some progress toward standardization is occurring. The European Union, for example, opened a trademark-protection office to police trademark infringement against firms that operate in any EU country.

Copyrights   **Copyrights** give creators of original works the freedom to publish or dispose of them as they choose. The existence of a copyright is typically denoted by inclusion of the well-known symbol ©, a date, and the copyright holder's name. A copyright holder has rights such as the following:

> **copyright**
> *Property right giving creators of original works the freedom to publish or dispose of them as they choose.*

- To reproduce the copyrighted work
- To derive new works from the copyrighted work
- To sell or distribute copies of the copyrighted work
- To perform the copyrighted work
- To display the copyrighted work publicly

Copyright holders include authors and publishers of literary works; composers of musical scores; developers of computer-software programs; and artists, photographers, and painters. Works created after January 1, 1978, are automatically copyrighted for the creator's lifetime plus 50 years. Publishing houses receive copyrights for either 75 years from the date of publication or 100 years after creation, whichever comes first. Copyrights are protected under the **Berne Convention** (www.wipo.int)—an international copyright treaty to which the United States is a member—and the 1954 Universal Copyright Convention. More than 50 countries abide by one or both of these treaties.

A copyright is granted for the *tangible expression* of an idea, not for the idea itself. For example, no one can copyright the idea of a movie about the sinking of the *Titanic*. However, once the film itself is made to express its creator's treatment of the subject, that film can be copyrighted.

Believe it or not, one of the most well-known songs around the world, "Happy Birthday to You," is actually protected by U.S. copyright law. The song was composed in 1859 and copyrighted in 1935. Although the copyright was set to expire in 2010, on the song's 75th copyright birthday, the U.S. Congress extended it until 2030. Who owns the copyright, and what do they stand to gain from the extension? The media empire AOL/Time Warner owns it, and perhaps as much as $20 million.[21]

A major problem for music companies is halting the illegal sharing of digital music files on the Internet. A landmark case of copyright infringement on the Internet was that of Napster (www.napster.com). Napster was at the center of the free, unrestricted swapping of digital music files online using so-called peer-to-peer technology. At its peak in February 2001, Napster had nearly 1.6 million users logged on worldwide simultaneously swapping music files. Meanwhile, the illegal swapping meant record companies and their artists received no royalties. The world's biggest record labels sued Napster

Berne Convention
International treaty that protects copyrights.

Contrary to popular belief, "Happy Birthday to You" is indeed a copyrighted song. Although originally set to expire in the year 2010, copyright protection was extended to 2030.

"We're OK, folks – 'Happy Birthday to You' isn't a copyright song."

for copyright infringement and won. But it was a rather hollow victory. Music lovers just continued their free swapping of music on the Web sites of Napster alternatives.[22]

PRODUCT SAFETY AND LIABILITY

Most countries have product safety laws that lay down standards to be met by manufactured products. **Product liability** holds manufacturers, sellers, and others, including individual company officers, responsible for damage, injury, or death caused by defective products. Injured parties can sue for both monetary compensation through *civil* lawsuits and fines or imprisonment through *criminal* lawsuits. Civil suits are frequently settled before cases go to court.

> **product liability**
> *Responsibility of manufacturers, sellers, and others for damage, injury, or death caused by defective products.*

The United States has the toughest product liability laws in the world, with Europe a close second. Less-developed and emerging countries have the weakest laws. By the same token, insurance premiums and legal expenses are greater in the nations with strong product liability laws. Damage awards tend to be several times larger in the United States than in other developed countries.

Enforcement of product liability laws differs from nation to nation. In the United States and Canada, for instance, tobacco companies are regularly under attack for their belated warnings about the health effects of tobacco and nicotine and their marketing tactics. In an unprecedented move, Canada's Health Minister Allan Rock announced in 2001 that he would introduce legislation that would ban tobacco companies from marketing cigarettes under the labels "light" or "mild," saying that they mislead consumers into a false sense of security.[23] But in countries like India and Sri Lanka, tobacco companies are practically free from any scrutiny whatsoever by public-welfare organizations. Because of far less stringent regulation, the biggest market for U.S. cigarette makers is Asia, followed closely by Eastern Europe.

TAXATION

National governments use income and sales taxes for many purposes. They use tax revenue to pay government salaries, build military capacity, and shift earnings from people with high incomes to the poor. They also pass indirect taxes called consumption taxes, which serve two main purposes:

1. To help pay for the consequences of using a particular product
2. To make imports more expensive

Consumption taxes on products such as alcohol and tobacco help pay the healthcare costs of treating the illnesses that result from the use of these products. Similarly, gasoline taxes help pay for the road and bridge repairs needed to counteract the effects of traffic and weathering. Taxes on imports give locally made products an advantage among price-sensitive consumers.

Unlike the United States, many countries employ a so-called **value added tax** (**VAT**)—a tax levied on each party that adds value to a product throughout its production and distribution. Supporters of the VAT system contend that it distributes taxes on retail sales more evenly between producers and consumers. Suppose, for instance, that a shrimper sells the day's catch of shrimp for $1 per kilogram and that the country's VAT is 10 percent (Table 3.2). The shrimper, processor, wholesaler, and retailer pay taxes of $0.10, $0.07, $0.11, and $0.10, respectively, for the value that each adds to the product as it makes its way to consumers. Because the government collects taxes from each party along this path, consumers pay no additional tax at the point of sale. However, because producers and distributors must increase prices to compensate for their tax burdens, consumers end up paying the tax. So that the poor are not overly burdened, many countries exclude the VAT on certain items such as children's clothing.

> **value added tax (VAT)**
> *Tax levied on each party that adds value to a product throughout its production and distribution.*

TABLE 3.2	Effect of Value-Added Taxes (VAT)			
Production Stage	Selling Price	Value Added	10% VAT	Total VAT
Shrimper	$1.00	$1.00	$0.10	$0.10
Processor	1.70	0.70	0.07	0.17
Wholesaler	2.80	1.10	0.11	0.28
Retailer	3.80	1.00	0.10	0.38

ANTITRUST REGULATIONS

antitrust (antimonopoly) laws
Laws designed to prevent companies from fixing prices, sharing markets, and gaining unfair monopoly advantages.

Laws designed to prevent companies from fixing prices, sharing markets, and gaining unfair monopoly advantages are called **antitrust (antimonopoly) laws.** Such laws try to provide consumers with a wide variety of products at fair prices. The United States has the world's strictest antitrust regulation and is its strictest enforcer. The European Union also has rather strict antitrust regulation. In Japan, the Fair Trade Commission enforces antitrust laws but is often ineffective because *absolute proof* of wrongdoing is needed to bring charges. To learn about the U.S. agency responsible for antitrust enforcement (and the activities of several other agencies), see the Entrepreneurial Focus titled "The Long Arm of the Law."

ENTREPRENEURIAL FOCUS

The Long Arm of the Law

Every government has agencies designed to monitor the national business environment and enforce its laws. Here are several important U.S. agencies that entrepreneurs and small businesses can consult for free legal information.

➡ **U.S. Patent and Trademark Office (USPTO).** The USPTO is a noncommercial federal bureau within the Department of Commerce. By issuing patents it provides incentives to invent, invest in, and disclose new technologies worldwide. By registering trademarks it protects business investment and safeguards consumers against confusion and deception. By disseminating patent and trademark information it facilitates the development and sharing of new technologies worldwide. To learn more visit the USPTO Web site at (**www.uspto.gov**).

➡ **U.S. International Trade Commission (USITC).** The USITC is an independent, quasi-judicial federal agency. It provides trade expertise to both the legislative and executive branches of government, determines the impact of imports on U.S. industries, and directs actions against certain unfair trade practices, such as patent, trademark, and copyright infringement. The agency has broad investigative powers on matters of trade and is a national resource where trade data are gathered and analyzed. Visit the USITC at (**www.usitc.gov**).

➡ **Federal Trade Commission (FTC).** The FTC enforces a variety of federal antitrust and consumer protection laws. It seeks to ensure that the nation's markets function competitively and are vigorous, efficient, and free of undue restrictions. The Commission also works to enhance the smooth operation of the marketplace by eliminating acts or practices that are unfair or deceptive. In general, the Commission's efforts are directed toward stopping actions that threaten consumers' opportunities to exercise informed choice. Learn more about the FTC at (**www.ftc.gov**).

➡ **U.S. Consumer Product Safety Commission (CPSC).** The CPSC is an independent federal regulatory agency created to protect the public from injury and death associated with some 15,000 types of consumer products, including car seats, bicycles and bike helmets, lawnmowers, toys, and walkers. It also provides information for businesses regarding the export of noncompliant, misbranded, or banned products. Learn more about the activities of the CPSC at (**www.cpsc.gov**).

Companies based in strict antitrust countries often argue that they are at a disadvantage against competitors whose home countries condone *market sharing*, whereby competitors agree to serve only designated segments of a certain market. That is why firms in strict antitrust countries often lobby for exemptions in certain international transactions. Small businesses also argue that they could better compete against large international companies if they could join forces without fear of violating antitrust laws.

In the absence of a global antitrust enforcement agency, international companies must concern themselves with the antitrust laws of each nation in which they do a significant amount of business. In fact, a nation (or group of nations) can block a merger or acquisition between two nondomestic companies if those companies do a good deal of business within it. This is exactly what happened to the proposed $43 billion merger between General Electric (GE) (**www.ge.com**) and Honeywell (**www.honeywell.com**) in 2001. GE wanted to marry their manufacture of airplane engines to Honeywell's production of advanced electronics for the aviation industry. Although both companies are based in the United States, together they employ 100,000 Europeans. GE alone earned $25 billion in Europe the year before the proposed merger's collapse. The European Union blocked the merger because it believed that the result would be higher prices for customers, particularly airlines.[24]

BUSINESS AND INTERNATIONAL RELATIONS

The political relations between a company's home country and those in which it does business affects its international business activities. Favorable political relationships foster stable business environments and increase international cooperation in many areas, including the development of international communications and distribution infrastructures. In turn, a stable environment requires a strong legal system through which disputes can be resolved quickly and fairly. In general, favorable political relations lead to increased business opportunities and lower risk.

To generate stable business environments, some countries have turned to *multilateral agreements*—treaties concluded among several nations, each of whom agrees to abide by treaty terms even if tensions develop. According to the European Union's founding treaty, goods, services, and citizens of member nations are free to move across members' borders. Every nation must continue to abide by such terms even if it has a conflict with another member. Thus, although Britain and France disagree on many issues, neither can treat goods, services, and citizens moving from one country to the other any differently than it treats those of any other EU nation. See Chapter 8 for a detailed presentation of the European Union.

THE UNITED NATIONS

Although individual nations sometimes have the power to influence the course of events in certain parts of the world, they cannot monitor political activities everywhere at once. The **United Nations (UN)** (**www.un.org**) was formed after the Second World War to provide leadership in fostering peace and stability around the world. The UN and its many agencies provide food and medical supplies, educational supplies and training, and financial resources to poorer member nations. The UN receives its funding from member contributions based primarily on gross national product (GNP). Practically all nations in the world are UN members—except for several small countries and territories that have observer status.

Figure 3.3 gives an overview of the UN system. A Secretary General who is elected by all members and serves for a 5-year term heads the UN. The UN system consists of six main organs:

United Nations (UN)
International organization formed after World War II to provide leadership in fostering peace and stability around the world.

FIGURE 3.3   The United Nations System

The UNITED NATIONS system

UNITED NATIONS

PRINCIPAL ORGANS OF THE UNITED NATIONS

INTERNATIONAL COURT OF JUSTICE	SECURITY COUNCIL	GENERAL ASSEMBLY	ECONOMIC AND SOCIAL COUNCIL	TRUSTEESHIP COUNCIL	SECRETARIAT

Military Staff Committee
Standing Committee and ad hoc bodies
International Criminal Tribunal for the Former Yugoslavia
International Criminal Tribunal for Rwanda
UN Monitoring, Verification and Inspection Commission (Iraq)
United Nations Compensation Commission
Peacekeeping Operations and Missions

Main committees
Other sessional committees
Standing committees and ad hoc bodies
Other subsidiary organs

PROGRAMMES AND FUNDS

UNCTAD
United Nations Conference on Trade and Development

ITC
International Trade Centre (UNCTAD/WTO)

UNDCP
United Nations Drug Control Programme

UNEP
United Nations Environment Programme

UNHSP
United Nations Human Settlements Programme (UN-Habitat)

UNDP
United Nations Development Programme

UNIFEM
United Nations Development Fund for Women

UNV
United Nations Volunteers

UNFPA
United Nations Population Fund

UNHCR
Office of the United Nations High Commissioner for Refugees

UNICEF
United Nations Children's Fund

WFP
World Food Programme

UNRWA**
United Nations Relief and Works Agency for Palestine Refugees in the Near East

OTHER UN ENTITIES

OHCHR
Office of the United Nations High Commissioner for Human Rights

UNOPS
United Nations Office for Project Services

UNU
United Nations University

UNSSC
United Nations System Staff College

RESEARCH AND TRAINING INSTITUTES

INSTRAW
International Research and Training Institute for the Advancement of Women

UNICRI
United Nations Interregional Crime and Justice Research Institute

UNITAR
United Nations Institute for Training and Research

UNRISD
United Nations Research Institute for Social Development

UNIDIR**
United Nations Institute for Disarmament Research

FUNCTIONAL COMMISSIONS

Commission for Social Development
Commission on Human Rights
Commission on Narcotic Drugs
Commission on Crime Prevention and Criminal Justice
Commission on Science and Technology for Development
Commission on Sustainable Development
Commission on the Status of Women
Commission on Population and Development
Statistical Commission

REGIONAL COMMISSIONS

Economic Commission for Africa (ECA)
Economic Commission for Europe (ECE)
Economic Commission for Latin America and the Caribbean (ECLAC)
Economic and Social Commission for Asia and the Pacific (ESCAP)
Economic and Social Commission for Western Asia (ESCWA)

United Nations Forum on Forests

Sessional and Standing Committees
Expert, ad hoc and related bodies

RELATED ORGANIZATIONS

IAEA
International Atomic Energy Agency

WTO (trade)
World Trade Organization

WTO (tourism)
World Tourism Organization

CTBTO Prep.com
PrepCom for the Nuclear-Test-Ban-Treaty Organization

OPCW
Organization for the Prohibition of Chemical Weapons

SPECIALIZED AGENCIES*

ILO
International Labour Organization

FAO
Food and Agriculture Organization of the United Nations

UNESCO
United Nations Educational, Scientific and Cultural Organization

WHO
World Health Organization

WORLD BANK GROUP

IBRD International Bank for Reconstruction and Development
IDA International Development Association
IFC International Finance Corporation
MIGA Multilateral Investment Guarantee Agency
ICSID International Centre for Settlement of Investment Disputes

IMF
International Monetary Fund

ICAO
International Civil Aviation Organization

IMO
International Maritime Organization

ITU
International Telecommunication Union

UPU
Universal Postal Union

WMO
World Meteorological Organization

WIPO
World Intellectual Property Organization

IFAD
International Fund for Agricultural Development

UNIDO
United Nations Industrial Development Organization

SECRETARIAT

OSG
Office of the Secretary-General

OIOS
Office of Internal Oversight Services

OLA
Office of Legal Affairs

DPA
Department of Political Affairs

DDA
Department for Disarmament Affairs

DPKO
Department of Peacekeeping Operations

OCHA
Office for the Coordination of Humanitarian Affairs

DESA
Department of Economic and Social Affairs

DGAACS
Department of General Assembly Affairs and Conference Services

DPI
Department of Public Information

DM
Department of Management

OIP
Office of the Iraq Programme

UNSECOORD
Office of the United Nations Security Coordinator

ODCCP
Office for Drug Control and Crime Prevention

UNOG
UN Office at Geneva

UNOV
UN Office at Vienna

UNON
UN Office at Nairobi

*Autonomous organizations working with the United Nations and each other through the coordinating machinery of the Economic and Social Council.
**Report only to the General Assembly.

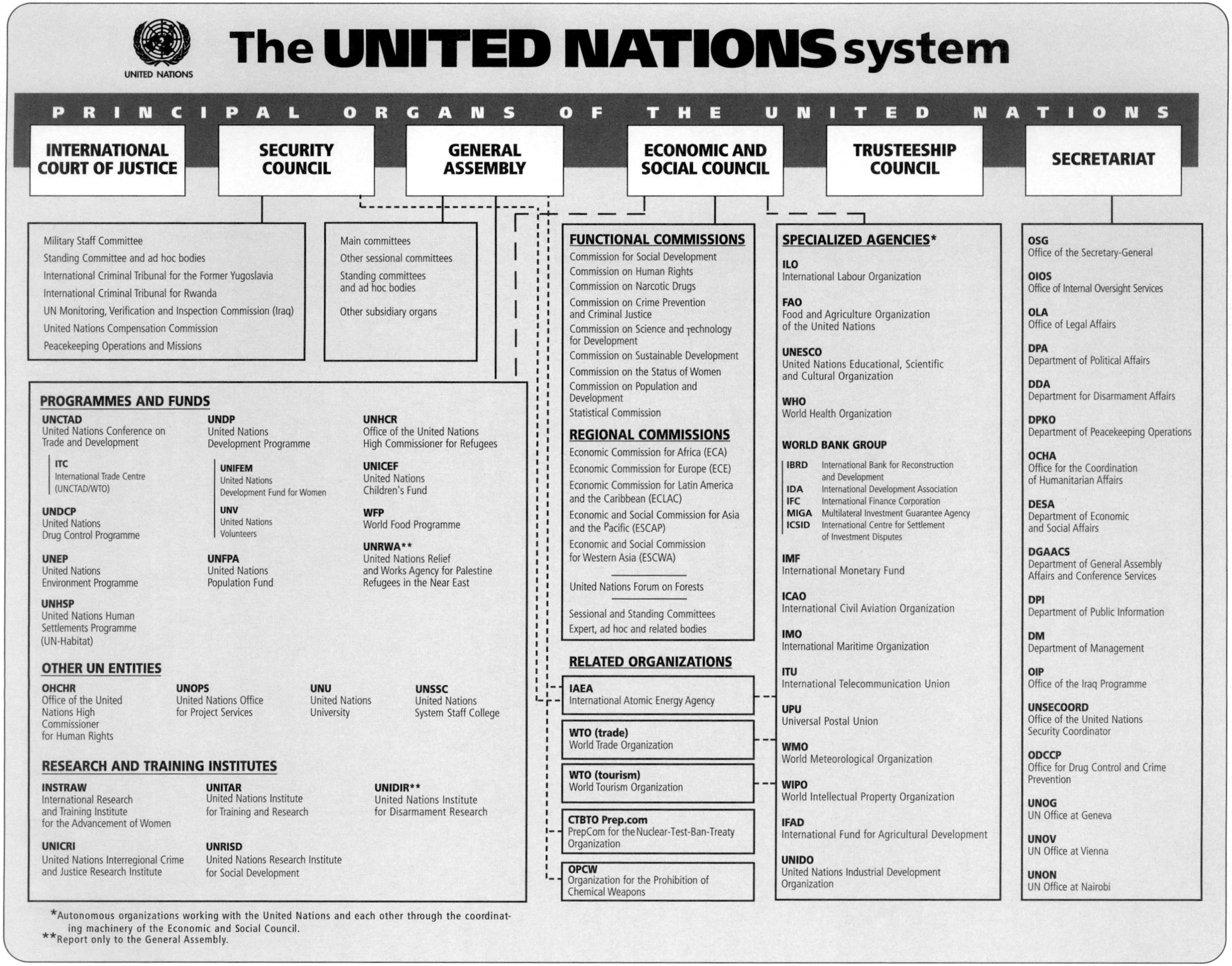

- All members have an equal vote in the *General Assembly*, which discusses and recommends action on any matter that falls within the UN Charter. It approves the UN budget and the makeup of the other bodies.
- The *Security Council* consists of 15 members. Five (China, France, the United Kingdom, Russia, and the United States) are permanent. Ten others are elected by the General Assembly for 2-year terms. The Council is responsible for ensuring international peace and security, and all UN members are supposed to be bound by its decisions.
- As you see in Figure 3.3, the *Economic and Social Council*, which is responsible for economics, human rights, and social matters, administers a host of smaller organizations and specialized agencies.
- The five permanent members of the Security Council make up the *Trusteeship Council*, which administers all trustee territories under UN custody.
- The *International Court of Justice* consists of 15 judges elected by the General Assembly and Security Council. It can hear disputes only between nations, not cases brought against individuals or corporations. It has no compulsory jurisdiction, and its decisions can be, and have been, disregarded by specific nations.
- Headed by the Secretary General, the *Secretariat* administers the operations of the UN.

An important body within the UN Economic and Social Council is the United Nations Conference on Trade and Development (UNCTAD) (www.unctad.org). The organization has a broad mandate in the areas of international trade and economic development. One recent conference focused on how developing nations' musical traditions can alert young people worldwide to pressing development issues, including AIDS, poverty, and national debt. The conference proposed a new initiative designed to develop the business management skills of individuals in developing nations so they can profit from the rich cultural assets they behold. A success story is that of an artist/entrepreneur named Youssou N'Dour. He set up his own music company to record musicians from all over Africa and export the music directly from Dakar, Senegal.[25]

A FINAL WORD

Differences in political and legal systems present both opportunities and risks for international companies. Because of the intricate connections among politics, law, and culture, gaining complete control over events is extremely difficult in even the most stable national business environment. Nevertheless, understanding differences in culture, politics, and law is the first step for any company that hopes to manage the risks of doing business in unfamiliar environments. Managers of international companies also need to understand how global legal issues, including intellectual property, product safety, and antitrust laws, affect operations and strategy. In the next chapter, we will continue our discussion of national business environments by examining the different ways in which *economic systems* function.

There is a variety of additional material available on the Companion Website that accompanies this textbook. You can access this information by visiting the Website at (www.prenhall.com/wild).

summary

① Describe each main type of *political system*. A *political system* consists of the structures, processes, and activities by which a nation governs itself. Today, two main types of political systems are most common. In a *democratic system*, leaders are elected directly by the wide participation of the people or the people's representatives. Most democracies take the form of a *representative democracy*, in which citizens nominate individuals from their groups to represent their political needs and views. Typically, democracies strive to guarantee five rights: (1) freedom of expression, (2) periodic elections, (3) full civil and property rights, (4) minority rights, and (5) nonpolitical bureaucracies.

In a *totalitarian system*, individuals govern without the support of the people, maintain control over nearly all aspects of people's lives, and do not tolerate opposing viewpoints. Under *theocratic totalitarianism*, a country's religious leaders are also its political leaders, who enforce laws and regulations based on religious and totalitarian beliefs. Under *secular totalitarianism*, political leaders rely on military and bureaucratic power. There are three forms of secular totalitarianism. Under *communist totalitarianism*, the government aims for social equality by planning all types of economic activity. Under *tribal totalitarianism*, one tribe imposes its will on other populations in the country. *Right-wing totalitarianism* is characterized by capitalist economics but denies most political freedoms.

② Identify the origins of *political risk* and how managers can reduce its effects. *Political risk* is the likelihood that a government or society will undergo political changes that negatively affect local business activity. It arises from a variety of sources, including (1) corrupt or poor political leadership; (2) frequent changes in the form of government; (3) political involvement of religious or military leaders; (4) an unstable political system; (5) conflict among races, religions, or ethnic groups; and (6) poor relations with other countries. *Macro risk* threatens all companies in a nation regardless of industry. *Micro risk* threatens firms within a particular industry or even smaller groups.

There are at least five different forms of political risk: (1) conflict and violence, (2) terrorism and kidnapping, (3) property seizure, (4) policy changes, and (5) local content requirements. *Property seizure*—the taking of a company's assets by a local government—may take one of three forms: *confiscation* (forced transfer of assets without compensation); *expropriation* (forced transfer with compensation); or *nationalization* (forced takeover of an entire industry). *Local content requirements* are regulations that require manufacturers to use local resources.

In managing political risk, companies can adopt one or more of four strategies: (1) *avoidance* (not investing in a country); (2) *adaptation* (incorporating risk into business strategy); (3) *information gathering* (monitoring local political events); and (4) *political influence* (such as by *lobbying*—hiring people to represent the firm's views on local political matters).

③ List the main types of *legal systems* and explain how they differ. A *legal system* is a country's set of laws and regulations, including the processes by which its laws are enacted and enforced and the ways in which its courts hold parties accountable for their actions. There are three categories of legal systems. Under *common law*, the justice system decides cases by interpreting the law on the basis of *tradition* (legal history), *precedent* (past cases), and *usage* (application of laws in specific situations). *Civil law* is based on a detailed set of written rules and statutes that constitute a legal *code*. All obligations, responsibilities, and privileges follow directly from the written code. *Theocratic law* is based on religious teachings.

④ Describe the major *legal issues* facing international companies. Laws around the world adhere to widely varying standards, and there is no well-defined body of international law. There are, however, some efforts being made to achieve *standardization*—uniformity in interpreting and applying laws in more than one country.

Chief among the legal issues affecting international business are (1) protection of *property rights* (legal rights to resources and any income they generate); (2) protection of *intellectual property*, including *patents*, *trademarks*, and *copyrights* that result from intellectual talent and ability; (3) *product liability* standards applying to companies responsible for damage, injury, or death caused by defective products; (4) *taxation* policies (which may discourage the use of a product or increase the prices of imports); and (5) *antitrust regulations* designed to prevent companies from fixing prices, sharing markets, and gaining unfair monopoly advantages.

5 Explain how *international relations* affect **international business activities**. Political relations between a company's home country and those with which it does business strongly affect its international activities. In general, favorable political relations lead to increased opportunity and stable business environ-

ments. The mission of the *United Nations (UN)* is to provide leadership in fostering peace and stability around the world. Although its global peacekeeping efforts have had mixed results, its many agencies continue to aid poorer nations by providing food and medical supplies, educational supplies and training, and financial resources.

questions **for review**

1. What is a *political system*? Explain the relation between a "political system" and a "culture."

2. Distinguish between *wide* and *narrow political participation*.

3. What is *democracy*? Describe the effects of a democratic environment on business activities.

4. What is the difference between a *pure democracy* and a *representative democracy*?

5. What is a *coalition government*?

6. What is *totalitarianism*? Explain the different forms of totalitarianism.

7. What is *political risk*? Identify the five main types of political risk and explain how each can affect international business activities.

8. Distinguish between *confiscation*, *expropriation*, and *nationalization*.

9. List four different methods that businesses use to manage political risk.

10. Describe the three main types of *legal systems*. Identify the differences among them and give examples of countries employing each type.

11. How does the *standardization* of laws benefit international companies?

12. Identify the different categories and subcategories of *intellectual property*.

13. What are *property rights*?

14. What are *product liability* laws? Describe how product liability laws can differ from country to country.

15. Why do countries collect *taxes*? What are the ramifications for international business?

16. How does the enforcement of *antitrust (antimonopoly) laws* benefit consumers?

17. How do *international relations* between countries affect the activities of international companies?

questions **for discussion**

1. The Internet is forcing politicians to change their governing methods. How might the Internet affect change in totalitarian political systems like China and North Korea? What might the Net's future expansion mean for nations with theocratic systems (for example, Iran)? What changes might technology bring to the way that democracies function?

2. Under a totalitarian political system, the Indonesian economy grew strongly for 30 years. In India, meanwhile, the economic system of the world's largest functioning democracy has been relatively poor over the past 40 years. Relying on what you

learned in this chapter, do you think the Indonesian economy grew despite or because of a totalitarian regime? What might explain India's relatively poor performance under a democratic political system?

3. Consider the following statement: "Democratic political systems, as opposed to totalitarian ones, provide international companies with more stable environments in which to do business." Do you agree? Why or why not? Support your argument with specific country examples.

in practice

Read the brief article below and then answer the questions that follow.

China's High-Tech Role

LINKOU, Taiwan—A corporate exodus from Taiwan to China is having profound implications for U.S. companies and their government.

Companies such as Dell Computer Corp. and Compaq Computer Corp. rely on Taiwanese companies to make parts and computers for them. But as Taiwan's subcontractors migrate to China, the main source of personal computers (PCs) and other information technology (IT) products to the United States will likely be its main adversary—China.

"There is a question of economic security," said Morris Chang, chairman of Taiwan Semiconductor Manufacturing Corp. If China were to someday stop supplying the U.S. market with IT products, he said, "that could shut down a large part of the IT industry in the United States."

Mr. Chang and other executives say that with China becoming a critical link in the global supply chain, political skirmishes could have costly economic fallout. But such an event in a global economy is unlikely. "It is the computing equivalent of mutually assured destruction," said Andrew Grove, chairman of Intel Corp. "You can't hurt the other party without hurting yourself."

1. This chapter discussed policy changes in the context of business between Taiwan and China. Locate recent articles on the investment climate between Taiwan and China. Has the "active opening, effective management" change proposed by Taiwan in fact been implemented?

2. What has been the amount of flows from Taiwan to China in recent years? What is it that makes China such an attractive location for Taiwanese firms in the first place? Identify as many contributing factors as you can.

3. What role do you think globalization has played in diminishing the ability of governments to use economic weapons to settle political disputes? Do you believe this trend will continue or decline?

projects

1. Two groups of four students each will debate the ethics of doing business in countries with totalitarian governments. After the first student from each side has spoken, the second student will question the opposing side's arguments, looking for holes and inconsistencies. The third student will attempt to answer these arguments. A fourth student will present a summary of each side's arguments. Finally, the class will vote to determine which team has offered the more compelling argument.

2. Select two recent articles from business magazines (in print or on their Web sites). One article should discuss the political element of a country's business environment, the other a legal element of the same environment. Potential topics include corruption and pending legislation relevant to international companies. Summarize both articles and explain what businesses can do to prepare for, or respond to, any special problems the articles discuss.

3. Select a country that interests you. What type of political and legal systems does the country have? Do free elections take place? Is the government heavily involved in the economy? Is the legal system effective and impartial? Do political and legal conditions suggest that it should be further considered as a potential market? Present your findings to the class.

As we saw in this chapter, the piracy of intellectual property—computer software, films, books, music CDs, and pharmaceutical drugs—is a common problem. Due to piracy, companies doing business in Asian countries (including China, India, Indonesia, Japan, the Philippines, South Korea, Taiwan, and Thailand) lose more than $3 billion in sales every year. Often, criminals are connected to political leaders and receive legal protection from prosecution.

The following two examples are illustrative:

➡ Indian law gives international pharmaceutical firms five- to seven-year patents on *processes used to manufacture drugs*—but *not on the drugs themselves*. Local companies pirate this property of the international pharmaceutical companies by slightly modifying production processes in order to arrive at the finished drugs.

➡ In China, political protection for pirates of intellectual property is common. In fact, government officials, people working for the government, and even the People's Liberation Army (China's national army) operate many factories churning out pirated products. Many operate on government-owned land.

Despite high piracy rates, because of expanding markets and rapid economic growth, Asian countries remain attractive to international companies. Although the U.S. government complains about China's piracy practices, it tends to renew normal trading relations status (formerly known as most favored nation [MFN] trading status) to China annually.

thinking globally

1. What actions can companies and governments take to ensure that products cannot be easily pirated? Be specific.

2. Do you think that the international business community is being too lax about the abuse of intellectual property rights in China and other Asian countries? Are international companies simply afraid to speak out for fear of jeopardizing access to the markets of these countries?

3. The Internet is making it easier to transmit digital information around the world. This increased trade in digital communication poses a threat to intellectual property because digital technology allows the manufacture of perfect clones of original works. How might the Internet affect intellectual-property laws?

a question of ethics

1. Small street-side stalls and tabletop vendors in developing countries around the world sell illegal copies of desktop software, sometimes at one-tenth the price of the authentic version. Sophisticated business application software that normally sells for hundreds of dollars in developed nations can be had for just a few dollars. Authorities in such countries sometimes have different attitudes toward software pirates than their counterparts in developed nations. Why such a casual attitude toward theft on a billion-dollar scale? They might welcome a certain amount of piracy because very few people can afford software at free-market prices.

    Imagine that you're the proprietor of a fledging computer graphics company in Shanghai, China. With an income of only a few thousand dollars a year, you cannot afford to buy the original packaged graphics software that you need to get your business off the ground. Are you being unethical by buying pirated software? Despite its illegality, is it justified because it will help facilitate economic development in your country?

2. Pharmaceutical makers such as Merck hold worldwide patents on many of the powerful anti-AIDS drugs. But the company recently came under pressure from competitors such as India's Cipla, which offers cheaper alternatives, and from politicians and nongovernmental groups to supply AIDS drugs at reduced prices to poor nations. But a company invests heavily to develop such drugs because a patent allows it to recoup its investment. If a company is forced to give away, or sell at reduced prices, a drug that combats diseases that afflict poor nations disproportionately, they might turn their attention to diseases that occur largely in relatively wealthy nations, such as heart disease and cancer.

    Do you think companies in Merck's position are being unethical by enforcing their hold on patents? AIDS, cancer, and heart disease all kill their victims. In your opinion, where do we draw the line in terms of which diseases allow us to ignore a drug company's patent?

4

economic systems and development

LEARNING OBJECTIVES

After studying this chapter, you should be able to

1 Describe what is meant by a *centrally planned economy,* and explain why its use is declining.

2 Identify the main characteristics of a *mixed economy,* and explain the emphasis on *privatization.*

3 Explain how a *market economy* functions, and identify its distinguishing features.

4 Describe the different ways to measure a nation's level of *development.*

5 Describe the process of *economic transition,* and identify the remaining obstacles for businesses.

BEACONS

A Look Back

CHAPTER 3 discussed ways in which different political and legal systems affect international business activities. We also explored some of the ways managers can cope with the risks presented by political and legal uncertainties.

A Look at This Chapter

This chapter explains different types of economic systems and examines the effect that economics has on international business. We also discuss economic development and the difficulties facing countries undergoing transition to market economies.

A Look Ahead

CHAPTER 5 introduces us to a major form of international business activity—international trade. We examine the patterns of international trade and outline several theories that attempt to explain why nations conduct trade.

Drilling for Progress

PORT GENTIL, Gabon—Royal Dutch/Shell Group (**www.shell.com**) employs over 90,000 employees and operates in more than 130 countries around the world. The global company even splits its headquarters between London, England, and The Hague, The Netherlands.

The firm engages in a broad array of businesses, including oil/gas exploration and production, chemical production, gas and power generation, sales and marketing of oil products, and renewable sources of energy. The nature of its activities means that Royal Dutch/Shell has to operate in some of the harshest conditions on the planet. The company's oil drilling and exploration activities take it from the North Sea's icy waters to the steamy rainforest of Gabon. Below is a photo of a Shell Oil employee overseeing operations on an oil-drilling platform off the coast of Brunei Darussalam, Malaysia.

Shell's activities also take the company's operations to both the world's least-developed nations and its most-developed economies. The company needs to adapt itself to doing business in communist nations that still sometimes use central planning and in democratic nations that rely on the "invisible hand" of the free market. It also works with local communities and governments to make progress on both economic and human development. For example, the company operates programs for women at risk in Slovakia and Romania to help them start businesses. As you read this chapter, think about the disparity in the development of nations and how companies can work with nations in improving standards of living.[1]

ike culture and systems of politics and law, economic systems differ from one country to another. In Chapter 2, we saw that one defining element of a culture is its tendency toward *individualism* or *collectivism*. Economic systems in individualist cultures tend to provide incentives and rewards for individual business initiative. Collectivist cultures tend to offer fewer such incentives and rewards. For example, in individualist cultures *entrepreneurs*—businesspeople who accept the risks and opportunities involved in creating and operating new business ventures—tend to be rewarded with relatively low tax rates that encourage their activities.

Furthermore, national culture can have a strong impact on a nation's economic development. In turn, the development of a country's economy can dramatically affect many aspects of its culture. In this chapter, we introduce the world's different economic systems and examine the link between culture and economics. We begin by explaining each main type of economic system. Then we explore economic development and ways of classifying nations using several indicators of development. We conclude by looking at how countries are implementing market-based economic reforms and the challenges they face.

ECONOMIC SYSTEMS

economic system
Structure and processes that a country uses to allocate its resources and conduct its commercial activities.

A country's **economic system** consists of the structure and processes that it uses to allocate its resources and conduct its commercial activities. No nation is either completely individualist or completely collectivist in its cultural orientation. Likewise, no economic system reflects a completely individual or group orientation. The economies of all nations display a blend of individual and group values (the latter of which are often reflected in government involvement in business activities). In other words, no economy is entirely focused on individual reward at the expense of social well-being. Nor is any economy so completely focused on social well-being that it places no value on individual incentive and enterprise.

Every economy displays a *tendency* toward individualist or collectivist economic values. This allows us to organize systems along a continuum that characterizes them as *centrally planned, mixed,* or *market economies* (see Figure 4.1). Let's now take a look at each of these three types of economic systems.

CENTRALLY PLANNED ECONOMY

centrally planned economy
Economic system in which a nation's land, factories, and other economic resources are owned by the government, which plans nearly all economic activity.

A **centrally planned economy** is a system in which a nation's land, factories, and other economic resources are owned by the government. The government makes nearly all economy-related decisions—including who produces what and the prices of products, labor, and capital. Central planning agencies specify production goals for factories and other production units and even decide prices. In the former Soviet Union, for instance, communist officials set prices for such staples as milk, bread, eggs, and other essential goods. The ultimate goal is to achieve a wide range of political, social, and economic objectives by taking complete control over production and distribution of the nation's resources.

FIGURE 4.1

Continuum of Economic Systems

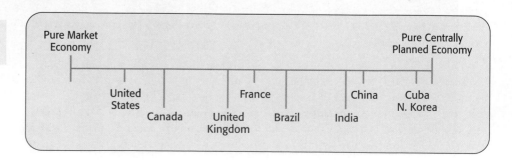

Origins of the Centrally Planned Economy   Central planning is rooted in the ideology that the welfare of the group is more important than individual well-being. Just as collectivist cultures emphasize group over individual goals, a centrally planned economy strives to achieve economic and social equality.

The German philosopher Karl Marx popularized the idea of central economic planning in the nineteenth century. Marx formulated his ideas while witnessing the hardship endured by working people in Europe during and after the Industrial Revolution. Marx argued that the economy could not be reformed, but that it must be overthrown and replaced with a more equitable "communist" system.

Different versions of Marx's ideas were implemented in the twentieth century by means of violent upheaval. Revolutions installed totalitarian (see Chapter 3) economic and political systems in Russia in 1917, China and North Korea in the late 1940s, and Cuba in 1959. By the 1970s, central planning was the economic law in lands stretching across Central and Eastern Europe (Albania, Bulgaria, Czechoslovakia, East Germany, Hungary, Poland, Romania, and Yugoslavia), Asia (Cambodia, China, North Korea, and Vietnam), Africa (Angola and Mozambique), and Latin America (Cuba and Nicaragua).

Decline of Central Planning   In the late 1980s, nation after nation began to dismantle communist central planning in favor of market-based economies. Economists, historians, and political scientists attribute the collapse of centrally planned economies to a combination of several factors.

Failure to Create Economic Value   Central planners paid little attention to the task of producing quality goods and services at the lowest possible cost. In other words, they failed to see that commercial activities succeed when they create economic value for customers. Along the way, scarce resources were wasted in the pursuit of commercial activities that were not self-sustaining.

Failure to Provide Incentives   Government ownership of economic resources drastically reduced incentives for people and organizations to maximize the benefits obtained from those resources. There were few incentives to create new technologies, new products, and new production methods (except in the areas of aerospace, nuclear power, and other sciences, in which government scientists excelled). The result was little or no economic growth and consistently low standards of living. Government policies that eliminate incentives to create wealth and develop effective production techniques impair development.

Even today, for example, North Korea remains perhaps the most closed economy in the world. For the most part, the policy of *juche* (self-reliance) is causing extreme hardship for its people. The combination of recurring floods and droughts, a shortage of fertilizers, and a lack of farm machinery pose a continual roadblock to the nation reaching its peak food production potential.[2] That is why the North Korean government has to rely on aid from abroad to feed its people.

Failure to Achieve Rapid Growth   Leaders in communist nations took note of the high rates of economic growth in countries like Hong Kong, Singapore, South Korea, and Taiwan—the so-called four tigers. The realization that a once-poor region of the world had achieved such growth awakened central planners. They realized that an economic system based on private ownership fosters growth much better than one hampered by central planning. This belief persists despite the economic difficulties that have occurred in Asia since 1997.

Failure to Satisfy Consumer Needs   Would-be consumers in many centrally planned economies were tired of standards of living that had slipped far below those of their counterparts in predominantly market economies. Ironically, although central planning was conceived as a means for creating a more equitable system for distributing wealth, too many central planners failed to provide even basic necessities such as adequate

While farming in other nations today is a highly mechanized and even computerized endeavor, it is labor-intensive and inefficient in North Korea. The government's failed communist economic policies have hampered development and are at the root of its inability to afford fertilizers and modern machinery that could boost food production. Famine and general economic collapse throughout the 1990s cut the life expectancy by more than six years.

food, housing, and medical care. Underground economies (black markets) for all kinds of goods and services flourished and in some cases even outgrew "official" economies. Prices on the black markets were much higher than the official prices set by governments.

Focus on China   China began its experiment with central planning in 1949, when communists defeated the nationalists in a long and bloody civil war. Today, the country's leaders describe its economic philosophy as "socialism with Chinese characteristics." There is possibly no country on earth that has done more for its people economically over the past two decades than China. Glistening skyscrapers dominate the Shanghai and Beijing cityscapes. Although rural China continues to look and function much as it has for centuries, today many people in large cities have good job prospects. The country's immense population, rising incomes, and expanding opportunities are attracting new business ventures like never before.

The Early Years   From 1949 until reforms were initiated in the late 1970s, China had a unique economic system. Agricultural production was organized into groups of people who formed production "brigades" and production "units." Communes were larger entities responsible for planning agricultural production quotas and industrial production schedules. Rural families owned their own homes and parcels of land on which to produce particular crops. Production surpluses could be consumed by the family or sold at a profit on the open market. In 1979 the government initiated agricultural reforms that strengthened work incentives in this sector. Family units could then grow whatever crops they chose and sell the produce at market prices.

At about the same time, township and village enterprises (TVEs) began to appear. Each TVE relied on the open market for materials, labor, and capital and used a non-governmental distribution system. Each TVE employed managers who were directly responsible for profits and losses. Although the government initially regarded TVEs as illegal operations unrelated to the officially sanctioned communes, they were legalized in 1984, further laying the groundwork for a market economy.

Patience and **Guanxi**   Initially, and in line with communist ideology, outside companies were restricted from participating in the Chinese economy. But from the mid-1980s to the present, outside companies enjoy ever-greater opportunities to enter into joint ventures with Chinese partners. Nevertheless, non-Chinese companies must often endure a long and patient struggle to succeed in China. One of the most important factors in forming a successful venture in China is *guanxi*—the Chinese term for "personal relationships." For more on learning the secrets of *guanxi*, see this chapter's Global Manager titled "Guidelines for Good *Guanxi*."

Challenges Ahead Economic reforms are moving along very well in China, and the country continues to experience strong growth. However, political and social problems pose threats to China's future economic performance. Unrest continues in China in the form of skirmishes between secular and Muslim Chinese in western provinces and occasional terrorist attacks in Beijing. Meanwhile, for the most part political leaders continue to restrict democratic reforms.

Another potential problem is unemployment. Intensified competition and the entry of international companies into China are placing greater emphasis on efficiency and the cutting of payrolls in some industries. But the biggest contributor to the unemployed sector seems to be migrant workers. Hundreds of thousands of workers have left their farms and now go from city to city searching for better-paying factory work or construction jobs. Unhappiness with economic progress in the countryside and the misery of migrant workers are serious potential sources of social unrest for the Chinese government.

GLOBAL MANAGER

Guidelines for Good *Guanxi*

➡ **The Importance of Contacts, Not Contracts.** In China, face-to-face communication and personal relationships take priority over written contracts. Mu Dan Ping, a partner in the Chinese Business Group at Ernst & Young's (**www.ey.com**) Los Angeles office, offers the following diagram to show the different priorities:

United States: Reason → Law → Relationship
China: Relationship → Reason → Law

Managers from the United States look for the rationale or reason first, says Mu. Is there a market with profit potential? If so, they want a *legal contract* before they spend time on a business *relationship*. Conversely, explains Mu, the Chinese need to establish a *trust relationship* first. Then they look for common goals as a *reason* for doing business. In a way, the *legal contract* is just a formality, serving to ensure mutual understanding.

➡ **Pleasure before Business.** It seems impossible *not* to talk business when you've come to China for the express purpose of conducting business. But experts advise that you leave your sales pitches on the back burner and follow the lead of your Chinese hosts. Many companies seeking partnerships in China overlook the importance of personal relationships. They send their top performers to wow Chinese businesspeople with savvy sales pitches. But companies that send their salesperson of the year can return empty-handed—friendship comes before business.

➡ **Business Partners Are Family Members Too.** In China, family is extremely important. Visiting businesspeople should never turn down invitations to partake in a Chinese executive's family life. When Lauren Hsu was market analyst for Kohler Company (**www.kohler.com**), a manufacturer of plumbing fixtures, she was responsible for researching the Chinese market and identifying potential joint venture partners. Once, in the midst of negotiations, Hsu was invited to go bowling with the partner's daughter and then to a piano concert with the entire family. Such activities had little to do with promoting Kohler plumbing fixtures, but 2 years of meetings and visits to get acquainted eventually resulted in a joint venture deal.

➡ **Research, Research, Research.** China is not a single market, but many different regional markets with different cultures and even different languages. No one knows the importance of research more than Bob Wilner, director of international human resources for McDonald's Corporation (**www.mcdonalds.com**). Wilner went to China to learn as much as possible about the market, how people were managed, and the country's employment systems. "Unlike the way we cook our hamburgers exactly the same in all 101 countries," says Wilner, "the way we manage, motivate, reward and discipline is more sensitive to the culture." Wilner and other McDonald's managers were able to develop that sensitivity only through repeated visits.

In 1997 China regained control of Hong Kong after 99 years under British rule. For the most part, China has kept its promise of "one country, two systems." While the economic and political freedoms of people in Hong Kong would remain largely intact, the rest of China would continue along the lines drawn by the communist leadership. The southern coastal territory of Macao also returned to Chinese control in 1999. Only a one-hour ferry ride from Hong Kong, Macao was under Portuguese administration since it was founded in 1557. Although Macao's main function used to be that of trading post, today it serves mainly as a gambling outpost. In fact, it is commonly referred to as "Asia's Vegas."

It is important for China to manage its one country, two systems policy well to preserve order in China, Hong Kong, and Macao. The island of Taiwan is watching very closely. Any chance of its eventual reunification with the Chinese mainland depends on the successful integration of Hong Kong and Macao. For now at least, things appear to be going smoothly. Reunification seems more likely as economic ties between China and Taiwan grow steadily. For instance, Taiwan recently scrapped a 50-year ban that capped the size of investments in China and eased restrictions on direct financial flows between Taiwan businesses and the mainland.[3] Also, China's entry into the World Trade Organization (www.wto.org) in 2001 and Taiwan's entry in 2002 will encourage further integration of their two economies.[4]

MIXED ECONOMY

mixed economy
Economic system in which land, factories, and other economic resources are more equally split between private and government ownership.

A **mixed economy** is a system in which land, factories, and other economic resources are more equally split between private and government ownership. In a mixed economy, the government owns fewer economic resources than does the government in a centrally planned economy. In a mixed economy, the government tends to control the economic sectors that it considers important to national security and long-term stability. Such sectors usually include iron and steel manufacturing (for building military equipment), oil and gas production (to guarantee continued manufacturing and availability), and automobiles (to guarantee employment for a large portion of the workforce). Many mixed economies also maintain generous welfare systems to support the unemployed and provide health care for the general population.

Mixed economies are found all around the world: Denmark, France, Germany, Norway, Spain, and Sweden in Western Europe; India, Indonesia, Malaysia, Pakistan, and Sri Lanka in Asia; Argentina in Latin America; and South Africa. Although all the governments of these nations do not centrally plan their economies, they all influence economic activity by means of special incentives, including subsidies to key industries.

Origins of the Mixed Economy
Proponents of mixed economies contend that a successful economic system must be not only efficient and innovative, but also should protect society from the excesses of unchecked individualism and organizational greed. The goal is to achieve low unemployment, low poverty, steady economic growth, and an equitable distribution of wealth by means of the most effective policies.

Proponents point out that throughout the 1990s, European and U.S. rates of productivity and growth were almost identical. Although the United States has created more jobs, it has done so at the cost of widening social inequality, proponents say. They argue that nations with mixed economies should not dismantle their social-welfare institutions but modernize them so that they contribute to national competitiveness. Austria, The Netherlands, and Sweden are taking this route. In The Netherlands, labor unions and the government agreed to an epic deal involving wage restraint, shorter working hours, budget discipline, new tolerance for part-time and temporary work, and the trimming of social benefits.[5] As a result, Dutch unemployment today tends to hover between 2 and 3 percent. By comparison, unemployment in next-door Belgium is around 11 percent and the average jobless rate for all European Union nations is around 9 percent.[6]

Decline of Mixed Economies   Many mixed economies are converting to market-based systems. The reasons for the decline of mixed economies are similar to those for centrally planned economies. When assets are owned by the government there seems to be less incentive to eliminate waste or to practice innovation. Extensive government ownership tends to result in a lack of responsibility and accountability, rising costs, defective products, and slow economic growth. Many government-owned businesses in mixed economies needed large infusions of taxpayers' money to survive as world-class competitors. That is why taxes and prices were higher and standards of living lower. Underpinning the move toward more market-based systems is large-scale *privatization*.

    Move toward Privatization   The selling of government-owned economic resources to private operators is called **privatization**. The main goal of privatization is to increase economic efficiency. It also removes subsidies formerly paid to government-owned companies and curtails the practice of appointing managers for political reasons rather than for their managerial expertise. Because privatized companies compete in open markets for material, labor, and capital, they can go out of business if they do not produce competitive products at fair prices, which is extremely rare for government-owned companies.

    As discussed earlier, people in many European nations prefer a combination of rich benefits and high unemployment to the low jobless rates and smaller social safety net of the United States. In France, for instance, the French electorate continues to hold fast to a deeply embedded tradition of social welfare and job security in government-owned firms. "Here," reports Ernest Antoine-Seilliere, president of the French conglomerate CGIP (www.cgip.fr), "social security and social solidarity weigh more than efficiency."[7]

    Still, to improve competitiveness, governments across Europe have privatized companies worth many billions of dollars. But as Europe's economies began to experience slower growth in 2001 and faced elections in 2002, many projects aimed at further economic reform were delayed. For instance, because voters don't like pain, France put off the planned privatization of state-owned utility Gaz de France (www.gazdefrance.com), social spending was to increase $4.5 billion in 2002, and a new French law was pending that would force companies laying off workers to double severance pay.[8] Only time will tell if European governments will veer back to a more conservative stance as their economies recover.

> **privatization**
> *Policy of selling government-owned economic resources to private companies and individuals.*

Piccadilly Circus in central London buzzes with activity on a sunny spring afternoon. The U.K. government began selling off state-owned companies in the 1980s in an effort to improve efficiency. Today, the U.K. economy lies somewhere between the more collectivist economies of continental Europe and the more individualist one of the United States. What is your personal view regarding the balance between individualist and collectivist government policies?

MARKET ECONOMY

In a **market economy**, the majority of a nation's land, factories, and other economic resources are privately owned, either by individuals or businesses. Nearly all economy-related decisions—including who produces what and the prices of products, labor, and capital—are determined by the interplay of two forces:

➡ **Supply**—the quantity of a good or service that producers are willing to provide at a specific selling price.

➡ **Demand**—the quantity of a good or service that buyers are willing to purchase at a specific selling price.

As supply and demand change for a good or service, so does its selling price. The lower the price, the more people will demand the product; the higher the price, the less people will demand it. Likewise, the lower the price, the smaller the quantity that producers will supply; the higher the price, the more they will supply. In this respect, what is called the "price mechanism" (or "market mechanism") dictates supply and demand.

Many market forces and uncontrollable natural forces can affect the price for many products, particularly commodities. Chocolate lovers, for example, should consider how the interplay of several forces affects the price of cocoa, the principal ingredient in chocolate. Suppose that consumption suddenly rises in large cocoa-consuming nations such as Britain, Japan, and the United States. Suppose further that disease and pests plague crops in cocoa-producing countries such as Brazil, Ghana, and the Ivory Coast. As worldwide consumption of cocoa begins to outstrip production, market pressure is felt on both the demand side (consumers) and the supply side (producers). Falling worldwide reserves of cocoa forces the price of cocoa higher.

Origins of the Market Economy   Market economics is rooted in the belief that individual concerns should be placed above group concerns. In this view, the group benefits when individuals receive incentives and rewards to act in certain ways. If people are allowed to own their homes, for example, they are more likely to take care of the property. Conversely, under a system of publicly owned property, individuals have little incentive to care for property.

Laissez-Faire Economics   For many centuries the world's dominant economic philosophy supported government control of a significant portion of a society's assets and government involvement in its international trade. But in the mid-1700s a new approach to national economics called for less government interference in commerce and greater individual economic freedom. This approach became known as a *laissez-faire* system, loosely translated from French as "allow them to do [without interference]."

Canada and the United States are examples of contemporary market economies. It is no accident that both these countries have individualist cultures. As much as an emphasis on individualism fosters a democratic form of government, it also supports a market economy.

Features of a Market Economy   To function smoothly and properly, a market economy requires three things: *free choice*, *free enterprise*, and *price flexibility*.

➡ *Free choice* gives individuals access to alternative purchase options. In a market economy, few restrictions are placed on consumers' ability to make their own decisions and exercise free choice. For example, a consumer shopping for a new car is guaranteed a variety from which to choose. The consumer can choose among dealers, models, sizes, styles, colors, and mechanical specifications such as engine size and transmission type.

➡ *Free enterprise* gives companies the ability to decide which goods and services to produce and the markets in which to compete. They are free to enter new and different lines of business, select geographic markets and customer segments to pursue, hire workers, and advertise their products. They are, therefore, guaranteed the right to pursue interests profitable to them.

→ *Price flexibility* allows most prices to rise and fall to reflect the forces of supply and demand. In contrast, nonmarket economies often set and maintain prices at stipulated levels. Interfering with the price mechanism violates a fundamental principle of the market economy.

Government's Role in a Market Economy   In a market economy, the government has relatively little direct involvement in business activities. Even so, it usually plays an important role in four areas: *enforcing antitrust laws, preserving property rights, providing a stable fiscal and monetary environment*, and *preserving political stability*. Let's look briefly at each of these areas.

Enforcing Antitrust Laws   When one company is able to control a product's supply—and, therefore, its price—it is considered a *monopoly*. The goal of *antitrust (or antimonopoly) laws* is to encourage the development of industries with as many competing businesses as the market will sustain. (These laws are explained fully in Chapter 3.) In such industries, prices are kept low by the forces of competition. By enforcing antitrust laws, governments prevent monopoly businesses and combinations that restrain trade from exploiting consumers and constraining the growth of commerce through competition.

The Federal Trade Commission (FTC) of the U.S. government seeks to ensure the competitive and efficient functioning of the nation's markets. But the FTC (**www.ftc.gov**) can also evaluate proposed deals outside the United States when the U.S. market is likely to be affected. For instance, the FTC reviewed a proposed acquisition of Sweden's Svedala Industri (**www.svedala.com**) by Finland's Metso Oyj (**www.metsocorporation.com**) for about $1.6 billion. Metso and Svedala are the world's two largest suppliers of rock-processing equipment. In response to FTC concerns over potential anticompetitive effects in the global market for rock-processing equipment, the two companies agreed to sell parts of their businesses to third parties.[9]

Preserving Property Rights   A smoothly functioning market economy rests on a legal system that safeguards individual property rights. By preserving and protecting individual property rights, governments encourage individuals and companies to take risks such as investing in technology, inventing new products, and starting new businesses. Strong protection of property rights ensures entrepreneurs that their claims to assets and future earnings are legally safeguarded. This protection also supports a healthy business climate in which a market economy can flourish.

Providing a Stable Fiscal and Monetary Environment   Unstable economies are often characterized by high inflation and unemployment. These forces create general uncertainty about the nation's suitability as a place to do business. Governments can help control inflation through effective *fiscal policies* (policies regarding taxation and government spending) and *monetary policies* (policies controlling money supply and interest rates). A stable economic environment helps companies to make better forecasts of costs, revenues, and the future of the business in general. Such conditions reduce the risks associated with future investments such as product development and business expansion.

Preserving Political Stability   A market economy depends on a stable government for its smooth operation and, indeed, for its future existence. Political stability helps businesses engage in activities without worrying about terrorism, kidnappings, and other political threats to their operations. (See Chapter 3 for extensive coverage of political risk and stability.)

Economic Freedom   So far we have discussed the essence of market economies as being grounded in freedom: free choice, free enterprise, free prices, and freedom from direct intervention by government. Map 4.1 shows how countries rank according to their levels of economic freedom. Some of the factors involved in the rankings include trade policy, government intervention in the economy, property rights, black markets, and wage and price controls. Of the 155 countries ranked, 74 are either free or mostly free, whereas 81 are mostly not free or repressed.

Recall that in Chapter 3 we said that the connection between political freedom and economic growth is not at all certain. Likewise, we can say only that countries with the greatest economic freedom *tend to have* the highest standards of living, whereas those with the lowest freedom tend to have the lowest standards of living. Figure 4.2 (on page 120) shows that the more economic freedom a country has, the higher its per capita income is. It also demonstrates that economic freedom does not *guarantee* a high per capita income. You can see that some countries rank very low on economic freedom yet have higher per capita incomes than some countries with far greater freedom. But, on average, once an economy moves from the "mostly not free" category to the "mostly free" category, per capita income increases nearly four times.[10]

MAP 4.1

Economic Freedom around the World

This map classifies countries according to their levels of economic freedom. Only 12 countries and territories are considered completely "free," whereas 62 nations are "mostly free." But the scale tips in favor of a lack of economic freedom: There are 66 nations labeled "mostly not free" and 15 nations labeled "repressed."

The economic well-being of one nation's people as compared with that of another nation's people is reflected in the country's level of **economic development**. Level of economic development reflects several economic and human indicators, including a nation's economic output (agricultural and industrial), infrastructure (power and transportation facilities), and people's physical health and level of education. Cultural, political, legal, and economic differences between nations can cause great differences in economic development from one country to another.

Economic development is an increasingly important topic for international businesspeople. Today international businesses, like Royal Dutch/Shell in our opening company profile, commonly conduct business in countries that are low on the economic-development scale. Although these countries tend to be poor, they can have ambitious development programs. A fuller understanding of economic development should help managers to accomplish their objectives more effectively.

DEVELOPMENT OF NATIONS

economic development
Measure for gauging the economic well-being of one nation's people as compared with that of another nation's people.

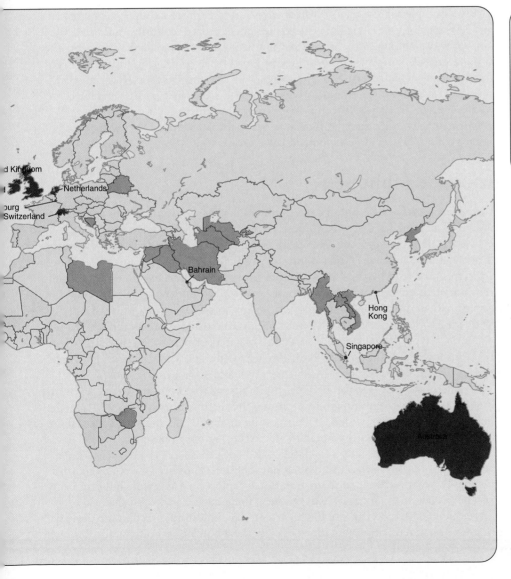

FIGURE 4.2

Economic Freedom and Wealth

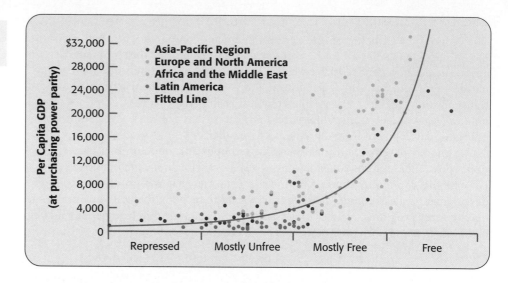

Businesspeople can use many different measures to estimate a country's level of economic development. One Hong Kong–based investment research company, Jardine Fleming Securities (www.jfleming.com), has a rather unusual way of estimating development. The firm monitors Nike's (www.nike.com) production patterns to gauge industrial and economic development in Asian nations. The company takes its theory seriously, arguing that as companies follow Nike into a country, workers' paychecks and skills increase and the country's currency grows stronger—encouraging yet more investment and development.[11]

Anyone uneasy with such an indicator has many other more formal methods of gauging a country's level of development. Let's take a look at several of these.

NATIONAL PRODUCTION

gross national product (GNP)

Value of all goods and services produced by a country during a 1-year period, including income generated by both domestic and international activities.

gross domestic product (GDP)

Value of all goods and services produced by a country's domestic economy over a 1-year period.

GDP or GNP per capita

Nation's GDP or GNP divided by its population.

The broadest measure of economic development is **gross national product (GNP)**—the value of all goods and services produced by a country during a one-year period. This figure includes income generated both by domestic production and by the country's international activities. **Gross domestic product (GDP)** is the value of all goods and services produced by the domestic economy over a 1-year period. GDP is a narrower figure that excludes a nation's income generated from exports, imports, and the international operations of its companies. A country's **GDP per capita** is simply its GDP divided by its population. GNP per capita is calculated similarly. Both GDP per capita and GNP per capita measure a nation's income per person. Map 4.2 (on pages 122–123) shows how the World Bank (www.worldbank.org) classifies countries according to their Gross National Income per Capita (a term it uses).

Marketers often use GDP or GNP per capita figures to determine whether a country's population is wealthy enough to begin purchasing its products. For instance, the Asian nation of Myanmar, with a GDP per capita of about $120 per year, is very poor. Here, you won't find computer companies marketing laptops or designer-apparel firms selling expensive clothing. Yet several large makers of personal-care products are staking out territory in Myanmar. Companies like Colgate-Palmolive (www.colgate.com) and Unilever (www.unilever.com) are traditional explorers of uncertain but promising markets in which they can offer relatively cheap items such as soap and shampoo.

Although GDP and GNP are the most popular indicators of economic development, they have several important drawbacks. In the following sections, we discuss each of these in some detail.

Uncounted Transactions   Many of a nation's transactions are not counted in either GDP or GNP. Some of the activities not included are:

➡ Volunteer work
➡ Unpaid household work
➡ Illegal activities such as gambling and black market (underground) transactions
➡ Unreported transactions conducted in cash

In many cases, the underground economy is so large and prosperous that official statistics such as GDP per capita are almost meaningless. In the case of Myanmar, for instance, economists report that official numbers mask a thriving underground economy spurred by differences between official and black-market currency exchange rates.

The unofficial economy accounts for a large percentage of overall GDP in several central and eastern European countries. In Ukraine, according to official statistics, GDP has *shrunk* by more than 60 percent since the break from Moscow in 1991.[12] Why, then, do kids in Reeboks (**www.reebok.com**) dash through Kiev streets snarled with Jeeps and shiny Mercedes-Benzes (**www.mercedes.com**)? The answer is that roughly half of the GDP flows through the country in unreported cash. Who generates this cash? There's little incentive for a small Kiev manufacturer to go the official route when faced with a gauntlet of 14 regulatory and permit steps just to export a batch of socks to neighboring Poland. It is much simpler for the company to do business in the underground economy.[13]

In addition, *barter* (the exchange of goods and services for other goods and services instead of money) regularly occurs in many developing countries. Barter is a popular alternative for buyers who lack the hard currency needed to pay for imports. In one well-known case, Pepsi-Cola (**www.pepsi.com**) traded soft drinks in the former Soviet Union for 17 submarines, a cruiser, a frigate, and a destroyer. Pepsi then converted its payment into cash by selling the military goods as scrap metal.[14] Because of their lack of currency, Russians still make extensive use of barter. In one classic incident, the Russian government paid 8,000 teachers in the Altai republic (1,850 miles east of Moscow) their monthly salaries with 15 bottles of vodka each. Teachers had previously refused an offer to receive part of their salaries in toilet paper and funeral accessories.[15]

Question of Growth   Because gross product figures are a snapshot of one year's economic output, they do not tell us whether a nation's economy is growing or shrinking. In predicting a country's future output, its expected economic growth rate should be examined. Thus, even a nation with moderate GDP or GNP figures will inspire greater investor confidence and international investment if growth rates are high.

Problem of Averages   Remember that per capita numbers give an average figure for an entire country. Although these numbers can be broadly helpful in estimating the quality of life and level of economic development, averages do not tell the story in much detail. In most countries, urban areas are more developed than rural areas and have higher per capita income. In less-advanced countries, regions surrounding good harbors or other transportation facilities are usually more developed than interior regions. Sometimes industrial parks boasting companies with advanced technology in production or design can generate a disproportionate share of a country's earnings.

Because Shanghai and other coastal regions of China are far more developed than the country's interior, GDP or GNP per capita figures for the country as a whole are quite misleading. Mercedes-Benz does a fair amount of business in Shanghai, whereas many agricultural regions deep inside China still rely on bicycles and animals for a good deal of their transportation.

Pitfalls of Comparison   Country comparisons using gross product figures can be misleading. In order to compare gross product per capita, each currency involved must be translated into a single currency unit (usually the dollar) at official exchange rates. But official exchange rates provide only limited data. Although they tell us how many units of one currency it takes to buy one unit of another, they do not tell us what that unit of local currency can buy in its home country. Thus, to understand the value of a currency in its home country, we must apply the concept of *purchasing power parity*.

purchasing power
Value of goods and services that can be purchased with one unit of a country's currency.

purchasing power parity (PPP)
Relative ability of two countries' currencies to buy the same "basket" of goods in those two countries.

PURCHASING POWER PARITY

Using gross product figures to compare production across countries does not account for the different cost of living in each country. **Purchasing power** is the value of goods and services that can be purchased with one unit of a country's currency. **Purchasing power parity (PPP)** is the relative ability of two countries' currencies to buy the same "basket" of goods in those two countries. This basket of goods is representative of ordinary, daily-use

MAP 4.2

Country Classification by Gross National Income per Capita

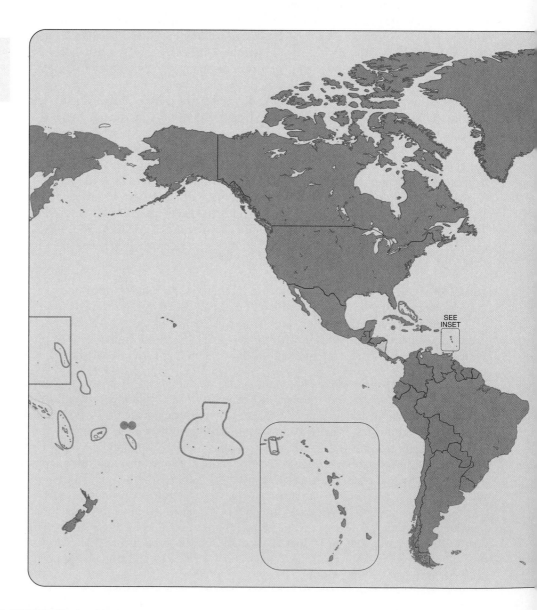

items such as apples, rice, soap, toothpaste, and so forth. Estimates of gross product per capita at PPP allow us to see what a currency can actually buy in real terms.

Using purchasing power parity to compare the wealth of nations produces some interesting results. Table 4.1, for instance, shows how several countries compare to the United States when their respective GDPs per capita are adjusted to reflect PPP. Thus, if we convert Swiss francs to dollars at official exchange rates, we estimate Swiss GDP per capita at $36,247. However, if we estimate Switzerland's GDP per capita at PPP, we realize that it is actually lower than that of the United States—$28,697, as compared with $33,836. Why the difference? GDP per capita at PPP is lower in Switzerland because of its higher cost of living. This means that it costs more to buy the same basket of goods in Switzerland than it does in the United States. The opposite phenomenon occurs in the case of the Czech Republic. Because the cost of living there is lower than in the United States, the Czech Republic's GDP per capita rises from $5,156 to $13,203 when PPP is considered. We will discuss PPP in far greater detail in Chapter 10.

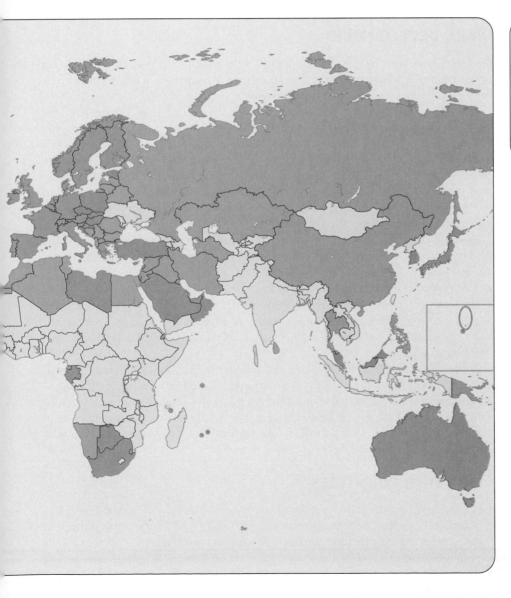

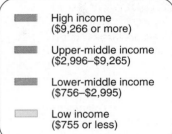

High income
($9,266 or more)

Upper-middle income
($2,996–$9,265)

Lower-middle income
($756–$2,995)

Low income
($755 or less)

TABLE 4.1	Estimates of GDP per Capita at PPP (Selected Countries)	
Country	GDP per Capita (U.S. $)	PPP Estimate of GDP per Capita (U.S. = 100)
United States	33,836	33,836
Switzerland	36,247	28,697
Canada	20,822	26,423
Australia	21,492	25,721
Japan	35,517	25,590
United Kingdom	24,228	22,882
Czech Republic	5,156	13,203
Hungary	4,772	11,232
Mexico	4,921	8,383
Turkey	2,809	6,338

HUMAN DEVELOPMENT

The purchasing power parity concept does a fairly good job in revealing differences between nations' levels of economic development. Unfortunately, it leaves much to be desired *as an indicator of a people's total well-being.*

Table 4.2 shows how selected countries rank according to the United Nations' **human development index (HDI)**—the measure of the extent to which a people's needs are satisfied and the extent to which these needs are addressed equally across a nation's entire population. As such, the HDI goes beyond calculations of a country's financial wealth. It measures the extent to which a people's needs are satisfied along three dimensions: (1) a long and healthy life, (2) an education, and (3) a decent standard of living. The three factors the HDI incorporates to evaluate success along these dimensions are life expectancy, educational attainment, and income.

Table 4.2 also illustrates the disparity that can be present between wealth and the HDI. For example, we see that the United States ranks second in terms of GDP per capita but ranks sixth in providing health care, education, and a decent standard of living. A conspicuous example in the table is the entry for Botswana. The country ranks 114th in terms of HDI but ranks 59th in terms of GDP per capita. Perhaps most striking in Table 4.2 is the column showing each nation's life expectancy at birth. We see that the people of first-ranked Norway have a life expectancy that is more than twice that of last-ranked Sierra Leone.

Unlike the other measures we have discussed, the HDI looks beyond financial wealth. By stressing the human aspects of economic development, the HDI demonstrates that high national income alone does not guarantee human progress. However, the importance of national income should not be underestimated. Countries need money to build good schools, provide quality health care, support environmentally friendly industries, and underwrite other programs designed to improve quality of life.

CLASSIFYING COUNTRIES

Nations are commonly classified as being *developed, newly industrialized,* or *developing.* These classifications are based on national indicators such as GDP per capita, portion of the economy devoted to agriculture, amount of exports in the form of industrial goods, and overall economic structure. However, there are no consensus lists of countries in

human development index (HDI)
Measure of the extent to which a people's needs are satisfied and the extent to which these needs are addressed equally across a nation's entire population.

TABLE 4.2	Human Development Index (HDI)			
HDI Rank	Country	HDI Value	GDP per Capita Rank	Life Expectancy at birth (years)
High Human Development				
1	Norway	0.939	3	78.4
3	Canada	0.936	6	78.7
6	United States	0.934	2	76.8
9	Japan	0.928	11	80.8
11	Switzerland	0.924	5	78.8
14	United Kingdom	0.923	19	77.5
17	Germany	0.921	14	77.6
24	Hong Kong, China	0.880	20	79.4
33	Czech Republic	0.844	39	74.7
39	Chile	0.825	48	75.2
Medium Human Development				
51	Mexico	0.790	51	72.4
55	Russia	0.775	55	66.1
69	Brazil	0.750	57	67.5
87	China	0.718	94	70.2
94	South Africa	0.702	45	53.9
114	Botswana	0.577	59	41.9
Low Human Development				
127	Pakistan	0.498	122	59.6
140	Tanzania	0.436	161	51.1
152	Rwanda	0.395	144	39.9
162	Sierra Leone	0.258	162	38.3

any category, and borderline countries are often classified differently in different listings. Let's take a closer look at each of these classifications.

Developed Countries   Countries that are highly industrialized, highly efficient, and whose people enjoy a high quality of life are **developed countries**. People in developed countries usually receive the finest health care and benefit from the best educational systems in the world. Most developed nations also support aid programs for helping poorer nations to improve their economies and standards of living. Countries in this category include Australia, Canada, Japan, New Zealand, the United States, all western European nations, and Greece.

Newly Industrialized Countries   Countries that recently increased the portion of their national production and exports derived from industrial operations are **newly industrialized countries (NICs)**. The NICs are located primarily in Asia and Latin America. Most listings of NICs include Asia's "four tigers" (Hong Kong, South Korea, Singapore, and Taiwan), Brazil, China, India, Malaysia, Mexico, South Africa, and Thailand. Depending on the pivotal criteria that we use for classification, a number of other countries could be placed in this category, including Argentina, Brunei, Chile, the Czech Republic, Hungary, Indonesia, the Philippines, Poland, Russia, Slovakia, Turkey, and Vietnam.

When we combine newly industrialized countries with countries that have the potential to become newly industrialized, we arrive at a category often called **emerging markets**. Generally, emerging markets have developed some (but not all) of the operations and

developed country
Country that is highly industrialized, highly efficient, and whose people enjoy a high quality of life.

newly industrialized country (NIC)
Country that has recently increased the portion of its national production and exports derived from industrial operations.

emerging markets
Newly industrialized countries plus those with the potential to become newly industrialized.

export capabilities associated with NICs.[16] However, debate continues over the defining characteristics of such classifications as *newly industrialized country* and *emerging market.*

Developing Countries   Nations with the poorest infrastructures and lowest personal incomes are called **developing countries** (also called *less-developed countries*). These countries often rely heavily on one or a few sectors of production, such as agriculture, mineral mining, or oil drilling. They might show potential for becoming newly industrialized countries, but typically lack the necessary resources and skills to do so. Most lists of developing countries include many nations in Africa, the Middle East, and the poorest formerly communist nations in Eastern Europe and Asia.

Developed countries employ the latest technological advances in their manufacturing sectors. However, developing countries (and NICs as well) are sometimes characterized by a high degree of **technological dualism**—use of the latest technologies in some sectors of the economy coupled with the use of outdated technologies in others.

> **developing country (also called less-developed country)**
> Nation that has a poor infrastructure and extremely low personal incomes.

> **technological dualism**
> Use of the latest technologies in some sectors of the economy coupled with the use of outdated technologies in other sectors.

ECONOMIC TRANSITION

> **economic transition**
> Process by which a nation changes its fundamental economic organization and creates new free-market institutions.

Over the past two decades, countries with centrally planned economies have been remaking themselves in the image of stronger market economies. This process, called **economic transition**, involves changing a nation's fundamental economic organization and creating entirely new free-market institutions. Some nations take transition further than others do, but the process typically involves five reform measures:[17]

1. Macroeconomic stabilization to reduce budget deficits and expand credit availability
2. Liberalization of economic activity that is decided by prices reflecting supply and demand
3. Legalization of private enterprises and privatization of state-owned enterprises in accord with an effective system of individual property rights
4. Removal of trade and investment barriers in goods and services, and removal of controls on convertibility of the nation's currency
5. Development of a social-welfare system designed to ease the transition process

OBSTACLES TO TRANSITION

There is little doubt that transition from central planning to free-market economics is generating tremendous international business opportunities. But difficulties arising from years of socialist economic principles have hampered progress from the start. Some countries that emerged from behind the iron curtain of the former Soviet Union still endure high unemployment rates. Some of the highest unemployment rates are in Bulgaria (19 percent), Croatia (22 percent), and Slovakia (18 percent).[18] Concerns about employment affect children as well as adults. A recent survey found that when children in transition countries were asked what kind of country they want to live in, employment and the economy were primary concerns. For details, see this chapter's World Business Survey titled "Young Voices."

Let's now take a look at the key remaining obstacles that are hindering former socialist and communist countries in their transition to free-market economies; *lack of managerial expertise, shortage of capital, cultural differences,* and *environmental degradation.*

Lack of Managerial Expertise   One challenge facing companies in transitional economies is a lack of managers qualified to conduct operations in a highly competitive global economy. Because central planners formerly decided nearly every aspect of the nation's commercial activities, there was little need for production, distribution, and marketing plans or strategies—or for the trained individuals to devise them.

Likewise, because the types of goods and services to be offered were decided by central planning committees, there was little need to investigate consumer wants and

WORLD BUSINESS SURVEY

Young Voices

The United Nations Children's Fund (Unicef) has just produced a huge survey gathering the views of over 15,000 young people across Europe and Central Asia as part of its Young Voices campaign. The question below asked what kind of country they want to live in. Western children wanted less crime and violence, while Central European, Central Independent States (CIS), and Baltic children wanted jobs, a better economy, and peace.

I would like my country to be a place where. . .

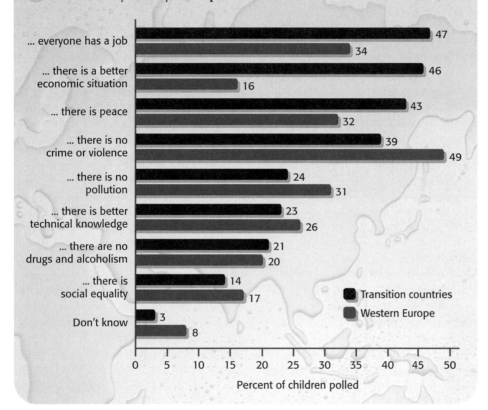

Percent of children polled

- ... everyone has a job — Transition countries: 47, Western Europe: 34
- ... there is a better economic situation — Transition countries: 46, Western Europe: 16
- ... there is peace — Transition countries: 43, Western Europe: 32
- ... there is no crime or violence — Transition countries: 39, Western Europe: 49
- ... there is no pollution — Transition countries: 24, Western Europe: 31
- ... there is better technical knowledge — Transition countries: 23, Western Europe: 26
- ... there are no drugs and alcoholism — Transition countries: 21, Western Europe: 20
- ... there is social equality — Transition countries: 14, Western Europe: 17
- Don't know — Transition countries: 3, Western Europe: 8

■ Transition countries
■ Western Europe

needs—or for specialists who were capable of conducting such research. Because central planners set prices, very little thought was given to strategies for delivering competitively priced products—or to the need for experts in operations, inventory, distribution, or logistics. Because all products were basically the same, there was no need for marketers with advertising skills.

Factory managers at government-owned firms had only to meet production requirements already set by central planners. In fact, some products rolled off assembly lines merely to be stacked outside the doors of the factory. After all, knowing where they went after that—and who took them there—was not the factory manager's job.

Signs of Progress   Although managers in transitional countries tend to lack expertise in some areas of business management, the situation is improving. "The gap in education and experience between managers from advanced countries and those of the former socialist bloc has narrowed dramatically," says Thomas Allgäuer, managing partner at Egon Zehnder International (**www.zehnder.com**), an executive search company. The reasons he cites for this trend are improved education, opportunities to study and work abroad, and changes in work habits caused by companies investing locally.[19]

Some managers from former communist nations are even finding managerial opportunities in Western Europe and the United States with some of the largest multinationals. One such success story is that of 30-year-old Vanda Wolfová. She is employed by Ogilvy EMEA marketing agency (**www.ogilvy.com**) in Paris, France. This journalist with a bachelor's degree in mass communication became Ogilvy & Mather's first employee in Prague. After establishing and running O&M Focus, a subsidiary specializing in public relations, she took an offer to work on global projects in Paris. "Of course, they looked at me differently from the way they would had I been from England," she admits. "I had to prove that I could do it."[20]

Shortage of Capital   Not surprisingly, transition is very expensive. To facilitate the process and ease the pain, governments must usually spend a great deal of money in three areas:

1. Developing a telecommunications and infrastructure system, including highways, bridges, rail networks, and sometimes subways
2. Setting up financial institutions, including stock markets and a banking system
3. Educating people in the ways of market economics

Unfortunately, governments of transition economies still cannot afford all the required investment. Usually they lack capital because of the same financial management practices that they are trying to replace. However, outside sources of capital are available, including national and international companies, other governments, and international financial institutions, such as the World Bank, the International Monetary Fund (IMF), and the Asian Development Bank. But another problem facing many transition countries is that they already owe substantial amounts of money to international lenders.

Cultural Differences   Economic transition and reform make deep cultural impressions on a nation's people. As we saw in Chapter 2, cultures differ greatly, with some more open to change than others. Likewise, certain cultures welcome economic change more easily than others. Transition often replaces dependence on the government with greater emphasis on individual responsibility, incentives, and rights. In some cultures such changes can be traumatic. Deep cuts in welfare payments, unemployment benefits, and guaranteed government jobs can present a major shock to a nation's people. Importing modern management practices without tailoring them to the local culture can also have serious consequences.

South Korea's Daewoo Motors (**www.dm.co.kr**) faced a culture clash when it entered Central Europe. Korea's management system is based on a rigid hierarchical structure and an obsessive work ethic. Managers at Daewoo's domestic car plant in Pupyong-Gu were expected to arrive an hour early for work to stand at the company gates and greet workers—who arrive singing the company anthem. But implementing the Korean work ethic in its Czech Republic factory proved tricky. Korean managers could not understand why employees want holidays that coincide with their children's school breaks or why European managers so frequently switch companies. So Daewoo tried to bridge the cultural and workplace gaps. At any one time, 500 Romanians, Poles, and Uzbeks were studying their Korean colleagues' work habits and methods by staffing assembly lines at Daewoo Motors' plant in Korea for 6-month stretches. Traveling in the other direction were Korean managers and technicians who specialized in assembly-line efficiency.[21]

Environmental Degradation   The economic and social policies of former communist governments in Central and Eastern Europe were disastrous for the natural environment. The direct effects of environmental destruction are evident in increased levels of sickness and disease, including asthma, blood deficiencies, and cancer—the result of which is lower productivity in the workplace. Countries in transition often suffer periods during which the negative effects of a market economy seem to outweigh its benefits. It's hard to enjoy a larger paycheck when the streets are choked with smog and the parks and rivers are polluted. Commuters can suffer carbon monoxide poisoning, children can get lead poisoning from flaking house paint, smokestacks pollute the air, and toxic chemicals often flow down the rivers.

FOCUS ON RUSSIA

Russia's experience with communism dates back to 1917. For the next 75 years, factories, distribution, and all other facets of operations, as well as the prices of labor, capital, and products, were controlled by the government. While China was experimenting with private farm ownership and a limited market-price system, the Soviet Union remained staunchly communist under a system of complete government ownership. This total absence of market institutions meant that, unlike China, Russia endured massive political and economic reforms at the same time.

Rough Transition   In the 1980s the former Soviet Union entered a new era of freedom of thought, freedom of expression, and economic restructuring. For the first time since the communist takeover, people were allowed to speak freely about their lives under economic socialism. And speak freely they did—venting their frustrations over a general lack of consumer goods, poor-quality products, and long lines at banks and grocery stores.

But the transition from government ownership and central planning has been challenging for ordinary Russians. Except for criminals and wealthy businesspeople, whom the Russians call the "oligarchs," people are having difficulty maintaining their standard of living and affording many basic items such as food and clothing. Today, some Russians are surviving because they were factory managers under the old system and retained their jobs in the new system. Others have turned to the black market, creating organized-crime syndicates and relying on extortion payments to amass personal wealth. Still others are working hard to build legitimate companies but find themselves forced into making "protection" payments to organized crime.

Challenges Ahead for Russia   Several challenges lie ahead for Russia. As in so many other transitional economies, managerial talent needs to be fostered. Years of central planning hampered development of the managerial skills needed to operate companies in a market-based economy. Russian managers must improve their skills in every facet of management practice, including financial control, research and development, employee hiring and training, marketing, and pricing.

Political instability, especially in the form of intensified nationalist sentiment, is another potential threat to further progress toward transition. Also, some experts worry about the future disposition of Russia's nuclear weapons stockpiles. Almost everyone in Russia is badly in need of currency, and sales of such stockpiles can earn large sums of hard currency. Although the temptation to sell weapons to other nations is particularly great, in the wrong hands they can threaten global security, even that of Russia itself.

One Bright Spot   Russia needs tax revenue to establish the institutions that are essential to the functioning of a market economy, such as well-running stock markets, a strong central bank, and an effective tax system. But without being able to collect taxes from individuals and corporations, the government cannot afford to establish these institutions or to pay coal miners, teachers, and the pensions of the elderly and to invest in education and infrastructure. Payment for goods and services through barter, not cash, exacerbates this problem because such transactions are not taxed.

FIGURE 4.3
Back to Cash

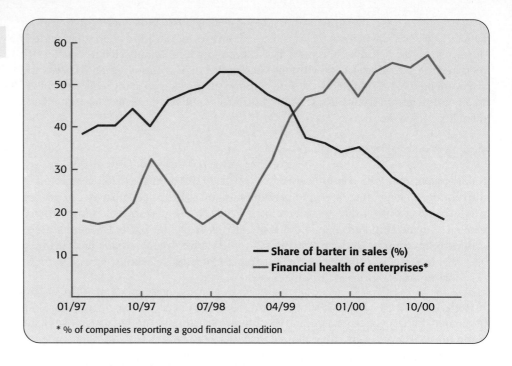

* % of companies reporting a good financial condition

Legend: Share of barter in sales (%); Financial health of enterprises*

Before the Russian currency (the ruble) collapsed in 1998, large sums of international aid covered up the hole in the budget caused by the lack of tax revenues, which resulted in part from extensive barter. But afterward, a lack of international aid forced the government to crack down. The government and energy suppliers began demanding that companies pay their energy bills in cash. Faced with a threat of disconnection, and sometimes bankruptcy, firms suddenly found the cash to pay up. The move caused a ripple effect throughout the economy as firms began demanding cash payments from their customers.[22] As Figure 4.3 shows, although barter remains a problem in Russia, it accounts for much less of the nation's economic activity than it did earlier.

A FINAL WORD

Ongoing market reforms in formerly centrally planned and mixed economies are having a profound effect on international business. Freer markets are spurring major shifts in manufacturing activity. Lured by incentives such as low wages and growing markets, international companies are forging ties in newly industrialized countries and exploring opportunities in developing nations. Global capital markets are making it easier for these companies to set up factories abroad, and some newly industrialized countries are even producing world-class competitors of their own.

International companies are keenly aware that many countries that are experiencing difficulties have immense potential for growth. Some experts, for instance, estimate that the middle class in India will soon climb to over 300 million people—more than the entire U.S. population. As long as one-time centrally planned economies continue down the path toward free markets, they will spur domestic entrepreneurial activity and attract international investors. This chapter completes our coverage of national business environments. The next chapter introduces Part 3 of the book—the international trade and investment environment.

There is a variety of additional material available on the Companion Website that accompanies this book. You can access this information by visiting the Website at (www.prenhall.com/wild).

summary

❶ Describe what is meant by a *centrally planned economy,* and explain why its use is declining. An *economic system* consists of the structure and processes that a country uses to allocate its resources and conduct its commercial activities. In a *centrally planned economy*, the government owns land, factories, and other economic resources, and plans nearly all economic-related activities. The philosophy of central planning stresses the group over individual well-being and strives for economic and social equality.

The use of central planning is declining for several reasons. First, scarce resources were wasted because central planners paid little attention to product quality and buyers' needs. Second, a lack of incentives to innovate resulted in little or no economic growth and consistently low standards of living. Third, central planners realized that other economic systems were achieving far higher growth rates for other countries. Fourth, consumers became fed up with a lack of basic necessities such as adequate food, housing, and health care.

❷ Identify the main characteristics of a *mixed economy,* and explain the emphasis on *privatization.* In a *mixed economy*, land, factories, and other economic resources are split between private and government ownership, with governments tending to control the economic sectors crucial to national security and long-term stability. Proponents of mixed economies contend that a successful economic system not only must be efficient and innovative, but also should protect society from the excesses of unchecked individualism and organizational greed.

However, attempting to become more efficient in their use of scarce resources, many mixed economies are engaging in *privatization*—the sale of government-owned economic resources to private operators. Because privatized companies compete in open markets for material, labor, and capital, they can go out of business if they do not produce competitive products at fair prices. This is nearly unheard of for many state-owned companies.

❸ Explain how a *market economy* functions, and identify its distinguishing features. In a *market economy*, private individuals or businesses own the majority of land, factories, and other economic resources. Economic decisions are influenced by the interplay of *supply* (the quantity of a product that producers are willing to provide at a specific selling price) and *demand* (the quantity of a product that buyers are willing to purchase at a specific selling price). Market economics is rooted in the belief that individual concerns are paramount and that the group benefits when individuals receive proper incentives and rewards.

This approach, whereby there is less government interference in commerce and greater individual economic freedom, is known as a laissez-faire system. To function smoothly, the market economy requires (1) *free choice* (in buyers' purchasing options), (2) *free enterprise* (in producers' competitive decisions), and (3) *price flexibility* (reflecting supply and demand). The government's role in a market economy centers on (1) *enforcing antitrust laws*, (2) *preserving property rights*, (3) *providing a stable fiscal and monetary environment*, and (4) *preserving political stability*.

❹ Describe the different ways to measure a nation's level of *development.* *Economic development* refers to the economic well-being of one nation's people compared with that of another nation's people. Formal methods for gauging economic development include the following. (1) *National production* includes measures such as *gross national product (GNP)* (the value of all goods and services produced in one year by a country) and *gross domestic product (GDP)* (the value of all goods and services produced in one year by the domestic economy). (2) *Purchasing power parity (PPP)* refers to the relative ability of two countries' currencies to buy the same "basket" of goods in those two countries. This index is used to correct comparisons that are made at official exchange rates, which, therefore ignore different costs of living in different nations. (3) The United Nations' *human development index (HDI)* goes beyond estimates of financial wealth in order to measure the extent to which a people's needs are satisfied and addressed equally across the population.

❺ Describe the process of *economic transition,* and identify the remaining obstacles to businesses. The process whereby a nation changes its fundamental economic organization in order to create free-market institutions is called *economic transition*. Typically, five reform measures are involved: (1) macroeconomic stabilization, (2) liberalization of economic activity, (3) legalization of private enterprises and privatization of state-owned enterprises, (4) removal of barriers to free trade, investment, and currency flows, and (5) development of a social welfare system.

There are four major obstacles to successful economic transition. First, there is a *lack of managerial expertise* because central planners made virtually all operations, pricing, and sales decisions. Second, there is a *shortage of capital* to pay for new communications and infrastructure, new financial institutions, and the education of people about the working of a market economy. Third, *cultural differences* between transition economies and the West can make it difficult to introduce modern management practices. Fourth, *environmental degradation* has caused lower workforce productivity due to substandard health conditions.

questions **for review**

1. What is an *economic system*? Explain the relation between culture and economics.

2. What is a *centrally planned economy*? Describe the link between central planning and communism. Name two countries that have now or have had centrally planned economies.

3. Describe China's experience with central planning. What is the importance of *guanxi*?

4. What is a *mixed economy*? Explain the origin of mixed economies, and name three countries with mixed economies.

5. Define *market economy*. What are the three requirements of a market economy?

6. Define *economic development*.

7. Describe three *measures of economic development*. What are the advantages and disadvantages of each?

8. How does *GNP* differ from *GDP*?

9. Explain the concept of *purchasing power parity*. What are its implications for income per capita relative to other nations?

10. Explain the value of the *Human Development Index (HDI)*.

11. Which three broad categories are used to *classify* countries according to level of economic development? Name three countries in each category.

12. What are the main characteristics of *developed countries*? *Newly industrialized countries*? *Developing countries*?

13. What types of countries tend to be characterized by *technological dualism*?

14. List the five reform measures involved in making the *transition* from a centrally planned or mixed economy to a market economy.

15. What is *privatization*? Explain its importance to economic transition.

16. What are the four main *obstacles* to businesses in transitional economies? Briefly describe each.

17. Explain Russia's experience with economic transition.

questions **for discussion**

1. The Internet has penetrated many aspects of business and culture in developed countries, but it is barely available in many poor countries. Do you think that this technology is going to widen the economic development gap between rich and poor countries? Why or why not? Is there a way that developing countries can use such technologies as a tool for economic development?

2. Imagine that you are the director of a major international lending institution supported by funds from member countries. What one area in newly industrialized and developing economies would be your priority for receiving development aid? Do you suspect that any member countries will be politically opposed to aid in this area? Why or why not?

3. Two students are discussing the pros and cons of different measures of economic development. "GDP per capita," declares the first, "is the only true measure of how developed a country's economy is." The second student counters: "I disagree. The only true measure of a country's economic development is its people's quality of life, regardless of its GDP." Why is each of these students incorrect? Respond to each with a one-paragraph comment.

in practice

Read the article below and answer the questions that follow.

Light Years Ahead

TALLINN, Estonia—More than a decade since casting off the chains of communism, Estonians are enjoying their freedoms.

Today the country's political system broadly represents the population, the economy is wide open, and foreign investment is flowing in. In fact, a European Union report released Tuesday put Estonia among a select few that could become members within three years.

The capital, Tallinn has been especially prosperous. Half of the city's residents have a mobile phone and average monthly wages are 22 percent higher than the nation as a whole. Founded as a fortress by the Danes in the thirteenth century, the city still enjoys strong ties to Scandinavia. A magnet for Finnish tourists, who take a brief ferry ride to drink and shop cheaply, Tallinn is sometimes called a suburb of Helsinki.

The tiny nation is light years ahead of some others that have clearly veered off the road to free markets. Belarus, for one, is under authoritarian rule, lacks civil and political freedoms, and is isolationist.

1. Why do you think some nations (such as Estonia, Hungary, and Poland) outperformed others (such as Belarus and Ukraine) during their postcommunist transitions? Identify as many possible economic factors and social/cultural factors as you can for at least two countries. Briefly describe why you think each was important in each nation's case.

2. Some nations, including the Baltic States, experienced high growth rates while enduring large increases in alcoholism and suicide rates during their transitions. Why do you think a nation's people can be so depressed when the economy is performing so well?

3. Companies explicitly or implicitly supplement their analysis of a nation's attractiveness as a new market or production base with human development indicators. Do you think this is appropriate? List several human development issues that can affect company operations in a nation and, therefore, the decision to enter the market.

projects

1. In this project, two groups of four students debate the benefits and drawbacks of both market and mixed economies. After the first student from each side has spoken, the second student questions the opponent's arguments, looking for holes and inconsistencies. The third student attempts to answer these arguments. The fourth student presents a summary of each side's arguments. Finally, the class will vote on which team has offered the more compelling argument.

2. Select a recent article from a business magazine or Web site discussing some economic issue within a particular country. Potential topics include privatization of state-owned companies, the influence of a capital shortage on transition, and investment in advancing human development such as public health programs. Summarize the article and explain how local and international companies will be affected by, and respond to, the issue.

3. Select a country that interests you. What type of economic system does it have? Has it always had this type of economic system? Is it developed, newly industrializing, or developing? How does it rank on the various measures of economic development? Has it undergone any form of economic transition within the past 15 years? If so, what have been the effects of that transition on the culture and the country's political, legal, and economic systems? Present a brief report to the class.

Like M.B.A. students all over the world, students in Havana University's M.B.A. program take courses ranging from accounting to international trade. Yet for HU's graduates, applying the principles of capitalist business in communist Cuba is another matter. Still, the mere existence of an M.B.A. program in Cuba, plus the recent influx of investment, are signs that the aging dictator, Fidel Castro, may be loosening his iron grip on the island's planned economy.

When the Soviet Union collapsed in 1989, Cuba had to kiss Soviet subsidies good-bye. With state-owned industrial dinosaurs wheezing away and the economy under immense strain, Castro opened up key state industries to non-Cuban investment. As a result, joint ventures have become a key plank in the effort to prop up Cuba through limited economic reforms. The money comes chiefly from Canada, Mexico, and Europe—all of whom benefit from the absence of Cuba's neighbor and nemesis, the United States, which has maintained a trade embargo against Cuba since 1960. One of the biggest players in Cuba today is Canada's Sherritt International Corporation (www.sherritt.com). Sherritt's flag flutters outside the island's biggest nickel mine, and Sherritt rigs are reviving output from old oil fields. After turning around the ailing nickel mine at Moa, Sherritt received Castro's go-ahead to develop beach resorts and beef up communications and transport networks.

Although international concerns like Sherritt are free to invest in Cuba, they face some harsh realities and a number of restrictions. For instance, Ricardo Elizondo came to Cuba from Mexico to help manage his company's stake in ETECSA, Cuba's national telecommunications firm. Elizondo reports that anyone who wants to do business in Cuba must accept the reality of partnership with a socialist state. Cuba lacks a legal system to enforce commercial contracts; it lacks a banking system to offer credit; and there are no private-property rights. One thing the government doesn't lack is plenty of labor laws—and these are onerous. Non-Cuban partners cannot hire, fire, or even pay workers directly. They must pay the government to provide laborers who, in turn, are paid only a fraction of these payments.

Why do companies investing in Cuba put up with such restrictions? For one thing, they are getting a great return on their investment. "Cuba's assets are incredibly cheap, and the potential return is huge," says Frank Mersch, VP at Toronto's Altamira

Management (www.altamira.com), which holds 11 percent of Sherritt. Castro, say analysts, is offering outsiders deals with rates of return up to 80 percent a year. Moreover, international investors tend to agree with the widespread belief that the Castro regime won't last very long. Once Castro loses his hold on Cuba, whether through capitulation, exile, or death, the United States will likely end its embargo. In that case, property prices will soar. Companies like Sherritt and ETECSA, who stepped in first, will have gained a valuable toehold in what could be a vibrant market economy.

thinking globally

1. Sherritt pays the Cuban government $9,500 per year per worker. According to Frank Calzon of Freedom House, a New York–based human rights group, the government then pays workers only $120 to $144 per year. Why do you think the Cuban government requires non-Cuban businesses to hire and pay workers only through the government? Do you think it is ethical for non-Cuban businesses to enter into partnerships with the Cuban government? Why or why not?

2. "See Cuba before Castro dies," is the chant of some young travelers who are reacting to reports that 75-year-old Fidel Castro is in poor health. Do some research on Cuba, and describe a scenario for economic transition in the event that the Castro regime collapses. How do you think that the transition to a market economy in Cuba would be the same as or different from the transitions now taking place in Russia and China?

3. The United States not only has maintained a trade embargo against Cuba since 1960 but also has enacted a law permitting U.S. companies to sue companies from other nations that traffic in the property of U.S. firms nationalized by Castro when he took over. It also empowers the U.S. government to deny entry visas to the executives of such firms as well as their families. Given the fact that the Cold War is over, why do you think the United States maintains such a hard line against doing business with Cuba? Do you think this embargo is in the United States' best interests? Why or why not?

a question of ethics

1. China's People's Liberation Army (PLA) has built a sprawling network of businesses—enterprises that do everything from raise pigs to run airlines and hospitals, mine coal, manage hotels, and operate paging and cellular networks. As a business conglomerate, of course, the PLA partners with international investors. Some argue that a large portion of foreign investment going to China is with companies and cartels controlled by the Chinese military. Others argue that it's easy to read too much into the PLA's foray into business. They point out that there is little centralized coordination among the thousands of businesses with military affiliations, and that some companies are run by retired officers, others by civilians.

   If you were looking for a joint venture partner in China, would you have any ethical concerns about partnering with the PLA? If so, what would those be? Suppose you were managing a Canadian–Chinese joint venture involving the PLA, when a clash between pro-democracy demonstrators and the PLA turns bloody. How would this turn of events affect business relations with your PLA partner? Are the ethical issues of partnering with the Chinese military any different from those that arise from exporting to China? Why or why not?

2. The social-welfare states of Western Europe were founded after the Second World War with specific ethical considerations in mind: reduce social and economic inequality, improve living standards for the poor, and provide health care for everyone. Now many of these countries have trimmed social-welfare provisions and increased their reliance on market forces. Do you think that the ethical concerns of half a century ago are a thing of the past, or do you feel that market reforms will simply re-create the conditions that motivated the development of the welfare state in the first place? Argue the merits of each case.

5 international trade

LEARNING OBJECTIVES

After studying this chapter, you should be able to

1. Describe the relation between *international trade volume* and *world output*, and identify overall *trade patterns*.

2. Describe *mercantilism*, and explain its impact on the world powers and their colonies.

3. Identify the differences between *absolute advantage* and *comparative advantage*.

4. Explain the *factor proportions* and *international product life cycle* theories.

5. Explain the *new trade* and *national competitive advantage* theories.

BEACONS

A Look Back

Chapters 2, 3, and 4 examined the ways in which cultural, political, legal, and economic differences between countries influence international business activities.

A Look at This Chapter

This chapter begins our study of the international trade and investment environment. We explore the oldest form of international business activity—international trade. We discuss the benefits and volume of international trade and explore the major theories that attempt to explain why trade occurs.

A Look Ahead

Chapter 6 explains business-government trade relations. We explore both the motives and methods of government intervention and how the global trading system works to promote free trade.

Trade Tastes Good

MPUMALANGA, South Africa—Although the twentieth century meant civil and regional war for much of Africa, a new age seems to be dawning for some nations. In addition to South Africa, countries that show promise include Botswana, Ghana, Nigeria, Mozambique, and Uganda. U.S. trade with Africa is more than $10 billion annually and rising.

Coca-Cola (**www.cocacola.com**) is one company riding the wave of growing trade and investment in Africa. Coca-Cola has been operating in countries south of the Sahara desert since 1938 and recently came back to Angola, which it left in 1975. In fact, the only two countries in which Coca-Cola does not have operations are Libya and Sudan, which were made off limits to U.S. firms by the U.S. government. Although sales in Africa and the Middle East account for just 2 percent of Coke's profits, the continent's growth potential is what lures the company.

Typically, a salesperson starts by selling Coke by the case on a street corner and then moves up to selling from a kiosk. Two brothers from Mpumalanga, South Africa, started selling Coke years ago out of a "spaza shop"—a small store run out of the back of a tin and cinderblock house. Now they own a multimillion-dollar Coca-Cola bottling business. It is this sort of entrepreneurial drive that could raise living standards across the African continent. As you read this chapter, consider explanations for the pattern of trade flows around the world.[1]

Today, people around the world are accustomed to purchasing goods and services from companies in other countries. In fact, many consumers get their first taste of another country's culture through merchandise purchased from that country. Chanel No. 5 (www.chanel.com) perfume evokes the romanticism of France. The fine artwork on Imari porcelain conveys the Japanese attention to detail and quality. And Levi's jeans (www.levi.com) portray the casual lifestyle of people in the United States.

In this chapter, we explore international trade in goods and services. We begin by examining the benefits, volume, and patterns of international trade. We then explore a number of important theories that attempt to explain why nations trade with one another.

OVERVIEW OF INTERNATIONAL TRADE

The purchase, sale, or exchange of goods and services across national borders is called **international trade**. This is in contrast to domestic trade, which occurs between different states, regions, or cities within a country.

Over the past decade a majority of the world's economies have seen an increase in the importance of trade. One way to measure the importance of trade to a nation is to

MAP 5.1

The Importance of Trade
This map shows each nation's trade volume as a share of its GDP, adjusted for purchasing power parity (PPP).

Trade as a share of GDP at PPP is defined as the sum of merchandise exports and imports measured in current U.S. dollars divided by the value of GDP converted to international dollars using PPP conversion factors.

This is a conservative measure: Because the GDP of many developing countries is larger in PPP terms than when converted at official exchange rates, the resulting ratios tend to be lower.

examine the volume of an economy's trade relative to its total output. As Map 5.1 demonstrates, the value of trade passing through some nations' borders actually exceeds the amount of goods and services that they produce (the 100.1% and above category).

international trade
Purchase, sale, or exchange of goods and services across national borders.

BENEFITS OF INTERNATIONAL TRADE

As we saw in our opening company profile, international trade is opening doors to new entrepreneurial opportunity across Africa. It also provides a country's people with a greater choice of goods and services. For example, because Finland has a cool climate, it cannot be expected to grow cotton. But it can sell paper and other products made from lumber (which it has in abundance) to the United States. It can then use the proceeds from the sale to buy Pima cotton from the United States. Thus, people in Finland get cotton they would otherwise not have. Although the United States has vast forests, the wood-based products from Finland might be of a certain quality or price that fills a gap in the U.S. marketplace.

International trade is an important engine for job creation in many countries. The Department of Commerce of the United States (**www.doc.gov**) estimates that for every $1 billion increase in exports, 22,800 jobs are created in the country.[2] Moreover, it has

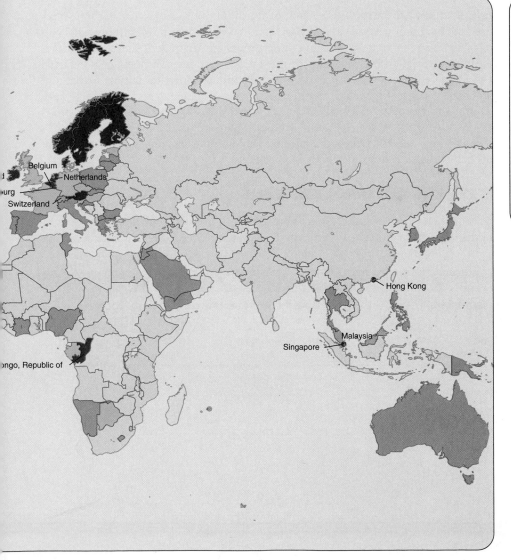

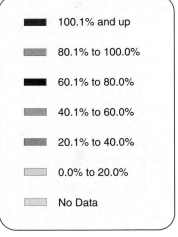

	100.1% and up
	80.1% to 100.0%
	60.1% to 80.0%
	40.1% to 60.0%
	20.1% to 40.0%
	0.0% to 20.0%
	No Data

been estimated that 12 million U.S. jobs depend on exports and that these jobs pay on average from 13 to 18 percent more than jobs not related to international trade.[3] Expanded trade often benefits other countries similarly.

VOLUME OF INTERNATIONAL TRADE

The value and volume of international trade continues to increase. Today, world merchandise exports are roughly $5.5 trillion and service exports are approaching the $1.4 trillion mark. Table 5.1 shows the world's largest exporters of merchandise and services. Perhaps not surprisingly, the United States dominates the rest of the world in the export of both merchandise and commercial services.

Most of world merchandise trade is comprised of trade in manufactured goods. The dominance of manufactured goods in the trade of merchandise has persisted over time and will likely continue to do so. Figure 5.1 shows the impressive growth in the volume of world trade in manufactures, mining products, and agricultural products. Although the importance of trade in services is growing for many nations, it tends to be relatively more important for the world's richest countries. Trade in services makes up roughly 20 percent of total world trade.

Trade and World Output The level of world output in any given year influences the level of international trade in that year. Slower world economic output slows the volume of international trade, and higher output spurs greater trade. Trade slows in times of economic recession because when people are less certain about their own financial futures they buy fewer domestic and imported products. Another reason output and trade move together is that a country in recession also often has a currency that is weak relative to other nations. This makes imports more expensive relative to domestic products. (We discuss the relation between currency values and trade fully in Chapter 10.) As shown in Figure 5.2, in addition to trade and world output moving in lockstep fashion, trade has consistently grown faster than output.

INTERNATIONAL TRADE PATTERNS

Exploring the volume of international trade and world output provides useful insights into the international trade environment. However, it does not tell us who trades with

TABLE 5.1 *World's Top Exporters*

World's Top Merchandise Exporters				World's Top Commercial Service Exporters			
Rank	Exporter	Value (U.S. billions)	Share of World Total (%)	Rank	Exporter	Value (U.S. billions)	Share of World Total (%)
1	United States	695.2	12.4	1	United States	253.4	18.8
2	Germany	541.5	9.6	2	United Kingdom	101.5	7.5
3	Japan	419.4	7.5	3	France	82.6	6.1
4	France	300.4	5.3	4	Germany	79.3	5.9
5	United Kingdom	269.0	4.8	5	Italy	61.2	4.5
6	Canada	238.4	4.2	6	Japan	60.3	4.5
7	Italy	230.6	4.1	7	Netherlands	54.2	4.0
8	Netherlands	200.4	3.6	8	Spain	53.0	3.9
9	China	195.2	3.5	9	Belgium/Luxembourg	39.0	2.9
10	Belgium	176.3	3.1	10	Hong Kong, China	34.9	2.6

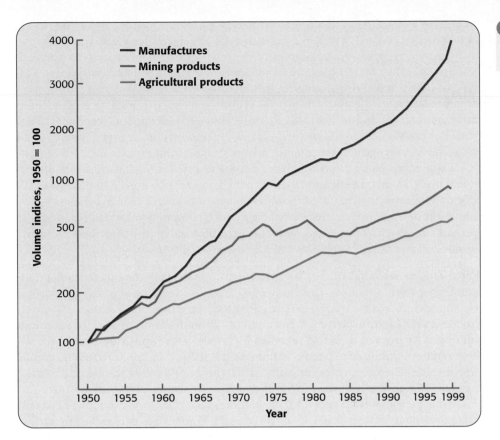

FIGURE 5.1

**Breakdown of World
Merchandise Exports**

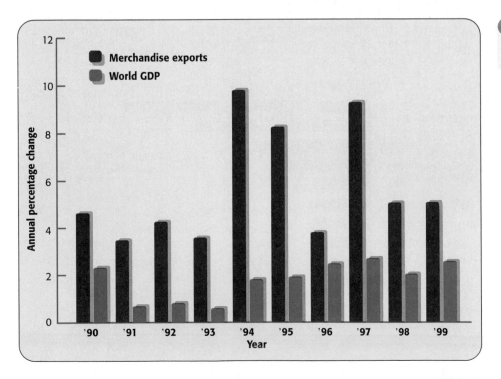

FIGURE 5.2

**Growth of World Merchandise
Exports and GDP**

whom. For instance, it does not reveal whether trade occurs primarily between the world's richest nations or whether there is significant trade activity involving poorer nations.

Customs agencies in most countries record the destination of exports, the source of imports, and the physical quantities and values of goods crossing their borders. This type of data is revealing, although it is sometimes misleading. For example, governments sometimes deliberately distort the reporting of trade in military equipment or other sensitive goods. In other cases, extensive trade in underground economies (black markets) can distort the real picture of trade between nations. Nevertheless, customs data tend to reflect general trade patterns among nations rather well.

Large ocean-going cargo vessels are needed to support these patterns in international trade. In fact, Greek and Japanese merchant ships own over 30 percent of the world's total capacity (measured in tons shipped, or tonnage) of merchant ships. As a whole, the developing countries' share of the total is rising and today stands at nearly 20 percent.[4] To see a list of the top 10 countries according to capacity owned, see the World Business Survey titled "Who Owns The High Seas?"

Who Trades with Whom?   Not surprisingly, a broad pattern of merchandise trade among the world's nations tends to persist. Trade between the world's high-income economies accounts for roughly 60 percent of total world merchandise trade. Two-way trade between high-income countries and low- and middle-income nations accounts for about 34 percent of world merchandise trade. Meanwhile, merchandise trade between low- and middle-income nations accounts for only about 6 percent of total world trade. These figures reveal the low purchasing power of the world's poorest nations and indicate their general lack of economic development.[5]

Table 5.2 shows trade data for the major regions of the world economy. The number representing intraregional exports for Western Europe (which is at the intersection

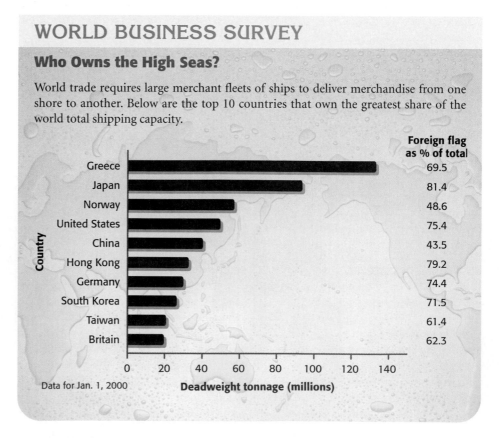

WORLD BUSINESS SURVEY

Who Owns the High Seas?

World trade requires large merchant fleets of ships to deliver merchandise from one shore to another. Below are the top 10 countries that own the greatest share of the world total shipping capacity.

Country	Foreign flag as % of total
Greece	69.5
Japan	81.4
Norway	48.6
United States	75.4
China	43.5
Hong Kong	79.2
Germany	74.4
South Korea	71.5
Taiwan	61.4
Britain	62.3

Data for Jan. 1, 2000   Deadweight tonnage (millions)

TABLE 5.2	Intra- and Inter-Regional Merchandise Trade (U.S. $ billions)							
Origin	**North America**	**Latin America**	**Western Europe**	**C./E. Europe/ Baltic States/CIS**	**Africa**	**Middle East**	**Asia**	**World**
North America	370	146	181	6	11	22	197	934
Latin America	183	47	38	3	3	3	18	297
Western Europe	232	57	1,625	120	59	57	176	2,353
C./E. Europe/Baltic States/CIS	9	4	120	56	3	4	16	214
Africa	17	3	57	1	11	2	15	112
Middle East	25	2	34	1	8	14	73	170
Asia	367	35	252	13	21	37	650	1,394
World	1,203	294	2,307	200	116	139	1,145	5,473

of the row and column titled "Western Europe") immediately stands out. This number tells us that over $1.6 trillion (nearly 70 percent) of Western Europe's exports are destined for other nations in Western Europe. In contrast, intraregional exports account for 47 percent of all exports in Asia and 40 percent of exports in North America. These data underscore the rationale behind, and results of, efforts toward European regional integration called the European Union—discussed fully in Chapter 8.

Data in the table also reveal why headlines in the United States often complain that Asia's markets are not open to goods from North America. The value of North American exports to Asia, $197 billion, is only slightly more than half the value of Asian exports to North America, $367 billion. But as economies across Asia develop, these figures should adjust to reflect their greater purchasing power. Some economists call this century the "Pacific century," referring to the expected future growth of Asian economies and the resulting shift in trade flows from the Atlantic Ocean to the Pacific. As these nations' economies grow, it will become increasingly important for managers to fully understand how to do business in Asia. See this chapter's Global Manager titled "Building Good Relations in the Pacific Rim" for some pointers on doing business in Pacific Rim nations.

TRADE DEPENDENCE AND INDEPENDENCE

All countries fall on a continuum of trade interdependencies, with total dependence on another country at one end, and total independence from other countries at the other. Complete independence was considered desirable from the sixteenth century through much of the eighteenth. Some remote island nations were completely independent simply because they lacked methods of transportation to engage in trade. However, today this is far less common, and isolationism is generally considered undesirable.

Effect on Developing and Transition Nations Developing and transition nations that share borders with developed countries are often dependent on their wealthier neighbors. Trade dependency has been a blessing for many central and eastern European nations. A large number of joint ventures now bridge the borders between Germany and its neighbors—Germany has more than 6,000 joint ventures in Hungary alone. Germany also is central Europe's mightiest trading partner, accounting for more than half of the European Union's (www.europa.eu.int) total trade with the 12 central and eastern European countries that have applied to join the group. By combining German technology with lower Central European production costs, German companies gain an edge over the competition. Opel (www.opel.com), the German arm of General Motors

GLOBAL MANAGER

Building Good Relations in the Pacific Rim

To do business in Pacific Rim countries (those that rim the Pacific Ocean in Asia), start by recognizing two facts: (1) Asian customers can be as diverse as their individual cultures, and (2) aggressive salesmanship doesn't work in the land of the "four tigers." Cultural nuances and business etiquette demand a little homework before you visit these countries. Some general rules apply, however. Here are five:

1. **Count on third-party contacts.** Asians prefer to do business with people they know. Cold calls—in which you call a company with no prior contact—and other direct-contact methods seldom work. Meeting the right people in an Asian company almost always depends on having the right introduction. Use a proper intermediary. If the person with whom you hope to do business respects your intermediary, chances are he or she will respect you.

2. **Carry a bilingual business card.** To make a good first impression, have bilingual cards printed even though many Asians speak English—the international language of business. It shows both respect for the language and commitment to doing business in a particular country. It also translates your title into the local language. Asians generally are not comfortable until they know your position and whom you represent.

3. **Leave the hard sell at home.** Asian businesspeople are tough negotiators, but they dislike argumentative exchanges. Harmony and consensus are the bywords. Be prepared to be patient but firm.

4. **Go easy with legalese.** Legal documents are not as important as personal relationships. Most Asians do not like detailed contracts and will often insist that agreements be left flexible so that adjustments can be made easily to fit changing circumstances. It's very important to foster good relations based on mutual trust and benefit. The importance of a contract in many Asian societies is not what it stipulates, but rather who signed it.

5. **Build personal rapport.** Social ease and friendship are prerequisites to doing business. Accept invitations and be sure to reciprocate. As much business is transacted in informal dinner settings as in corporate settings.

Corporation (www.gm.com), built a $440 million plant in Szentgotthard, Hungary, to use lower-cost labor to make parts for and assemble its Astra hatchbacks for export.[6]

Dangers of Trade Dependency   Trade dependency can be dangerous. If the nation that is depended on experiences economic recession or political turmoil, the dependent nation can experience serious economic problems. Trade dependency is causing concern today in Mexico. For the past 25 years, Mexico has seen rising investment by U.S. companies, assembling products such as refrigerators, calculators, laptop computers, and mobile phones. Since the free trade agreement (NAFTA) between Canada, Mexico, and the United States came into effect in 1994, Mexico's exports have tripled and inward investment has totaled $85 billion. But poor education, rampant corruption, red tape, relatively high taxes compared to similar markets, and an outdated infrastructure are forcing some companies to abandon Mexico for locations in Asia and Europe—leaving many unemployed in their wake. Mexico's garment industry recently lost 22,000 jobs, many of them going to China and the Caribbean. Thus, although trade dependency was a blessing for Mexico for many years, it may now feel the pain as companies shift jobs out of the country.[7]

Balance between Dependence and Independence   Today trade between most nations is characterized by a certain degree of interdependency. Companies in the developed countries do a great deal of business with those in other developed nations. In addition, the level of interdependency between certain pairs of countries often reflects the amount of trade that occurs between a company's subsidiaries in the two nations. For example, transactions between subsidiaries of international companies account for about one third of U.S. exports and about two fifths of U.S. imports. The Mercedes-Benz (www.mercedes.com) plant in Tuscaloosa, Alabama, imports most of

Shown here, employees in Mexico churn out all of General Electric's gas ranges and most of its electric stoves sold in the United States. For over 25 years, companies flocked to Mexico to set up assembly plants that brought jobs to ordinary Mexicans. But some companies are moving production of price-sensitive goods to cheaper locations such as China. As a result, Mexico is experiencing some negative aspects of its dependence on U.S. trade.

its components for production of its Mercedes-Benz sport utility vehicle from Germany. The completed vehicle is then sent back to Germany or to affiliates in other countries.

THEORIES OF INTERNATIONAL TRADE

Trade between different groups of people has occurred for many thousands of years. But it was not until the fifteenth century that people tried to explain why trade occurs and how trade can benefit both parties to an exchange. Figure 5.3 shows a timeline of when the main theories of international trade were proposed. Today, efforts to refine existing trade theories and to develop new ones continue. Let's now discuss the first theory that attempts to explain why nations should engage in international trade—*mercantilism*.

MERCANTILISM

The trade theory that nations should accumulate financial wealth, usually in the form of gold, by encouraging exports and discouraging imports is called **mercantilism**. It states that other measures of a nation's well-being, such as living standards or human develop-

mercantilism
Trade theory that holds that nations should accumulate financial wealth, usually in the form of gold, by encouraging exports and discouraging imports.

FIGURE 5.3 **Trade Theory Timeline**

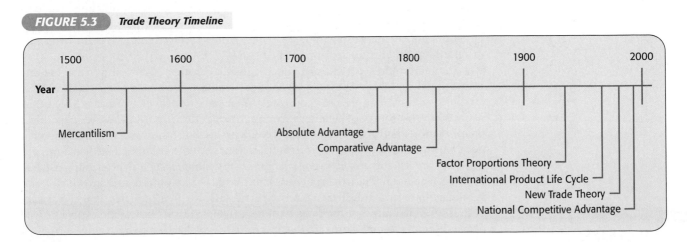

ment, are irrelevant. Nation-states in Europe followed this economic philosophy from about 1500 to the late 1700s. The most prominent mercantilist nations included Britain, France, The Netherlands, Portugal, and Spain.

How Mercantilism Worked   When navigation was a fairly new science, Europeans explored the world by sea, claiming the lands they encountered in the name of the European monarchy that was financing their voyage. Early exploration led them to Africa, Asia, and North, South, and Central America where they established colonies. Colonial trade was conducted for the benefit of mother countries, and colonies were generally treated as exploitable resources.

In recent times, former colonies have struggled to diminish their reliance on the former colonial powers. For example, in an effort to decrease their dependence on their former colonial powers, African nations are welcoming trade relationships with partners from Asia and North America. But due to geographic proximity, the European Union is still often preferred as a trading partner.

Trade Surpluses   Just how did countries implement mercantilism? First, nations believed they could increase their wealth by maintaining a **trade surplus**—the condition that results when the value of a nation's exports is greater than the value of its imports. In mercantilism, a trade surplus meant that a country was taking in more gold on the sale of its exports than it was paying out for its imports. A **trade deficit** is the opposite condition—one that results when the value of a country's imports is greater than the value of its exports. In mercantilism, trade deficits were to be avoided at all costs. (We discuss the importance of national trade balance more fully in Chapter 7.)

Intervention   Second, national governments actively intervened in international trade to maintain a trade surplus. According to mercantilism, the accumulation of wealth depended on increasing a nation's trade surplus, not necessarily expanding its total value or volume of trade. The governments of mercantilist nations did this by either banning certain imports or imposing various restrictions on them, such as tariffs or quotas. At the same time, they subsidized home-based industries to expand exports. Governments also typically outlawed the removal of their gold and silver to other nations.

Colonization   Third, mercantilist nations acquired less-developed territories (colonies) around the world to serve as sources of inexpensive raw materials and as markets for higher-priced finished goods. Colonies were the source of many essential raw materials, including tea, sugar, tobacco, rubber, and cotton. These resources would be shipped to the mercantilist nation, where they were incorporated into finished goods such as clothing, cigars, and other products. These finished goods would then be sold to the colonies. Trade between mercantilist countries and their colonies were a huge source of profits for the mercantilist powers. The colonies received low prices for basic raw materials but paid high prices for finished goods.

The mercantilist and colonial policies greatly expanded the wealth of the nations employing them. This wealth allowed nations to build armies and navies to control their far-flung colonial empires and to protect their shipping lanes from attack by other nations. It was a source of a nation's economic power that in turn increased its political power relative to other countries. Today, countries seen by others as trying to maintain a trade surplus and expanding their national treasuries at the expense of other nations are accused of practicing *neo-mercantilism* or *economic nationalism*. Fairly or not, Japan has often been accused of practicing neo-mercantilism because of its consistently high trade surplus with several industrial nations—particularly the United States. France has also been labeled neo-mercantilist by its trading partners when it has tried to export its way out of difficult economic times in the past.

trade surplus
Condition that results when the value of a nation's exports is greater than the value of its imports.

trade deficit
Condition that results when the value of a country's imports is greater than the value of its exports.

Flaws of Mercantilism Despite its seemingly positive benefits for any nation implementing it, mercantilism is inherently flawed. Mercantilist nations believed that the world's wealth was limited and that a nation could increase its share of the pie only at the expense of its neighbors—called a *zero-sum game*. The main problem with mercantilism is that if all nations were to barricade their markets from imports and push their exports onto others, international trade would be severely restricted. In fact, trade in all nonessential goods would likely cease altogether.

In addition, paying colonies little for their exports but charging them high prices for their imports impaired their economic development. Thus, their appeal as markets for goods was less than it would have been if they were allowed to accumulate greater wealth. These negative aspects of mercantilism were made apparent by a trade theory developed in the late 1700s—*absolute advantage*.

ABSOLUTE ADVANTAGE

Scottish economist Adam Smith first put forth the trade theory of absolute advantage in 1776.[8] The ability of a nation to produce a good more efficiently than any other nation is called an **absolute advantage**. In other words, a nation with an absolute advantage can produce a greater output of a good or service than other nations using the same amount of, or fewer, resources.

> **absolute advantage**
> Ability of a nation to produce a good more efficiently than any other nation.

Among other things, Smith reasoned that international trade should not be banned or restricted by tariffs and quotas, but allowed to flow according to market forces. If people in different countries were able to trade as they saw fit, no country would need to produce all the goods it consumed. Instead, a country could concentrate on producing the goods in which it holds an absolute advantage. It could then trade with other nations to obtain the goods it needed but did not produce.

Suppose Barry Bonds (baseball's single-season home run king) needs to install a hot tub in his family's home during the baseball season. Should he do the job himself or hire a professional installer to do it for him? Suppose Bonds (who has never installed a hot tub before) would have to take 1 month off from playing baseball and forgo roughly $800,000 in salary to complete the job. On the other hand, the professional installer (who does not play professional baseball) can complete the job for $10,000 and do it in 2 weeks. Whereas Bonds has an absolute advantage in playing major league baseball, the installer has an absolute advantage in installing hot tubs. It takes Bonds 1 month to do the job the installer can do in 2 weeks. Thus, Bonds should hire the professional to install the hot tub to save himself both time and money resources.

Let's now apply the absolute advantage concept to an example of two trading countries to see how trade can increase production and consumption in both nations.

Case: Riceland and Tealand Suppose that we live in a world of just two countries (Riceland and Tealand), two products (rice and tea), and transporting goods between these two countries costs nothing. Riceland and Tealand currently produce and consume their own rice and tea. The table below shows the number of units of resources (labor) each country expends in creating rice and tea. In Riceland, just 1 resource unit is needed to produce a ton of rice, but 5 units of resources are needed to produce a ton of tea. In Tealand, 6 units of resources are needed to produce a ton of rice, whereas 3 units are needed to produce a ton of tea.

	Rice	Tea
Riceland	1	5
Tealand	6	3

Another way of stating each nation's efficiency in the production of rice and tea is:

➡ In Riceland, 1 unit of resources = 1 ton of rice *or* ½ ton of tea
➡ In Tealand, 1 unit of resources = ⅙ ton of rice *or* ⅓ ton of tea

These numbers also tell us one other thing about rice and tea production in these two countries. Because one unit of resources produces 1 ton of rice in Riceland compared to Tealand's output of only ⅙ ton of rice, Riceland has an absolute advantage in rice production—it is the more efficient rice producer. However, because one resource unit produces ⅓ ton of tea in Tealand compared to Riceland's output of just ⅕ ton, Tealand has an absolute advantage in tea production.

Gains from Specialization and Trade   Suppose now that Riceland specializes in rice production to maximize the output of rice in our two-country world. Likewise, Tealand specializes in tea production to maximize world output of tea. Although each country now specializes and world output increases, both countries face a problem. Riceland can consume only its rice production and Tealand can consume only its tea production. The problem can be solved if the two countries trade with each other to obtain the good that it needs but does not produce.

Suppose that Riceland and Tealand agree to trade rice and tea on a one-to-one basis—a ton of rice costs a ton of tea and *vice versa*. Thus, Riceland can produce 1 extra ton of rice with an additional resource unit and trade with Tealand to get 1 ton of tea. This is a lot better than the ⅕ ton of tea that Riceland would have gotten by investing that additional resource unit in making tea for itself. Thus, Riceland definitely benefits from the trade. Likewise, Tealand can produce ⅓ extra ton of tea with an additional resource unit and trade with Riceland to get ⅓ ton of rice. This is twice as much as the ⅙ ton of rice it could have produced using that additional resource unit to make its own rice. Thus, Tealand also benefits from the trade. The gains resulting from this simple trade are shown in Figure 5.4.

Although Tealand does not gain as much as Riceland does from the trade, it does get more rice than it would without trade. The gains from trade for actual countries

FIGURE 5.4

Gains from Specialization and Trade: Absolute Advantage

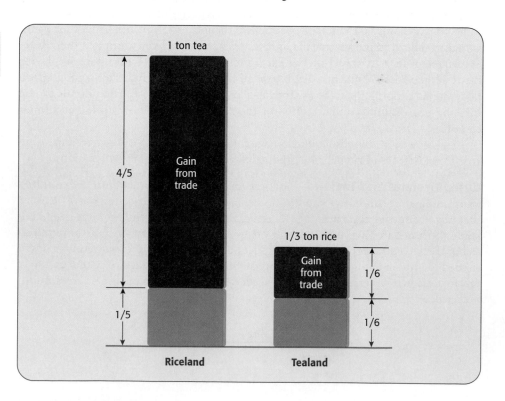

would depend on the total number of resources each country had at its disposal. Another important determinant of the actual benefits from trade is the demand for each good in each country.

As this example shows, the theory of absolute advantage destroys the mercantilist idea that international trade is a zero-sum game. Instead, because there are gains to be had by both countries party to an exchange, international trade is a *positive-sum game*. The theory also calls into question the objective of national governments to acquire wealth through restrictive trade policies. It argues that nations should instead open their doors to trade so their people can obtain a greater quantity of goods more cheaply. Thus, the theory does not measure a nation's wealth by how much gold and silver it has on reserve, but by the living standards of its people.

Despite the power of the theory of absolute advantage in showing the gains from trade, there is one potential problem. What happens if one country does not hold an absolute advantage in the production of any product? Are there still benefits to trade, and will trade even occur? To answer these questions, let's take a look at an extension of absolute advantage, the theory of *comparative advantage*.

COMPARATIVE ADVANTAGE

An English economist named David Ricardo developed the theory of comparative advantage in 1817.[9] He proposed that if one country (in our example of a two-country world) held absolute advantages in the production of both products, specialization and trade could still benefit both countries. A country has a **comparative advantage** when it is unable to produce a good more efficiently than other nations, but produces the good more efficiently than it does any other good. In other words, *trade is still beneficial even if one country is less efficient in the production of two goods, as long as it is less inefficient in the production of one of the goods.*

> **comparative advantage**
> *Inability of a nation to produce a good more efficiently than other nations, but an ability to produce that good more efficiently than it does any other good.*

Let's return to our hot tub example. Now suppose that Barry Bonds has previously installed many hot tubs and can do the job in 1 week—twice as fast as the hot tub installer. Thus, Barry Bonds now holds absolute advantages in both baseball and hot tub installation. Although the professional installer is at an absolute disadvantage in both hot tub installation and baseball, he is less inefficient in hot tub installation. However, despite his absolute advantage in both areas, Bonds would still have to give up $200,000 to take time off from playing baseball to complete the work. Is this a wise decision? No. Bonds should hire the professional installer. The installer earns money he would not earn if Bonds did the job himself, and Bonds earns more money continuing to play baseball than he would save if he installed the hot tub himself.

Gains from Specialization and Trade   To see how the theory of comparative advantage works with international trade, let's return to our example of Riceland and Tealand. In our earlier discussion, Riceland had an absolute advantage in rice production and Tealand had an absolute advantage in tea production. Suppose that Riceland now holds absolute advantages in the production of both rice *and* tea. The table below shows the number of units of resources each country now expends in creating rice and tea. Riceland still needs to expend just 1 resource unit to produce a ton of rice, but now it needs to invest only 2 units of resources (instead of 5) to produce a ton of tea. Tealand still needs 6 units of resources to produce a ton of rice and 3 units to produce a ton of tea.

	Rice	Tea
Riceland	1	2
Tealand	6	3

Another way of stating each nation's efficiency in the production of rice and tea is:

➡ In Riceland, 1 unit of resources = 1 ton of rice *or* ⅓ ton of tea
➡ In Tealand, 1 unit of resources = ⅙ ton of rice *or* ⅓ ton of tea

Thus, for every unit of resource employed Riceland can produce more rice and tea than Tealand can—it has absolute advantages in the production of both goods. But if Riceland has absolute advantages in the production of both goods, it can't possibly gain from trading with a less-efficient producer, right? Wrong, because although Tealand has absolute disadvantages in both rice and tea production, it has a *comparative* advantage in tea. In other words, although it is unable to produce either rice or tea more efficiently than Riceland, Tealand produces tea more efficiently than it produces rice.

Assume once again that Riceland and Tealand decide to trade rice and tea on a one-to-one basis. Tealand could use 1 unit of resources to produce ⅙ ton of rice. But it would do better to produce ⅓ ton of tea with this unit of resources and trade with Riceland to get ⅓ ton of rice. Thus, by specializing and trading, Tealand gets twice as much rice than it could if it were to produce the rice itself. There are also gains from trade for Riceland despite its dual absolute advantages. Riceland could invest 1 unit of resources in the production of ½ ton of tea. However, it would do better to produce 1 ton of rice with the 1 unit of resources and trade that rice for 1 ton of tea. Thus, Riceland gets twice as much tea through trade than if it were to produce the tea itself. This is in spite of the fact that it is a more efficient producer of tea than Tealand.

The benefits for each country from this simple trade are shown in Figure 5.5. Again, the benefits from trade for actual countries depends on the amount of resources at their disposal and each market's desired level of consumption of each product.

Assumptions and Limitations   Throughout the discussion of absolute and comparative advantage, we made several important assumptions that limit the real-world application of the theories. First, we assumed that countries are driven only by the maximization of production and consumption. This is often not the case. In fact, govern-

FIGURE 5.5

Gains from Specialization and Trade: Comparative Advantage

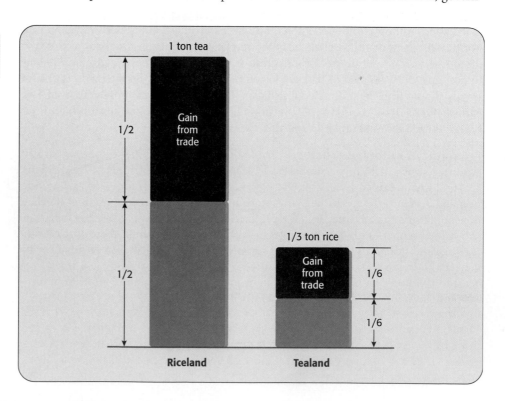

ments of most nations involve themselves in international trade issues out of a concern for workers or consumers. (The role of government in international trade is discussed in detail in Chapter 6.)

Second, the theories assume that there are only two countries engaged in the production and consumption of just two goods. This is obviously not the situation that exists in the real world. There currently are more than 180 countries and literally a countless number of products being produced, traded, and consumed worldwide.

Third, it is assumed that there are no costs for transporting traded goods from one country to another. In reality, transportation costs are a major expense of international trade for some products. If transportation costs for a good are higher than the savings generated through specialization, trade will not occur.

Fourth, the theories consider labor the only kind of resource for the production process because labor accounted for a very large portion of the total production cost of most goods at the time the theories were developed. Moreover, it is assumed that resources are mobile within each nation but cannot be transferred between them. Labor, and especially natural resources, can be difficult and costly to transfer between nations. However, this is definitely changing. For example, people from a nation that belongs to the European Union are allowed to live and work in any other member nation.

Finally, it is assumed that specialization in the production of one particular good does not result in gains in efficiency. But we know that specialization results in increased knowledge of a task and perhaps even future improvements in how that task is performed. Thus, the amount of resources needed to produce a specific amount of a good should decrease over time.

Despite the assumptions made in the theory of comparative advantage, research reveals that it appears to be supported by a substantial body of evidence.[10] Nevertheless, economic researchers continue to develop and test new theories to explain the international purchase and sale of products. Let's now examine one of these, the theory of *factor proportions*.

FACTOR PROPORTIONS THEORY

In the early 1900s, an international trade theory emerged that focused attention on the proportion (supply) of resources in a nation. The cost of any resource is simply the result of supply and demand: Factors in great supply relative to demand will be less costly than factors in short supply relative to demand. **Factor proportions theory** states that countries produce and export goods that require resources (factors) that are abundant and import goods that require resources in short supply.[11] The theory resulted from the research of two economists, Eli Heckscher and Bertil Ohlin, and is therefore sometimes called the Heckscher–Ohlin theory.

Factor proportions theory differs considerably from the theory of comparative advantage. Recall that the theory of comparative advantage states that countries specialize in producing the good that it can produce more efficiently than any other good. Thus, the focus of the theory (and absolute advantage as well) is on the *productivity* of the production process for a particular good. In contrast, factor proportions theory says that a country specializes in producing and exporting goods using the factors of production that are most *abundant*, and thus *cheapest*—not the goods in which it is most productive.

Labor versus Land and Capital Equipment   Factor proportions theory breaks a nation's resources into two categories: labor on the one hand, land and capital equipment on the other. It predicts that a country will specialize in products that require labor if the cost of labor is low relative to the cost of land and capital. Alternatively, a country will specialize in products that require land and capital equipment if their cost is low relative to the cost of labor.

factor proportions theory
Trade theory holding that countries produce and export goods that require resources (factors) that are abundant and import goods that require resources in short supply.

Factor proportions theory is conceptually appealing. For example, Australia has a great deal of land (nearly 60 percent of which is meadows and pastures) and a small population relative to its size. Australia's exports consist largely of mined minerals, grain, beef, lamb, and dairy products—products that require a great deal of land and natural resources. Australia's imports, on the other hand, consist mostly of manufactured raw materials, capital equipment, and consumer goods—things needed in capital-intensive mining and modern agriculture. But instead of looking only at anecdotal evidence, let's see how well factor proportions theory stands up to scientific testing.

Evidence on Factor Proportions Theory: The Leontief Paradox Despite its conceptual appeal, factor proportions theory is not supported by studies that examine the trade flows of nations. The first large-scale study to document such evidence was performed by a researcher named Wassily Leontief in the early 1950s.[12] Leontief tested whether the United States, which uses an abundance of capital equipment, exports goods requiring capital-intensive production and imports goods requiring labor-intensive production. Contrary to the predictions of the factor proportions theory, his research found that U.S. exports require more labor-intensive production than its imports. This apparent paradox between the predictions using the theory and the actual trade flows is called the *Leontief paradox*. Leontief's findings are supported by more recent research on the trade data of a large number of countries.

What might account for the paradox? One possible explanation is that factor proportions theory considers a country's production factors to be homogeneous—particularly labor. But we know that labor skills vary greatly within a country—more highly skilled workers emerge from training and development programs. When expenditures on improving the skills of labor are taken into account, the theory seems to be supported by actual trade data. Further studies examining international trade data will help us better understand what reasons actually account for the Leontief paradox.

Because of the drawbacks of each of the international trade theories mentioned so far, researchers continue to propose new ones. Let's now examine a theory that attempts to explain international trade on the basis of the life cycle of products.

INTERNATIONAL PRODUCT LIFE CYCLE

Raymond Vernon put forth an international trade theory for manufactured goods in the mid-1960s. His **international product life cycle theory** says that a company will begin by exporting its product and later undertake foreign direct investment as the product moves through its life cycle. The theory also says that for a number of reasons a country's export eventually becomes its import.[13]

Although Vernon developed his model around the United States, we can generalize it today to apply to any of the developed and innovative markets of the world, such as Australia, the European Union, Japan, and North America. Let's now examine how his theory attempts to explain international trade flows.

Stages of the Product Life Cycle International product life cycle theory follows the path of a good through its life cycle (from new to maturing to standardized product) to determine where it will be produced (see Figure 5.6). In the *new product stage*, stage 1, the high purchasing power and demand of buyers in an industrialized country spur a company to design and introduce a new product concept. Because the exact level of demand in the domestic market is highly uncertain at this point, the company keeps its production volume low and based in the home country. Keeping production where initial research and development occurred and staying in contact with customers allows managers to monitor buyer preferences and to modify the product as needed.

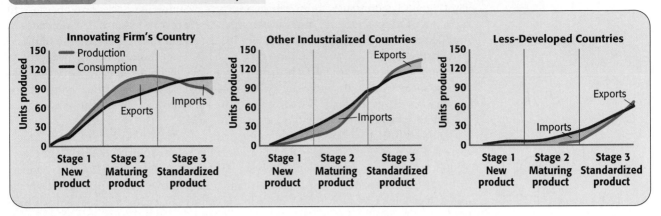

FIGURE 5.6 *International Product Life Cycle*

Although initially there is virtually no export market, exports do begin to pick up late in the new product stage.

In the *maturing product stage*, stage 2, the domestic market and markets abroad become fully aware of the existence of the product and its benefits. Demand rises and is sustained over a fairly lengthy period of time. As exports begin to account for an increasingly greater share of total product sales, the innovating company introduces production facilities in the countries with the highest demand. Near the end of the maturity stage, the product begins generating sales in developing nations, and perhaps some manufacturing presence is established there.

In the *standardized product stage*, stage 3, competition from other companies selling similar products pressures companies to lower prices in order to maintain sales levels. As the market becomes more price-sensitive, the company begins searching aggressively for low-cost production bases in developing nations to supply a growing worldwide market. Furthermore, as most production now takes place outside the innovating country, demand in the innovating country is supplied with imports from developing countries and other industrialized nations. Late in this stage, domestic production might even cease altogether.

Limitations of the Theory Vernon developed his theory at a time when most of the new products being developed in the world were originating and being sold first in the United States. One reason U.S. companies were strong globally in the 1960s was that their domestic production bases were not destroyed during the Second World War, as was the case in Europe (and to some extent Japan). In addition, during the war the production of many durable goods in the United States, including automobiles, was shifted to the production of military transportation and weaponry. This laid the foundation for an enormous demand for new capital-intensive consumer goods following the war, such as autos and home appliances. Furthermore, advances in technology that were originally developed with military purposes in mind were integrated into consumer goods. A wide range of new and innovative products like televisions, photocopiers, and computers, met the seemingly insatiable appetite of consumers in the United States.

Thus, the theory seemed to explain world trade patterns quite well when the United States dominated world trade. But today its ability to depict the trade flows of nations accurately is weak. The United States is no longer the sole innovator of products in the world. New products seem to be springing up everywhere as the research and development activities of companies continue to globalize.

Furthermore, companies today design new products and make product modifications at a very quick pace. The result is quicker product obsolescence and a situation in which companies "cannibalize" their existing products with new product introductions. This is forcing companies to introduce products in many markets simultaneously to recoup a product's research and development costs before its sales decline and it is dropped from the product line. The theory has a difficult time explaining the resulting trade patterns.

In fact, older theories might better explain today's global trade patterns. Much production in the world today more closely resembles what is predicted by the theory of comparative advantage. Boeing's (www.boeing.com) assembly plant in Everett, Washington, constructs its wide-body aircraft—the 747, 767, and 777. The shop floor has wooden crates marked "Belfast, Ireland" containing nose landing-gear doors. On a metal rack, there is a stack of outboard wing flaps from Italy. The entire fuselage of the 777 has traveled in quarter sections from Japan. Its wing tip assembly comes from Korea, its rudders from Australia, and so on.[14] This pattern resembles the theory of comparative advantage in that a product's components are made in the country that can produce them at a high level of productivity. Components are later assembled in a chosen location.

Finally, the theory is challenged by the fact that more companies are operating in international markets from their inception.[15] Many small companies are teaming up with companies in other markets to develop new products or production technologies. This strategy is particularly effective for small companies that would otherwise be unable to participate in international production or sales. Ingenico of France (www.ingenico.com) is now the number one world supplier of secure transaction systems, including terminals and their associated software. But the company began small and worked with a global network of entrepreneurs scattered around the world, who acted as Ingenico's agents by giving the company a local face and helping it to conquer local markets. Managing Director Gerard Compain explained the usefulness of its global network, "These people know their countries better than we do. And they know how to design and sell products for those markets."[16] Also, the Internet has made it easier for small companies to reach a global audience from its inception. For a discussion of several pitfalls small companies can avoid in fulfilling their international orders taken on the Internet, see the Entrepreneurial Focus titled "Five Common Fulfillment Mistakes."

The international product life cycle theory does retain some explanatory power when applied to technology-based products that are eventually mass-produced. However, other more powerful international trade theories continue to emerge.

NEW TRADE THEORY

new trade theory
Trade theory holding that (1) there are gains to be made from specialization and increasing economies of scale, (2) the companies first to market can create barriers to entry, and (3) government may play a role in assisting its home companies.

During the 1970s and 1980s, a new theory emerged to explain trade patterns.[17] The **new trade theory** states that (1) there are gains to be made from specialization and increasing economies of scale, (2) the companies first to enter a market can create barriers to entry, and (3) government may play a role in assisting its home-based companies. Because the theory emphasizes productivity rather than a nation's resources, it is in line with the theory of comparative advantage but at odds with factor proportions theory.

First-Mover Advantage According to the new trade theory, as a company increases the extent to which it specializes in the production of a particular good, output rises because of gains in efficiency. Regardless of the amount of a company's output, it has fixed production costs such as the cost of research and development, and the plant and equipment needed to produce the product. The theory states that as specialization and output increase, companies can realize economies of scale, thereby pushing the unit costs of production lower. That is why as many companies expand, they lower prices to buyers and force potential new competitors to produce at a similar level of output if they want to be competitive in their pricing. Thus, the presence of large economies of scale can create an industry that supports only a few large firms.

A **first-mover advantage** is the economic and strategic advantage gained by being the first company to enter an industry. This first-mover advantage can create a formidable barrier to entry for potential rivals. The new trade theory also states that a country may dominate in the export of a certain product because it has a firm that has acquired a first-mover advantage.[18]

Because of the potential benefits of being the first company to enter an industry, some businesspeople and researchers make a case for government assistance. They say that by working together to target potential new industries, a government and its home-based companies can take advantage of the benefits of being the first mover in an industry. Government involvement has always been widely accepted in undertakings such as space exploration, for national security reasons, but less so in purely commercial ventures. But the fear that governments of other countries might participate with industry to gain first-mover advantages spurs many governments into action.

The theory is still too fresh, and not enough evidence is yet available to judge its accuracy or value. Let's now look at the last major theory of international trade—*national competitive advantage*.

> **first-mover advantage**
> *Economic and strategic advantage gained by being the first company to enter an industry.*

NATIONAL COMPETITIVE ADVANTAGE

Michael Porter put forth a theory in 1990 to explain why certain countries are leaders in the production of certain products.[19] His **national competitive advantage theory** states that a nation's competitiveness in an industry depends on the capacity of the industry to innovate and upgrade. Porter's work incorporates certain elements of previous international trade theories but also makes some important new discoveries.

> **national competitive advantage theory**
> *Trade theory holding that a nation's competitiveness in an industry depends on the capacity of the industry to innovate and upgrade.*

This Tablet PC prototype developed by Microsoft demonstrates the concept of tablet computing. The company believes it represents the natural evolution of the laptop computer. The new product might give Microsoft a first-mover advantage, a potentially formidable barrier to entry for rival computer makers. Can you think of a recently introduced product that might give its manufacturer a first-mover advantage?

Porter is not preoccupied with explaining the export and import patterns of nations, but with explaining why some nations are more competitive in certain industries. He identifies four elements present in every nation to varying degrees that form the basis of national competitiveness. Figure 5.7 shows the *Porter diamond*, which consists of: (1) factor conditions; (2) demand conditions; (3) related and supporting industries; and (4) firm strategy, structure, and rivalry. Let's take a look at each of these elements and see how they all interact to support national competitiveness.

Factor Conditions Factor proportions theory considers a nation's resources, such as a large labor force, natural resources, climate, or surface features, as paramount factors in what products a country will produce and export. Porter acknowledges the value of such resources, which he terms *basic* factors, but also discusses the significance of what he calls *advanced* factors.

Advanced Factors Advanced factors include things such as the skill levels of different segments of the workforce and the quality of the technological infrastructure in a nation. Advanced factors are the result of investments in education and innovation such as worker training and technological research and development. Whereas the basic factors can be the initial spark for why an economy begins producing a certain product, advanced factors account for the sustained competitive advantage a country enjoys in that product.

Today for example, Japan has an advantage in auto production and the United States in the manufacture of airplanes. In the manufacture of computer components, Taiwan reigns supreme, although China is an increasingly important competitor. These countries did not attain their status in their respective areas because of basic factors. For example, Japan did not acquire its advantage in autos because of its natural resources of iron ore—it has virtually none and must import most of the iron it needs. These countries developed their productivity and advantages in producing these products through deliberate efforts, including worker training and development, and improvements in technology and work processes.

Demand Conditions Sophisticated buyers in the home market are also important to national competitive advantage in a product area. A sophisticated domestic market

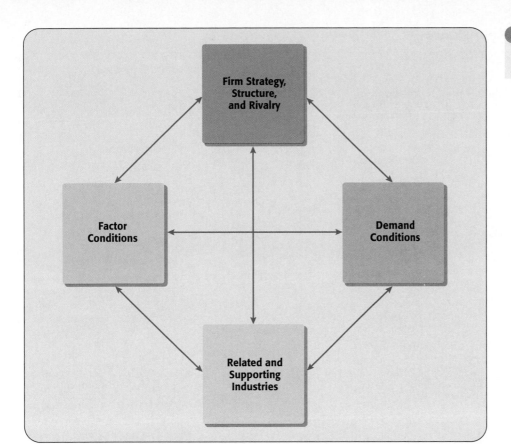

FIGURE 5.7

Determinants of National Competitive Advantage

drives companies to modify existing products to include new design features and develop entirely new products and technologies. Companies in markets with sophisticated buyers should see the competitiveness of the entire group improve. For example, the sophisticated U.S. market for computer software has helped give companies based in the United States an edge in developing new software products.

Related and Supporting Industries   Companies that belong to a nation's internationally competitive industries do not exist in isolation. Rather, supporting industries spring up to provide the inputs required by the industry. How does this happen? Companies that can benefit from the product or process technologies of an internationally competitive industry begin to form clusters of related economic activities in the same geographic area. The presence of these clusters serves to reinforce the productivity, and therefore competitiveness, of each industry within the cluster. For example, Italy is home to a successful cluster in the footwear industry that greatly benefits from the country's closely related leather-tanning and fashion-design industries. Map 5.2 shows the locations of some important clusters in the United States. Looking at the cluster in Colorado, we see that mining and the exploration of oil and gas depend heavily on the provision of engineering services, which in turn require advanced computer hardware and software.

A relatively small number of clusters usually account for a major share of regional economic activity. They also often account for an overwhelming share of the economic activity that is "exported" to other locations. *Exporting clusters*—those that export products or make investments to compete outside the local area—are the primary source of an area's long-term prosperity. Although the demand for a local industry is inherently limited by the size of the local market, an exporting cluster can grow far beyond that limit.[20]

MAP 5.2   *Mapping Selected U.S. Clusters*

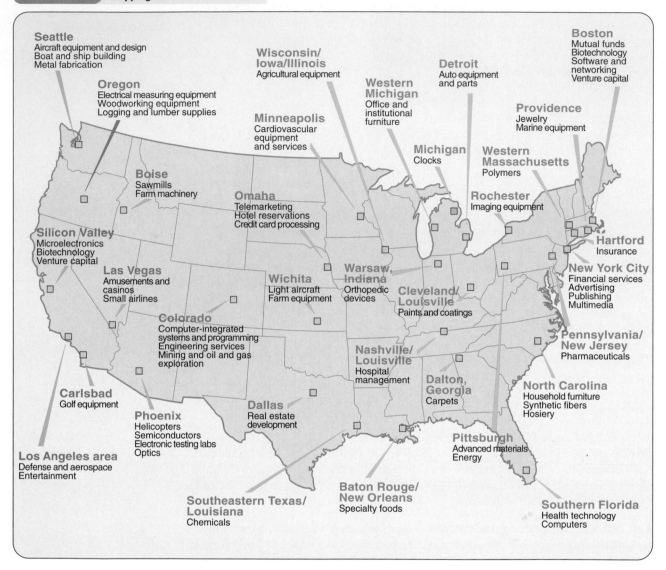

Seattle
Aircraft equipment and design
Boat and ship building
Metal fabrication

Oregon
Electrical measuring equipment
Woodworking equipment
Logging and lumber supplies

Boise
Sawmills
Farm machinery

Wisconsin/ Iowa/Illinois
Agricultural equipment

Minneapolis
Cardiovascular equipment and services

Western Michigan
Office and institutional furniture

Detroit
Auto equipment and parts

Boston
Mutual funds
Biotechnology
Software and networking
Venture capital

Providence
Jewelry
Marine equipment

Michigan
Clocks

Western Massachusetts
Polymers

Rochester
Imaging equipment

Omaha
Telemarketing
Hotel reservations
Credit card processing

Silicon Valley
Microelectronics
Biotechnology
Venture capital

Las Vegas
Amusements and casinos
Small airlines

Wichita
Light aircraft
Farm equipment

Warsaw, Indiana
Orthopedic devices

Cleveland/ Louisville
Paints and coatings

Hartford
Insurance

New York City
Financial services
Advertising
Publishing
Multimedia

Colorado
Computer-integrated systems and programming
Engineering services
Mining and oil and gas exploration

Nashville/ Louisville
Hospital management

Dalton, Georgia
Carpets

Pennsylvania/ New Jersey
Pharmaceuticals

Carlsbad
Golf equipment

Phoenix
Helicopters
Semiconductors
Electronic testing labs
Optics

Dallas
Real estate development

North Carolina
Household furniture
Synthetic fibers
Hosiery

Pittsburgh
Advanced materials
Energy

Los Angeles area
Defense and aerospace
Entertainment

Southeastern Texas/ Louisiana
Chemicals

Baton Rouge/ New Orleans
Specialty foods

Southern Florida
Health technology
Computers

Firm Strategy, Structure, and Rivalry   The strategic decisions of firms have lasting effects on their future competitiveness. Managers committed to producing quality products that are valued by buyers while maximizing the firm's market share and/or financial returns are essential. But highly skilled managers are not all that are needed. Equally as important is the industry structure and rivalry between a nation's companies. The more intense the struggle is to survive between a nation's domestic companies, the greater will be their competitiveness. This heightened competitiveness helps them to compete against imports and against companies that might develop a production presence in the home market.

Government and Chance   Apart from the four factors identified as part of the diamond, Porter identifies the roles of government and chance in fostering the national competitiveness of industries.

By their actions, governments can often increase the competitiveness of firms and perhaps even entire industries. For example, a report by McKinsey & Company (www.mckinsey.com), an international consultancy, discussed how the Indian government could increase GDP growth from 6 percent per year to 10 percent. Among other things, it placed the blame on the government's slow pace of privatization. The report argues that the government should reduce its sky-high ownership of 43 percent of India's capital stock to increase productivity. In a dozen "modern sectors" of the economy, labor productivity is, on average, 15 percent of that of the United States. Although productivity is 44 percent of the U.S. average in software, it is as low as 1 percent in electricity distribution. Privatization of government-owned assets would force companies to become more competitive in world markets if they are to survive.[21]

Although chance events can help the competitiveness of a firm or an industry, it can also threaten it. McDonald's (www.mcdonalds.com) holds a clear competitive advantage worldwide in the fast-food industry. But its overwhelming dominance was threatened by the discovery of Mad Cow Disease. To keep customers from flocking to the non-beef substitute products of competitors, McDonald's introduced the McPork sandwich.

Porter's theory holds promise but has just begun to be subjected to research using actual data on each of the factors involved and national competitiveness. There are important implications for companies and governments if the theory accurately identifies the important drivers of national competitiveness. For instance, government policies should not be designed to protect national industries that are not internationally competitive, but develop the components of the diamond that contribute to increased competitiveness. Support for or against this latest and influential theory will accumulate over time as research into its value continues.

A FINAL WORD

This chapter introduced and explained a number of concepts regarding international trade. We explored the benefits of international trade and its volume and pattern in the world today. As we saw in this chapter's opening example, trade can free a nation's entrepreneurial spirit and bring economic development. As the value and volume of trade continues to expand worldwide, new theories will likely emerge to explain why countries trade and why they have advantages in producing certain products. In the next chapter we will discuss business-government trade relations and how they influence the volume and pattern of international trade.

There is a variety of additional material available on the Companion Website that accompanies this book. You can access this information by visiting the Website at (www.prenhall.com/wild).

summary

1 Describe the relation between *international trade volume* and *world output*, and identify overall *trade patterns*. *International trade* is the purchase, sale, or exchange of goods and services across national borders. International trade provides a country's people with a greater choice of goods and services and is an important engine for job creation in many countries. Most of world merchandise trade is comprised of trade in manufactured goods. Service exports make up roughly 20 percent of total world trade annually. Slower world economic output slows the volume of international trade, and higher output spurs greater trade. Also, trade has consistently grown faster than output.

The pattern of international trade in merchandise is dominated by flows among the high-income economies of the world (60 percent), followed by trade among high-income countries and low- and middle-income nations (34 percent). Trade among the low- and middle-income nations is just 6 percent of the total. A large amount of trade in Western Europe is intraregional, meaning that it largely occurs between Western European nations.

2 Describe *mercantilism* and explain its impact on the world powers and their colonies. The trade theory that nations should accumulate financial wealth, usually in the form of gold, by encouraging exports and discouraging imports is called *mercantilism*. Nation-states in Europe followed this economic philosophy from about 1500 to the late 1700s.

Countries implemented mercantilism by doing three things. First, they increased their wealth by maintaining a *trade surplus*—the condition that results when the value of a nation's exports is greater than the value of its imports. Second, national governments actively intervened in international trade to maintain a trade surplus. Third, mercantilist nations acquired less-developed territories (colonies) around the world to serve as sources of inexpensive raw materials and as markets for higher-priced finished goods. Mercantilism assumes that a nation increases its wealth only at the expense of other nations—a *zero-sum game.*

3 Identify the differences between *absolute advantage* and *comparative advantage*. The ability of a nation to produce a good more efficiently than any other nation is called an *absolute advantage*. According to this theory, international trade should be allowed to flow according to market forces. A country can concentrate on producing the goods in which it holds an absolute advantage and then trade with other nations to obtain the goods it needs but does not produce. Because there are gains to be had by both countries party to an exchange, international trade is shown to be a *positive-sum game*. The theory measures a nation's wealth by the living standards of its people.

A nation holds a *comparative advantage* in the production of a good when it is unable to produce the good more efficiently than other nations, but can produce it more efficiently than it can any other good. As a result, trade is still beneficial even if one country is less efficient in the production of two goods, so long as it is less inefficient in the production of one of the goods.

4 Explain the *factor proportions* and *international product life cycle* theories. The *factor proportions theory* states that countries produce and export goods that require resources (factors) that are abundant and import goods that require resources that are in short supply. The factor proportions theory predicts that a country will specialize in products that require labor

if its cost is low relative to the cost of land and capital. Alternatively, a country will specialize in products that require land and capital equipment if their cost is low relative to the cost of labor. The apparent paradox between predictions of the theory and actual trade flows is called the *Leontief paradox*.

The *international product life cycle theory* says that a company will begin exporting its product and later undertake foreign direct investment as the product moves through its life cycle. In the *new product stage* production volume is low and remains based in the home country. In the *maturing product stage* the company introduces production facilities in the countries with the highest demand. In the *standardized product stage* competition forces an aggressive search for low-cost production bases in developing nations to supply a worldwide market.

5 Explain the *new trade* and *national competitive advantage* theories. The *new trade theory* argues that as a company increases the extent to which it specializes in the production of a particular good, output rises because of gains in efficiency. As specialization and output increase, companies can realize economies of scale, thereby pushing the unit costs of production lower. The presence of large economies of scale can allow a firm to gain a *first-mover advantage*—the economic and strategic advantage gained by being the first company to enter an industry. The theory says that by working together, governments and home-based companies can target potential new industries in which to become first movers. It also argues that the government may play a role in assisting its home companies.

National competitive advantage theory states that a nation's competitiveness in an industry (and, therefore, trade flows) depends on the capacity of the industry to innovate and upgrade. The *Porter diamond* identifies four elements that form the basis of national competitiveness: (1) *Factor conditions* including the skill levels of different segments of the workforce and the quality of the technological infrastructure; (2) *demand conditions* such as a sophisticated domestic market; (3) *related and supporting industries* that spring up and form clusters of related economic activities; and (4) *firm strategy, structure, and rivalry* conditions that are present in an industry. Finally, the actions of *governments* and the occurrence of *chance events* can also affect the competitiveness of a nation's companies.

questions for review

1. What is *international trade*?

2. Identify how important trade is to the economies of five nations.

3. What are some of the *benefits* of international trade?

4. Of the 10 countries responsible for much of the world's merchandise trade, how many are from Africa? Asia? Europe? North America? South America?

5. What portion of total world trade occurs in merchandise? In services?

6. Explain the relation between trade and *world output*.

7. Describe the broad *pattern* of international trade.

8. Why is a nation's level of *dependence* or *independence* important?

9. What is *mercantilism*? Explain how mercantilism worked, and describe its flaws.

10. How does a *trade surplus* differ from a *trade deficit*?

11. What types of policies might a country have in place to be called *neo-mercantilist*?

12. What is an *absolute advantage*? Describe how it works using a numerical example.

13. What is meant by a *comparative advantage*? Explain why countries can gain from trade despite not having an absolute advantage.

14. What is the *factor proportions theory*? Identify the two categories of national resources.

15. Describe the *international product life cycle theory* including its three stages.

16. What is the *new trade theory*? Explain what is meant by the term *first-mover advantage*.

17. Describe *national competitive advantage theory*. What are the four elements of the *Porter diamond* and the two other factors influencing competitiveness?

questions for discussion

1. If the nations of the world were to suddenly cut off all trade with one another, what products might you no longer be able to obtain in your country? Choose one other country and identify the products it would need to do without.

2. Many economists predict the eventual rise of China as a "superpower" because of economic reform, along with the work ethic and high education of its population. How do you think trade between Asia, Europe, and North America will be affected by China's continued development?

3. Because of its abundance of natural resources, Brazil was once considered a nation certain to attain advanced economic status quickly. Yet over the past two decades Brazil has sometimes been referred to as an economic "basket case." What forces do you think are preventing Brazil's economic progress?

in practice

Among other things, the theory of national competitive advantage states that a country gains a competitive advantage in an industry when its home-based companies form a cluster of activities that support one another. Read the article on the right and answer the following questions.

1. Identify the various participants (public and private) mentioned in the article. What do you think each party has to offer the cluster to encourage the cross-fertilization of ideas and innovations?

2. Why is it that today governments often try to create clusters around groundbreaking research in high-technology products and processes?

3. Two recent, influential theories (new trade theory and the theory of national competitive advantage) emphasize a role for governments in helping domestic companies become strong internationally. Do you think governments should undertake such efforts or let markets, on their own, decide who should succeed or fail?

4. Can you identify a cluster that exists in your hometown or city, or that of your college or university? If so, identify the members of the cluster and what each one has to offer.

Genetic Valley

Unique in Europe, "Genopole" (www.genopole.org) is a designated area for genetic research and development. It is a joint effort by the French government and private companies to thrust France to the forefront of life sciences research. The site of the venture is in Évry, France, about 20 miles south of Paris.

Public centers already established in Genopole include Genoscope (the National Gene Sequencing Center), Genethon (laboratories for gene research), the National Genotyping Center, and the French Muscular Dystrophy Association. Private firms active in Genopole include Genset, Rhône-Poulenc, and Euro Sequence Gene Services.

The Université d'Évry/Val d'Essone, which is located near Genopole, provides special courses related to the activities of Genopole. The courses are centered on genetics, genomics, and their associated disciplines, including scientific instrumentation, nanotechnology, robotics, and bioinformatics. Among other things, Genopole offers researchers and private companies a ready-made infrastructure, available land, public and private financing, the creation of an international conference center, and high-speed Internet access.

projects

1. Select a recent business periodical and find an article that discusses the advantages and/or disadvantages of international trade. Write a summary of the points made in the article and express why you agree or disagree with them.

2. Locate the annual report (or other information) from a large international firm in your library or on the Internet. To what extent does the company rely on imports to supply its production facilities in various countries? How much of the company's total sales are outside its home country? Does the company import from and export to mostly high-income countries only or low- and middle-income countries as well? Is the company's export revenue increasing or decreasing, and at what rate? Supply other information you think is relevant and write a one- or two-page report of your findings.

3. Select a recent business periodical and find an article that discusses the deteriorating export situation of a country. Has it tried to export its way out of slow economic growth? If so, what forces led it to resort to increasing exports to stimulate its economy? If not, why hasn't it? What is the forecast for the recovery of its export sector in the near term? Write a short report on your findings.

business case 5

DHL WORLDWIDE EXPRESS: FIRST IN ASIA AND THE WORLD

What company is the leading international express carrier? If you answered Federal Express (www.fedex.com), UPS (www.ups.com), or Airborne Express (www.airborne.com) you're wrong. Try DHL Worldwide Express (www.dhl.com). This company, based in San Francisco, California, actually carved out the niche for international express service in 1969 when it began shipping bills of lading and other documents from San Francisco to Honolulu. Soon the company got requests to deliver and pick up in Japan and other Asian countries, and the whole business of international express delivery was born.

Today the company delivers and picks up from 120,000 destinations in 228 countries and territories and employs 69,000 employees worldwide, many of them based in Asia, the company's first and most important international market. Customer service and reliability are what DHL prides itself on most. The company hires DHL personnel in the countries in which it operates and sees this practice as key to forging relationships with customers in its overseas markets. "Unlike many of our competitors," says one DHL executive, "we don't take a package and hand it off to an agent. We ensure that our deliveries and pick-ups are made by DHL personnel and that we can manage business locally by using local people who know local customs." Because relationships are the name of the game in service businesses, DHL is currently cultivating relationships with customs agents. The archaic customs clearance procedures in many countries are the biggest obstacle to speedy international deliveries.

Express air delivery is now a huge business in Asia, but DHL has several formidable competitors snapping at its heels. These include Federal Express, which offers competitive rates, and local players like Hong Kong Delivery, whose small size makes it highly flexible. DHL cannot simply rest on its number-one position or boast of its long years of experience to stay ahead. The dangers of complacency were brought home to the company in the mid-1980s, when its DHL Japan office faced customer resistance to a price hike. DHL employees had simply assumed that the firm would always be number one and had grown lax on service. In fact, an objective "shipment test" revealed that DHL Japan provided the worst service at what were already the highest prices. Japanese customers had simply continued to use DHL because it was the first in the business and because loyalty was important. Yet, the proposed price hike might have been the decisive factor in convincing formerly compliant customers to defect. Fortunately, DHL Japan's then-president, Shinichi Momose, was able to get the affiliate back on track through aggressive initiatives.

Today DHL's customer service record is winning repeated kudos in Asia and around the world. For example, a DHL division called DHL Logistics earned a gold medal for excellence in 2001 for the second consecutive year in the eighteenth annual Quest for Quality survey conducted by the industry's Logistics Management and Distribution Report. It is also often voted the "Best Express Service" at the annual Asian Freight Industry Awards. "We operate in an increasingly competitive business," explains DHL Far East Regional Managing Director John A. Kerr, "and our customers are demanding both increased levels of services and sophisticated logistics solutions. . . . We cannot afford to be so complacent in the years ahead. We will continue to listen to our customers, understand their needs, and work to meet their requirements."

thinking globally

1. As the first to set up an international air express business in 1969, DHL had the first-mover advantage over other companies. Is being a first mover as advantageous for a service company, such as DHL Worldwide Express, as it is for a manufacturing company, such as Boeing? Explain.

2. When it comes to global expansion and setting up affiliates abroad, how is a service company's focus different from that of a manufacturing company? What elements do you think

are necessary for a service company to achieve global success? What are the obstacles to global expansion?

3. DHL prides itself on having its own staff of 69,000 people spread out across the globe instead of relying on local agents. Discuss the merits and drawbacks of this international staffing approach.

4. After reading the above case, what do you think are the dangers, if any, of being a first mover?

a question of ethics

1. In the actual practice of international trade, both physical resources and capital cross international borders freely, whereas labor is heavily restricted. In fact, it is very difficult in many nations for someone to get a permit to allow them to be gainfully employed within that country. Thus, while companies are free to set up production in markets where labor is cheap, labor cannot move to markets where wages are higher. Why do you think this situation prevails? Is it ethical that of all the components of production, labor is the one most subject to restrictions on its international mobility? Discuss.

2. Recent international trade theories propose that protectionist actions that restrict imports harm a nation's standard of living—an argument for free trade. Yet, think about what happens when free trade and global competition spur companies to move production to cheaper locations abroad, thereby eliminating jobs in their home countries. The gains and losses of free trade are not always distributed evenly across the population. Argue either for or against the necessity of measures that protect domestic production and, therefore, jobs at home.

3. In 2001 the European Union and the United States ended a 9-year battle over trade in bananas. The European Union was giving preferential treatment to banana exporters from Africa, the Caribbean, and the Pacific island nations. But the United States challenged what it saw as unfair trading practices, and the World Trade Organization (www.wto.org) agreed. Large global fruit companies such as Dole (www.dole.com), Chiquita (www.chiquita.com), and Del Monte (www.delmonte.com)—which alone account for nearly two thirds of the fruit traded worldwide—supported the U.S. action. The European Union argued it was trying to support these struggling economies, where bananas make up a large portion of their income. Discuss the ethics of managing trade in the interests of countries that are seen as vulnerable in the global economy. Would you have argued on behalf of the United States or the European Union? Why?

6

business–government trade relations

LEARNING OBJECTIVES

After studying this chapter, you should be able to

1 Describe the, *political*, *economic*, and *cultural motives* behind governmental intervention in trade.

2 List and explain the methods governments use to *promote* international trade.

3 List and explain the methods governments use to *restrict* international trade.

4 Discuss the importance of the *World Trade Organization* in promoting free trade.

BEACONS

A Look Back

CHAPTER 5 explored theories that have been developed to explain the pattern that international trade should take. We examined the important concept of comparative advantage and the conceptual basis for how international trade benefits nations.

A Look at This Chapter

This chapter discusses the active role of national governments in international trade. We examine the motives for government intervention and the tools that nations use to accomplish their goals. We then explore the global trading system and show how it promotes free trade.

A Look Ahead

CHAPTER 7 continues our discussion of the international business environment. We explore recent patterns of foreign direct investment, theories that try to explain why it occurs, and the role of governments in influencing investment flows.

Spreading Their Magic

HOLLYWOOD, California—The merger of AOL and Time Warner in early 2000 created a sprawling global enterprise with 90,000 employees working in a wide variety of businesses. The merger was designed to blend the promise of the interactive "new media" with the strength of "old media."

AOL Time Warner (**www.aoltimewarner.com**) is a media goliath with businesses including cable television (Turner Broadcasting, HBO), publishing (Time, Sports Illustrated), music (Warner Music Group), Internet services (America Online), and film (Warner Bros., New Line Cinema). The media creations of the AOL Time Warner group of companies, to the dismay of some, affect the lives of people in practically every nation on the planet.

One of those film creations, *Harry Potter and the Sorcerer's Stone*, was based on the novel by former British schoolteacher J.K. Rowling and produced by New Line Cinema. After first snatching up the book in every major language, kids from Tampa to Tokyo and from Buffalo to Buenos Aires poured into cinemas to be awed by young Harry on the silver screen. Another huge hit for the group was the *The Lord of The Rings: The Fellowship of the Ring* that was produced by Warner Bros. and based on the tale by J.R.R. Tolkien.

AOL Time Warner is literally marching across the globe. America Online is the undisputed global leader in Internet services—it has over 34 million subscribers worldwide that surf the Web more than 1 billion hours each month. The old media units of the company also continue to extend their reach abroad. Warner Home Video, a unit of AOL Time Warner, recently struck a deal with a company in India to market the media giant's home video products including classic films and cartoons in both India and neighboring Bangladesh.

But media companies like AOL Time Warner must tread carefully as they spread the influence of their magical kingdoms around the world. Some governments fear that their own nations' writers, actors, directors, and producers will be drowned out by such big-budget Hollywood productions as *Harry Potter* and *The Lord of the Rings*. Others fear the replacement of their traditional values with those depicted in the imported entertainment. As you read this chapter, think about the nature of different products and the reasons governments get involved in international trade.[1]

Chapter 5 discussed theories that describe what the patterns of international trade *should* look like. The theory of comparative advantage states that the country that has a comparative advantage in the production of a certain goodwill produce that good when barriers to trade do not exist. However, this ideal does not accurately characterize trade in today's global marketplace. Despite efforts by organizations such as the World Trade Organization (www.wto.org) and smaller groups of countries, nations still retain many barriers to trade.

In this chapter we look in detail at business–government trade relations. We first explain why nations erect barriers to trade, exploring the cultural, political, and economic motives for such barriers. We then examine the instruments countries use to restrict both imports and exports. We then discuss efforts of the global trading system to promote trade by reducing trade barriers. In Chapter 8 we cover how smaller groups of countries are eliminating barriers to trade and investment.

WHY DO GOVERNMENTS INTERVENE IN TRADE?

free trade
Pattern of imports and exports that would result in the absence of trade barriers.

The pattern of imports and exports that would result in the absence of trade barriers is called **free trade**. Despite the advantages of free trade that we discussed in Chapter 5, national governments have long intervened in the trade of goods and services. Why do governments impose restrictions on free trade? In general, they do so for reasons that are political, economic, or cultural—or some combination of the three. Countries often intervene in trade by strongly supporting their domestic companies' exporting activities. But the more emotionally charged trade intervention occurs when a nation's economy is underperforming. In tough economic times businesses and workers will often lobby their governments to protect them from imports that are reducing work and eliminating jobs in the domestic market. Let's now take a closer look at government involvement in trade by examining the political, economic, and cultural motives for intervention.

POLITICAL MOTIVES

Government officials often make trade-related decisions based on political motives. Why? Because a politician's very survival might depend on pleasing voters and getting reelected. However, a trade policy based purely on political motives is seldom the wisest policy in the long run. The main political motives behind government intervention in trade include protecting jobs, preserving national security, responding to other nations' unfair trade practices, and gaining influence over other nations.

To Protect Jobs   Short of an unpopular war, nothing will oust a government faster than high rates of unemployment. Thus, practically all governments become involved when trade threatens jobs at home. For example, the president of Guyana, in South America, urged her fellow citizens to buy local goods instead of imports saying, "A foreign product does not mean it's better. Local goods are quite good. I use them all the time." Making her case on her weekly radio talk show, she went so far as to ask importers to act "as patriots and not bring things that are not needed into the country to crowd locally made products off the shelves."[2]

But efforts to protect jobs typically receive less publicity. Fuji (www.fujifilm.com) of Japan and Kodak (www.kodak.com) of the United States control large shares of the market for photographic film in China. This caused Chinese nationalists to urge the government to support China Lucky Film, the struggling state-owned company whose market share recently plunged to 7 percent. Fearing the death of yet another major Chinese brand, the government considered whether to prohibit a proposed joint venture between Kodak and Lucky. China's National Association of Light Industry urged the government to provide $240 million in cash and low-interest loans to rescue Lucky while maintaining a ban on joint ventures in film manufacturing.[3]

To Preserve National Security   Industries considered essential to national security often receive government-sponsored protection. This is true for both imports and exports.

National Security and Imports   Preserving national security by restricting certain imports is supported by the argument that a government must have access to a domestic supply of certain items—such as weapons, fuel, and air, land, and sea transportation—in the event that war could restrict their availability. For example, many nations (particularly the United States) continue to search for oil within their borders in case war disrupts the flow of oil from outside sources. Legitimate national security reasons for intervention can be difficult to argue against, particularly when they have the support of most of a country's people.

Some countries fiercely protect their agricultural sector for national security reasons because a nation that imports its food supplies could face starvation in times of war. France has come under attack by other European nations as well as countries outside Europe for protecting its agricultural sector. French agricultural subsidies are intended to provide a fair financial return for French farmers, who traditionally operate on a small scale and therefore have high production costs and low profit margins. But many developed nations are exposing agribusiness to market forces, prompting farms to increase

Greenpeace activists in Hong Kong denounce the possible inclusion of genetically modified (GM) organisms in McDonald's products. But food companies today often have little choice because many crops, including corn, soybeans, and wheat are grown with genetically enhanced seed technology to resist insects and disease. European nations continue to fiercely resist U.S. efforts to export GM crops to their shores. Do you believe the Europeans are right to refuse the importation of genetically modified crops?

their efficiency. As a result, farmers are discovering new ways to manage risk and improve efficiency. Other farmers are experimenting with alternating crops, more intensive land management, high-tech "precision farming," and greater use of biotechnology.[4]

However, protection from import competition does have its drawbacks. Perhaps the main one is the added cost of continuing to produce a good or provide a service that could be supplied more efficiently by an international supplier. Also, once a policy of protection is adopted it may remain in place much longer than necessary. Thus, policy makers should consider whether the trade policy decision is truly a matter of national security before intervening.

National Security and Exports Governments also have national security motives for banning certain defense-related goods from export to other nations. Most industrialized nations have agencies that review requests to export technologies or products that are said to have *dual uses*—meaning they have both industrial and military applications. Products designated as dual use are classified as such and require special governmental approval before export can take place. Bans on the export of dual-use products were strictly enforced during the years of the Cold War between the Western powers and the former Soviet Union. Some countries have relaxed enforcement of these controls since the early 1990s. However, because of the continued presence of terrorist threats and rogue nations that badly want weapons of mass destruction, such bans are receiving renewed support.

For example, several years ago it was revealed that technology transfers to China fell into the dual-use category. It was alleged that two U.S. firms—Hughes Electronics Corporation (**www.hughes.com**) and Loral Space and Communications (**www.loral.com**)—helped China improve its long-range ballistic missile capabilities. The companies used Chinese rockets to launch satellites and helped Chinese scientists improve their rocket technology after the failure of some launches. Both companies denied wrongdoing and acted only after receiving approval for the technology transfers from the government. Loral responded to the charges in a written statement, saying "We believe we demonstrated that any material exchanged with the Chinese was from open sources, readily available in standard engineering textbooks."[5] This situation worries officials who fear that China (as it has in the past) might sell the missile technology to India's longtime foe Pakistan, thus disrupting the balance of power in the region.

To Respond to "Unfair" Trade
Many observers argue that it makes no sense for one nation to allow free trade if other nations actively protect their own industries. Governments often threaten to close their ports to another nation's ships or to impose extremely high tariffs on its goods if the other nation does not concede on some trade issue that is seen as being unfair. In other words, if one government thinks another nation is not "playing fair," it will often threaten to play unfairly unless certain concessions are agreed.

To Gain Influence
Governments of the world's largest nations may become involved in trade to gain influence over smaller nations. For example, Japan has a good deal of influence in Asia. Japan accounts for a large portion of the imports and exports of many countries throughout Asia and Southeast Asia, and lent the region a large amount of money to help it recover from recent financial crises. No doubt the Japanese government expects to generate goodwill among its neighbors through such deals.

Similarly, the United States goes to great lengths to gain and maintain control over events in all of Central, North, and South America as well as the Caribbean basin. This is one reason behind the free trade initiatives in the Americas that are strongly supported by the United States. The potential to exert influence on internal politics is also a primary reason why the United States is keeping its embargo on communist Cuba.

The United States has maintained a trade embargo on Cuba since 1961 in the hope of exerting political influence against Fidel Castro's communist regime. Although some observers believe the embargo is punishing ordinary Cubans, the Cuban government claims it is having minimal effect on daily life. Meanwhile, dangerous, illegal migration to the United States using homemade rafts, human smugglers, or fake visas continues. How do you feel about the embargo: Is it working or should it be lifted?

ECONOMIC MOTIVES

Although governments intervene in trade for highly charged cultural and political reasons, they also have economic motives for their intervention. The most common economic reasons given for nations' attempts to influence international trade are the protection of young industries from competition and the promotion of a strategic trade policy.

To Protect Infant Industries   According to the *infant industry argument*, a country's emerging industries need protection from international competition during their development phase until they become sufficiently competitive internationally. This argument is based on the idea that infant industries need protection because of a steep learning curve. In other words, only as an industry grows and matures, does it gain the knowledge it needs to become more innovative, efficient, and competitive.

Although this argument is conceptually appealing, it does have several problems. First, the argument requires governments to distinguish between industries that are worth protecting and those that are not. This is very difficult, if not impossible, to do. For years, Japan has targeted infant industries for protection, low-interest loans, and other benefits. Its performance on assisting these industries was very good from the 1950s to the early 1980s but has been less successful since then. Until the government achieves future success in identifying and targeting industries, supporting this type of policy remains questionable.

Second, protection from international competition can cause domestic companies to become complacent toward innovation. This can limit a company's incentives to obtain the knowledge it needs to become more competitive. The most extreme examples of complacency are industries within formerly communist nations. When their communist protections collapsed in the late 1980s and early 1990s, practically all the state-run companies were decades behind their international competitors. Indeed, many required financial assistance in the form of infusions of capital or outright purchase to survive.

Third, protection can do more economic harm than good. Consumers often end up paying more for products because a lack of competition typically creates fewer incentives to cut production costs or improve quality. Meanwhile, companies become more reliant on protection. For example, protection of domestic industries in Japan has caused a two-tier economy to emerge. In one tier are protected and noncompetitive domestic industries; in the other are highly competitive multinationals. In the flagging domestic industries of banking, property, construction, retailing, and local manufacturing, higher costs are the result of protected markets, high wages, overregulation, and barriers to imports. In contrast, the large multinationals enjoy low-cost advantages because of their efficient production facilities in East Asia, Europe, Latin America, and the United States. Because these multinationals regularly face rivals in overseas markets, they've learned to be strong competitors in order to survive.[6]

Fourth, the infant industry argument also holds that it is not always possible for small, promising companies to obtain funding in capital markets, and thus they need financial support from their government. However, international capital markets today are far more sophisticated than in the past, and promising business ventures can normally obtain funding from private sources.

To Pursue Strategic Trade Policy   Recall from our discussion in Chapter 5 that new trade theorists believe government intervention can help companies take advantage of economies of scale and be the first movers in their industries. First-mover advantages result because economies of scale in production limit the number of companies that an industry can sustain.

Benefits of Strategic Trade Policy   Supporters of strategic trade policy argue that it results in increased national income. Companies should earn a good profit if they obtain first-mover advantages and solidified positions in their markets around the world. They also claim that strategic trade policies helped South Korea build global conglomerates (called *chaebol*) that dwarf the competition. For example, Korean shipbuilders over many years received a variety of government subsidies, including low-cost financing. The *chaebol* made it possible for companies to survive poor economic times because of the wide range of industries in which they competed. Such policies also had spinoff effects on related industries such as transportation. By the mid-1990s one of the country's largest shipping firms, Hanjing Shipping, had become the largest cargo transporter between Asia and the United States.[7]

Drawbacks of Strategic Trade Policy   Although it sounds as if strategic trade policy has only benefits, there can be drawbacks as well. Lavish government assistance to domestic companies caused inefficiency and high costs for both South Korean and Japanese companies in the late 1990s. For example, because of high wages at home attributable to large government concessions to local labor unions, Korea's *chaebol* were operating under very low profit margins. When the Asian currency crisis hit in the summer of 1997, the *chaebol* were not prepared for the consequences. The government realized it had given away too much in the good times and pulled back some of its support by, for one thing, passing a law to make it easier for companies to fire employees.[8]

In addition, when governments decide to support specific industries, their choice is often subject to political lobbying by the groups seeking government assistance. It is possible that special-interest groups could capture all the gains from assistance with no benefit for consumers. If this were to occur, consumers could end up paying more for lower-quality goods than they could otherwise obtain.

CULTURAL MOTIVES

Nations often restrict trade in goods and services to achieve cultural objectives, the most common being protection of national identity. In Chapter 2 we saw how culture and trade are intertwined and significantly affect one another. The cultures of countries are slowly altered by exposure to the people and products of other cultures. Unwanted cultural influence in a nation can cause great distress and cause governments to block imports that it believes are harmful—recall our discussion of *cultural imperialism* in Chapter 2.

The French try to keep their language free of such alien English words as *jeans* and *hamburger*. French law bans foreign-language words from virtually all business and government communications, radio and TV broadcasts, public announcements, and advertising messages—at least whenever a suitable French alternative is available. You can't advertise a *best-seller*; it has to be a *succès de librairie*. You can't sell *popcorn* at *le cinéma*; French moviegoers must snack on *mais soufflé*. A select group of individuals comprising the Higher Council on French Language works against the inclusion of such so-called "Franglais" phrases as *le marketing*, *le cash flow*, and *le brainstorming* into commerce and other areas of French culture.

Canada is another country making headlines for its attempts to mitigate the cultural influence of entertainment products imported from the United States. Canada requires at least 35 percent of music played over Canadian radio to be by Canadian artists. In fact, many countries are considering laws to protect their media programming for cultural reasons. The problem with such restrictions is that they reduce the selection of products available to consumers.

Cultural Influence of the United States Certainly, the United States, more than any other nation, is seen as a threat to national cultures around the world. Why is this? The reason is the global strength of the United States in entertainment and media (such as movies, magazines, and music) and consumer goods. Such products are highly visible to all consumers and cause groups of various kinds to lobby government officials for protection from their cultural influence. Because the rhetoric of protectionism tends to receive widespread public support, domestic producers of competing products find it easy to join in the calls for protection.

How does the English language so easily infiltrate the cultures of other nations? Despite the grand conspiracy theories put forth by some individuals and groups, it is the natural result of international trade. International trade in all sorts of goods and services is exposing people around the world to new words, ideas, products, and ways of life. But as international trade continues to expand, many governments try to limit potential adverse effects on their cultures and economies. This is where the theory of international trade meets the reality of international business today.

METHODS OF PROMOTING TRADE

In the previous discussion we alluded to the types of instruments available to governments in their efforts at promoting or restricting trade with other nations. The most common instruments that governments use are shown in Table 6.1. In this section we examine each specific method of trade promotion. We cover methods of trade restriction in the next section.

SUBSIDIES

Financial assistance to domestic producers in the form of cash payments, low-interest loans, tax breaks, product price supports, or some other form is called a **subsidy**. Regardless of the form a subsidy takes, it is intended to assist domestic companies in fending off international competitors. This can mean becoming more competitive in the home market or increasing competitiveness in international markets through exports. Because of the many forms a subsidy can take, it is virtually impossible to calculate the amount of subsidies any country offers its producers. In fact, the World Trade Organization is often called on to settle arguments over charges of unfair subsidies, doing so only after a long and arduous investigation. Even then, the losing party gener-

subsidy
Financial assistance to domestic producers in the form of cash payments, low-interest loans, tax breaks, product price supports, or some other form.

TABLE 6.1	Methods of Promoting and Restricting Trade	
Trade Promotion	**Trade Restriction**	
Subsidies	Tariffs	
Export financing	Quotas	
Foreign trade zones	Embargoes	
Special government agencies	Local content requirements	
	Administrative delays	
	Currency controls	

ally disagrees with the verdict but is bound to accept the organization's ruling (the World Trade Organization is discussed in detail shortly).

Subsidies in Media and Entertainment   As mentioned earlier, media and entertainment are commonly subsidized in many nations. However, France does stand out as being very generous with its subsidies to entertainment. The French film authority, *Le Centre National de la Cinématographie* (www.cnc.fr), subsidizes many films each year. In one recent year, some French films received "automatic" subsidies to the tune of about $54 million while others benefited from about $20 million a year in advances against box-office receipts. The French government argues that such subsidies are necessary to counteract the influence of Hollywood films and TV programs. Whereas Hollywood films are privately financed and driven by market demand, critics contend that France's films are less competitive because they have to satisfy bureaucratic agendas for funding.[9] However, the fact that many French films are critically acclaimed worldwide might present one argument against removing subsidies that apparently stoke artistic inspiration.

Drawbacks of Subsidies   Critics charge that subsidies cover costs that truly competitive industries should be able to absorb on their own. In this sense, it is argued, subsidies simply encourage inefficiency and complacency. Because governments generally pay for subsidies with funds obtained from income and sales taxes, it is widely believed that subsidies benefit companies and industries that receive them but harm consumers. Thus, although subsidies provide short-term relief to companies and industries, the idea that government subsidies help the nation's citizens in the long term is highly questionable.

One fact that has recently caught the attention of policy makers concerned with the environmental consequences of government policies is that subsidies lead to an overuse of resources. For example, subsidies in developing nations to cover the high cost of energy total more than $230 billion a year—more than four times the total amount of financial assistance to developing countries. Such wasteful spending deprives developing countries of resources that could be invested in other more productive ways, including the transition to more sustainable forms of energy.[10]

EXPORT FINANCING

Governments often promote exports by helping companies finance their export activities. They can offer loans that a company could otherwise not obtain or charge them an interest rate that is lower than the market rate. Another option is for a government to guarantee that it will repay the loan of a company if the company should default on repayment; this is called a *loan guarantee*.

Many nations have special agencies dedicated to helping their domestic companies gain export financing. For example, a very well known institution is called the *Export-Import Bank of the United States*—or *Ex-Im Bank* for short. The Ex-Im Bank (www.exim.gov) finances the export activities of companies in the United States and offers them reasonably priced cargo insurance. Another U.S. government agency, the *Overseas Private Insurance Corporation (OPIC)*, also provides insurance services. Through OPIC (**www.opic.gov**), both exporters and companies that invest abroad can insure against losses due to three factors: (1) expropriation, (2) currency inconvertibility, and (3) war, revolution, and insurrection.

Receiving financing from government agencies is often crucial to the success of small businesses that are just beginning to export. In fact, taken together, the "little guys" account for over 80 percent of all transactions handled by the Ex-Im Bank. According to Lalitha Swart, senior vice president at Silicon Valley Bank (**www.svb.com**) in Santa Clara, California, most of the customers that her bank links up with the Ex-Im Bank are small to medium-size exporters. "I would describe them as emerging high-growth companies," says Swart. "They tend to be in industries such as telecommunications, life sciences, software, computer peripherals, [and] managed healthcare."[11]

In recent years, the Ex-Im Bank has launched several programs to fuel growth in small business exporting. For instance, a revolving loan to Lynch Machinery of Bainbridge, Georgia, allowed the firm to hire 60 new employees and fill orders for $50 million in glass presses for computers and high-definition TVs for export to China and other Asian markets.[12] Changes for 1999 and beyond include creating a new system that makes it easier for the Ex-Im Bank to approve small loan requests. Another new program is designed to reach small businesses that are owned by minorities and women, are in depressed urban and rural areas, and that produce environmentally beneficial products. For a survey of ways in which the Ex-Im Bank helps businesses gain export financing, see the Entrepreneurial Focus titled "Ex-Im Bank: Experts in Export Financing."

ENTREPRENEURIAL FOCUS

Ex-Im Bank: Experts in Export Financing

What follows are some of the ways that the Ex-Im Bank helps businesses. For more information, visit (**www.exim.gov**) or call toll-free 1-800-565-EXIM.

City/State Program. This program brings the Ex-Im Bank's financing services to small and medium-size U.S. companies that are ready to export. These partnership programs currently exist with 38 state and local government offices and private sector organizations.

Working Capital Guarantee Program. This program helps small and medium-size businesses that have exporting potential but lack the needed funds by encouraging commercial lenders to loan them money. The bank guarantee covers 90 percent of the loan's principal and accrued interest. The exporter may use the guaranteed financing to purchase finished products for export or pay for raw materials, for example.

Credit Information Services. The bank's repayment records provide credit information to U.S. exporters and commercial lenders. The bank can provide information on a specific country or individual company abroad. But the bank does not divulge confidential financial data on non-U.S. buyers to whom it has extended credit, nor confiden-

tial information regarding particular credits or conditions in other countries.

Export Credit Insurance. This program helps U.S. exporters develop and expand their overseas sales by protecting them against loss should a non-U.S. buyer or other non-U.S. debtor default for political or commercial reasons. The insurance policy can make obtaining export financing easier because, with approval by the bank, the proceeds of the policy can be used as collateral.

Guarantee Program. This program provides repayment protection for private-sector loans made to creditworthy buyers of U.S. capital equipment, projects, and services. The bank guarantees that, in the event of default, it will repay the principal and interest on the loan. The non-U.S. buyer must make a cash payment of at least 15 percent. Most guarantees provide comprehensive coverage against political and commercial risks.

Loan Program. The bank makes loans directly to non-U.S. buyers of U.S. exports and intermediary loans to creditworthy parties that provide loans to non-U.S. buyers. The program provides fixed-interest-rate financing for export sales of U.S. capital equipment and related services.

However, export-financing programs are not immune to controversy. In general, few criticize government support of small business exporting activities. But support for large multinational corporations is often controversial. The Ex-Im Bank's financing of large companies has angered critics, who contend that subsidizing large private companies at taxpayer expense amounts to corporate welfare. Furthermore, the Ex-Im Bank's original mandate was to support domestic employment; it thus offered low-cost financing only for exports whose content was 100 percent domestic. But companies pressured the Ex-Im Bank to relax this restriction, and now it will finance exports with at least 50 percent domestic content.[13]

FOREIGN TRADE ZONES

foreign trade zone (FTZ)
Designated geographic region in which merchandise is allowed to pass through with lower customs duties (taxes) and/or fewer customs procedures.

Most countries promote trade with other nations by creating what is called a **foreign trade zone (FTZ)**—a designated geographic region in which merchandise is allowed to pass through with lower customs duties (taxes) and/or fewer customs procedures. Often, the intended purpose of foreign trade zones is increased employment, with increased trade a by-product. Figure 6.1 is an ad for Turkey's "Aegean Free Zone," in which the Turkish government allows companies to conduct manufacturing operations free of taxes.

Customs duties increase the total amount of a good's production cost and increase the time it takes to get it to market. Companies can reduce such costs and time by establishing a facility inside a foreign trade zone. A common purpose of many companies' facilities in such zones is final product assembly. For example, Japanese car plants in Indiana, Kentucky, Ohio, and Tennessee are designated as foreign trade zones that are administered by the U.S. Department of Commerce (**www.doc.gov**). The car companies are allowed to import parts from other production facilities around the world at 50 percent of the normal duty charged on such parts. After assembly the vehicles are sold within the United States market with no further duties being charged. Thus, state governments offer lower customs duties in return for the jobs created by having the assembly take place in the United States.

China has established a number of large foreign trade zones to reap the employment advantages they offer. Goods imported into these zones do not require import licenses or other documents, nor are they subject to import duties. International companies can also store goods in these zones before shipping them on to other countries

FIGURE 6.1

The Aegean Free Zone

without incurring taxes in China. Moreover, five of these zones are located within specially designated economic zones in which local governments can offer additional opportunities and tax breaks to international investors.[14]

Another country that has enjoyed the beneficial effects of foreign trade zones is Mexico. As early as the 1960s, Mexico established such a zone along its northern border with the United States. Creation of the zone caused development of companies called *maquiladoras* along the border inside Mexico. The *maquiladoras* import materials or parts from the United States without duties, perform some processing on them, and export them back to the United States, which charges duties only on the value added to the product in Mexico. The program has expanded rapidly over the three decades since its inception, employing hundreds of thousands of people from all across Mexico who come north looking for work.

SPECIAL GOVERNMENT AGENCIES

The governments of most nations have special agencies responsible for promoting exports. Such agencies can be particularly helpful to small and midsize businesses that have limited financial resources. Government trade-promotion agencies often organize trips for trade officials and businesspeople to visit other countries to meet potential business partners and generate contacts for new business. They also typically open trade offices in other countries. These offices are designed to promote the home country's exports and introduce businesses to potential business partners in the host nation. Government trade-promotion agencies typically do a great deal of advertising in other countries to promote the nation's exports. Figure 6.2 is an ad for ProChile—the government of Chile's Trade Commission, which has 35 commercial offices worldwide and a Web site (**www.chileinfo.com**).

Governments not only promote trade by encouraging exports but also can encourage imports that the nation does not or cannot produce. For example, the Japan External Trade Organization (JETRO) (**www.jetro.go.jp**) is a trade-promotion agency of the government. The agency coaches small and midsize overseas businesses on the protocols of Japanese deal making, arranges meetings with suitable Japanese distributors and partners, and even assists in finding temporary office space for first-time visitors.

FIGURE 6.2

Promoting Chile to the World

Town & Country (T&C) Cedar Homes (**www.cedarhomes.com**), based in Petoskey, Michigan, manufactures prefabricated homes. The company credits JETRO for making Japan indispensable to its livelihood. Says T&C president Stephan Biggs: "JETRO's office in Michigan received requests from Japan, searched their database, and put our hand in theirs. And that was it. It has to do with relationships, and we couldn't have done it without JETRO." By linking with the Intercontinental Trading Corporation, a Japanese distributor, T&C has introduced a new style of home to affluent Japanese. Now sales to Japan comprise 20 percent of T&C's total sales.[15]

For all companies, and particularly small ones with fewer resources, just finding out about the wealth of government regulations in other countries is a daunting task. What are the tariffs charged on a product? Are quotas placed on certain products? Fortunately, it is now possible to get answers to questions like these through the Internet. For a list of some very informative Web sites, see the Global Manager titled "Surfing the Regulatory Seas."

METHODS OF RESTRICTING TRADE

tariff
Government tax levied on a product as it enters or leaves a country.

We saw earlier in this chapter some of the political, economic, and cultural reasons why governments intervene in trade. In this section we discuss the methods governments can employ to restrict unwanted trade. There are two general categories of trade barrier available to governments: *tariffs* and *nontariff barriers*. A **tariff** is a government tax levied on a product as it enters or leaves a country. Tariffs add to the cost of imported products and therefore tend to lower the quantity sold of the products levied with a tariff. Nontariff barriers limit the quantity of an imported product. In turn, the lower quantity of the product available in the market tends to increase its price and thus decrease sales. Let's now take a closer look at tariffs and the various types of nontariff barriers.

TARIFFS

We can classify tariffs into three categories according to the country that levies the tariff. First, a tariff levied by the government of a country that is exporting a product is called an *export tariff*. Countries can use export tariffs when they think that the price of an export is lower than it should be. Developing nations whose exports consist mostly of low-priced natural resources often levy export tariffs. Second, a tariff levied by the government of a country that a product is passing through on its way to its final destination is called a *transit tariff*. Transit tariffs have been almost entirely eliminated worldwide through international trade agreements. Third, a tariff levied by the government in a country that is importing a product is called an *import tariff*. The import tariff is by far the most common tariff used by governments today.

We can further break down the import tariff into three subcategories based on the manner in which it is calculated. First, an **ad valorem tariff** is levied as a percentage of the stated price of an imported product. Second, a **specific tariff** is levied as a specific fee for each unit (measured by number, weight, etc.) of an imported product. Third, a **compound tariff** is levied on an imported product and calculated partly as a percentage of its stated price and partly as a specific fee for each unit. There are two main reasons why countries levy tariffs.

To Protect Domestic Producers   First, tariffs are a way of protecting domestic producers of a product. Because import tariffs raise the effective cost of an imported good, domestically produced goods can appear more attractive to buyers. In this way, domestic producers gain a protective barrier against imports. Although producers that receive tariff protection can gain a price advantage, in the long run protection can keep them from increasing efficiency. A protected industry can be devastated if protection encourages complacency and inefficiency and it is later thrown into the lion's den of international competition. For example, Mexico began reducing tariff protection in the mid-1980s as a prelude to NAFTA negotiations. Although Mexican producers struggled to become more efficient, many were forced into bankruptcy.

To Generate Revenue   Second, tariffs are a source of government revenue. Using tariffs to generate government revenue is most common among relatively less developed nations. The main reason is that less-developed nations tend to have less formal domestic economies that lack the capability to record domestic transactions accurately. The lack of accurate record keeping makes collection of sales taxes within the country extremely difficult. Nations solve the problem by simply raising their needed revenue through import and export tariffs. As countries develop, however, they tend to generate a greater portion of their revenues from taxes on income, capital gains, and other economic activity.

The discussion so far leads us to question: "Who benefits from tariffs?" We've already mentioned the two principle reasons for tariff barriers—protecting domestic producers and raising government revenue. Thus, on the surface it appears that governments and domestic producers benefit. We also discussed that tariffs raise the effective price of a product because importers typically must charge buyers a higher price to recover the cost of this additional tax. Thus, it appears on the surface that consumers do not benefit. As we also mentioned earlier, there is the danger that tariffs will create inefficient domestic producers that may go out of business once protective import tariffs are removed. Analysis of the total cost to a country is far more complicated and goes beyond the scope of our discussion. Suffice it to say that tariffs tend to exact a cost on countries as a whole because they lessen the gains from trade to a nation's people.

ad valorem tariff
Tariff levied as a percentage of the stated price of an imported product.

specific tariff
Tariff levied as a specific fee for each unit (measured by number, weight, etc.) of an imported product.

compound tariff
Tariff levied on an imported product and calculated partly as a percentage of its stated price and partly as a specific fee for each unit.

QUOTAS

quota
Restriction on the amount (measured in units or weight) of a good that can enter or leave a country during a certain period of time.

A restriction on the amount (measured in units or weight) of a good that can enter or leave a country during a certain period of time is called a **quota**. After tariffs, a quota is the second most common type of trade barrier. Governments typically administer their quota systems by granting quota licenses to the companies or governments of other nations (in the case of import quotas), and domestic producers (in the case of export quotas). Governments normally grant such licenses on a year-by-year basis.

Reason for Import Quotas   A government may impose an *import quota* to protect its domestic producers by placing a limit on the amount of goods allowed to enter the country. This helps domestic producers maintain their market shares and prices because competitive forces are restrained. In this case, domestic producers win because of the protection of their markets. Consumers lose because of higher prices and limited selection attributable to lower competition. Other losers include domestic producers whose own production requires the import subjected to a quota. Companies relying on the importation of so-called intermediate goods will find the final cost of their own products increase.

A few years ago, China had in place an import quota system in its filmmaking industry. One year, state-run China Film Corporation imported just 10 blockbuster movies—all through revenue-sharing agreements with international distributors. The agreement resulted in Buena Vista International (www.bvimovies.co.uk) earning a mere $500,000 in China on its immensely popular Disney film *The Lion King*, although the film grossed more than $1.3 million in Shanghai alone. "[Chinese] taxes are unlike [those] anywhere else in the world," reports Buena Vista executive Larry Kaplan. "A hit there brings in less than in a small central European country." Under international pressure China later abolished its quota system.[16]

Countries historically have placed import quotas on the textiles and apparel products of other countries under what is called the Multi-Fiber Arrangement. Countries affected by this arrangement account for over 80 percent of world trade in textiles and clothing each year. Although the 1974 arrangement was originally planned to last just 4 years, it has since been continually revised and extended. However, all quotas in this industry are expected to be phased out completely by 2005.

International pressure forced China to abandon its import quota system in the filmmaking industry. In the mid-1990s, when the system was still in effect, Buena Vista International earned a mere $500,000 from the showing of the popular Disney film, *The Lion King*, although the film grossed more than $1.3 million in Shanghai alone. Under what circumstances, if any, do you think nations should be allowed to impose import quotas?

Reasons for Export Quotas There are at least two reasons why a country imposes *export quotas* on its domestic producers. First, it may wish to maintain adequate supplies of a product in the home market. This motive is most common among countries that export natural resources that are essential to domestic business or the long-term survival of a nation.

Second, a country may restrict export of a good to restrict its supply on world markets, thereby increasing the international price of the good. This is the motive behind the formation and activities of the Organization of Petroleum Exporting Countries (OPEC) (www.opec.org). This group of nations from the Middle East and Latin America attempts to restrict the world's supply of crude oil to earn greater profits. Although OPEC was quite successful in its early years, the 1970s, it is finding it difficult to get a consensus among its members to restrict oil production in recent years.

Voluntary Export Restraints A unique version of the export quota is called a **voluntary export restraint (VER)**—a quota that a nation imposes on its own exports, usually at the request of another nation. Countries normally self-impose a voluntary export restraint in response to the threat of an import quota or total ban on the product by an importing nation. The classic example of the use of a voluntary export restraint is the automobile industry in the 1980s. Japanese carmakers were making significant market share gains in the U.S. market. The closing of U.S. carmakers' production facilities in the United States was creating a volatile anti-Japan sentiment among the population and the U.S. Congress. Fearing punitive legislation in Congress if Japan did not limit its automobile exports to the United States, the Japanese government and its carmakers self-imposed a voluntary export restraint on cars headed for the United States.

If domestic producers do not curtail production, consumers in the country that imposes an export quota benefit from lower prices due to a greater supply. Producers in an importing country benefit because the goods of producers from the exporting country are restrained, which may allow them to increase prices. Export quotas hurt consumers in the importing nation because of reduced selection and perhaps higher prices. However, export quotas might allow these same consumers to retain their jobs if imports were threatening to put domestic producers out of business. Again, detailed economic studies are needed to determine the winners and losers in any particular export quota case.

Tariff-Quotas A hybrid form of trade restriction is called a **tariff-quota**—a lower tariff rate for a certain quantity of imports and a higher rate for quantities that exceed the quota. Figure 6.3 shows how a tariff-quota actually works. Imports entering a nation

voluntary export restraint (VER)
Unique version of export quota that a nation imposes on its exports, usually at the request of an importing nation.

tariff-quota
Lower tariff rate for a certain quantity of imports and a higher rate for quantities that exceed the quota.

FIGURE 6.3

How a Tariff-Quota Works

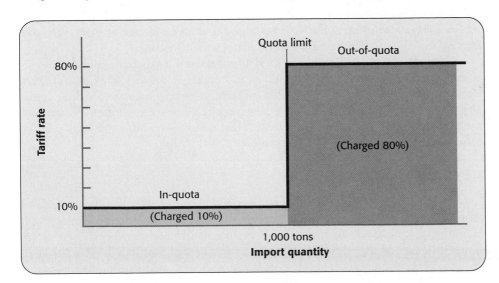

under a quota limit of, say, 1,000 tons are charged a 10 percent tariff. But subsequent imports that do not make it under the quota limit of 1,000 tons are charged a tariff of 80 percent. Tariff-quotas are used extensively in the trade of agricultural products. Many countries implemented tariff-quotas in 1995 after their use was permitted by the international trade agency known as the GATT (now part of the World Trade Organization).

EMBARGOES

A complete ban on trade (imports and exports) in one or more products with a particular country is called an **embargo**. An embargo may be placed on one or a few goods or it may completely ban trade in all goods. It is the most restrictive nontariff trade barrier available, and it is typically applied to accomplish political goals. Embargoes can be decreed by individual nations or by supranational organizations such as the United Nations. Because they can be very difficult to enforce, embargoes are used less today than they have been in the past. One example of a total ban on trade with another country is the United States' embargo on trade with Cuba. In fact, U.S. tourists are not legally able to vacation in Cuba.

After a military coup ousted elected President Aristide of Haiti in the early 1990s, restraints were applied to force the military junta either to reinstate Aristide or to hold new elections. One restraint was an embargo by the Organization of American States. Because of difficulties in actually enforcing the embargo and after two years of fruitless United Nations diplomacy, the embargo failed. Then the United Nations stepped in with a ban on trade in oil and weapons. Despite some smuggling through the Dominican Republic, which shares the island of Hispaniola with Haiti, the embargo was generally effective, and Aristide was eventually reinstated.

LOCAL CONTENT REQUIREMENTS

Recall from Chapter 3 that *local content requirements* are laws stipulating that producers in the domestic market must supply a specified amount of a good or service. These requirements can state that a certain portion of the end product consists of domestically produced goods or that a certain portion of the final cost of a product has domestic sources.

The purpose of local content requirements is to force companies from other nations to employ local resources in their production processes—particularly labor. Similar to other restraints on imports, such requirements help protect domestic producers from the price advantage of companies based in other, low-wage, countries. Today, many developing countries use local content requirements as a strategy to boost industrialization. Yet, companies can circumvent local content requirements by locating production facilities inside the nation that stipulates such restrictions.

Although many people consider music the universal language, not all cultures are equally open to the world's diverse musical influences. To prevent Anglo-Saxon music from "corrupting" French culture, French law requires radio programs to include at least 40 percent French content. Such local content requirements are intended to protect both the French cultural identity and the jobs of French artists against other nations' pop culture that regularly washes up on French shores.

ADMINISTRATIVE DELAYS

Regulatory controls or bureaucratic rules designed to impair the rapid flow of imports into a country are called **administrative delays**. This nontariff barrier includes a wide range of government actions, such as requiring international air carriers to land at inconvenient airports, requiring product inspections that damage the product itself, purposely understaffing customs offices to cause unusual time delays, and requiring special licenses that take a long time to obtain. The objective of all such administrative delays for a country is to discriminate against imported products—in a word, protectionism.

Although Japan has removed some of its trade barriers, many subtle obstacles to imports remain. Products ranging from cold pills and vitamins to farm products and building materials find it hard to penetrate the Japanese market. One journalist visiting Japan reports that because her cold tablets contained more pseudoephedrine sulfate than Japanese law allows, she had to hand them over to customs agents—they were considered narcotics![17]

Saudi Arabia opened its markets further to imports when it simplified its customs clearance process. Government agencies eliminated the annual review of product registration and lowered registration fees that it charges importers. They also began allowing 60 product-testing facilities and more than 180 laboratories located outside Saudi Arabia to provide certification testing services for conformity to Saudi laws. Some of the products covered by the changes include children's toys and playground equipment.[18]

CURRENCY CONTROLS

Restrictions on the convertibility of a currency into other currencies are called **currency controls**. A company that wishes to import goods generally must pay for those goods in a common, internationally acceptable currency such as the U.S. dollar, European Union euro, or Japanese yen. Generally, it must also obtain the currency from its nation's domestic banking system. Governments can require that companies that desire such a currency apply for a license to obtain it. Thus, a country's government can discourage imports by restricting who is allowed to convert the nation's currency into the internationally acceptable currency.

Another way governments apply currency controls to reduce imports is by stipulating an exchange rate that is unfavorable to potential importers. Because the unfavorable exchange rate can force the cost of imported goods to an impractical level, many potential importers simply give up on the idea. Meanwhile, the country will often allow exporters to exchange the home currency for an international currency at favorable rates to encourage exports.

currency controls
Restrictions on the convertibility of a currency into other currencies.

GLOBAL TRADING SYSTEM

The global trading system certainly has seen its ups and downs. World trade volume reached a peak in the late 1800s, only to be devastated when the United States passed the Smoot–Hawley Act in 1930. The act represented a major shift in U.S. trade policy from one of free trade to one of protectionism. The act set off round after round of competitive tariff increases among the major trading nations. Other nations felt that if the United States was going to restrict its imports, they were not going to give exports from the United States free access to their domestic markets. The Smoot–Hawley Act, and the global trade wars that it helped to usher in, crippled the economies of the industrialized nations and helped spark the Great Depression. Living standards around the world were devastated throughout most of the 1930s.

We begin this section by looking at early attempts to develop a global trading system, the *General Agreement on Tariffs and Trade*, and then examine its successor, the *World Trade Organization*.

GENERAL AGREEMENT ON TARIFFS AND TRADE (GATT)

Attitudes toward free trade changed markedly in the late 1940s. In the previous 50 years, extreme economic competition among nations and national quests to increase their resources for production helped create two world wars and the worst global economic recession ever. As a result, economists and policy makers proposed that the world band together and agree on a trading system that would help to avoid similar calamities in the future. A system of multilateral agreements was developed that became known as the **General Agreement on Tariffs and Trade (GATT)**—a treaty designed to promote free trade by reducing both tariff and nontariff barriers to international trade. The GATT was formed in 1947 by 23 nations—12 developed and 11 developing economies—and came into force in January 1948.[19]

The GATT was highly successful throughout its early years. Between 1947 and 1988, it helped to reduce average tariffs from 40 percent to 5 percent and multiply the volume of international trade by 20 times. But by the middle to late 1980s, rising nationalism worldwide and trade conflicts led to a nearly 50 percent increase in nontariff barriers to trade. Also, services (not covered by the original GATT) had become increasingly important—accounting for between 25 and 30 percent of total world trade. It was clear that a revision of the treaty was necessary, and in 1986 a new round of trade talks began.

Uruguay Round of Negotiations   The ground rules of the GATT resulted from periodic "rounds" of negotiations between its members. Though relatively short and straightforward in the early years, negotiations became protracted as the issues grew more complex. Table 6.2 shows the eight negotiating rounds that occurred under the auspices of the GATT. Note that whereas tariffs were the only topic of the first five rounds of negotiations, other topics were added in subsequent rounds.

The Uruguay Round of GATT negotiations, began in 1986 in Punta del Este, Uruguay (hence its name), was the largest trade negotiation in history. It was the eighth round of GATT talks within a span of 40 years and took more than 7 years to complete. The Uruguay Round made significant progress in reducing trade barriers by revising and updating the 1947 GATT. In addition to developing plans to further reduce barriers to merchandise trade, the negotiations modified the original GATT treaty in several important ways.

TABLE 6.2   The Rounds of GATT

Year	Site	Number of Countries Involved	Topics Covered
1947	Geneva, Switzerland	23	Tariffs
1949	Annecy, France	13	Tariffs
1951	Torquay, England	38	Tariffs
1956	Geneva	26	Tariffs
1960–1961	Geneva (Dillon Round)	26	Tariffs
1964–1967	Geneva (Kennedy Round)	62	Tariffs, antidumping measures
1973–1979	Geneva (Tokyo Round)	102	Tariffs, nontariff measures, "framework agreements"
1986–1994	Geneva (Uruguay Round)	123	Tariffs, nontariff measures, rules, services, intellectual property, dispute settlement, investment measures, agriculture, textiles and clothing, natural resources, creation of the WTO

Agreement on Services   Because of the ever-increasing importance of services to the total volume of world trade, nations wanted to include GATT provisions for trade in services. The General Agreement on Trade in Services (GATS) extended the principle of nondiscrimination to cover international trade in all services, although talks regarding some sectors were more successful than were others. The problem is that although trade in goods is a straightforward concept—goods are exported from one country and imported to another—it can be difficult to define exactly what a service is. Nevertheless, the GATS created during the Uruguay Round identifies four different forms that international trade in services can take:

1. *Cross-border supply*: Services supplied from one country to another (for example, international telephone calls).
2. *Consumption abroad*: Consumers or companies using a service while in another country (for example, tourism).
3. *Commercial presence*: A company establishing a subsidiary in another country to provide a service (for example, banking operations).
4. *Presence of natural persons*: Individuals traveling to another country to supply a service (for example, business consultants).

Agreement on Intellectual Property   Like services, products consisting entirely or largely of intellectual property are accounting for an increasingly large portion of international trade. Recall from Chapter 3 that *intellectual property* refers to property that results from people's intellectual talent and abilities. Products classified as intellectual property are supposed to be legally protected by copyrights, patents, and trademarks.

Although international piracy continues, the Uruguay Round took an important step toward getting it under control. It created the Agreement on Trade-Related Aspects of Intellectual Property (TRIPS) to help standardize intellectual-property rules around the world. The TRIPS Agreement concurs that protection of intellectual-property rights benefits society because it encourages the development of new technologies and other creations. It supports the articles of both the Paris Convention and the Berne Convention (see Chapter 3) and in certain instances takes a stronger stand on intellectual-property protection.

Agreement on Agricultural Subsidies   Trade in agricultural products has long been a bone of contention for most of the world's trading partners at one time or another. Some of the more popular barriers countries use to protect their agricultural sectors include import quotas and subsidies paid directly to farmers. The Uruguay Round addressed the main issues of agricultural tariffs and nontariff barriers in its Agreement on Agriculture. The result is increased exposure of national agricultural sectors to market forces and increased predictability in international agricultural trade. The agreement forces countries to convert all nontariff barriers to tariffs—a process called "tariffication." It then calls on developed and developing nations to cut agricultural tariffs significantly, but places no requirements on the least-developed economies.

WORLD TRADE ORGANIZATION (WTO)

Perhaps the greatest achievement of the Uruguay Round was the creation on January 1, 1995, of the *World Trade Organization (WTO)*—the international organization that regulates trade between nations. The three main goals of the WTO (**www.wto.org**) are to help the free flow of trade, to help negotiate further opening of markets, and to settle trade disputes between its members. One key component of the WTO that was carried over from GATT is the principle of nondiscrimination called **normal trade relations** (formerly called "most favored nation status")—a requirement that WTO members

normal trade relations (formerly "most favored nation status")
Requirement that WTO members extend the same favorable terms of trade to all members that they extend to any single member.

extend the same favorable terms of trade to all members that they extend to any single member. For example, if Japan were to reduce its import tariff on German automobiles to 5 percent, it must reduce the tariff it levies against auto imports from all other WTO nations to 5 percent.

The newly formed WTO replaced the *institution* of GATT but absorbed the GATT *agreements* (such as on services, intellectual property, and agriculture) into its own agreements. Thus, the GATT institution no longer officially exists. As of early 2002 the WTO recognized 144 members and over 30 "observer" members.

Dispute Settlement in the WTO   The power of the WTO to settle trade disputes is what really sets it apart from the GATT. Under the GATT, nations could file a complaint against another member and a committee would investigate the matter. If appropriate, the GATT would identify the unfair trade practices and member countries would pressure the offender to change its ways. But in reality, GATT rulings (usually given only after very long investigative phases that sometimes lasted years) were likely to be ignored.

In contrast, the various WTO agreements are essentially contracts between member nations that commit them to maintaining fair and open trade policies. When one WTO member files a complaint against another, the Dispute Settlement Body of the WTO moves into action swiftly. Decisions are to be rendered in less than 1 year—9 months if the case is urgent, 15 months if the case is appealed. The WTO dispute settlement system is not only faster and automatic, but its rulings cannot be ignored or blocked by members. Offenders must realign their trade policies according to WTO guidelines or suffer financial penalties and perhaps trade sanctions. Because of its ability to penalize offending member nations, the WTO's dispute settlement system is the spine of the global trading system.

Dumping and the WTO   The WTO also gets involved in settling disputes that involve "dumping" and the granting of subsidies. When a company exports a product at a price that is either lower than the price normally charged in its domestic market, or lower than the cost of production, it is said to be **dumping**. Charges of dumping are made (fairly or otherwise) against almost every nation at one time or another and can occur in any type of industry. For example, Western European plastic producers considered retaliating against Asian competitors whose prices were substantially lower in European markets than at home. More recently, U.S. steel producers and their powerful union charged that steelmakers in Brazil, Japan, and Russia were dumping steel on the U.S. market at low prices. The problem arose as nations tried to improve their economies (through exporting) in the wake of continued reverberations from the Asian financial crisis.

Because dumping is an act by a company, not a country, the WTO cannot punish the country in which the company accused of dumping is based. Rather, it can only respond to the steps taken by the country that retaliates against the company. The WTO allows a nation to retaliate against dumping if it can show that dumping is actually occurring, can calculate the damage to its own companies, and can show that the damage is significant. The normal way a country retaliates is to charge an **antidumping duty**—an additional tariff placed on an imported product that a nation believes is being dumped on its market. But such measures must expire within 5 years of the time they are initiated unless a country can show that circumstances warrant their continued existence. This chapter's World Business Survey, titled "Striking Back," shows the number of antidumping investigations initiated by members of the World Trade Organization in 2 recent years. Gary Horlick, an antidumping lawyer in Washington, D.C., says that the reliance on antidumping investigations looks like "Smoot–Hawley in slow motion."[20]

dumping
Practice of exporting a product at a price either lower than the price that the product normally commands in its domestic market or lower than the cost of production.

antidumping duty
Additional tariff placed on an imported product that a nation believes is being dumped on its market.

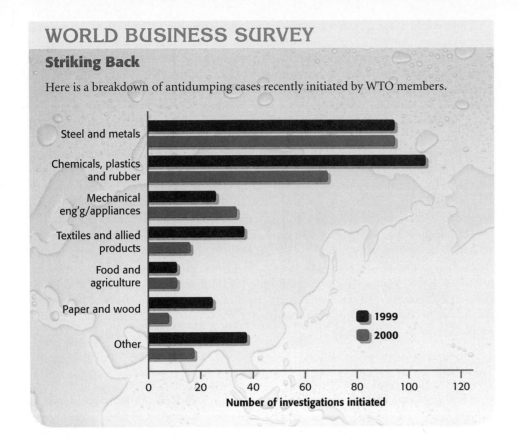

WORLD BUSINESS SURVEY

Striking Back

Here is a breakdown of antidumping cases recently initiated by WTO members.

Number of investigations initiated

- 1999
- 2000

Subsidies and the WTO Governments often retaliate when the competitiveness of their companies is threatened by a subsidy that another country pays its own domestic producers. Like antidumping measures, nations can retaliate against product(s) that receive an unfair subsidy by charging a **countervailing duty**—an additional tariff placed on an imported product that a nation believes is receiving an unfair subsidy. Unlike dumping, because payment of a subsidy is an action by a country, the WTO regulates the actions of the government that reacts to the subsidy as well as those of the government that originally paid the subsidy.

countervailing duty
Additional tariff placed on an imported product that a nation believes is receiving an unfair subsidy.

New Round of Negotiations A new round of negotiations to lower trade barriers further still was agreed to at the WTO meeting in Doha, Qatar, in late 2001. The new round of negotiations could bring particular benefits for developing nations. Agricultural subsidies in the world's rich countries are worth $1 billion per day—more than six times the value of their combined aid budgets. Poor countries should also obtain greater access to rich countries' textile markets and other markets that are labor intensive. The potential benefits are enormous considering that over 70 percent of poor nations' exports are agriculture and textiles. The Doha round also will prompt poor nations to reduce tariffs among themselves. Finally, poor nations are to receive help from rich nations in integrating themselves into the global trading system.[21]

The WTO and The Environment Steady gains in global trade and rapid industrialization in many developing and emerging economies have generated environmental concerns among both governments and special-interest groups. Of concern to many people are levels of carbon dioxide emissions—the principal greenhouse gas, believed to contribute to global warming. Most carbon dioxide emissions are created from the burning of fossil fuels and the manufacture of cement.

The World Trade Organization has no separate agreement that deals with environmental issues. The WTO explicitly states that it is not to become a global environmental agency responsible for setting environmental standards. It leaves such tasks to national governments and the many intergovernmental organizations that already exist for such purposes. The WTO works alongside the roughly 200 international agreements on the environment. Some of these include the Montreal Protocol for protection of the ozone layer, the Basel Convention on international trade or transport of hazardous waste, and the Convention on International Trade in Endangered Species.

Nevertheless, the preamble to the agreement that established the WTO does mention the objectives of environmental protection and sustainable development. The WTO also has an internal committee called the Committee on Trade and Environment. The committee's responsibility is to study the relationship between trade and the environment and to recommend possible changes in the WTO trade agreements.

In addition, the WTO does take explicit positions on some environmental issues related to trade. First, although the WTO supports national efforts at labeling "environmentally friendly" products as such, it states that labeling requirements or policies cannot discriminate against the products of other WTO members. Second, the WTO supports policies of the least-developed countries that require full disclosure of potentially hazardous products entering their markets for reasons of public health and environmental damage.

A FINAL WORD

Despite the theoretical benefits of trade that we discussed in Chapter 5, nations do not simply throw open their doors to free trade and force all their domestic businesses to sink or swim. This chapter has discussed reasons why national governments continue to protect all or some of their industries and how they go about it. The global trading system through the World Trade Organization tries to strike a balance between national desires for protection and international desires for free trade. In the next chapter we continue our discussion of the international trade and investment environment by discussing foreign direct investment. We look at recent patterns in foreign direct investment flows, examine theories that try to explain why it occurs, and discuss how governments intervene in these flows.

 There is a variety of additional material available on the Companion Website that accompanies this book. You can access this information by visiting the Website at (**www.prenhall.com/wild**).

summary

1 **Describe the _political, economic,_ and _cultural_ _motives_ behind governmental intervention in trade.** Despite the advantages of _free trade_, government intervention is common. The main _political_ motives behind government intervention in trade include (a) protecting jobs, (b) preserving national security, (c) responding to other nations' unfair trade practices, and (d) gaining influence over other nations.

The most common _economic_ reasons given for nations' attempts to influence international trade are

(a) protection of young industries from competition and (b) promotion of a strategic trade policy. According to the _infant industry argument_, a country's emerging industries need protection from international competition during their development phase until they become sufficiently competitive internationally. Although conceptually appealing, this argument can cause domestic companies to become noncompetitive, and inflate prices. Believers in _strategic trade policy_ argue that government intervention can help companies take advantage of economies of scale and be first movers in their industries. But government assistance to domestic companies can result in inefficiency, higher costs, and even trade wars between nations.

Perhaps the most common *cultural* motive for trade intervention is protection of national identity. Unwanted cultural influence can cause a government to block imports that it believes are harmful.

❷ **List and explain the methods governments use to *promote* international trade.** A *subsidy* is financial assistance to domestic producers in the form of cash payments, low-interest loans, tax breaks, product price supports, or some other form. It is intended to assist domestic companies in fending off international competitors. Critics charge that subsidies amount to corporate welfare and are detrimental in the long term.

Governments also can offer *export financing*— loans to exporters that they would not otherwise receive or loans at below-market interest rates. Another option is to guarantee that the government will repay a company's loan if the company should default on repayment—called a *loan guarantee.*

Most countries promote trade with other nations by creating what is called a *foreign trade zone (FTZ)*—a designated geographic region in which merchandise is allowed to pass through with lower customs duties (taxes) and/or fewer customs procedures. Finally, most nations have *special government agencies* responsible for promoting exports. These agencies organize trips abroad for trade officials and businesspeople and open offices abroad to promote home country exports.

❸ **List and explain the methods governments use to *restrict* international trade.** A *tariff* is a government tax levied on a product as it enters or leaves a country. An *export tariff* is one that is levied by the government of a country that is exporting a product. A tariff levied by the government of a country that a product is passing through on its way to its final destination is called a *transit tariff.* An *import tariff* is one that is levied by the government of a country that is importing a product. Three categories of import tariff are *ad valorem tariffs, specific tariffs,* and *compound tariffs.*

A restriction on the amount (measured in units or weight) of a good that can enter or leave a country during a certain period of time is called a *quota.* Governments may impose *import quotas* to protect domestic producers or *export quotas* to maintain adequate supplies in the home market or increase prices of a product on world markets.

A complete ban on trade (imports and exports) in one or more products with a particular country is called an *embargo.* Laws stipulating that a specified amount of a good or service be supplied by producers in the domestic market are called *local content requirements.* Governments can also discourage imports by causing *administrative delays* (regulatory controls or bureaucratic rules to impair imports) or *currency controls* (restrictions on the convertibility of a currency).

❹ **Discuss the importance of the *World Trade Organization* in promoting free trade.** The *General Agreement on Tariffs and Trade (GATT)* was a treaty designed to promote free trade by reducing both tariff and nontariff barriers to international trade. The *Uruguay Round* of GATT negotiations that ended in 1994 made significant progress in several areas: (1) International trade in services was included for the first time; (2) intellectual property rights were clearly defined; (3) tariff and nontariff barriers in agricultural trade were reduced significantly; and (4) the *World Trade Organization (WTO)* was created—an international organization to regulate trade.

The three main goals of the WTO are to help the free flow of trade, to help negotiate further opening of markets, and to settle trade disputes between its members. A key component of the WTO is the principle of nondiscrimination called *normal trade relations* that requires WTO members to treat all members equally.

When a company exports a product at a price either lower than the price it normally charges in its domestic market or lower than the cost of production, it is said to be *dumping.* The WTO allows a nation to retaliate against dumping if it can show that dumping is actually occurring, can calculate the damage to its own companies, and can show that the damage is significant.

questions for review

1. Identify the *political motives* for government intervention in trade. Explain how national security concerns affect exports and imports.

2. What are the main *economic motives* for government trade intervention? Explain the drawbacks of each approach.

3. Identify the *cultural motives* for nations to intervene in free trade.

4. List the methods governments can use to *promote* international trade.

5. What is a *subsidy*? Identify the drawbacks of using subsidies.

6. Explain how *export financing* helps promote trade. Why is it especially important to small and midsize businesses?

7. What is a *foreign trade zone*? Explain how it promotes trade, and illustrate with an example.

8. How can *special government agencies* help promote trade?

9. Identify methods governments can use to *restrict* international trade.

10. Explain the difference between a *tariff* and a *quota*.

11. What is a *voluntary export restraint*? Explain how it is used and how it differs from a quota.

12. Explain what an *embargo* is and why it is seldom used today.

13. What is the purpose of a *local content requirement*?

14. Explain how *administrative delays* and *currency controls* are used to restrict trade.

15. What is the *General Agreement on Tariffs and Trade (GATT)*?

16. What was the *Uruguay Round*? What were its main accomplishments?

17. What is the *World Trade Organization (WTO)*? Describe how the WTO settles trade disputes.

18. Explain what it means for a nation to have *normal trade relations* (or most favored nation status).

19. Explain the difference between an *antidumping duty* and a *countervailing duty*.

20. Identify efforts at protecting the *environment* from international trade and rapid industrialization.

questions for discussion

1. Imagine that the people in your nation are convinced that international trade is harmful to their wages and jobs and that your task is to change their minds. What kinds of programs would you implement to educate your people about the benefits of trade? Describe how each would help change people's attitudes.

2. Most countries create a list of "hostile" countries and require potential exporters to those nations to apply for special permission before they are allowed to proceed. Which countries would you place on such a list for your nation, and why? Which products are you most concerned about, and why?

3. Two students are discussing efforts within the global trading system to reduce trade's negative effects on the environment. One student says, "Sure, there may be pollution effects, but they're a small price to pay for a higher standard of living." The other student agrees saying, "Yeah, those 'tree-huggers' are always exaggerating those effects anyway. Who cares if some little toad in the Amazon goes extinct? I sure don't." What counterarguments can you offer to these students?

in practice

Read the article below and answer the questions that follow.

WTO Rules Against United States

WASHINGTON, D.C.—The World Trade Organization (WTO) today ruled against a U.S. law that gives tax breaks to American exporters, a decision that could open the way for the European Union (EU) to impose billions of dollars in retaliatory duties.

The WTO ordered the United States to repeal $4 billion of tax breaks for U.S. exporters who operate through off-shore subsidiaries, or face possible sanction. If the United States fails to comply, the matter goes to an arbitration panel, which would set the level of penalties the EU can impose.

Analysts say the EU is likely to use the decision as leverage. If the U.S. imposes a new set of steel tariffs, the EU could respond with duties on selected U.S. goods from steel-producing states such as Pennsylvania or Indiana.

But many European companies are ambivalent about the U.S. tax breaks because they have U.S. subsidiaries that benefit from them.

1. Do you think the United States is being singled out unfairly by the WTO? Explain your answer.

2. What cultural, political, or economic reasons do you think motivates the United States to maintain its tax breaks for U.S. exporters? List as many as you can.

3. Do you think that the WTO should have the power to dictate the trade policies of individual nations and punish them if they do not comply? Why or why not?

4. The United States (in fact, much of the industrialized world) was in recession when the WTO made its ruling. Do you think countries experiencing economic difficulties should be allowed to erect temporary tariff and nontariff barriers? Why or why not? What effect do you think such an allowance would have on the future of the global trading system?

projects

1. Select a recent business periodical in print or online and find an article that discusses government intervention in promoting or restricting trade. Write a short summary (about 800 words) of what motivated the action, which industries or individual companies are affected, and the reaction of other nations or the World Trade Organization.

2. Select a company involved in importing or exporting in your city or town. Make an appointment to interview the owner or a manager. Your goal is to understand how government involvement in international trade has helped or harmed the company's business activities. Be sure to inquire about specific past examples and the future potential impacts of government intervention. Write a short report of your interview and present a brief talk in which you present your findings to the class.

3. In this project, two groups of four students each will debate the case for or against protectionism surrounding a recent dramatic rise in the import of coffee into your country. One team represents businesspeople in your country who welcome the imports because they benefit their livelihood. The other group represents businesspeople who oppose the imports because it hurts their livelihood. The goal is to try to convince your government to introduce or not introduce protection for domestic coffee growers. After the first student from each side has spoken, the second student questions the opponent's arguments, looking for holes and inconsistencies. The third student attempts to answer these arguments. The fourth student presents a summary of each side's arguments. Finally, the class votes on which team has offered the more compelling argument.

"Canada Launches WTO Challenge to U.S. . . . Mexico Widens Anti-dumping Measure. . . China to Begin Probe of Synthetic Rubber Imports. . . Steel Dispute Raises Issue of Free-Trade Credibility. . . It Must Be Stopped," scream headlines around the world.

International trade theories argue that nations should open their doors to trade. Conventional free-trade wisdom says that by trading with others, a country can offer its citizens a greater quantity and selection of goods at cheaper prices than it could in the absence of trade. Nevertheless, truly free trade still does not exist because national governments intervene. Despite the efforts of the World Trade Organization (WTO) and smaller groups of nations, governments still cry foul in the trade game. Worldwide, the number of antidumping cases initiated averaged 234 per year over the past 7 years; cases peaked at 356 in 1999 but fell to 272 cases in 2000 and 134 in 2001.

In the past, the world's richest nations would typically charge a developing nation with dumping. But today, emerging markets, too, are jumping into the fray. China recently launched an inquiry to determine whether synthetic rubber imports (used in auto tires and footwear) from Japan, South Korea, and Russia are being dumped in the country. Mexico expanded coverage of its Automatic Import Advice System. The system requires importers (from a select list of countries) to notify Mexican officials of the amount and price of a shipment 10 days prior to its expected arrival in Mexico. The 10-day notice gives domestic producers advanced warning of low-priced products so they can report dumping before the products clear customs and enter the marketplace. India set up a new government agency to handle antidumping cases. Even Argentina, Indonesia, South Africa, South Korea, and Thailand are using this recently popular tool of protectionism.

Why is dumping so popular? Oddly enough, the WTO allows it. The WTO has made major inroads on the use of tariffs, slashing them across almost every product category in recent years. But it does not have authority to punish companies, only governments. Thus, the WTO cannot make judgments against individual companies that are dumping products in other markets. It can only pass rulings against the government of the country that imposes an antidumping duty. But the WTO allows countries to retaliate against nations whose producers are suspected of dumping when it can be shown that (1) the alleged offenders are significantly hurting domestic producers, and (2) the export price is lower than the cost of production or lower than the home-market price.

Alternatives to bringing antidumping cases before the WTO do exist. United States President George W. Bush relied on a Section 201 or "global safeguard" investigation under U.S. trade law in 2002 to slap tariffs of up to 30 percent on steel imports. The U.S. steel industry had been suffering under an onslaught of steel imports from many nations, including Brazil, the European Union, Japan, and South Korea. Yet, nations still brought complaints about the action before the WTO.

Supporters of antidumping tariffs claim that they prevent dumpers from undercutting the prices charged by producers in a target market, driving them out of business. Another claim in support of antidumping is that it is an excellent way of retaining some protection against the potential dangers of totally free trade. Detractors of antidumping tariffs charge that once such tariffs are imposed they are rarely removed. They also claim that it costs companies and governments a great deal of time and money to file and argue their cases. It is also argued that the fear of being charged with dumping causes international competitors to keep their prices higher in a target market than would otherwise be the case. This would allow domestic companies to charge higher prices and not lose market share—forcing consumers to pay more for their goods.

thinking globally

1. "You can't tell consumers that the low price they are paying for that fax machine or automobile is somehow unfair. They're not concerned with the profits of some company. To them, it's just a great bargain and they want it to continue." Do you agree with this statement? Do you think that people from different cultures would respond differently to this statement? Explain your answers.

2. As we have seen, currently the WTO cannot get involved in punishing individual companies—its actions can only be directed toward governments of countries. Do you think this is a wise policy? Why or why not? Why do you think the WTO was not given authority to charge individual companies with dumping? Explain.

3. Identify a recent antidumping case that was brought before the WTO. Locate as many articles in the press as you can that discuss the case. Identify the nations, product(s), and potential punitive measures involved. Supposing you were part of the WTO's Dispute Settlement Body, would you vote in favor of the measures taken by the retaliating nation? Why or why not? *Hint*: A good Web site to visit is that of the World Trade Organization (www.wto.org).

a question **of ethics**

1. Since the early 1980s the United States has drawn fire from the business community for imposing economic sanctions (similar to an embargo) against Iran for primarily political reasons. Those sanctions disallow international trade and investment between U.S. and Iranian businesspeople. Business leaders in the United States would like the sanctions removed so they can be included in lucrative Iranian oil and gas deals in which firms from other countries are engaging. Other sanction opponents wonder if a policy of offering "all stick and no carrot" is undermining social and political change in Iran since the offending regime goes largely unpunished.

   Do you think sanctions can be effective at changing the behavior of governments? Why or why not? Do you think that one country acting alone can bring about reforms through the use of economic sanctions or embargoes? Assuming that ordinary people suffer the brunt of sanctions most, what do think about the morality of their use?

2. A nonprofit trade and industry group, the National Foreign Trade Council (NFTC) (**www.nftc.org**), based in Washing-

ton, D.C., won a court battle in 2000 against the State of Massachusetts. In a unanimous decision, the U.S. Supreme Court sided with the NFTC and struck down a Massachusetts law that was designed to deny state contracts to any company doing business in Myanmar. The Court ruled that the Massachusetts law intruded on the federal government's authority and was preempted by federal law regarding Myanmar. In fact, the U.S. Constitution states that, "foreign policy is exclusively reserved for the federal government." The NFTC says it shares concern over human rights abuses occurring in Myanmar, but believes that a coordinated, multinational effort would be most effective at instilling change in the nation.

Do you think that companies should be penalized in their domestic business dealings because of where they do business abroad? Do you think that the World Trade Organization should get into domestic/international political matters? Why or why not? What do you think would be the effect on domestic firms if every state were allowed to punish firms based on their own foreign policy ideals?

7 foreign direct investment

LEARNING OBJECTIVES

After studying this chapter, you should be able to

1. Describe the worldwide patterns of *foreign direct investment (FDI)* and the reasons for these patterns.

2. Describe each of the *theories* that attempt to explain why foreign direct investment occurs.

3. Discuss the important *management issues* in the foreign direct investment decision.

4. Explain why *governments* intervene in the free flow of foreign direct investment.

5. Discuss the *policy instruments* that governments use to promote and restrict foreign direct investment.

BEACONS

A Look Back

CHAPTER 6 explained business–government relations in the context of trade in goods and services. We explored the motives and methods of government intervention. We also examined the global trading system and how it promotes free trade.

A Look at This Chapter

This chapter examines another significant form of international business, foreign direct investment (FDI). Again, we are concerned with the patterns of FDI and the theories on which it is based. We also explore why and how governments intervene in FDI activity.

A Look Ahead

CHAPTER 8 explores the trend toward greater regional integration of national economies. We explore the benefits of closer economic cooperation and examine prominent regional trading blocs that exist around the world.

VW: Untouchable

FRANKFURT, Germany—The Volkswagen Group (**www.vw.com**) owns some of the most prestigious and best-known automotive brands in the world, including Audi, Bentley, Bugatti, Lamborghini, Rolls-Royce, Seat, Skoda, and Volkswagen. From its 43 production facilities worldwide it produces five million cars annually. The company has sales in more than 150 countries and currently holds a 12 percent share of the world market.

But Volkswagen, like companies everywhere, is not doing it entirely on its own. Governments around the world zealously defend their biggest firms because of the economic ramifications of failure. German Chancellor Gerhard Schröder is heavily involved in promoting Volkswagen abroad. In fact, Mr. Schröder once served on Volkswagen's supervisory board when he was governor of the state of Lower Saxony. Mr. Schröder recently opened a new assembly line at the Volkswagen plant in Anchieta, near São Paulo, Brazil. Then during a stay in New York in 2002, he could be seen driving the new Volkswagen Phaeton, the first public use of the new luxury model from Volkswagen.

No less effort is expended in supporting Volkswagen in its home neighborhood. In Germany, the carmaker is still protected by its own law known as "Lex VW" that gives the government special voting rights that allow it to block a takeover. In 2001, Germany single-handedly killed a takeover reform proposal by the European Union (EU), partly over concerns about the effect on Volkswagen. Then while campaigning in 2002, Chancellor Schröder told a crowd of cheering auto workers in central Germany, "Any efforts by the commission in Brussels to smash the VW culture will meet the resistance of the federal government as long as we are in power."

Germany's defense of Volkswagen's special treatment is rooted in the carmaker's importance to jobs in the domestic economy and in the close ties between government and management. Volkswagen employs tens of thousands of people and symbolizes the postwar resurgence of the German economy. While reading this chapter, think about the foreign direct investments that companies make and the relations between businesses and local, regional, and national governments everywhere.[1]

Many early trade theories were created at a time when most production factors (such as labor, financial capital, capital equipment, and land or natural resources) either could not be moved or could not be moved easily across national borders. But today, all of the above except land are internationally mobile. In fact, inequities in the distribution of these factors among countries often propel resources toward those countries where scarcity exists. Companies can easily finance expansion from international financial institutions and whole factories can be picked up and moved to another country. Even labor is more mobile than in years past, although many barriers restrict the complete mobility of labor.

foreign direct investment
The purchase of physical assets or a significant amount of the ownership (stock) of a company in another country to gain a measure of management control.

Foreign direct investment (FDI) is the purchase of physical assets or a significant amount of the ownership (stock) of a company in another country to gain a measure of management control. Thus, at the core of foreign direct investment are international flows of capital. But there is wide disagreement on what exactly constitutes foreign direct investment. Nations set different thresholds at which they classify an international capital flow as FDI. Most governments set the threshold at anywhere from 10 to 25 percent of stock ownership in a company abroad—the U.S. Commerce Department sets it at 10 percent. In contrast, an investment that does not involve obtaining a degree of control in a company is called a **portfolio investment**.

portfolio investment
Investment that does not involve obtaining a degree of control in a company.

In this chapter, we examine the importance of foreign direct investment to the operations of international companies. We begin by exploring the growth of FDI in recent years and—investigating its sources and destinations. We then take a look at several theories that attempt to explain foreign direct investment flows. Next, we turn our attention to several important management issues that arise in most decisions about whether a company should undertake FDI. We then focus on the reasons why governments try to encourage or restrict foreign direct investment and the methods they employ to accomplish these goals.

PATTERNS OF FOREIGN DIRECT INVESTMENT

Just as international trade displays distinct patterns, so too does foreign direct investment. In this section we first take a look at the factors that have led to robust growth in FDI over the past decade. We then turn our attention to the destinations and sources of foreign direct investment.

GROWTH OF FOREIGN DIRECT INVESTMENT

Foreign direct investment (FDI) continues to expand rapidly, though not at the pace of the 1990s. After growing about 20 percent per year in the first half of the 1990s, FDI grew by about 40 percent per year in the second half of the decade. Although the global economic slowdown in 2000 caused FDI to grow just 18 percent that year, it did reach a record $1.3 trillion. FDI also continues to grow faster than both world production and trade.[2]

At one time, Boeing aircraft were made entirely in the United States. But today Boeing can source its landing-gear doors from Northern Ireland, outboard wing flaps from Italy, wing tip assemblies from Korea, rudders from Australia, and fuselages from Japan. Sometimes, Boeing buys a large portion of their international suppliers' physical assets or traded stock (called foreign direct investment) to gain some decision-making power in supplier organizations.

There are two main reasons that account for the rising tide of FDI flows over the past decade or so—*globalization* and *mergers and acquisitions*.

Globalization   Recall from Chapter 6 that in the 1980s old barriers to trade were not being reduced and new, creative barriers seemed to be popping up in many nations. This presented a problem for companies that were trying to export their products to markets around the world. This resulted in a wave of FDI as many companies entered promising markets to get around growing trade barriers. But then the Uruguay Round of GATT negotiations (see Chapter 6) created renewed determination to further reduce barriers to trade. As countries lowered their trade barriers, companies realized that they could now produce in the most efficient and productive locations around the world, and simply export to their markets worldwide. This set off another wave of FDI flows into low-cost newly industrialized and emerging nations worldwide—one that continues today. Therefore, the forces that are causing globalization to occur are part of the reason for growth in foreign direct investment.

Increasing globalization is also causing a growing number of international companies from emerging markets to undertake FDI. For example, companies from Taiwan began investing heavily in other nations in the mid-1980s. Acer (**www.acer.com**), headquartered in Singapore but founded in Taiwan, manufactures personal computers and computer components. Just 20 years after it opened for business, Acer had spawned 10 subsidiaries worldwide and became the dominant industry player in many emerging markets.

Mergers and Acquisitions   The number of *mergers and acquisitions (M&A)* and their exploding values also underlie the growth in foreign direct investment flows. Throughout the 1980s and 1990s, all M&A activity (domestic and international) grew at 42 percent annually, numbering more than 26,000 per year at the end of the 1990s. Over that period of time, the value of all M&A activity as a share of GDP rose from 0.3 percent to 8 percent. In fact, cross-border M&As increased 35 percent in 1999, reaching $720 billion in over 6,000 deals (see Figure 7.1). The total value of cross-border M&A activity is expected to rise above the $1 trillion mark in the near future.[3]

FIGURE 7.1

Value of Cross-Border M&As

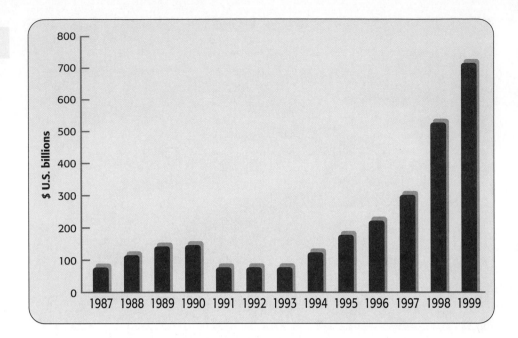

The power of the largest multinationals seems to be multiplying every year. The largest deal ever was the $203 billion takeover of Mannesmann of Germany by Vodafone Group (www.vodafone.com) of Britain. Their growing confidence is apparent in the comments of an executive during a meeting over the merger of Travelers Group (www.travelers.com) and Citicorp (www.citicorp.com). At one point in the merger talks, a director apparently asked the question: "Can anyone stop us?" After a brief silence, someone replied, "NATO" (the military alliance between the United States, Canada, and nations across Europe). Such confidence is fueling the continuation of mergers worldwide.[4]

Many cross-border M&A deals are driven by the desire of companies to do any or all of the following:

➡ Get a foothold in a new geographic market
➡ Increase a firm's global competitiveness
➡ Fill gaps in companies' product lines in a global industry
➡ Reduce costs in areas such as research and development, production, or distribution

But large global companies and the mergers and buyouts occurring among them do not comprise all foreign direct investment. Entrepreneurs and small businesses also play important roles in the expansion of FDI flows.

Role of Entrepreneurs and Small Businesses   Data does not exist that specifically states the portion of worldwide FDI that is contributed by entrepreneurs and small businesses. Nevertheless, we know from anecdotal evidence that these companies are engaged in FDI.

Consider the case of Brian Bowen and a few adventurous buddies from Perry, Georgia. When Uzbekistan (a former Soviet Union republic) opened its borders to investment in the 1990s, Bowen and five fellow entrepreneurial friends took their savings and went in to set up cellular phone service in Tashkent, Uzbekistan. Tashkent was almost entirely leveled by an earthquake in 1966 and the surviving landline telephone service dated from the 1920s. But today, the country would shut down without the cellular service provided by Bowen's company, International Communication Group (ICG). Bowen and his friends share ownership of the company with the Uzbekistan government. Bowen admits that the arrangement did present some difficulties: "I don't have any experience dealing with the KGB, the mafia, or the family connections in the bureaucracy here." In addition to learning the ins and outs of the government bureaucracy, Bowen has learned to eat horsemeat, drink vodka toasts, and enjoy *plov*—a dish of pilaf rice and mutton. The company has 7,000 subscribers, 240 employees, and could be worth as much as $100 million by some industry estimates.[5]

Unhindered by many of the constraints of a large company, entrepreneurs investing in other markets often demonstrate an inspiring can-do spirit mixed with ingenuity and bravado. For a day-in-the-life look at a young entrepreneur who is realizing his dreams in China, see the Entrepreneurial Focus titled "Cowboy Candy Rides into Manchuria."

WORLDWIDE FLOWS OF FDI

More than 60,000 multinational companies with over 800,000 affiliates abroad are driving the FDI flows.[6] Developed countries remain the prime destination for FDI because cross-border M&As are concentrated in developed nations. Developed countries account for more than three-quarters of global FDI inflows, which were a little over $1 trillion in 2000. In comparison, FDI inflows to developing countries were valued at $240 billion. But their share in world FDI flows declined to 19 percent, compared to the peak of 41 percent in 1994. Countries in Central and Eastern Europe accounted for 2 percent of global FDI or $27 billion. Meanwhile, the world's 49 poorest nations attracted just 0.3 percent of world inflows in 2000.

Among developed countries, European Union nations, the United States, and Japan accounted for over 70 percent of world inflows and 82 percent of outflows in 2000. The United States remains the world's largest FDI recipient country with inflows of $281 billion, and accounted for $139 billion of outflows. Increasing regional integration among

ENTREPRENEURIAL FOCUS

Cowboy Candy Rides into Manchuria

Tom Kirkwood, at just 28 years old, turned his dream of introducing his grandfather's taffy to China into a fast-growing, if still unprofitable, business. Kirkwood's story—his hassles and hustling—provides some lessons on the purest form of global investing. The basics that small investors in China can follow are as basic as they get. Find a product that's easy to make, widely popular, and cheap to sell and then choose the least expensive, investor-friendliest place to make it.

Kirkwood, whose family runs the Shawnee Inn, a ski and golf resort in Shawnee-on-Delaware, Pennsylvania, decided to make candy in Manchuria—China's gritty, heavily populated, industrial northeast. Chinese often give individually wrapped candies as a gift, and Kirkwood reckoned that China's rising, increasingly prosperous urbanites would have a lucrative sweet tooth. "You can't be M&Ms, but you don't have to be penny candy, either," Kirkwood says. "You find your niche. Because a niche in China is an awful lot of people."

Kirkwood decided early on that he wanted to do business in China. In the mid-1980s after prep school, he spent a year in Taiwan and China learning Chinese and working in a Shanghai engineering company. The experience gave him a taste for adventure capitalism on the frontier of China's economic development. In 1991, while in China advising other firms on how to set up business, Kirkwood set up a partnership with Bulgarian student Peter S. Moustakerski. The two eventually came up with what they considered a sure-fire idea—candy. Using $400,000 of Kirkwood's family money, they bought equipment and rented a factory in Shenyang, a city of 6 million people in the heart of Manchuria. Roads and rail transport were convenient, and wages were low. The local government seemed amenable to a 100 percent foreign-owned factory, and the Shenyang Shawnee Cowboy Food Company was born.

Although it's a small operation with only 51 employees, Kirkwood is determined to make it a success. As he boarded a flight to Beijing for a meeting with a distributor recently, he realized he had a bag full of candy. He offered one to a flight attendant. When lunch is over, he vowed, "Everybody on this plane will know Cowboy Candy."

EU nations resulted in record inflows of $617 billion. In 2000, the United Kingdom was the top worldwide source of FDI, and Germany was the largest recipient of FDI in Europe.

Developing nations had varying experiences in 2000. FDI inflows to developing nations in Asia hit a record $143 billion in 2000, with Hong Kong itself attracting $64 billion. Meanwhile, FDI flows to China were stable at $41 billion. More FDI into China is sure to come following its entry into the World Trade Organization in 2002. Outward FDI from developing nations in Asia doubled in 2000 to $85 billion with $63 billion coming from Hong Kong alone—more than half of that was to China. Inflows to the Southeast Asian nations were 10 percent of the world total in 2000—compared to over 30 percent in the mid-1990s. India, the largest recipient in the subcontinent, received $2 billion.

Elsewhere, FDI inflows to all of Africa accounted for about 1 percent of the world total in 2000. FDI to Africa declined from about $10 billion to slightly more than $9 billion in 2000—the first decline since the mid-1990s. After tripling during the second half of the 1990s, FDI flows into Latin America and the Caribbean also fell in 2000, by 22 percent, to $86 billion. Privatization continues to be an important driver of inward FDI there. FDI inflows to Central and Eastern Europe hit a record $27 billion in 2000. Again, privatization of state-owned assets was a driving force behind the inflows.

EXPLANATIONS FOR FOREIGN DIRECT INVESTMENT

So far we have examined the flows of foreign direct investment but have not investigated explanations for why FDI occurs. There are four main theories that attempt to explain why companies engage in foreign direct investment: *international product life cycle*, *market imperfections (internalization)*, *eclectic theory*, and *market power*. Let's now look at each of these in detail.

INTERNATIONAL PRODUCT LIFE CYCLE

international product life cycle theory
Theory stating that a company will begin by exporting its product and later undertake foreign direct investment as a product moves through its life cycle.

Although we introduced the international product life cycle in Chapter 5 in the context of international trade, it also has been used to explain foreign direct investment.[7] The theory of the **international product life cycle** states that a company will begin by exporting its product and later undertake foreign direct investment as a product moves through its life cycle. In the *new product stage*, a good is produced in the home country because of uncertain domestic demand and to keep production close to the research department that developed the product. In the *maturing product stage*, the company directly invests in production facilities in countries where demand is great enough to warrant its own production facilities. In the final *standardized product stage*, increased competition creates pressures to reduce production costs. In response, a company builds production capacity in low-cost developing nations to serve its markets around the world.

Despite its conceptual appeal, the international product life cycle theory is limited in its power to explain why companies choose FDI over other forms of market entry. A local firm in the target market could pay for the right (license) to use the special assets needed to manufacture a particular product. In this way, a company could avoid the additional risks associated with direct investments in the market. The theory also fails to explain why firms choose FDI over exporting activities. It might be less expensive to serve a market abroad by increasing output at the home-country factory rather than by building additional capacity within the target market.

The theory explains why the FDI of some firms follows the international product life cycle of their products. But it does not explain why other market entry modes are inferior or less advantageous options. Let's now look at a more recently developed theory—*market imperfections (internalization)* theory.

MARKET IMPERFECTIONS (INTERNALIZATION)

A market that is said to operate at peak efficiency (prices are as low as they can possibly be) and where goods are readily and easily available is said to be a *perfect market*. However, perfect markets are rarely, if ever, seen in business because of factors that cause a breakdown in the efficient operation of an industry—called *market imperfections*. **Market imperfections** theory states that when an imperfection in the market makes a transaction less efficient than it could be, a company will undertake foreign direct investment to internalize the transaction and thereby remove the imperfection. There are two market imperfections that are relevant to this discussion—trade barriers and specialized knowledge.

Trade Barriers   One common market imperfection in international business is trade barriers, such as tariffs. For example, the North American Free Trade Agreement stipulates that a sufficient portion of a product's content must originate within Canada, Mexico, or the United States in order for the product to escape tariff charges when it is imported to any of these three markets. That is why a large number of Korean manufacturers of video-cassette recorders (VCRs) invested in production facilities in Tijuana, Mexico, just south of Mexico's border with California. By investing in production facilities in Mexico, the Korean companies were able to skirt the North American tariffs that would have been levied if they were to export VCRs from Korean factories. The presence of a market imperfection (tariffs) caused those companies to undertake foreign direct investment.

Specialized Knowledge   The unique competitive advantage of a company sometimes consists of specialized knowledge. This knowledge could be the technical expertise of engineers or the special marketing abilities of managers. When the knowledge is technical expertise, companies can charge a fee to companies in other countries for use of the knowledge in producing the same or a similar product. But when a company's specialized knowledge is embodied in its employees, the only way to exploit a market opportunity in another nation may be to undertake FDI.

The possibility that a company will create a future competitor by charging another company for access to its knowledge is another market imperfection that can encourage FDI. Rather than trade a short-term gain (the fee charged another company) for a long-term loss (lost competitiveness), a company will prefer to undertake investment. For example, as Japan rebuilt its industries in the 1950s following the Second World War, many Japanese companies paid Western firms for access to the special technical knowledge embodied in their products. Those Japanese companies became adept at revising and improving many of these technologies and became leaders in their industries, such as electronics and automobiles.

ECLECTIC THEORY

The **eclectic theory** states that firms undertake foreign direct investment when the features of a particular location combine with ownership and internalization advantages to make a location appealing for investment.[8] A *location advantage* is the advantage of locating a particular economic activity in a specific location because of the characteristics (natural or acquired) of that location.[9] These advantages have historically been natural resources such as oil in the Middle East, timber in Canada, and copper in Chile. However, they can also be acquired advantages, such as a productive workforce. An *ownership advantage* is the advantage that a company has due to its ownership of some special asset, such as brand recognition, technical knowledge, or management ability. An *internalization advantage* is the advantage that arises from internalizing a business activity rather than leaving it to a relatively inefficient market. This theory states that when all these advantages are present, a company will undertake FDI.

market imperfections
Theory stating that when an imperfection in the market makes a transaction less efficient than it could be, a company will undertake foreign direct investment to internalize the transaction and thereby remove the imperfection.

eclectic theory
Theory stating that firms undertake foreign direct investment when the features of a particular location combine with ownership and internalization advantages to make a location appealing for investment.

MARKET POWER

market power
Theory stating that a firm tries to establish a dominant market presence in an industry by undertaking foreign direct investment.

vertical integration
Extension of company activities into stages of production that provide a firm's inputs (backward integration) or absorb its output (forward integration)

Firms often seek the greatest amount of power possible in their industries relative to rivals. The **market power** theory states that a firm tries to establish a dominant market presence in an industry by undertaking foreign direct investment. The benefit of market power is greater profit because the firm is far better able to dictate the cost of its inputs and/or the price of its output.

One way a company can achieve market power (or dominance) is through **vertical integration**—the extension of company activities into stages of production that provide a firm's inputs (*backward integration*) or absorb its output (*forward integration*). Sometimes a company can effectively control the world supply of an input needed by its industry if it has the resources or ability to integrate backward into supplying that input. Companies may also be able to achieve a great deal of market power if they can integrate forward to increase control over output. For example, they could perhaps make investments in distribution to leapfrog channels of distribution that are tightly controlled by competitors.

MANAGEMENT ISSUES IN THE FDI DECISION

Decisions about whether to engage in foreign direct investment involve several important issues regarding management of the company and its market. Some of these issues are grounded in the inner workings of firms that undertake FDI, such as the control desired over operations abroad or the firm's cost of production. Others are related to the market and industry in which a firm competes, such as the preferences of customers or the actions of rivals. Let's now examine each of these important issues.

CONTROL

Many companies investing abroad are greatly concerned with controlling the activities that occur in the local market, for a variety of reasons. Perhaps the company wants to be certain that its product is being marketed in the same way in the local market as it is at home. Or maybe it wants to ensure that the selling price remains the same in both markets. Some companies try to maintain ownership of a large portion of the local operations, say even up to 100 percent, in the belief that greater ownership gives them greater control.

However, for a variety of reasons even complete ownership does not *guarantee* control. For example, the local government might intervene and require a company to hire some local managers rather than bringing them all in from the home office. Companies may need to prove a scarcity of skilled local managerial talent before the government will let them bring managers in from the home country. Governments might also require that all goods produced in the local facility be exported so they do not compete with products of the country's domestic firms.

Partnership Requirements Because of the importance of control, many companies have strict policies regarding how much ownership they will take in firms in other nations. In fact, prior to the 1990s IBM (**www.ibm.com**) had the strict policy that international subsidiaries needed to be 100 percent owned by the home office. However, companies must sometimes abandon such policies when a country demands shared ownership in return for access to its market.

Governments saw such requirements as a way to shield their workers and industries from what they perceived as exploitation or domination by large international firms. Companies would sometimes sacrifice control to pursue a market opportunity but frequently did not. By the 1980s, most countries retreated from such a hard-line stance and began to open their doors to investment by multinationals. For example, in the 1980s

Employees pass in front of the IBM office building in Johannesburg, South Africa. In order to maintain control over their operations abroad, many companies demand some minimal level of ownership before they will engage in foreign direct investment. IBM used to have the policy that all international subsidiaries needed to be 100 percent owned by the home office. What benefits/drawbacks do you think are associated with such a "go solo" approach?

Mexico was making its decisions on investment by multinationals on a case-by-case basis. IBM was trying to negotiate for 100 percent ownership of a facility in Guadalajara and got the go-ahead after the company made numerous concessions in other areas.

Benefits of Cooperation   Recent years have seen greater harmony between governments and international companies, though the business press still tends to highlight the controversies. The reason is that governments of many developing and newly industrialized countries have come to realize the benefits of investment by multinationals, including decreased unemployment, increased tax revenues, training to create a more highly skilled workforce, and the transfer of technology. A country with a reputation for overly restricting the operations of multinational enterprises can see its inward investment flow dry up. Indeed, restrictive policies of India's government continue to deny the nation the foreign direct investment flows in the proportions that neighboring Southeast Asian nations are receiving.

Cooperation also frequently opens important communication channels that help firms to maintain positive relationships in the host country. Both parties tend to walk a fine line—cooperating most of the time, but holding fast on occasions when the stakes are especially high.

Cooperation with a local partner and respect for national pride in Central Europe contributed to the successful acquisition of Hungary's Borsodi brewery (formerly a state-owned enterprise) by Belgium's Interbrew (www.interbrew.com). From the start, Interbrew wisely insisted it would move ahead provided (1) the local brand would receive total backing, (2) local management would be in charge, and (3) Interbrew would assist local management with technical, marketing, sales, distribution, and general management training. Borsodi eventually became one of the parent company's key subsidiaries and is now run entirely by Hungarian managers.

PURCHASE-OR-BUILD DECISION

Another important matter for managers is whether to purchase an existing business or to build a subsidiary abroad from the ground up—called a *greenfield investment*. An acquisition generally provides the investor with an existing plant and equipment as well as personnel. The acquiring firm may also benefit from the goodwill the existing company has built up over the years and, perhaps, brand recognition of the existing firm. The purchase of an existing business may also allow for alternative methods of financing the purchase, such as an exchange of stock ownership between the companies. Factors that can reduce the appeal of purchasing existing facilities include obsolete equipment, poor relations with workers, and an unsuitable location.

Mexico's Cemex, S.A. (www.cemex.com), is a multinational company that made a fortune by buying struggling, inefficient plants around the world and reengineering them. Chairman Lorenzo Zambrano has long figured that it was "Buy big globally, or be bought." The success of Cemex in using FDI has confounded, even rankled, its competitors in developed nations. An example is when Cemex borrowed money and carried out a $1.8 billion purchase of Spain's two largest cement companies, Valenciana and Sanson. Of the company's $8 billion in assets at the time, nearly half of the total was international.

But adequate facilities are sometimes simply unavailable and a company must go ahead with a greenfield investment. Because Poland is a source of skilled and inexpensive labor, it is an appealing location for car manufacturers. But the country had little in the way of advanced car-production facilities when General Motors (www.gm.com) was considering investing there. So, GM built a $320 million facility in Poland's Silesian region. The factory has the potential to produce 200,000 units annually—some of which are designated for export to profitable markets in Western Europe. However, greenfield investments can have their share of headaches—obtaining the necessary permits and financing and hiring local personnel can be a real problem in some markets.

We have only addressed some of the issues important to managers when considering purchasing or building in a market abroad. We will have more to say on this topic in Chapter 15 when we see how companies actually take on such an ambitious goal. In the meantime, for additional insight into the concerns of managers in this situation see the Global Manager titled "Investing Abroad? Be Prepared for Surprises."

PRODUCTION COSTS

There are many factors that affect the cost of production in any national market. For example, labor regulations can increase the hourly cost of production severalfold. Companies may be required to provide benefits packages for their employees that are over and above hourly wages. More time than was planned for might be required to train workers adequately to bring productivity up to an acceptable standard. Although the cost of land and the tax rate on profits can be lower in the local market (or purposely lowered to attract multinationals), it cannot be assumed that they will remain constant. Companies from around the world using Taiwan as a production base have witnessed rising wages and land prices that erode profits as the economy continues to industrialize. Companies are instead finding that China is their low-cost location of choice.

Rationalized Production   One approach companies use to contain production costs is **rationalized production**—a system of production in which each of a product's components are produced where the cost of producing that component is lowest. All the components are then brought together at one central location for assembly into the final product. Consider the typical stuffed animal made in China whose components are all imported to China (with the exception of the polycore thread with which it's sewn). The stuffed animal's eyes are molded in Japan. Its outfit is imported from France. The polyester-fiber stuffing comes from either Germany or the United States, and the pile-fabric "fur" is produced in Korea. Only final assembly of these components occurs in China.

Although highly efficient, a potential problem with this production model is that a work stoppage in one country can bring the entire production process to a standstill. For example, production of automobiles is highly rationalized, with parts coming in

rationalized production
System of production in which each of a product's components are produced where the cost of producing that component is lowest.

GLOBAL MANAGER

Investing Abroad? Be Prepared for Surprises

The decision of whether to build facilities in a market abroad or to purchase the existing operations of a company already in the local market can be a difficult task. Managers can minimize their risk by preparing themselves and their company for any number of surprises that their firms might face, including the following:

➡ **Human Resource Policies.** This aspect of FDI often holds the biggest surprise. Many managers erroneously assume the policies they use at home can simply be imported into the local culture with minimal revision. Unfortunately, these policies seldom address local customs and abide by local regulations. For example, many European countries require government approval for a plant to run a continuous operation in several shifts and have regulations governing shift work for women in certain manufacturing operations.

➡ **Labor Costs.** This factor of production is often higher than expected. For instance, Denmark has a minimum wage of about $13 an hour—more than twice as high as that of the United States. Mexico has a minimum daily rate of only $3. But the effective rate is nearly double because of government-mandated benefits and employment practices.

➡ **Mandated Benefits.** These often cover elements totally alien to managers and can include things such as company-supplied clothing and meals, required profit sharing, guaranteed employment contracts, and generous dismissal policies. Costs of these programs can top 100 percent of an employee's wages. Such programs are typically nonnegotiable and strictly enforced. Violations can result in government seizure of company property, assessment of large fines, and even prison terms for executives.

➡ **Unions.** These differ a great deal from country to country. In some countries organized labor is present at almost every company, although relations can be more or less hostile than in the home market and strikes at individual plants can be frequent or seldom. In Scandinavia, rather than dealing with a single union at its plant, an employer may have to negotiate with five or six—each representing a different skill or profession.

➡ **Economic-Development Incentives.** Existing in most countries these can be substantial and can change constantly. For example, the European Union is trying to standardize incentives based on unemployment levels. But some member countries continually stretch the rules and several have been penalized for exceeding guidelines.

➡ **Information.** Comprehensive and comparable data on vital factors such as the availability of labor, utility services, and plant sites simply do not exist in some countries. Such information, although varying in quality and availability, is generally good in developed countries; in undeveloped countries it is suspect at best. Therefore, any firm considering international expansion must perform careful research early in the decision process.

➡ **Personal and Political Contacts.** These types of contacts can be extremely important—especially in developing and emerging nations—and are sometimes the only way to get operations established. But using them can be difficult. Moreover, complying with practices that are common in the local market can create ethical dilemmas for managers.

from a multitude of countries for assembly. When the United Auto Workers (www.uaw.com) union held a strike for many weeks against General Motors (www.gm.com) several years ago, many of GM's international assembly plants were threatened. The plant at which that the UAW chose to launch their strike supplied brake pads to virtually all of GM's plants throughout North America.

Case: The Mexican Maquiladora   Stretching 2,000 miles from the Pacific Ocean to the Gulf of Mexico, the 130-mile-wide strip along the U.S.–Mexican border may well be North America's fastest-growing region. With 11 million people and $150 billion in output, the region's economy is larger than that of Poland's and close to the size of Thailand's. The combination of a low-wage regional economy nestled next to a prosperous giant is now becoming a model for other regions that are split by wage or technology gaps. Some analysts compare the U.S.–Mexican border region to that between Hong Kong and its manufacturing realm, China's Guangdong Province. Officials from cities along the border between Germany and Poland are also studying the U.S.–Mexican experience. Yet, ethical dilemmas have arisen over the wide gap between Mexican and U.S. wages and over the loss of U.S. union jobs to *maquiladora* nonunion jobs. *Maquiladoras* also do not operate under the same stringent environmental regulations to which companies across the border must adhere.

Cost of Research and Development   As the role of technology as a powerful competitive factor continues to grow, the soaring cost of developing subsequent stages of technology has led multinationals to engage in cross-border alliances and acquisitions. For instance, huge multinational pharmaceutical companies are intensely interested in the pioneering biotechnology work done by smaller, entrepreneurial start-ups. Cadus Pharmaceutical Corporation of Tarrytown, New York, is using yeast to determine the function of 400 genes that are related to so-called receptor molecules. Many disorders are associated with the improper functioning of these receptors—making them good targets for drug development. A few years ago, Cadus invested up to $68 million with the United Kingdom's SmithKline Beecham to allow it access to its yeast work. Glaxo, another British pharmaceutical giant, cut a deal with Sequana Therapeutics Inc., a genomics firm in La Jolla, California, for access to its work on nematodes.[10] (Note: Glaxo and SmithKline Beecham have since merged, (**www.gsk.com**).)

One indicator of the significance of technology in foreign direct investment is the amount of R&D being conducted by affiliates of parent companies in other countries. The globalization of innovation and the phenomenon of foreign direct investment in R&D are not necessarily motivated by demand factors such as the size of local markets. Instead, foreign direct investment in R&D appears more likely to be spurred by supply factors such as gaining access to high-quality scientific and technical human capital.[11]

CUSTOMER KNOWLEDGE

The behavior of buyers is frequently an important issue in the decision of whether to undertake foreign direct investment. A local presence can help companies gain valuable knowledge about customers that could not be obtained in the home market. For example, when customer preferences for a product differ a great deal from country to country, a local presence might help companies to better understand such preferences and tailor their products accordingly.

Some countries have quality reputations in certain product categories. German automotive engineering, Italian shoes, French perfume, and Swiss watches impress customers as being of superior quality. Because of these perceptions, it can be profitable for a firm to produce its product in the country with the quality reputation although the company is based in another country. For example, a cologne or perfume producer might want to bottle its fragrance in France and give it a French name. Such image appeal can be strong enough to encourage foreign direct investment.

FOLLOWING CLIENTS

Firms commonly engage in foreign direct investment when doing so puts them close to firms for which they act as a supplier. This practice of "following clients" can be expected in industries in which many component parts are obtained from suppliers with whom a manufacturer has a close working relationship. It also tends to result in clusters in which companies that supply one another's inputs congregate in a certain geographic region (see Chapter 5). For example, when Mercedes (**www.mercedes.com**) opened its first international plant just outside Tuscaloosa, Alabama, as many as nine automobile-parts suppliers also moved to the area from Germany—bringing with them additional investment in the millions of dollars.

FOLLOWING RIVALS

FDI decisions frequently resemble a "follow the leader" scenario in industries with a limited number of large firms. In other words, many of these firms believe that choosing not to make a move parallel to that of the "first mover" might result in being shut out of a potentially lucrative market. For example, when firms based in industrial countries moved back into South Africa after the end of apartheid, their competitors followed. Of course, each market can sustain only a certain number of rivals. Firms that cannot compete will choose the "least damaging option." This seems to have been the case for Pepsi (**www.pepsi.com**), which went back into South Africa in 1994, but withdrew in 1997 after being crushed by Coke (**www.cocacola.com**).

GOVERNMENT INTERVENTION IN FOREIGN DIRECT INVESTMENT

Nations often intervene in the flow of FDI to protect their cultural heritages, domestic companies, and, of course, jobs. Thus, nations frequently enact laws, create regulations, or construct administrative hurdles with which companies from other nations must deal if they wish to invest in the nation.

In a general sense, a bias toward protectionism or openness is rooted in a nation's culture, history, and politics. Values, attitudes, and beliefs form the basis for much of a government's position regarding foreign direct investment. For example, South American nations with strong cultural ties to a European heritage (such as Argentina) are generally enthusiastic about investment received from European nations. South American nations with stronger indigenous influences (such as Ecuador) are generally less enthusiastic.

Opinions vary widely on the appropriate amount of foreign direct investment a country should allow. At one extreme are those who favor complete economic self-sufficiency and oppose any form of FDI. At the other extreme are those who favor free markets with no government intervention at all. However, most countries believe that

The French government, wanting to preserve its national culture, provides strong financial backing for projects promoting French culture. Asterix and Obelix, the Gallic warriors loved by comic fans worldwide, came to life in the most expensive film in French history: $48.2 million. Also receiving investment from Germany and Italy, the film provided an "image of resistance to American cinematographic imperialism," as French newspaper, *Le Monde*, put it.

a certain amount of FDI is desirable to raise national output and enhance the standard of living for their peoples. Thus, in between the two extremes are those who believe that the decision of whether to allow investment depends on the particular situation. Besides philosophical ideals, countries intervene in FDI for a host of far more practical reasons. But before we take a look at those reasons, we must understand what is meant by a country's *balance of payments*.

BALANCE OF PAYMENTS

balance of payments
A national accounting system that records all payments to entities in other countries and all receipts coming into the nation.

A country's **balance of payments** is a national accounting system that records all payments to entities in other countries and all receipts coming into the nation. International transactions that result in payments (outflows) to entities in other nations are reductions in the balance of payments accounts and therefore recorded with a minus sign. International transactions that result in receipts (inflows) from other nations are additions to the balance of payments accounts and thus recorded with a plus sign. For example, when a U.S. company buys 40 percent of the publicly traded stock of a Mexican company on Mexico's stock market, the U.S. balance of payments records the transaction as an outflow of capital and it is recorded with a minus sign. Table 7.1 shows the balance of payments accounts for the United States. As shown in the table, any nation's balance of payments consists of two major components—the *current account* and *capital account*. Let's now describe each of these accounts and discuss how to read Table 7.1.

current account
A national account that records transactions involving the import and export of goods and services, income receipts on assets abroad, and income payments on foreign assets inside the country.

Current Account   The **current account** is a national account that records transactions involving the import and export of goods and services, income receipts on assets abroad, and income payments on foreign assets inside the country. The *merchandise*

TABLE 7.1	U.S. Balance of Payments Accounts, 2000 (U.S. $ millions)	
Current Account		
Exports of goods and services and income receipts	1,418,568	
Merchandise	772,210	
Services	293,492	
Income receipts on U.S. assets abroad	352,866	
Imports of goods and services and income payments		−1,809,099
Merchandise		−1,224,417
Services		−217,024
Income payments on foreign assets in U.S.		−367,658
Unilateral transfers		−54,136
Current account balance		−444,667
Capital Account		
Increase in U.S. assets abroad (capital outflow)		−580,952
U.S. official reserve assets		−290
Other U.S. government assets		−944
U.S. private assets		−579,718
Foreign assets in the U.S. (capital inflow)	1,024,218	
Foreign official assets	37,619	
Other foreign assets	986,599	
Capital account balance	443,266	
Statistical discrepancy	55,537	

account in Table 7.1 includes exports and imports of tangible goods such as computer software, electronic components, and apparel. The *services* account includes exports and imports of services such as tourism, business consulting, and banking services. Suppose a company in the United States receives payment for consulting services provided to a company in another country. The receipt is recorded as an "export of services" and assigned a plus sign in the services account in the balance of payments.

The *income receipts* account includes income earned on U.S. assets held abroad. When a U.S. company's subsidiary in another country remits profits back to the parent in the United States, the receipt is recorded in the income receipts account and given a plus sign. The *income payments* account includes income paid to entities in other nations that is earned on assets they hold in the United States. For instance, when a French company's U.S. subsidiary sends profits earned in the United States back to the parent company in France, the transaction is recorded in the income payments account as an outflow and given a minus sign.

A **current account surplus** occurs when a country exports more goods and services and receives more income from abroad than it imports and pays abroad. Conversely, a **current account deficit** occurs when a country imports more goods and services and pays more abroad than it exports and receives from abroad. Table 7.1 shows that the United States had a current account deficit in 2000. See the World Business Survey, titled "Ups and Downs of Current Accounts," to see which nations are piling up the biggest surpluses and debts with the rest of the world.

Capital Account   The **capital account** is a national account that records transactions involving the purchase or sale of *assets*. Suppose a U.S. citizen buys shares of stock in a

current account surplus
When a country exports more goods and services and receives more income from abroad than it imports and pays abroad.

current account deficit
When a country imports more goods and services and pays more abroad than it exports and receives from abroad.

capital account
A national account that records transactions involving the purchase or sale of assets.

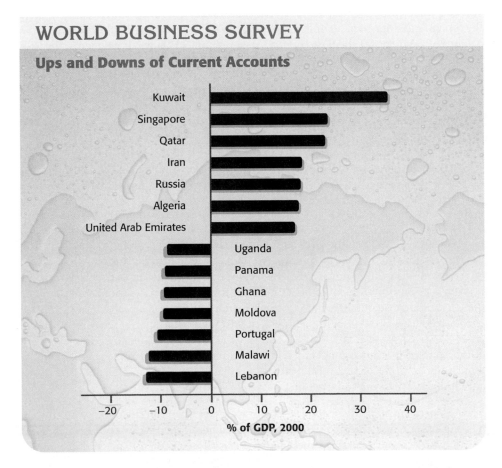

WORLD BUSINESS SURVEY

Ups and Downs of Current Accounts

Mexican company on Mexico's stock market. The transaction would show up on the capital accounts of both the United States and Mexico—as an outflow of assets from the United States and an inflow of assets to Mexico. Conversely, suppose a Mexican investor buys real estate in the United States. That transaction also shows up on the capital accounts of both nations—as an inflow of assets to the United States and as an outflow of assets from Mexico. Although the balances of the current and capital accounts should be the same, there commonly is error due to recording methods. This figure is recorded in Table 7.1 as a *statistical discrepancy*.

REASONS FOR INTERVENTION BY THE HOST COUNTRY

A number of reasons underlie a government's decisions regarding foreign direct investment by international companies. Let's now look at the two main reasons countries intervene in FDI flows—the *balance-of-payments* and *to obtain resources and benefits*.

Balance of Payments   Many governments see intervention as the only way to keep their balance of payments under control. First, because foreign direct investment inflows are recorded as additions to the balance of payments, a nation gets a balance-of-payments boost from an initial FDI inflow. Second, as we saw in Chapter 6, countries can impose local content requirements on investors from other nations coming in for the purpose of local production. This gives local companies the chance to become suppliers to the production operation. This can help to reduce the nation's imports and thereby improve its balance of payments. Third, exports (if any) generated by the new production operation can have a favorable impact on the host country's balance of payments.

But when companies repatriate profits back to their home countries, they deplete the foreign exchange reserves of their host countries. These capital outflows decrease the balance of payments of the host country. To shore up its balance of payments, the host nation may prohibit or restrict the nondomestic company from removing profits to its home country.

Alternatively, host countries conserve their foreign exchange reserves when international companies reinvest their earnings. Reinvesting in local manufacturing facilities can also improve the competitiveness of local producers and boost a host nation's exports—thus improving its balance-of-payments position.

Obtain Resources and Benefits   Beyond balance-of-payments reasons, governments might intervene in FDI flows to acquire resources and benefits such as *technology* and *management skills and employment*.

Access to Technology   Investment in technology, whether in products or processes, tends to increase the productivity and competitiveness of individual nations. That is why host nations have a strong incentive to encourage the importation of technology. For years, developing countries in Asia were introduced to expertise in industrial processes as multinationals set up factories within their borders. But today some of them are trying to acquire and develop their own technological expertise. Singapore has been particularly successful in gaining access to high technology. German industrial giant Siemens (www.siemens.com) chose Singapore as the site for an Asia-Pacific microelectronics design center employing 60 people. Singapore has also gained valuable semiconductor technology by joining with U.S.-based Texas Instruments (www.ti.com) and others to set up the country's first wafer-fabrication plant.

Management Skills and Employment   As we saw in Chapter 4, many once-communist nations suffer from a lack of the management skills needed to succeed in the global economy. By encouraging FDI, these nations can allow talented managers to come in who can train locals so that, over time, the international competitiveness of their domestic companies will improve. Furthermore, locals who are trained in modern management techniques may eventually leave the firm to start their own local businesses—further expanding employment opportunities. However, detractors argue that although FDI may create jobs, it may also destroy jobs because less competitive local firms may be forced out of business.

REASONS FOR INTERVENTION BY THE HOME COUNTRY

Home nations (those from which international companies launch their investments) may also seek to encourage or discourage *outflows* of FDI for a variety of reasons. However, there generally tend to be fewer concerns among home nations because they tend to be prosperous, industrialized nations. For these countries, an outward investment seldom has a national impact—unlike the impact on developing or emerging nations that receive the FDI. Nevertheless, among the most common reasons for discouraging outward FDI are the following:

➡ *Investing in other nations sends resources out of the home country.* As a result, fewer resources are used for development and economic growth at home. On the other hand, profits on assets abroad that are returned home increase both a home country's balance of payments and its available resources.

➡ *Outgoing FDI may ultimately damage a nation's balance of payments by taking the place of its exports.* This can occur when a company creates a production facility in a market abroad, the output of which replaces exports that used to be sent there from the home country. For example, if a Volkswagen (www.vw.com) plant in the United States fills a demand that U.S. buyers would otherwise satisfy with purchases of German-made autos, Germany's balance of payments is correspondingly decreased. But although the investment has an initial negative balance-of-payments effect, the nation's balance of payments is positively affected when companies repatriate profits earned abroad. Thus, despite the initial negative impact, an international investment might make a positive contribution to the balance-of-payments position of the country in the long term.

➡ *Jobs resulting from outgoing investments may replace jobs at home.* This is often the most contentious issue for home countries. The relocation of production to a low-wage nation can have a strong impact on a locale or region. However, the impact is rarely national and its effects are often muted by other job opportunities in the economy. In addition, there may be an offsetting improvement in home-country employment if additional exports are needed to support the activity that was represented by the outgoing FDI. For example, if Hyundai (www.hyundai.com) of South Korea builds an automobile manufacturing plant in Brazil, Korean employment may increase in order to supply the Brazilian plant with parts.

But foreign direct investment is not always a negative influence on home nations. In fact, under certain circumstances they actually might encourage it. Specifically, countries promote outgoing FDI for the following reasons:

➡ *Outward FDI can increase long-term competitiveness.* Today, businesses frequently compete on a global scale. The most competitive firms tend to be those that conduct business in the most favorable location anywhere in the world, continuously improve their performance relative to competitors, and derive technological advantages from alliances formed with other companies. Japanese companies have become masterful at benefiting from FDI and cooperative arrangements with companies from other nations. The key to their success is that Japanese companies see every cooperative venture as a learning opportunity.

➡ *Nations may encourage FDI in industries that they have determined to be "sunset" industries.* Sunset industries are those that use outdated and obsolete technologies or employ low-wage workers with few skills. These jobs are not greatly appealing to countries that have industries that pay skilled workers high wages. By allowing some of these jobs to go abroad and retraining workers in higher-paying skilled work, they can upgrade their economies toward "sunrise" industries. This represents a trade-off for governments between a short-term loss of jobs and the long-term benefit of developing workers' skills.

GOVERNMENT POLICY INSTRUMENTS AND FDI

Over time, both host and home nations have developed a range of methods to either promote or restrict FDI (see Table 7.2). Governments use these tools for many reasons, including improving balance-of-payments positions, acquiring resources, and, in the case of outward investment, keeping jobs at home. Let's now take a look at these methods.

HOST COUNTRIES: RESTRICTION

Host countries have a variety of methods to restrict incoming FDI. These take two general forms—*ownership restrictions* and *performance demands*.

Ownership Restrictions   Governments can impose *ownership restrictions* that prohibit nondomestic companies from investing in certain industries or from owning certain types of businesses. Most often, such prohibitions apply to businesses in cultural industries and companies vital to national security. For instance, as India and some Islamic countries in the Middle East try to protect traditional values, accepting investment by Western companies is a controversial issue between purists and moderates. Also, most nations do not allow FDI in their domestic weapons or national defense firms.

Another ownership restriction is a requirement that nondomestic investors hold less than a 50 percent stake in local firms when they undertake foreign direct investment. This requirement was popular in earlier times when host countries thought that 51 percent local ownership gave them control over a local subsidiary.

But nations are eliminating such restrictions because companies today often can choose another location that has no such restriction in place. For example, when GM was deciding whether to invest in an aging automobile plant in Jakarta, Indonesia, the Indonesian government scrapped its ownership restriction of an eventual forced sale to Indonesians. Indonesia's action was no doubt prompted by the fact that China and Vietnam were also courting GM for its financial investment.

TABLE 7.2	Methods of Promoting and Restricting FDI	
	FDI Promotion	**FDI Restriction**
Host Countries	Tax incentives Low-interest loans Infrastructure improvements	Ownership restrictions Performance demands
Home Countries	Insurance Loans Tax breaks Political pressure	Differential tax rates Sanctions

Performance Demands   More common than ownership requirements are *performance demands* that influence how international companies operate in the host nation. Although typically viewed as intrusive, most international companies allow for them in the same way they allow for home-country regulations. Performance demands include ensuring that a portion of the product's content originates locally, stipulating the portion of output that must be exported, or requiring that certain technologies be transferred to local businesses.

HOST COUNTRIES: PROMOTION

Host countries also offer a variety of incentives to encourage inflows of FDI. Again, these take two general forms—*financial incentives* and *infrastructure improvements*.

Financial Incentives   Host governments of all nations grant companies financial incentives if they will invest within their borders. One method includes *tax incentives* such as lower tax rates or offers to waive taxes on local profits for a period of time—extending as far out as five or more years. A country may also offer *low-interest loans* to investors.

However, the downside of incentives such as these is that it can allow multinationals to create bidding wars between locations that are vying for the investment. In such cases, the company eventually invests in the most appealing region after the locations endure rounds of escalating incentives. Companies have even been accused of engaging other governments in negotiations so as to force concessions from locations already selected for investment. The cost to taxpayers of snaring FDI can be several times what the actual jobs themselves pay—especially in the case of a bidding war.

Infrastructure Improvements   Because of the problems associated with financial incentives, some governments are taking an alternative route to luring investment. Lasting benefits for communities surrounding the investment location can result from making local *infrastructure improvements*—better seaports suitable for containerized shipping, improved roads, and increased telecommunications systems. For instance, Malaysia is carving a $40 billion Multimedia Super Corridor (MSC) into a region's forested surroundings. The region has planned a paperless government, an intelligent city called Cyberjaya, two telesuburbs, a technology park, a multimedia university, and an intellectual-property-protection park. The MSC is dedicated to creating the most advanced technologies in telecommunications, medicine, distance learning, and remote manufacturing.

HOME COUNTRIES: RESTRICTION

To limit the effects of outbound FDI on the national economy, home governments may exercise either of the following two options:

➡ Impose *differential tax rates* that charge income from earnings abroad at a higher rate than domestic earnings.
➡ Impose outright *sanctions* that prohibit domestic firms from making investments in certain nations.

HOME COUNTRIES: PROMOTION

On the other hand, to encourage outbound FDI, home-country governments can do any of the following:

➡ Offer *insurance* to cover the risks of investments abroad, including, among others, insurance against expropriation of assets, losses from armed conflict, kidnappings, and terrorist attacks.

➡ Grant *loans* to firms wishing to increase their investments abroad. A home-country government may also guarantee the loans that a company takes from financial institutions.

➡ Offer *tax breaks* on profits earned abroad or negotiate special tax treaties. For example, several multinational agreements reduce or eliminate the practice of double taxation—profits earned abroad being taxed both in the home and host countries.

➡ Apply *political pressure* on other nations to get them to relax their restrictions on inbound investments. Non-Japanese companies often find it very difficult to invest inside Japan. The United States, for one, repeatedly pressures the Japanese government to open its market further to FDI. But because such pressure has achieved little success, many U.S. companies cooperate with local Japanese businesses.

A FINAL WORD

In this chapter, we learned about the second major way of conducting international business—foreign direct investment (FDI). We saw that, like trade decisions, many factors influence a company's decision about whether to invest in markets abroad. Companies can be thwarted in their efforts or encouraged to invest in a nation, depending on the philosophies of the home and host governments. The balance-of-payments positions of both home and host nations are also important because FDI flows affect the economic health of both nations. We learned that companies ranging from massive global corporations to adventurous entrepreneurs all contribute to FDI flows.

The next chapter will conclude our study of the trade and investment aspects of the international business environment. Specifically, we see how groups of nations, anywhere from just a few to several dozen, are joining forces to integrate their economies and thereby facilitate international trade and investment.

There is a variety of additional material available on the Companion Website that accompanies this book. You can access this information by visiting the Website at (**www.prenhall.com/wild**).

summary

❶ Describe the worldwide patterns of *foreign direct investment (FDI)* and the reasons for these patterns.
Foreign direct investment (FDI) continues to expand rapidly, though not at the pace of the 1990s. After growing about 20 percent per year in the first half of the 1990s, FDI grew by about 40 percent per year in the second half of the decade. Although the global economic slowdown in 2000 caused FDI to grow just 18 percent that year, it did reach a record $1.3 trillion. FDI also continues to grow faster than both world production and trade.

Developed countries account for more than three-quarters of global FDI inflows. In comparison, developing countries' share of world FDI flows declined to 19 percent, compared to the peak of 41 percent in 1994. The world's 49 poorest nations attracted just 0.3 percent of world inflows in 2000.

Among developed countries, European Union nations, the United States, and Japan accounted for over 70 percent of world inflows and 82 percent of outflows in 2000. The United States remains the world's largest FDI recipient country. In 2000, the United Kingdom was the top worldwide source of FDI. FDI inflows to all of Africa accounted for about 1 percent of the world total in 2000.

Globalization and a growing number of *mergers and acquisitions* account for the growth in FDI. This growth pattern and its causes are expected to continue well into the future.

❷ Describe each of the *theories* that attempt to explain why foreign direct investment occurs. The *international product life cycle* states that a company will begin by exporting its product and later undertake foreign direct investment as a product moves through its life cycle. In the new product stage, a good is produced in the home country. But in the maturing product stage, the company directly invests in production facilities in the countries in which demand is high. In the final standardized product stage, a company builds production capacity in low-cost nations to serve its markets around the world.

Market imperfections theory states that when an imperfection in the market makes a transaction less efficient than it could be, a company will undertake foreign direct investment to internalize the transaction and thereby remove the imperfection.

The *eclectic theory* states that firms undertake foreign direct investment when the features of a particular location combine with ownership and internalization advantages to make a location appealing for investment. When all these advantages are present, a company will undertake FDI.

The *market power* theory states that a firm tries to establish a dominant market presence in an industry by undertaking foreign direct investment. One way a company achieves market power is through backward or forward *vertical integration.*

3 **Discuss the important *management issues* in the foreign direct investment decision.** Companies investing abroad are often concerned with *controlling* activities in the local market. But local governments might require a company to hire local managers or require that all goods produced in a local facility be exported so they do not compete with products of domestic firms.

Another matter of concern is whether to *purchase an existing business or to build an international subsidiary from the ground up.* An acquisition generally provides the investor with an existing plant and equipment as well as personnel. On the other hand, factors that reduce the appeal of purchasing existing facilities include obsolete equipment, poor relations with workers, and an unsuitable location. But adequate facilities are sometimes simply unavailable and a company must go ahead with a *greenfield investment.*

Labor regulations can increase the hourly *cost of production* several times. One approach companies use to contain production costs is *rationalized production*—a system of production in which each of a product's components are produced in the location in which the cost of producing that component is lowest.

A local market presence might help companies gain valuable knowledge about the *behavior of buyers*

that it could not obtain from the home market. Firms commonly engage in foreign direct investment when doing so puts them close to both *client* firms and *rival* firms.

4 **Explain why *governments* intervene in the free flow of foreign direct investment.** Both host and home countries interfere in the free flow of FDI for a variety of reasons. One reason that governments of *host* countries intervene in foreign direct investment flows is to protect their *balance of payments*. Allowing FDI to come in gives a nation a balance-of-payments boost. Countries also improve their balance-of-payments position from the exports of local production operations created by FDI. However, when direct investors send profits made locally back to the parent company in the home country, the balance of payments decreases. Local investment in *technology* also tends to increase the productivity and competitiveness of the nation. By encouraging FDI, nations can also bring in people with *management skills* who can train locals and thus improve the competitiveness of local companies. Furthermore, many local *jobs* are also created as a result of incoming FDI.

Home countries also intervene in FDI flows. For one thing, investing in other nations sends resources out of the home country—lowering the balance of payments. On the other hand, profits on assets abroad that are returned home increase a home country's balance of payments. Also, outgoing FDI may ultimately damage a nation's balance of payments by taking the place of its exports. In addition, jobs that result from outgoing investments may replace jobs at home that were based on exports to the host country.

5 **Discuss the *policy instruments* that governments use to promote and restrict foreign direct investment.** Host-country governments can impose *ownership restrictions* that prohibit nondomestic companies from investing in businesses in cultural industries and those vital to national security. They can also create *performance demands* that influence how international companies operate in the host nation.

They can also grant companies *tax incentives* such as lower tax rates or offer to waive taxes on local profits for a period of time. A country may also offer *low-interest loans* to investors. Some governments prefer to lure investment by making local *infrastructure improvements*—better seaports suitable for containerized shipping, improved roads, and increased telecommunications systems.

To limit the effects of outbound FDI on the national economy, home governments may impose *differential tax rates* that charge income from earnings abroad at a higher rate than domestic earnings. Or they can impose outright *sanctions* that prohibit domestic firms from making investments in certain nations. On the other hand, to encourage outbound FDI home-country governments can offer *insurance* to cover the risks of investments abroad. They can also grant *loans* to firms that wish to increase their investments abroad. A home-country government may also guarantee the loans that a company takes from financial institutions. They might also offer *tax breaks* on profits earned abroad or negotiate special tax treaties. Finally, they may apply *political pressure* on other nations to get them to relax their restrictions on inbound investments.

questions **for review**

1. What is *foreign direct investment (FDI)*? Explain how FDI differs from *portfolio investment*.

2. What are three factors that contribute to the growth in FDI?

3. Identify at least three motivations behind companies' decisions to engage in FDI.

4. What are the main destinations and sources of FDI? Describe how each is changing.

5. Describe how the *international product life cycle* explains FDI. What are the three product stages?

6. How does the theory of *market imperfections (internalization)* explain FDI?

7. Explain the *eclectic theory*. Identify the three advantages that must be present for FDI to occur, according to the theory.

8. How does the theory of *market power* explain the occurrence of FDI? Describe the importance of *vertical integration* to the theory.

9. Why is control important to the FDI decision?

10. Describe the role of production costs in the FDI decision. What is *rationalized production*?

11. How does the need for customer knowledge, following clients, and following rivals impact the FDI decision?

12. What is a country's *balance of payments*? Explain its usefulness briefly.

13. Identify the difference between the *current account* and the *capital account*.

14. For what reasons do *host* countries intervene in FDI?

15. For what reasons do *home* countries intervene in FDI?

16. Identify the main methods *host* countries use to restrict and promote FDI.

17. What methods do *home* countries use to intervene in FDI?

questions **for discussion**

1. You overhear your superior tell another manager in the company, "I'm fed up with this nation's companies always leaving the country to hire low-wage workers elsewhere. Don't any of them have any national pride?" The other manager responds, "I disagree. It is every company's duty to make as much profit as possible for its owners. If that means going abroad to reduce costs, so be it." Do you agree with either of these managers? Why or why not? Now step into the conversation and give a description of where you stand on the issue.

2. The global carmaker you work for is investing in an automobile assembly facility in Costa Rica with a local partner. Explain the potential reasons for this investment. Will your company want to exercise a great deal of control over this operation? Why or why not? What areas might your company want to exercise control over and what areas might it cede control to the partner?

3. This chapter presented several theories that have been proposed to explain the flow of foreign direct investment. Which of these theories seems most appealing to you? Why is it appealing? Can you think of one or more companies that seem to fit the pattern described by the theory? In your opinion, what faults do the alternative theories have?

in practice

Read the article below and answer the questions that follow.

Intel Ups Investment

MANILA, The Philippines—Intel Corp. plans to invest between $80 million and $100 million this year to upgrade and consolidate its semiconductor-assembly facilities in the Philippines, one of Intel's lowest-cost locations.

The investment primarily is aimed at supporting the company's push to increase production volumes of its high-end microprocessors for personal computers, which have been in tight supply in recent months because of manufacturing bottlenecks.

Following the upgrade, the factory in the Philippines' Cavite province will become Intel's largest global facility for assembly and final testing of its microprocessors and flash-memory chips, including state-of-the-art Pentium 4 processors, said Chit Ventura, an Intel spokeswoman in the Philippines. The additional cash injection will bring Intel's total investment in the Philippines, where the company has been operating for 27 years, to about $1.3 billion, said Ms. Ventura.

1. Investigate the economy of the Philippines and its neighbors. In what economic sectors is each country strong? Do the strengths of each country really complement one another or do they compete directly with one another? If you were considering investing in the Philippines, what management issues would concern you? Be specific.

2. This story tells of investment into the Philippines. But many Southeast Asian governments fear they are losing ground to China in the race to attract investments from multinational corporations. What do you think those governments could do to increase the attractiveness of their homelands for multinationals?

3. We live in an era of intense national competition to attract investment from abroad to create jobs and raise living standards. Find a recent article in the business press or on the World Wide Web that describes a company's action to relocate some or all of its business operations. What reasons are stated for the relocation? Has any consideration been given to the plight of the employees being put out of work?

projects

1. In the business press, locate at least two articles that discuss a cross-border merger or acquisition that has taken place within the past year. What reasons did each company give for the merger or acquisition? Was it a marriage of equals or did a larger partner absorb a far smaller one? Do the articles identify any internal issues that managers had to deal with following the merger or acquisition? What is the performance of the new company? Write a one- to two-page report of your findings.

2. With several of your classmates, select a country that interests you. For the most recent data you can find, what is its balance-of-payments position? What is its current account balance? What is its capital account balance? What are some possible causes for the surplus or deficit you see? What are some of the effects on the nation of this surplus or deficit? Prepare a brief report and present it to the class.

3. With one or two of your classmates, visit your city's chamber of commerce office and/or its economic development office. Does the city have a practice of offering incentives to lure companies into the area? Does it try to attract international companies and, if so, how? Does it try to persuade companies in certain industries to invest in the region? Ask other questions you feel are pertinent. Present your findings to the class.

MERCEDES-BENZ: FOOTLOOSE IN TUSCALOOSA

"Aloof." "Serious." "Not youthful." Definitely "not fun." These were the unfortunate epithets applied to Mercedes-Benz by a market research firm that assesses product personalities. Research among American dealers also revealed that consumers felt so intimidated by Mercedes that they wouldn't sit in the cars at the showroom. In order to increase sales and broaden the market to a more youthful and value-conscious consumer, Mercedes-Benz (www.mercedes.com) of North America came up with a series of inventive, free-spirited ads featuring stampeding rhinos and bobbing aliens. Although the new ads boosted sales, the company needed more than a new marketing message to ensure its future growth. What it needed was an all-new Mercedes. Enter the Mercedes M-Class, a sports utility vehicle (SUV). With a base price of $35,000 and a luxury lineage, Mercedes placed its M-Class to compete squarely against the Ford Explorer and Jeep Grand Cherokee.

Not only was the M-Class Mercedes' first SUV, but it was also the first car that Mercedes had manufactured outside of Germany—in the heart of Dixie, no less. The rough-hewn town of Vance, Alabama (population 400), where people hang out at the local barbecue joint, is the last place you'd expect to find button-down engineers from Stuttgart, Germany. But this small town outside of Tuscaloosa appealed to Mercedes for several reasons. Labor costs in the U.S. Deep South are 50 percent lower than in Germany. Also, Alabama offered an attractive $250 million in tax refunds and other incentives to win the much-needed Mercedes jobs. Mercedes also wanted to be closer to the crucial U.S. market and to create a plant from the ground up, one that would be a model for its future international operations.

The gleaming, E-shaped Mercedes plant is the brainchild of engineer-turned-CEO, Andreas Renschler. When Japanese carmakers entered the U.S. market in the 1980s, they reproduced their car-building philosophies, cultures, production practices, and management styles in the United States. But Mercedes started with the proverbial blank sheet of paper. In order to appeal to U.S. workers, Mercedes knew it had to abandon the rigid hierarchy of the typical Mercedes production line and create a more egalitarian shop floor. Thus, administrative offices in the Vance plant run through the middle of the manufacturing area, and although it is all glassed in, team members still have easy access to administrators. The plant is also designed so that workers can unilaterally stop the assembly line to correct manufacturing problems. So far, the system has been a catalyst to communication among the Alabama plant's 1,500 U.S. workers, German trainers, and diverse management team that includes executives from both Detroit and Japan. Even so, Mercedes spent an enormous amount of time and effort to train its U.S. workforce. Explains Sven Schoolman, a 31-year-old trainer from Sindelfingen, "In Germany, we don't say we build a car. We say we build a Mercedes. We had to teach that."

So far the Mercedes' M-class is competing very well against the entrenched competition. The company is also gaining valuable experience in how to set up and operate a plant in another country. "It was once sacrosanct to talk about our cars being 'Made in Germany,'" said Jurgen E. Schrempp, CEO of Mercedes' parent, DaimlerChrysler (www.daimlerchrysler.com). "We have to change that to 'Made by Mercedes,' and never mind where they are assembled."

thinking globally

1. What were the chief factors involved in Mercedes' decision to undertake FDI in the United States?

2. Why do you think Mercedes decided to build the plant from the ground up in Alabama rather than buying an existing plant in, say Detroit?

3. Do you think Mercedes risks diluting its "Made in Germany" reputation for engineering quality by building its M-class in Alabama? Why or why not?

4. What do you see as the pros and cons of Mercedes' approach to managing FDI—abandoning the culture and some of the practices of its home country? What are the pros and cons of the approach of the Japanese carmakers—trying to duplicate the culture and production practices of the home country?

a question of ethics

1. It is becoming more common for companies to promise manufacturing contracts to overseas suppliers in exchange for entry into that country's market. Labor union representatives argue that these kinds of deals are made at the expense of jobs at home. After all, if a company can have parts made in China at lower wages, why keep factories going at home? They also are concerned that the transfer of technology will breed strong competitors in other nations and thereby threaten even more domestic jobs. However, others argue that the increase in sales abroad actually helps create more jobs at home. Discuss the ethics of companies contracting out production to factories abroad in exchange for sales contracts.

2. In order to become a major export platform for the semiconductor industry, Malaysia's government not only offered tax breaks but also guaranteed that electronics workers would be prohibited from organizing independent labor unions. The government decreed that the goal of national development required a "union-free" environment for the "pioneers" of semiconductors. Under pressure from U.S. labor unions, the Malaysian government offered a weak alternative to industry unions—company-by-company "in-house" unions. Yet as soon as workers organized one at a Harris Electronics plant, the 21 union leaders were fired and the new union disbanded. In another instance, when French-owned Thomson Electronics inherited a Malaysian factory with a union of 3,000, it closed the plant and moved the work to Vietnam.

Newly industrialized nations such as Malaysia feel that their futures depend on investment by multinationals. Their governments are acutely aware that in the absence of incentives such as a "union-free" workforce, international companies can easily take their investment elsewhere. Discuss the problems that these governments face in balancing the needs of their citizens with the long-term quest for economic development.

8 regional economic integration

LEARNING OBJECTIVES

After studying this chapter, you should be able to

1. Define *regional economic integration,* and identify its five levels.

2. Discuss the *benefits* and *drawbacks* associated with regional economic integration.

3. Describe regional integration in *Europe,* and discuss its future enlargement.

4. Discuss regional integration in the *Americas,* and analyze its future prospects.

5. Characterize regional integration in *Asia,* and discuss how it differs from integration elsewhere.

6. Describe regional integration in the *Middle East* and *Africa,* and explain why progress there has been slow.

BEACONS

A Look Back

CHAPTER 7 examined recent patterns of foreign direct investment. We explored the theories that try to explain why it occurs and saw how governments influence investment flows.

A Look at This Chapter

This chapter explores the trend toward greater integration of national economies. We first examine the reasons why nations are making significant efforts at regional integration. We then study the most prominent regional trading blocs in place around the world today.

A Look Ahead

CHAPTER 9 begins our inquiry into the international financial system. We describe the structure of the international capital market and explain how the foreign exchange market operates.

Think Global, Act Regional?

VEVEY, Switzerland—The products of Switzerland-based Nestlé (**www.nestle.com**) are available in nearly every country on the planet, even in North Korea. The company has brilliantly turned humdrum products like bottled water and pet food into well-known global brands.

Nestlé, as the world's largest food company, does business across cultural borders 24 hours a day—earning just 2 percent of its sales at home. Yet food is an integral part of the social fabric of every nation. That is why Nestlé tries to respect the cultural and political traditions of countries in which its products are produced and sold. Years ago, Nestlé was blamed for the deaths of infants in Africa because mothers were inadequately instructed and used impure water to mix Nestlé's infant formulas. When it markets its infant foods today, Nestlé tries to be more sensitive to the traditional ways in which babies are fed. Companies like Nestlé also need to watch for changes in attitudes that result from greater cross-cultural contact caused by regional integration.

The laws of regional trading blocs also affect the business activities of Nestlé. When Nestlé and Coca-Cola (**www.cocacola.com**) announced a joint venture to develop coffee and tea drinks, they first had to show the European Union (EU) Commission that they would not stifle competition across the region. Firms operating within the EU also have to abide by EU environmental protection laws. Nestlé minimizes the amount of packaging waste that results from use of its products and works closely with Germany, for example, to develop and manage waste-recovery programs.

As you read this chapter, think of all the ways business activities are affected when groups of nations band together in regional trading blocs.[1]

Regional trade agreements are changing the landscape of the global marketplace. Companies like Nestlé of Switzerland are finding that these agreements are lowering trade barriers and opening up new markets for goods and services. Markets otherwise off-limits because tariffs made imported products too expensive can become quite attractive once tariffs are lifted. But trade agreements can be double-edged swords for many companies. Not only do they allow domestic companies to seek new markets abroad, but they also let competitors from other nations enter the domestic market. Such mobility increases competition in every market that takes part in an agreement.

Trade agreements can allow a company to alter their strategies, sometimes radically. Nations in the Americas are working to create a free-trade area that runs from the northern tip of Alaska to the southern tip of South America. Some U.S. companies doing business in Latin America are pushing strongly for completion of this so-called Free Trade Area of the Americas (FTAA). United States–based Eastman Kodak (www.kodak.com) manufactures cameras, film, photographic paper, and chemicals in Brazil, Canada, Mexico, and the United States. The company estimates that it could save $25 million annually on import duties under the agreement. "If you've got tariff-free trade, you can use your factories in new and different ways," says Christopher Padilla, Eastman's director for international trade relations. In the absence of tariffs, multinationals can save money by supplying entire regions from just a few plants, rather than plants in each nation.[2]

We began Part Three of this book by discussing the gains resulting from specialization and trade. We now close by showing how groups of countries are cooperating to dismantle barriers that threaten these potential gains. In this chapter, we focus on regional efforts to encourage freer trade and investment. We begin by defining *regional economic integration* and describing its five different levels. Then we examine the benefits and drawbacks of regional trade agreements. Finally, we explore in detail several long-established trade agreements and several agreements that are in the earliest stages of development.

WHAT IS REGIONAL ECONOMIC INTEGRATION?

regional economic integration (regionalism)
Process whereby countries in a geographic region cooperate with one another to reduce or eliminate barriers to the international flow of products, people, or capital.

free-trade area
Economic integration whereby countries seek to remove all barriers to trade between themselves, but each country determines its own barriers against nonmembers.

The process whereby countries in a geographic region cooperate with one another to reduce or eliminate barriers to the international flow of products, people, or capital is called **regional economic integration** (also called *regionalism*). A group of nations in a geographic region undergoing economic integration is called a *regional trading bloc*.

The goal of nations undergoing economic integration is not only to increase cross-border trade and investment but also to raise living standards for their people. We saw in Chapter 5, for instance, how specialization and trade create real gains in terms of greater choice, lower prices, and increased productivity. Regional trade agreements are designed to help nations accomplish these objectives. Regional economic integration sometimes has additional goals, such as protection of intellectual property rights or the environment, or even eventual political union.

LEVELS OF REGIONAL INTEGRATION

Since the development of theories demonstrating the potential gains available through international trade, nations have tried to reap these benefits in a variety of ways. Figure 8.1 shows five potential levels (or degrees) of economic and political integration for regional trading blocs. A *free-trade area* is the lowest extent of national integration, *political union* the greatest. Each level of integration incorporates the properties of those levels that precede it.

Free-Trade Area   Economic integration whereby countries seek to remove all barriers to trade between themselves, but each country determines its own barriers against nonmembers is called a **free-trade area**. A free-trade area is the lowest level of economic

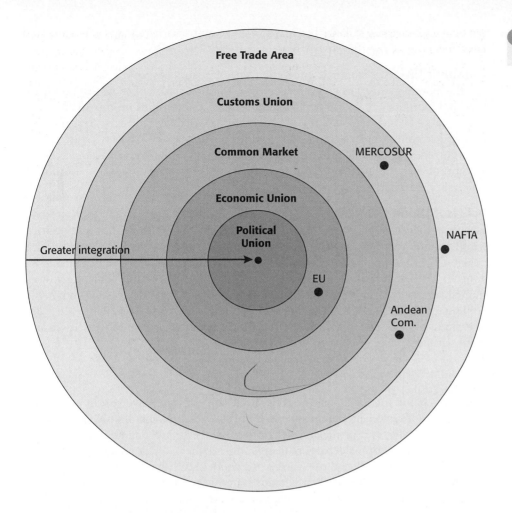

FIGURE 8.1

Levels of Regional Integration

integration that is possible between two or more countries. Countries belonging to the free-trade area strive to remove all tariffs and nontariff barriers, such as quotas and subsidies, on international trade in goods and services. However, each country is able to maintain whatever policy it sees fit against nonmember countries. These policies can differ widely from country to country. Countries belonging to a free-trade area also typically establish a process by which trade disputes can be resolved.

Customs Union Economic integration whereby countries remove all barriers to trade among themselves, but erect a common trade policy against nonmembers is called a **customs union**. Thus, the main difference between a free-trade area and a customs union is that the members of a customs union agree to treat trade with all nonmember nations in a similar manner. Countries belonging to a customs union might also negotiate as a single entity with other supranational organizations, such as the World Trade Organization.

Common Market Economic integration whereby countries remove all barriers to trade and the movement of labor and capital between themselves but erect a common trade policy against nonmembers is called a **common market**. Thus, a common market integrates the elements of free-trade areas and customs unions and adds the free movement of important factors of production—people and cross-border investment. Because it requires at least some cooperation in economic and labor policy, this level of integration is very difficult to attain. Furthermore, the benefits to individual countries

customs union
Economic integration whereby countries remove all barriers to trade between themselves but erect a common trade policy against nonmembers.

common market
Economic integration whereby countries remove all barriers to trade and the movement of labor and capital between themselves but erect a common trade policy against nonmembers.

can be uneven because skilled labor may move to countries where wages are higher, and investment capital may flow to where returns are greater.

Economic Union Economic integration whereby countries remove barriers to trade and the movement of labor and capital, erect a common trade policy against nonmembers, and coordinate their economic policies is called an **economic union**. An economic union goes beyond the demands of a common market by requiring that member nations harmonize their tax, monetary, and fiscal policies and that they create a common currency. Economic union requires that member countries concede a certain amount of their national autonomy (or sovereignty) to the supranational union of which they are a part.

Political Union Economic and political integration whereby countries coordinate aspects of their economic *and* political systems is called a **political union**. A political union requires member nations to accept a common stance on economic and political policies regarding nonmember nations. However, nations are allowed a degree of freedom in setting certain political and economic policies within their territories. Individually, Canada and the United States provide early examples of political unions. In both these nations smaller states and provinces combined to form larger entities. A group of nations currently taking steps in this direction is the European Union—discussed later in this chapter.

---

economic union
Economic integration whereby countries remove barriers to trade and the movement of labor and capital, erect a common trade policy against nonmembers, and coordinate their economic policies.

political union
Economic and political integration whereby countries coordinate aspects of their economic and political systems.

EFFECTS OF REGIONAL ECONOMIC INTEGRATION

Few topics in international business are as hotly contested and involve as many groups as the effects of regional trade agreements on people, jobs, companies, cultures, and living standards. The topic often spurs debate over the merits and demerits of such agreements. On one side of the debate are people who see the bad that regional trade agreements cause—on the other, those who see the good. Each party to the debate cites data on trade and jobs that bolster their position. They point to companies that have picked up and moved to another country where wages are lower after a new agreement was signed or companies that have stayed at home and kept jobs there. The only thing made clear as a result of such debates is that both sides are right some of the time.

Then there is the cultural aspect of such agreements: Some people argue that they will lose their unique cultural identity if their nation cooperates too much with other nations. As we saw in this chapter's opening company profile, Nestlé tries to be as sensitive as possible to cultural differences across markets. But such large global companies are often lightning rods for those warning of cultural homogenization. Let's now take a closer look at the main benefits and drawbacks of regional integration.

BENEFITS OF REGIONAL INTEGRATION

Recall from Chapter 5 that nations engage in specialization and trade because of the gains in output and consumption. Greater specialization, increased efficiency, greater consumption, and higher standards of living all should result from higher levels of trade between nations.

Trade Creation As we have seen, economic integration removes barriers to trade and/or investment for nations belonging to a trading bloc. The increase in the level of trade between nations that results from regional economic integration is called **trade creation**. One result of trade creation is that consumers and industrial buyers in member nations are faced with a wider selection of goods and services not available before. For example, the United States has many popular brands of bottled water, including Coke's Dasani (**www.dasani.com**) and Pepsi's (**www.pepsi.com**) Aquafina (the number-

---

trade creation
Increase in the level of trade between nations that results from regional economic integration.

one best-seller). But grocery and convenience stores inside the United States stock a wide variety of lesser-known brands of bottled water imported from Canada, including Stonepoint's Classic Selection Spring Water (www.mystonepoint.com). No doubt, the free-trade agreement between Canada, Mexico, and the United States (discussed below) created export opportunities for these Canadian brands.

Another result of trade creation is that buyers can acquire goods and services at lower cost after trade barriers such as tariffs are lowered. Furthermore, lower costs tend to lead to higher demand for goods because people have more money left over after a purchase to buy other products.

Greater Consensus   In Chapter 6 we saw how the World Trade Organization (WTO) works to lower barriers on a global scale. Efforts at regional economic integration differ in that they comprise smaller groups of nations—ranging from several countries to as many as 30 or more. The benefit of trying to eliminate trade barriers in smaller groups of countries is that it can be easier to gain consensus from fewer members as opposed to, say, the 144 countries that comprise the WTO.

Political Cooperation   There can also be *political* benefits from efforts toward regional economic integration. A group of nations can have significantly greater political weight than each nation has individually. Thus, the group, as a whole, can have more say when negotiating with other countries in forums such as the WTO or perhaps even the United Nations. Moreover, integration involving political cooperation can reduce the potential for military conflict between member nations. In fact, peace was at the center of early efforts at integration in Europe in the 1950s. The devastation of two world wars in the first half of the twentieth century caused Europe to see integration as one way of preventing further armed conflicts.

Employment Opportunities   Regional integration can also expand employment opportunities by enabling people to move from one country to another to find work, or simply to earn a higher wage. Regional integration has opened doors for young people in Europe. Vincent Wauters is a 26-year-old Belgian who has a degree in history and speaks three languages. His willingness to pick up and move made him a good catch for French catalog retailer La Redoute (www.laredoute.fr). "I have a vision that is clearly European," says Wauters. "I have a sense of our common history, our cultural diversity, and I'm used to the kind of flexibility that's needed for people to adapt to one another." Anne-Marie Ronayne, a consultant with the international recruiting firm EMDS (www.emdsnet.com), agrees. "Companies," she says, "are looking for their future leaders. That means finding people with good attitudes, who can think across borders."[3] In this way regional integration can help improve the quality of life and living standards for a nation's people.

DRAWBACKS OF REGIONAL INTEGRATION

Although regional integration tends to benefit countries, it can also have substantial negative effects. Let's now examine the more important of these.

Trade Diversion   The flip side of trade creation is **trade diversion**—the diversion of trade away from nations not belonging to a trading bloc and toward member nations. Trade diversion can occur after formation of a trading bloc because of the lower tariffs charged between member nations. It can actually result in increased trade with a less-efficient producer within the trading bloc and reduced trade with a more-efficient non-member producer. In this sense, economic integration can unintentionally reward a less-efficient producer within the trading bloc. Unless there is other internal competition for the producer's good or service, buyers will likely pay more after trade diversion due to the inefficient production methods of the producer.

trade diversion
Diversion of trade away from nations not belonging to a trading bloc and toward member nations.

A World Bank report caused a stir over the results of the free-trade bloc between Latin America's largest countries, MERCOSUR (discussed later in this chapter). The report suggested that the bloc's formation only encouraged free trade in the lowest-value products of local origin, while deterring competition for more sophisticated goods manufactured outside the market. Closer analysis showed that while imports from one member state to another tripled during the period studied, imports from the rest of the world also tripled. Thus, the net effect of the agreement was trade creation, not trade diversion as critics had charged.[4] Also, the Australian Department of Foreign Affairs and Trade released results of a study that examined the impact of the North American Free Trade Agreement on Australia's trade with and investment in North America. The study found no evidence of trade diversion in the 5 years following the agreement's formation.[5]

Shifts in Employment

Perhaps the most controversial aspect of regional economic integration is how people's jobs are affected. Because the formation of trading blocs significantly reduces or eliminates barriers to trade among members, the producer of a particular good or service is likely to be the most productive producer. Industries requiring mostly unskilled labor, for example, will tend to shift production to low-wage nations within a trading bloc. But figures on the numbers of jobs lost or gained vary depending on the source.

By mid-2001, the U.S. government contended that rising U.S. exports to Mexico and Canada created 900,000 jobs.[6] But the AFL-CIO (www.aflcio.org), the federation of U.S. unions, disputes these figures and claims a loss of jobs due to NAFTA. Trade agreements do cause dislocations in labor markets—some jobs are lost while others are gained. For instance, some jobs were no doubt gained as a result of expanding transportation and warehousing industries on the U.S. side of the border. But U.S. jobs also were lost in some manufacturing sectors.

It is highly likely that once trade and investment barriers are removed, countries protecting low-wage domestic industries from competition will see these jobs move to the country where wages are lower. But this is also an opportunity for workers to upgrade their skills and gain more advanced job training. This can help nations increase their competitiveness, because a more educated and skilled workforce attracts higher-paying jobs than does a less skilled workforce. However, an opportunity for a nation to improve some abstract "factors of production" is little consolation to people finding themselves suddenly out of work.

Loss of National Sovereignty

Successive levels of integration require that nations surrender more of their national sovereignty. The least amount of sovereignty that must be surrendered to the trading bloc occurs in a free-trade area. Countries are allowed to set their own barriers to trade against all nonmember nations. However, a political union requires nations to give up a high degree of sovereignty in foreign policy. This is why a political union is so hard to achieve. Long histories of cooperation or animosity between nations do not disappear when a group of countries forms a union. Because one member nation may have very delicate ties with a nonmember nation with which another member may have very strong ties, the setting of a common foreign policy can be extremely tricky.

Because of the benefits and despite the drawbacks of regional trade agreements, economic integration is taking place throughout the world. Europe, the Americas, Asia, the Middle East, and Africa are all undergoing integration to some degree. In the remaining sections of this chapter we examine the most prominent efforts at integration in each of these regions. We begin by looking at the region with the longest history and highest level of integration—Europe.

The most sophisticated and advanced example of regional integration that we can point to today is occurring in Europe. European efforts at integration began shortly after the Second World War as a cooperative effort between a small group of countries and involved a few select industries. Regional integration now encompasses practically all of Western Europe and all industries. Let's now explore integration in Europe, beginning with its earliest attempts at cooperation.

EUROPEAN UNION

In the middle of the twentieth century, many would have scoffed at the idea that the European countries, which had spent so many years at war with one another, could present a relatively unified whole by the close of the century. How did Europe come so far in such a relatively short time?

The Early Years   A war-torn Europe emerged from the Second World War in 1945 facing two challenges. First, it needed to rebuild itself and avoid further armed conflict. Second, it needed to increase its industrial strength to stay competitive with an increasingly powerful United States. Cooperation seemed to be the only way of facing these challenges. Belgium, France, West Germany, Italy, Luxembourg, and the Netherlands signed the Treaty of Paris in 1951, creating the *European Coal and Steel Community*. These nations were determined to remove barriers to trade in coal, iron, steel, and scrap metal so as to coordinate coal and steel production among themselves, thereby controlling the postwar arms industry.

The members of the European Coal and Steel Community signed the Treaty of Rome in 1957, creating the *European Economic Community* (see Map 8.1). The Treaty of Rome outlined a future common market for these nations. It also aimed at establishing common transportation and agricultural policies among members. In 1967 the Community's scope was broadened to include additional industries, notably atomic energy, and changed its name to the *European Community*. As the goals of integration continued to expand, so too did the bloc's membership. Waves of enlargement occurred in 1973, 1981, 1986, and 1995. In 1994 the bloc once again changed its name, to the *European Union (EU)*. Today the 15-member European Union (**www.europa.eu.int**) has a population of about 370 million people and a GDP of over $6 trillion.

Over the past two decades two important milestones contributed to the EU's continued progress: the *Single European Act* and the *Maastricht Treaty*.

Single European Act   By the mid-1980s, EU member nations were frustrated by remaining trade barriers and a lack of harmony on several important matters, including taxation, law, and regulations. The important objective of harmonizing laws and policies was beginning to appear unachievable. A commission that was formed to analyze the potential for a common market by the end of 1992 put forth several proposals. The goal was to remove remaining barriers, increase harmonization, and thereby enhance the competitiveness of European companies. The proposals became the *Single European Act (SEA)* and went into effect in 1987.

As companies positioned themselves to take advantage of the opportunities that the SEA offered, a wave of mergers and acquisitions swept across Europe. Large firms combined their special understanding of European needs, capabilities, and cultures with their advantage of economies of scale. Small and medium-size companies were encouraged through EU institutions to engage in networking with one another to offset any negative consequences resulting from, for example, changing product standards.

MAP 8.1 *Regional Integration in Europe*

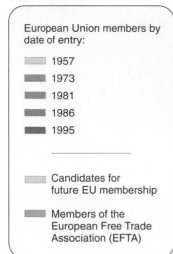

European Union members by date of entry:

- 1957
- 1973
- 1981
- 1986
- 1995

_____

- Candidates for future EU membership
- Members of the European Free Trade Association (EFTA)

Maastricht Treaty Some members of the EU wanted to take European integration further still. A 1991 summit meeting of EU member nations took place in Maastricht, The Netherlands. The meeting resulted in the *Maastricht Treaty*, which went into effect in 1993.

The Maastricht Treaty had three aims. First, it called for banking in a single, common currency after January 1, 1999, and circulation of coins and paper currency on January 1, 2002. Today a common currency clearly benefits firms doing business in the EU. The costs (commissions) inherent in converting from the currency of one member nation to another can be avoided. Business owners also need not worry about the potential loss of money due to shifting exchange rates between national currencies on cross-border deals in the EU. And not having to cover such costs and risks frees up capital for greater investment. Monetary union is discussed in much greater detail in Chapter 10.

Second, the treaty set up monetary and fiscal targets for countries that wished to take part in monetary union. Third, the treaty called for political union of the member nations—including development of a common foreign and defense policy and common citizenship. Progress on political integration will wait until the countries gauge the success of the final stages of economic and monetary union.

Enlargement of the European Union   One of the most hotly debated topics across the European Union today is the issue of enlargement. For negotiation purposes and eventual accession, applicant countries have been divided into two groups. The first-wave countries include Cyprus, the Czech Republic, Estonia, Hungary, Poland, and Slovenia. The second wave includes Bulgaria, Latvia, Lithuania, Malta, Romania, and Slovakia (see Map 8.1). These countries are to become members after they meet certain demands laid down by the EU. These so-called *Copenhagen Criteria* require each country to demonstrate that it:

➡ Has stable institutions, which guarantee democracy, the rule of law, human rights, and respect for and protection of minorities.
➡ Has a functioning market economy, capable of coping with competitive pressures and market forces within the European Union.
➡ Is able to assume the obligations of membership, including adherence to the aims of economic, monetary, and political union.
➡ Has the ability to adopt the rules and regulations of the Community, the rulings of the European Court of Justice, and the Treaties.

One country that has applied for membership, but with whom membership negotiations have not begun is Turkey. One reason for the failure of Turkey to win support in the EU is charges (fair or not) by member nations of human rights abuses. Another reason is intense opposition by Greece, Turkey's longtime foe. However, Turkey does have a customs union with the EU, and this is increasing trade between the two. Despite disappointment for some countries that are EU hopefuls and despite intermittent setbacks in the enlargement process, integration is going forward.

Structure of the European Union   Five EU institutions play important roles in monitoring and enforcing economic and political integration (see Figure 8.2).

European Parliament   The European Parliament consists of more than 600 members elected by popular vote within each member nation every 5 years. As such, they are expected to voice their particular political views on EU matters. The European Parliament fulfills its role of adopting EU law by debating and amending legislation proposed by the European Commission. It exercises political supervision over all EU institutions—giving it the power to supervise commissioner appointments and to censure the commission. It also has veto power over some laws (including the annual budget of the EU). There is a call for increased democratization within the EU, and some believe this could be achieved by strengthening the powers of the Parliament. The Parliament

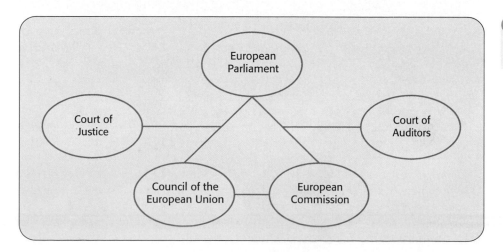

FIGURE 8.2

Institutions of the European Union

conducts its activities in Belgium (in the city Brussels), France (in the city Strasbourg), and Luxembourg.

Council of the European Union The Council is the legislative body of the EU. When it meets it brings together representatives of member states at the ministerial level. The makeup of the council changes depending on the topic under discussion. For instance, when the topic is agriculture, the Council comprises the ministers of agriculture of each member nation. No proposed legislation becomes EU law unless the Council votes it into law. Although passage into law for sensitive issues such as immigration and taxation still requires a unanimous vote, some legislation today requires only a simple majority to win approval. The Council also concludes, on behalf of the EU, international agreements with other nations or international organizations. The Council is headquartered in Brussels, Belgium.

European Commission The Commission is the executive body of the EU. It comprises commissioners appointed by each member country—larger nations get two commissioners, smaller countries get one. Member nations appoint the president and commissioners after being approved by the European Parliament. It has the right to draft legislation, is responsible for managing and implementing policy, and monitors member nations' implementation of, and compliance with, EU law. Each commissioner is assigned a specific policy area, such as competitive policy or agricultural policy. Although commissioners are appointed by their national governments, they are expected to behave in the best interest of the EU as a whole, not in the interest of their own country. The European Commission is headquartered in Brussels, Belgium.

Court of Justice The Court of Justice is the court of appeals of the EU and is composed of one justice from each member country. One type of case that the Court of Justice hears is one in which a member nation is accused of not meeting its treaty obligations. Another type is one in which the commission or council is charged with failing to live up to their responsibilities under the terms of a treaty. Like the commissioners, justices are required to act in the interest of the EU as a whole, not in the interest of their own countries. The Court of Justice is located in Luxembourg.

The European Union (EU) began as a grouping of just 6 member nations, expanded to 15 today, and may have twice that many within a decade. In order to balance what are sometimes diverging national interests, the EU designed a one-of-kind system of government. It also designed the role of each EU institution to reflect this balancing act. But some question whether the EU will function effectively following further enlargement.

Court of Auditors   The Court of Auditors comprises 15 members (one from each member nation) appointed for 6-year terms. The Court is assigned the duty of auditing the EU accounts and implementing its budget. It also aims to improve financial management in the EU and report to member nations' citizens on the use of public funds. As such, it issues annual reports and statements on implementation of the EU budget. The Court has roughly 250 auditors and 300 additional staff to assist it in carrying out its functions. The Court of Auditors is based in Luxembourg.

EUROPEAN FREE TRADE ASSOCIATION (EFTA)

Certain European nations were reluctant to join in the ambitious goals of the EU, fearing destructive rivalries and a loss of national sovereignty. Some of these nations did not want to be part of a common market but instead wanted the benefits of a free-trade area. That is why in 1960 several countries banded together and formed the *European Free Trade Association (EFTA)* to focus on trade in industrial, not consumer, goods. Because some of the original members joined the EU and some new members joined EFTA (www.efta.int), today the group consists of only Iceland, Liechtenstein, Norway, and Switzerland (see Map 8.1).

The population of EFTA is slightly less than 12 million, and it has a combined GDP of $409 billion. Despite its relatively small size, members remain committed to free-trade principles and raising standards of living for their people. The EFTA and EU created the *European Economic Area (EEA)* to cooperate on matters such as the free movement of goods, persons, services, and capital among the 19 nations. The two groups also cooperate in other areas, including the environment, social policy, and education.

CENTRAL EUROPEAN FREE-TRADE AREA

To prepare them for eventual European Union membership, the EU encouraged candidate countries to establish their own free-trade area. To this end Bulgaria, the Czech Republic, Hungary, Poland, Romania, Slovakia, and Slovenia formed the *Central European Free Trade Area (CEFTA)*. Among other aims, CEFTA (www.cefta.org) is to remove customs duties and other barriers to trade in industrial products and agriculture. But because of the difficulties experienced by farmers in some of these nations, complete abolition of trade barriers in agriculture is unlikely. Also, as part of their efforts to join the EU, Croatia, Estonia, Latvia, Lithuania, and Ukraine have applied for CEFTA membership. To learn a bit more about how entrepreneurs can do business in one CEFTA country, see this chapter's Entrepreneurial Focus titled "Czech List."

Let's now examine the progress of economic integration in the Americas and see how far it has come and where it is headed.

INTEGRATION IN THE AMERICAS

Europe's success at economic integration caused other regions to consider the benefits of forming their own regional trading blocs. Latin American countries began forming regional trading arrangements in the early 1960s but made substantial progress only in the 1980s and 1990s. North America was about three decades behind Europe in taking major steps toward economic integration. Let's now explore the major efforts toward economic integration in North, South, and Central America, beginning with North America.

NORTH AMERICAN FREE TRADE AGREEMENT (NAFTA)

There has always been a good deal of trade between Canada and the United States. In fact, the two nations are each other's largest trading partners. Canada and the United States had in the past established trade agreements in several industrial sectors of their

The demise of communism in Eastern Europe means more opportunity. Those opportunities were apparent to Howard Woffinden, and Greg Gold, soon after filming a series of Claudia Schiffer fitness videos in Prague, Czech Republic. They joined Prague partner Tomas Krejci in 1996 and formed Los Angeles–based Milk & Honey Films (**www.milkandhoneyfilms.com**) to support U.S. filmmakers who were shooting abroad and overseas shops who were shooting in the United States. Yet they admit that working in the Czech Republic can be challenging. Here's their advice:

➡ **Don't rush familiarity**. Czech society is very formal. "Unless you know people well, use a formal manner of speaking," says Woffinden. This includes using titles like "doctor" and "mister." It's rarely appropriate to use first names unless you're close friends.

➡ **Build relationships**. What matters most isn't money, says Gold, but "being referred by someone you've done business with, building personal relationships or [cashing in] favors owed."

➡ **Find a Czech partner**. Because the Republic was communist for 40 years before becoming a capitalist democracy, Woffinden says, "The method for getting things done is different from ours." You'll need a local to deal with the still-prevalent communist attitudes.

➡ **Expect limited resources**. Woffinden points out that the country's infrastructure, though improving, is still underdeveloped. "When we arrived five years ago, the phone system was archaic. Often, you can't call someone—you have to physically locate them." The Internet also facilitates communication in the absence of personal phones.

➡ **Hire local professionals**. Milk & Honey Films uses a Czech accountant to handle the paperwork required by Czech taxes (including a VAT tax of 17 to 22 percent) and red tape. It also employs a bilingual attorney to interpret differences between Czech and U.S. law.

➡ **Establish who's in charge**. Companies must have a "responsible person" (*jednatel*), who is in charge of all aspects of the business. Woffinden notes that Czechs often want to work directly with this *jednatel* rather than company reps.

---

economies, including automotive products. In January 1989 the *U.S.–Canada Free Trade Agreement* went into effect. The goal was to eliminate all tariffs on bilateral trade between Canada and the United States by 1998.

But accelerating progress in Europe in the late 1980s and early 1990s caused new urgency in the task of creating a North American trading bloc that included Mexico. Mexico joined what is now the World Trade Organization in 1987 and began privatizing state-owned enterprises in 1988. Talks between Canada, Mexico, and the United States in 1991 eventually resulted in the formation of the *North American Free Trade Agreement (NAFTA)*. NAFTA (**www.nafta-sec-alena.org**) became effective in January 1994 and superseded the U.S.–Canada Free Trade Agreement. Today NAFTA comprises a market with 410 million consumers and a GDP of about $11 trillion (see Map 8.2).

As a free-trade agreement, NAFTA seeks to eliminate most tariffs and nontariff trade barriers on most goods originating from within North America by 2008. The agreement also calls for liberalized rules regarding government procurement practices, the granting of subsidies, and the imposition of countervailing duties (see Chapter 6). Other provisions deal with issues such as trade in services, intellectual property rights, and standards of health, safety, and the environment.

Local Content Requirements and Rules of Origin   Manufacturers and distributors are finding that while NAFTA encourages free trade between Canada, Mexico, and the United States, the resulting trade is anything but hassle-free. Local content requirements and rules of origin are among the agreement's most complex criteria. These rules create special problems for producers and distributors. Although they rarely know the precise origin of every part or component in a piece of industrial equipment, they are responsible for determining whether a product has sufficient North American content

MAP 8.2   *Regional Integration in North America*

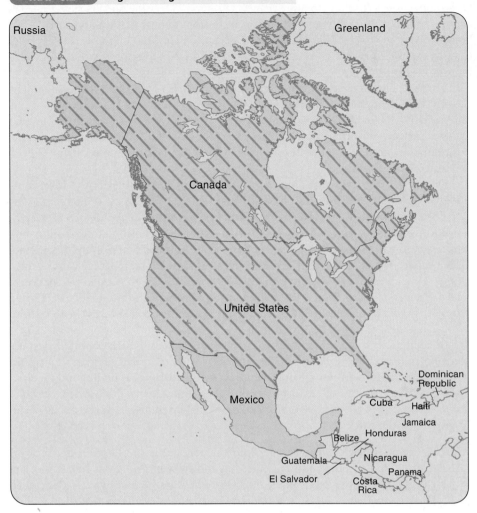

to qualify for tariff-free status. The producer or distributor must also provide a NAFTA "certificate of origin" to an importer to claim an exemption from tariffs. Four criteria determine whether a good meets NAFTA rules of origin:[7]

➡ Goods wholly produced or obtained in the NAFTA region
➡ Goods containing nonoriginating inputs but meeting Annex 401 origin rules (which covers regional input)
➡ Goods produced in the NAFTA region wholly from originating materials
➡ Unassembled goods and goods classified in the same harmonized system category as their parts that do not meet Annex 401 rules but have sufficient North American regional value content

Effects of NAFTA   Between 1993 and 2000 trade among the three nations increased markedly, with the greatest gains occurring between Mexico and the United States. Today the United States exports more to Mexico than it does to Britain, France, Germany, and Italy combined. In fact, in 1997 Mexico became the second largest export market for the United States for the first time ever.

In the first 7 years of NAFTA, Mexico's exports to the United States jumped an astonishing 240 percent, from almost $40 billion to nearly $136 billion (an average annual rate of 34 percent). Meanwhile, U.S. exports to Mexico grew nearly 170 percent, from a little over $41 billion to more than $111 billion.[8] Over the same period, Canada's exports to the United States more than doubled, from almost $117 billion to $242 billion, while U.S. exports to Canada grew 76 percent, from $100 billion to $176 billion. Canada exported very little to Mexico before NAFTA, but afterward exports grew 114 percent in seven years from $640 million to nearly $1.4 billion.[9]

The agreement's effect on employment and wages is not as easy to determine. The U.S. Trade Representative Office claims that exports to Mexico and Canada support 2.9 million U.S. jobs (900,000 more than in 1993), which pay 13 to 18 percent more than national averages for production workers.[10] But the AFL-CIO group of unions dispute this claim; they argue that since its formation NAFTA has cost the United States 750,000 jobs and job opportunities.[11]

Despite the disparity in the numbers referenced by different groups, it is certainly true that some U.S. companies headed for the border after NAFTA came into being. One U.S. firm that made a massive manufacturing commitment to Mexico is Delphi Automotive Systems (www.delphiauto.com). Delphi has 70,000 employees in its 45 facilities in Mexico—many along the border with the United States. Delphi manufactures a variety of lighting, electric, and steering assemblies for many of the world's automotive companies. The company cemented its commitment to Mexico by opening a Tech Center in Ciudad Juarez, its first major engineering effort outside the United States. By siting this center closer to manufacturing facilities, the company benefits from reduced lead times and start-up costs.[12]

In addition to claims of job losses, opponents claim that NAFTA has damaged the environment, particularly along the United States–Mexico border. Although the agreement included provisions for environmental protection, Mexico is finding it difficult to deal with the environmental impact of greater economic activity. But Mexico's *Instituto Nacional de Ecologia* (www.ine.gob.mx) has developed an industrial-waste-management program, including an incentive system to encourage waste reduction and recycling.

Expansion of NAFTA   Continued ambivalence about the long-term effects of NAFTA, including the concerns of union leaders and environmental watchdogs, is delaying its expansion. Chile's significant economic progress in the past two decades caused business leaders to argue for its integration into NAFTA. The slender nation of 14 million

Air pollution from increased industrialization mixes with fog over Mexico City, Mexico. On the day this photo was taken, visibility was so poor that the city's airport had to close. NAFTA provisions for waste reduction, recycling, and disposal of hazardous materials were inspired in part by such damage to air and water. To read more about NAFTA's provisions, go to its Web site at (**www.nafta-sec-alena.org**).

people is no economic giant, but it might be a model for economic reform in other South American nations. Chile began its market reforms about 15 years ahead of Brazil (the largest economy in South America), and today is largely open to trade and investment.[13]

The pace at which NAFTA expands will depend to a large extent on whether the U.S. Congress grants successive U.S. presidents trade-promotion ("fast-track") authority. Trade-promotion authority allows a U.S. administration to engage in all necessary talks surrounding a trade deal without the official involvement of Congress. After the deal's details are decided, Congress then simply votes yes or no on the deal and cannot revise the treaty's provisions.

But there is little doubt that future integration will occur among nations in the Americas. In fact, it is even possible that the North American economies will one day adopt a single currency. As the former deputy managing director of the International Monetary Fund, Stanley Fischer, said, "As trade relations between Mexico and the U.S. strengthen and as the economies open up to each other, I think having two currencies won't make a great deal of sense." Fischer noted that although this could be difficult for both Canada and Mexico to stomach politically, in the long run he expects to see one currency for all of North America.[14]

ANDEAN COMMUNITY

Attempts at integration among Latin American countries had a rocky beginning. The first try, the *Latin American Free Trade Association (LAFTA)*, was formed in 1961. The agreement first called for the creation of a free-trade area by 1971 but then extended that date to 1980. Yet because of a crippling debt crisis in South America and a reluctance of member nations to do away with protectionism, the agreement was doomed to an early demise. Disappointment with LAFTA led to the creation of two other regional trading blocs—the Andean Community and the Latin American Integration Association.

Formed in 1969, the *Andean Community* (originally the Andean Pact) today includes five South American countries located in the Andes mountain range—Bolivia, Colombia, Ecuador, Peru, and Venezuela (see Map 8.3). The group comprises a market of more than 105 million consumers and a combined GDP of about $500 billion. The main objectives of the group included tariff reduction for trade among member nations, a common external tariff, and common policies in both transportation and certain industries. But political ideology was somewhat hostile to the concept of free markets and favored a good deal of government involvement in business affairs. Also, inherent distrust among members made lower tariffs and more open trade hard to achieve.

The Andean Community had the ambitious goal of establishing a common market by 1995, but delays mean that it remains a somewhat incomplete customs union. The group now hopes to have the common market in place by 2005. The Andean countries posted nearly 30 percent annual gains in trade from 1990 to 1997 but experienced recession in the late 1990s. Furthermore, political violence in Colombia continues to threaten the stability of its government and the nation's economy is experiencing its worst problems in decades. Meanwhile, according to official estimates as much as 80 percent of Venezuelans have fallen below the poverty line.

The common market will be difficult to implement within the framework of the Andean Community. One reason is that each country has been given significant exceptions in the tariff structure that they have in place for trade with nonmember nations. Another reason is that countries continue to sign agreements with just one or two countries outside the Andean Community framework. Such independent action impairs progress internally and hurts the credibility of the Andean Community with the rest of the world. Furthermore, Bolivia and Chile have gained associate membership in the trading bloc known as MERCOSUR (discussed shortly), which indicates a lack of confidence in the future success of the Andean Community.

MAP 8.3   *Regional Integration in Latin America*

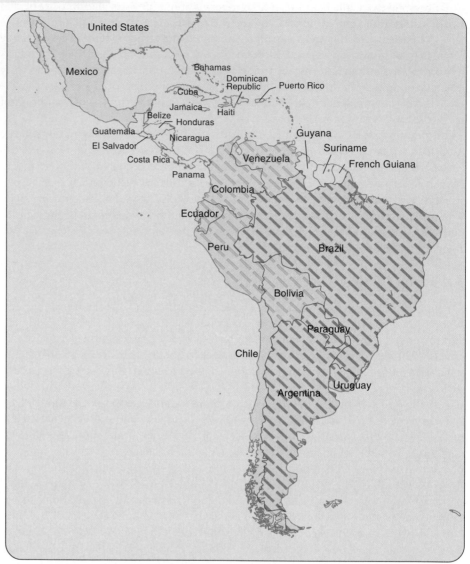

Andean Community

Latin American Integration Association (ALADI)

Southern Common Market (MERCOSUR)

LATIN AMERICAN INTEGRATION ASSOCIATION (ALADI)

The *Latin American Integration Association (ALADI)* was formed in 1980. Map 8.3 shows the countries that belong to the ALADI trading bloc. Because of the failure of the first attempt at integration (LAFTA), the objectives of ALADI were scaled back significantly. The ALADI agreement calls for preferential tariff agreements to be made between pairs of member nations (called *bilateral* agreements) that reflect the economic development of each nation. Although the agreement resulted in roughly 24 bilateral agreements and 5 subregional pacts, the agreements did not accomplish a great deal of cross-border trade. Dissatisfaction with progress once again caused certain nations to form a trading bloc of their own—MERCOSUR.

SOUTHERN COMMON MARKET (MERCOSUR)

The *Southern Common Market (MERCOSUR)* was established in 1988 between just Argentina and Brazil, but it expanded to include Paraguay and Uruguay in 1991. In 1996

MERCOSUR (www.mercosur.org) underwent another expansion when Bolivia and Chile became associate, but not full, members of the bloc (see Map 8.3). Peru and Venezuela are also showing interest in MERCOSUR.

Today MERCOSUR acts as a customs union and boasts a market of more than 220 million consumers (nearly half of Latin America's total population) and 60 percent of its total economic output. Its first years of existence were very successful—trade between members grew nearly fourfold during the 1990s. MERCOSUR is progressing on trade and investment liberalization and is emerging as the most powerful trading bloc in all of Latin America. It may even incorporate all the countries of South America into a South American Free Trade Agreement, after which it would link up with NAFTA to form a Free Trade Area of the Americas (discussed shortly). But the bloc's pace of integration has been hampered by (1) differing trade agendas and macroeconomic policy frameworks and (2) the economic problems being experienced by Argentina and Brazil.[15]

Regional economic integration in Latin America has certainly caught the eye of European businesses as well. Some notable European companies in Latin America include Germany's Volkswagen (www.vw.com) and Italy's Fiat (www.fiat.com) in autos, France's supermarket chain Carrefour (www.carrefour.com), and the British/Dutch personal-care products group Unilever (www.unilever.com). As European companies continue making inroads into Latin America, U.S. companies are pressuring their government to move more quickly in integrating Chile into NAFTA and accelerating the creation of the Free Trade Area of the Americas. Latin America's large consumer base and its potential as a low-cost production platform for worldwide export appeal to both the European Union and the United States.[16]

CENTRAL AMERICA AND THE CARIBBEAN

Attempts at economic integration in Central American countries and throughout the Caribbean basin have been much more modest than efforts elsewhere in the Americas. Nevertheless, let's look at two efforts at integration in these two regions—CARICOM and CACM.

Caribbean Community and Common Market (CARICOM) The *Caribbean Community and Common Market (CARICOM)* trading bloc was formed in 1973. Map 8.4 shows the members of CARICOM (www.caricom.org). Although the Bahamas is a member of the Community it does not belong to the Common Market and the Republic of Haiti is likely to gain membership soon. As a whole, CARICOM has a combined GDP of nearly $30 billion and a market of almost 6 million people.

In early 2000, CARICOM members signed an agreement calling for the establishment of the CARICOM Single Market, calling for the free movement of factors of production including goods, services, capital, and labor. However, several members have yet to ratify the agreement.[17] The main difficulty CARICOM will continue to face is that most members trade more with nonmembers than they do with one another simply because members do not have the imports each needs.

Central American Common Market (CACM) The *Central American Common Market (CACM)* was formed in 1961 to create a common market between Costa Rica, El Salvador, Guatemala, Honduras, and Nicaragua (see Map 8.4). Together, the members of CACM (www.sieca.org.gt) comprise a market of 33 million consumers and have a combined GDP of about $120 billion. However, the common market was never realized because of a long and bloody war between El Salvador and Honduras and guerrilla conflicts in several countries. But renewed peace is creating more business confidence and optimism, which is driving double-digit growth in trade between members.

Furthermore, the group has not yet created a customs union. External tariffs among members range anywhere from 4 percent to 12 percent. And the tentative nature of

MAP 8.4 *Regional Integration in Central America and the Caribbean*

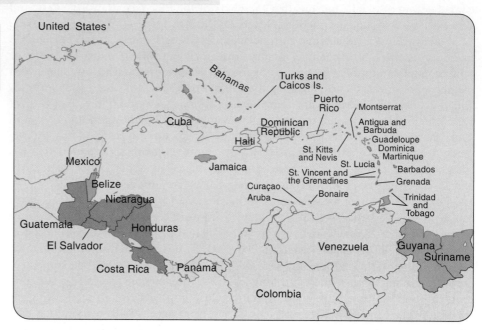

Caribbean Community and Common Market (CARICOM)

Central American Common Market (CACM)

cooperation was obvious in 2000 when Honduras and Nicaragua slapped punitive tariffs on each other's goods during a dispute over a patch of water. But officials remain positive, saying that their ultimate goal is European-style integration, closer political ties, and adoption of a single currency—probably the dollar. In fact, El Salvador adopted the U.S. dollar as its official currency in 2000, and Guatemala already uses the dollar alongside it quetzal.[18]

FREE TRADE AREA OF THE AMERICAS (FTAA)

Sure to dominate future discussion of regional trading blocs in the Americas is creation of a *Free Trade Area of the Americas (FTAA)*(www.alca-ftaa.org). The objective of the FTAA is to create the largest free-trade area on the planet, stretching from the northern tip of Alaska to the southern tip of Tierra del Fuego, in South America. The FTAA would comprise 34 nations and 800 million consumers and have a collective GDP of more than $12 trillion. The only Western Hemisphere nation that would not be part of the FTAA is Cuba. The FTAA would work alongside the different trading blocs such as NAFTA, MERCOSUR, the Andean Community, and CACM. After going into effect, the FTAA would remove tariffs and nontariff barriers between all member countries over the course of a decade or more.

The first official meeting, the 1994 Summit of the Americas, created the broad blueprint for the agreement. Government representatives reaffirmed their commitment to the FTAA at the Second Summit of the Americas in April 1998. Actual negotiations began in September 1998 and are scheduled to finish no later than 2005. The Third Summit of the Americas was held in April 2001 and met with protests by labor organizations, environmentalists, and others protesting increased globalization. In an effort to placate the concerns of some of these groups, leaders attending the summit declared that they would halve the number of people living in extreme poverty by 2015.[19]

The reasons for a renewed U.S. quest for completing the FTAA are apparent when we consider the fact that the United States participates in just 2 free-trade agreements out of 130 worldwide. In the Western Hemisphere, it participates in just 1 of 30.[20] One businessperson supporting the FTAA is William Weiller, chairman and CEO of Purafil,

Inc. (www.purafil.com) of Atlanta, Georgia. In 2000, this maker of air-purification systems exported just 15 percent of its $22 million in sales to Latin America because of the cost added to the products by existing tariffs. Weiller believes that removing tariffs could cause his exports south of the border to leap to 25 percent of sales. Says Weiller, "If there's a level playing field, we'll be more aggressive."[21]

Corruption is an area of contention for Canada and the United States, who fear that closer cooperation could mean more piracy and lost sales to counterfeit goods. Latin America has long been identified as a market for pirated merchandise, particularly music on CD-ROMs and computer software. Some music is even produced in Macao, China, and sent for sale in Latin America.[22] See the World Business Survey titled "Corruption Perceptions in the FTAA" to see corruption rankings for some FTAA countries.

WORLD BUSINESS SURVEY

Corruption Perceptions in the FTAA

Corruption is a problem throughout Latin America for all firms doing business there. If the FTAA is going to be a success, corruption will have to be rooted out. The figure below shows the results of a survey on how businesspeople perceive corruption in some countries involved in the FTAA.

* Corresponds to rank in worldwide survey of 85 countries
** Ranges between 10 = *highly clean* and 0 = *highly corrupt*
   Data is for 2000

TRANSATLANTIC ECONOMIC PARTNERSHIP (TEP)

The *Transatlantic Economic Partnership (TEP)* between the United States and the European Union surfaced in May 1998 at the EU–United States summit meeting. In addition to the goal of forging closer economic ties between the EU and the United States, the partnership aims to contribute to stability, democracy, and development worldwide. Although the EU and the United States differ in important ways, the partnership is one of equals in terms of the size of their economies.

There is good reason for partnership. Together, the United States and the European Union have a combined population of 650 million, account for half the world's GDP, and have trade and investment flows that amount to nearly $1 billion every day! Moreover, each is the other's largest single trading partner (considering all the EU countries as a whole) and most important source of, and destination for, foreign investment.[23]

MAP 8.5
Regional Integration in Asia

Efforts outside Europe and the Americas at economic and political integration have tended to be looser arrangements. Let's take a look at two important coalitions in Asia and among Pacific Rim nations—the Association of Southeast Asian Nations and the organization for Asia Pacific Economic Cooperation.

ASSOCIATION OF SOUTHEAST ASIAN NATIONS (ASEAN)

Indonesia, Malaysia, the Philippines, Singapore, and Thailand formed the *Association of Southeast Asian Nations (ASEAN)* in 1967. Brunei joined in 1984, Vietnam in 1995, Laos and Myanmar in 1997, and Cambodia in 1998 (see Map 8.5). Together, the ASEAN (www.aseansec.org) countries comprise a market of about 500 million consumers and a GDP of more than $800 billion. The three main objectives of the alliance are to (1)

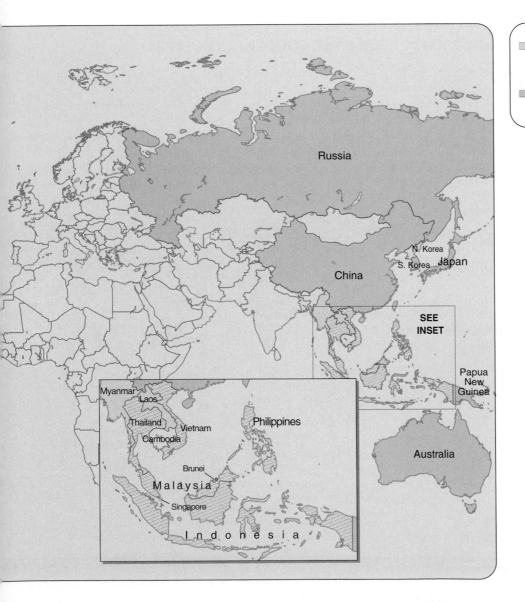

promote economic, cultural, and social development in the region; (2) safeguard the region's economic and political stability; and (3) serve as a forum in which differences can be resolved fairly and peacefully.

The intention to admit Cambodia, Laos, and Myanmar (formerly Burma) was met with criticism from some Western nations. The concern regarding Laos and Cambodia being admitted stems from their roles in supporting the communists during the Vietnam War. The quarrel with Myanmar centers on evidence cited by the West of its continued human rights violations. Nevertheless, ASEAN felt that by adding these countries to the coalition, it could counter China's rising strength and its resources of cheap labor and abundant raw materials.[24]

Companies involved in Asia's developing economies are likely to be doing business with an ASEAN member. This is even a more likely prospect as China, Japan, and South Korea speed up their efforts at joining ASEAN as soon as 2008. The new arrangement would allow China to act "as a bridge between the less advanced and more advanced economies," said Supachai Panitchpakdi, deputy prime minister of Thailand.[25] Some key facts about ASEAN that companies must consider are contained in the Global Manager titled "The Ins and Outs of ASEAN."

ASIA PACIFIC ECONOMIC COOPERATION (APEC)

The organization for *Asia Pacific Economic Cooperation (APEC)* was formed in 1989. Begun as an informal forum among 12 trading partners, APEC (www.apecsec.org.sg) now has 21 members (see Map 8.5). Together, the APEC nations account for more than half of world trade and a combined GDP of more than $16 trillion.

The stated aim of APEC is not to build another trading bloc. Instead, it desires to strengthen the multilateral trading system and expand the global economy by simplifying and liberalizing trade and investment procedures among member nations. In the

GLOBAL MANAGER

The Ins and Outs of ASEAN

Businesses that are unfamiliar with operating in ASEAN do need to exercise caution in their dealings. Some inescapable facts about ASEAN that warrant consideration are the following:

➡ **Diverse cultures and politics.** The Philippines is a representative democracy, Brunei is an oil-rich sultanate, and Vietnam is a state-controlled communist country. Business policies and protocol must be adapted to each country.

➡ **Economic difficulties.** Many ASEAN nations are still feeling the effects of the economic crisis of 1997. Before then ASEAN attracted 30 percent of foreign direct investment into Asia's developing economies. In 2000 it attracted just 15 percent.

➡ **Corruption and black markets.** Bribery and black markets are common in many ASEAN countries, including Indonesia, Myanmar, the Philippines, and

Vietnam. One corruption study placed Indonesia fourth from the bottom of 91 nations surveyed.

➡ **Political change and turmoil.** Several nations in the region recently elected new leaders. Indonesia in particular went through presidents at a fast clip recently. Companies must remain alert to shifting political winds and laws regarding trade and investment.

➡ **Border disputes.** Parts of Thailand's borders with Cambodia and Laos are tested frequently. Hostilities break out sporadically between Thailand and Myanmar over border alignment and ethnic Shan rebels operating along the border.

➡ **Lack of common tariffs and standards.** Doing business in ASEAN nations can be costly. Harmonized tariffs, quality and safety standards, customs regulations, and investment rules would cut transaction costs significantly.

long term, APEC hopes to have free trade and investment throughout the region by 2010 for developed nations and 2020 for developing ones.

The Record of APEC APEC has succeeded in halving members' tariff rates from an average of 15 percent to 7.5 percent. The early years saw the greatest progress, but further liberalization has been hampered since the Asian financial crisis of 1997. For instance, members have not yet specified complete timetables for eliminating trade barriers and subsidies by 2010 and 2020.[26] APEC is at least as much a political body as it is a movement toward freer trade. After all, APEC certainly does not have the focus or the record of accomplishments of NAFTA or the EU. Nonetheless, open dialogue and attempts at cooperation should continue to encourage progress toward APEC goals, however slow.

Further progress may create some positive benefits for people doing business in APEC nations. It is changing the granting of business visas so businesspeople can travel throughout the region without obtaining multiple visas. It is recommending mutual recognition agreements on professional qualifications so that engineers, for example, could practice in any APEC country, regardless of nationality. And it is ready to simplify and harmonize customs procedures. Eventually, businesses could use the same customs forms and manifests for all APEC economies.[27]

INTEGRATION IN THE MIDDLE EAST AND AFRICA

Economic integration has not left out the Middle East and Africa, although progress there is more limited than in any other geographic region. Its limited success is due mostly to the small size of the countries involved and their relatively low level of development. The largest of these coalitions are the Gulf Cooperation Council and the Economic Community of West African States.

GULF COOPERATION COUNCIL (GCC)

Several Middle Eastern nations formed the *Gulf Cooperation Council (GCC)* in 1980. Members of the GCC are Bahrain, Kuwait, Oman, Qatar, Saudi Arabia, and the United Arab Emirates (see Map 8.6). The primary purpose of the GCC at its formation was to cooperate with the increasingly powerful trading blocs in Europe at the time—the EU and EFTA. However, as it has evolved the GCC has become as much a political as an economic entity. Its cooperative thrust allows citizens of member countries to travel freely in the GCC without visas. It also permits citizens of one member nation to own land, property, and businesses in any other member nation without the need for local sponsors or partners.

ECONOMIC COMMUNITY OF WEST AFRICAN STATES (ECOWAS)

The *Economic Community of West African States (ECOWAS)* was formed in 1975 but relaunched its efforts at economic integration in 1992 because of a lack of early progress (see Map 8.6). One of the most important goals of ECOWAS (www.ecowas.int) is the formation of a customs union and eventual common market and monetary union. Together, the ECOWAS nations comprise a large portion of the economic activity in sub-Saharan Africa.

Progress on market integration is almost nonexistent. In fact, the value of trade occurring among ECOWAS nations is just 11 percent of the value of the trade members undertake with third parties. But ECOWAS has made progress in the free movement of people, construction of international roads, and development of international telecommunication links. Some of the main problems ECOWAS has encountered arise because of political instability, poor governance, weak national economies, poor infrastructure, and poor economic policies.

MAP 8.6   *Regional Integration in the Middle East and Africa*

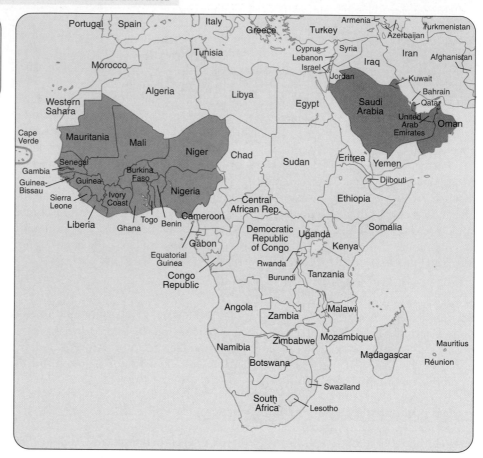

Gulf Cooperation Council (GCC)

Economic Community of West African States (ECOWAS)

A FINAL WORD

This chapter has described the main regional integration efforts that are occurring throughout the world today. Table 8.1 summarizes the members of each regional trading bloc presented in this chapter. We saw that there is a great deal of debate about the merits or demerits of regional trade agreements. We also learned about some of the ethical elements of such agreements and the actions of governments and independent organizations to counter the negative effects of integration. Although there are drawbacks to integration, governments will continue to be enticed by the potential gains from increased trade and by the desire to raise their peoples' standard of living. Thus, despite its negative aspects, it is likely that regional economic integration will continue to roll back the barriers to trade between nations and between existing trading blocs of nations.

There is a variety of additional material available on the Companion Website that accompanies this textbook. You can access this information by visiting the Website at (**www.prenhall.com/wild**).

summary

① Define *regional economic integration*, and identify its five levels. The process whereby countries in a geographic region cooperate with one another to reduce or eliminate barriers to the international flow

of products, people, or capital is called *regional economic integration*. A group of nations in a geographic region undergoing economic integration is called a *regional trading bloc*. There are five potential levels (or

TABLE 8.1   The World's Main Regional Trading Blocs

EU	**European Union**
	Austria, Belgium, Britain, Denmark, Finland, France, Germany, Greece, Ireland, Italy, Luxembourg, Netherlands, Portugal, Spain, Sweden
EFTA	**European Free Trade Association**
	Iceland, Liechtenstein, Norway, Switzerland
NAFTA	**North American Free Trade Agreement**
	Canada, Mexico, United States
Andean	**Andean Community**
	Bolivia, Colombia, Ecuador, Peru, Venezuela
ALADI	**Latin American Integration Association**
	Argentina, Bolivia, Brazil, Chile, Colombia, Ecuador, Mexico, Paraguay, Peru, Uruguay, Venezuela
MERCOSUR	**Southern Common Market**
	Argentina, Brazil, Paraguay, Uruguay (Bolivia and Chile are associate members)
CARICOM	**Caribbean Community and Common Market**
	Antigua and Barbuda, Bahamas, Barbados, Belize, Dominica, Grenada, Guyana, Jamaica, Montserrat, St. Kitts and Nevis, St. Lucia, St. Vincent and the Grenadines, Suriname, Trinidad and Tobago
CACM	**Central American Common Market**
	Costa Rica, El Salvador, Guatemala, Honduras, Nicaragua
FTAA	**Free Trade Area of the Americas**
	Caribbean, Central America, North America, South America
TEP	**Transatlantic Economic Partnership**
	European Union (15 countries), United States
ASEAN	**Association of Southeast Asian Nations**
	Brunei, Cambodia, Indonesia, Laos, Malaysia, Myanmar, Philippines, Singapore, Thailand, Vietnam
APEC	**Asia Pacific Economic Cooperation**
	Australia, Brunei, Canada, Chile, China, Hong Kong, Indonesia, Japan, South Korea, Malaysia, Mexico, New Zealand, Papua New Guinea, Peru, Philippines, Russia, Singapore, Taiwan, Thailand, United States, Vietnam
GCC	**Gulf Cooperation Council**
	Bahrain, Kuwait, Oman, Qatar, Saudi Arabia, United Arab Emirates
ECOWAS	**Economic Community of West African States**
	Benin, Burkina Faso, Cape Verde, Gambia, Ghana, Guinea, Guinea-Bissau, Ivory Coast, Liberia, Mali, Mauritania, Niger, Nigeria, Senegal, Sierra Leone, Togo

degrees) of integration for regional trading blocs. Each level of integration incorporates the properties of those preceding it. (1) A *free-trade area* is an economic integration in which countries seek to remove all barriers to trade between themselves, but each country determines its own barriers against nonmembers. (2) A *customs union* is an economic integration in which countries remove all barriers to trade between themselves but erect a common trade policy against nonmembers. (3) A *common market* is an economic integration in which countries remove all barriers to trade and the movement of labor and capital between themselves but erect a common trade policy against nonmembers. (4) An *economic union* is an economic integration in which countries remove barriers to trade and the movement of labor and capital, erect a common trade policy against nonmembers, and coordinate their economic policies. (5) A *political union* is an economic and political integration in which countries coordinate aspects of their economic *and* political systems.

2 Discuss the *benefits* and *drawbacks* associated with regional economic integration. The resulting increase in the level of trade between nations as a result of regional economic integration is called *trade creation*. One result of trade creation is that consumers and industrial buyers in member nations are faced with a wider selection of goods and services that were not available before. Also, buyers can acquire goods and services at lower cost following the lowering of trade barriers such as tariffs. A political benefit is that a smaller, regional group of nations can find it easier to reduce trade barriers than can larger groups of nations. Nations can also have more say when negotiating with other countries or organizations, can reduce the potential for military conflict, and expand employment opportunities.

The flip side of trade creation is *trade diversion*—the diversion of trade away from nations not belonging to a trading bloc and toward member nations. Trade diversion can actually result in increased trade with a less-efficient producer within the trading bloc. Regional integration also forces some people out of work. Finally, political union requires nations to give up a high degree of sovereignty in foreign policy.

3 Describe regional integration in *Europe* and discuss its future enlargement. The *European Coal and Steel Community* was formed in 1951 to remove trade barriers for coal, iron, steel, and scrap metal among the member nations. Following several waves of expansion, broadenings of its scope, and name changes, the Community is now known as the European Union (EU). Today the EU consists of 15 nations. There are two sets of six nations from Central, Eastern, and Southern Europe awaiting future EU expansion as soon as they meet the so-called *Copenhagen Criteria* that relate to their political, legal, and economic systems. Five institutions that form the main institutional framework of the EU are the European Parliament, European Commission, Council of the European Union, Court of Justice, and Court of Auditors.

Other European nations created the *European Free Trade Association (EFTA)* to focus on trade in industrial, not consumer, goods. Today EFTA has just four members. The EFTA and EU created the *European Economic Area (EEA)* to cooperate on trade matters.

To prepare for eventual EU membership, candidate countries established the *Central European Free Trade Area (CEFTA)*. The aim is to remove customs duties and other barriers to trade in industrial products and agriculture.

4 Discuss regional integration in the *Americas* and analyze its future prospects. The *North American Free Trade Agreement (NAFTA)* between Canada, Mexico, and the United States became effective in January 1994. As a free-trade agreement, NAFTA seeks to eliminate most tariffs and nontariff trade barriers on most goods originating from within North America by 2008.

The *Andean Community* was formed in 1969 and calls for tariff reduction for trade among member nations, a common external tariff, and common policies in transportation and certain industries. The *Latin American Integration Association (ALADI)* formed in 1980 between Mexico and 10 South American nations has had little impact on cross-border trade. The *Southern Common Market (MERCOSUR)* was established in 1988. Today MERCOSUR acts as a customs union and is emerging as the most powerful trading bloc in all of Latin America.

The *Caribbean Community and Common Market (CARICOM)* trading bloc was formed in 1973. The main difficulty CARICOM faces is that most members trade more with nonmembers than they do with each other. The *Central American Common Market (CACM)* was formed in 1961 but protracted conflicts have hampered progress for the CACM.

The objective of the *Free Trade Area of the Americas (FTAA)* is to create a trading bloc encompassing all of Central, North, and South America (excluding Cuba). The goal of the *Transatlantic Economic Partnership (TEP)* between the United States and the European Union is to contribute to stability, democracy, and development worldwide, in addition to forging closer economic ties between the two.

5 Characterize regional integration in *Asia* and discuss how it differs from integration elsewhere. The *Association of Southeast Asian Nations (ASEAN)*, formed in 1967, has three main objectives: (1) to promote economic, cultural, and social development in the region; (2) to safeguard the region's economic and political stability; and (3) to serve as a forum in which differences can be resolved fairly and peacefully. Today ASEAN has 10 members but China, Japan, and South Korea may join in the future.

The organization for *Asia Pacific Economic Cooperation (APEC)* was formed in 1989. Begun as an informal forum among 12 trading partners, APEC now has 21 members. Together, the APEC nations account for more than half of world trade and a combined GDP of more than $16 trillion. The stated aim of APEC is not to build another trading bloc. Instead, it desires to strengthen the multilateral trading system and expand the global economy by simplifying and liberalizing trade and investment procedures among member nations. In the long term, APEC hopes to have free trade and investment throughout the region by 2010 for developed nations and 2020 for developing ones.

6 **Describe regional integration in the *Middle East* and *Africa* and explain why progress there has been slow.** Several Middle Eastern nations formed the *Gulf Cooperation Council (GCC)* in 1980. Members of the GCC are Bahrain, Kuwait, Oman, Qatar, Saudi Arabia,

and the United Arab Emirates. The primary purpose of the GCC at its formation was to cooperate with the increasingly powerful trading blocs in Europe at the time—the EU and EFTA. Today its thrust is to allow citizens of member countries to travel freely without visas and to permit citizens of member nations to own properties in another member nation without the need for local sponsors or partners.

The *Economic Community of West African States (ECOWAS)* was formed in 1975 but relaunched its efforts at economic integration in 1992 because of a lack of early progress. One of the most important goals of ECOWAS is the formation of a customs union and eventual common market. The group's lack of progress on economic integration largely reflects each nation's lack of economic development.

questions for review

1. What is the ultimate goal of *regional economic integration*?

2. What are the *five levels*, or degrees, of regional integration? Briefly describe each one.

3. Identify three potential *benefits* of regional economic integration and three potential *drawbacks*.

4. Explain the difference between *trade creation* and *trade diversion*. Why are these two concepts important?

5. Identify at least two reasons for Europe's initial desires to form a regional trading bloc.

6. What is the *European Union (EU)*? Explain its plans for enlargement.

7. Identify the five main institutions of the European Union. Briefly describe the function each performs.

8. What is the *European Free Trade Association (EFTA)*?

9. What is the *Central European Free Trade Area (CEFTA)*? What is its purpose?

10. What three countries belong to the *North American Free Trade Agreement (NAFTA)*?

11. What effect has NAFTA had on trade between member nations?

12. What is the *Andean Community*? Give one reason why it is behind schedule.

13. Who are the members of the *Southern Common Market (MERCOSUR)* trading bloc? Briefly describe how it has performed.

14. List the five nations that belong to the *Central American Common Market (CACM)*.

15. What is the *Free Trade Area of the Americas (FTAA)*?

16. What is the *Transatlantic Economic Partnership (TEP)*? Identify its main goals.

17. What are the three main objectives of the *Association of Southeast Asian Nations (ASEAN)*?

18. How do the goals of the organization for *Asia Pacific Economic Cooperation (APEC)* differ from those of other regional blocs?

19. What is the *Gulf Cooperation Council*? Identify its six members.

20. What is the *Economic Community of West African States (ECOWAS)*? Explain why it has had limited success.

questions for discussion

1. It is likely that the proliferation and growth of regional trading blocs will continue into the foreseeable future. At what point do you think the integration process will stop (if ever)? Explain your answer.

2. Some people believe that the rise of regional trading blocs threatens free-trade progress made by the World Trade Organization (WTO). Do you agree? Why or why not?

3. Certain groups of countries, particularly in Africa, are far less economically developed than other regions, such as Europe and North America. What sort of integration arrangement do you think developed countries could create with less-developed nations to improve living standards? Be as specific as you can.

in practice

In this chapter, you read about the proposed Free Trade Area of the Americas (FTAA). Read the following article and answer the questions that follow.

Building Blocs

LA PAZ, Bolivia—An eventual FTAA could cause the region to experience a huge increase in trade. "I think it's reasonable to expect that within a few years you would get at least a doubling of trade" in Latin America, said Gary Hufbauer, senior fellow at the Institute for International Economics.

But some smaller countries are concerned how much they would benefit. Says Jamaica's ambassador to the United States, "Let's say we all produce sugar, so you will have competition between the smallest, poorest country and the largest, richest country."

Such fears could result in the formation of subregional blocs—trade blocs formed among small groups of nations that then harmonize rules with each other. Says Jaime Garcia, Peru's former vice minister of industry, "The FTAA brings together countries and economies of all shapes and sizes. That lends itself toward subregional trading blocs."

---

1. Small companies typically have difficulty competing against large multinationals when their governments take part in regional trading blocs. What could governments do to help their small companies compete after the formation of such blocs?

2. Do you think that by forming subregional trading blocs small countries can really strengthen their negotiating positions against large nations? Why or why not? Do you think that very small nations should even participate in regional trade agreements with very large nations? Why or why not?

3. Do you think that the FTAA will help lift the living standards for people in the smallest countries (such as Ecuador or Nicaragua), or will it only be a boon for the largest nations such as Brazil, Canada, and the United States?

4. Do you think that subregional or regional trade agreements cause instability on a subregional, regional, or global scale, or do you believe they foster cooperation? Explain your answer.

5. After all you've read in this chapter about regional trade agreements, what is your assessment of their value? Should their progress continue or be rolled back?

projects

1. Some analysts believe that NAFTA can extend its current arrangement to more advanced levels of economic integration. In small groups of several students or more, discuss the obstacles that NAFTA nations might face as they seek to bring other nations into their fold. Discuss whether political integration is a possibility.

2. Go to your library or link to a business information service on the Internet. Locate articles that describe how a large international company is coping with regional economic integration. Write a one-page report on how the company is responding to the integration. Are the company's strategies paying off or are there problems? Describe the factors behind the company's success or problems.

3. In this project, two groups of four students debate the advantages and disadvantages of regional economic integration. After the first student from each side has spoken, the second student questions the opponent's arguments, looking for holes and inconsistencies. The third student attempts to answer these arguments. The fourth student presents a summary of each side's arguments. Finally, the class votes on which team offered the more compelling argument.

business case 8

TAINTED TRADE: INCREASING IMPORTS BRINGS INCREASE IN ILLNESS

Today, U.S. citizens in the dead of a Minnesota winter can indulge their cravings for summer-fresh raspberries. Europeans who are thousands of miles away from North America can put Mexican mangoes in their breakfast cereal. Japanese shoppers can buy radishes that were grown from seeds cultivated in Oregon. Eating fresh and natural produce is a growing consumer trend, and globalization of the food industry, falling barriers to trade, and formation of regional trading blocs make it possible for people to choose from produce grown all over the world. Unfortunately, these forces have also made it more likely that these same consumers will get debilitating—and even deadly—illnesses from foodborne pathogens.

In the United States several outbreaks linked to the burgeoning global trade in produce have made headlines in recent years. One very serious case occurred several years ago when 2,300 people were victims of a parasite called cyclospora that had hitched a ride on raspberries grown in Guatemala. Outbreaks of hepatitis A and salmonella from tainted strawberries and alfalfa sprouts, respectively, have also alarmed consumers. Although health officials say there is no evidence that imports are inherently more dangerous, they do cite some real reasons for worry. For one thing, imported produce often comes from countries where food hygiene and basic sanitation are less advanced. For another, some microbes that cause no damage in their home country are deadly when introduced on foreign soil. Finally, the longer the journey from farm to table, the greater is the chance of contamination. Just consider the journey taken by the salmonella-ridden alfalfa sprouts: The seeds for the sprouts were bought from Uganda and Pakistan, among other nations, shipped through the Netherlands, flown into New York, and trucked all around the United States.

Incidences of food contamination show no signs of abating. Since the passage of NAFTA, cross-border trade in food among Canada, Mexico, and the United States has skyrocketed. Meanwhile, federal inspections of U.S. imports by the Food and Drug Administration have dropped significantly. The increase in imports has clearly strained the U.S. food-safety system, which was built 100 years ago for a country contained within its own borders. Although it isn't feasible for the United States to plant FDA inspectors in every country, options are available. The U.S. Congress could tighten further the ban on importing fruit and vegetables from countries that do not meet expanded U.S. food-safety standards. More money could be given to the FDA to enable it to hire investigators to inspect more fully not just produce but also farming methods and government safety systems in other countries. Countries that blocked the new inspections would be forbidden to sell fruit and vegetables in the United States. Although such measures would irk trading partners of the United States, it most certainly would fuel the worldwide debate on food safety and trade.

thinking globally

1. How do you think countries with a high volume of exports to the United States, such as Mexico, would respond to stricter food-safety rules? Do you think such measures are a good way to stem the tide of food-related illnesses? Why or why not?

2. Sue Doneth of Marshall, Michigan, is a mother of one of the schoolchildren who was exposed to the hepatitis A virus after eating tainted frozen strawberry desserts. Speaking before Congress she said, "We are forcing consumers to trade the health and safety of their families for free trade. That is not fair trade. NAFTA is not a trade issue: it is a safety issue." Do you think food-safety regulations should be built into an extension of NAFTA? Why or why not? What are the benefits and drawbacks of putting food-safety regulations into international trade pacts?

3. The lack of harmonized food-safety practices and standards is just one of the challenges faced by the food industry as it becomes more global. What other challenges face the food industry in an era of economic integration and opening markets?

a question of ethics

1. Some argue that the term *free trade agreement* in describing NAFTA or the European Union is misleading. They say these agreements are really "preferential trade agreements" that offer free trade only to members and relative protection against nonmembers. This may be happening to the Caribbean nations that were excluded from NAFTA. Some argue that from apparel factories in Jamaica to sugar cane fields in Trinidad, NAFTA has cost jobs, market share, and income for the vulnerable island nations of the region. They say that jobs have migrated from these nations to Mexico as a result of NAFTA. Given the impact on nonmember nations, do you think such trade agreements are ethical? Why do you think islands in the Caribbean basin were not invited to be part of NAFTA? Imagine yourself as a member of the U.S. Congress. Make an argument for including the Caribbean or excluding it from an expansion of NAFTA.

2. Pan-European marketing is inhibited not only by different cultural preferences in each EU country but also by various restrictions each country places on advertising. For instance, Greece and Sweden have bans on advertising aimed at children, and France outlaws alcohol and tobacco advertising. Some business leaders see national advertising restrictions as measures designed to protect countries' domestic industries.

How is it possible to know whether such restrictions are the result of ethical concerns or are really protective measures? Do you think that a nation's ethical concerns, such as the impact of advertising on children or the promotion of tobacco and alcohol, should be superseded by regional trade agreements that strive for unified standards and more open trade? Why or why not?

3. Labor unions and environmentalists in the United States aren't the only ones speaking out against the effects of NAFTA. There continues to be opposition in Mexico by those who complain of a loss of national sovereignty and who feel that the income gap between the two countries will never be narrowed. Average hourly wages on the U.S. side of the border can be six times that on the Mexican side. Mexican critics fear that their entire country will be subsumed by companies from the United States that do not contribute to Mexico's higher standard of living, but who instead use Mexico as a low-cost assembly site while keeping high-paying, high-skilled jobs at home. Do you think that there is a way for trade agreements to help close the economic gap between poor and wealthy partners? Or will the interests of poorer nations always be subordinate to wealthier countries within regional trading blocs?

9 international financial markets

After studying this chapter, you should be able to

1 Discuss the purposes, development, and financial centers of the *international capital market.*

2 Describe the *international bond, international equity,* and *Eurocurrency markets.*

3 Discuss the four primary functions of the *foreign exchange market.*

4 Explain how currencies are *quoted* and the different *rates* given.

5 Identify the main *instruments* and *institutions* of the foreign exchange market.

6 Explain why and how governments restrict *currency convertibility.*

BEACONS

A Look Back

CHAPTER 8 introduced the most prominent efforts at regional economic integration occurring around the world. We saw how international companies are responding to the challenges and opportunities that regional integration is creating.

A Look at This Chapter

This chapter introduces us to the international financial system by describing the structure of international financial markets. We learn first about the international capital market and its main components. We then turn to the foreign exchange market, explaining how it works and outlining its structure.

A Look Ahead

CHAPTER 10 concludes our study of the international financial system. We discuss the factors that influence exchange rates and explain why and how governments and other institutions try to manage exchange rates. In so doing, we focus on recent monetary problems in emerging markets worldwide.

A Yen for Nintendo

KYOTO, Japan—In a *New Yorker* cartoon, a boy recites his latest book report before his classmates. The caption below: "Game Boy: A Memoir of Addiction, by Ronald Markowitz." Since 1989, the Nintendo Company, (**www.nintendo.com**) has been feeding the addiction of Game Boy fanatics worldwide.

Nintendo traces its roots to 1889 when Fusajiro Yamauchi began manufacturing *Hanafuda* Japanese playing cards in Kyoto, Japan. Today, Nintendo produces and sells video game systems, including Nintendo 64, Game Boy Advance, and GameCube. To date, the company has sold more than one billion video games worldwide. In fact, more than 40 percent of U.S. households own a Nintendo game system. The company created such icons as Mario, Donkey Kong, and Pokémon, which pop up in cultures worldwide. Practically everywhere Nintendo characters adorn licensed merchandise, including children's furniture, backpacks, coloring books, mugs, T-shirts, potato chip bags, and canned soda.

But Nintendo's game-design and marketing talents are not all that affect its performance—so do exchange rates between the Japanese yen (¥) and other currencies. The earnings of Nintendo's 40 subsidiaries and affiliates worldwide are integrated into the consolidated financial statements at the end of the year. Translating subsidiaries' earnings from other currencies into yen when it is relatively weak increases Nintendo's stated earnings in yen. In fact, the firm reported record net income in 2001 of ¥ 96.6 billion ($779 million). But Nintendo also reported that this was in part due to a foreign exchange gain of ¥ 66.3 billion ($535 million). The gain resulted from a sharp drop in the yen against foreign currencies shortly before the company translated its subsidiaries' earnings into Japanese yen.

The potential existed for Nintendo to get a similar boost in 2002 because the company is forecasting an exchange rate of 121 yen to the dollar for the year. But industry analysts figure that if it continues to trade around 135 to the dollar, the weak yen could add ¥ 54 billion ($436 million) to Nintendo's operating profit in 2002. As you read this chapter, keep in mind all the ways that shifting currency values affect a company's performance and what companies can do to shield themselves from adverse changes.[1]

Well-functioning financial markets are an essential element of the international business environment. They funnel money from organizations and economies with excess funds to those with shortages. International financial markets also allow companies to exchange one currency for another. Such exchanges, as well as the rates at which currencies are exchanged, are critical to international business.

For example, suppose you purchase a CD player imported from a company based in the Philippines. Whether you realize it or not, the price you paid for that CD player was affected by the *exchange rate* between your country's currency and the Philippine peso. Ultimately, the Filipino company that sold you the CD player must convert the purchase made in your currency into Philippine pesos. Thus, the profit earned by the Filipino company is also influenced by the exchange rate between your currency and the peso. Managers must understand how changes in currency values—and thus in exchange rates—affect the profitability of their international business activities. Among other things, managers at our hypothetical company in the Philippines must know how much to charge you for their CD player.

In this chapter, we launch our study of the international financial system by exploring the structure of the international financial markets. The two interrelated systems that comprise the international financial markets are (1) the international capital market and (2) the foreign exchange market. We start by examining the purposes of the international capital market and tracing its recent development. We then take a detailed look at the international bond, equity, and Eurocurrency markets, each of which helps companies to borrow and lend money internationally. Following that, we take a look at the functioning of the foreign exchange market—an international market for currencies that facilitates international business transactions. Finally, we explore how currency convertibility affects international transactions.

INTERNATIONAL CAPITAL MARKET

capital market
System that allocates financial resources in the form of debt and equity according to their most efficient uses.

A **capital market** is a system that allocates financial resources in the form of debt and equity according to their most efficient uses. Its main purpose is to provide a mechanism through which those who wish to borrow or invest money can do so efficiently. Individuals, companies, governments, mutual funds, pension funds, and all types of nonprofit organizations participate in capital markets. For example, an individual might want to buy her first home; a midsize company might want to add production capacity; and a government might want to develop a new fiber optic telecommunications system. Sometimes these individuals and organizations have excess cash to lend; at other times, they need funds.

PURPOSES OF NATIONAL CAPITAL MARKETS

There are two primary means by which companies obtain external financing: *debt* and *equity*. Capital markets function to help them obtain both types of financing. However, to understand the international capital market fully we need to review the purposes of capital markets in domestic economies. Quite simply, national capital markets help individuals and institutions borrow the money that other individuals and institutions want to lend. Although in theory borrowers could search individually for various parties who are willing to lend or invest, this would be a time-consuming process. Consequently, intermediaries of all kinds exist to facilitate financial exchanges. Most of us are familiar with the most common capital-market intermediaries:

➡ *Commercial banks* lend borrowers their investors' deposits at a specific rate of interest. They provide loans for new investment projects and may help to finance a firm's import or export activities.
➡ *Investment banks* help clients to invest excess capital and to borrow needed capital. They act as *agents*, introducing clients to organizations that provide either investment or borrowing opportunities.

Role of Debt   **Debt** consists of loans in which the borrower promises to repay the borrowed amount (the *principal*) plus a predetermined rate of *interest*. Company debt normally takes the form of **bonds**—instruments that specify the timing of principal and interest payments. The holder of a bond (the *lender*) can force the borrower into bankruptcy if the borrower fails to pay on a timely basis. Bonds issued for the purpose of funding investments are commonly issued by private-sector companies and by municipal, regional, and national governments.

Role of Equity   **Equity** is part ownership of a company, in which the equity holder participates with other part owners in the company's financial gains and losses. Equity normally takes the form of **stock**—shares of ownership in a company's assets that give *shareholders* (*stockholders*) a claim on the company's future cash flows. Shareholders may be rewarded with *dividends*—payments made out of surplus funds—or by increases in the value of their shares. Of course, they may also suffer losses due to poor company performance—and thus decreases in the value of their shares. Dividend payments are not guaranteed; they are determined by the company's board of directors and based on financial performance. In capital markets, shareholders can either sell one company's stock for that of another or *liquidate*

debt
Loans in which the borrower promises to repay the borrowed amount (the principal) plus a predetermined rate of interest.

bond
Debt instrument that specifies the timing of principal and interest payments.

equity
Part ownership of a company in which the equity holder participates with other part owners in the company's financial gains and losses.

stock
Shares of ownership in a company's assets that give shareholders a claim on the company's future cash flows.

Large financial institutions benefit borrowers and lenders worldwide in many ways. As investment banks, they underwrite debt and equity securities and advise corporations, governments, and institutions. As asset managers, they are caretakers of the personal financial savings of individuals. In fact, Merrill Lynch has a truly global reach, with offices in 38 countries and total client assets exceeding $1.5 trillion.

them—exchange them for cash. **Liquidity,** which is a feature of both debt and equity markets, refers to the ease with which bondholders and shareholders may convert their investments into cash.

PURPOSES OF THE INTERNATIONAL CAPITAL MARKET

The **international capital market** is a network of individuals, companies, financial institutions, and governments that invest and borrow across national boundaries. It consists of both formal exchanges (in which buyers and sellers meet to trade financial instruments) and electronic networks (in which trading occurs anonymously). This market makes use of unique and innovative financial instruments specially designed to fit the needs of investors and borrowers located in different countries who are doing business with one another. Large international banks play a central role in the international capital market. They gather the excess cash of investors and savers around the world and then channel this cash to borrowers across the globe.

Expanding the Money Supply for Borrowers
The international capital market is a conduit for joining borrowers and lenders in different national capital markets. Thus, a company that is unable to obtain funds from investors in its own nation can seek financing from investors elsewhere, making it possible for the company to undertake an otherwise impossible project. The option of going outside the home nation is particularly important to firms in countries with small or developing capital markets of their own—particularly those with emerging stock markets. An expanded supply of money also benefits small but promising companies that might not otherwise get financing if there is intense competition for capital.

Reducing the Cost of Money for Borrowers
An expanded money supply reduces the cost of borrowing. Like the prices of potatoes, wheat, and other commodities, the "price" of money is determined by supply and demand. If its supply increases, its price—in the form of interest rates—falls. That is why excess supply creates a buyer's (borrower's) market, forcing down interest rates and the cost of borrowing. Projects regarded as infeasible because of low expected returns might be viable at a lower financing cost.

Reducing Risk for Lenders
The international capital market expands the available set of lending opportunities. In turn, an expanded set of opportunities helps reduce risk for lenders (investors) in two ways:

1. *Investors enjoy a greater set of opportunities from which to choose.* They can thus reduce overall portfolio risk by spreading their money over a greater number of debt and equity instruments. In other words, if one investment loses money, the loss can be offset by gains elsewhere.
2. *Investing in international securities benefits investors because some economies are growing while others are in decline.* For example, the prices of bonds in Thailand do not follow bond-price fluctuations in the United States, which are independent of prices in Hungary. In short, investors reduce risk by holding international securities whose prices move independently.

Unfortunately, small would-be borrowers still face some serious problems in trying to secure loans. In particular, interest rates are often high and many entrepreneurs have nothing to put up as collateral. But as you can see from the Entrepreneurial Focus titled "Where Microcredit Is Due," some unique methods are available for getting capital into the hands of small businesspeople—particularly in developing nations.

Where Microcredit Is Due

Obtaining capital challenges the entrepreneurial spirit in many developing countries. If a person is lucky enough to obtain a loan, it is typically from a loan shark, whose inordinate interest rates devour most of the entrepreneur's profits. However, an alternative money-lending practice is growing in popularity. In obtaining microcredit, small groups of low-income entrepreneurs borrow money at competitive rates without having to put up collateral. Besides being collateral-free, microcredit offers the following advantages:

Borrowers Sink or Swim Together. For better or worse, group members are joined at the economic hip: If a member fails to pay off a loan, everyone may lose future credit. Often, however, peer pressure and support help to defend against this contingency. In addition, strong family ties in developing countries tend to furnish important support networks.

Most Loans Go to Women. Although the outreach to male borrowers is increasing, most microcredit borrowers are women. Women tend to be better at funneling profits into family nutrition, clothing, and education, as well as into business expansion. The successful use of microcredit in Bangladesh has increased wages, community income, and the status of women. One local bank that has already loaned $450 million to 2.1 million borrowers enjoys a 98 percent on-time payback record.

It Might Even Work in Developed Countries. The microcredit concept was pioneered in developed countries as a way for developing countries to create the foundation for a market economy. Nowadays, the use of microcredit within developed nations might be a way to spur economic growth in depressed geographic areas, such as inner cities. But whereas microcredit loans in developing countries typically average less than $100, those in developed nations average a minimum of at least $500.

FORCES EXPANDING THE INTERNATIONAL CAPITAL MARKET

Around 40 years ago, national capital markets functioned largely as independent markets. But since that time, the amount of debt, equity, and currencies traded internationally has increased dramatically. This rapid growth can be traced to three main factors:

➡ *Information Technology*. Information is the lifeblood of every nation's capital market because investors need information about investment opportunities and their corresponding risk levels. Large investments in information technology over the past two decades have drastically reduced the costs, in both time and money, of communicating around the globe. Investors and borrowers can now respond in record time to breaking news in the international capital market. The introduction of electronic trading after the daily close of formal exchanges also facilitates faster response times.

➡ *Deregulation*. Deregulation of national capital markets has been instrumental in the expansion of the international capital market. The need for deregulation became apparent in the early 1970s when heavily regulated markets in the largest countries were facing fierce competition from less regulated markets in smaller nations. Deregulation increased competition, lowered the cost of financial transactions, and opened many national markets to global investing and borrowing. Continued growth in the international capital market depends on further deregulation. For instance, although Japan opened its banking industry to outsiders somewhat in the late 1990s, more needs to be done to spur greater competition there.

➡ *Financial Instruments*. Greater competition in the financial industry is creating the need to develop innovative financial instruments. One result of the need for new types of financial instruments is **securitization**—the unbundling and repackaging of hard-to-trade financial assets into more liquid, negotiable, and marketable financial instruments (or *securities*). For instance, a mortgage loan from a bank is not liquid or negotiable because it is a customized contract between the bank and the borrower: Banks cannot sell loans and thus raise capital for further investment because each loan differs from

securitization
Unbundling and repackaging of hard-to-trade financial assets into more liquid, negotiable, and marketable financial instruments (or securities).

every other loan. But agencies of the U.S. government, such as the Federal National Mortgage Association (**www.fanniemae.com**), guarantee mortgages against default and thus accumulate them as pools of assets. They then sell securities in capital markets that are backed by these mortgage pools. When mortgage bankers participate in this process, they are able to raise capital for further investment.[2]

WORLD FINANCIAL CENTERS

The world's three most important financial centers are London, New York, and Tokyo. But officials at traditional exchanges worry that information technology may make formal stock exchanges obsolete. Indeed, unless they continue to modernize, cut costs, and provide new customer services, they might be rendered obsolete by trading on the Internet and other new electronic systems.

Offshore Financial Centers   An **offshore financial center** is a country or territory whose financial sector features very few regulations and few, if any, taxes. These centers tend to be characterized by economic and political stability and usually provide access to the international capital market through an excellent telecommunications infrastructure. As we will see in Chapter 10, most governments protect their own currencies by restricting the amount of activity that domestic companies can conduct in foreign currencies. That is why companies often find it hard to borrow funds in foreign currencies and so turn to offshore centers, which offer large amounts of funding in currencies other than their own. In short, offshore centers are sources of (usually cheaper) funding for companies with multinational operations.

offshore financial center
Country or territory whose financial sector features very few regulations and few, if any, taxes.

Offshore financial centers fall into two categories:

➡ *Operational centers* see a great deal of financial activity. Prominent operational centers include London (which does a good deal of currency trading) and Switzerland (which supplies a great deal of investment capital to other nations).
➡ *Booking centers* are usually located on small island nations or territories with favorable tax and/or secrecy laws. Little financial activity takes place here. Rather, funds simply pass through on their way to large operational centers. In fact, booking centers are typi-

cally home to offshore branches of domestic banks that use them merely as bookkeeping facilities to record tax and currency-exchange information.[3] Some important booking centers are the Cayman Islands and the Bahamas in the Caribbean; Gibraltar, Monaco, and the Channel Islands in Europe; Bahrain in the Middle East; and Singapore in Southeast Asia.

Increasingly, offshore centers are attracting attention in the rapidly expanding world of electronic commerce. Anguilla, a small Caribbean island that belongs to the United Kingdom, is attempting to become a center for Internet-based companies. How? In Anguilla, such firms are allowed to do all the electronic commerce they want via the Internet and pay no taxes on their profits. To meet one "Webpreneur" who is working to attract business to Anguilla, see his Web site at (**www.offshore.com.ai**).

MAIN COMPONENTS OF THE INTERNATIONAL CAPITAL MARKET

Now that we have covered the basic features of the international capital market, let's take a closer look at its main components: the international bond, international equity, and Eurocurrency markets.

INTERNATIONAL BOND MARKET

The **international bond market** consists of all bonds sold by issuing companies, governments, or other organizations *outside their own countries*. Issuing bonds internationally is an increasingly popular way to raise needed funding. Typical buyers include medium- to large-size banks, pension funds, mutual funds, and governments with excess financial reserves. Large international investment banks, such as Morgan Stanley (**www.ms.com**) and JPMorgan Chase (**www.jpmorganchase.com**), typically manage the sales of new international bond issues for corporate and government clients.

Types of International Bonds   One instrument used by companies to access the international bond market is called a **Eurobond**—a bond issued outside the country in whose currency it is denominated. In other words, a bond issued by a Venezuelan company, denominated in U.S. dollars, and sold in Britain, France, Germany, and the Netherlands (but not available in the United States or to its residents) is a Eurobond. Because this Eurobond is denominated in U.S. dollars, the Venezuelan borrower both receives the loan and makes its interest payments in dollars.

Eurobonds are popular (accounting for 75 to 80 percent of all international bonds) because the governments of countries in which they are sold do not regulate them. The absence of regulation substantially reduces the cost of issuing a bond. Unfortunately, it increases its risk level—a fact that may discourage some potential investors. The traditional markets for Eurobonds are Europe and North America.

Companies also obtain financial resources by issuing so-called **foreign bonds**— bonds sold outside the borrower's country and denominated in the currency of the country in which they are sold. For instance, a yen-denominated bond issued by the German carmaker BMW in Japan's domestic bond market is a foreign bond. Foreign bonds account for about 20 to 25 percent of all international bonds.

Foreign bonds are subject to the same rules and regulations as the domestic bonds of the country in which they are issued. Countries typically require issuers to meet certain regulatory requirements and to disclose details about company activities, owners, and upper management. Thus BMW's *samurai bonds* (the name for foreign bonds issued in Japan) would need to meet the same disclosure and other regulatory requirements that Toyota's bonds in Japan must meet. Foreign bonds in the United States are called *yankee bonds*, and those in the United Kingdom *bulldog bonds*. Foreign bonds issued and traded in Asia outside Japan (and normally denominated in dollars) are called *dragon bonds*.

international bond market
Market consisting of all bonds sold by issuing companies, governments, or other organizations outside their own countries.

Eurobond
Bond issued outside the country in whose currency it is denominated.

foreign bond
Bond sold outside the borrower's country and denominated in the currency of the country in which it is sold.

Interest Rates: A Driving Force   Today, low interest rates (the cost of borrowing) are fueling growth in the international bond market. Low interest rates in developed nations are resulting from low levels of inflation but also mean that investors earn little interest on bonds issued by governments and companies in domestic markets. Thus, banks, pension funds, and mutual funds are seeking higher returns in the newly industrialized and developing nations, where higher interest payments reflect the greater risk of the bonds. At the same time, corporate and government borrowers in developing countries badly need capital to invest in corporate expansion plans and public works projects. As the demand for money outstrips the supply, interest rates in these markets might go even higher.

This situation raises an interesting question: How can investors who are seeking higher returns and borrowers who are seeking to pay lower interest rates both come out ahead? The answer, at least in part, lies in the international bond market:

➡ By issuing bonds in the international bond market, borrowers from newly industrialized and developing countries can borrow money from other nations where interest rates are lower.

➡ By the same token, investors in developed countries buy bonds in newly industrialized and developing nations in order to obtain higher returns on their investments (although they also accept greater risk).

Despite the attraction of the international bond market, many emerging countries see the need to develop their own national markets. Volatility in the global currency market—such as the drop in value of several major Southeast Asian currencies in the late 1990s—can wreak havoc when projects that earn funds in Indonesian rupiahs or Filipino pesos must pay off debts in dollars. Why? A drop in a country's currency forces borrowers to shell out more local currency to pay off the interest owed on bonds denominated in an unaffected currency.

INTERNATIONAL EQUITY MARKET

international equity market
Market consisting of all stocks bought and sold outside the issuer's home country.

The **international equity market** consists of all stocks bought and sold outside the issuer's home country. Both companies and governments frequently sell shares in the international equity market. Buyers include other companies, banks, mutual funds, pension funds, and individual investors. The stock exchanges that list the greatest number of companies from outside their own borders are Frankfurt, London, and New York. Large international companies frequently list their stocks on several national exchanges simultaneously and sometimes offer new stock issues only outside their country's borders. Four factors are responsible for much of the past growth in the international equity market.

Spread of Privatization   With many countries continuing to abandon central planning and socialist-style economics, the worldwide pace of privatization is accelerating. A single privatization often places billions of dollars of new equity on stock markets. When the government of Peru sold its 26 percent share of the national telephone company, Telefonica del Peru (www.telefonica.com.pe), it raised $1.2 billion. Of the total value of the sale, 48 percent was sold in the United States, 26 percent to other international investors, and another 26 percent to domestic retail and institutional investors in Peru.

Increased privatization in Europe is also expanding worldwide equity. Although historically Europe has been more devoted to debt as a means of financing, an "equity culture" is taking root. As the European Union becomes more thoroughly integrated, investors will become more willing to invest in the stocks of companies from other European nations.

Economic Growth in Developing Countries   Continued economic growth in newly industrialized and developing countries is also contributing to growth in the international equity market. As companies based in emerging economies succeed and grow, they require greater investment. Because only a limited supply of funds is available in these nations, the international equity market is a major source of funding.

Activity of Investment Banks   Investment banks facilitate the sale of a company's stock worldwide by bringing together sellers and large potential buyers. Increasingly, investment banks are searching for investors outside the national market in which a company is headquartered. In fact, this method of raising funds is becoming more common than listing a company's shares on another country's stock exchange. The World Business Survey titled "Ranking the Top Investment Banks" conveys borrowers' satisfaction with the capital-raising abilities of the world's top banks.

Advent of Cybermarkets   The automation of stock exchanges is encouraging growth in the international equity market. The term *cybermarkets* denotes stock markets that have no central geographic locations. Rather, they consist of global trading activities conducted on the Internet. Cybermarkets (consisting of supercomputers, high-speed data lines, satellite uplinks, and individual personal computers) match buyers and sellers in nanoseconds. They allow companies to list their stocks worldwide through an electronic medium in which trading takes place 24 hours a day.[4]

EUROCURRENCY MARKET

All the world's currencies that are banked outside their countries of origin are referred to as *Eurocurrency* and traded on the **Eurocurrency market.** Thus, U.S. dollars deposited in a bank in Tokyo are called *Eurodollars* and British pounds deposited in New York are called *Europounds*. Japanese yen deposited in Frankfurt are called *Euroyen*, and so forth.

> **Eurocurrency market**
> *Market consisting of all the world's currencies (referred to as Eurocurrency) that are banked outside their countries of origin.*

WORLD BUSINESS SURVEY

Ranking the Top Investment Banks

Companies rely on investment banks to locate investors who will provide the firm with capital to finance its projects. Investment banks underwrite new issues of international bonds and equities (among other instruments) on the international capital market. Shown here are the findings of a recent poll asking borrowers what banks provide the best service in the raising of capital and managing risk.

Rank	Institution
1	Deutsche
2	Citibank/Salomon Smith Barney
3	JPMorgan
4	Merrill Lynch
5	Barclays Capital
6	Morgan Stanley Dean Witter
7	Goldman Sachs
8	UBS Warburg
9	Credit Suisse First Boston
10	Lehman Brothers

Because the Eurocurrency market is characterized by very large transactions, only the very largest companies, banks, and governments are typically involved. Deposits originate primarily from four sources:

➡ Governments with excess funds generated by a prolonged trade surplus
➡ Commercial banks with large deposits of excess currency
➡ International companies with large amounts of excess cash
➡ Extremely wealthy individuals

Eurocurrency originated in Europe during the 1950s—hence the "*Euro*" prefix. Communist governments of eastern European nations feared that they might forfeit dollar deposits made in U.S. banks if claims were filed against them by U.S. citizens. To protect their dollar reserves, they deposited them in banks across Europe. Banks in the United Kingdom began lending these dollars to finance international trade deals, and banks in other countries (including Canada and Japan) followed suit. The Eurocurrency market is valued at around $6 trillion, with London accounting for about 20 percent of all deposits. Other important markets include Canada, the Caribbean, Hong Kong, and Singapore.

Appeal of the Eurocurrency Market   Typically, governments strictly regulate commercial banking activities in their own currencies within their borders. For example, they often force banks to pay deposit insurance to a central bank, where they must keep a certain portion of all deposits "on reserve" in non-interest-bearing accounts. Although such restrictions protect investors, they add costs to banking operations.

The main appeal of the Eurocurrency market is the complete absence of regulation. The absence of regulation and its resulting lower costs mean that banks can charge borrowers less, pay investors more, and still earn healthy profits. In addition, extremely large transactions considerably reduce transaction costs. Moreover, **interbank interest rates**—rates that the world's largest banks charge one another for loans—are determined by the free market. The most commonly quoted rate in the Eurocurrency market is the *London Interbank Offer Rate (LIBOR)*—the interest rate that London banks charge other large banks that borrow Eurocurrency. The *London Interbank Bid Rate (LIBID)* is the interest rate offered by London banks to large investors for Eurocurrency deposits.

An unappealing feature of the Eurocurrency market is greater risk: Government regulations that protect depositors in national markets are nonexistent. However, despite the greater risk of default, Eurocurrency transactions are fairly safe because of the size of the banks involved.

interbank interest rates
Interest rates that the world's largest banks charge one another for loans.

FOREIGN EXCHANGE MARKET

foreign exchange market
Market in which currencies are bought and sold and their prices determined.

exchange rate
Rate at which one currency is exchanged for another.

Unlike domestic transactions, international transactions involve the currencies of two or more nations. To exchange one currency for another in international transactions, companies rely on a mechanism called the **foreign exchange market**—a market in which currencies are bought and sold and their prices determined. Financial institutions convert one currency into another at a specific **exchange rate**—the rate at which one currency is exchanged for another. Rates depend on the size of the transaction, the trader conducting it, general economic conditions and, sometimes, government mandate.

In many ways, the foreign exchange market is like the markets for commodities such as cotton, wheat, and copper. The forces of supply and demand determine currency prices, and transactions are conducted through a process of *bid* and *ask quotes*. If someone asks for the current exchange rate of a certain currency, the bank does not know whether it is dealing with a prospective buyer or seller. Thus, it quotes two rates: The *bid quote* is the price at which it will buy, the *ask quote* is the price that it will pay. For example, say that the British pound is quoted in U.S. dollars at $1.6296. The bank may then bid $1.6294 to *buy* British pounds and offer to *sell* them at $1.6298. The difference between the two rates is the *bid–ask spread*. Naturally, banks always buy low and sell high, earning their profits from the bid–ask spread.

FUNCTIONS OF THE FOREIGN EXCHANGE MARKET

The foreign exchange market is not really a source of corporate finance. Rather, it facilitates corporate financial activities and international transactions. Investors use the foreign exchange market for four main reasons.

Currency Conversion   Companies use the foreign exchange market to convert one currency into another. Suppose a Malaysian company sells a large number of computers to a customer in France. The French customer wishes to pay for the computers in euros, the European Union currency, whereas the Malaysian company wants to be paid in its own ringgit. How do the two parties resolve this dilemma? They turn to banks to exchange the currencies for them.

Companies also must convert to local currencies when they undertake foreign direct investment. Later, when a firm's international subsidiary earns a profit and the company wishes to return some of it to the home country, it must convert the local money into the home currency.

Currency Hedging   The practice of insuring against potential losses that result from adverse changes in exchange rates is called **currency hedging.** International companies commonly use hedging for one of two purposes:

> **currency hedging**
> *Practice of insuring against potential losses that result from adverse changes in exchange rates.*

1. To lessen the risk associated with international transfers of funds
2. To protect themselves in credit transactions in which there is a time lag between billing and receipt of payment.

Suppose a South Korean carmaker has a subsidiary in Britain. The parent company in Korea knows that in 30 days—say, on February 1—its British subsidiary will be sending it a payment in British pounds. Because the parent company is concerned about the value of that payment in South Korean *won* one month in the future, it wants to insure against the possibility that the pound's value will fall over that period—meaning, of course, that it will receive less money. Therefore, on January 2 the parent company contracts with a financial institution, such as a bank, to exchange the payment in one month at an agreed-upon exchange rate specified on January 2. In this way, as of January 2 the Korean company knows exactly how many won the payment will be worth on February 1.

Currency Arbitrage   **Currency arbitrage** is the instantaneous purchase and sale of a currency in different markets for profit. For instance, assume that a currency trader in New York notices that the value of the European Union euro is lower in Tokyo than in New York. Therefore, the trader can buy euro in Tokyo, sell them in New York, and earn a profit on the difference. High-tech communication and trading systems allow the entire transaction to occur within seconds. However, if the difference between the value of the euro in Tokyo and the value of the euro in New York is not greater than the cost of conducting the transaction, it is not worth making.

> **currency arbitrage**
> *Instantaneous purchase and sale of a currency in different markets for profit.*

Currency arbitrage is a common activity among experienced traders of foreign exchange, very large investors, and companies in the arbitrage business. Firms whose profits are generated primarily by another economic activity, such as retailing or manufacturing, take part in currency arbitrage only if they have very large sums of cash on hand.

Interest Arbitrage   **Interest arbitrage** is the profit-motivated purchase and sale of interest-paying securities denominated in different currencies. Companies use interest arbitrage to find better interest rates abroad than those that are available in their home countries. The securities involved in such transactions include government treasury

> **interest arbitrage**
> *Profit-motivated purchase and sale of interest-paying securities denominated in different currencies.*

Ordinary citizens across Southeast Asia suffered badly after the values of their nations' currencies collapsed in the late 1990s. An Indonesian protester with a fistful of rupiah banknotes shouts during a demonstration in front of the central bank as riot police look on in Jakarta. He was one of a group of people that was protesting rising food prices as Indonesia battled its worst economic crisis in three decades. The sign behind the man reads "The country's debt—why should the people pay?"

bills, corporate and government bonds, and even bank deposits. Suppose a trader notices that the interest rates paid on bank deposits in Mexico are higher than those paid in Sydney, Australia (after adjusting for exchange rates). He can convert Australian dollars to Mexican pesos and deposit the money in a Mexican bank account for, say, one year. At the end of the year, he converts the pesos back into Australian dollars and earns more in interest than the same money would have earned had it remained on deposit in an Australian bank.

currency speculation
Purchase or sale of a currency with the expectation that its value will change and generate a profit.

Currency Speculation   **Currency speculation** is the purchase or sale of a currency with the expectation that its value will change and generate a profit. The shift in value might be expected to occur suddenly or over a longer period. The foreign exchange trader may bet that a currency's price will go either up or down in the future. Suppose a trader in London believes that the value of the Japanese yen will increase over the next three months. Therefore, today she buys yen with pounds at the current price, intending to sell them in 90 days. If the price of yen rises in that time, she earns a profit; if it falls, she takes a loss. Speculation is much riskier than arbitrage because the value, or price, of currencies is quite volatile and is affected by many factors. Like arbitrage, currency speculation is commonly the realm of foreign exchange specialists rather than the managers of firms engaged in other endeavors.

A classic example of currency speculation unfolded in Southeast Asia in 1997. After news emerged in May about Thailand's slowing economy and political instability, currency traders sprang into action. They responded to poor economic growth prospects and an overvalued currency, the Thai baht, by dumping the baht on the foreign exchange market. When the supply glutted the market, the value of the baht plunged. Meanwhile, traders began speculating that other Asian economies were also vulnerable. From the time the crisis first hit until the end of 1997, the value of the Indonesian rupiah fell by 87 percent, the South Korean won by 85 percent, the Thai baht by 63 percent, the Philippine peso by 34 percent, and the Malaysian ringgit by 32 percent.[5] Although many currency speculators made a great deal of money, the resulting hardship experienced by these nations' citizens caused some to question the ethics of currency speculation on such a scale. (We cover the Asian crisis and currency speculation in detail in Chapter 10.)

Because of the importance of foreign exchange to trade and investment, businesspeople must understand how currencies are quoted in the foreign exchange market. Managers must understand the financial instruments available to help them protect the profits earned by their international business activities. They must also be aware of government restrictions that may be imposed on the convertibility of currencies and know how to work around these and other obstacles.

QUOTING CURRENCIES

There are two components to every quoted exchange rate: the quoted currency and the base currency. If an exchange rate quotes the number of Japanese yen needed to buy one U.S. dollar (¥/$), the yen is the **quoted currency** and the dollar the **base currency**. When you designate any exchange rate, the quoted currency is always the *numerator* and the base currency the *denominator*. For example, if you were given a yen/dollar exchange rate quote of 120/1 (meaning that 120 yen are needed to buy 1 dollar), the numerator is 120 and the denominator 1. We can also designate this rate as ¥ 120/$.

Direct and Indirect Rate Quotes   Table 9.1 lists exchange rates between the U.S. dollar and a number of other currencies as reported by the *Wall Street Journal.* There is one important thing to note about this table. The currencies of those nations that are participating in the single currency (*euro*) of the European Union are already out of public circulation. However, the business press continues to quote exchange rates for the national currencies alongside the euro. For example, you can see in Table 9.1 a quote for the Netherlands' former currency, the guilder, and the euro, which now circulates.

The second column of numbers in Table 9.1, under the heading "Currency per U.S. $," tells us *how many units of each listed currency can be purchased with one U.S. dollar.* For example, find the row labeled "Japan (Yen)." The number 134.70 in the second column tells us that 134.70 Japanese yen can be bought with 1 U.S. dollar. We state this exchange rate as ¥ 134.70/$. Because the yen is the quoted currency, we say that this is a *direct quote* on the yen and an *indirect quote* on the dollar. This method of quoting exchange rates is called *European terms* because it is typically used outside the United States.

The first column of numbers in Table 9.1, under the heading "U.S. $ equivalent," tells us how many U.S. dollars it costs to buy one unit of each listed currency. The first column following the words "Japan (Yen)," tells us that it costs $0.007424 to purchase 1 yen (¥)—less than one U.S. cent. We state this exchange rate as $0.007424/¥. In this case, because the dollar is the quoted currency, we have a *direct quote* on the dollar and an *indirect quote* on the yen. The practice of quoting the U.S. dollar in direct terms is called *U.S. terms* because it is used mainly in the United States.

Whether we use a direct or an indirect quote, it is easy to find the other: simply divide the quote into the numeral 1. The following formula is used to derive a direct quote from an indirect quote:

$$\text{Direct quote} = \frac{1}{\text{Indirect quote}}$$

And for deriving an indirect quote from a direct quote:

$$\text{Indirect quote} = \frac{1}{\text{Direct quote}}$$

For example, suppose we are given an indirect quote on the U.S. dollar of ¥ 134.70/$. To find the direct quote, we simply divide ¥ 134.70 into $1:

$$\$1 \div \text{¥} \, 134.70 = \$0.007424 / \text{¥}$$

quoted currency
In a quoted exchange rate, the currency with which another currency is to be purchased.

base currency
In a quoted exchange rate, the currency that is to be purchased with another currency.

TABLE 9.1 **Exchange Rates, Friday, February 8, 2002**

Country	U.S. $ equiv.	Currency per U.S. $	Country	U.S. $ equiv.	Currency per U.S. $
Argentina (Peso)	0.4819	2.0750	Japan (Yen)	0.007424	134.70
Australia (Dollar)	0.5104	1.9594	1 Month Forward	0.007435	134.51
Austria (Schilling)	0.06344	15.763	3 Months Forward	0.007457	134.09
Bahrain (Dinar)	2.6525	0.3770	6 Months Forward	0.007496	133.41
Belgium (Franc)	0.02164	46.211	Jordan (Dinar)	1.4104	0.7090
Brazil (Real)	0.4067	2.4590	Kuwait (Dinar)	3.2478	0.3079
Britain (Pound)	1.4143	0.7071	Lebanon(Pound)	0.0006605	1,514.0
1 Month Forward	1.4120	0.7082	Malaysia (Ringitt)[b]	0.2632	3.8000
3 Months Forward	1.4070	0.7107	Malta (Lira)	2.1896	0.4567
6 Months Forward	1.3997	0.7144	Mexico (Peso)	0.1102	9.0750
Canada (Dollar)	0.6258	1.5980	Netherland (Guilder)	0.3961	2.5244
1 Month Forward	0.6257	1.5982	New Zealand (Dollar)	0.4183	2.3906
3 Months Forward	0.6254	1.5989	Norway (Krone)	0.1114	8.9799
6 Months Forward	0.6251	1.5997	Pakistan (Rupee)	0.01663	60.150
Chile (Peso)	0.001460	685.15	Peru (New Sol)	0.2865	3.4900
China (Renminbi)	0.1208	8.2767	Philippines (Peso)	0.01952	51.225
Colombia (Peso)	0.0004383	2,281.8	Poland (Zloty)	0.2375	4.2100
Czech Republic (Koruna)			Portugal (Escudo)	0.004354	229.66
Commercial Rate	0.02748	36.384	Russia (Ruble)[c]	0.03252	30.752
Denmark (Krone)	0.1175	8.5084	Saudi Arabia (Riyal)	0.2666	3.7504
Ecuador (US Dollar)[a]	1.0000	1.0000	Singapore (Dollar)	0.5451	1.8344
Finland (Markka)	0.1468	6.8111	Slovak Republic (Koruna)	0.02059	48.557
France (Franc)	0.1331	7.5143	South Africa (Rand)	0.08753	11.425
1 Month Forward	0.1329	7.5231	South Korea (Won)	0.0007603	1,315.2
3 Months Forward	0.1326	7.5425	Spain (Peseta)	0.005247	190.60
6 Months Forward	0.1321	7.5678	Sweden (Krona)	0.09440	10.593
Germany (Mark)	0.4463	2.2405	Switzerland (Franc)	0.5918	1.6897
1 Month Forward	0.4458	2.2431	1 Month Forward	0.5919	1.6894
3 Months Forward	0.4447	2.2489	3 Months Forward	0.5921	1.6889
6 Months Forward	0.4432	2.2565	6 Months Forward	0.5926	1.6875
Greece (Drachma)	0.002562	390.30	Taiwan (Dollar)	0.02855	35.030
Hong Kong (Dollar)	0.1282	7.7993	Thailand (Baht)	0.02275	43.965
Hungary (Forint)	0.003579	279.44	Turkish (Lira)	0.00000071	1,402,500
India (Rupee)	0.02055	48.650	United Arab (Dirham)	0.2723	3.6730
Indonesia (Rupiah)	0.0000976	10,250	Uruguay (Peso) Financial	0.06885	14.525
Ireland (Punt)	1.1084	0.9022	Venezuela (Bolivar)	0.001257	795.50
Israel (Shekel)	0.2143	4.6660			
Italy (Lira)	0.0004508	2,218.1	Special Drawing Rights	1.2450	0.8032
			Euro	0.8730	1.1455

Special Drawing Rights (SDR) are based on exchange rates for the U.S., German, British, French, and Japanese currencies.
[a] Adopted U.S. dollar as of 9/11/00. [b] Government rate. [c] Russian Central Bank rate.

Note that our solution matches the number in the first column of Table 9.1 following the words "Japan (Yen)." Conversely, to find the indirect quote, we divide the direct quote into 1. In our example, we divide $0.007424 into ¥ 1:

$$¥\ 1 \div \$0.007424 = ¥\ 134.70\,/\$$$

This solution matches the number in the second column of Table 9.1 following the words "Japan (Yen)."

Calculating Percent Change   Why are businesspeople and foreign exchange traders interested in tracking currency values over time as measured by exchange rates? Because changes in currency values can benefit or harm current and future international transactions. **Exchange-rate risk** (also known as **foreign exchange risk**) is the risk of adverse changes in exchange rates. Managers develop strategies to minimize this risk by tracking percent changes in exchange rates. For example, take P_N as the exchange rate at the end of a period (the currency's *new* price), and P_O as the exchange rate at the beginning of that period (the currency's *old* price). Now we can calculate percent change in the value of a currency with the following formula:

$$\text{Percent change (\%)} = \frac{Pn - Po}{Po} \times 100$$

Note: This equation yields the percent change in the base currency, not in the quoted currency.

Let's illustrate the usefulness of this calculation with a simple example. Suppose that on February 1 of the current year, the exchange rate between the Polish zloty (PLZ) and the U.S. dollar was PLZ 5/$. On March 1 of the current year, the exchange rate stood at PLZ 4/$. What is the change in the value of the base currency—the dollar? If we plug these numbers into our formula, we arrive at the following change in the value of the dollar:

$$\text{Percent change (\%)} = \frac{4 - 5}{5} \times 100 = -20\%$$

Thus, the value of the dollar has fallen 20 percent. In other words, one U.S. dollar buys 20 percent fewer Polish zloty on March 1 than it did on February 1.

To calculate the change in the value of the Polish zloty, we must first calculate the indirect exchange rate on the zloty; this is necessary because we want to make the zloty our base currency. Using the formula presented earlier, we obtain an exchange rate of $.20/PLZ (1 ÷ PLZ 5) on February 1 and an exchange rate of $.25/PLZ (1 ÷ PLZ 4) on March 1. Plugging these rates into our percent-change formula, we get:

$$\text{Percent change (\%)} = \frac{.25 - .20}{.20} \times 100 = 25\%$$

Thus, the value of the Polish zloty has risen 25 percent. One Polish zloty buys 25 percent more U.S. dollars on March 1 than it did on February 1.

How important is this difference to businesspeople and exchange traders? Consider the fact that the typical trading unit in the foreign exchange market (called a *round lot*) is $5 million. Therefore, a $5 million purchase of zlotys on February 1 would yield PLZ 25 million. But because the dollar has lost 20 percent of its buying power by March 1, a $5 million purchase would get us only 20 million Polish zloty—5 million fewer zloty than a month earlier.

Cross Rates   International transactions between two currencies other than the U.S. dollar often use the dollar as a vehicle currency. For instance, a retail buyer of merchandise in the Netherlands might convert its euros (recall that the Netherlands now uses the EU currency) to U.S. dollars and then pay its Japanese supplier in U.S. dollars. The Japanese supplier may then take those U.S. dollars and convert them to Japanese yen. This process was more common years ago, when fewer currencies were freely convertible and when the United States greatly dominated world trade. Today, a Japanese sup-

In the right margin:

exchange-rate risk (foreign exchange risk)
Risk of adverse changes in exchange rates.

plier may want payment in euros. In this case, both the Japanese and the Dutch companies need to know the exchange rate between their respective currencies. To find this rate using their respective exchange rates with the U.S. dollar, we calculate what is called their **cross rate**—an exchange rate calculated using two other exchange rates.

cross rate
Exchange rate calculated using two other exchange rates.

Cross rates between two currencies can be calculated using either currency's indirect or direct exchange rates with another currency. For example, suppose we want to know the cross rate between the currencies of the Netherlands and Japan. If we return to Table 9.1 we see that the *direct* quote on the euro is € 1.1455/$. The *direct* quote on the Japanese yen is ¥ 134.70/$. To find the cross rate between the euro and the yen, with the yen as the base currency, we simply divide € 1.1455/$ by ¥ 134.70/$:

$$\text{€ } 1.1455/\$ \div \text{¥ } 134.70/\$ = \text{€ } 0.0085/\text{¥}$$

Thus, it costs 0.0085 euros to buy 1 yen.

We can also calculate the cross rate between the euro and the yen by using the indirect quotes for each currency against the U.S. dollar. Again, we see in Table 9.1 that the *indirect* quote on the euro to the dollar is $0.8730/€. The *indirect* quote on the yen to the dollar is $0.007424/¥. To find the cross rate between the euro and the yen, again with the yen as the base currency, we divide $0.8730/€ by $0.007424/¥:

$$\$0.8730/\text{€} \div \$0.007424/\text{¥} = \text{€}117.59/\text{¥}$$

We must then perform an additional step to arrive at the same answer as we did earlier. Because *indirect* quotes were used in our calculation, we must divide our answer into 1:

$$1 \div \text{€ } 117.59/\text{¥} = \text{€ } 0.0085/\text{¥}$$

Again (as in our earlier solution), we see that it costs 0.0085 euros to buy 1 yen.

Table 9.2 shows the cross rates for major world currencies. When finding cross rates using direct quotes, currencies down the left-hand side represent quoted currencies; those across the top represent base currencies. Conversely, when finding cross rates using indirect quotes, currencies down the left-hand side represent base currencies; those across the top represent quoted currencies. Look at the intersection of the "Euro" row (the quoted currency in our example) and the "Yen" column (our base currency). Note that our solutions for the cross rate between euro and yen match the listed rate of 0.0085 euros to the yen.

TABLE 9.2 | **Key Currency Cross Rates**

	Dollar	Euro	Pound	SFranc	Guilder	Peso	Yen	Lira	D-Mark	FFranc	CdnDlr
Canada	1.5980	1.3951	2.2601	0.9457	0.6330	0.1761	0.0119	0.0007	0.7132	0.2127	—
France	7.5143	6.5600	10.627	4.4471	2.9767	0.8280	0.0558	0.0034	3.3538	—	4.7023
Germany	2.2405	1.9560	3.1687	1.3260	0.8875	0.2469	0.0166	0.0010	—	0.2982	1.4021
Italy	2,218.1	1,936.4	3,137.0	1,312.7	878.66	244.42	16.467	—	989.99	295.18	1,388.0
Japan	134.70	117.59	190.51	79.718	53.359	14.843	—	0.0607	60.121	17.926	84.293
Mexico	9.0750	7.9225	12.835	5.3708	3.5949	—	0.0674	0.0041	4.0504	1.2077	5.6790
Netherlands	2.5244	2.2038	3.5703	1.4940	—	0.2782	0.0187	0.0011	1.1267	0.3359	1.5797
Switzerland	1.6897	1.4751	2.3897	—	0.6693	0.1862	0.0125	0.0008	0.7542	0.2249	1.0574
United Kingdom	0.7071	0.6173	—	0.4185	0.2801	0.0779	0.0052	0.0003	0.3156	0.0941	0.4425
Euro	1.1455	—	1.6200	0.6779	0.4538	0.1262	0.0085	0.0005	0.5113	0.1524	0.7168
United States	—	0.8730	1.4143	0.5918	0.3961	0.1102	0.0074	0.0005	0.4463	0.1331	0.6258

Naturally, the exchange rate between the euro and the yen is quite important to both our Japanese supplier and the Dutch retailer. If the value of the euro falls relative to the yen, the Dutch company must pay more in euros for its Japanese products. This situation will force the Dutch company to take one of two steps: either increase the price at which it resells the Japanese product (perhaps reducing sales) or keep prices at current levels (thus reducing its profit margin). Ironically, the Japanese supplier will suffer if the yen rises too much. Why? Under such circumstances, the Japanese supplier can do one of two things: allow the exchange rate to force its euro prices higher (thus maintaining profits) or reduce its yen prices to offset the decline of the euro (thus reducing its profit margin). Both the Japanese supplier and the Dutch buyer can absorb exchange rate changes by squeezing profits—but only to a point. Once that point is passed, they will no longer be able to trade. The Dutch buyer will be forced to look for a supplier in a country with a more favorable exchange rate or for a supplier in its own country (or another that uses the euro).

SPOT RATES

All the exchange rates we've discussed so far are called **spot rates**—exchange rates that require delivery of the traded currency within 2 business days. Exchange of the two currencies is said to occur "on the spot," and the **spot market** is the market for currency transactions at spot rates. The spot market assists companies in performing any one of three functions:

1. Converting income generated from sales in another country into their home-country currency
2. Converting funds into the currency of an international supplier
3. Converting funds into the currency of a country in which they wish to invest

spot rate
Exchange rate requiring delivery of the traded currency within 2 business days.

spot market
Market for currency transactions at spot rates.

Buy and Sell Rates The spot rate is available only for trades worth millions of dollars. That is why it is available only to banks and foreign exchange brokers. If you are traveling to another country and want to exchange currencies at your bank before departing, you will not be quoted the spot rate. Rather, banks and other institutions will give you a *buy rate* (the exchange rate at which the bank will buy a currency) and an *ask rate* (the rate at which it will sell a currency). In other words, you will receive what we described when introducing the foreign exchange market as *bid* and *ask* quotes. These rates reflect the amounts that large currency traders are charging, plus a markup.

For example, suppose that you are leaving Mexico for a business trip to Canada and need to buy some Canadian dollars (C$). The bank will quote you exchange rate terms, such as Peso 5.6785/95 per C$. In other words, the bank will buy Canadian dollars at the rate of Peso 5.6785/C$ and sell them at the rate of Peso 5.6795/C$.

FORWARD RATES

When a company knows that it will need a certain amount of foreign currency on a certain future date, it can exchange currencies using a **forward rate**—an exchange rate at which two parties agree to exchange currencies on a specified future date. Forward rates represent the expectations of currency traders and bankers regarding a currency's future spot rate. Reflected in these expectations are a country's present and future economic conditions (including inflation rate, national debt, taxes, trade balance, and economic growth rate) as well as its social and political situation. The **forward market** is the market for currency transactions at forward rates.

forward rate
Exchange rate at which two parties agree to exchange currencies on a specified future date.

forward market
Market for currency transactions at forward rates.

Companies commonly use the forward market to insure themselves against unfavorable exchange-rate changes. It can be used for all types of transactions that require future payment in other currencies, including credit sales or purchases, interest receipts or payments on investments or loans, and dividend payments to stockholders in other countries. However, not all currencies are traded in the forward market. In particular, these include the currencies of countries with high inflation rates or currencies that generate little demand on international financial markets.

Forward Contracts   Suppose a Brazilian bicycle maker imports parts from a Japanese supplier. Under the terms of their contract, the Brazilian importer must pay 100 million Japanese yen in 90 days. The Brazilian firm can wait until one or two days before payment is due, buy yen in the spot market, and pay the Japanese supplier. Unfortunately, in the 90 days between the contract and the due date, the exchange rate will probably change. What if the value of the Brazilian *real* goes down? In that case, the Brazilian importer will have to pay more reals to get the same 100 million Japanese yen. Therefore, our importer may want to pay off the debt before the 90-day term. But what if it does not have the cash on hand? What if it needs those 90 days to collect accounts receivable from its own customers?

To decrease its exchange-rate risk, our Brazilian importer can enter into a **forward contract**—a contract that requires the exchange of an agreed-upon amount of a currency on an agreed-upon date at a specific exchange rate. Forward contracts are commonly signed for 30, 90, and 180 days into the future, but customized contracts (say, for 76 days) are possible. Note that a forward contract *requires* exchange of an agreed-upon amount of a currency on an agreed-upon date at a specific exchange rate: The bank must deliver the yen, and the Brazilian importer must buy them at the prearranged price. Forward contracts belong to a family of financial instruments called **derivatives**—instruments whose values *derive* from other commodities or financial instruments. These include not only forward contracts, but also currency swaps, options, and futures (which we discuss below).

In our example, the Brazilian importer can use a forward contract to pay yen to its Japanese supplier in 90 days. It is always possible, of course, that in 90 days, the value of the real will be lower than its current value. But by locking in at the forward rate, the Brazilian firm protects itself against the less favorable spot rate at which it would have to buy yen in 90 days. In this case, the Brazilian company protects itself from paying more to the supplier at the end of 90 days than if it were to pay at the spot rate in 90 days. Thus, it protects its profit from further erosion if the spot rate becomes even more unfavorable over the next three months. Remember, too, that such a contract prevents the Brazilian importer from taking advantage of any increase in the value of the real in 90 days that would reduce what the company owed its Japanese supplier.

Premiums and Discounts   As we have already seen, a currency's forward exchange rate can be higher or lower than its current spot rate. If its forward rate is higher than its spot rate, the currency is trading at a *premium*. If its forward rate is lower, it is trading at a *discount*. Return once again to Table 9.1. Locate the row under "Britain (Pound)" labeled "1 Month Forward." This is the 30-day forward exchange rate for the British pound (GBP). Note that the rate of $1.4120/GBP is *less* than the spot rate of $1.4143/GBP (the spot rate quoted in the previous row of Table 9.1). The pound, therefore, is trading at a *discount* on the 1-month forward contract. We know, then, that a contract to deliver British pounds in 30 days costs $0.0023 less per pound in 30 days than it does today. Likewise, the 3- and 6-month forward rates tell us that pounds cost $0.0073 and $0.0146 less in 90 and 180 days, respectively. Clearly, the pound is also trading at a discount on 3- and 6-month forward contracts.

forward contract
Contract that requires the exchange of an agreed-upon amount of a currency on an agreed-upon date at a specific exchange rate.

derivative
Financial instrument whose value derives from other commodities or financial instruments.

SWAPS, OPTIONS, AND FUTURES

In addition to forward contracts, three other types of currency instruments are used in the forward market: currency swaps, options, and futures.

Currency Swaps A **currency swap** is the simultaneous purchase and sale of foreign exchange for two different dates. Currency swaps are an increasingly important component of the foreign exchange market. Suppose a Swedish carmaker imports parts from a subsidiary in Turkey. The Swedish company must pay the Turkish subsidiary in Turkish lira for the parts when they are delivered tomorrow. It also expects to receive Turkish liras for cars sold in Turkey in 90 days. Our Swedish company exchanges krona for lira in the spot market today to pay its subsidiary. At the same time, it agrees to a forward contract to sell Turkish lira (and buy Swedish krona) in 90 days at the quoted 90-day forward rate for lira. In this way, the Swedish company uses a swap both to reduce its exchange-rate risk and to lock in the future exchange rate. In this sense, we can think of a currency swap as a more complex forward contract.

Currency Options Recall that a forward contract *requires* exchange of an agreed-upon amount of a currency on an agreed-upon date at a specific exchange rate. In contrast, a **currency option** is a right, or *option*, to exchange a specific amount of a currency on a specific date at a specific rate. In other words, whereas forward contracts require parties to follow through on currency exchanges, currency options do not.

Suppose a company buys an option to purchase Swiss francs at SF 1.67/$ in 30 days. If, at the end of the 30 days, the exchange rate is SF 1.70/$, the company would *not* exercise its currency option. Why? It could get 0.03 more Swiss francs for every dollar by exchanging at the spot rate in the currency market rather than at the stated rate of the option. Companies often use currency options to hedge against exchange rate risk or to obtain foreign currency.

Currency Futures Contracts Similar to a currency forward contract is a **currency futures contract**—a contract requiring the exchange of a specific amount of currency on a specific date at a specific exchange rate. All of these conditions are fixed and not adjustable.

FOREIGN EXCHANGE MARKET TODAY

The foreign exchange market is actually an electronic network that connects the world's major financial centers. In turn, each of these centers is a network of foreign exchange traders, currency trading banks, and investment firms. In a single day, the volume of trading on the foreign exchange market (comprising currency swaps and spot and forward contracts) totals more than $1.2 trillion—roughly the yearly gross domestic product of Italy.[6] Several major trading centers and several currencies dominate the foreign exchange market.

TRADING CENTERS

Most of the world's major cities participate in trading on the foreign exchange market. However, in recent years, just three countries have come to account for slightly more than half of all global currency trading: the United Kingdom, the United States, and Japan. Accordingly, most of this trading takes place in the financial capitals of London, New York, and Tokyo.

London dominates the foreign exchange market for historic and geographic reasons. The United Kingdom was once the world's largest trading nation. British merchants needed to exchange currencies of different nations, and London naturally assumed the role of financial trading center. London quickly came to dominate the market and still does so because of its location halfway between North America and Asia. A key factor is its time zone. Because of differences in time zones, London is opening for business as markets in Asia close trading for the day. When New York opens for trading in the morning, trading continues in London for several hours.

Map 9.1 shows why it is possible to trade foreign exchange 24 hours a day (except weekends and major holidays). At least one of the three major centers (London, New York, and Tokyo) keeps the market open for 21 hours each day. Moreover, trading does not stop during the three hours they are closed because other trading centers (including San Francisco and Sydney, Australia) remain open. Also, most large banks that are active in foreign exchange ensure continuous trading by employing overnight traders.

IMPORTANT CURRENCIES

vehicle currency
Currency used as an intermediary to convert funds between two other currencies.

Although the United Kingdom is the major location of foreign exchange trading, the U.S. dollar is the currency that dominates the foreign exchange market. Because the U.S. dollar is so widely used in world trade, it is considered a **vehicle currency**—a currency used as an intermediary to convert funds between two other currencies. The currencies most often involved in currency transactions are the U.S. dollar, British pound, Japanese yen, and European Union euro.

The U.S. dollar is a vehicle currency for two main reasons. First, the United States is the world's largest trading nation. Because the United States is so heavily involved in international trade, many international companies and banks maintain dollar deposits, making it easy to exchange other currencies with dollars. Second, following World War II, all of the world's major currencies were tied indirectly to the dollar because it was the

MAP 9.1 *Financial Trading Centers, by Time Zone*

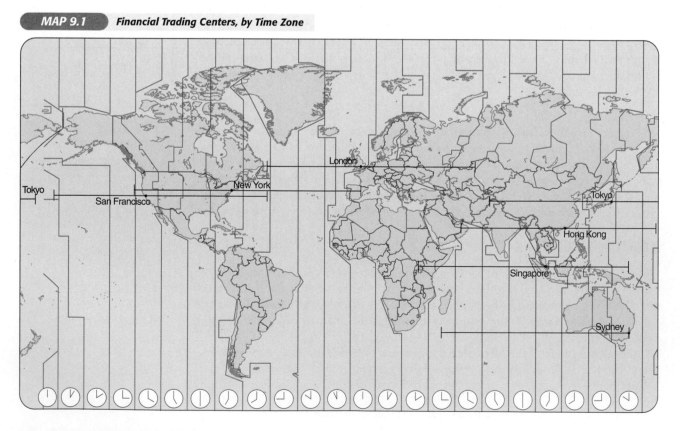

most stable currency. In turn, the dollar's value was tied to a specific value of gold—a policy that held wild currency swings in check. Although world currencies are no longer linked to the value of gold (see Chapter 10), the stability of the dollar, along with its resistance to inflation, helps people and organizations maintain their purchasing power better than their own national currencies. Even today, people in many countries convert extra cash from national currencies into dollars.

INSTITUTIONS OF THE FOREIGN EXCHANGE MARKET

So far, we have discussed the foreign exchange market only in general terms. We now look at the three main components of the foreign exchange market: the interbank market, securities exchanges, and the over-the-counter market.

Interbank Market It is in the **interbank market** that the world's largest banks exchange currencies at spot and forward rates. Many companies receive their foreign exchange services from the banks with which they do most of their business. Each bank satisfies client requests for exchange quotes by obtaining them from other banks in the interbank market. For transactions that involve commonly exchanged currencies, the largest banks often have sufficient currency on hand. But rarely exchanged currencies are not typically kept on hand and may in fact not be obtainable from another bank. In such cases, banks turn to *foreign exchange brokers*, who maintain vast networks through which to obtain seldom traded currencies.

> **interbank market**
> Market in which the world's largest banks exchange currencies at spot and forward rates.

In the interbank market, then, banks act as agents for client companies. In addition to locating and exchanging currencies, banks commonly offer advice on trading strategy, supply a variety of currency instruments, and provide other risk-management services. They also help clients manage exchange-rate risk by providing information on rules and regulations around the world.

Large banks in the interbank market have significant power in currency markets and use their influence to get better rates than smaller players. Of course, clients benefit when banks pass on savings in the form of lower fees. However, small firms often find it difficult to get favorable bank rates because they deal only in small volumes of currencies and do so rather infrequently. For this reason, a small company might choose a discount international payment service to provide it with better quotes.

Clearing Mechanisms Clearing mechanisms are an important element of the interbank market. Banks continuously perform foreign exchange transactions with other banks and foreign exchange brokers. These accounts are not settled after each individual trade in a single currency. Rather, they are settled after a number of transactions have been processed. The process of aggregating the currencies that one bank owes another and then carrying out that transaction is called **clearing.** In the past, clearing was normally done each day or once every 2 days and involved the actual transportation of currencies from one bank to another. But nowadays clearing is performed more frequently and handled through computerized clearing mechanisms.

> **clearing**
> Process of aggregating the currencies that one bank owes another and then carrying out the transaction.

Securities Exchanges **Securities exchanges** specialize in currency futures and options transactions. Buying and selling currencies on these exchanges entails the use of securities *brokers*, who facilitate transactions by transmitting and executing clients' orders. Transactions on securities exchanges are much smaller than those in the interbank market and vary with each currency. The world's largest futures and options exchange is the Chicago Board of Trade (www.cbt.com). The exchange has 3,600 members trading in 48 different futures and options products.[7] The second-largest futures exchange is the Chicago Mercantile Exchange (www.cme.com), a company with 2,725 members—mostly banks, investment firms, brokers, and independent traders. That exchange deals in a variety of financial futures, including futures for most major currencies.[8]

> **securities exchange**
> Exchange specializing in currency futures and options transactions.

The third-largest exchange is the London International Financial Futures Exchange (www.liffe.com), on which trades futures and options for major currencies. In the United States, trading in currency *options* occurs only on the Philadelphia Stock Exchange (www.phlx.com), the leading currency options exchange in the world. It deals in both standardized options and customized options, allowing investors flexibility in designing currency option contracts.[9]

over-the-counter (OTC) market
Exchange consisting of a global computer network of foreign exchange traders and other market participants.

Over-the-Counter Market   The **over-the-counter (OTC) market** is an exchange with no central trading location: It consists of a global computer network of foreign exchange traders and other market participants. All foreign exchange transactions can be performed in the OTC market. The major players are large financial institutions and investment banks, including Goldman Sachs (www.gs.com) and Merrill Lynch (www.ml.com).

The over-the-counter market has grown rapidly because it offers several benefits for business. First, it allows businesspeople to search freely for the institution that provides the best (lowest) price for conducting a transaction. Second, it offers greater opportunities for designing customized transactions. See the Global Manager titled "Five Strategies

GLOBAL MANAGER

Five Strategies for More Effective Foreign Exchange Management

1. **Analyze your foreign exchange activities and choose service providers who best fit your needs.** Analyze your needs. What is the nature of your foreign exchange activity? What types of transactions do you undertake and in which currencies? How frequent and how large are your wire transfers? Could repetitive transfers be consolidated? Next, take a close look at the range of service providers available to you. Many businesspeople automatically turn to local bankers when they need to transfer funds abroad, but this may not be the best choice. In some cases, a mix of service providers might offer the best solution.

2. **Trade with major players in the foreign exchange market.** In terms of cost and service, money-center banks—those located in financial centers—who participate directly in the foreign exchange market may have some advantages over local banks. Often, dealing directly with a large trading institution is more cost effective than dealing with a local bank because it avoids the additional markup that the local bank charges for its services.

3. **Consolidate transactions to boost your buying power and realize economies of scale.** Depending on your circumstances, you may want to time international payments in order to consolidate multiple transfers into one large transaction. If you find yourself making multiple smaller payments in the same currency, consider opening a local-currency account

abroad against which you can write drafts. Likewise, allowing foreign receivables to accumulate in an interest-bearing local account until they can be repatriated in a lump sum may prove more advantageous than exchanging each payment individually.

4. **Encourage competition between providers and be an aggressive negotiator.** If your foreign exchange activity is substantial, work to develop relationships with at least two money-center banks. Then you can play one against the other to get the best rates. You should also monitor the rates you're getting over time. Some institutions raise rates gradually, especially if they sense you're not shopping around. To monitor your exchange rates accurately, you'll need access to real-time market rates provided by firms like Reuters, Telerate, and Bloomberg. A word of caution: Beware of less expensive, time-delayed services that delay data by 15 minutes or more—an eternity in the foreign exchange market where rates can change by the second.

5. **Automate your operations for greater accuracy and efficiency.** Every phone call, fax, or transmittal opens the door to human error and delays in getting funds where and when you need them. That is why it makes sense to harness the power of computers to your international wire transfers and drafts. Widely available from banks and specialized service providers, automated software programs greatly reduce the potential for errors and miscommunication while speeding the execution of transfers.

for More Effective Foreign Exchange Management" for other ways that companies can become more adept in their foreign exchange activities.

Our discussion of the foreign exchange market so far assumes that all currencies can be readily converted to another in the foreign exchange market. A **convertible currency** (also called **hard currency**) is traded freely in the foreign exchange market, with its price determined by the forces of supply and demand. Countries that allow full convertibility are those that are in strong financial positions and have adequate reserves of foreign currencies. Such countries have no reason to fear that people will sell their own currency for that of another. However, many newly industrialized and developing countries do not permit the free convertibility of their currencies. Let's now take a look at why governments place restrictions on the convertibility of currencies and how they do it.

GOALS OF CURRENCY RESTRICTION

Governments impose currency restrictions to achieve several goals. One goal is to preserve a country's reserve of hard currencies with which to repay debts owed to other nations. Developed nations, emerging markets, and some countries that export natural resources tend to have the greatest amounts of foreign exchange. Without sufficient reserves (liquidity), a country could default on its loans and thereby discourage future investment flows. This is precisely what happened to Argentina in January of 2002. Three months following the default, the economy seemed to be sinking into chaos further still.

A second goal of currency restriction is to preserve hard currencies to pay for imports and to finance trade deficits. Recall from Chapter 5 that a country runs a *trade deficit* when the value of its imports exceeds the value of its exports. Currency restrictions help governments maintain inventories of foreign currencies with which to pay for such trade imbalances. They also make importing more difficult because local companies cannot obtain foreign currency to pay for imports. The resulting reduction in imports directly improves the country's trade balance.

A third goal is to protect a currency from speculators. For instance, in the wake of the 1997–1998 Asian financial crisis, some Southeast Asian nations considered the control of their currencies as an option to limit the damage done by economic downturns. For example, Malaysia stemmed the outflow of foreign money by preventing local investors from converting their Malaysian holdings into other currencies. The move also curtailed currency speculation but, in the process, effectively cut off Malaysia from investors elsewhere in the world.

A fourth (less common) goal is to keep resident individuals and businesses from investing in other nations. These policies are designed to generate more rapid economic growth by forcing investment in the home country. Unfortunately, although this might work in the short term, it normally slows long-term economic growth. The reason is that there is no guarantee that domestic funds held in the home country will be invested there. Instead, they might be saved or even spent on consumption. Ironically, increased consumption can mean further increases in imports, making the balance-of-trade deficit even worse.

POLICIES FOR RESTRICTING CURRENCIES

Certain government policies are frequently used to restrict currency convertibility. Governments can require that all foreign exchange transactions be performed at or approved by the country's central bank. They can also require import licenses for some or all import transactions. These licenses help the government control the amount of foreign currency leaving the country.

convertible currency (hard currency)
Currency that trades freely in the foreign exchange market, with its price determined by the forces of supply and demand.

Some governments implement systems of *multiple exchange rates*, specifying a higher exchange rate on the importation of certain goods or on imports from certain countries. The government can thus reduce importation while ensuring that important goods still enter the country. It also can use such a policy to target the goods of countries with which it is running a trade deficit.

Other governments issue *import deposit requirements* that require businesses to deposit certain percentages of their foreign exchange funds in special accounts before being granted import licenses. In addition, *quantity restrictions* limit the amount of foreign currency that residents can take out of the home country when traveling to other countries as tourists, students, or medical patients.

Countertrade   Finally, one way to get around national restrictions on currency convertibility is **countertrade**—the practice of selling goods or services that are paid for, in whole or part, with other goods or services. One simple form of countertrade is a *barter* transaction, in which goods are exchanged for others of equal value. Parties exchange goods and then sell them in world markets for hard currency. For instance, Cuba once exchanged $60 million worth of sugar for cereals, pasta, and vegetable oils from the Italian firm Italgrani, and Boeing (**www.boeing.com**) has sold aircraft to Saudi Arabia in return for oil. The many different forms of countertrade are covered in detail in Chapter 13.

> **countertrade**
> *Practice of selling goods or services that are paid for, in whole or part, with other goods or services.*

A FINAL WORD

This chapter surveyed the most important components of international financial markets. We learned about the international bond, equity, and Eurocurrency markets. Despite the problems in Asia and Russia and in other emerging markets of Latin America, continued growth in the international capital market is expected. We also learned the fundamentals of exchange rates and saw how the foreign exchange market is structured. In the next chapter, we extend our coverage of the international financial system to see how market forces (including interest rates and inflation) have an impact on exchange rates. We will then conclude our study of the international financial system by looking at the roles of government and international institutions in managing movements in exchange rates.

 There is a variety of additional material available on the Companion Website that accompanies this book. You can access this information by visiting the Website at (**www.prenhall.com/wild**).

summary

❶ Discuss the purposes, development, and financial centers of the *international capital market*. The international capital market has three main purposes. First, it provides an expanded supply of capital for borrowers because it joins together borrowers and lenders in different nations. Second, it lowers the cost of money for borrowers because a greater supply of money lowers the cost of borrowing (interest rates). Third, it lowers risk for lenders because it makes available a greater number of investments.

Growth in the international capital market is due mainly to three factors. First, advances in *information technology* allow borrowers and lenders to do business more quickly and cheaply. Second, the *deregulation* of capital markets is opening the international capital market to increased competition. Third, innovation in *financial instruments* is increasing the appeal of the international capital market.

The world's most important financial centers are London, New York, and Tokyo. These cities conduct a large number of financial transactions daily. Other locations, called *offshore financial centers*, handle less business but have few regulations and few, if any, taxes.

2 **Describe the *international bond, international equity,* and *Eurocurrency markets.*** The *international bond market* consists of all bonds sold by issuers outside their own countries. It is experiencing growth primarily because investors in developed markets are searching for higher rates from borrowers in emerging markets and vice versa. The *international equity market* consists of all stocks bought and sold outside the home country of the issuing company. The four factors primarily responsible for the growth in international equity are *privatization*, greater issuance of stock by *companies in newly industrialized and developing nations*, greater *international reach of investment banks*, and *global electronic trading*. The *Eurocurrency market* consists of all the world's currencies that are banked outside their countries of origin. The appeal of the Eurocurrency market is its lack of government regulation and, therefore, lower cost of borrowing.

3 **Discuss the four primary functions of the *foreign exchange market.*** The foreign exchange market is the market in which currencies are bought and sold and in which currency prices are determined. It has four primary functions. First, individuals, companies, and governments use it, directly or indirectly, to convert one currency into another. Second, it offers tools with which investors can *insure against adverse changes in exchange rates*. Third, it is used to earn a profit from *arbitrage*—the purchase and sale of a currency, or other interest-paying security, in different markets. Finally, it is used to *speculate about a change in the value of a currency*.

4 **Explain how currencies are *quoted* and the different rates given.** Currencies are quoted in a number of different ways. An *exchange-rate quote* between currency A and currency B (A/B) of 10/1 means that it takes 10 units of currency A to buy 1 unit of currency B. This example reflects a *direct quote* of currency A and an *indirect quote* of currency B. The exchange rate in this example is calculated using their actual values. We can also calculate an exchange rate between two currencies by using their respective exchange rates with a common currency; the resulting rate is called a *cross rate*. A *spot rate* is an exchange rate that requires delivery of the traded currency within two business days. This rate is normally obtainable only by large banks and foreign exchange brokers. The *forward rate* is the rate at which two parties agree to exchange currencies on a specified future date. Forward exchange rates represent the market's expectation of what the value of a currency will be at some point in the future.

5 **Identify the main *instruments* and *institutions* of the foreign exchange market.** Companies involved in international business make extensive use of certain financial instruments in order to reduce exchange-rate risk. A *forward contract* requires the exchange of an agreed-upon amount of a currency on an agreed-upon date at a specific exchange rate. A *currency swap* is the simultaneous purchase and sale of foreign exchange for two different dates. A *currency option* is the right to exchange a specific amount of a currency on a specific date at a specific rate. It is sometimes used to acquire a needed currency. Finally, a currency *futures contract* requires the exchange of a specific amount of currency on a specific date at a specific exchange rate. It is similar to a forward contract except that none of the terms is negotiable.

The world's largest banks exchange currencies in the *interbank market*. These banks locate and exchange currencies for companies and sometimes provide additional services. *Securities exchanges* are physical locations at which currency futures and options are bought and sold (in smaller amounts than those traded in the interbank market). The *over-the-counter (OTC)* market is an exchange that exists as a global computer network linking traders to one another.

6 **Explain why and how governments restrict *currency convertibility.*** There are four main goals of currency restriction. First, a government may be attempting to preserve the country's hard currency reserves for repaying debts owed to other nations. Second, convertibility might be restricted to preserve hard currency to pay for needed imports or to finance a trade deficit. Third, restrictions might be used to protect a currency from speculators. Finally, such restrictions can be an attempt to keep badly needed currency from being invested abroad. Policies used to enforce currency restrictions include government approval for currency exchange, imposed import licenses, a system of multiple exchange rates, and imposed quantity restrictions.

questions for review

1. Distinguish between *debt* and *equity*.

2. What are the three main benefits of the *international capital market*? Explain each briefly.

3. Name three factors responsible for growth in the international capital market.

4. Define and explain *securitization*.

5. Which three cities are considered the most important financial centers in the international capital market?

6. What is an *offshore financial center*? Why are these appealing to business?

7. What is the single most important factor fueling growth in the *international bond market*? Explain the role and influence of this factor.

8. What is the *international equity market*? Explain the factors responsible for its expansion.

9. What is the *Eurocurrency market*? Explain how it functions.

10. For what four reasons do investors use the *foreign exchange market*?

11. Distinguish between *currency arbitrage* and *interest arbitrage*.

12. What is a *direct exchange-rate quote*? An *indirect quote*?

13. Explain how to calculate percent changes in currency prices.

14. What are *cross rates*? Why are they important?

15. Distinguish between *spot rate* and *forward rate*. How is each used in the foreign exchange market?

16. Explain the differences among *currency swaps, options*, and *futures*.

17. Where are the world's main foreign exchange trading centers located? Which three currencies are used most in the foreign exchange market?

18. What is a *vehicle currency*?

19. Describe the three main institutions in the *foreign exchange market*.

20. Why are restrictions placed on *currency conversion*? What policies can governments use to restrict currency conversion?

questions for discussion

1. What factors do you think are holding back the creation of a truly *global* capital market? How might a truly global capital market function differently from the present-day international market? (*Hint:* Some factors to consider are interest rates, currencies, regulations, and financial crises for some countries.)

2. The use of different national currencies creates a barrier to further growth in international business activity. What are the pros and cons, among companies *and* governments, of replacing national currencies with regional currencies? Do you think a global currency is someday possible? Why or why not?

3. Governments dislike the fact that offshore financial centers facilitate money laundering. Do you think that electronic commerce makes it easier or harder to launder money and camouflage other illegal activities? Do you think offshore financial centers should be allowed to operate as freely as they do now, or do you favor regulation? Explain your answers.

in practice

Read the article below and answer the questions that follow.

Dollar-Yen Volatility

Last week, the dollar ranged from 135.85 to 111.45 yen. While analysts used to see four-yen moves of the dollar as volatile, a repeat of last week's ranges won't come as a surprise this week.

Late Friday in New York, the dollar was trading at 116.68 yen, down from 119.45 Thursday. The U.S. currency also traded at 1.6368 marks, up from 1.6350. Sterling was at $1.7065, down from $1.7110.

1. Is the exchange rate quote for the U.S. dollar a direct or indirect quote on the (a) yen? (b) mark? (c) sterling (British pound)?

2. (a) From Thursday to Friday, what percentage change in the value of the dollar occurred against the yen? (b) sterling? (*Remember to mind your quoted and base currencies!*)

3. Using the mark as the base currency, what is Friday's cross rate between the yen and the mark?

4. Using sterling as the base currency, what is Friday's cross rate between the mark and the sterling?

projects

1. This chapter taught us that information technology, deregulation, and innovative financial instruments have been behind the growth in the international capital market. Write a short report (about 800 words) on the ways in which recent advances in one of these three areas is helping to grow the international capital market. You might want to focus on a specific technology, nation (other than your own), international organization, or new financial instrument. Report your findings to the class in a brief presentation.

2. With several of your classmates, select a country that interests you. Does the country have a city that is an important financial center? What volume of bonds is traded on the country's bond market? What is the total value of stocks traded on its stock exchange(s)? Does it have an emerging stock market? How has its stock market performed over the past year? What is the exchange rate between its currency and that of your own country? What factors are responsible for the stability or volatility in that exchange rate? Are there any restrictions on the exchange of the nation's currency? How is the forecast for the country's currency likely to influence business activity in its major industries? Present a brief summary of your findings to the class. *Hint:* Two good sources to begin your research are the monthly *International Financial Statistics* and the annual *Exchange Arrangements and Exchange Restrictions,* both published by the International Monetary Fund (www.imf.org).

3. Suppose your company has $10 million in excess cash to invest for one month. Your task is to invest this money in the foreign exchange market to earn a profit—holding dollars is not an option. Select the currencies that you wish to buy at today's spot rate, but do not buy less than $2.5 million of any single currency. Track the spot rate for each of your currencies over the next month in the business press. At the end of the month, exchange your currencies at that day's spot rate. Calculate your gain or loss over the one-month period. (Your instructor will determine whether, and how often, you may trade currencies throughout the month.)

business case 9
ARGENTINA STARES INTO THE ABYSS

Argentina's President, Eduardo Duhalde, summed it up perfectly. "Argentina is bust. It's bankrupt. Business is halted, the chain of payments is broken, there is no currency to get the economy moving and we don't have a peso to pay Christmas bonuses, wages, or pensions," said Mr. Duhalde in a speech to Argentina's Congress.

Although it was the star of Latin America in the 1990s, Argentina defaulted on its $155 billion of public debt in early 2002, the largest default by any country ever. After taking office in January, President Duhalde implemented many measures to keep the country's fragile economy from complete collapse after 4 years of recession. For 10 years the Argentine peso was fixed at parity to the dollar through a currency board. The president cut those strings immediately. But when it was allowed to float freely on currency markets, Argentina's peso quickly lost two-thirds of its value and was trading at 3 pesos to the dollar. Then, strapped for cash, the government seized the savings accounts of its citizens and restricted how much they could withdraw at a time. When street protesters turned violent they beat up several politicians and attacked dozens of banks. Michael Smith, manager of HSBC's Argentine subsidiary (www.hsbc.com.ar), addressed people's feelings of distrust. "We're somewhat less popular than serial killers," said Smith.

Local companies were having an equally difficult time. Many companies blamed their defaults on the requirement that they get authorization from the central bank to send money abroad. Stiff restrictions on foreign-currency exchange forced importers to wait several months or more while the government authorized payments in dollars. Companies also struggled with new rules that raised taxes on exporters and other cash-rich firms to help the government pay for social services. Local firms also had a hard time obtaining funds to pay their debts to foreign suppliers. But the loss of confidence among non-Argentine businesses was more difficult to quantify. Many entered Argentina during a wave of free-market changes and privatizations in the 1990s. "If the government can just arbitrarily change contracts," said a foreign diplomat in Buenos Aires, "how can you feel safe about any business relationship here in the coming months?"

The declining peso intensified problems for U.S. companies that fought to manage soaring debts and mounting losses from their Argentine operations. Argentine units of U.S. companies, which tend to collect revenues in pesos, had an increasingly difficult time repaying their dollar-denominated debts as the peso's value fell. The government decreed that electricity and gas companies switch their contracts from dollars to less valuable pesos and then froze utility rates to protect consumers. But parent companies were not likely to rescue their ailing operations because many operations in Argentina were independent entities. AES Corp. (www.aes.com) of Arlington, VA. invested hundreds of millions of dollars in the Argentine electricity sector. It said in a statement that most of its Argentine businesses are in default on their project-financing arrangements but that AES "is not generally required to support the potential cash flow or debt service obligations of these businesses."

The government, trying to lighten its debt load and restore credibility with the International Monetary Fund (www.imf.org), ordered $50 billion in dollar-denominated government debt (mostly domestic) swapped into pesos. The swap was aimed at unlocking $10 billion in IMF loans that were frozen in December 2001 when Argentina failed to meet certain economic targets. U.S. and European investors owned another $46 billion in government bonds, which were to be restructured in a separate transaction. Argentina's government spent the previous decade amassing debts in dollars and other foreign currencies. But when the government cut loose the peso from the dollar in January 2002, the weak peso made the debt far more expensive to repay.

Previous crises in emerging-market nations seemed to infect other emerging economies. There was Mexico and its "tequila effect" on Latin America, Thailand's currency collapse caused the Asian "flu," and Russia's default was felt worldwide among industrialized nations. So why wasn't Argentina's default felt more widely? The only neighbor sharing the pain seemed to be Uruguay in tourism and banking. Some argue that it is due to improved information. Mohamed El-Erian, managing director at Pacific Investment Management Co. (www.pimco.com), says,

"Now we have better information. We all went out and hired more analysts. Now, we have lot more understanding," he said. Others say that markets simply anticipated the crisis and money managers adjusted portfolios early on in the economic debacle. Regardless of any potential lack of contagion, the effect on Argentina's economy is real. In 2002, the economy was expected to shrink anywhere from 5 to 10 percent while unemployment hovered around 25 percent.

thinking globally

1. Update the economic situation in Argentina to reflect recent events. Did the peso lose even more of its value than it had by early 2002? Do you think it was wise to cut the ties between the peso and the dollar? Why did Argentina peg its currency to the dollar in the first place? Do you think that the peso-dollar link contributed to Argentina's problems? Explain your answers.

2. How did local and international companies adapt to the new business environment in Argentina? Did they pursue similar courses of action or design distinct strategies to deal with the effects of the crisis? Be specific in your answer by giving as many examples as you can.

3. What was the impact on ordinary citizens immediately after the default and later as the government tried to recover? What do the after effects of the crisis mean for ordinary citizens' spending power? What has it done to the value of their savings? In your opinion, has international aid helped or hurt the ordinary people of Argentina? Explain your answer.

a question of ethics

1. Bank deposits in offshore financial centers (OFCs) grew from the tens of billions of dollars a few decades ago to more than $1 trillion today. "*Dirty money*" obtained through drug trafficking, gambling, and other illicit activities uses offshore financial centers to escape the same thing as respectable "*clean capital*": national taxation and government regulations. Some experts argue that such things as international currency markets and offshore tax havens are destabilizing and hostile to public interest. They say that people use such institutions to get beyond the reach of the long arm of the law and undermine what they consider to be

inefficient and bureaucratic attempts to impose a certain morality on people.

Do you agree or disagree with such a view? Explain. Do you think that corporate use of OFCs to avoid home-country bureaucracies and taxes is ethical? Why or why not?

2. The goal of government *regulation* of financial-services industries is to maintain the integrity and stability of financial systems, thereby protecting both depositors and investors. For instance, regulations include prohibitions against insider trading, against lending by management to itself or to closely related entities (a practice called "self-dealing"), and against

other transactions in which there is a conflict of interest. However, in less than two decades *deregulation* has transformed the world's financial markets. It spurred competition and growth in financial sectors and allowed capital to flow freely across borders, which boosted the economies of developing countries.

But what do you see as the "dark side" of deregulation, in terms of business ethics? What do you think Adam Smith, one of the first philosophers of capitalism, meant when he warned against the dangers of "colluding producers"? How do you think this warning applies to the financial-services sector today?

10

international monetary system

LEARNING OBJECTIVES

After studying this chapter, you should be able to

1 Explain how *exchange rates* influence the activities of domestic and international companies.

2 Identify the factors that help determine exchange rates and their impact on business.

3 Describe the primary methods of *forecasting exchange rates*.

4 Discuss the evolution of the current *international monetary system* and explain how it operates.

BEACONS

A Look Back

CHAPTER 9 examined how the international capital market and foreign exchange market operate. We also explained how exchange rates are calculated and how different rates are used in international business.

A Look at This Chapter

This chapter extends our knowledge of exchange rates and international financial markets. We examine factors that help determine exchange rates and explore rate-forecasting techniques. We discuss international attempts to manage exchange rates and review recent currency problems in Russia, Argentina, and other emerging markets.

A Look Ahead

CHAPTER 11 introduces the topic of the last part of this book—international business management. We will explore the specific strategies and organizational structures that companies use in accomplishing their international business objectives.

The Point of No Return

BRUSSELS, Belgium—"Europe's Big Idea . . . Ready, Set, Euros!," screamed headlines worldwide surrounding January 1, 2002. That was the day the *euro* began circulating in Europe. Posing with a giant euro coin, Romano Prodi, President of the European Commission, proclaimed, "The euro is your money, it is our money. It's our future. It is a piece of Europe in our hands."

Not since the time of the Roman Empire had a currency circulated so widely in Europe. The Greek gave up their *drachma*, a currency they had used for nearly 3,000 years. In Italy, multizeroed lire disappeared as billionaires became mere millionaires. Yet, the unprecedented changeover of national currencies went smoother than many thought possible. In fact, within just two weeks 95 percent of all cash transactions involved the receipt of euros for payment and the return of euros as change. After only two months, many of the so-called legacy currencies were no longer legal tender on the street.

Some companies were better suited than others to take advantage of the introduction of paper and coins than were others. Security transport company, Securicor PLC (**www.securicor.com**), was fully booked from September 2001 through March 2002—the company was forecasting bumper earnings. Some companies were even able to tie new products to the euro launch. For example, Italy's Gucci Group (**www.gucci.com**) saw the occasion as an opportunity to outfit Italians with new wallets that accommodate the euro notes, which are larger than the old lira.

But apart from such short-term benefits, the euro holds some very real, long-term benefits for Europe. For one thing, the euro eliminates exchange-rate risk for companies in the euro zone, making the financial aspects of business more predictable. Also, growth in the Eurobond market created a cheaper and deeper source of funding that paved the way for corporate

investment and growth. Mergers and acquisitions soared as companies prepared for intensified competition.

But some questioned whether the euro would ever be strong enough to challenge the U.S. dollar in world trade. When the euro began its existence as a virtual currency in 1999, it bought around $1.17. Yet, when it began circulating 3 years later, it bought just 90 U.S. cents. Some pointed to this fact as evidence that the U.S. dollar will continue to reign supreme in world trade. But the relative weakness of the euro was not all bad news—it supported exports and fueled growth among nations in the euro zone. As you read this chapter, keep in mind how events in the international monetary system affect the decisions of managers and the performance of their companies.[1]

In Chapter 9, we explained the fundamentals of how exchange rates are calculated and how different types of exchange rates are used. This chapter extends our understanding of the international financial system by exploring factors that determine exchange rates and various international attempts to manage them. We begin by learning how exchange-rate movements affect a company's activities. We then examine the factors that help determine currency values and in turn exchange rates. Next, we learn about different methods of forecasting exchange rates. We conclude this chapter by exploring the international monetary system and its performance.

HOW EXCHANGE RATES INFLUENCE BUSINESS ACTIVITIES

Movement in a currency's exchange rate affects many activities of both domestic and international companies. For one thing, exchange rates affect the demand for a company's products in the global marketplace. When a country's currency is *weak* (valued low relative to other currencies), the price of its exports on world markets declines and the price of imports increases. Lower prices make the country's exports more appealing on world markets. They also give companies the opportunity to take market share away from companies whose products are priced high in comparison.

Furthermore, a company that is selling in a country with a *strong* currency (one that is valued high relative to other currencies) while paying workers in a country with a weak currency improves its profits. For example, Dell Computer (www.dell.com) makes nearly all of its products in Penang, Malaysia, and prices everything it exports in dollars. But at the same time, Dell pays its Malaysian workers and suppliers in the local currency, ringgits. In the late 1990s, Malaysia's currency lost a great deal of its value. The result for Dell was that revenue was being generated in a strong currency, whose value was climbing steadily, while expenses were being paid in a weak currency, whose value kept falling. On the downside, companies with such a price advantage might grow complacent about reducing production costs. Further, if managers view the temporary price advantage caused by exchange rates as permanent, long-term competitiveness could be impaired.[2]

The intentional lowering of the value of a currency by the nation's government is called **devaluation.** The reverse, the intentional raising of its value by the nation's government, is called **revaluation.** These concepts are not to be confused with the terms *weak currency* and *strong currency,* although their effects are similar.

Devaluation lowers the price of a country's exports on world markets and increases the price of imports because the country's currency is now worth less on world markets. Thus, a government might devalue its currency to give its domestic

devaluation
Intentional lowering of the value of a nation's currency.

revaluation
Intentional raising of the value of a nation's currency.

companies an edge over competition from other countries. However, devaluation reduces consumers' buying power. It might also allow inefficiencies to persist in domestic companies because there is now less pressure to be concerned with production costs. Revaluation has the opposite effects: It increases the price of exports and reduces the price of imports.

Figure 10.1 shows exchange rates between the U.S. dollar and several major world currencies. We can see that the Japanese yen fell steadily throughout the late 1980s. But in the early 1990s, a strong yen began to hurt Japan's automobile exports by adding about $3,300 to the cost of every Japanese auto sold in the United States. But the situation reversed in the middle to late 1990s, when the dollar rose against the yen. Japan's carmakers were once again able to price their exports attractively in the United States. U.S. carmakers were forced to reduce their own prices in order to stay competitive, thus hurting their profit margins. Even so, Japan's carmakers increased their U.S. market share by nearly 10 percent in 1997 alone. Meanwhile, U.S. domestic carmakers were trying to persuade U.S. policy makers that a weaker dollar was important for their short-term survival because it increased the price of imported autos.[3]

There are steps companies can take to counter the negative effects that too strong a currency can have on exports. For example, a strong dollar can cause U.S. companies to become more aggressive in boosting exports. For a look at some of these approaches, see the Global Manager titled "Exporting Against the Odds: Key Strategies for Success."

Exchange rates also affect the amount of profit a company earns from its international subsidiaries. The earnings of international subsidiaries are typically integrated into the parent company's financial statements *in the home currency*. Translating subsidiary earnings from a weak *host* country currency into a strong *home* currency *reduces* the amount of these earnings when stated in the home currency. Likewise, translating earnings into a weak home currency increases stated

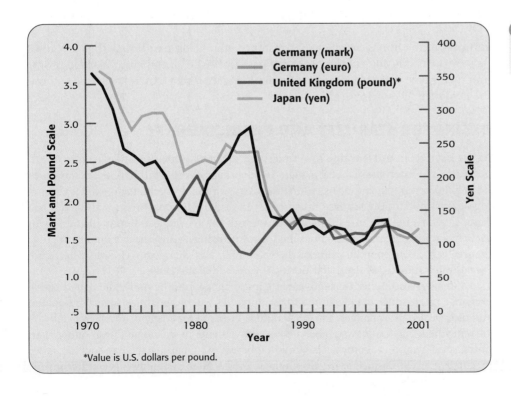

FIGURE 10.1

Exchange Rates of Major World Currencies

earnings in the home currency. For instance, many companies saw their earnings hurt by the fall in value of the Argentine peso in 2002. When firms translated profits into their home currencies, profits were far lower than they would have been without the peso's fall in value.

DESIRE FOR STABILITY AND PREDICTABILITY

As we have seen, unfavorable movements in exchange rates can be costly for both domestic and international companies. *Stable* exchange rates improve the accuracy of financial planning, including cash flow forecasts. Although methods do exist for insuring against potentially adverse movements in exchange rates, most of these are too expensive for small and medium-sized businesses. Moreover, as the unpredictability of exchange rates increases, so too does the cost of insuring against the accompanying risk. Figure 10.2 shows how the value of the U.S. dollar has changed over time. The figure reveals the instability of the dollar during the decade of the 1980s.

Managers also prefer that movements in exchange rates be *predictable*. Predictable exchange rates reduce the likelihood that companies will be caught off-guard by sudden and unexpected rate changes. They also reduce the need for costly insurance (usually by currency hedging) against possible adverse movements in exchange rates. Rather than purchasing insurance, companies would be better off spending their money on more productive activities, such as developing new products or designing more efficient production methods.

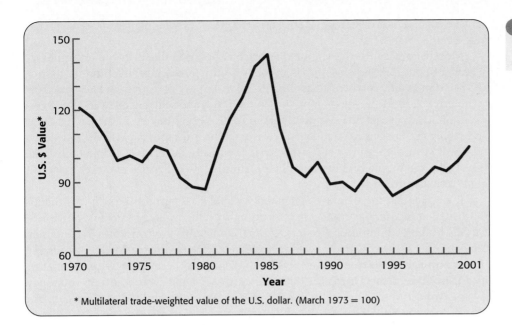

FIGURE 10.2

Value of the U.S. Dollar over Time

* Multilateral trade-weighted value of the U.S. dollar. (March 1973 = 100)

WHAT FACTORS DETERMINE EXCHANGE RATES?

To improve our knowledge of the factors that help determine exchange rates, we must first understand two important concepts: the law of one price and purchasing power parity. Each of these concepts tells us the level at which an exchange rate *should* be. While discussing these concepts, we will examine some of the many factors that affect the actual levels of exchange rates.

LAW OF ONE PRICE

An exchange rate tells us how much of one currency we must pay to receive a certain amount of another. But it does not tell us whether a specific product will actually cost us more or less in a particular country (as measured in our own currency). When we travel to another country, we discover that our own currency buys more or less than it does at home. In other words, we quickly learn that exchange rates do not guarantee or stabilize the buying power of our currency. Thus, we can lose purchasing power in some countries while gaining it in others. For example, a restaurant meal for you and a friend that costs 60 euros in France might cost you 11,000 yen (about 80 euros) in Japan and 22,000 bolivar (about 30 euros) in Venezuela. Thus, compared to your meal in France, you've suffered a loss of purchasing power in Japan but benefited from increased purchasing power in Venezuela.

The **law of one price** stipulates that an identical product must have an identical price in all countries when the price is expressed in a common-denominator currency. For this principle to apply, products must be identical in quality and content in all countries, and must be entirely produced within each particular country.

For example, suppose coal mined within the United States and Germany is of similar quality in each country. Suppose further that a kilogram of coal costs € 1.5 in Germany and $1 in the United States. Therefore, the law of one price calculates the *expected* exchange rate between the euro and dollar to be € 1.5/$. However, suppose the *actual* euro/dollar exchange rate as witnessed on currency markets is € 1.2/$. A kilogram of coal still costs $1 in the United States and € 1.5 in Germany. But in order to pay for German coal *with dollars denominated after the change in the exchange rate*, one must convert not just $1 into euros, but $1.25 (the expected exchange rate divided by the

law of one price
Principle that an identical item must have an identical price in all countries when the price is expressed in the same currency.

actual exchange rate, or € 1.5 ÷ $1.2). Thus, the price of coal is higher in Germany than in the United States.

Moreover, because the law of one price is being violated in our example, an *arbitrage* opportunity arises—that is, an opportunity to buy a product in one country and sell it in a country where it has a higher value. For example, one could earn a profit by buying coal at $1 per kilogram in the United States and selling it at $1.25 (€ 1.5) per kilogram in Germany. However, note that as traders begin buying in the United States and selling in Germany, greater demand drives *up* the price of U.S. coal, whereas greater supply drives *down* the price of German coal. Eventually, the price of coal in both countries will settle somewhere between the previously low U.S. price and the previously high German price.

If it seems that the arbitrage opportunity would disappear for the same reason that it arose, that is essentially the case. According to William Louis Dreyfus, one of the world's leading commodities traders, companies like his are constantly seeking new opportunities as they themselves arbitrage old ones out of existence. In other words, it is the nature of arbitrage to even out excessive fluctuation by destroying its own profitability. An arbitrageur, says Dreyfus, is "like a microbe. While the microbe attacks your body, it has a wonderful time living, but it ends up killing your body and dies as a result. The arbitrageur is exactly the same. When he sees a market inefficiency, he goes to it and makes it efficient. As a consequence, his profit margin disappears."[4]

Big MacCurrencies   The usefulness of the law of one price is that it helps us determine whether a currency is overvalued or undervalued. Each year *The Economist* publishes what it calls its "Big MacCurrencies" exchange-rate index (see Table 10.1). This index uses the law of one price to determine the exchange rate that should exist between the U.S. dollar and other major currencies. It employs the McDonald's Big Mac as its single product to test the law of one price. Why the Big Mac? Because each one is fairly identical in quality and content across national markets and almost entirely produced within the nation in which it is sold. According to the Big Mac index, the average price of a Big Mac was $2.54 in the United States. The cheapest Big Mac was found in the Philippines at a dollar-equivalent price of $1.17, the most expensive in Switzerland at $3.65. Therefore, according to the Big Mac index the Philippines' peso was undervalued by 54 percent ({[(50.3 − 23.2) / 50.3] × −100} = − 54 percent). On the other hand, the Swiss franc is overvalued by 44 percent ({[(1.73 − 2.48) / 1.73] × −100} = 44 percent).

Such large discrepancies between a currency's exchange rate on currency markets and the rate predicted by the Big Mac index are not surprising for several reasons. For one thing, the selling price of food is affected by subsidies for agricultural products in most countries. Also, a Big Mac is not a "traded" product in the sense that one can buy Big Macs in low-priced countries and sell them in high-priced countries. Prices can also be affected because Big Macs are subject to different marketing strategies in different countries. Finally, countries impose different levels of sales tax on restaurant meals.

The drawbacks of the Big Mac index reflect the fact that applying the law of one price to a single product is too simplistic a method for estimating exchange rates. Nonetheless, academic studies find that currency values tend to change in the direction suggested by the Big Mac index.[5]

PURCHASING POWER PARITY

We were introduced to the purchasing power parity concept in Chapter 4 when we discussed economic development. The purchasing power parity concept is also useful in determining at what level an exchange rate should be. Recall that *purchasing power parity (PPP)* is the relative ability of two countries' currencies to buy the same "basket" of

TABLE 10.1 Burgers and Exchange Rates

Country	Big Mac Prices		Implied PPP* of the dollar	Actual $ exchange rate 04/17/01	Under(-)/ over(+) valuation against the dollar, %
	in local currency	in dollars			
United States [†]	$2.54	2.54	–	–	–
Argentina	Peso2.50	2.50	0.98	1.00	−2
Australia	A$3.00	1.52	1.18	1.98	−40
Brazil	Real3.60	1.64	1.42	2.19	−35
Britain	£1.99	2.85	1.28[‡]	1.43[‡]	12
Canada	C$3.33	2.14	1.31	1.56	−16
Chile	Peso1260	2.10	496	601	−17
China	Yuan9.90	1.20	3.90	8.28	−53
Czech Rep.	Koruna56.00	1.43	22.0	39.0	−44
Denmark	DKr24.75	2.93	9.74	8.46	15
Euro area	€2.57	2.27	0.99[§]	0.88[§]	−11
France	FFr18.5	2.49	7.28	7.44	−2
Germany	DM5.10	2.30	2.01	2.22	−9
Italy	Lire4300	1.96	1693	2195	−23
Spain	Pta395	2.09	156	189	−18
Hong Kong	HK$10.70	1.37	4.21	7.80	−46
Hungary	Forint399	1.32	157	303	−48
Indonesia	Rupiah14700	1.35	5787	10855	−47
Japan	¥294	2.38	116	124	−6
Malaysia	M$4.52	1.19	1.78	3.80	−53
Mexico	Peso21.9	2.36	8.62	9.29	−7
New Zealand	NZ$3.60	1.46	1.42	2.47	−43
Philippines	Peso59.00	1.17	23.2	50.3	−54
Poland	Zloty5.90	1.46	2.32	4.03	−42
Russia	Rouble35.00	1.21	13.8	28.9	−52
Singapore	S$3.30	1.82	1.30	1.81	−28
South Africa	Rand9.70	1.19	3.82	8.13	−53
South Korea	Won3000	2.27	1181	1325	−11
Sweden	SKr24.0	2.33	9.45	10.28	−8
Switzerland	SFr6.30	3.65	2.48	1.73	44
Taiwan	NT$70.0	2.13	27.6	32.9	−16
Thailand	Baht55.0	1.21	21.7	45.5	−52

*Purchasing-power parity: local price divided by price in United States
[†]Average of New York, Chicago, San Francisco and Atlanta [‡]Dollars per pound [§]Dollars per euro

goods in those two countries. Thus, although the law of one price holds for single products, PPP is meaningful only when applied to a *basket* of goods. Let's look at an example to see why this is so.

Suppose 650 baht in Thailand will buy a bag of groceries that costs $30 in the United States. What do these two numbers tell us about the economic conditions of people in Thailand as compared with people in the United States? First, they help us compare the *purchasing power* of a Thai consumer with that of a consumer in the United States. But the question is: Are Thai consumers better off or worse off than their counterparts in the United States? In order to address this question, we first need to know the *GNP per capita* of both countries:

Thai GNP/capita = 122,277 baht
U.S. GNP/capita = 26,980 dollars

Suppose the *exchange rate* between the two currencies is 41.45 baht = 1 dollar. With this figure, we can translate 122,277 baht into dollars: 122,277/41.45 = \$2,950. We can now restate our question: Do prices in Thailand enable a Thai consumer with \$2,950 to buy more or less than a consumer in the United States with \$26,980?

We already know that 650 baht will buy in Thailand what \$30 will buy in the United States. Thus, 650/30 = 21.67 baht per dollar. Note, then, that whereas the exchange rate on currency markets is 41.45 baht/\$, the *purchasing power parity rate* of the baht is 21.67/\$. Let's now use this figure to calculate a different comparative rate between the two currencies. We can now recalculate Thailand's GNP per capita at PPP as follows: 122,277/21.67 = \$5,643. Clearly, Thai consumers, on average, are not nearly as affluent as their counterparts in the United States. But when we consider the *goods and services that they can purchase with their baht*—not the amount of U.S. dollars that they can buy—we see that a GNP per capita at PPP of \$5,643 more accurately portrays the real purchasing power of Thai consumers.

Therefore, our new calculation considers *price levels* in adjusting the relative values of the two currencies. Thus, in the context of exchange rates, the principle of purchasing power parity can be interpreted as the exchange rate between two nations' currencies is equal to the ratio of their price levels (in our example, 21.67 instead of 41.45). In other words, in our example, PPP tells us how many units of Thai currency a consumer in Thailand needs in order to buy the same amount of products as a consumer in the United States can buy with 1 dollar.

As we can see in the above example, the exchange rate at PPP (21.67/\$) is normally different from the actual exchange rate in financial markets (41.45/\$). However, PPP states that economic forces will push the actual market exchange rate toward that determined by purchasing power parity. If not, arbitrage opportunities would arise. Purchasing power parity holds for internationally traded products that are not restricted by trade barriers and that entail few or no transportation costs. In order to earn a profit, arbitrageurs must be certain that the basket of goods purchased in the low-cost country would still be lower-priced in the high-cost country *after adding transportation costs, tariffs, taxes, and so forth*. Let's now see what impact inflation and interest rates have on exchange rates and purchasing power parity.

Role of Inflation Inflation is the result of the supply and demand for a currency. If additional money is injected into an economy that is not producing greater output, people will have more money to spend on the same amount of products as before. As growing demand for products outstrips stagnant supply, prices will rise and devour any increase in the amount of money that consumers have to spend. Therefore, inflation erodes people's purchasing power.

Impact of Money-Supply Decisions Because of the damaging effects of inflation, governments try to manage the supply of and demand for their currencies. They do this through the use of two types of policies designed to influence a nation's money supply. *Monetary policy* refers to activities that directly affect a nation's interest rates or money supply. Selling government securities reduces a nation's money supply because investors pay money to the government's treasury to acquire the securities. Conversely, when the government buys its own securities on the open market, cash is infused into the economy and the money supply increases.

Fiscal policy involves using taxes and government spending to influence the money supply indirectly. For instance, to reduce the amount of money in the hands of con-

Turkey tried, failed, and then tried again to launch a disinflation program backed by international lending agencies. At one point in 2001, inflation was running at an annual rate of 200 percent. Then, the government took a stab at what was considered the soft underbelly of the entire economy—a corrupt banking system. Here, a security guard blocks the entrance to a state-owned bank that was seized by authorities and restaffed before it was allowed to reopen. What are some of the ways that inflation hurts a nation's economy?

sumers, governments increase taxes—people are forced to pay money to the government coffers. Conversely, lowering taxes increases the amount of money in the hands of consumers. Governments can also step up their own spending activities to increase the amount of money circulating in the economy, or cut government spending to reduce it.

Impact of Unemployment and Interest Rates Many industrialized countries are very effectively controlling inflation (see Figure 10.3). Some economists claim that

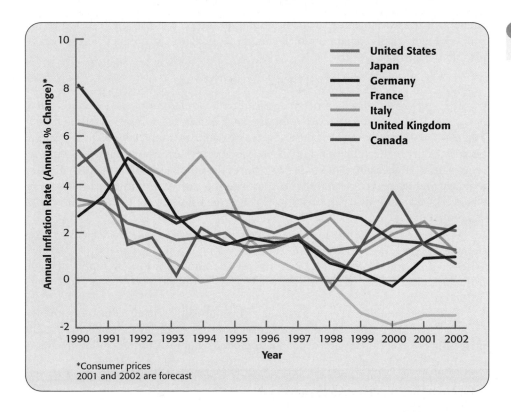

FIGURE 10.3

How Low Can They Go?

international competition is responsible for keeping inflation under control. The logic (called "the new paradigm") runs as follows: Global competition and the mobility of companies to move anywhere that costs are lowest, keeps a lid on wages. Because wages are kept under control, companies do not raise prices on their products, thus containing inflation. More research and time will be needed to see whether this is in fact the case.

Other key factors in the inflation equation are a country's unemployment and interest rates. When unemployment rates are low, there is a shortage of labor and employers pay higher wages to attract employees. Then, in order to maintain reasonable profit margins with higher labor costs, they usually raise the prices of their products, passing off the cost of higher wages to the consumer—thus causing inflation.

Interest rates (discussed in detail below) affect inflation because they affect the cost of borrowing money. Low interest rates encourage people to take out loans to buy items such as new homes and cars and to run up debt on their credit cards. High interest rates prompt people to cut down on the amount of debt they carry because higher rates mean larger monthly payments on debt. Thus, one way to cool off an inflationary economy is to raise interest rates because raising the cost of debt reduces consumer spending and makes it more costly for businesses to expand.

How Exchange Rates Adjust to Inflation An important component of the concept of purchasing power parity is that exchange rates adjust to different rates of inflation in different countries. Such adjustment is necessary to maintain purchasing power parity between nations. For example, suppose that at the beginning of the year the exchange rate between the Mexican peso and the U.S. dollar is 8 pesos/$ (or $.125/peso). Also suppose that inflation is pushing consumer prices higher in Mexico at an annual rate of 20 percent whereas prices are rising just 3 percent per year in the United States. To find the new exchange rate (E_e) at the end of the year, we use the following formula:

$$E_e = E_b(1 + i_1)/(1 + i_2)$$

where E_b is the exchange rate at the beginning of the period, i_1 is the inflation rate in country 1 and i_2 is the inflation rate in country 2. Plugging the numbers for this example into the formula, we get:

$$E_e = 8_{pesos/\$}[(1 + 0.20)/(1 + 0.03)] = 9.3_{pesos/\$}$$

It is important to remember that *because the numerator of the exchange rate is pesos, the inflation rate for Mexico must also be placed in the numerator for the ratio of inflation rates*. Thus, we see that the exchange rate adjusts from 8 pesos/$ to 9.3 pesos/$ because of the higher inflation rate in Mexico and the corresponding change in currency values. Higher inflation in Mexico reduces the number of U.S. dollars that a peso will buy and increases the number of pesos that a dollar will buy. In other words, whereas it had cost only 8 pesos to buy a dollar at the beginning of the year, it now costs 9.3 pesos.

In our example, tourists from the United States can now take less expensive vacations in Mexico, but Mexicans will find the cost of U.S. vacations more expensive. Whereas companies based in Mexico must pay more in pesos for any supplies bought from the United States, U.S. companies will pay less, in dollar terms, for supplies bought from Mexico.

This discussion illustrates at least one of the difficulties facing countries with high rates of inflation. Both consumers and companies in countries experiencing rapidly increasing prices see their purchasing power eroded. Figure 10.4 shows inflation rates in several developing countries and countries in transition—those most often plagued by rocketing prices. Notice the difference between these inflation rates and those we saw earlier in Figure 10.3 for developed nations.

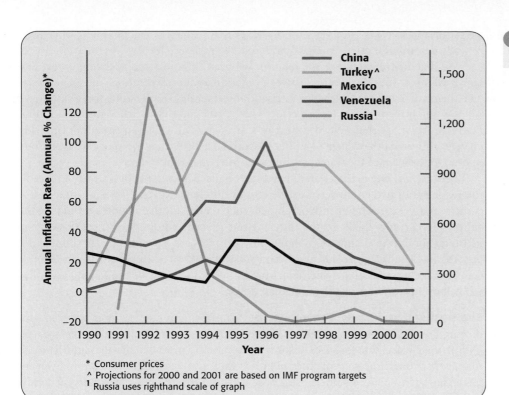

FIGURE 10.4
The Curse of Inflation

* Consumer prices
^ Projections for 2000 and 2001 are based on IMF program targets
¹ Russia uses righthand scale of graph

Role of Interest Rates In order to see how interest rates affect exchange rates between two currencies, we must first review the connection between inflation and interest rates within a single economy. We distinguish between two types of interest rates: *real interest rates* and *nominal interest rates*. Let's say that your local banker quotes you an interest rate on a new-car loan. The quoted rate charged by the bank is the nominal interest rate, which consists of the real interest rate plus an additional charge for inflation. The reasoning behind this principle is simple. Recall from our earlier discussion that because inflation erodes the purchasing power of currencies, the lender must be compensated for this erosion during the loan period.

Fisher Effect Now suppose instead that your bank lends you money to buy a delivery van for your home-based business. Let's say that, given your credit-risk rating, the bank would normally charge you 5 percent annual interest. But if inflation is expected to be 2 percent over the next year, your annual rate of interest will be 7 percent: 5 percent real interest plus 2 percent to cover inflation. This principle that relates inflation to interest rates is called the **Fisher effect:** the principle that the nominal interest rate is the sum of the real interest rate and the expected rate of inflation over a specific period. We write this relation between inflation and interest rates as:

Nominal Interest Rate = Real Interest Rate + Inflation Rate

If money were free from all controls when transferred internationally, the real rate of interest should be the same in all countries. To see why this is true, suppose that real interest rates are 4 percent in Canada and 6 percent in the United States. This situation creates an arbitrage opportunity: Investors could borrow money in Canada at 4 percent, lend it in the United States at 6 percent, and earn a profit on the 2 percent spread in interest rates. If enough people took advantage of this opportunity, interest rates would go up in Canada, where demand for money would become heavier, and down in the United States, where the money supply was growing. Again, the arbitrage opportunity

Fisher effect
Principle that the nominal interest rate is the sum of the real interest rate and the expected rate of inflation over a specific period.

would disappear because of the same activities that made it a reality. That is why, theoretically, real interest rates remain equal across countries.

We demonstrated earlier the relation between inflation and exchange rates. The Fisher effect clarifies the relation between inflation and interest rates. Now, let's investigate the relation between exchange rates and interest rates. To illustrate this relation, we refer to the **international Fisher effect**—the principle that a difference in nominal interest rates supported by two countries' currencies will cause an equal but opposite change in their *spot exchange rates*. Recall from Chapter 9 that the spot rate is the rate quoted for delivery of the traded currency within two business days.

Because real interest rates are theoretically equal across countries, any difference in interest rates in two countries must be due to different expected rates of inflation. A country that is experiencing inflation higher than that of another country should see the value of its currency fall. If so, the exchange rate must be adjusted to reflect this change in value. For example, suppose nominal interest rates are 5 percent in Australia and 3 percent in Canada. Expected inflation in Australia, then, is 2 percent higher than in Canada. The international Fisher effect predicts that the value of the Australian dollar will fall by 2 percent against the Canadian dollar.

Evaluating Purchasing Power Parity   Purchasing power parity is better at predicting long-term exchange rates (more than 10 years) than short-term rates. Unfortunately, accurate forecasts of short-term rates are most beneficial to international managers because most companies plan less than five years into the future. Even so, most short-term plans assume a great deal about future economic and political conditions in different countries. Among common considerations are added costs, trade barriers, and even investor psychology.

Impact of Added Costs   There are many possible reasons for the failure of PPP to predict exchange rates accurately. For one thing, PPP assumes no transportation costs. Suppose that the same basket of goods costs $100 in the United States and 1,350 krone ($150) in Norway. Seemingly, one could make a profit through arbitrage by purchasing these goods in the United States and selling them in Norway. However, if it costs another $60 to transport the goods to Norway, the total cost of the goods once they arrive in Norway will be $160. Obviously, no shipment will occur. Because no arbitrage opportunity exists after transportation costs are added, there will be no leveling of prices between the two markets and the price discrepancy will persist. Thus, even if PPP predicts that the Norwegian krone is overvalued, the effect of transportation costs will keep the dollar/krone exchange rate from adjusting. In a world in which transportation costs exist, PPP does not always correctly predict shifts in exchange rates.

Impact of Trade Barriers   PPP also assumes no barriers to international trade. However, such barriers certainly do exist. Governments establish trade barriers for many reasons, including helping domestic companies remain competitive and preserving jobs for their citizens. Suppose the Norwegian government in our earlier example imposes a 60 percent tariff on the $100 basket of imported goods or makes its importation illegal. Because no leveling of prices or exchange-rate adjustment will occur, PPP will fail to predict exchange rates accurately.

Impact of Business Confidence and Psychology   Finally, PPP overlooks the human aspect of exchange rates: the role of people's confidence and beliefs about a nation's economy and its currency's value. Many countries gauge confidence in their economies by conducting a *business confidence survey*. The largest survey of its kind in Japan is called the tankan survey. It gauges business confidence four times each year among 10,000 companies.

Investor confidence in the value of a currency plays an important role in determining its exchange rate. Suppose several currency traders believe that the Indian rupee will increase in value. They will buy Indian rupees at the current price, sell them if the value increases, and earn a profit. However, suppose that all traders share the same belief and all follow the same course of action. The activity of the traders themselves will be sufficient to push the value of the Indian rupee higher. It does not matter why traders believed the price would increase. As long as enough people act on a similar belief regarding the future value of a currency, its value will change accordingly.

That is why nations try to maintain the confidence of investors, businesspeople, and consumers in their economies. Lost confidence causes companies to put off investing in new products and technologies and to delay the hiring of additional employees. Consumers tend to increase their savings and not increase their debts if they have lost confidence in an economy. These kinds of behaviors act to weaken a nation's currency.

FORECASTING EXCHANGE RATES

Before undertaking any international business activity, managers must consider the impact that currency values will have on financial results. Therefore, they must try to make the best possible guess at future exchange rates. This section explores two distinct views regarding how accurately future exchange rates can be predicted by forward exchange rates—the rate agreed upon for foreign exchange payment at a future date. We also take a brief look at different techniques for forecasting exchange rates.

EFFICIENT MARKET VIEW

A great deal of debate revolves around the issue of whether markets themselves are efficient or inefficient in forecasting exchange rates. A market is *efficient* if prices of financial instruments quickly reflect new public information made available to traders. The **efficient market view** thus holds that prices of financial instruments reflect all publicly available information at any given time. As applied to exchange rates, this means that forward exchange rates are accurate forecasts of future exchange rates.

Recall from Chapter 9 that a *forward exchange rate* reflects a market's expectations about the future values of two currencies. In an efficient currency market, forward exchange rates reflect all relevant publicly available information at any given time. Therefore, they are considered the best possible predictors of exchange rates. Proponents of this view hold that there is no other publicly available information that could improve the forecast of exchange rates over that provided by forward rates. If one accepts this view, companies waste time and money collecting and examining information believed to affect future exchange rates. But there is always a certain amount of deviation between forward and actual exchange rates. The fact that forward exchange rates are less than perfect inspires companies to search for more accurate forecasting techniques.

> **efficient market view**
> View that prices of financial instruments reflect all publicly available information at any given time.

INEFFICIENT MARKET VIEW

The **inefficient market view** holds that prices of financial instruments do not reflect all publicly available information. Proponents of this view believe that companies can search for new pieces of information to improve forecasting. However, the cost of searching for further information must not outweigh the benefits of its discovery.

Naturally, the inefficient market view is more compelling when the existence of *private* information is considered. Suppose a single currency trader holds privileged information regarding a future change in a nation's economic policy—information that she believes will affect its exchange rate. Because the market is unaware of this informa-

> **inefficient market view**
> View that prices of financial instruments do not reflect all publicly available information.

tion, it is not reflected in forward exchange rates. Our trader will no doubt earn a profit by acting on her store of private information.

Now that we understand the two basic views related to market efficiency, let's look at the specific methods that companies use to forecast exchange rates.

FORECASTING TECHNIQUES

The debate about whether markets are efficient or inefficient forecasters of exchange rates leads to the question of whether experts can improve on the forecasts of forward exchange rates in *either* an efficient or inefficient market. As we have already seen, some analysts believe that forecasts of exchange rates can be improved by uncovering information not reflected in forward exchange rates. In fact, companies exist to provide exactly this type of service. There are two main forecasting techniques based on this belief in the value of added information—fundamental analysis and technical analysis.

fundamental analysis
Technique using statistical models based on fundamental economic indicators to forecast exchange rates.

Fundamental Analysis   **Fundamental analysis** employs statistical models based on fundamental economic indicators to forecast exchange rates. These models are often quite complex, with many variations reflecting different possible economic conditions. Economic variables used in these models include factors such as inflation, interest rates, money supply, tax rates, and government spending. Such analyses also often consider a country's balance-of-payments situation (see Chapter 7) and government intervention in foreign exchange markets to influence a currency's value.

technical analysis
Technique using charts of past trends in currency prices and other factors to forecast exchange rates.

Technical Analysis   Another method of forecasting exchange rates is **technical analysis**—a technique that employs charts of past trends in currency prices and other factors to forecast exchange rates. Using highly statistical models and charts of past data trends, analysts estimate the conditions prevailing during changes in exchange rates and try to estimate the timing, magnitude, and direction of future changes. Many forecasters combine the techniques of both fundamental and technical analyses to arrive at potentially more accurate forecasts.

DIFFICULTIES OF FORECASTING

The business of forecasting exchange rates is a rapidly growing industry. This trend seems to provide evidence that a growing number of people believe it is possible to improve on the forecasts of exchange rates embodied in forward rates. However, difficulties remain. Despite highly sophisticated statistical techniques in the hands of well-trained analysts, forecasting is not a pure science. Few forecasts are ever 100 percent accurate because of unexpected events that occur throughout the forecast period.

Over and above the problems associated with the data used by these techniques, failings can be traced to the human element involved in forecasting. For example, people might miscalculate the importance of economic news becoming available to the market, placing too much emphasis on some elements and ignoring others.

EVOLUTION OF THE INTERNATIONAL MONETARY SYSTEM

So far in this chapter, we have discussed how companies are affected by changes in exchange rates and why managers prefer exchange rates to be stable and predictable. We saw how inflation and interest rates affect currency values, and in turn exchange rates, in different countries. We also learned that despite attempts to forecast exchange rates accurately, difficulties remain.

For all these reasons, governments develop systems designed to manage exchange rates between their currencies. Groups of nations have created both formal and informal agreements to control exchange rates between their currencies. The present-day

international monetary system is the collection of agreements and institutions that govern exchange rates. In this section, we briefly trace the evolution of the current international monetary system and examine its performance.

EARLY YEARS: THE GOLD STANDARD

In the earliest days of international trade, gold was the internationally accepted currency for payment of goods and services. Using gold as a medium of exchange in international trade has several advantages. First, its limited supply made it a commodity in high demand. Second, because gold is highly resistant to corrosion, it can be traded and stored for hundreds of years. Third, because it can be melted into either small coins or large bars, gold is a good medium of exchange for both small and large purchases.

But gold also has its disadvantages. First, its weight made transporting it expensive. Second, when a transport ship sank at sea, the gold sank to the ocean floor and was lost. Thus, merchants wanted a new way to make their international payments without the need to haul large amounts of gold around the world. The solution was found in the **gold standard**—an international monetary system in which nations linked the value of their paper currencies to specific values of gold. Britain was the first nation to implement the gold standard in the early 1700s—it remained intact until the First World War.

Par Value   The gold standard required a nation to fix the value (price) of its currency to an ounce of gold. The value of a currency expressed in terms of gold is called its *par value*. Each nation must then guarantee to convert its paper currency into gold for anyone demanding it at its par value. The calculation of each currency's par value was based on the concept of purchasing power parity. This provision made the purchasing power of gold the same everywhere and maintained the purchasing power of currencies across nations.

All nations fixing their currencies to gold also indirectly linked their currencies to one another. Because the gold standard *fixed* nations' currencies to the value of gold, it is called a **fixed exchange-rate system**—one in which the exchange rate for converting one currency into another is fixed by international governmental agreement. This system and the use of par values made calculating exchange rates between any two currencies a very simple matter. For example, under the gold standard the U.S. dollar was originally fixed at $20.67/oz of gold and the British pound at £ 4.2474/oz. The exchange rate between the dollar and pound was $4.87/£ ($20.67 ÷ £ 4.2474).

Advantages of the Gold Standard   The gold standard was quite successful in its early years of operation. In fact, this early record of success is causing some economists and policy makers to call for its rebirth today. Three main advantages of the gold standard underlie its early success.

First, the gold standard drastically *reduces the risk in exchange rates* because it maintains highly fixed exchange rates between currencies. Deviations that do arise are much smaller than they would be under a system of freely floating currencies. The more stable that exchange rates are, the less companies are affected by actual or potential adverse changes in them. Because the gold standard significantly reduced the risk in exchange rates and, therefore, the risks and costs of trade, international trade grew rapidly following its introduction.

Second, the gold standard *imposes strict monetary policies* on all countries that participate in the system. Recall that the gold standard requires governments to convert paper currency into gold if demanded by holders of the currency. If all holders of a nation's paper currency decided to trade it for gold, the government must have an equal amount of gold reserves to pay them. That is why a government cannot allow the volume of its paper currency to grow faster than the growth in its reserves of gold. By lim-

What's wrong with just printing more money when your country is in debt? It causes inflation. Germany learned that lesson the hard way in 1923 when it printed huge quantities of money to support workers in the Ruhr River valley. Prices spiraled 9,439 percent in just 1 year. At one point, the German mark had an exchange rate of DM 4.2 trillion to the dollar! Life savings were wiped out. A postage stamp cost billions of marks. Banks conducted transactions by the cartful and much daily business was done through barter.

iting the growth of a nation's money supply, the gold standard also was effective in controlling inflation.

Third, the gold standard can *help correct a nation's trade imbalance*. Suppose Australia is importing more than it is exporting (experiencing a trade deficit). As gold flows out of Australia to pay for imports, its government must decrease the supply of paper currency in the domestic economy because it cannot have paper currency in excess of its gold reserves. As the money supply falls, so do prices of goods and services in Australia because demand is falling (consumers have less to spend) whereas the supply of goods is unchanged. Meanwhile, the falling prices of Australian-made goods causes Australian exports to become cheaper on world markets. Exports will rise until Australia's international trade is once again in balance. The exact opposite occurs in the case of a trade surplus: The inflow of gold supports an increase in the supply of paper currency, which increases demand for, and therefore the cost of, goods and services. Thus, exports will fall in reaction to their higher price until trade is once again in balance.

Collapse of the Gold Standard   Nations involved in the First World War needed to finance their enormous war expenses, and they did so by printing more paper currency. Of course, this violated the fundamental principle of the gold standard and forced nations to abandon the standard. The aggressive printing of paper currency caused rapid inflation for these nations. When the United States returned to the gold standard in 1934, it adjusted its par value from $20.67/oz of gold to $35.00/oz to reflect the lower value of the dollar that resulted from inflation. Thus, the U.S. dollar had undergone a devaluation. However, Britain returned to the gold standard several years earlier at its previous level, which did not reflect the effect inflation had on its currency.

Because the gold standard links currencies to one another, devaluation of one currency in terms of gold affects the exchange rates between currencies. The decision of the United States to devalue its currency and Britain's decision not to do so lowered the price of U.S. exports on world markets and increased the price of British goods imported into the United States. For example, whereas it had previously required $4.87 to purchase one British pound, it now required $8.24 ($35.00 ÷ £ 4.2474). This forced the cost of a £ 10 tea set exported from Britain to the United States to go from $48.70

before devaluation to $82.40 after devaluation. This drastically increased the price of imports from Britain (and other countries), lowering its export earnings. As countries devalued their currencies in retaliation, a period of "competitive devaluation" resulted. To improve their trade balances, nations chose arbitrary par values to which they devalued their currencies. People quickly lost faith in the gold standard because it was no longer an accurate indicator of a currency's true value. By 1939, the gold standard was effectively dead.

BRETTON WOODS AGREEMENT

In 1944, representatives from 44 nations met in the New Hampshire resort town of Bretton Woods to lay the foundation for a new international monetary system. The resulting **Bretton Woods Agreement** was an accord among nations to create a new international monetary system based on the value of the U.S. dollar. The new system was designed to balance the strict discipline of the gold standard with the flexibility that countries needed to deal with temporary domestic monetary difficulties. Let's now take a brief look at the most important features of that system.

Bretton Woods Agreement
Agreement (1944) among nations to create a new international monetary system based on the value of the U.S. dollar.

Fixed Exchange Rates The Bretton Woods Agreement incorporated fixed exchange rates by tying the value of the U.S. dollar directly to gold and the value of other currencies to the value of the dollar. The par value of the U.S. dollar was fixed at $35/oz of gold. Other currencies were then given par values against the U.S. dollar instead of gold. For example, the par value of the British pound was established as $2.40/£. Member nations were expected to keep their currencies from deviating more than 1 percent above or below their par values. The Bretton Woods Agreement also improved on the gold standard by extending the right to exchange gold for dollars only to national governments, rather than anyone who demanded it.

Built-In Flexibility The new system also incorporated a degree of built-in flexibility. For example, although competitive currency devaluation was ruled out, large devaluation was allowed under the extreme set of circumstances called **fundamental disequilibrium**—an economic condition in which a trade deficit causes a permanent negative shift in a country's balance of payments. In this situation, a nation can devalue its currency more than 10 percent. Yet, devaluation under these circumstances should accurately reflect a permanent economic change for the country in question, not temporary misalignments.

fundamental disequilibrium
Economic condition in which a trade deficit causes a permanent negative shift in a country's balance of payments.

World Bank To provide funding for countries' efforts toward economic development, the Bretton Woods Agreement created the **World Bank**—officially called the International Bank for Reconstruction and Development (IBRD). The immediate purpose of the World Bank (www.worldbank.org) was to finance European reconstruction following the Second World War. It later shifted its focus to the general financial needs of developing countries. The Bank finances many types of economic development projects in Africa, South America, and Southeast Asia. The World Bank also offers funds to countries that are unable to obtain capital from commercial sources for certain projects that are considered too risky. The Bank often undertakes projects to develop transportation networks, power facilities, and agricultural and educational programs.

World Bank (International Bank for Reconstruction and Development)
Agency created by the Bretton Woods Agreement to provide funding for national economic development efforts.

International Monetary Fund The Bretton Woods Agreement established the International Monetary Fund (IMF) as the agency to regulate the fixed exchange rates and enforce the rules of the international monetary system. At the time of its formation, the IMF (www.imf.org) had just 29 members—today 183 countries belong. Included among the main purposes of the IMF are:[6]

International Monetary Fund (IMF)
Agency created by the Bretton Woods Agreement to regulate fixed exchange rates and enforce the rules of the international monetary system.

- Promoting international monetary cooperation
- Facilitating expansion and balanced growth of international trade
- Promoting exchange stability, maintaining orderly exchange arrangements, and avoiding competitive exchange devaluation
- Making the resources of the Fund temporarily available to members
- Shortening the duration and lessening the degree of disequilibrium in the international balance of payments of member nations

Special Drawing Right (SDR)   World financial reserves of dollars and gold grew scarce in the 1960s, at a time when the activities of the IMF demanded greater amounts of dollars and gold. The IMF reacted by creating what is called a **special drawing right** (**SDR**)—an IMF asset whose value is based on a "basket" of its five biggest members' currencies (France, Germany, Japan, the United Kingdom, and the United States). Figure 10.5 shows the "weight" each currency contributes to the overall value of the SDR. The value of the SDR is set daily and changes with increases and declines in the values of its underlying currencies. Today there are more than 21 billion SDRs in existence that were worth about $29 billion in 2001 (1SDR equaled about $1.26 at the time).

The significance of the SDR is that it is the unit of account for the IMF. Each nation is assigned a quota based on the size of its economy when it enters the IMF. Payment of this quota by each nation provides the IMF with the funds it needs to make short-term loans to members.

Collapse of the Bretton Woods Agreement   The system developed at Bretton Woods worked quite well for about 20 years—an era that boasted unparalleled stability in exchange rates. However, in the 1960s the Bretton Woods system began to falter. The main problem was that the United States was experiencing a trade deficit (imports were exceeding exports) and a budget deficit (expenses were outstripping revenues). Governments that were holding dollars began to doubt that the U.S. government had an adequate amount of gold reserves to redeem all its paper currency held outside the country. When they began demanding gold in exchange for dollars, a large sell-off of dollars on world financial markets followed.

Smithsonian Agreement   In August 1971 the U.S. government held less than one-fourth of the amount of gold needed to redeem all U.S. dollars in circulation. In late 1971

FIGURE 10.5

Valuation of the SDR

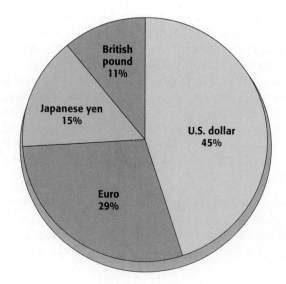

the United States and other countries reached the so-called **Smithsonian Agreement** to restructure and strengthen the international monetary system. The three main accomplishments of the Smithsonian Agreement were: (1) the value of the dollar in terms of gold was lowered to $38/oz of gold, (2) other countries increased the values of their currencies against the dollar, and (3) the 1 percent band within which currencies were allowed to float was increased to 2.25 percent.

Final Days   The success of the Bretton Woods system relied on the U.S. dollar remaining a strong reserve currency. However, high inflation and a persistent trade deficit had kept the dollar weak and so demonstrated a fundamental flaw in the system. The weak U.S. dollar strained the abilities of central banks in Japan and most European countries to maintain exchange rates with the dollar. Because these nations' currencies were tied to the U.S. dollar, as the dollar continued to fall, so too did their currencies. Britain left the system in the middle of 1972 and allowed the pound to float freely against the dollar. The Swiss abandoned the system in early 1973. In January 1973 the dollar was again devalued, this time to around $42/oz of gold. But even this move was not enough. As nations began dumping their reserves of the dollar on a massive scale, currency markets were temporarily closed to prevent further selling of the dollar. When markets reopened, the values of most major currencies were floating against the U.S. dollar. The era of an international monetary system based on *fixed* exchange rates was over.

A MANAGED FLOAT SYSTEM EMERGES

The Bretton Woods system collapsed because it depended so heavily on the stability of the dollar. As long as the dollar remained strong, it worked well. But when the dollar weakened, it failed to perform properly. Originally, the new system of *floating* exchange rates was viewed as a temporary solution to the shortcomings of the Bretton Woods and Smithsonian agreements. However, no new coordinated international monetary system was forthcoming. Rather, there emerged several independent efforts to manage exchange rates.

Jamaica Agreement   By January 1976 returning to a system of fixed exchange rates seemed unlikely. Therefore, world leaders met to draft the so-called **Jamaica Agreement**—an accord among members of the IMF to formalize the existing system of floating exchange rates as the new international monetary system. The Jamaica Agreement contained several main provisions. First, it endorsed a **managed float system** of exchange rates—that is, a system in which currencies float against one another, with governments intervening to stabilize their currencies at particular target exchange rates. This is in contrast to a **free float system**—a system in which currencies float freely against one another without governments intervening in currency markets.

Second, gold was no longer the primary reserve asset of the IMF. Member countries could retrieve their gold from the IMF if they so desired. Third, the mission of the IMF was augmented: Rather than being the manager of a fixed exchange-rate system only, it was now a "lender of last resort" for nations with balance-of-payment difficulties. Member contributions were increased to support the newly expanded activities of the IMF.

Later Accords   Between 1980 and 1985 the U.S. dollar rose dramatically against other currencies, pushing up prices of U.S. exports and adding once again to a U.S. trade deficit. In September 1985 the world's five largest industrialized nations, known as the "G5" (Britain, France, Germany, Japan, and the United States), arrived at a solution. The *Plaza Accord* was a 1985 agreement among the G5 nations to act together in forcing down the value of the U.S. dollar. The Plaza Accord caused traders to sell the dollar and its value fell.

By February 1987 the industrialized nations were concerned that the value of the U.S. dollar was now in danger of falling too low. Meeting in Paris, leaders of the "G7" nations (the G5 plus Italy and Canada) drew up another agreement. The *Louvre Accord* was a 1987 agreement among the G7 nations that affirmed that the U.S. dollar was appropriately valued and that they would intervene in currency markets to maintain its current market value. Once again, currency markets responded and the dollar stabilized.

TODAY'S EXCHANGE-RATE ARRANGEMENTS

Today's international monetary system remains in large part a managed float system whereby most nations' currencies float against one another and governments engage in limited intervention to realign exchange rates. However, within the larger monetary system certain countries try to maintain more stable exchange rates by tying their currencies to other currencies. Let's take a brief look at two ways nations attempt to do this.

Pegged Exchange-Rate Arrangement   Think of one country as a small lifeboat tethered to a giant cruise ship as it navigates choppy monetary waters. Many economists argue that rather than let their currencies face the tides of global currency markets alone, developing economies should tie them to other, more stable currencies. Pegged exchange-rate arrangements "peg" a country's currency to a more stable and widely used currency in international trade. Countries then allow the exchange rate to fluctuate within a specified margin (usually 1 percent) around a central rate.

Many small countries peg their currencies to the U.S. dollar, European Union euro, the special drawing right (SDR) of the IMF, or other individual currency. Belonging to this category are the Bahamas, El Salvador, Iran, Malaysia, Netherlands Antilles, and Saudi Arabia. Other nations peg their currencies to groups, or "baskets," of currencies. For example, Bangladesh and Burundi tie their currencies (the *taka* and *Burundi franc*, respectively) to those of its major trading partners. Other members of this group are Botswana, Fiji, Kuwait, Latvia, Malta, and Morocco.

currency board
Monetary regime that is based on an explicit commitment to exchange domestic currency for a specified foreign currency at a fixed exchange rate.

Currency Board   A **currency board** is a monetary regime that is based on an explicit commitment to exchange domestic currency for a specified foreign currency at a fixed exchange rate. The government with a currency board is legally bound to hold an amount of foreign currency that is at least equal to the amount of domestic currency. Because a currency board restricts a government from issuing additional domestic currency unless it has the foreign reserves to back it, it helps cap inflation.

Thanks to a currency board, Bosnia and Herzegovina has built itself a strong and stable currency. However, observers remark that the currency board's survival depends on sound budget policies.[7] Argentina had a currency board from 1991 until it was abandoned in early 2002 when the peso was allowed to float freely on currency markets. Other nations with currency boards include Brunei Darussalam, Bulgaria, Hong Kong, Djibouti, Estonia, and Lithuania.

EUROPEAN MONETARY SYSTEM

Following the collapse of the Bretton Woods system, leaders of many European Union (EU) nations did not give up hope for a system that could stabilize currencies and reduce exchange-rate risk. Their efforts became increasingly important as trade between EU nations continued to expand. In 1979, these nations created the *European monetary system (EMS)*. The EMS was established to stabilize exchange rates, promote trade among nations, and keep inflation low through monetary discipline. As planned, the system ceased to exist in 1999 when 12 EU member nations adopted a single currency.

How The System Worked   The mechanism that limited the fluctuations of European Union members' currencies within a specified trading range (or *target zone*) was called the *exchange rate mechanism (ERM)*. Members were required to keep their currencies within 2.25 percent of the highest- and lowest-valued currencies. To illustrate, suppose that a weakening French franc were about to reach the 2.25 percent variation in its exchange rate with the German mark. The central banks of both France and Germany were to drive the value of the French franc higher—forcing the exchange rate away from the 2.25 percent band limit. How did they do so? By buying up French francs on currency markets, thereby increasing demand for the franc and forcing its value higher.

The EMS was quite successful in its early years. Currency realignments were infrequent and inflation was fairly well controlled. But in late 1992, both the British pound and the Italian lira had been on the lower fringe of the allowable 2.25 percent fluctuation band with the mark for some time. Currency speculators began unloading their pounds and lira. The central banks of neither Britain nor Italy had enough money to buy their currencies on the open market. As their currencies' values plummeted, they were forced to leave the ERM. The EMS was revised in late 1993 to allow currencies to fluctuate 15 percent up or down from the midpoint of the target zone. Although the Italian lira returned to the ERM in November 1996, the British pound remained outside the ERM.

European Monetary Union   Despite the speculative attacks in the 1990s, EU leaders remained determined to merge their currencies. **European monetary union** is the European Union plan that established its own central bank and currency in January 1999. Signed in 1991, the *Maastricht Treaty* stated the economic criteria with which member nations must comply in order to partake in the single currency, the *euro*. First, consumer price inflation must be below 3.2 percent and must not exceed that of the three best-performing countries by more than 1.5 percent. Second, the debt of government must be 60 percent of GDP or lower. An exception is made if the ratio is diminishing and approaching the 60 percent mark. Third, the general government deficit must be at or below 3 percent of GDP. An exception is made if the deficit is close to 3 percent, or if the deviation is temporary and unusual. Fourth, interest rates on long-term government securities must not exceed by more than 2 percent those of the three countries with the lowest inflation rates. Meeting these criteria better aligned countries' economies and paved the way for smoother policy making under a single European Central Bank.

> **European monetary union** European Union plan establishing its own central bank and currency as of January 1999.

Of the 15 EU members, the nations that adopted the single currency are Austria, Belgium, Finland, France, Germany, Greece, Ireland, Italy, Luxembourg, the Netherlands, Portugal, and Spain. The only EU countries that opted out of transition to the euro (at least for now) are Britain, Denmark, and Sweden. People across Europe had differing opinions on the euro's impact shortly before circulation of euro coins and paper. See the World Business Survey titled "Euro Attitudes" for whether the euro will make people feel more "European."

Of the three nations opting out of the euro, Denmark is the only one participating in what is called the *exchange rate mechanism II (ERM II)*. The ERM II (in which membership is voluntary) was introduced January 1, 1999, and continues to function today. The aim of ERM II is to support nations that seek future membership in EMU by linking their currencies to the euro. The euro acts as an *anchor* of a *hub and spokes* model, to which a currency is linked on a bilateral basis. The currencies of participating countries have a central rate against the euro with acceptable fluctuation margins of 15 percent, although narrower margins can be arranged. Future accession countries to the EU will be obliged to join the single currency once they satisfy the criteria of the Maastricht Treaty.[8]

Management Implications of the Euro   The move to a single currency influences all the activities of companies within the European Union. First, the euro completely eliminates exchange-rate risk for business deals between member nations using the euro.

WORLD BUSINESS SURVEY

Euro Attitudes

Below are responses to the statement: When we use the euro instead of our national currencies, we will probably feel a little more European than now.

Country	Strongly agree	Quite agree	Quite disagree	Strongly disagree	Don't know
Austria	10%	28%	29%	27%	6%
Belgium	23	28	20	29	1
Finland	11	34	17	36	3
France	25	28	19	27	1
Germany	14	37	31	15	4
Greece	11	21	34	25	8
Ireland	29	36	20	11	4
Italy	33	30	19	13	5
Luxembourg	30	29	19	19	3
Netherlands	6	25	19	48	2
Portugal	5	40	31	11	12
Spain	20	25	15	33	7

It reduces transaction costs by eliminating the cost of converting from one currency to another. In fact, the EU leadership estimates the financial gains to Europe could eventually be 0.5 percent of GDP. The efficiency of trade between participating members resembles that of interstate trade in the United States because only a single currency is involved.

Second, the euro makes prices between markets more transparent, making it more difficult to charge different prices in different markets. This should help end the need for shoppers to flock to other countries to save on high-ticket items. For instance, shortly before monetary union a Mercedes-Benz S320 (**www.mercedes.com**) cost $72,614 in Germany but only $66,920 in Italy. A Renault Twingo (**www.renault.com**) that sold for $13,265 in France cost $11,120 in Spain. Car brokers and shopping agencies even sprang up specifically to help European consumers reap such savings.

RECENT FINANCIAL CRISES

Despite the best efforts of nations to head off financial crises within the international monetary system, the world has experienced several wrenching crises in recent years. Let's now take a look at the most prominent of these.

Developing Nations' Debt Crisis   By the early 1980s certain developing countries (especially in Latin America) had amassed huge debts payable not only to large international commercial banks but also to the IMF and the World Bank. In 1982 Mexico, Brazil, and Argentina announced that they would be unable to pay interest on their loans. At the same time, many of these countries were also experiencing runaway inflation. Many countries in Africa were facing similar problems.

To prevent a meltdown of the entire financial system, international agencies stepped in with a number of temporary solutions to the crisis. Repayment schedules were revised to put off repayment until further into the future. Then, in 1989, U.S.

Treasury Secretary Nicholas Brady unveiled the Brady Plan. The Brady Plan called for large-scale reduction of the debt owed by poorer nations, the exchange of old loans for new low-interest loans, and the making of debt instruments (based on these loans) that would be tradable on world financial markets. This last feature allowed a debtor country to receive a loan from an institution and then use it to buy special securities (called "Brady Bonds") on financial markets. Funds for these new loans came from private commercial banks and were backed by the IMF and the World Bank.

Mexico's Peso Crisis   Armed rebellion in the poor Mexican state of Chiapas and assassination of a presidential candidate shook investors' faith in Mexico's financial system in 1993 and 1994. Capital flowing into Mexico was mostly in the form of stocks and bonds (portfolio investment) rather than factories and equipment (foreign direct investment). Portfolio investment fled Mexico for the United States as the Mexican peso grew weak and U.S. interest rates rose. A lending spree by Mexican banks, coupled with weak banking regulations, also played a role in delaying the government's response to the crisis. In late 1994 the Mexican peso was devalued, forcing a loss of purchasing power on the Mexican people.

In response to the crisis, the IMF and private commercial banks in the United States stepped in with about $50 billion in loans to shore up the Mexican economy. Thus, Mexico's peso crisis contributed to an additional boost in the level of IMF loans. Mexico repaid the loans ahead of schedule and once again has a sizable reserve of foreign exchange.

Southeast Asia's Currency Crisis   The roar of the "four tiger" economies and those of other high-growth Asian nations suddenly fell silent in the summer of 1997. For 25 years the economies of five Southeast Asian countries—Indonesia, Malaysia, the Philippines, Singapore, and Thailand—had wowed the world with growth rates twice those of most other countries. Even though many analysts projected continued growth for the region, and even though billions of dollars in investment flooded in from the West, savvy speculators were pessimistic.

When South Korea was in shambles a few years ago, the International Monetary Fund (IMF) helped bail out its economy. But ordinary Koreans strongly protested the IMF's policy prescriptions that, among other things, called for high interest rates to prevent the remaining foreign investors from fleeing. As people lost their jobs and savings were being wiped out by a falling currency, people could not afford such high-interest-rate loans. Do you think that the IMF should have the power it has in dictating government policies in countries that need aid?

On July 11, 1997, the speculators struck, selling off Thailand's baht on world currency markets. The selling forced an 18 percent drop in the value of the baht before speculators moved on to the Philippines and Malaysia. By November the baht had plunged another 22 percent and every other economy in the region was in a slump. The shock waves of Asia's crisis could be felt throughout the global economy.

Suddenly, countries thought to be strong emerging market economies—"tigers" even to be emulated by other developing countries—were in need of billions of dollars to keep their economies from crumbling. When the dust settled, Indonesia, South Korea, and Thailand all needed IMF and World Bank funding. As incentives for these countries to begin the long process of economic restructuring, IMF loan packages came with a number of strings attached. For example, the Indonesian loan package involved three long-term goals to help put the Indonesian economy on a stronger footing: (1) to restore the confidence of international financial markets; (2) to restructure the domestic financial sector; and (3) to support domestic deregulation and trade reforms.

What caused the crisis in the first place? Well, it depends on whom you ask. Some believe it was caused by an Asian style of crony capitalism. They say that poor regulation, the practice of extending loans to friends and relatives who are poor credit risks, and a lack of transparency regarding the financial health of banks and companies are to blame. Others point to currency speculators and panicking investors as the main causes. Still others argue that persistent current account deficits in these countries are what caused the large dumping of these nations' currencies. What really caused the crisis is probably a combination of all these forces.[9]

Russia's Ruble Crisis   Russia had a whole host of problems throughout the 1990s—some were constant, others were intermittent. For starters, Russia was not immune to the events unfolding across Southeast Asia in the late 1990s. As investors became wary of potential problems in other emerging markets worldwide, stock market values in Russia plummeted. Another problem contributing to Russia's problems was depressed oil prices. Because Russia depends on oil production for a large portion of its GDP, the low price of oil on world markets cut into the government's reserves of hard currency. Also cutting into the government's coffers was an unworkable tax collection system and a large underground economy—meaning that most taxes went uncollected.

Then there was the problem of inflation. We learned earlier in this chapter how an expanded amount of money chasing the same amount of goods forces prices higher. This is exactly what happened when Russia released prices in 1992. As prices skyrocketed, people dug beneath their mattresses where they had stashed their rubles during times when there were no goods to purchase. We also saw earlier how inflation eats away at the value of a nation's currency. Russia saw inflation take its exchange rate from less than 200 rubles to the dollar in early 1992 to more than 5,000 to the dollar in 1995.

Then in early 1996 as currency traders dumped the ruble, the Russian government found itself attempting to defend the ruble on currency markets. As its foreign exchange reserves dwindled in a hopeless effort, the government asked for, and received, a $10 billion aid package from the IMF. In return, Russia promised to reduce its debt (which was averaging about 7 percent of GDP), collect taxes owed it, cease printing inflation-stoking sums of currency, and peg its currency to the dollar.

Things seemed to improve for a while, but then in mid-1998 the government found itself once again trying to defend the ruble against speculative pressure on currency markets. In a single day the government spent $1 billion trying to prop up the ruble's value, forcing its hard currency reserves to shrivel to $14 billion. As it grew obvious that the government would soon be bankrupt, the IMF stepped in and promised Russia another $11 billion. But when it was alleged that some of the IMF loan had been funneled into offshore bank accounts, the IMF held up distribution of the money. On August 17, 1998, badly strapped for cash, the government announced that it would allow the ruble to devalue by 34 percent by the end of the year. It also declared a 90-day foreign debt moratorium and announced a de-facto default on the government's domestic bond obligations. On August 26, the Russian Central Bank announced that it would no longer be able to support the ruble on currency markets. In less than 1 month, its value fell 300 percent. Inflation shot up to 15 percent a month in August from 0.2 percent in July and reached 30 percent in the first week of September.[10] By the time it was all over in late 1998, the IMF had lent Russia more than $22 billion.

Argentina's Peso Crisis   Argentina was the star of Latin America in the early and mid 1990s. Yet, by late 2001, Argentina had been in recession for nearly 4 years mainly due to Brazil's devaluation of its own currency in 1999—making Brazil's exports cheaper on world markets. Meanwhile, Argentina's goods remained relatively expensive because its own currency was linked to a very strong U.S. dollar through a currency board. As a result, Argentina saw much of its export business dry up and the economy slowed significantly.

Things came to a head when the country began running out of money to service its debt obligations. The country finally defaulted on its $155 billion of public debt in early 2002, the largest default by any country ever. The government scrapped its currency board that linked the peso to the U.S. dollar and the peso quickly lost about 70 percent of its value on currency markets. The government, strapped for cash, seized the savings accounts of its citizens and restricted how much they could withdraw at a time.

By late 2001, the IMF had already promised $48 billion to rescue Argentina. Yet, in April of 2002 the IMF was reviewing the reforms of the Argentine government before it would release more of that cash. The IMF wanted greater reductions in government spending and expressed concern over the existence of separate currencies issued by provincial governments that circulate locally alongside the peso.[11] In 2002, Argentina's economy was expected to shrink by as much as 10 percent while unemployment hovered around 25 percent.

FUTURE OF THE INTERNATIONAL MONETARY SYSTEM

Recurring crises in the international monetary system are raising calls for a new system that is designed to meet the challenges of a global economy. Many believe that the vestiges of the IMF created by the Bretton Woods Agreement are no longer adequate to insulate the world's economies from disruptions in a single country or small group of countries.

Meanwhile, leaders of many developing and newly industrialized countries are bemoaning what global capital has done to their economies. Indian Prime Minister Bihari Vajpayee said the "world is paying the price for the dogma of the invisible hand of market forces."[12] Malaysian Prime Minister Mahathir Mohamad echoed these sentiments: "The only system allowed is that of capitalist free markets, of globalization. That the unfettered, unregulated free market has destroyed the economies of whole regions and of many countries in the world does not matter," he wrote.[13]

Although some call for the elimination of the IMF and its replacement by institutions not yet clearly defined, more likely is revision of the IMF and its policy prescriptions. Efforts have already been taken to develop internationally accepted codes of good practice to allow comparisons of countries' fiscal and monetary practices. Countries have also been encouraged to be more open and clear regarding their financial policies. Transparency on the part of the IMF is also being increased to instill greater accountability on the part of its leadership. The IMF also is increasing its efforts at surveillance of member nations' macroeconomic policies and increasing its abilities in the area of financial sector analysis.

Yet, orderly ways must still be found to integrate international financial markets so that risks are better managed. Moreover, the private sector must become involved in the prevention and resolution of financial crises. Policy makers are concerned with the way money floods into developing economies when growth is strong and then just as quickly heads for the exits at the first sign of trouble. Furthermore, some argue that because the IMF bails out debtor countries, private-sector banks do not exercise adequate caution when loaning money in risky situations: After all, the IMF will be there to pay off the loans of debtor countries. Greater cooperation and understanding between the IMF, private-sector banks, and debtor nations is needed.

A FINAL WORD

The occurrence of recent financial crises, including Mexico, Southeast Asia, Russia, and Argentina, underscores the need for managers to fully understand the complexities of the international financial system. In Chapters 9 and 10, we have discussed the international financial markets and international monetary system in detail. Understanding this material improves our knowledge of financial risks in international business. But this knowledge must be paired with vigilance of financial market conditions to manage businesses in the global economy effectively.

The next chapter begins our in-depth look at the main aspects of managing an international business. As we saw in this chapter, not only are a company's financial decisions affected by events in international financial markets, but so too are production and marketing decisions. Our understanding of national business environments, international trade and investment, and the international financial system will serve us well as we embark on our tour of the nuances of international business management.

There is a variety of additional material available on the Companion Website that accompanies this book. You can access this information by visiting the Website at (**www.prenhall.com/wild**).

summary

① Explain how *exchange rates* influence the activities of domestic and international companies. Exchange rates influence many aspects of a firm's activities. For one thing, they affect demand for a company's products in the global marketplace. When a country's currency is *weak* (valued low relative to other currencies), the price of its exports on world markets declines and the price of imports increases. Lower prices make the

country's exports more appealing on world markets. Furthermore, a company that sells in a country with a *strong* currency (one that is valued high relative to other currencies) while paying workers at home in its own weak currency improves its profits.

The intentional lowering of the value of a currency by the nation's government is called *devaluation*. The reverse, the intentional raising of its value by the nation's government, is called *revaluation*. Devaluation lowers the price of a country's exports on world markets and increases the price of imports because the country's currency is now worth less on world markets. Revaluation has the opposite effects: It increases the price of exports and reduces the price of imports.

Exchange rates also affect the amount of profit a company earns from its international subsidiaries. Translating subsidiary earnings from a weak *host* country currency into a strong *home* currency *reduces* the amount of these earnings when stated in the home currency.

❷ Identify the factors that help determine exchange rates and their impact on business. Two concepts are used to determine the level at which an exchange rate *should* be. The *law of one price* stipulates that when price is expressed in a common-denominator currency, an identical product must have an identical price in all countries. For this principle to apply, products must be identical in quality and content in all countries and must be entirely produced within each particular country. The *purchasing power parity (PPP)* concept helps determine the relative ability of two countries' currencies to buy the same "basket" of goods in those two countries. Thus, although the law of one price holds for *single* products, PPP is meaningful only when applied to a *basket* of goods.

Two phenomena influence both exchange rates and PPP: inflation and interest rates. When additional money is injected into an economy that is not producing greater output, prices rise because more money chases the same amount of products. When unemployment is low, employers pay higher wages to attract or retain employees. Employers then typically raise prices to offset the additional labor costs to maintain profits.

In turn, *interest rates* affect inflation because they affect the cost of borrowing money. Low rates encourage people and businesses to increase spending by taking on debt. On the other hand, high rates prompt them to reduce the debt because higher rates mean greater debt payments. Because *real interest rates*—rates that do not account for inflation—are theoretically equal across countries, any difference in the rates of two countries must be due to different expected rates of inflation. A country that is experiencing inflation higher than that of another country should see the relative value of its currency fall.

❸ Describe the primary methods of *forecasting exchange rates.* There are two distinct views regarding how accurately future exchange rates can be predicted by *forward exchange rates*—that is, by the rate agreed upon for foreign exchange payment at a future date. The *efficient market view* holds that prices of financial instruments reflect all publicly available information at any given time. As applied to exchange rates, this means that forward exchange rates are accurate forecasts of future exchange rates. The *inefficient market view* holds that prices of financial instruments do not reflect all publicly available information. Proponents of this view believe that forecasts can be improved by information not reflected in forward exchange rates.

Two main forecasting techniques are based on this belief in the value of added information. *Fundamental analysis* uses statistical models based on fundamental economic indicators to forecast exchange rates. *Technical analysis* employs a technique using charts of past trends in currency prices and other factors to forecast exchange rates. Many forecasters combine the techniques of fundamental and technical analyses to arrive at potentially more accurate forecasts.

❹ Discuss the evolution of the current *international monetary system* and explain how it operates. The *Bretton Woods Agreement* (1944) was an accord among nations to create an international monetary system based on the value of the U.S. dollar. The system was designed to balance the strict discipline of the *gold standard*, which linked paper currencies to specific values of gold, with the flexibility that countries needed to deal with temporary domestic monetary difficulties. The most important features of the system were *fixed exchange rates, built-in flexibility, funds for economic development,* and an *enforcement mechanism.*

Bretton Woods created the *World Bank*, which funds poor nations' economic development projects such as the development of transportation networks, power facilities, and agricultural and educational programs. It also established the *International Monetary Fund (IMF)* to regulate fixed exchange rates and enforce the rules of the international monetary system.

Ultimately, the Bretton Woods Agreement collapsed because it depended so heavily on the stability of the dollar. As long as the dollar remained strong, it worked well. But when the dollar weakened, it failed to perform properly. The *Jamaica*

Agreement (1976) endorsed a *managed float system* of exchange rates—that is, a system in which currencies float against one another, with limited government intervention to stabilize currencies at a particular target exchange rate. This system differs from a *free float system* in which currencies float freely against one another without governments intervening in currency markets. But within the system, certain countries try to maintain more stable exchange rates by tying their currencies to another country's stronger currency.

The *European monetary system (EMS)* was a complex system designed by the European Union (EU) to stabilize exchange rates, promote trade, and control inflation through monetary discipline. The EU established a single currency in January 1999 through a plan called the *European monetary union*. The main benefit of a single currency, the *euro*, is the complete elimination of both exchange-rate risk and currency conversion costs within the euro zone.

questions **for review**

1. How are *exchange rates* important to managers' decisions? Provide several examples.

2. Why is it desirable for exchange rates to be stable and predictable?

3. What is the *law of one price*? Explain briefly.

4. What are the limitations of the law of one price?

5. What is meant by *purchasing power parity* in the context of exchange rates? Explain briefly.

6. How does *inflation* influence exchange rates? Describe the impact of money-supply decisions and unemployment on inflation.

7. What is the impact of *interest rates* on exchange rates? Explain the *international Fisher effect*.

8. What are the limitations of purchasing power parity?

9. What is the relation between business confidence and psychology on the one hand and exchange rates on the other?

10. What are the two market *views* regarding *exchange-rate forecasting*? Explain each briefly.

11. What are the two primary *methods* of forecasting exchange rates? Explain each briefly.

12. What was the *gold standard*? Briefly describe its evolution and collapse.

13. What was the *Bretton Woods Agreement*?

14. What factors led to the demise of the monetary system created by Bretton Woods?

15. Why did the world shift to a *managed float system* of exchange rates? Briefly describe the performance of this system.

16. What was the purpose of the *European monetary system*? Briefly describe how it functioned and describe its performance.

17. How did the *International Monetary Fund* assist countries during recent financial crises?

questions **for discussion**

1. There are benefits of both floating and fixed exchange-rate systems. Describe the advantages and disadvantages of each briefly. Do you think the world will move toward an international monetary system more characteristic of floating or fixed exchange rates in the future? Explain your answer.

2. Do you think that an international monetary system with currencies valued on the basis of gold would work today? Why or why not? Do you think implementing a system similar to the old European monetary system on a global scale would work? Why or why not?

3. The activities of the IMF and the World Bank largely overlap each other. Devise a plan to reduce the duplication of these institutions' services and to assign them responsibilities. Also, would you have them take a greater role on issues such as the environment and corruption? Describe your plan and justify your proposed solution.

in practice

Read the article below and answer the questions that follow.

Argentina's Continuing Crisis

BUENOS AIRES, Argentina—Seeking International Monetary Fund approval, Economy Minister Jorge Remes Lenicov presented a federal budget that imposes more austerity on crisis-wracked Argentina.

The spending cuts, along with floating the peso, which had been pegged at parity to the dollar since 1991, have been central demands from the IMF. Since being devalued in January the peso has lost more than half its value against the dollar. Argentina previously scrapped a dual exchange-rate system and ordered all dollar deposits and debts converted into pesos.

Mr. Remes said the economy is expected to contract 4.9% this year, after shrinking 3.7% in 2001. A raft of monthly indicators released Tuesday showed how a freeze on bank accounts and political disarray had hurt the economy. January car sales plunged more than 80% from a year earlier; retail sales tumbled between 35% and 90%, depending on the sector; and real-estate transactions fell 90%. Mr. Remes estimated that consumer prices will rise 14% this year.

1. Research the economic crisis that struck Argentina in late 2001 and early 2002. Identify as many potential contributing factors as you can. Do you think Argentina's involvement in the trading bloc MERCOSUR had anything to do with its problems?

2. Update the progress of Argentina's economy since this article was written. What are the current conditions in its exchange rate, inflation, and debt load? How involved did the IMF become in Argentina's economic policies? Was the IMF criticized once again for its policy prescriptions?

3. Update how Argentina's companies, investors, and citizens are faring since this article appeared. How were companies' earnings and future projects affected? Did investors have renewed confidence in Argentina and return? Did Argentines see the purchasing power of their currency rebound?

[*Hint:* Good sources of information to answer these questions include *The Economist* (www.economist.com), the *Financial Times* (www.ft.com), and *The Wall Street Journal* (www.wsj.com). Also good to consult are publications by international agencies including the International Monetary Fund (www.imf.org), the World Bank (www.worldbank.org), and the Organization for Economic Cooperation and Development (OECD) (www.oecd.org).]

projects

1. You are the production manager for a manufacturing company based in Japan. You are forecasting the exchange rate between the Japanese yen and Indian rupee to decide whether to build a new factory in India. The current spot exchange rate is .32 rupee/¥. Inflation is 10 percent in India and 2 percent in Japan. What is your forecast of the rupee/yen exchange rate for 1 year from today?

2. With several of your classmates, select a country that interests you. Is the nation a member of the IMF? Does it participate in a regional monetary system to manage exchange rates? How have inflation and interest rates affected the nation's exchange rate with other currencies? What impact has the country's exchange rate had on its imports and exports? How has the exchange rate recently affected the activities of companies operating in the country? What is the forecasted exchange rate for the coming weeks, months, and year?

[*Hint:* Good sources to consult include various issues of *International Financial Statistics* (Washington, DC: International Monetary Fund) and *Exchange Arrangements and Exchange Restrictions, Annual Reports* (Washington, DC: International Monetary Fund).]

3. Your company based in Brazil wants to estimate demand in the U.S. market for its newly developed product. The market research firm you hired requires $150,000 to perform a thorough study. However, you are informed that your total research budget for the year is 3 million Brazilian real and that no more than 20 percent of the budget can be spent on any one project.

a. If the current exchange rate is 5 real/$, will you have the market study conducted? Why or why not?

b. If the exchange rate changes to 3 real/$, will you have the study conducted? Why or why not?

c. At what exchange rate do you change your decision from rejecting the proposed research project to accepting the project?

BANKING ON FORGIVENESS

When James Wolfensohn became head of the World Bank in 1996, he bluntly admitted that the Bank had "screwed up" in Africa. Decades of loans had erected a vast modern infrastructure—dams, roads, and power plants—for Africa's poor, but the gap between rich and poor did not narrow. In fact, the policies of the Bank and global financial regulators had created a new crisis in sub-Saharan Africa: These nations were now mired in debt they could not possibly repay. Africa's total debt at the time almost equaled the annual gross national product of the entire continent. For instance, in Mozambique, where 25 percent of all children die before the age of 5 from infectious disease, the government was spending twice as much paying off debt as it was spending on health care and education.

For years, nongovernmental organizations (NGOs), such as the advocacy group Oxfam International, had lobbied the Bank and the International Monetary Fund (IMF) to write off loans to their poorest borrowers, calling for "debt forgiveness" or "debt relief." Fortunately for the African people and their advocates, the new head of the Bank put debt forgiveness at the top of his agenda. In the fall of 1996 the World Bank and IMF announced a plan to reduce the external debt of the world's poorest, most heavily indebted countries. The purpose of the plan, called the Heavily Indebted Poor Countries (HIPC) Debt Initiative, is to slash overall debt stocks by 50 percent, lower poor nations' debt service, and boost social spending in poor nations. The HIPC identified 42 countries (34 in Africa, 4 in Latin America, 3 in Asia, and 1 in the Middle East) that may qualify for debt reduction. But debt relief is not automatic. The international banking community is using debt as both a carrot and a stick: Whereas nations with good reform records will get relief, those who can point to little reform will not.

For instance, Uganda was the first country declared eligible for assistance in 1997 and was the first to receive debt relief under the HIPC Initiative in 1998. The decision to begin the program with Uganda was not an arbitrary one. While under the brutal dictatorship of Idi Amin, Uganda was treated as a pariah by creditors. But when Amin and his regime were toppled, new president Yoweri Musevini led the country through a decade-long process of economic reform. Uganda is now considered a model country, boasting a steady growth rate of around 5 percent, with coffee as its main export. By offering debt relief to Uganda, the World Bank and IMF are rewarding Uganda's exemplary track record by reducing its debt to the lowest possible level—about twice the value of its exports. Savings from the debt relief program are pledged to improve health care and to make primary education available to all Ugandan families. In addition to Uganda, Bolivia, Burkina Faso, Guyana, Ivory Coast, and Mozambique also qualified for early assistance.

But just when many countries were receiving debt relief under the HIPC Initiative, the debate over aid versus loans arose once again. In early 2002, 171 nations, the IMF, the World Bank, business leaders, and nongovernmental organizations attended the U.N. Conference on Financing for Development in Monterrey, Mexico. The group was discussing how to prevent economic collapses and debt problems in the developing world, and how to use dwindling aid more efficiently. A week prior to the conference, U.S. President George W. Bush pledged $5 billion more in foreign aid, but wanted the money given away in the form of grants to financially and politically stable nations. "Many have rallied to the idea of dropping the debt. I say let's rally to the idea of stopping the debt," he said, with U2 singer Bono at his side. Bush wanted 40 percent of all World Bank funds for poor nations to be distributed in the form of grants instead of loans they won't be able to repay.

Meanwhile, European Union (EU) leaders pledged to increase aid levels by $20 billion by 2006. But they feared that giving the money away as grants would drain the World Bank's coffers, as well as their own. EU Development Commissioner Poul Nielson said, "We may not be able to do as much for the least-developed countries. The role of the bank is a bank." For support, the EU pointed to World Bank data that showed more than 95 percent of all loans are repaid, and argued that poor nations are more careful with loans than handouts.

thinking globally

1. In negotiating the HIPC Debt Initiative, the World Bank and the IMF worked closely together. However, at one point the plan came to a standstill when the two organizations produced different figures for Uganda's coffee exports, with the IMF giving a more optimistic forecast and so arguing against the need for debt relief. In your opinion, is there any benefit to these organizations working together? Explain. Which organization do you think should play a greater role in aiding economic development? Why?

2. The World Bank and the IMF had once argued that the leniency of debt forgiveness would make it more difficult for the lenders themselves to borrow cheaply on the world's capital markets. If you were a World Bank donor, would you support the HIPC Debt Initiative or argue against it? Explain your answer.

3. At the time the HIPC Initiative was being developed, some critics contended that it fell short. For example, Harvard economist Jeffrey Sachs argued that the need for debt relief was obvious 10 years earlier. The carrot, said Sachs, is simply too little, too late, and he added that for some countries, the situation was so grim that entire external indebtedness, not just half, should be written off. Do you think the World Bank and the IMF should write off the entire debt of countries? What are the pros and cons of this approach for debt relief?

a question of ethics

1. When currency speculators turned their backs on Malaysia and forced a devaluation of the ringgit, Prime Minister Mahathir Mohamad denounced currency speculators as "immoral" and argued that currency trading should take place only to facilitate deals between countries. Although most observers dismiss these comments as coming from a man known for his outspoken tirades against Western investors, others contend that the prime minister's rhetoric voices a genuine concern.

   Is it ethical for global currency speculators to bet against national currencies, perhaps sending whole economies into a tailspin while they profit? Or, do you think that currency speculators perform a valuable service by correcting overvalued or undervalued currencies? What do you think would have happened to the economies of Southeast Asia if currency speculators had not forced devaluation? Support your answers with logical reasoning.

2. In recent years, the governments of industrialized nations have stepped in to bail out emerging nations in the midst of financial crises. Consider the bailouts of Mexico, Indonesia, and Thailand. The IMF then announced a plan to boost its lending capital by $285 billion in order to cope with the next crisis. Taxpayers in industrial countries would foot the bill. By late 2001, the IMF had cobbled together $48 billion in credit to help Argentina. That's on top of billions in emergency loans to Russia. Some critics call this system a kind of "remnant socialism" that rescues financial institutions and investors from their own mistakes with money from taxpayers. For instance, the financial crisis in Thailand was largely a private-sector affair. Thai banks and insurance companies were heavily in debt, and the central bank had recklessly pledged its foreign exchange reserves to shore up the currency.

   Do you think it is ethical that losses are *socialized* (that is, subsidized through government-sponsored bailouts) while profits are *privatized*? Why or why not? Explain exactly who does benefit from bailouts like the one in Thailand. What might be a good alternative to an IMF bailout?

11 planning and organizing international operations

LEARNING OBJECTIVES

After studying this chapter, you should be able to

1 Explain the stages of *identification* and *analysis* that precede strategy selection.

2 Identify the two *international strategies* and the *corporate-level strategies* that companies use.

3 Identify the *business-level strategies* of companies and the role of *department-level strategies*.

4 Discuss the important issues that influence the choice of *organizational structure*.

5 Describe each type of *international organizational structure* and explain the importance of *work teams*.

BEACONS

A Look Back

CHAPTER 10 explored the international monetary system. We examined the factors that affect the determination of exchange rates and discussed international attempts to create a system of stable and predictable exchange rates.

A Look at This Chapter

This chapter introduces us to planning and strategy in international companies. We explore the different types of strategies international companies employ and important factors in their selection. We also examine some organizational structures that companies devise to suit their international operations.

A Look Ahead

CHAPTER 12 explains how managers screen and research potential markets and sites for operations. We also identify the information required in the screening process and explain where managers can go to obtain such information.

Ryanair Is Flying High

DUBLIN, Ireland—"There's no one in Europe doing what Ryanair is doing," says Martin Borghetto, European transport analyst at Morgan Stanley in London. What exactly is Ryanair (**www.ryanair.com**) doing? It offers low-fare, no-frills flying to about 7 million passengers a year. Ryanair's fares are an average of 50 percent lower than Europe's big national carriers and sometimes one-tenth as much. Growing from one flight daily between Ireland and London in 1985, Ryanair now has 75 routes between 13 European nations.

Ryanair has successfully carved out a niche among the flying public. Describing his company's approach, CEO Michael O'Leary said, "It's very simple. We're like Wal-Mart in the U.S.—we pile it high and sell it cheap." The cornerstone of Ryanair's strategy is to use less-congested, secondary airports just outside Europe's biggest cities. For instance, instead of serving London's Heathrow or Gatwick, Ryanair flies into Stansted. Instead of using Frankfurt Main, Ryanair serivces Hahn, a former U.S. fighter base 60 miles west of Frankfurt. This strategy allows Ryanair to negotiate airport fees as low as $1.50 per passenger as opposed to the $15 to $22 per passenger charged by Europe's major airports. No expense stands in the way of Ryanair's achieving its mission. When its caterer could no longer provide free ice, Ryanair stopped serving it, a move that should save about $50,000 a year. Even water costs a few dollars, so bring your own.

Big national carriers such as British Airways and Lufthansa are facing their own D-day invasions—D as in discount. Ryanair is hot on their heels and chipping away at their profits. In fact, Ryanair is the only European airline to make a profit every year since 1990. O'Leary is confident that his strategy is going to be a success. "Ryanair is going to be a monster in Europe within the next 10 to 12 years," he says. As you read this chapter, think of all the strategies that firms use to serve their customers.[1]

Planning is the process of identifying and selecting an organization's objectives and deciding how the organization will achieve those objectives. In turn, **strategy** is the set of planned actions taken by managers to help a company meet its objectives. The key to developing an effective strategy, then, is to clearly define a company's objectives (or goals) and carefully plan how it will achieve those goals. This requires a company to undertake an analysis of its own capabilities and strengths to identify what it can do better than the competition. It also means that a company must carefully assess the competitive environment and the national and international business environments in which it operates.

A well-defined strategy helps a company to compete effectively in increasingly competitive international markets. It serves to coordinate a company's various divisions and departments so that it reaches its company-wide goals in the most effective and efficient manner possible. A clear, appropriate strategy focuses a company on the activities that it performs best and on the industries for which it is best suited and keeps it away from a future of mediocre performance or total failure. An inappropriate strategy can lead managers to take actions that cause internal tensions and pull a company in opposite directions, or take the firm into industries about which they know very little.

We begin this chapter by exploring important factors that managers consider when analyzing their companies' strengths and weaknesses. We examine the different international strategies and the corporate-, business-, and department-level strategies that companies employ. Finally, we explore the different types of organizational structures that companies use to coordinate their international activities.

INTERNATIONAL PLANNING AND STRATEGY

Many of the concerns facing managers when formulating a strategy are the same for both domestic and international companies. Firms must determine what products to produce, where to produce them, and where and how to market them. The biggest difference lies in complexity. Companies considering international production need to select from perhaps many potential countries, each likely having more than one possible location. Depending on its product line, a company that wants to market internationally might have an equally large number of markets to consider. Whether it is being considered as a site for operations or as a potential market, each international location has a rich mixture of cultural, political, legal, and economic traditions and processes. All these factors add to the complexity of planning and strategy for international managers.

STRATEGY FORMULATION

The strategy-formulation process involves both planning and strategy. Strategy formulation permits managers to step back from day-to-day activities and get a fresh perspective on the current and future direction of the company and its industry. As shown in Figure 11.1, this procedure can be regarded as a three-stage process. Let's now examine several important factors to consider in each stage of this process.

IDENTIFY COMPANY MISSION AND GOALS

Most companies have a general purpose for why they exist that they express in a **mission statement**—a written statement of why a company exists and what it plans to accomplish. For example, one company might set out to supply the highest level of service in a *market segment*—a clearly identifiable group of potential buyers. Another might be determined to be the lowest-cost supplier in its segment worldwide. The mission statement often guides decisions such as which industries to enter or exit and how to compete in chosen segments.

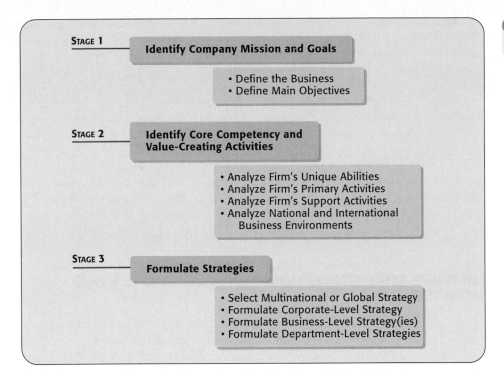

FIGURE 11.1
Strategy-Formulation Process

Types of Mission Statements Mission statements often spell out how a company's operations affect its **stakeholders**—all parties, ranging from suppliers and employees to stockholders and consumers, who are affected by a company's activities. For instance, some statements focus on the interests of consumers. Thus global eye-care company Bausch & Lomb (**www.bausch.com**) includes the customer in its statement of its goals and activities:

> As a global eye care company, we will help consumers see, look and feel better through innovative technology and design.[2]

Other companies issue very broad mission statements that recognize all their stakeholders. Britain's Cadbury Schweppes (**www.cadburyschweppes.com**) is a global company whose businesses in over 200 countries are beverages and confectionery (candies). Although most products in the confectionery group carry the Cadbury name, its beverage group includes well-known brands such as 7-Up, Dr. Pepper, Crush, and Mott's. The firm's mission statement reads as follows:

> Our task is to build on our traditions of quality and value to provide brands, products, financial results and management performance that meet the interests of our shareholders, consumers, employees, customers, suppliers and the communities in which we operate.[3]

Thus, the mission statement of an international business depends on (among other things) the type of business it is in, the stakeholders it is trying most to satisfy, and the aspect of the business that is most important to achieving its goals. However, companies must be sensitive to the needs of its different stakeholders in different nations. For instance, the need of a company's stockholders in one nation for financial returns must be balanced against the needs of buyers in another country or the public at large where it has production facilities. That is why a company cannot be irresponsible in its duties for proper waste disposal activities or excessive noise levels near residential areas, for example.

stakeholders
All parties, ranging from suppliers and employees to stockholders and consumers, who are affected by a company's activities.

Managers must also define the *objectives* they wish to achieve in the global marketplace. Objectives at the highest level in a company tend to be stated in the most general terms. An example of this type of objective would be:

> To be the largest global company in each industry in which we compete.

Objectives of individual business units in an organization tend to be more specific. They are normally stated in more concrete terms and sometimes even contain numerical targets. For example, such a mission statement could be stated as follows:

> To mass-produce a zero-pollution emissions automobile by 2008.

Objectives usually become even more precise at the level of individual departments and almost always contain numerical targets of performance. For example, the following could be the objective of a marketing and sales department:

> To increase market share by 5 percent in each of the next 3 years.

IDENTIFY CORE COMPETENCY AND VALUE-CREATING ACTIVITIES

Before managers formulate effective strategies, they must analyze the company, its industry (or industries), and the national business environments in which it is involved. They should also examine industries and countries being targeted for potential future entry. In this section we address the company and its industries. We examine the business environment in the next section.

Unique Abilities of Companies   Although large multinational companies are often involved in multiple industries, most perform one activity (or a few activities) better than any competitor does. A **core competency** is a special ability of a company that competitors find extremely difficult or impossible to equal.[4] It is not a skill; individuals possess skills. An architect's ability to design an office building in the Victorian style is a skill. A core competency refers to multiple skills that are coordinated to form a single technological outcome. Although skills can be learned through on-the-job training and personal experience, core competencies develop over longer periods of time and are difficult to teach.

For example, at one point Canon of Japan (**www.canon.com**) invested money to acquire expertise in optic technology. However, only later did Canon succeed in developing a variety of products based on optic technology—cameras, copiers, and semiconductor lithographic equipment. When the firm possessed the ability to create such products, it had fully developed a legitimate core competency.[5] Likewise, Sony's (**www.sony.com**) core competency in miniaturizing electronic components fortifies its global leadership position in consumer electronics.

How do managers actually go about analyzing and identifying their unique abilities? Let's take a look at a tool commonly used by managers to analyze their companies—*value-chain analysis*.

Value-Chain Analysis   Managers must select strategies consistent with both their company's particular strengths and the market conditions faced by their firm. Managers should also select company strategies based on what the company does that customers find valuable. This is why managers conduct a **value-chain analysis**—the process of dividing a company's activities into primary and support activities and identifying those that create value for customers.[6] As you can see from Figure 11.2, value-chain analysis divides a company's activities into primary activities and support activities that are central to creating customer value. *Primary activities* include inbound and outbound logis-

core competency
Special ability of a company that competitors find extremely difficult or impossible to equal.

value-chain analysis
Process of dividing a company's activities into primary and support activities and identifying those that create value for customers.

FIGURE 11.2   *Components of a Company's Value Chain*

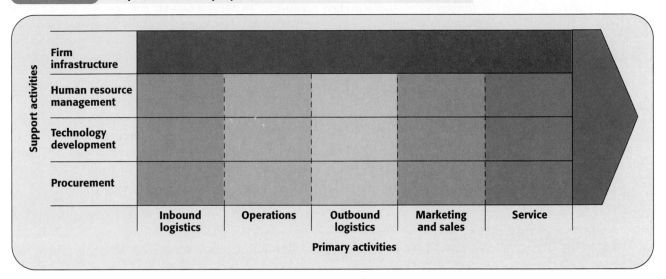

tics, manufacturing (or operations), marketing and sales, and customer service. Primary activities involve the physical creation of the product, its marketing and delivery to buyers, and its after-sales support and service. *Support activities* include firm infrastructure, human resource management, technology development, and procurement. Each of these activities provides the inputs and infrastructure required by the primary activities.

Each primary and support activity is a source of strength or weakness for a company. Managers determine whether each activity enhances or detracts from customer value and incorporate this knowledge into the strategy-formulation process. Analysis of primary and support activities often involves finding activities in which improvements can be made with large benefits. Let's take a look at how managers determine whether an activity enhances customer value.

Primary Activities   When analyzing primary activities, managers often look for areas in which the company can increase the value provided to its customers. For instance, managers might examine production processes and discover new, more efficient manufacturing methods to reduce production costs and improve quality. Customer satisfaction might be increased by improving logistics management that shortens the time it takes to get a product to the buyer or by providing better customer service.

Companies might also lower costs by introducing greater automation into the production process.[7] For example, Stan Shih, founder of computer maker Acer (www.global.acer.com), applied a fast-food production model to personal computer manufacturing. Rather than manufacture complete computers in Asia and ship them around the world, Acer builds components at plants scattered throughout the world. Those components are then shipped to assembly plants where computers are built according to customer specifications. Shih commented, "Today, there is no longer any value added in assembling computers—everyone can make a PC. To succeed, you have to gain a top position in component segments or else as a distribution leader in a country or region."[8] By altering its production and logistics processes, Acer created a business model that created value for customers.

Support Activities   Support activities assist companies in performing their primary activities. For example, the actions of any company's employees are crucial to its success. Manufacturing, logistics, marketing and sales, and customer service all benefit when employees are qualified and well trained. International companies can often improve the quality of their product by investing in worker training and management development. In turn, ensuring quality can increase the efficiency of a firm's manufacturing, marketing and sales, and customer service activities. Effective procurement can locate low-cost, high-quality raw materials or intermediate products and ensure on-time delivery to production facilities. Finally, a sophisticated infrastructure not only improves internal communication but also supports organizational culture and each primary activity.

Thus, the in-depth analysis of a company inherent in the strategy-formulation process helps managers to discover their company's unique core competency and abilities and the activities that create customer value. For some guidelines on how small companies can perform a self-analysis, see the Entrepreneurial Focus titled "Know Yourself, Know Your Product."

ENTREPRENEURIAL FOCUS

Know Yourself, Know Your Product

Going International. It's the most popular blueprint today for company growth. But if the blueprint is flawed, if the foundation isn't stable, if the materials aren't first class, international expansion could prove to be the tremor that takes down the temple. Here are some factors any small business should consider to be successful abroad.

➡ **Are you ready to go international?** Consider how long your company has been in business and whether it is stable enough to brave the rough international seas. Assess whether your product must be adapted for international markets and whether you can adapt successfully. Determine whether the expected sales volume abroad is worth the effort. Are you a success at home? Potential international partners will be more eager to partner with a company that is doing very well in its domestic market.

➡ **Have a thorough understanding of your product.** You must know how to capitalize on your product's strengths, minimize its weaknesses, correct its flaws, and modify it for other markets—or not modify it as the case may be. Beverly Hills Polo Club (BHPC) (**www.bhpc.com**) licenses its trademark in more than 75 countries. "We export the concept of America," says Don Garrison, vice president of international marketing for BHPC. "That's difficult to define sometimes, but there's a certain identification with Beverly Hills and Southern California that people around the world find very appealing." The company understands that to modify its product or what it represents would gut it of its essence.

➡ **Examine your company's internal activities.** Does your company have the infrastructure to take the company international? The effort will require a great deal of managerial and financial resources to tackle the job. Check that each department—procurement, production, marketing and sales, credit and collections, and so on—can devote the resources needed to the new international activities. The financial investment will be great, but early profits will be slim to none. Be certain that international activities will not overly burden the company's domestic business in the near- to mid-term. Also, make sure that everyone—from the CEO to the shipping room clerk—appreciates the commitment needed and the role each will play.

➡ **Ask important questions of strategy.** Does your company have an overall strategy into which your international business will fit? Have you developed a separate international strategy? Is it one that can successfully complement your domestic strategy? The answers to these questions reflect what you want to gain from going international, how quickly you want to achieve profits, and how long-term your commitment is. The question of strategy development is also vital to building on your success.

➡ **Finally, create the strategic plan.** Create a written strategic plan for your international ambitions. Include the commitment in time and money that you are willing to make and the resources you have available. Be certain of what resources you *can* devote to your international effort and what resources you *should* devote to it. They may well not be the same. Determine what kind of international partners you *want* to attract and what kind of international partners you *will* attract. These also may not be the same.

A company cannot identify its unique abilities in a vacuum separate from the environment in which it operates. The external business environment consists of all the elements outside a company that can affect its performance, such as cultural, political, legal, and economic forces; workers' unions; consumers; and financial institutions. Let's now explore some of the main environmental forces that have an impact on strategy formulation.

National and International Business Environments   National differences in language, religious beliefs, customs, traditions, and climate complicate strategy formulation. For example, language differences can increase the cost of operations and administration. Manufacturing processes must sometimes be adapted to the supply of local workers and to local customs, traditions, and practices. Marketing activities sometimes can result in costly mistakes if they do not incorporate cultural differences. For instance, a company once decided to sell its laundry detergent in Japan but did not adjust the size of the box in which it was sold. The company spent millions of dollars developing a detailed marketing campaign and was shocked when it experienced disappointing sales. It turns out that the company should have packaged the detergent in smaller containers for the Japanese market. Japanese shoppers prefer smaller quantities because they tend to walk home from the store and have smaller storage areas in tight living quarters.[9]

Differences in political and legal systems also complicate international strategies. Legal and political processes often differ in target countries to such an extent that firms must hire outside consultants to teach them about the local system. Such knowledge is important to international companies because the approval of the host government is almost always necessary for making direct investments. Companies need to know which ministry or department has the authority to grant approval for a big business deal—a process that can become extremely cumbersome. For example, non-Chinese companies in China must often get approval from several agencies, and the process is further complicated by the tendency of local government officials to interpret laws differently than do bureaucrats in Beijing (the nation's capital).

Different national economic systems further complicate strategy formulation. Negative attitudes of local people toward the impact of direct investment can generate political unrest. Economic philosophy affects the tax rates that governments impose. Whereas socialist economic systems normally levy high taxes on business profits, free-market economies tend to levy lighter taxes. The need to work in more than one currency also complicates international strategy. To minimize losses from currency fluctuations, companies must develop strategies to deal with exchange-rate risk.

Finally, apart from complicating strategy, the national business environment can affect the location that a company chooses to perform an activity. For instance, a nation that spends a high portion of its GDP on research and development attracts high-tech industries and high-wage jobs and, as a result, prospers. In contrast, countries that spend relatively little in the way of R&D tend to have lower levels of prosperity. This chapter's World Business Survey titled "Invest and Prosper" shows R&D spending for a selected group of nations.

FORMULATE STRATEGIES

As we've already seen, the strengths and special capabilities of international companies, along with the environmental forces they face, play a large role in the type of strategy that managers choose. Let's now examine this final stage in the planning and strategy-formulation process—formulating strategies.

Two International Strategies   Companies engaged in international business activities can approach the market using either a *multinational* or a *global* strategy. It is important to note that these two strategies do not include companies that export.

Invest and Prosper

Countries that don't spend much on R&D tend to be less prosperous. That is why for a nation to prosper, its companies must innovate in order to compete. Says Michael May, of consulting firm Accenture, "If competition intensifies as expected, businesses will place a premium on innovation and entrepreneurship. These same businesses are increasingly reliant on the application of technology as a means of strategic advantage." Here is how some countries are doing on their R&D spending.

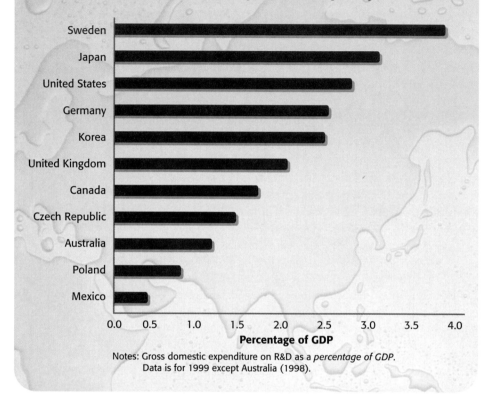

Notes: Gross domestic expenditure on R&D as a *percentage of GDP*.
Data is for 1999 except Australia (1998).

Exporters do not have foreign direct investments in other national markets and should instead devise an appropriate export strategy (see Chapter 13). Let's now examine what it means for a company to follow a multinational or a global strategy.

Multinational Strategy   Some international companies choose to follow a **multinational (multidomestic) strategy**—a strategy of adapting products and their marketing strategies in each national market to suit local preferences. In other words, a multinational strategy is just what its name implies—a separate strategy for each of the multiple nations in which a company markets its products. To implement a multinational strategy, companies often establish largely independent, self-contained units (or subsidiaries) in each national market. Typically, each subsidiary undertakes its own product research and development, production, and marketing. In many ways, each unit functions largely as an independent company. Multinational strategies are often appropriate for companies in industries in which buyer preferences do not converge across national borders, such as certain food products and some print media.

The main benefit of a multinational strategy is that it allows companies to monitor buyer preferences closely in each local market and to respond quickly and effectively as

multinational (multidomestic) strategy
Adapting products and their marketing strategies in each national market to suit local preferences.

new buyer preferences emerge. The result that companies hope for when offering a tailored product is that customers will perceive it as delivering greater value than do competitors' products, allowing a company using a multinational strategy to charge higher prices and/or gain market share.

The main drawback of a multinational strategy is that it does not allow companies to exploit scale economies in product development, manufacturing, or marketing. Thus, a multinational strategy typically increases the cost structure for international companies and forces them to charge higher prices to recover such costs. As such, a multinational strategy is usually poorly suited to industries in which price competitiveness is a key success factor. Furthermore, the high degree of independence with which each unit operates can reduce opportunities for sharing knowledge between units within a company.

Global Strategy   Other companies decide that what suits their operations is a **global strategy**—a strategy of offering the same products using the same marketing strategy in all national markets. Companies that follow a global strategy often take advantage of scale and location economies by producing entire inventories of products or components in a few optimal locations. They also tend to perform product research and development in one or a few locations and typically design promotional campaigns and advertising strategies at headquarters. So-called global products are most common in industries characterized by price competition and, therefore, pressure to contain costs. They include certain electronic components, a wide variety of industrial goods such as steel, and some consumer goods such as paper and writing instruments.

The main benefit of a global strategy is its cost savings due to product and marketing standardization. These cost savings can then be passed on to consumers to help the company gain market share in its market segment. A global strategy also allows managers to share lessons learned in one market with managers at other locations.

The main problem with a global strategy is that it may cause a company to overlook important differences in buyer preferences from one market to another. A global strategy does not allow a company to modify its products except for the most superficial features, such as the color of paint applied to a finished product or small add-on features. This can present an opportunity for a competitor to step in and satisfy unmet needs that local buyers might have, thereby creating a niche market.

In addition to deciding whether the company will follow a multinational or a global strategy, managers must formulate strategies for the corporation, each business unit, and each department. Let's now explore the three different levels of company strategy shown in Figure 11.3: *corporate-*, *business-*, and *department-level* strategies.

> **global strategy**
> *Offering the same products using the same marketing strategy in all national markets.*

Corporate-Level Strategies   Companies involved in more than one line of business must first formulate a *corporate-level strategy*. In part, this means identifying the national markets and industries in which the company will operate. It also involves developing overall objectives for the company's different business units and specifying the role that each unit will play in reaching those objectives. The four key approaches to corporate strategy are *growth*, *retrenchment*, *stability*, and *combination*.

Growth Strategy   A **growth strategy** is designed to increase the scale or scope of a corporation's operations. *Scale* refers to the *size* of a corporation's activities, *scope* to the *kinds* of activities it performs. Yardsticks commonly used to measure growth include geographic coverage, number of business units, market share, sales revenue, and number of employees. *Organic growth* refers to a corporate strategy of relying on internally generated growth. For example, management at 3M (**www.3m.com**) strongly encourages entrepreneurial activity, often spinning off business units to nurture the best ideas and carry them to completion. Microsoft (**www.microsoft.com**), too, generates much of its growth organically, especially through the effective use of work teams.[10]

> **growth strategy**
> *Strategy designed to increase the scale (size of activities) or scope (kinds of activities) of a corporation's operations.*

FIGURE 11.3

Three Levels of Company Strategy

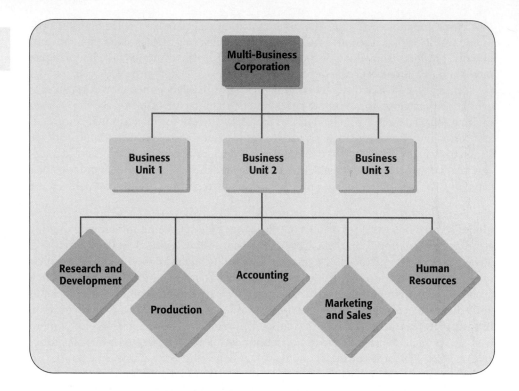

Other methods of growth include mergers and acquisitions, joint ventures, and strategic alliances (see Chapter 13). These tactics are used when companies do not wish to invest in developing certain skills internally or when other companies already do what managers are trying to achieve. Common partners in implementing these strategies include competitors, suppliers, and buyers. Corporations typically join forces with competitors to reduce competition, expand product lines, or expand geographically. A common motivation for joining forces with suppliers is to increase control over the quality, cost, and timing of inputs.

One corporation undertaking an aggressive global growth strategy is Intel (www.intel.com). Intel's goal is "to be the preeminent building block supplier to the worldwide Internet economy." Intel manufactures computer components (the "building blocks" of computing systems), including microprocessors, chipsets, motherboards, memory units, and software. It provides these components to manufacturers in the computer, automobile, and mobile-phone industries. Intel's growth strategy focuses not only on delivering "the high-performance processors that drive today's connected PCs and related products," but working "with other industry leaders to expand the PC's role as a consumer and business communications device, driving future PC sales."[11] Central to Intel's accomplishing its growth strategy are the huge potential in large emerging markets such as China and Brazil, and the increasing penetration of the World Wide Web there.

Retrenchment Strategy   The exact opposite of a growth strategy is a **retrenchment strategy**—a strategy designed to reduce the scale or scope of a corporation's businesses. Corporations often cut back the *scale* of their operations when economic conditions worsen or competition increases. They may do so by closing factories with unused capacity and laying off workers. Corporations can also reduce the scale of their operations by laying off managers and salespeople in national markets that are not generating adequate sales revenue. Corporations reduce the *scope* of their activities by selling unprofitable business

retrenchment strategy
Strategy designed to reduce the scale or scope of a corporation's businesses.

Retrenchment is often a painful strategy that can be met with considerable resistance, like that expressed by these protesting workers at Weirton Steel (**www.weirton.com**), in Weirton, West Virginia. In the late 1990s, a rising tide of imported steel depressed prices as much as 20 percent—forcing Weirton to shut down part of the plant. Then, in 2002, the U.S. imposed up to 30 percent tariffs on imported steel to give the industry time to "restructure." Do you think more consolidation and plant closings were on the way?

units or those no longer directly related to their overall aims. Weaker competitors often resort to retrenchment when national business environments grow more competitive.

Stability Strategy   A **stability strategy** is designed to guard against change. It is often employed by corporations trying to avoid either growth or retrenchment. Typically such corporations have met their stated objectives or are satisfied with what they have already accomplished. They believe that their strengths are being fully exploited and their weaknesses fully protected against. They also see the business environment as posing neither profitable opportunities nor threats. They have no interest in expanding sales, increasing profits, increasing market share, or expanding the customer base; at present, they want simply to maintain their present positions.

Combination Strategy   The purpose of a **combination strategy** is to mix growth, retrenchment, and stability strategies across a corporation's business units. For example, a corporation can invest in units that show promise, retrench in those for which less exposure is desired, and stabilize others. In fact, corporate combination strategies are quite common because international corporations rarely follow identical strategies in each of their business units.

Business-Level Strategies   In addition to stipulating the overall corporate strategy, managers must also formulate separate *business-level strategies* for each business unit. For some companies, this means creating just one strategy. This is the case when the business-level strategy and the corporate-level strategy are one and the same because the corporation is involved in just one line of business.

For other companies, this means creating anywhere from two to dozens of strategies. For example, as we saw earlier in this chapter, Cadbury Schweppes (www.cadburyschweppes.com) of Britain has two main business units—beverages and confectionery—each with its own strategy. The strategy of the beverages business unit is to "strengthen our soft drink's position worldwide and to be the largest and most successful non-cola brand owner." For the confectionery unit, strategy is "based on building viable positions in prioritised markets through organic growth and acquisitions."[12]

stability strategy
Strategy designed to guard against change and used by corporations to avoid either growth or retrenchment.

combination strategy
Strategy designed to mix growth, retrenchment, and stability strategies across a corporation's business units.

Thus, the beverages unit is focused on strengthening the position of its existing soft drink products, but the confectionery unit is attempting to create new products in promising markets through internal growth and by acquiring other firms.

The key to developing an effective business-level strategy is deciding on a *general competitive strategy in the marketplace*. Each business unit must decide whether to sell the lowest-price product in an industry or to integrate special attributes into its products. As you can see in Figure 11.4, a business unit can employ one of three generic business-level strategies for competing in its industry—*low-cost leadership*, *differentiation*, or *focus*.[13] Let's now explore each of these strategies in detail.

Low-Cost Leadership Strategy   A strategy in which a company exploits economies of scale to have the lowest cost structure of any competitor in its industry is called a **low-cost leadership strategy**. Companies that pursue the low-cost leadership position also try to contain administrative costs and the costs of its various primary activities, including marketing, advertising, and distribution. We saw in this chapter's opening company profile how Ryanair engages in aggressive cost cutting to be Europe's leading low-cost airline. Although cutting costs is the mantra for firms that pursue a low-cost leadership position, other important competitive factors such as product quality and customer service cannot be ignored. Factors underlying the low-cost leadership position (efficient production in large quantities) help guard against attack by competitors because of the large up-front cost of getting started. Also, because achieving low-cost leadership tends to rely on large-scale production to contain costs, the strategy typically requires the company to have a large market share. One negative aspect of the low-cost leadership strategy is low customer loyalty—all else equal, buyers will purchase from the low-cost leader regardless of who it is.

A low-cost leadership strategy works best with mass-marketed products aimed at price-sensitive buyers. This strategy is often well suited to companies with a standardized product and marketing promotions. Two global companies vying for the low-cost leadership position in their respective industries include Casio (**www.casio.com**) in sports watches and Texas Instruments (**www.ti.com**) in calculators and other electronic devices.

low-cost leadership strategy
Strategy in which a company exploits economies of scale to have the lowest cost structure of any competitor in its industry.

FIGURE 11.4

Three Generic Business-Level Strategies

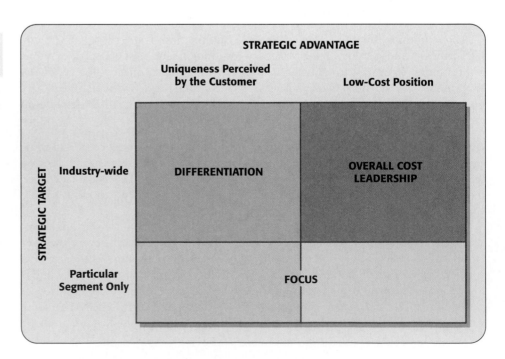

STRATEGIC ADVANTAGE

	Uniqueness Perceived by the Customer	Low-Cost Position
Industry-wide	DIFFERENTIATION	OVERALL COST LEADERSHIP
Particular Segment Only	FOCUS	

STRATEGIC TARGET

Differentiation Strategy A **differentiation strategy** is one in which a company designs its products to be perceived as unique by buyers throughout its industry. Because its buyers perceive the product as unique, a company that follows a differentiation strategy can charge a higher price and enjoys greater customer loyalty than does the low-cost leader. A differentiation strategy tends to force a company into a lower-market-share position because it generally involves the perception of exclusivity or as meeting the needs of only a certain group of buyers. Companies that use this strategy must develop loyal customer bases to offset smaller market shares and the higher costs of producing and marketing a unique product.

One way products can be differentiated is by improving their reputation for *quality*. Ceramic tableware for everyday use is found at department stores in almost every country. However, the ceramic tableware made by Japanese producer Noritake (www.noritake.com) differentiates itself from common tableware by emphasizing its superior quality. The perception of higher quality allows manufacturers to charge higher prices for their products worldwide.

Other products are differentiated by distinctive *brand images*. IZOD (www.izod.com) and Calvin Klein, for example, are relatively pricey global clothiers appealing to a young, fashionable clientele. Each is continually introducing new textures and colors that are at once stylish and functional. Another example is Italian carmaker Alfa Romeo (www.alfaromeo.com), which does not compete in the fiercely competitive mass-consumer segment of the global automobile industry. To do so, it would have to be price-competitive and offer a wider selection of cars. Instead, Alfa Romeo offers a high-quality product with a brand image that rewards the Alfa Romeo owner with status and prestige.

Another differentiating factor is *product design*—the sum of the features by which a product looks and functions according to customer requirements. For instance, the designs of Casio (www.casio.com) and other makers of mass-market sports watches stress functionality. On the other hand, the sports watches of TAG Heuer (www.tagheuer.com) from Switzerland offer classy, stylish designs in addition to performance. Special features differentiate both goods and services in the minds of consumers who value those features. Manufacturers can also combine several differentiation factors in formulating their strategies.

differentiation strategy
Strategy in which a company designs its products to be perceived as unique by buyers throughout its industry.

Internet retailer Amazon.com (**www.amazon.com**) differentiates itself by taking orders over the Internet and filling requests with reliability and speed. Amazon started out selling only books in 1995 but today offers all sorts of products, including CDs, DVDs, games, cameras, and computers. The company partners with traditional retailers including Circuit City, Target, and Toys "R" Us. In fact, even bricks-and-mortar bookseller, Borders, closed its own Web site and now partners with Amazon.

Focus Strategy   A **focus strategy** is one in which a company focuses on serving the needs of a narrowly defined market segment by being the low-cost leader, by differentiating its product, or both. Increasing competition often means more products distinguished by price or differentiated by quality, design, and so forth. In turn, a greater product range leads to the continuous refinement of market segments. Today many industries consist of large numbers of market segments and even smaller subsegments. For example, some firms try to serve the needs of one ethnic or racial group, whereas others, often entrepreneurs and small businesses, focus on a single geographic area.

For instance, Johnson & Johnson (**www.johnsonandjohnson.com**) is commonly thought of as being a single, large consumer-products company. In fact, it is a conglomerate consisting of more than 160 separately chartered companies that market an enormous variety of products to a wide array of market segments. Many of these individual J&J companies try to dominate their segments by producing specialty goods and services. In so doing, they focus on narrow segments using either low-cost leadership or differentiation techniques.

A focus strategy often means designing products and promotions aimed at consumers who are either dissatisfied with existing choices or who want something distinctive. Consider the highly fragmented gourmet coffee market. One brand of coffee called Luwak sells for around *$300 per pound*! Certainly the coffee is made from distinctive beans. Apparently, luwaks (weasels on the Indonesian island of Java) eat coffee berries containing coffee beans. The beans "naturally ferment" as they pass through the luwaks and are recovered from the animals' waste. The beans are then washed, roasted, and sold around the world as a specialty coffee (certainly having a distinctive taste).[14]

The strategies we've discussed here can be applied to practically all firms in all markets worldwide. However, companies in emerging markets often face special problems. See the Global Manager titled "Competing with Giants" to see how domestic companies in emerging markets can survive the onslaught by the major multinational companies.

Department-Level Strategies   Achieving corporate- and business-level objectives depends on effective departmental strategies that focus on the specific activities that transform resources into products. Formulation of *department-level strategies* brings us back to where we began our analysis of a company's capabilities that support its strategy—to the primary and support activities that create value for customers. After managers analyze these activities, they must then develop strategies that exploit their firm's value-creating strengths.

Primary and Support Activities   Each department is instrumental in creating customer value through lower costs or differentiated products. This is especially true of departments that conduct *primary activities*. Manufacturing strategies are obviously important in cutting the production costs of both standardized and differentiated products. They are also crucial to improving product quality. Effective marketing strategies allow companies to promote the differences in their products. A strong sales force and good customer service contribute to favorable images among consumers or industrial buyers and generate loyal customers of both kinds. Efficient logistics in bringing raw materials and components into the factory and getting the finished product out the factory door can result in substantial cost savings.

Support activities also create customer value. For example, research and development identifies market segments with unsatisfied needs and designs products to meet them. Human resource managers can improve efficiency and cut costs by hiring well-trained employees and conducting worker training and management-development programs. Procurement tasks provide operations with quality resources at a reasonable

GLOBAL MANAGER

Competing with Giants

Industries differ in the degree to which they are global—some, such as semiconductors or aircraft, are highly global, but others, such as retail banking, are not. However, most industries lie somewhere in between. Also, some emerging-market companies have a competitive edge that is germane to the local market, such as an extensive, strong distribution network. Others have a competitive advantage that is transferable to other markets, such as expertise in building efficient factories. By analyzing these two facets—industry globalization and asset transferability—emerging-market companies can choose one of four strategies to combat multinational giants.

➡ **Defender.** If globalization pressures are weak, and a company's own assets are not transferable, the company needs to concentrate on defending its home turf. For instance, when India opened its automotive sector to international competitors in the mid-1980s, the country's largest domestic manufacturer of motor scooters, Bajaj Auto (**www.bajajauto.com**), was petrified. Honda (**www.honda.com**) soon burst onto the scene with superior technology, quality, and brand appeal. But Bajaj beefed up its distribution and service network and improved the design of its low-cost, rugged scooters. In the fall of 1998, Honda announced it was pulling out of its scooter-manufacturing venture in India.

➡ **Extender.** If globalization pressures are weak, but a company's assets can be transferred abroad, the company may be able to extend its success to a limited number of other markets. For example, when McDonald's (**www.mcdonalds.com**) entered the Philippines, local fast-food company Jollibee Foods (**www.jollibee.com/ph**) upgraded its service and developed rival menus customized to local tastes. Using its battle-tested recipes from home, Jollibee established dozens of restaurants in markets with large Filipino populations, including Hong Kong, the Middle East, and California.

➡ **Dodger.** If globalization pressures are strong, but a company's assets are not transferable, the company will need to dodge its larger rivals by restructuring itself around links in the value chain that buyers value. When Russia liberalized its economy, Russian personal-computer maker Vist (**www.vist.ru**) side-stepped oblivion by redefining its core business. When the big guns such as IBM (**www.ibm.com**) came in with superior PCs, Vist focused on its strengths—distribution, service, and warranties. Although Vist's computers are unremarkable, all its manuals are in Russian and the company provides lengthy warranties—unlike its multinational rivals, which charge a fee for an extended service contract. Vist is the leading brand of PCs in Russia, with 20 percent of the market.

➡ **Contender.** If globalization pressures are strong, and a company's assets can be transferred abroad, the company may be able to compete head-to-head with its multinational rivals in world markets. For instance, when General Motors (**www.gm.com**) decided to purchase radiator caps for its North American autos rather than make them itself, Sundaram Fasteners (**www.sundaram.com**) of India bought an entire GM production line and shipped it home. One year later Sundaram was GM's sole North American supplier of 5 million radiator caps per year. What Sundaram learned as GM's supplier benefited its core fastener business and allowed the company to target markets in Japan and Europe. Sundaram is now capable of supplying markets worldwide.

---

cost. Accounting and finance (elements of a firm's infrastructure) must develop efficient information systems to assist managers in making decisions and maintaining financial control, thus having an impact on costs and quality in general.

There are important elements that drive the decisions of world-class companies with regard to strategy formulation. For example, the important *production* issues to consider are the number and dispersion of production facilities and whether to standardize production processes for all markets. The important *marketing* issue is whether to standardize either the physical features of products, or their marketing strategies, across markets. We will present the strategic considerations of production and marketing activities in later chapters.

INTERNATIONAL ORGANIZATIONAL STRUCTURE

organizational structure
Way in which a company divides its activities among separate units and coordinates activities between those units.

Organizational structure is the way in which a company divides its activities among separate units and coordinates activities between those units. If a company's organizational structure is appropriate for its strategic plans, it will be more effective in working toward its goals. In this section, we explore several important issues related to organizational structures and examine several alternative forms that an organization's structure can take.

CENTRALIZATION VERSUS DECENTRALIZATION

Managers must determine the degree to which decision making in the organization will be centralized or decentralized. *Centralized decision making* is when decision making is centralized at a high level in one location, such as headquarters. *Decentralized decision making* is when decisions are made at lower levels, such as in international subsidiaries.

Should managers at the parent company be actively involved in the decisions made by international subsidiaries? Or should they intervene relatively little, perhaps only in the most crucial decisions? Some decisions, of course, must be decentralized. If top managers involve themselves in the day-to-day decisions of every subsidiary, they are likely to be overwhelmed. For example, they cannot get directly involved in every hiring decision or assignment of people to specific tasks at each facility. On the other hand, overall corporate strategy cannot be delegated to subsidiary managers. Only top management has the appropriate perspective to formulate corporate strategy.

In our discussion of centralization versus decentralization of decision making, it is important to remember two points:

1. Companies rarely centralize or decentralize all decision making. Rather, they seek the approach that will result in the greatest efficiency and effectiveness.
2. International companies may centralize decision making in certain geographic markets while decentralizing it in others. Numerous factors influence this decision, including the need for product modification and the abilities of managers at each location.

With these points in mind, let's take a look at some of the specific factors that determine whether centralized or decentralized decision making is most appropriate.

When to Centralize Centralized decision making helps to coordinate the operations of international subsidiaries. This fact is important for companies that operate in multiple lines of business or in many international markets. It is also important when one subsidiary's output is another's input. In such situations, coordinating operations from a single, high-level vantage point is more efficient. Purchasing is often centralized if all subsidiaries use the same inputs in production. For example, a company that manufactures steel filing cabinets and desks will need a great deal of sheet steel. A central purchasing department will get a better bulk price on sheet steel than would subsidiaries negotiating their own agreements. Each subsidiary then benefits by being able to purchase sheet steel from central purchasing at a lower cost than it would pay in the open market.

Some companies maintain strong central control over financial resources by channeling all subsidiary profits back to the parent for redistribution to subsidiaries based on their needs. This practice reduces the likelihood that certain subsidiaries will undertake investment projects when more promising projects go without funding at other locations. Other companies centrally design policies, procedures, and standards in order to stimulate a single global organizational culture. This policy makes it more likely that all subsidiaries will enforce company rules uniformly. It is also beneficial when companies transfer managers from one location to another. If policies are uniform, the transition proceeds more smoothly for both managers and subordinates.

When to Decentralize Decentralized decision making is beneficial when fast-changing national business environments put a premium on local responsiveness. Because subsidiary managers are in closer contact with local culture, politics, laws, and economies, decentralized decisions can result in products that are better suited to the needs and preferences of local buyers. Local managers are more likely to perceive environmental changes that managers at headquarters would not notice. Even if central managers did perceive such changes, they are likely to get a secondhand account of local events. Delayed response and misinterpreted events can result in lost orders, stalled production, and weakened competitiveness. Similarly, decentralized decision making can save money because informed decisions can be made without flying executives around the world on fact-finding missions.

Participative Management and Accountability Decentralization can also help to foster participative management practices. The morale of employees is likely to be higher if subsidiary managers and subordinates are involved in decision making. When delegated to subsidiaries, decisions related to national strategy—including production, promotion, distribution, and pricing decisions—can generate greater commitment from both managers and workers.

Decentralization often improves personal accountability for business decisions. When local managers are rewarded (or punished) for their decisions, they are likely to invest more effort in making and executing them. Conversely, if local managers must do nothing but implement policies dictated from above, they can attribute poor performance to decisions that were ill-suited to the local environment. When managers are held accountable for decision making and implementation, they typically delve more deeply into research and debate and consider all available options. The results are often better decisions and improved performance.

COORDINATION AND FLEXIBILITY

When designing organizational structure, managers seek answers to certain key questions. What is the most efficient method of linking divisions to one another? Who should coordinate the activities of different divisions in order to achieve overall strategies? How should information be processed and delivered to managers when it is required? What sorts of monitoring mechanisms and reward structures should be established? How should the company introduce corrective measures, and whose responsibility should it be to execute them? To answer these types of questions, we must look at the issues of coordination and flexibility.

Structure and Coordination As we have seen, some companies have a presence in several or more national business environments—they manufacture and market products practically everywhere. Others operate primarily in one country and export to, or import from, other markets. Each type of company must design an appropriate organizational structure. Each needs a structure that clearly defines areas of responsibility and **chains of command**—the lines of authority that run from top management to individual employees and specify internal reporting relationships. Finally, every firm needs a structure that brings together areas that require close cooperation. For example, to avoid product designs that make manufacturing more difficult and costly than necessary, most firms ensure that R&D and manufacturing remain in close contact.

chains of command
Lines of authority that run from top management to individual employees and specify internal reporting relationships.

Structure and Flexibility Organizational structure is not permanent—it is often modified to suit changes both within a company and in its external environment. Because companies usually base organizational structures on strategies, changes in strategy usually require adjustments in structure. Similarly, because changes in national business environments can force changes in strategy, the same changes will influence company structure. It is especially important to monitor closely the conditions in countries characterized by rapidly shifting cultural, political, and economic environments. Let's now explore four organizational structures that have been developed to improve the responsiveness and effectiveness of companies conducting international business activities.

TYPES OF ORGANIZATIONAL STRUCTURE

There are many different ways in which a company can organize itself to carry out its international business activities. But four organizational structures tend to be most common for the vast majority of international companies—*division structure, area structure, product structure,* and *matrix structure.*

International Division Structure An **international division structure** separates domestic from international business activities by creating a separate international division with its own manager (see Figure 11.5). In turn, the international division is typically divided into units corresponding to the countries in which a company is active—say, China, Indonesia, and Thailand. Within each country, a general manager controls the manufacture and marketing of the firm's products. Each country unit typically carries out all of its own activities with its own departments such as marketing and sales, finance, and production.

    Because the international division structure concentrates international expertise in one division, divisional managers become specialists in a wide variety of activities such as foreign exchange, export documentation, and host-government lobbying. By consigning international activities to a single division, a firm can reduce costs, increase efficiency, and prevent international activities from disrupting domestic operations. These are important criteria for firms that are new to international busi-

international division structure
Organizational structure that separates domestic from international business activities by creating a separate international division with its own manager.

FIGURE 11.5

International Division Structure

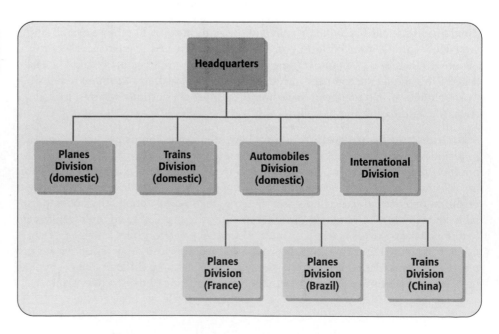

ness and whose international operations account for a small percentage of their total business.

However, an international division structure can also create two problems for companies. First, international managers must often rely on home-country managers for the financial resources and technical know-how that give the company its international competitive edge. Poor coordination between managers can hurt the performance not only of the international division but also of the entire company. Second, the general manager of the international division typically is responsible for operations in all countries. Although this policy facilitates coordination across countries, it reduces the authority of each country manager. Rivalries and poor cooperation between the general manager and country managers can be damaging to the company's overall performance.

International Area Structure   An **international area structure** organizes a company's entire global operations into countries or geographic regions (see Figure 11.6). The greater the number of countries in which a company operates, the greater the likelihood that it will organize into regions—say, Asia, Europe, and the Americas—instead of countries. Typically, a general manager is assigned to each country or region. Under this structure, each geographic division operates as a self-contained unit, with most decision making decentralized in the hands of the country or regional managers. Each unit has its own set of departments—purchasing, production, marketing and sales, R&D, and accounting. Each also tends to handle much of its own strategic planning. Management at the parent-company headquarters makes decisions regarding overall corporate strategy and coordinates the activities of various units.

The international area structure is best suited to companies that treat each national or regional market as unique. It is particularly useful when there are vast cultural, political, or economic differences between nations or regions. When they enjoy a great deal of control over activities in their own environments, general managers become experts on the unique needs of their buyers. On the other hand, because units act independently, allocated resources may overlap and cross-fertilization of knowledge from one unit to another may be less than desirable.

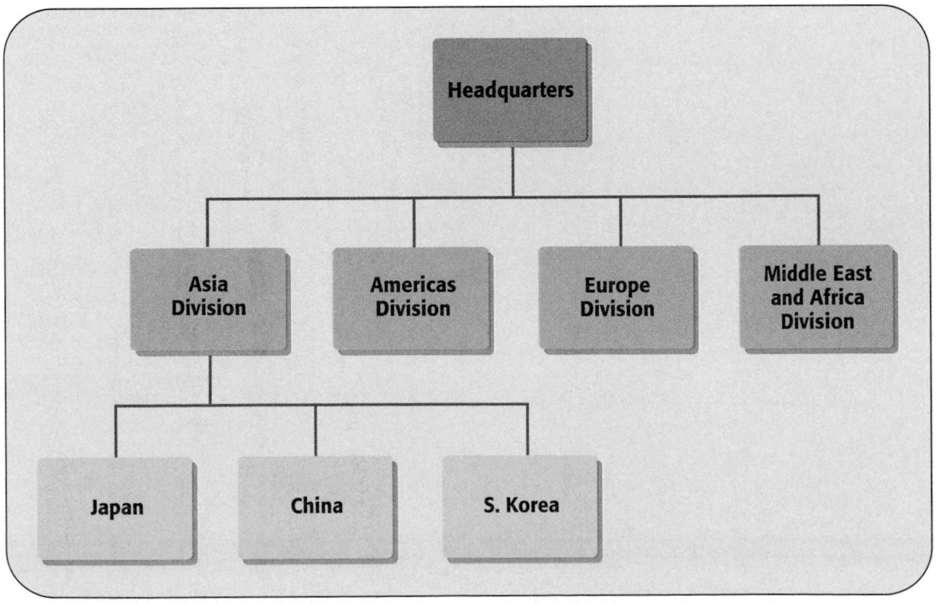

international area structure
Organizational structure that organizes a company's entire global operations into countries or geographic regions.

FIGURE 11.6
International Area Structure

global product structure
Organizational structure that divides worldwide operations according to a company's product areas.

Global Product Structure   A **global product structure** divides worldwide operations according to a company's product areas (see Figure 11.7). For example, divisions in a computer company might be Internet and Communications, Software Development, and New Technologies. Each product division is then divided into domestic and international units. Each function—R&D, marketing, and so forth—is thus duplicated in both the domestic and international units of each product division.

Because it overcomes some of the coordination problems of the international division structure, the global product structure is suitable for companies that offer diverse sets of products or services. Because the primary focus is on the product, both domestic and international managers for each product division must coordinate their activities so that they do not conflict.

global matrix structure
Organizational structure that splits the chain of command between product and area divisions.

Global Matrix Structure   A **global matrix structure** splits the chain of command between product and area divisions (see Figure 11.8). Each manager reports to two bosses—the president of the product division and the president of the geographic area. A main goal of the matrix structure is to bring together *geographic* area managers and *product* area managers in joint decision making. In fact, bringing together specialists from different parts of the organization creates a sort of team organization. The popularity of the matrix structure has grown among companies trying to increase local responsiveness, reduce costs, and coordinate worldwide operations.

The matrix structure resolves some of the shortcomings of other organizational structures, especially by improving communication between divisions and increasing the efficiency of highly specialized employees. At its best, the matrix structure can increase coordination while simultaneously improving agility and local responsiveness.

However, the global matrix structure suffers from two major shortcomings. First, the matrix form can be quite cumbersome. Numerous meetings are required simply to coordinate the actions of the various division heads, let alone the activities within divisions. In turn, the need for complex coordination tends to make decision making time-consuming and slows the reaction time of the organization. Second, individual responsibility and accountability can become foggy in the matrix organization structure. Because responsibility is shared, managers can attribute poor performance to the

FIGURE 11.7

Global Product Structure

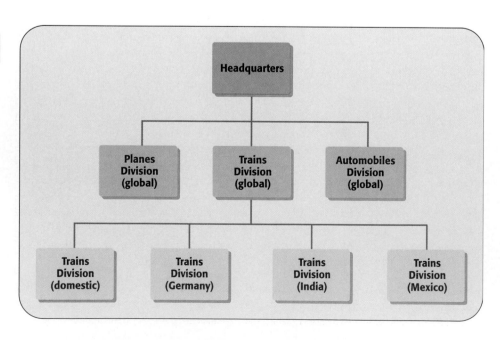

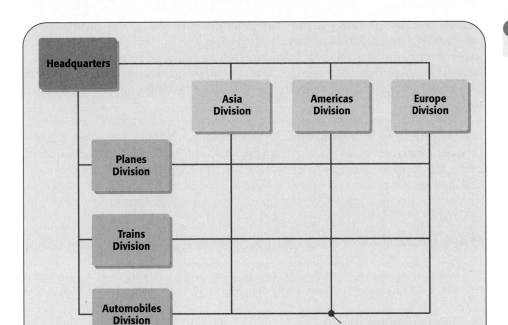

FIGURE 11.8
Global Matrix Structure

Headquarters

Asia Division

Americas Division

Europe Division

Planes Division

Trains Division

Automobiles Division

Bosses of this manager are:
Automobiles Division President
Americas Division President

actions of the other manager. Moreover, the source of problems in the matrix structure can be hard to detect and corrective action difficult to take.

There are other ways international companies can improve responsiveness and effectiveness. An increasingly popular method among international companies is implementation of work teams to accomplish goals and solve problems. In the next section we explore in detail the use of work teams.

WORK TEAMS

Forces of globalization demand that companies respond quickly to changes in all their business environments. The formation of teams can be highly useful in improving responsiveness by cutting across functional boundaries (such as that between production and marketing) that slow decision making in an organization. Although a matrix organization accomplishes this by establishing cross-functional cooperation, companies do not always want to change their entire organizational structure to reap the benefits that cross-functional cooperation provides. In such cases, companies can implement several different types of teams without changing the overall company structure.

Work teams are assigned the tasks of coordinating their efforts to arrive at solutions and implement corrective action. Today international companies are turning to work teams on an unprecedented scale to increase direct contact between different operating units. Apple Computer (www.apple.com), Federal Express (www.fedex.com), Motorola (www.motorola.com), and Volvo (www.volvo.com) are just some of the thousands of companies making extensive use of teams. Companies are even forming teams to design and implement their competitive strategies. Let's now take a look at several different types of teams—*self-managed teams*, *cross-functional teams*, and *global teams*.

Self-Managed Teams   A **self-managed team** is one in which the employees from a single department take on the responsibilities of their former supervisors. When used in production, such teams often reorganize the methods and flow of production processes.

self-managed team
Team in which the employees from a single department take on the responsibilities of their former supervisors.

Because they are "self-managed," they reduce the need for managers to watch over their every activity. The benefits of self-managed teams typically include increased productivity, product quality, customer satisfaction, employee morale, and company loyalty. In fact, the most common self-managed teams in many manufacturing companies are *quality-improvement teams*, which help reduce waste in the production process and, therefore, costs.

The global trend toward "downsizing" internal operations to make them more flexible and productive has increased the popularity of teams because they reduce the need for direct supervision. Companies around the world now employ self-managed teams in international operations. However, recent research indicates that cultural differences can affect resistance to the concept of self-management and the practice of using teams. Among other things, experts suggest that international managers follow some basic guidelines:[15]

➡ Use selection tests to identify the employees most likely to perform well in a team environment.
➡ Adapt the self-managed work-team concept to the national culture of each subsidiary.
➡ Adapt the process of integrating self-managed work teams to the national culture of each subsidiary.
➡ Train local managers at the parent company and allow them to introduce teams when resistance is expected to be great.

Similarly, the cultural differences discussed in Chapter 2 are important to managers who design teams in international operations. For example, certain cultures are less individualist and more collectivist. Some harbor greater respect for differences in status. In others, people tend to believe that the future is largely beyond their personal control, and other cultures reflect a so-called work to live mentality. Researchers say that in these cases conventional management should retain fairly tight authority over teams. But in cultures in which people are very hard working, teams are likely to be productive if given greater autonomy.[16] However, researchers stress that much more study is needed of this aspect of work teams.

Cross-Functional Teams   A **cross-functional team** is one composed of employees who work at similar levels in different functional departments. They work to develop changes in operations and are well suited to projects that require coordination across functions, such as reducing the time needed to get a product from the idea stage to the marketplace. International companies also use cross-functional teams to improve quality by having employees from purchasing, manufacturing, and distribution (among other functions) work together to address specific quality issues. For the same reason, cross-functional teams can help break down barriers between departments and reorganize operations around processes rather than by functional departments.

Global Teams   Finally, some very large international corporations are moving toward so-called **global teams**—groups of top managers from both headquarters and international subsidiaries who meet to develop solutions to company-wide problems. For example, Nortel Networks (**www.nortel.com**) of Canada created a global team of top executives from Britain, Canada, France, and the United States that traveled to Asia, Europe, and North America looking for ways to improve product-development practices.[17]

Depending on the issue at hand, team members can be drawn from a single business unit or assembled from several different units. While some teams are disbanded after resolving specific issues, others move on to new problems. The performance of global teams can be impaired by such matters as large distances between team members, lengthy travel times to meetings, and the inconvenience of working across time zones. Companies can sometimes overcome these difficulties, although doing so can be rather costly.

---

cross-functional team
Team that is composed of employees who work at similar levels in different functional departments.

global team
Team of top managers from both headquarters and international subsidiaries who meet to develop solutions to company-wide problems.

Managers have the important and complicated task of formulating international strategies at the levels of the corporation, business unit, and individual department. International managers must identify their companies' mission and the goals it is to achieve. Managers often analyze their companies' operations by viewing them as a chain of activities that create customer value (value-chain analysis). It is through this process that managers can identify and implement strategies suited to their companies' unique capabilities. The strategies that managers select then determine the firm's organizational structure. National business environments can affect managers' strategy and structure decisions, including whether to alter their products (standardization versus adaptation), where to locate facilities (centralized versus decentralized production), and what type of decision making to implement (centralized versus decentralized decision making).

The role of managers in formulating strategies and creating the overall organizational structure cannot be overstated. The strategies they choose will determine the market segments in which the firm will compete and whether it will go for low-cost leadership in its industry or differentiate its product and charge a higher price. These decisions are crucial to all later activities of corporations that are going international. They have an impact on how a company will enter international markets, employ its human resources, and manage its day-to-day production, marketing, and other operations.

There is a variety of additional material available on the Companion Website that accompanies this book. You can access this information by visiting the Website at (www.prenhall.com/wild).

summary

❶ Explain the stages of *identification* and *analysis* that precede strategy selection. The process of identifying and selecting an organization's objectives and deciding how the organization will achieve those objectives is called *planning*. In turn, *strategy* is the set of planned actions taken by managers to help a company meet its objectives.

As part of the strategy-formulation process, managers must undertake two important steps of *identification* and *analysis*. First, they *identify the company's mission and goals*. A *mission statement* is a written statement of why a company exists and what it plans to accomplish. Second, they *identify the company's core competency and value-creating activities*. A *core competency* is a special ability of a company that competitors find extremely difficult or impossible to equal.

Managers can analyze and identify their company's unique abilities that create value for customers by conducting a *value-chain analysis*—a procedure that divides a company's activities into primary activities and support activities that are central to creating value for customers. *Primary activities* include inbound and outbound logistics, manufacturing (or operations), marketing and sales, and customer service. *Support*

activities include firm infrastructure, human resource management, technology development, and procurement. Finally, managers must analyze the cultural, political, legal, and economic environments.

❷ Identify the two *international strategies* and the *corporate-level strategies* that companies use. Some companies choose to follow a *multinational (multidomestic) strategy*—adapting products and their marketing strategies in each national market to suit local preferences. Other companies decide that what suits their operations is a *global strategy*—offering the same products using the same marketing strategy in all national markets.

Companies involved in more than one line of business must formulate a *corporate-level strategy* that encompasses all of the company's different business units. A *growth strategy* is designed to increase the *scale* (*size* of activities) or *scope* (*kinds* of activities) of a corporation's operations. The exact opposite of a growth strategy is a *retrenchment strategy,* which is designed to reduce the scale or scope of a corporation's businesses. A *stability strategy* is designed to guard against change and is often employed by corporations that are trying to avoid either growth or retrenchment. The purpose of a *combination strategy* is to mix growth, retrenchment, and stability strategies across a corporation's business units.

❸ Identify the *business-level strategies* of companies and the role of *department-level strategies*. Managers formulate separate *business-level strategies* for each business unit. Most companies employ one of three generic business-level strategies for competing in an industry. A strategy in which a company exploits economies of scale to have the lowest cost structure of any competitor in its industry is called a *low-cost leadership strategy*. A *differentiation strategy* is one in which a company designs its products to be perceived as unique by buyers throughout its industry. A *focus strategy* is one in which a company focuses on serving the needs of a narrowly defined market segment by being the low-cost leader, by differentiating its product, or both.

Achieving corporate- and business-level objectives depends on effective *department-level strategies* that focus on the specific activities that transform resources into products. Each department is instrumental in creating customer value through lower costs or differentiated products. This is true of departments that conduct either *primary activities* or *support activities*.

❹ Discuss the important issues that influence the choice of *organizational structure*. *Organizational structure* is the way in which a company divides its activities among separate units and coordinates activities between those units. Important to organizational structure is the degree to which decision making in an organization will be centralized (made at a high level) or decentralized (made at a low level such as international subsidiaries). *Centralized decision making* helps to coordinate the operations of interna-

tional subsidiaries. *Decentralized decision making* is beneficial when fast-changing national business environments put a premium on local responsiveness.

When designing organizational structure, managers must consider the issues of *coordination* and *flexibility*. Every international company must design an organizational structure that clearly defines areas of responsibility and *chains of command*—the lines of authority that run from top management to individual employees and specify internal reporting relationships.

❺ Describe each type of *international organizational structure* and explain the importance of *work teams*. An *international division structure* separates domestic from international business activities by creating a separate division with its own manager. An *international area structure* organizes a company's entire global operations into countries or geographic regions, whereby each geographic division operates as a self-contained unit. A *global product structure* divides worldwide operations into product divisions that are then divided into domestic and international units. A *global matrix structure* splits the chain of command between product and area divisions. Each manager and employee reports to two bosses—the general manager of the product division and the general manager of the geographic area.

Work teams are assigned the tasks of coordinating their efforts to arrive at solutions and implement corrective action. A *self-managed team* is one in which the employees from a single department take on the responsibilities of their former supervisors. A *cross-functional team* is composed of employees who work at similar levels in different functional departments. A *global team* is composed of top managers from both headquarters and international subsidiaries who meet to develop solutions to company-wide problems.

questions **for review**

1. Define the terms *planning* and *strategy*. What is the importance of strategy to company performance?

2. Identify the three stages of the *strategy-formulation process*.

3. Define *mission statement*. How do companies incorporate *stakeholders* into the mission statement?

4. What is a *core competency*? Explain how it differs from a skill.

5. What is *value-chain analysis*? Describe the difference between primary and secondary activities.

6. How are national and international business environments important to strategy formulation? Give several examples.

7. Define *multinational strategy*. Under what circumstances is it appropriate?

8. What is a *global strategy*? Explain its primary appeal and main drawback.

9. What are the four *corporate-level strategies*? Identify the main characteristics of each.

10. Identify the three *business-level strategies*. Explain how each strategy differs from the other two.

11. Explain the importance of *department-level strategies* in helping a company achieve its goals.

12. Define *organizational structure*. What is the difference between *centralized* and *decentralized* decision making?

13. Why are *coordination* and *flexibility* important when designing organizational structure?

14. What is meant by the term *chains of command*?

15. What are the four types of *organizational structure* used by international companies? For each one, supply its definition and describe its main characteristics.

16. Identify the three different types of *work teams*. How does each help a company improve its responsiveness and effectiveness?

questions **for discussion**

1. The elements that affect strategy formulation are the same whether a company is domestic or international. Do you agree or disagree with this statement? Why? Support your argument with specific examples.

2. "Cultures around the world are becoming increasingly similar. Companies, therefore, should standardize both their products and global marketing efforts." Do you agree or disagree with this statement? Are there certain industries for which it might be more or less true? Provide specific examples.

3. Continuous advancements in technology are deeply affecting the way international businesses are managed. Do you think technology (the Internet, for example) should radically alter the fundamental strategies and organizational structures of international companies? Or do you think companies should simply graft new strategies and structures onto existing ones? Support your answers with specific examples.

in **practice**

Read the brief article below and answer the questions that follow.

Restructuring The Big Cheese

NORTHFIELD, IL—Kraft Foods today announced that it is to close two production facilities—one in Guatemala City, Guatemala, and the other in San Jose, Costa Rica.

The company stated that the move is part of a larger plan to restructure and consolidate its operations throughout Latin America. The two plants to close formerly belonged to Nabisco, with which Kraft merged several years ago. The plants make dry mix and baking powder.

Kraft's main businesses are snacks, beverages, cheese, grocery, and convenience meals. But with about three-quarters of its sales coming from the U.S. market, it is dwarfed abroad by the undisputed global food giant Nestle. The company also said that as part of its strategy to become more international, it plans to introduce additional brands abroad and make acquisitions in some markets.

1. What business-level strategy(ies) do you think Kraft is pursuing? Go to Kraft's Web site (www.kraft.com) and that of its parent company, Phillip Morris (www.philipmorris.com). What corporate-level strategy(ies) do you think Philip Morris is pursuing in its different businesses?

2. In June 2001, Philip Morris spun off Kraft with an initial public offering of 16 percent of Kraft's stock. Why do you think Philip Morris undertook this action? Do you think it has anything to do with the mix of businesses it is involved in? Why or why not?

3. Identify as many stakeholders of Philip Morris and Kraft as you can. Aside from smoking-related lawsuits, are there any trends that might have encouraged the company to spin off Kraft with the stock sale?

4. Japan Tobacco (www.jti.com) is a global company that, like Philip Morris, also owns food companies. Why do you think food and tobacco might not fit well together in a U.S. company, but seems to be fine in a Japanese company? In your answer consider as many cultural, legal, and ownership factors as you can.

projects

1. Select a recent periodical in the business press and identify several articles discussing changes taking place within a given industry over the past few months. Write a short summary of the articles. What changes are occurring, and how are companies responding? Are firms altering strategies, relocating production, or leaving or entering certain markets and/or lines of business? Are they altering their organizational structures in some way?

2. Working with several of your classmates, select and research an international company that interests you. (Annual reports can be obtained from companies' investor relations departments or their World Wide Web sites.) What is the company's mission statement or overriding objective? What are its corporate- and business-level strategies? In which nations does it produce and market its products? Are its production facilities centralized or decentralized? Does it standardize

products or adapt them for different markets? What type of organizational structure does it have? Which of the two types of international strategy does it seem to follow? Does the company make use of work teams?

3. Make a list of five products that you used or consumed within the past 24 hours. Your list might include such goods

as your toothpaste or your CD player and such services as an express mailing service, a cable/satellite TV program, and so forth. Which strategy does each product's or service's company employ—low-cost, differentiation, or focus? In one or two paragraphs, explain how you arrived at your answer for each company.

business case 11
THE IKEA KEY TO PRICING

IKEA (www.ikea.com) is a $10 billion global furniture powerhouse based in Sweden. With more than 150 stores in 29 countries, the company's success reflects founder Ingvar Kamprad's "social ambition" of selling a wide range of stylish, functional home furnishings at prices so low that the majority of people can afford to buy them. The story of Kamprad's success is detailed in a book titled *IKEA: The Entrepreneur, The Business Concept, The Culture.* The store exteriors are painted with Sweden's national colors, bright blue and yellow. Shoppers view furniture on the main floor in scores of realistic settings arranged throughout the cavernous showrooms.

In a departure from standard industry practice, IKEA's furniture bears names such as "Ivar" and "Sten" instead of model numbers. At IKEA, shopping is very much a self-service activity—after browsing and writing down the names of desired items in the showrooms, shoppers pick their furniture off shelves where they find boxes containing the furniture in kit form. In fact, one of the cornerstones of IKEA's strategy is having customers take their purchases home and assemble the furniture themselves. The typical IKEA store also contains a restaurant, a grocery store called the Swede Shop, a supervised play area for children, and a baby-care room.

IKEA's approach to the furniture business enables it to rack up impressive growth in an industry in which overall sales are flat. Sourcing furniture from more than 2,300 suppliers in 70 countries helps the company maintain its low-cost position. IKEA has also opened several stores in Central and Eastern Europe. Because many consumers in those regions have relatively low purchasing power, the stores offer a smaller selection of goods and some of the furniture was designed specifically for the cramped living styles typical in former Soviet bloc countries. Throughout Europe, IKEA benefits from the perception that Sweden is the source of high-quality products. In fact, one of the company's key selling points is its "Swedishness." In Western Europe, the United Kingdom represents IKEA's fastest-growing market—its London store has achieved annual sales growth of 20 percent. The company recently decided to increase the size of all 11 of its U.K. stores by up to 25 percent to keep up with demand in the face of delays in getting permission to build new stores. And IKEA plans an aggressive expansion in Italy—over the next couple of years it will double to 14 the number of stores it has there.

Industry observers predict that the United States will eventually be IKEA's largest market. The company opened its first U.S. store in Philadelphia in 1985 and today has dozens of outlets that generate over a billion dollars in sales annually. And IKEA's competitors are taking it seriously. Jeff Young, chief operating officer of Lexington Furniture Industries, says, "IKEA is on the way to becoming the Wal-Mart Stores of the home-furnishing industry. If you're in this business, you'd better take a look." However, some U.S. customers are irked to find popular items sometimes out of stock. Another problem is the long lines resulting from the company's no-frills approach. Complained one shopper, "Great idea, poor execution. The quality of much of what they sell is good, but the hassles make you question whether it's worth it."

Goran Carstedt, president of IKEA North America, responds to such criticism by referring to the company's mission. "If we offered more services, our prices would go up," he explains. "Our customers understand our philosophy, which calls for each of us to do a little in order to save a lot. They value our low prices. And almost all of them say they will come back again." To keep them coming back, IKEA is spending between $25 million and $35 million on advertising to get its message across. Whereas common industry practice is to rely heavily on newspaper and radio advertising, two thirds of IKEA's North American advertising budget is allocated for TV. John Sitnik, an executive at IKEA U.S. Inc., says, "We distanced ourselves from the other furniture stores. We decided TV is something we can own."

thinking globally

1. Has IKEA taken a standardization approach or an adaptation approach in its markets around the world? Do you think the company's approach is the right one?

2. Which retailers do you think will be IKEA's biggest competitors in the United States?

3. Company founder Kamprad recently decided to expand into China. Kamprad's decision was not based on market research but, rather, on his own intuition. Find a recent article or check IKEA's Web site to update the company's China strategy. Did Kamprad's decision pay off?

a question **of ethics**

1. Today, rapid changes in the international economy are causing the redrawing of geographical and political borders, especially in Europe. As a result, there is a growing interdependence of countries that are socially, politically, economically, and legally diverse. In response to these changes, multinational corporations are revising their operating policies and strategies. Many companies are also revising their approach to ethics as they adjust to the legal and moral atmosphere in which they operate. Given the complexity of the issues involved, do you think it would be possible to create a uniform code of ethics that is applicable to any business operating in any culture? What issues should such a code address?

2. In recent years, the U.S. government pursued an antitrust lawsuit against Microsoft Corporation (**www.microsoft.com**). One of the issues is whether Microsoft took unfair advantage of its powerful position in the computer industry by using "strong-arm tactics" on software customers throughout the world and by crushing weaker rivals. Regardless of whether or not Microsoft is guilty of anticompetitive acts in terms of the law, do you believe that Microsoft has conducted itself in an ethical manner in its business dealings? Has it abused its power in the industry, or is Microsoft simply a tough competitor?

analyzing international opportunities

LEARNING OBJECTIVES

After studying this chapter, you should be able to

1 Explain each of the four steps in the *market- and site-screening process.*

2 Describe the three primary difficulties of conducting *international market research.*

3 Identify the main sources of *secondary international data* and explain their usefulness.

4 Describe the main methods used to conduct *primary international research.*

BEACONS

A Look Back
CHAPTER 11 showed us how companies plan and organize themselves for international operations. We explored the different types of strategies and organizational structures that international companies use to accomplish their strategic goals.

A Look at This Chapter
This chapter begins with an explanation of how managers screen potential new markets and new sites for operations. We then describe the main difficulties of conducting international market research. We also identify the information required in the screening process and where managers can go to obtain such information.

A Look Ahead
CHAPTER 13 describes the selection and management issues surrounding the different entry modes available to companies going international. We examine the importance of an export strategy for exporters and the pros and cons of each entry mode.

Starbucks Creates a Global Buzz

BEIJING, China—"Per capita consumption of coffee in China is very small," admitted Howard Behar, president of Starbucks Coffee International (**www.starbucks.com**). "But what you have is a tremendous amount of people, so the market will grow." The company's objective is to establish Starbucks as the most recognized and respected brand in the world. Although the company has been highly successful in Japan, some observers question whether Starbucks can market coffee in a land of tea drinkers.

What doubters may not know is that long before its lively grand opening, complete with whirling lion dancers and the beating of Chinese drums, Starbucks was quietly but exhaustively researching the Chinese market. After careful study, the company was encouraged by the fact that one third of all Chinese households keep a jar of instant coffee on hand. Starbucks does not expect to change the tea-drinking habits of the older generation. It is targeting China's newly rich, trying to establish its coffee as the drink of choice for the average 18- to 45-year-old Chinese consumer.

At the same time, Starbucks is aggressively going after the European market. Although the company has been in Britain since the late 1990s, it steamed into Zurich, Switzerland, only in 2001. Again, Starbucks is taking a cautious approach. With its multicultural and multilingual population, the Swiss market gives Starbucks a "tremendous opportunity to learn how to operate elsewhere in Europe," reveals Mark McKeon, president of Starbucks Europe, Middle East, and Africa. As you read this chapter think about all the kinds of information and knowledge that companies must acquire before entering a new market.[1]

Traditionally, companies enter the international business arena by choosing familiar places—often by entering nearby countries first. Managers feel comfortable about entering nearby markets because they likely have already interacted with the people of those cultures and have at least some understanding of them. That's why companies in Canada, Mexico, and the United States often gain their initial international experiences in one another's markets. Likewise, firms in Asian countries often seek out opportunities in one another's markets before pursuing investment opportunities outside the region.

But today companies find themselves bridging the gaps presented by space and culture far more often. For one thing, technological advances in communication and transportation continue to open national markets around the globe. Today companies can realistically consider nearly every location on earth as either a potential market or as a site for business operations. In addition, the expansion of regional markets (such as the European Union) is causing companies to analyze opportunities farther from home. For example, companies are locating production facilities within regional markets because producing in one of a region's countries provides duty-free access to every consumer in the trade bloc.

Moreover, fast-paced change in the global marketplace is forcing companies to view business strategies from a global perspective. More than ever, they are formulating production, marketing, and other strategies as components of integrated plans. For instance, to provide a continuous flow of timely information into the production process, more and more firms are locating research and development (R&D) facilities near their production sites abroad. Managers also find themselves more often simultaneously screening and analyzing locations as potential markets *and* as potential sites for operations. When the M-class sport utility vehicle by Mercedes (www.mercedes.com) was introduced to the U.S. market, executives also decided to build the vehicle there. The company was obliged not merely to estimate the size of the potential market for the vehicle, but to decide at the same time on a suitable production site.

The attraction of companies to distant markets and the integrated nature of location decisions demand that companies approach the decision about location in a systematic manner. This chapter presents a systematic screening process for both markets and sites. After explaining the important cultural, political, legal, and economic forces affecting the screening process, we describe the difficulties of conducting international research. We then explore the main sources of existing data and the main methods for conducting international research firsthand.

SCREENING POTENTIAL MARKETS AND SITES

Two important issues concern managers during the market- and site-screening process. First, they want to keep the cost of the search as low as possible. Second, they want to examine every potential market and every possible location. To accomplish these two goals, managers typically approach the screening of markets and sites in a systematic way. We can break this *screening process* down into the following four steps:

1. Identify basic appeal
2. Assess the national business environment
3. Measure market or site potential
4. Select the market or site

Figure 12.1 shows that this screening process involves spending more time, money, and effort on the markets and sites that remain in the later stages of screening. Thus, expensive feasibility studies (conducted later in the process) are performed on a few markets and sites that hold the greatest promise. Therefore, this screening process is cost effective yet does not overlook potential locations. Let's now discuss each of these four steps in detail.

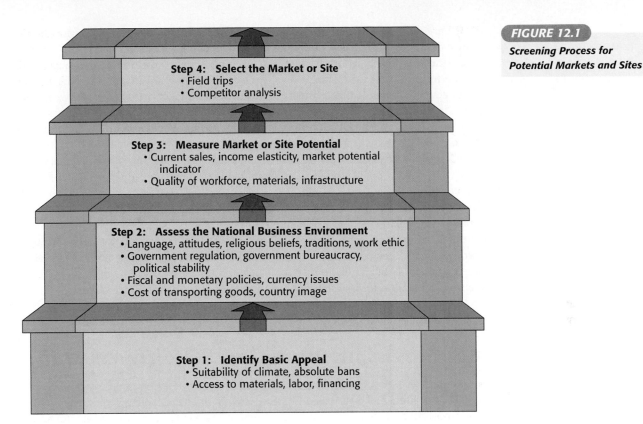

FIGURE 12.1

Screening Process for Potential Markets and Sites

Step 4: Select the Market or Site
- Field trips
- Competitor analysis

Step 3: Measure Market or Site Potential
- Current sales, income elasticity, market potential indicator
- Quality of workforce, materials, infrastructure

Step 2: Assess the National Business Environment
- Language, attitudes, religious beliefs, traditions, work ethic
- Government regulation, government bureaucracy, political stability
- Fiscal and monetary policies, currency issues
- Cost of transporting goods, country image

Step 1: Identify Basic Appeal
- Suitability of climate, absolute bans
- Access to materials, labor, financing

STEP 1: IDENTIFY BASIC APPEAL

We have already seen that companies go international either to increase sales (and thus profits) or to access resources. Therefore, the first step in identifying potential markets is to assess the basic demand for a product. Similarly, the first step in selecting a site for a facility to undertake production, R&D, or some other activity is to explore the availability of the resources required.

Determining Basic Demand   The first step in searching for potential markets means finding out whether there is a basic demand for a company's product. Important in determining this basic appeal is a country's climate. For example, no company would try to market snowboards in Indonesia, Sri Lanka, or Central America because they receive no snowfall. The same product, on the other hand, is well suited for markets in the Canadian Rockies, northern Japan, and the Swiss Alps. This stage may seem quite simple, but it cannot be taken too lightly. During its initial forays into international business, Wal-Mart (www.walmart.com) found itself stocked with ice-fishing huts in Puerto Rico and out of snowshoes in Ontario, Canada.[2]

Certain countries also ban certain goods. Islamic countries, for instance, forbid the importation of alcoholic products, and the penalties for smuggling are stiff. Also, although alcohol is available on the planes of international airlines such as British Airways (www.ba.com) and KLM (www.klm.com), it cannot leave the airplane and consumption cannot take place until the plane has left the airspace of the country operating under Islamic law.

Determining Availability of Resources   Companies that need certain resources to carry out local business activities must be sure that they are available. The raw materials needed for manufacturing must either be found in the national market or imported. However, imported inputs may encounter tariffs, quotas, or other government barriers. Therefore, managers must consider the additional costs of importing to ensure that total product cost does not rise to unacceptable levels.

The availability of labor is essential to production in any country. Many companies choose to relocate to countries where workers' wages are lower than they are in the home country. This practice is most common among makers of labor-intensive products—those for which labor accounts for a large portion of total cost. Companies that are considering local production must determine whether there is enough labor available locally for production operations.

Companies that hope to secure financing in a market abroad must determine the availability and cost of local capital. If local interest rates are too high, a company might be forced to obtain financing in its home country or in other markets in which it is active. On the other hand, access to low-cost financing may provide a powerful inducement to a company that is seeking to expand internationally. For example, British entrepreneur Richard Branson opened several of his Virgin (www.virgin.com) Megastores in Japan despite its reputation as a tough market to crack. One reason for Branson's initial attraction to Japan was a cost of capital of only 2.5 percent—roughly one-third its cost in Britain. As the finance director for Virgin commented, "If resources are available locally, it would be silly for us not to utilize them."[3]

Markets and sites that fail to meet a company's requirements for basic demand or resource availability in step 1 are removed from further consideration.

STEP 2: ASSESS THE NATIONAL BUSINESS ENVIRONMENT

If the cultures, politics, laws, and economies of all countries were the same, deciding where to market or produce products would be rather straightforward. Managers could rely on data that report the performance of the local economy and analyze expected profits from proposed investments. But as we learned in Chapters 2, 3, and 4, national business environments differ greatly from one country to another. Thus, international managers must work to understand these differences and to incorporate that understanding into market and site selection decisions. To see how some nations rate according to their overall business climates, see the World Business Survey titled "Global Business Climates." Let's now examine how domestic forces in the business environment actually affect the location selection process.

Cultural Forces   Although some countries display cultural similarities, most differ in many ways, including language, attitudes toward business, religious beliefs, traditions, and customs. Some products can be sold in markets worldwide with little or no modification. Some of these products are industrial machinery such as packaging equipment and consumer products such as toothpaste and soft drinks. However, other products must undergo extensive adaptation to suit local preferences, including certain types of ready-to-eat meals and, sometimes, books and magazines.

Cultural elements can influence what kinds of products are sold and how they are sold. Managers must assess how local culture will affect the salability of its product if the location is a candidate as a market. For instance, consider the experience of Coca-Cola (www.cocacola.com) in China, where many people take a traditional medicine to fight off flu and cold symptoms. As it turns out, the taste of this traditional medicine—which most people do not find appealing—is similar to that of Coke. Because of Coca-Cola's global marketing policy of one taste worldwide, the company had to overcome the aversion to the taste of Coke among Chinese consumers. It did so by creating a marketing campaign that associated buying Coke with experiencing a piece of America. What initially looked like an unattractive market for Coke became very successful through a carefully tailored marketing campaign.

Cultural elements in the business environment can also affect site-selection decisions. When substantial product modifications are needed for cultural reasons, a company might choose to establish production facilities in the target market itself.

WORLD BUSINESS SURVEY

Global Business Climates

The Netherlands is expected to be the best place in the world to conduct business in the next five years, according to the Economist Intelligence Unit. A stable political environment and attractive policies towards foreign investment contribute to its healthy business climate. Eastern European countries are expected to improve their relative standing the most in the coming years.

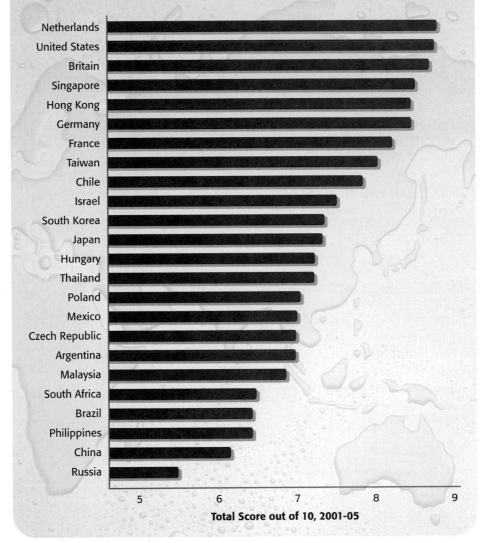

Total Score out of 10, 2001-05

However, better serving customers' special needs in a target market must be offset against any potential loss of economies of scale due to producing in several locations rather than just one. But today companies can minimize such losses through the use of flexible manufacturing methods. For example, although cellular phone manufacturer Nokia (**www.nokia.com**) produces in locations worldwide, it ensures that each one of its facilities can start producing any one of its mobile phones for its different markets within 24 hours.[4]

Having a qualified workforce is important for a company, whatever activity it is to undertake at a particular site. Also, a strong work ethic among the local workforce is essential to having productive operations. Managers must assess whether an appropriate work ethic exists in each potential country for the purposes of production, service, or any other business activity. An adequate level of educational attainment among the local workforce for the planned business activity is also very important. Although product-assembly operations may not require an advanced education, R&D, high-tech production, and certain services normally will require extensive higher education. If a potential site does not display an appropriate work ethic or educational attainment, it will be ruled out for further consideration.

Political and Legal Forces   Political and legal forces also influence the market and site-location decision. Important factors include government regulation, government bureaucracy, and political stability. Let's take a brief look at each of these.

Government Regulation   As we saw in earlier chapters, nations differ in their attitudes toward trade and investment, which is rooted in culture, history, and current events. Some governments take a strongly nationalistic stance, whereas others are quite receptive to international trade and investment. A government's attitude toward trade and investment is reflected in the quantity and types of restrictions it places on imports, exports, and investment in its country.

Government regulations can quickly eliminate a market or site from further consideration. First of all, they can create investment barriers to ensure domestic control of a company or industry. One way in which a government can accomplish this is by imposing investment rules on matters such as business ownership—for instance, forcing nondomestic companies into joint ventures. India's government originally forced PepsiCo (**www.pepsico.com**) to entrust 51 percent of its local ownership with Indian investors. PepsiCo was also required to give a certain portion of its revenue from sales in India to the Indian treasury.

Governments also can extend investment rules to bar international companies entirely from competing in certain sectors of the domestic economy. The practice is usually defended as a matter of national security. Economic sectors commonly declared off-limits include television and radio broadcasting, automobile manufacturing, aircraft manufacturing, energy exploration, military-equipment manufacturing, and iron and steel production. Such industries are protected either because they are culturally impor-

Governments can increase the cost of doing business within their borders by throwing up barriers to entry. Rather than give the Indian government its secret Coke formula, Coca-Cola (**www.cocacola.com**) actually gave up its battle against Pepsi (**www.pepsi.com**) there until the government dropped its demand. How did Pepsi fare in India? Well, among other things, the government initially required Pepsi to award Indian investors with 51 percent ownership of its local operations.

tant, are engines for economic growth, or are essential to any potential war effort. Host governments often fear (rightly or wrongly) that losing control in these economic sectors means placing their fate in the hands of international companies.

Second, governments can restrict international companies from freely removing profits earned in the nation. This policy can force a company either to hold cash in the host country or to reinvest it in new projects there. Such policies are normally rooted in the inability of the government in the host country to earn the foreign exchange needed to pay for badly needed imports. For example, Motorola's (www.motorola.com) Chinese subsidiary is required to convert the local currency (renminbi) to U.S. dollars before remitting profits back to the parent company in the United States. Motorola can satisfy this stipulation only as long as the Chinese government agrees to provide it with the needed U.S. dollars.

Third, governments can impose very strict environmental regulations. In most industrial countries, factories that produce industrial chemicals as their main output or as by-products must adhere to strict pollution standards. Regulations typically demand the installation of expensive pollution-control devices and the close monitoring of nearby air, water, and soil quality. While protecting the environment, such regulations also increase short-term production costs. Many developing and emerging markets have far less strict environmental regulations. Regrettably, some companies are alleged to have moved production of toxic materials to emerging markets to take advantage of lax environmental regulations and, in turn, lower production costs. Although such behavior is roundly criticized as highly unethical, it will occur less often as nations continue cooperating to formulate common environmental protection policies.

Finally, governments also can require that companies divulge certain information. Coca-Cola (www.cocacola.com) actually left India when the government demanded that it disclose its secret Coke formula as a requirement for doing business there. Coca-Cola returned only after the Indian government dropped its demand.

Government Bureaucracy A lean and smoothly operating government bureaucracy can make a market or site more attractive. But a bloated and cumbersome system of obtaining approvals and licenses from government agencies can make it less appealing. In many developing countries, the relatively simple matter of obtaining a license to establish a retail outlet often means acquiring numerous documents from several agencies. The bureaucrats in charge of these agencies generally are little concerned with high-quality service. Managers must be prepared to deal with administrative delays and a maze of rules. For instance, country managers for Millicom International Cellular (www.millicom.com) in Tanzania must wait 90 days to get customs clearance on the monthly import of roughly $1 million in cellular telephone equipment. But the size of the local market makes enduring such bureaucratic obstacles bearable: Several thousand cellular subscribers in Tanzania use their phones an average of 400 minutes per month.[5]

Thus, companies will endure a cumbersome bureaucracy if the opportunity is sufficient to offset any potential delays and expenses. Companies entering China cite the patience needed to navigate a maze of government regulations that often contradict one another and complain about the large number of permissions required from different agencies. The trouble stems from the fact that China is continually revising and developing its system of business law as its economy develops. But an unclear legal framework and inefficient bureaucracy are not deterring investment in China because the opportunities for both marketers and manufacturers are simply too great to ignore.

Political Stability Every nation's business environment is affected to some degree by political risk. As we saw in Chapter 3, political risk is the likelihood that a nation will undergo political changes that affect business activities negatively. Political risk can threaten the market of an exporter, the production facilities of a manufacturer, or the ability of a company to remove profits from the country in which they were earned.

The key element of political risk that concerns companies is *unforeseen political change*. If a company cannot estimate the future political environment with a fair degree of accuracy, political risk is increased. That is why an event with a negative impact that is expected to occur in the future is not, in itself, bad for companies because the event can be planned for and necessary precautions taken. Instead, unforeseen negative events are what create political risk for companies.

The perception of a market's political risk is often affected by managers' memories of past political unrest in a nation. However, managers cannot let past events blind them to future opportunities. International companies must try to monitor and predict political events that threaten operations and future earnings' potential. By investigating the political environment proactively, managers can focus on political risk and develop action plans for dealing with it.

But where do managers get the information to answer such questions? They may assign company personnel to gather information on the level of political risk in a country, or they may obtain it from independent agencies that specialize in providing political-risk services. The advice of country and regional specialists who are knowledgeable about the current political climate of a market can be especially helpful. Such specialists can include international bankers, political consultants, reporters, country-risk specialists, international relations scholars, political leaders, union leaders, embassy officials, and other local businesspeople currently working and living in the country in question.

Economic and Financial Forces Managers must carefully analyze a nation's economic policies before selecting it as a new market or site for operations. The poor fiscal and monetary policies of a nation's central bank can cause high rates of inflation, increasing budget deficits, a depreciating currency, falling productivity levels, and flagging innovation. Such consequences typically lower investor confidence and force international companies to scale back or cancel proposed investments. For example, restrictive trade and investment policies by the government of India finally gave way to more open policies in the early 1990s. Specifically, new investment policies encouraged investment in both production facilities and R&D centers, especially in the computer-software industry.

Political instability is an unpredictable factor in many markets, yet it remains one that companies must consider when they invest abroad. These Indonesian students clashed with police in Jakarta over how the government was handling the nation's worst economic crisis in decades. The protests continued on and off for months until, first the president, then his successor, resigned. What other unpredictable factors do you think can affect a company's investments abroad?

Currency and liquidity problems pose special challenges for international companies. Volatile currency values make it difficult for firms to predict future earnings accurately in terms of the home-country currency. Wildly fluctuating currency values also make it difficult to calculate how much capital a company needs for a planned investment. Unpredictable changes in currency values can also make liquidating assets more difficult because the greater uncertainty will likely reduce liquidity in capital markets—especially in countries with relatively small capital markets, such as Bangladesh and Bulgaria.

In addition to their home government's resources, managers can obtain information about economic and financial conditions from institutions such as the World Bank, the International Monetary Fund, and the Asian Development Bank. Other information sources include business and economic publications such as the *Far Eastern Economic Review* (www.feer.com), the annual country-risk guide published by *Euromoney* (www.euromoney.com), and the series of reports called *Economic Outlook* published by *The Economist* (www.economist.com).

Other Forces   A country's image and the cost of transporting materials and goods also play important roles in the assessment of national business environments. Let's now take a brief look at each of these forces.

Cost of Transporting Materials and Goods   The cost of transporting materials and finished goods affects any decision about where to locate manufacturing facilities. Some products cost very little to transport through the production and distribution process whereas others cost a great deal. **Logistics** refers to the management of the physical flow of products from the point of origin as raw materials to end users as finished products. Logistics weds production activities to the activities needed to deliver products to buyers. It includes all modes of transportation, storage, and distribution.

> **logistics**
> *Management of the physical flow of products from the point of origin as raw materials to end users as finished products.*

To realize the importance of efficient logistics, consider that global logistics is a $400 billion industry. We often consider the United States an efficient logistics market because of its extensive interstate road system and rail lines that stretch from east to west. But because of overcrowded highways, 2 billion people-hours are lost to gridlock each year. That translates into $48 billion in lost productivity![6] Because of the financial cost to businesses of inefficient logistics, many transport companies and cargo ports strenuously advertise their services.

Country Image   Because *country image* embodies every facet of a nation's business environment, it is highly relevant to the selection of sites for production, R&D, or any other activity. For example, country image affects the location of manufacturing or assembly operations because products must typically be stamped with labels identifying where they were made or assembled—such as "Made in China" or "Assembled in Brazil." Although such labels do not affect all products to the same degree, they can present important positive or negative images and boost or dampen sales.

Products made in relatively more developed countries tend to be evaluated more positively than those from less developed countries.[7] This relation can often be traced to the perception among consumers that the workforces of certain nations have superior skills in making particular products. For example, Procter & Gamble (www.pg.com) and Unilever (www.unilever.com), intense rivals in consumer products, both have manufacturing facilities in Vietnam. But Vietnamese consumers tend to shun locally made Close-Up toothpaste and Tide detergent and seek out the identical products produced in neighboring countries, such as Thailand. As one young Vietnamese shopper explained, "Tide from Thailand smells nicer." A general perception among Vietnamese consumers is that goods from Japan or Singapore are the best, followed by Thai goods. Unfortunately for Procter & Gamble and Unilever in Vietnam, many goods from these other countries are smuggled in and sold on the black market, thereby denying the companies of sales revenue.[8]

A country's image can be positive in one product class but negative in another. For example, consumers happily pay a premium for Corona (www.corona.com) beer imported from Mexico. Also, the fact that Volkswagen's (www.volkswagen.com) new Beetle is made in Mexico for the U.S. market has not hurt the Beetle's sales one bit. But would affluent consumers buy a hand-built Rolls-Royce (www.rrmc.co.uk) automobile if it were produced in Mexico? Because Rolls-Royce buyers pay for the image of a brilliantly crafted luxury car, the Rolls-Royce image probably would not survive intact if the company were to produce its cars in Mexico.

Finally, note that country image can and does change over time. For example, "Made in India" has traditionally been associated with low-technology products such as soccer balls and many types of textile products. But today world-class computer-software companies increasingly rely on the software-development skills of engineers located in and around Madras and Bangalore in southern India.

Throughout our discussion of step 2 of the screening process (assessing the national business environment), we have presented many factors central to traditional business activities. However, there are many issues that are specific to entering international markets successfully over the Internet. The Global Manager titled "Global E-Commerce Issues" addresses some of these.

STEP 3: MEASURE MARKET OR SITE POTENTIAL

Markets and sites passing the first two steps in the screening process undergo further analysis to arrive at a more manageable number of potential locations. Despite the presence of a basic need for a product and an adequately stable national business environment, potential customers might not be ready or able to buy a product for a variety of reasons. Despite the availability of resources, certain sites may be unable to supply a given company with the *level* of resources it needs. Let's now explore the factors that further influence the potential suitability of markets and sites for operations.

Measuring Market Potential   As barriers to trade continue to fall around the world, companies are looking to increase sales in industrialized and emerging markets worldwide. But companies can seldom create one marketing plan for every market in which they sell their products. Nations enjoy different levels of economic development, which affect what kinds of goods are sold, the manner in which they are sold, and the features they have. Likewise, the different levels of economic development require varying approaches to researching market potential. But how do managers estimate potential demand for particular products? Let's take a look at the factors managers consider when analyzing industrialized markets and then examine a special tool for analyzing emerging markets.

Industrialized Markets   The information needed to estimate the market potential for a product in industrialized nations tends to be more readily available than in emerging markets. In fact, for the most developed markets, research agencies exist for the sole purpose of supplying market data to companies. Euromonitor (www.euromonitor.com) is one such company with an extensive global reach in consumer goods. The company sells reports and does company-specific studies for many international corporations and entrepreneurs. Some of the information in a typical industry analysis includes:

- Names, production volumes, and market shares of the largest competitors
- Volume of exports and imports of the product
- Structure of the wholesale and retail distribution networks

GLOBAL MANAGER

Global E-Commerce Issues

Generating sales in new geographic markets over the Internet is an increasingly popular method of expansion for large multinationals and entrepreneurs alike. Managers around the globe who wish to learn more about entering new markets through the Internet can visit the e-commerce Web site of the U.S. Department of Commerce (**www.ecommerce.gov**). Here are some additional issues managers should consider when entering new markets over the Internet:

Infrastructure and Market Access Issues

➡ **Telecommunications infrastructure and information technology**. Before investing heavily in e-commerce, be sure to investigate whether your potential customers have easy access to the Internet. It should also be determined whether their government's telecommunications policies hinder the development of advanced digital networks.

➡ **Content**. Issues of content include topics such as truth in advertising, fraud prevention, and violent, seditious, or pornographic materials. Companies must be informed about the different policies of each country through which their information travels in order to avoid liability.

➡ **Standards**. It is not yet clear which country has the power to establish standards of operations for e-commerce. Also, standards can be established to act as non-tariff trade barriers to keep international companies out of a domestic market.

Legal Issues

➡ **Privacy**. One of the strengths of e-commerce is that information on consumers can be easily collected and used to generate more sales. But consumer groups and others, particularly in the European Union, are concerned that collecting such data is an invasion of privacy. They are particularly vehement about this issue if consumers are not aware that this information is collected, how it is used, and if it is passed on to third parties.

➡ **Security**. Companies must ensure that their data communications are safe from unauthorized access or modification. While the technology exists to provide security—encryption, password controls, and firewalls, for example—it needs to be supported by a global infrastructure.

➡ **Intellectual property protection**. Protection of copyrights, databases, patents, and trademarks is governed by international agreements. But because a legal framework for the Internet has not yet been developed, these issues remain a global trade concern for managers of e-businesses.

Financial Issues

➡ **Electronic payments**. Although secure encryption services in the credit card industry are well established, consumers remain concerned about security when it comes to their own credit card. Global electronic payment systems such as stored-value, smart cards, and other systems are still in various stages of development. Their increased use will alleviate many security issues for consumers.

➡ **Tariffs and taxation**. International policies regarding who should pay taxes on international e-commerce and to what nation they should be paid are not yet fully developed. Countries have widely different views on how these matters should be treated.

➡ Background on the market, including population figures, important social trends, and a description of the kinds of marketing approaches used
➡ Total expenditure on the product (and similar products) in the market
➡ Retail sales volume and market prices of the product
➡ Future outlook for the market and potential opportunities

The value of such information supplied by specialist agencies is readily apparent—these reports provide a quick overview of the size and structure of a nation's market for a product. Reports vary in their cost (depending on the market and product), but many can be had for around $750 to $1,500. The company also allows online purchase of reports in small segments for as little as $20 each. We discuss other sources for this type of market data later in this chapter.

income elasticity
Sensitivity of demand for a product relative to changes in income.

Thus, companies that enter the market in industrialized countries often have a great deal of data available on that particular market. What becomes important then is the forecast for the growth or contraction of a potential market. One way of forecasting market demand is determining a product's **income elasticity**—the sensitivity of demand for a product relative to changes in income. The income-elasticity *coefficient* for a product is calculated by dividing a percentage change in the quantity of a product demanded by a percentage change in income. A coefficient greater than 1.0 conveys an *income-elastic* product, or one for which demand increases in a greater proportion to growth in income. These products tend to be discretionary purchases, such as computers, video games, jewelry, or expensive furniture—generally not considered essential items. A coefficient less than 1.0 conveys an *income-inelastic* product, or one for which demand increases less relative to an increase in income. These products are considered essential and include food, utilities, and beverages. To illustrate, if the income-elasticity coefficient for carbonated beverages is 0.7, the demand for carbonated beverages will increase 0.7 percent for every 1.0 percent increase in income. Conversely, if the income-elasticity coefficient for DVD video players is 1.3, the demand for DVD players will increase 1.3 percent for every 1.0 percent increase in income.

Emerging Markets   Nearly every large company engaged in international business today is either already in or is considering entering the big emerging markets in China, India, and Brazil. With their large consumer bases and rapid growth rates, they whet the appetite of marketers around the world. Although these markets are sure to experience speed bumps along their paths of economic development, in the long term they cannot be ignored. Table 12.1 shows the enormous consumption gap between China, India, and Brazil, on the one hand, and the United States on the other, in several key industries.

Companies considering entering emerging markets often face special problems related to a lack of information. Data on market size or potential may not be available, for example, due to undeveloped methods for collecting such data in a country. But there are ways companies can assess potential in emerging markets. One way is for them to rank different locations by developing a so-called *market-potential indicator* for each. However, this method is useful only to companies considering exporting. Companies considering investing in an emerging market must look at other factors that we examine next in the discussion of measuring site potential. The main variables commonly included in market-potential analyses are:[9]

➡ *Market size.* This variable provides a snapshot of the size of a market at any point in time. It does not estimate the size of a market for a particular product, but rather the size of the overall economy. Market-size data allow managers to rank countries from largest to smallest, regardless of a particular product. Market size is typically estimated from a nation's total population or the amount of energy it produces and consumes.

TABLE 12.1 *Market Size: Emerging Markets versus the United States*				
Product	**China**	**India**	**Brazil**	**United States**
Televisions (million units)	13.6	5.2	7.8	23.0
Detergent (kilograms per person)	2.5	2.7	7.3	14.4
(million tons)	3.5	2.3	1.1	3.9
Shampoo (in billions of dollars)	1.0	0.8	1.0	1.5
Pharmaceuticals (in billions of dollars)	5.0	2.8	8.0	60.6
Automotive (million units)	1.6	0.7	2.1	15.5
Power (megawatt capacity)	236,542	81,736	59,950	810,964

➡ *Market growth rate.* This variable reflects the fact that although the overall size of the market (economy) is important, so too is its rate of growth. It helps managers avoid markets that are large but shrinking and target those that are small but rapidly expanding. It is generally obtained through estimates of growth in gross domestic product (GDP) and energy consumption.

➡ *Market intensity.* This variable estimates the wealth or buying power of a market from the expenditures of both individuals and businesses. It is estimated from per capita private consumption and/or per capita gross domestic product (GDP) at purchasing power parity (see Chapter 4).

➡ *Market consumption capacity.* The purpose of this variable is to estimate spending capacity. It is often estimated from the percentage of a market's population in the middle class, thereby concentrating on the core of an economy's buying power.

➡ *Commercial infrastructure.* This factor attempts to assess channels of distribution and communication. Variables may include the number of telephones, televisions, fax machines, or personal computers per capita; the density of paved roads or number of vehicles per capita; and the population per retail outlet. An increasingly important variable for businesses relying on the Internet for sales is the number of Internet hosts per capita. But because these data become outdated quickly, care must be taken to ensure accurate information from the most current sources.

➡ *Economic freedom.* This variable attempts to estimate the extent that free-market principles predominate. It is typically a summary of government trade policies, government involvement in business, the enforcement of property rights, and the strength of the black market. An index of political freedom, such as the annual *Freedom in the World* report published by Freedom House (**www.freedomhouse.org**), can be a useful resource.

➡ *Market receptivity.* This variable attempts to estimate market "openness." One way it can be estimated is by determining a nation's volume of international trade as a percent of gross domestic product (GDP). If a company wishes to see how receptive a market is to goods from its home country, it can ascertain the amount of per capita imports into the market from the home country. Managers can also examine the growth (or decline) in these imports.

➡ *Country risk.* This variable attempts to estimate the total risk of doing business, including political, economic, and financial risks. Some market-potential estimation techniques include this variable in the market-receptivity variable. This factor is typically obtained from one of the many services that rate the risk of different countries, such as Political Risk Services (**www.prsgroup.com**).

After each of these factors is analyzed, they are assigned values according to their importance to the demand for a particular product. Then potential locations are ranked (assigned a market-potential indicator value) according to their appeal as a new market. As you may recall, we discussed several of these variables earlier under the topics of national and international business environments. For example, *country-risk* levels are shown in Map 3.2 (pages 86–87); *economic freedom* is shown in Map 4.1 (pages 118–119), and *market receptivity* (or openness) in Map 5.1 (pages 138–139). Map 12.1 captures one other variable, *commercial infrastructure*, by showing the telephone lines per 1,000 people of each nation. This variable is an important indicator of a nation's overall economic development. Other variables that are also good proxies for this variable include the portion of a nation's roads that are paved or the number of personal computers, fax machines, and Internet hosts it has. However, one note of caution is important: Emerging markets often either lack such statistics, or in the case of paved roads, international comparison is difficult.

Measuring Site Potential   In this step of the site-screening process, managers must carefully assess the quality of the resources that they will employ locally. For many

MAP 12.1

**Nations' Commercial
Infrastructures**

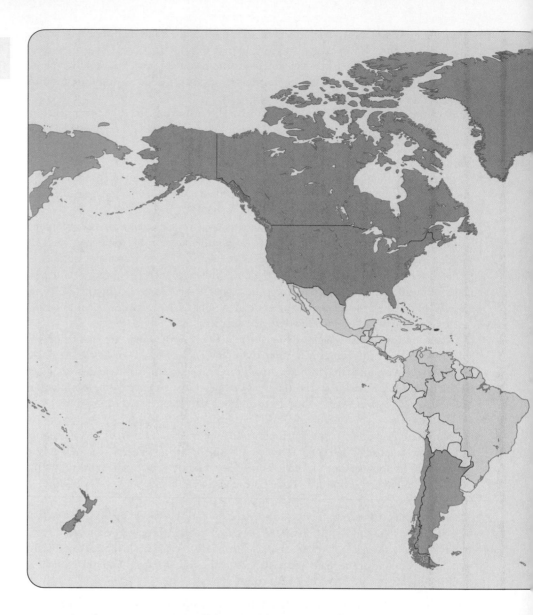

companies, the most important of these will be human resources—both labor and management. Wages are lower in certain markets because labor is abundant, relatively less skilled (though perhaps well-educated), or both. Employees may or may not be adequately trained to manufacture a given product or to perform certain R&D activities. If workers are not adequately trained, the site-selection process must consider the additional money and time needed to train them.

Training local managers also requires a substantial investment of time and money. A lack of qualified local managers sometimes forces companies to send managers from the home market to the local market. This adds to costs because home-country managers must often receive significant bonuses for relocating to the local market. Companies must also assess the productivity of local labor and managers. After all, low wages may reflect low productivity levels among the workforce.

Managers should also examine the local infrastructure, including roads, bridges, airports, seaports, and telecommunications systems when assessing site potential. Each of these systems can have a major impact on the efficiency with which a company transports materials and products. Of chief importance to many companies today is

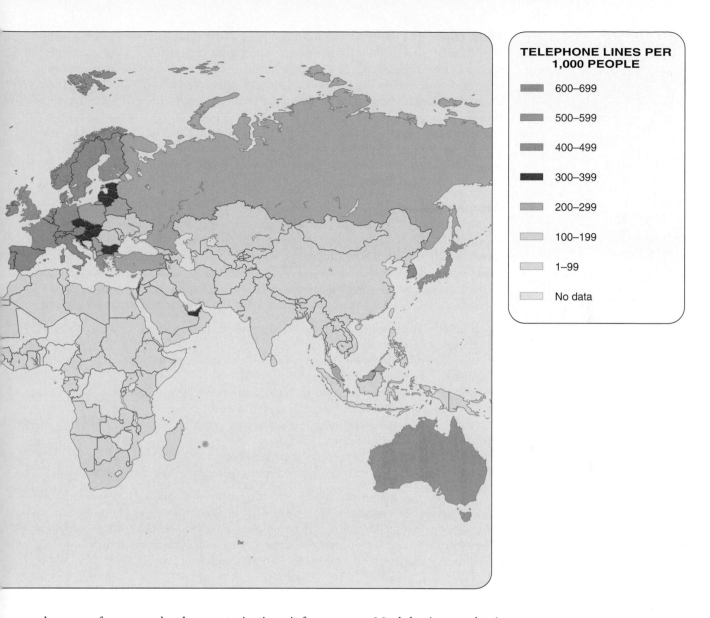

TELEPHONE LINES PER 1,000 PEOPLE

- 600–699
- 500–599
- 400–499
- 300–399
- 200–299
- 100–199
- 1–99
- No data

the state of a country's telecommunications infrastructure. Much business today is conducted through e-mail, and many businesses electronically relay information on matters such as sales orders, inventory levels, and production strategies that must be coordinated among subsidiaries in different countries. Therefore, managers must examine each potential site to determine how well it is prepared for contemporary communications.

STEP 4: SELECT THE MARKET OR SITE

This final step in the screening process involves the most intensive efforts yet of assessing remaining potential markets and sites—typically less than a dozen, sometimes just one or two. At this stage, managers normally want to visit each remaining location to confirm earlier expectations and perform a competitor analysis. In the final analysis, managers normally evaluate each potential location's contribution to cash flows by undertaking a financial evaluation of a proposed investment. The specialized and technical nature of this analysis can be found in most textbooks on corporate finance.

Field Trips   The importance of top managers making a personal visit to each remaining potential market or site cannot be overstated. Such trips typically involve attending strings of meetings and engaging in tough negotiations. The trip represents an opportunity for managers to see firsthand what they have so far seen only on paper. It gives them an opportunity to experience the culture, observe in action the workforce that they might soon employ, or make personal contact with potential new customers and distributors. Any issues remaining tend to be thoroughly investigated during field trips so that the terms of any agreement are known precisely in the event that a particular market or site is chosen. Managers can then usually return to the chosen location to put the terms of the final agreement in writing.

Competitor Analysis   Because competitor analysis was covered in detail in Chapter 11, we offer only a few comments here. Intensely competitive markets typically put downward pressure on the prices that firms can charge their customers. In addition, intensely competitive sites for production and R&D activities often increase the costs of doing business. Naturally, lower prices and higher costs due to competitive forces must be balanced against the potential benefits offered by each market and site under consideration. At the very least, then, competitor analysis should address the following issues:

➡ Number of competitors in each market (domestic and international)
➡ Market share of each competitor
➡ Whether each competitor's product appeals to a small market segment or has mass appeal
➡ Whether each competitor focuses on high quality or low price
➡ Whether competitors tightly control channels of distribution
➡ Customer loyalty commanded by competitors
➡ Potential threat from substitute products
➡ Potential entry of new competitors into the market
➡ Competitors' control of key production inputs (such as labor, capital, and raw materials)

So far we have examined a model that many companies follow when selecting new markets or sites for operations. We've seen what steps companies take in the screening process but have yet to learn how they undertake such a complex task. Let's now explore the types of situations companies encounter when conducting research in an international setting, and the specific tools used in their research.

CONDUCTING INTERNATIONAL RESEARCH

market research
Collection and analysis of information in order to assist managers in making informed decisions.

Today, increased global competition forces companies to engage in high-quality research and analysis before selecting new markets and sites for operations. Companies are finding that such research helps them to better understand both buyer behavior and business environments abroad. **Market research** is the collection and analysis of information in order to assist managers in making informed decisions. We define market research here to apply to the assessment of both potential markets and sites for operations. International market research provides information on national business environments, including cultural practices, politics, regulations, and the economy. It also informs managers about a market's potential size, buyer behavior, logistics, and distribution systems.

Conducting market research on new markets is helpful in designing all aspects of marketing strategy and understanding buyer preferences and attitudes. What works in France, for example, might not work in Singapore. Market research also lets managers learn about aspects of local business environments such as employment levels, wage rates, and the state of the local infrastructure before committing to the new location. It supplies managers with timely and relevant market information to anticipate market shifts, changes in current regulations, and the potential entry of new competitors.

In this section, we first learn about several common problems that confront companies when conducting international research. Then we explore some actual sources that managers use to assess potential new locations. We then examine some methods commonly used for conducting international research firsthand.

DIFFICULTIES OF CONDUCTING INTERNATIONAL RESEARCH

Market research serves essentially the same function in all nations. However, unique conditions and circumstances present certain difficulties that often force adjustments in the *way* research is performed in different nations. It is important for companies that are conducting market research themselves to be absolutely aware of potential obstacles so that their results are reliable. Companies that hire outside research agencies must also be aware of such difficulties. After all, they must evaluate the research results and assess their relevance to the location-selection decision. The three main difficulties associated with conducting international market research that we will now examine are:

1. Availability of data
2. Comparability of data
3. Cultural differences.

Availability of Data When trying to target specific population segments, marketing managers require highly detailed information. Fortunately, companies are often spared the time, money, and effort of collecting firsthand data for the simple reason that it has already been gathered. This is particularly true in the highly industrialized countries, including Australia, Canada, Japan, those in Western Europe, and the United States, where both government agencies and private research firms supply information. Information Resources Incorporated (www.infores.com), Survey Research Group (www.surveyresearchgroup.com), and ACNielsen (www.acnielsen.com) are just three of these types of information suppliers.

In many emerging and developing countries, however, previously gathered quality information is hard to obtain. Even when market data are available, their reliability is questionable. For example, analysts sometimes charge the governments of certain emerging markets (particularly China) with trying to lure investors by overstating estimates of gross income and consumption levels. In addition to deliberate misrepresentation, tainted information can also result from improper local collection methods and analysis techniques. But research agencies in emerging and developing markets that specialize in gathering data for clients in industrialized countries are developing higher-quality techniques of collection and analysis. For example, information supplier and pollster Gallup (www.gallup.com) is aggressively expanding its operations throughout Southeast Asia in response to the need among Western companies for more accurate market research.

Comparability of Data Likewise, data obtained from other countries must be interpreted with great caution. Because terms such as *poverty*, *consumption*, and *literacy* differ greatly from one country to another, such data must be accompanied by precise definitions. In the United States, for example, a family of four is said to be below the poverty line if its annual income is less than about $17,500. The equivalent income for a Vietnamese family of four would place it in the high upper class.

The different ways in which countries measure data also affect comparability across borders. For instance, some countries state the total quantity of foreign direct investment in their nations in terms of its *monetary value*. Others specify it in terms of the number of *investment projects* implemented during the year. But a single foreign direct investment into an industrialized nation can be worth many times what several or more projects are worth in a developing nation. Thus, to gather a complete picture of a nation's investments, researchers will often need to obtain both figures. Moreover, reported statistics may not distinguish between foreign direct investment (accompanied by managerial control) and portfolio investment (which is not accompanied by managerial control). Misinterpreting data because one does not know how it is compiled or measured can sabotage even the best marketing plans and production strategies.

Cultural Problems   Marketers who conduct research in unfamiliar markets must pay attention to the ways that cultural variables influence information. Perhaps the single most important variable is language. For example, if researchers are unfamiliar with a language in the market they are investigating, they might be forced to rely on interpreters. Interpreters might unintentionally misrepresent certain comments or be unable to convey the sentiment with which statements are made.

Researchers might also need to survey potential buyers through questionnaires written in the local language. To avoid any misstatement of questions or results, questionnaires must be translated into the language of the target market and the responses then translated back into the researcher's language. Written expressions must be highly accurate so that results do not become meaningless or, far worse, misleading. The potential to conduct written surveys is also affected by the illiteracy rates among the local population. A written survey is generally impossible to conduct in countries with high illiteracy rates such as Egypt (45 percent), Haiti (50 percent), and Pakistan (54 percent).[10] Researchers would probably need to choose a different information-gathering technique, such as personal interviews or observing retail purchases.

Companies that have little experience in an unfamiliar market often hire local agencies to perform some or all of their market research. Local researchers know the cultural terrain; they understand which practices are acceptable and which types of questions can be asked. They also typically know whom to approach for certain types of information. Perhaps most importantly, they realize how to interpret the information they gather and are likely to know its reliability. But a company that decides to conduct its own market research must, if necessary, adapt its research techniques to the local market. Many cultural elements that are taken for granted in the home market must be reassessed in the host business environment.

SOURCES OF SECONDARY INTERNATIONAL DATA

secondary market research
Process of obtaining information that already exists within the company or that can be obtained from outside sources.

Companies can consult a variety of sources to obtain information on a nation's business environment and markets. The particular source that managers should consult depends on the company's industry, the national markets it is considering, and how far along it is in its location-screening process. The process of obtaining information that already exists within the company or that can be obtained from outside sources is called **secondary market research**. Managers often use information gathered from secondary research activities to broadly estimate market demand for a product or to form a general impression of a nation's business environment. Secondary data are relatively inexpensive because they have already been collected, analyzed, and summarized by another party. Let's now take a look at the main sources of secondary data that help managers make more informed location–selection decisions.

International Organizations   A variety of international organizations are excellent sources of much free and inexpensive information about product demand in particular countries. For example, the *International Trade Statistics Yearbook* published by the United Nations (www.un.org) lists the export and import volumes of different products for each country. It also furnishes information on the value of exports and imports on an annual basis for the most recent 5-year period. The International Trade

Center (www.intracen.org), based in Geneva, Switzerland, also provides current import and export figures for more than 100 countries.

International development agencies, such as the World Bank (www.worldbank.org), the International Monetary Fund (www.imf.org), and the Asian Development Bank (www.adb.org), also provide valuable secondary data. For example, the World Bank publishes annual data on each member nation's population and economic growth rate. Today most secondary sources supply data on CD-ROM and through the Internet in addition to traditional printed versions.

Government Agencies   The commerce departments and international trade agencies of most countries typically supply information about import and export regulations, quality standards, and the sizes of various markets. These data are normally available directly from these departments, from agencies within each nation, and from the commercial attaché in each country's embassy abroad. In fact, visiting embassies and attending their social functions while visiting a potential location are excellent ways of making contacts with potential future business partners.

Granted, the attractively packaged information supplied by host nations often ignores many potential hazards in a nation's commercial environment—governments typically try to present their country in the best possible light. By the same token, such sources are prone to paint incomplete or one-sided portraits of the home market. Thus, it is important for managers to seek out additional sources that take a more objective view of a potential location.

One source that takes a fairly broad view of markets is the Central Intelligence Agency's *World Factbook* (www.odci.gov/cia/publications/factbook). This source can be a useful tool throughout the entire market- or site-screening process because of its wealth of facts on each nation's business environment. It identifies each nation's geography, climate, terrain, natural resources, land use, and important environmental issues in some detail. It also examines each nation's culture, system of government, and economic conditions, including government debt and exchange-rate conditions. It also provides an overview of the quality of each country's transportation and communications systems.

The Trade Information Center (TIC) (www.trade.gov/td/tic) operated by the U.S. Department of Commerce is a first stop for many importers and exporters. The TIC details product standards in other countries and offers advice on opportunities and best prospects for U.S. companies in individual markets. It also offers information on federal export-assistance programs that can be essential for first-time exporters. Other TIC information includes:

➡ National trade laws and other regulations
➡ Trade shows, trade missions, and special events
➡ Export counseling for specific countries
➡ Import tariffs and customs procedures
➡ The value of exports to other countries

The Chilean Trade Commission within Chile's Ministry of Foreign Affairs has been particularly aggressive in recent years in promoting Chile to the rest of the world. ProChile (www.chileinfo.com) has 35 commercial offices worldwide. The organization assists in developing the export process, establishing international business relationships, fostering international trade, attracting investment, and forging strategic alliances. It offers a wealth of information on all of Chile's key industries and provides business environment information such as risk ratings. It also provides details on important trade regulations and standards of which exporters, importers, and investors must be aware.[11]

Commercial offices of the states and provinces of many countries also typically have offices in other countries to promote trade and investment. These offices usually encourage investment in the home market by companies from other countries and will sometimes even help companies in other countries export to the home market. For instance, the Lorraine Development Corporation (www.lorrainedc.com) in Atlanta is the investment-promotion office of the Lorraine region of France. This corporation helps U.S. companies evaluate location opportunities in the Lorraine region—a popular area for industrial investment. It supplies information on sites, buildings, financing options, and conditions in the French business environment and conducts 10 to 20 site-selection studies per year for specific companies. "We've been in the U.S.A. since 1988," says director Frederic Mot. "Our main goal is to identify potential U.S. investors, and we contact about 2,000 American companies each year."[12] Figure 12.2 shows the U.S. states that have the most investment-promotion and trade offices abroad and the most popular locations for such offices.

Finally, many governments open their research libraries to businesspeople from all countries. For example, the Japanese External Trade Organization (JETRO) (www.jetro.go.jp) in central Tokyo has a large library full of trade data available to international companies already in Japan. In addition, the JETRO Web site can be useful for companies screening the potential of the Japanese market for future business activities from any location. The organization is dedicated to serving companies interested in exporting to or investing in Japan in addition to assisting Japanese companies in going abroad.

Industry and Trade Associations   Companies often join associations composed of firms within their own industry or trade. In particular, companies trying to break into new markets join such associations in order to make contact with others in their field. The publications of these organizations keep members informed about current events and help managers to keep abreast of important issues and opportunities. Many associations publish special volumes of import and export data for domestic markets. Frequently they compile directories that list each member's top executives, geographic scope, and contact information such as phone numbers and addresses. Today, many associations also maintain informative Web sites. Two interesting examples are the sites of the National Pasta Association (www.ilovepasta.org) and the National Onion Association (www.onions-usa.org).

Sometimes industry and trade associations will commission specialized studies of their industries and offer them to members at subsidized prices. Such studies typically address particularly important issues or explore new opportunities for international growth. For example, the Chocolate Manufacturers Association (www.nca-cma.org) of

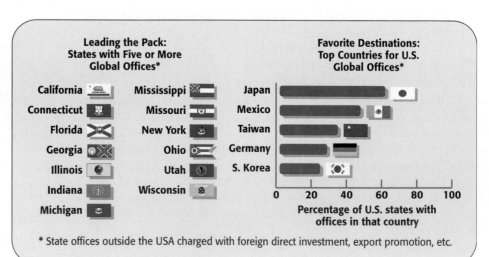

FIGURE 12.2

U.S. States' Global Development Offices

the United States and the state of Washington's Washington Apple Commission (www.bestapples.com) hired a research firm to study the sweet tooth of Chinese consumers.[13] The findings of the study were then made available to each organization's members to act on as they saw fit.

Service Organizations Many international service organizations in fields such as banking, insurance, management consulting, and accounting offer information to their clients on cultural, regulatory, and financial conditions in a market. For example, the accounting firm of Ernst & Young (www.ey.com) publishes a "Doing Business In" series for most countries. Each booklet contains information on a nation's business environment, regulations regarding foreign investment, legal forms of businesses, labor force, taxes, and culture.

Another service that provides information on world markets is MARKET: newsletters (see Figure 12.3). This company supplies specialized reports on market demographics, lifestyles, and consumer data and trends. Newsletters for each world region cover trends in areas such as population growth, consumer spending, purchase behavior, media, and advertising.

Internet and World Wide Web Companies engaged in international business are quickly realizing the wealth of secondary research information available on the Internet and the World Wide Web. These electronic resources are usually user-friendly and have vast amounts of information.

LEXIS-NEXIS (www.lexis-nexis.com) is a leading online provider of market information. The LEXIS-NEXIS database of full-text news reports from around the world is updated continuously. It also offers special services such as profiles of executives and

FIGURE 12.3 *Market: Newsletters*

products and information on the financial conditions, marketing strategies, and public relations of many international companies. Knight-Ridder (www.knightridder.com), CompuServe (www.compuserve.com), DIALOG (www.dialog.com), and Dow Jones (www.dj.com) are other popular online providers of global information. Internet search engines such as Ask Jeeves (www.askjeeves.com), Lycos (www.lycos.com), Overture (www.overture.com), and Yahoo! (www.yahoo.com) are quite helpful in narrowing down the plethora of information available electronically.

The Internet can be especially useful in seeking information about potential production sites. Because field trips to most likely candidates are expensive, online information can be enormously helpful in saving both time and money. For instance, you can begin a search for information on a particular country or region with most large online information providers. Narrowing your search to a more manageable list of subjects— say, culture, economic conditions, or perhaps a specific industry—can yield clues about sites that are promising and those that are not.

METHODS OF CONDUCTING PRIMARY INTERNATIONAL RESEARCH

Although secondary information is very informative and useful in the early stages of the screening process, sometimes more tailored data on a location are needed. Under such circumstances, it might be necessary to conduct **primary market research**—the process of collecting and analyzing original data and applying the results to current research needs. This type of research is very helpful in filling in the blanks left by secondary research. However, it is often more expensive to obtain than secondary research data because studies must be conducted in their entirety. Let's now explore some of the more common methods of primary research used by companies in the location-screening process.

Trade Shows and Trade Missions An exhibition at which members of an industry or group of industries showcase their latest products, see what rivals are doing, and learn about recent trends and opportunities is called a **trade show**. They are held on a continuing basis in virtually all markets and normally attract companies from around the globe. They are typically held by national or global industry trade associations or by government agencies. An excellent source of trade shows and exhibitions worldwide is EXPOguide, Inc. (www.expoguide.com).

Not surprisingly, the format and scope of trade shows differ from country to country. For example, because of its large domestic market, shows in the United States tend to be oriented toward business opportunities within the U.S. market. In line with U.S. culture, the atmosphere tends to be fairly informal, and business cards are handed out to all the contacts one meets—no matter how briefly. Conversely, because of the relatively smaller market of Germany and its participation in the European Union, trade shows there are more international in focus, showcasing business opportunities in markets all across Europe. They also tend be quite formal, and business cards are given to a contact only when a business relationship is highly desirable.[14] See this chapter's Entrepreneurial Focus titled "Is the World Your Oyster?" for how small companies can use trade shows and other tools to be successful abroad.

On the other hand, a **trade mission** is an international trip by government officials and businesspeople that is organized by agencies of national or provincial governments for the purpose of exploring international business opportunities. Businesspeople who attend trade missions are typically introduced both to important business contacts and well-placed government officials.

Small and medium-size companies often find trade missions very appealing for two reasons. First, the support of government officials gives them additional clout in the target country as well as access to officials and executives whom they would otherwise have

---

primary market research
Process of collecting and analyzing original data and applying the results to current research needs.

trade show
Exhibition at which members of an industry or group of industries showcase their latest products, see what rivals are doing, and learn about recent trends and opportunities.

trade mission
International trip by government officials and businesspeople that is organized by agencies of national or provincial governments for the purpose of exploring international business opportunities.

ENTREPRENEURIAL FOCUS

Is the World Your Oyster?

How can an entrepreneur or small business succeed in international markets? How can they compete with the more competitive pricing and sales efforts of large multinationals? It isn't easy, but it can be done. First, small companies must do lots of homework before jumping into the global marketplace. Going international is a long-term investment and preparedness is a critical success factor. They also must plan on investing a good deal of cash. A typical small business can expect to pay anywhere from $10,000 to $20,000 to perform some basic market research, to attend a trade show, and to visit one or two countries. Here are the tales of how two small companies are exploiting international opportunities at different stages of going international.

➡ Lucille Farms, Inc. of Montville, New Jersey, produces and markets cheese products. Alfonso Falivene, Lucille's chief executive, is taking a cautious approach to going international. He recently joined the U.S. Dairy Export Council that offers members, among other things, international trips to study new business opportunities and the compe-

tition. The Council also offers its members a great deal of free information on international markets. Notes Falivene, "I have stacks of information in my office. If I had to go out and get the information on my own, it would cost me thousands and thousands of dollars."

➡ Meter-Man, Inc. of Winnebago, Minnesota, manufactures agricultural measuring devices. When Meter-Man decided to go international, it saw trade shows as a great way to gain market intelligence and establish contacts. At a 5-day agricultural fair in Paris, company executives held 21 meetings with potential customers and sealed an agreement with a major distributor that covers the Parisian market for Meter-Man's products. James Neff, Meter-Man's sales and marketing director, was on a flight to a trade show in Barcelona, Spain, and struck up a conversation with the man next to him. The man wound up ordering $200,000 of Meter-Man's products and is today a major South American distributor for the company.

little opportunity to meet. Second, although such trips can sometimes be expensive for the smallest of businesses, they are generally worth the money because they almost always reap cost-effective rewards. Trade missions to faraway places sometimes involve visits to several countries to maximize the return for the time and money invested. For instance, a trade mission for European businesspeople to Latin America may include stops in Argentina, Brazil, Chile, and Mexico. A trade mission to Asia for North American or European companies might include stops in China, Hong Kong, Japan, South Korea, and Thailand.

Interviews and Focus Groups   Although industry data are very useful to companies early in the screening process for potential markets, subsequent steps must assess buyers' emotions, attitudes, and cultural beliefs. Industry data cannot tell us how individuals feel about a company or its product. Deciding whether to enter a market and the subsequent development of an effective marketing plan require this type of buyer information. Therefore, many companies supplement the large-scale collection of country data with other types of research, such as interviews with prospective customers. Interviews, of course, must be conducted carefully if they are to yield reliable and unbiased information. Respondents in some cultures might be unwilling to answer certain questions or may intentionally give vague or misleading answers to avoid getting too personal. For example, although individuals in the United States are renowned for their willingness to divulge all sorts of information about their shopping habits and even their personal lives, this is very much the exception as one goes around the world.

An unstructured but in-depth interview of a small group of individuals (8 to 12 people) by a moderator to learn the group's attitudes about a company or its product is called a **focus group**. Moderators guide a discussion on a topic but interfere as little as possible with the free flow of ideas. The interview is recorded for later evaluation to identify recurring or prominent themes among the participants. This type of research

focus group
Unstructured but in-depth interview of a small group of individuals (8 to 12 people) by a moderator to learn the group's attitudes about a company or its product.

helps marketers to uncover negative perceptions among buyers and to design corrective marketing strategies. Because subtle differences in verbal and body language could go unnoticed, focus group interviews tend to work best when moderators are natives of the countries in which the interview is held. Ironically, it is sometimes difficult to conduct focus groups in collectivist cultures (see Chapter 2) because people have a tendency to agree with others in the group. In such instances, it might be advisable to use a **consumer panel**—research in which people record in personal diaries, information on their attitudes, behaviors, or purchasing habits.

Surveys   Research in which an interviewer asks current or potential buyers to answer written or verbal questions to obtain facts, opinions, or attitudes is called a **survey**. For example, if Reebok (www.reebok.com) wants to learn about consumer attitudes toward its latest women's aerobics shoe in Britain, it could ask a sample of British women about their attitudes toward the shoe. Verbal questioning could be done in person or over the telephone, whereas written questioning could be done in person, through the mail, or through forms completed at Reebok's Web site. The results would then be tabulated, analyzed, and applied to the development of a marketing plan.

The single greatest advantage of survey research is the ability to collect vast amounts of data in a single sweep. But as a rule, survey methods must be adapted to local markets. For example, survey research can be conducted by any technological means in industrialized markets, such as over the telephone or the Internet. But telephone interviewing would yield poor results in Bangladesh because only a small percentage of the general population has telephones. Also, although a survey at a Web site is an easy way to gather data, it must be remembered that even in industrialized nations users still tend to represent only the middle- to upper-income households.

Written surveys can also be hampered by other problems. Some countries' postal services are unreliable to the point that parcels are delivered weeks or months after arriving at post offices, or never arrive at all because they are stolen or simply lost. Naturally, written surveys are impractical to conduct in countries with high rates of illiteracy, although this problem can perhaps be overcome by obtaining verbal responses to verbally asked questions.

Environmental Scanning   An ongoing process of gathering, analyzing, and dispensing information for tactical or strategic purposes is called **environmental scanning**. The environmental scanning process entails obtaining both factual and subjective information on the business environments in which a company is operating or considering entering. The continuous monitoring of events in other locations keeps managers aware of potential opportunities and threats to minimize financial losses and maximize returns. Environmental scanning contributes to making well-informed decisions and the development of effective strategies. It also helps companies develop contingency plans for a particularly volatile environment.

A FINAL WORD

In order to keep pace with an increasingly hectic and competitive global business environment, companies should follow a systematic screening process that incorporates high-quality research methods. This chapter provided a systematic way to screen potential locations as new markets or sites for business operations. However, these issues constitute only the first step in the process of "going international." The next step involves actually accomplishing the task of entering selected markets and establishing operations abroad. In the following chapters, we survey the types of entry modes available to companies, how they acquire the resources needed to carry out their activities, and how they manage their sometimes far-flung international business operations.

---

consumer panel
Research in which people record in personal diaries, information on their attitudes, behaviors, or purchasing habits.

survey
Research in which an interviewer asks current or potential buyers to answer written or verbal questions to obtain facts, opinions, or attitudes.

environmental scanning
Ongoing process of gathering, analyzing, and dispensing information for tactical or strategic purposes.

There is a variety of additional material available on the Companion Website that accompanies this book. You can access this information by visiting the Website at (www.prenhall.com/wild).

summary

1 **Explain each of the four steps in the *market- and site-screening process*.** To keep the cost of searching markets and sites as low as possible yet not overlook potentially attractive locations, managers can approach the *screening process* in a systematic four-step manner. Step 1 involves identifying basic appeal. For potential markets, this means assessing a location's basic product demand. For production, it means assessing the availability of required resources, such as raw materials, labor, and capital.

Step 2 of the screening process is to assess the national business environment of the market or site. This involves examining cultural, political, legal, and economic forces. Cultural forces can influence the kinds of products sold and how they are marketed. Important political and legal forces include government regulation, government bureaucracy, and political stability. The fiscal and monetary policies of a nation's central bank are also important.

Step 3 of the screening process is to measure the potential of each market or site for operations. Companies evaluating industrialized countries must forecast the size and growth of the market. Companies can rank emerging markets by developing a so-called *market-potential indicator* for each. As a site for potential business operations, a location must be examined for the availability of workers and managers, raw materials, and an adequate local infrastructure.

In Step 4 of the screening process, managers normally visit each remaining location to confirm earlier expectations and perform a competitor analysis. In the final analysis, managers normally evaluate each potential location's contribution to overall company cash flows by undertaking a financial evaluation of a proposed investment.

2 **Describe the three primary difficulties of conducting *international market research*.** The collection and analysis of information in order to assist managers in making informed decisions is called *market research*. Unique conditions and circumstances present three main difficulties that often force adjustments in the *way* research is performed in different nations.

First, managers can face problems with regard to the availability of data. In many developing countries pre-

viously gathered quality information is hard to obtain. Even when market data are available, their reliability is questionable. In addition to deliberate misrepresentation, tainted information can also result from improper local collection methods and analysis techniques.

Second, managers can face problems with the comparability of data across markets. Because terms such as *poverty*, *consumption*, and *literacy* differ greatly from one nation to another, such data must be accompanied by precise definitions. The different ways in which countries measure statistics also affect the comparability of data across borders.

Finally, managers can face problems rooted in cultural differences. Companies entering unfamiliar markets often hire local agencies to perform their market research for them. Local researchers know the cultural terrain; they understand which practices are acceptable and which types of questions can be asked. Also, they realize how to interpret the information they gather and are likely to know its reliability.

3 **Identify the main sources of *secondary international data* and explain their usefulness.** The process of obtaining information that already exists within the company or that can be obtained from outside sources is called *secondary market research*. Managers often use information from secondary research to broadly estimate market demand for a product or to form a general impression of a nation's business environment.

International organizations are excellent sources of much free and inexpensive information about demand for a product in a particular country. International development agencies, such as the World Bank, the International Monetary Fund, and the Asian Development Bank, also provide valuable secondary data. *Government agencies*—especially the commerce departments and international trade agencies of most countries—typically supply information about import and export regulations, quality standards, and the sizes of various markets. Commercial offices of the states and provinces of many countries also typically have offices in other countries to promote trade and investment.

Companies often join *industry and trade associations* composed of firms within their own industries or trades. The publications of these organizations help managers to keep abreast of important issues and opportunities. Many international *service organizations* in fields such as banking, insurance, management consulting, and accounting offer information to their clients on cultural, regulatory, and financial conditions in a market.

4 **Describe the main methods used to conduct** *primary international research*. The process of collecting and analyzing original data and applying the results to current research needs is called *primary market research*. However, primary research data are often more expensive to obtain than secondary research data because studies must be conducted in their entirety. Exhibitions at which members of an industry or group of industries showcase their latest products, see what rivals are doing, and learn about recent trends and opportunities are

called *trade shows*. A *trade mission* is an international trip by government officials and businesspeople that is organized by agencies of national or provincial governments for the purpose of exploring international business opportunities.

Companies can use *interviews* to assess potential buyers' emotions, attitudes, and cultural beliefs. An unstructured but in-depth interview of a small group of individuals by a moderator to learn the group's attitudes about a company or its product is called a *focus group*. In *surveys*, interviewers obtain facts, opinions, or attitudes by asking current or potential buyers to answer written or verbal questions. An ongoing process of gathering, analyzing, and dispensing information for tactical or strategic purposes is called *environmental scanning*.

questions **for review**

1. What are the four steps in the *screening process*?

2. Identify the main factors to investigate when identifying the basic appeal of a market or site for operations.

3. What are the key *cultural*, *political*, *legal*, *economic*, and *financial forces* that should be taken into consideration when assessing the national business environment?

4. How do the cost of transport and country image affect the location decision?

5. Define *income elasticity* and explain how it is interpreted. What is its importance in measuring market potential?

6. Identify the main components of a *market-potential indicator*. Why is it useful in assessing emerging markets?

7. What are the most important factors to consider in measuring site potential?

8. Describe the usefulness of undertaking a field trip and competitor analysis in the final stage of the screening process.

9. Define *market research*. What are some of the benefits associated with conducting international market research?

10. Identify the three main difficulties of conducting research in international markets. Explain each briefly.

11. Define *secondary market research*. When are secondary research data useful?

12. What are the main sources of secondary research data?

13. Define *primary market research*. How does it differ from secondary market research?

14. What is the difference between a *trade show* and a *trade mission*?

15. What are some of the issues that arise when using *focus groups* in international marketing research?

16. How does a *consumer panel* differ from a *survey*? Explain why it is sometimes difficult to conduct a survey in international markets.

17. Explain the usefulness of *environmental scanning*.

questions **for discussion**

1. For many global companies, China represents a very attractive market in terms of size and growth rate. However, because China has a communist government, it ranks lower in terms of economic freedom and higher in political risk than other country markets. Despite these risks, Volkswagen (www.volkswagen.com), Isuzu (www.isuzu.com), and Boeing (www.boeing.com) are just a few of the hundreds of companies that have established manufacturing operations in China. In large part, this is because the Chinese government makes selling in China contingent on a company's willingness to locate production there. The government wants

Chinese companies to learn modern management skills from non-Chinese companies and to acquire technology. Some observers believe that when Western companies agree to such conditions, they are bargaining away important industry know-how in exchange for sales today. Should Boeing and other companies go along with China's terms, or should they risk losing sales by refusing to transfer technology?

2. When Sony (www.sony.com) mounted its third official attempt to launch its MiniDisc recorder/player in the United States, it thought it finally had the right formula. Although the product was a success in Japan, response to the MiniDisc

in the U.S. market was lukewarm. A Sony executive noted, "This time around, we've done our homework, and we've found out what's in consumers' heads." What type of research do you think Sony used to "get inside the heads" of its target market? Do you think different cultures rely on different types of market research? Explain.

in practice

Read the article below and answer the questions that follow.

A Site to Ponder?

MEXICO CITY, Mexico—One year after Vicente Fox won the presidency, education spending remains too low, the energy sector remains closed to competition, and the police, army, and justice system still need reform.

Yet civil and political liberties have expanded, and it is becoming easier to start a business. Although Mexico is sliding into recession behind the United States, for the first time in 30 years it is not accompanied by a financial crisis. Mexico's fate is tied to that of the United States because the U.S. market absorbs nine tenths of Mexico's exports.

Yet in late 2001 Mexico's government struck high-wage settlements with auto workers, flight attendants, and oil workers to avoid strikes, causing wages to outpace inflation. If this continues, warns Finance Secretary Francisco Gil, "...We'll quickly price ourselves out of the market." Volkswagen spokesman Thomas Karig concurred saying, "Mexico definitely is no longer a low-wage country."

3. What are some of the benefits of "soft" market research data gathered using techniques such as focus groups and observation. What are the benefits of using "hard" data such as statistics on consumers' buying habits and figures on market size? As a manager, explain when each kind of data would be preferred and tell why.

1. First, update the performance of Mexico's economy and government using resources such as the business press and statistical databases. If wages are rising, why are companies still investing in Mexico? Are wages rising across the board or just in specific sectors? What sectors are investments still flowing in to Mexico?

2. Select a country that competes with Mexico for foreign direct investment. What characteristics make Mexico a better production base? A worse production base? List as many direct and relevant comparisons as you can—you might want to use this chapter's screening process as a guide.

3. Finally, Mexico is leading the hemisphere in trade agreements. It has agreements with nearly every country in the Western Hemisphere and Europe. In addition to the EU, it has a new trade agreement with the European Free Trade Association (see Chapter 8). Research what these agreements entail. What additional benefits (if any) could these agreements offer international companies producing in Mexico? *Note:* Remember to distinguish between the different benefits that different agreements provide.

projects

1. Visit the library at your college or university and consult the *Encyclopedia of Associations*. Select one or two associations that pertain to an industry that is of interest to you. Write or call the association and request an information packet. Compile a summary of the information you receive. Compare this information with that of your fellow students. Rank the trade associations in terms of the usefulness of their available information.

2. Select an emerging market that you would like to learn more about. Start by compiling fundamental country data. Then do additional research to flesh out the nature of the market opportunity offered by this country or its suitability as a manufacturing site. Structure your report using the steps identified in this chapter. Make a list of the international companies that are pursuing market opportunities in the country, and identify the products or brands that the compa-

nies are marketing. Are their reasons for doing business in the country consistent with the market opportunity as you have researched it? Determine whether these companies have established facilities for manufacturing, sales, or both.

3. A great deal of market information can be found in business-oriented magazines and journals. However, depending on where the magazine is published, the editorial point of view or emphasis may vary. For a particular country market, find a recent feature article in magazines from at least two different countries. As a starting point, look for articles in *The Economist* (Europe), *Far Eastern Economic Review* (Asia), and *Business Week* (North America). Write a brief summary of each article in which you compare and contrast issues such as content coverage, point of view, and editorial tone in the different magazines. How might a manager's opinion of a market be shaped by the views expressed?

RESEARCHING VIETNAM'S POTENTIAL

In 1990, Vietnam's communist government announced that non-Vietnamese manufacturers were welcome to set up shop in the Southeast Asian country. South Korea's Daewoo (www.dm.co.kr) quickly established itself as the number-one investor in Vietnam. Other well-known companies, including Toshiba (www.toshiba.co.jp), Peugeot (www.peugeot.com), and British Petroleum (www.bp.com), also took Hanoi up on its invitation. However, the absence of trade and diplomatic relations between the United States and Vietnam meant that U.S. companies had to sit on the sidelines. Nearly 4 years later, the U.S. government lifted the trade embargo with Vietnam, paving the way for a host of U.S. companies to pursue opportunities in Vietnam.

Experts agree that the Vietnamese market holds tremendous potential over the long term. However, it may be two decades before Vietnam reaches the level of economic development found even in Thailand today. Meanwhile, the country's location in the heart of Asia and the presence of a literate, low-wage workforce could be powerful magnets for international companies. But investment in Vietnam has lagged well behind that of other countries.

There are many challenges for investors in Vietnam. The population of 76 million is very poor, with an annual per capita income of only about $200. The infrastructure is undeveloped: Only 10 percent of roads are paved; electricity sources are unreliable; there is roughly one telephone per 100 people; and the banking system is undeveloped. Nevertheless, an emerging entrepreneurial class in Vietnam has developed a taste for expensive products such as Nikon (www.nikon.co.jp) cameras and Ray Ban (www.rayban.com) sunglasses—both of which are available in stores. Says Do Duc Dinh of the Institute on the World Economy, "There is a huge unofficial economy. For most people, we can live only 5 days or 10 days a month on our salary. But people build houses. Where does the money come from? Even in government ministries, there are two sets of books—one for the official money and one for unofficial."

The Communist Party of Vietnam (CPV) is struggling to adapt to the principles of a market economy, and the layers of bureaucracy built up over decades of communist rule slow the pace of change. A key agency is the State Committee for Cooperation and Investment; as Vu Tien Phuc, a deputy director of the agency, explained, "Every authority would like to have the last say. We have to improve the investment climate." Despite such statements, the government continues to conduct itself in a way that leaves international investors scratching their heads. In one incident Hanoi embarked on a "social evils crackdown" that included pulling down or painting over any sign or billboard printed in a language other than Vietnamese.

In the early 2000s, euphoria over Vietnam's potential is waning. Part of the problem is continuing economic difficulties across much of Southeast Asia. Asian countries that had been major investors scaled back their activities in Vietnam. More generally, many companies are finding it difficult to make a profit. Cross-border smuggling from Thailand depresses the legitimate sales of products produced locally. The Hanoi bureaucracy is also a major impediment because laws concerning taxes and foreign exchange are in constant flux. As a Western investment lawyer in Ho Chi Minh City said, "People are tired of waiting for economic reforms that come too little, too late."

Nevertheless, trade deals are going forward. In late 2001 Vietnam and the United States signed a new trade deal that gives Vietnam normal trade status with the United States. This means that Vietnam can now ship goods to the U.S. market at the lowest possible tariff rates. Meanwhile, U.S. companies will gain continually greater access to Vietnam. Almost immediately, Boeing announced that it had sold Vietnam Airlines four of its 777 jets for $440 million. If Vietnam can maintain its strong growth rate and expand its middle class, things will gradually improve.

thinking globally

1. Update the political, legal, and economic situation in Vietnam. Select a product and assess Vietnam's potential both as a market and as a manufacturing site.

2. What, if anything, can Western countries do to help improve the political climate for doing business in Vietnam?

3. What problems might a company encounter while conducting market research in Vietnam?

4. What would be your perception of a product with the label "Made in Vietnam"? Do you think the type of product would play a role in forming your perception?

a question **of ethics**

1. In his book, *One World, Ready or Not*, editor and journalist William Greider argues that multinational corporations from wealthy countries are seriously endangering the global economic system by investing capital in developing countries and laying off workers at home. In essence, Greider argues, globalization pits the interests of the older, more prosperous workers in wealthy countries against the interests of newly recruited, lower-paid workers in developing countries. Moreover, the disbursal of production and capital flight that Greider describes pits developing nations against one another as multinational companies move from one developing country to another in search of lower wages or bigger market opportunities. Greider believes that multinationals have an ethical obligation to try to preserve jobs for workers in their home-country markets. Do you agree? Explain your answer.

2. As the CEO of a large international company, you are proud of the fact that you have built a profitable business by investing in a Latin American country. As a key catalyst in mobilizing the nation's low-cost labor force, your company has helped the nation achieve double-digit economic growth. Following a political upheaval, however, a military government takes control. Workers' rights are being violated, as are those of individual citizens. As CEO, it is up to you to decide on a course of action. Should you pull out of the country, effectively abandoning your employees? Should you publicly and directly confront the leaders of the new government and insist that they respect workers' rights? Should you proceed more discreetly and pursue diplomacy out of the public's eye? Or, would another course of action be advisable? Can you make an ethical decision that is also a good business decision?

3. Many marketing research organizations and associations have codes of ethics that promote high standards of integrity for researchers working in the field or with clients. For example, members of the Qualitative Research Consultants Association (QRCA) agree to abide by a nine-point code of ethics that forbids such practices as discriminating in respondent recruitment and offering kickbacks or other favors in exchange for business. The code also calls for research to be conducted for legitimate research purposes, and not as a front for product promotion. Why do you think the QRCA and other market research organizations create such codes? Do you believe they are helpful in reducing unethical research practices? Why or why not?

13

selecting and managing entry modes

LEARNING OBJECTIVES

After studying this chapter, you should be able to

1 Explain why and how companies use *exporting, importing,* and *countertrade*.

2 Explain the various *means of financing* export and import activities.

3 Describe the different *contractual entry modes* that are available to companies.

4 Explain the various types of *investment entry modes*.

5 Discuss the important *strategic factors* in selecting an entry mode.

BEACONS

A Look Back
CHAPTER 12 explained how companies analyze international business opportunities. We learned how managers screen and research both potential markets and sites for operations.

A Look at This Chapter
This chapter introduces the different entry modes companies use to "go international." We discuss the important issues surrounding the selection and management of: (1) exporting, importing, and countertrade; (2) contractual entry modes; and (3) investment entry modes.

A Look Ahead
CHAPTER 14 explains the international marketing efforts of companies. We identify the key elements that influence how companies promote, price, and distribute their products.

Wal around the World

BENTONVILLE, Arkansas—With an astounding 1.2 million-strong staff, Wal-Mart (www.walmart.com) is the world's number one private-sector employer. With $216 billion in sales, it is the world's second-largest company—one based in a state in which chickens outnumber people. As it expands all around the world, Wal-Mart relies on its signature "Everyday Low Prices" policy to win over local customers.

When Wal-Mart first enters a market abroad or expands its presence there, it has many potential entry modes at its disposal, including joint ventures, acquisitions, and creating new subsidiaries from the ground up. Wal-Mart first became an international company in 1991 when it built a new store near Mexico City, Mexico. Today the company has more than 1,100 stores abroad.

Wal-Mart can also use the joint venture form of entry to learn the local culture and ways of doing business. When it first set foot in Brazil, Wal-Mart created a joint venture with a local company named Lojas Americanas. The company became a great asset to Wal-Mart in learning the ropes in Brazil. As Bob L. Martin, president and CEO of Wal-Mart International, said, "Lojas Americanas has been a valuable partner in helping us to achieve so much so fast in this new market . . . . They have helped us build a solid foundation which will serve as a springboard for additional expansion . . . ."

Wal-Mart expanded its presence in Korea using a mix of entry modes. The company bought four existing stores previously operated by Korea Makro and purchased six undeveloped sites on which it will build new stores. Its quest for profits growth is driving Wal-Mart's aggressive global expansion. The company expects international operations to account for one-third of its overall profits growth by 2006. As you read this chapter, think about why companies go international, the different market entry modes available to them, and when each mode is appropriate.[1]

entry mode
Institutional arrangement by which a firm gets its products, technologies, human skills, or other resources into a market.

The decision of how to enter a new market abroad is influenced by many factors, including the local business environment and a company's own core competency. An **entry mode** is the institutional arrangement by which a firm gets its products, technologies, human skills, or other resources into a market.[2] Companies thus seek entry to new marketplaces for the purpose of manufacturing and/or selling products within them. As we saw in this chapter's opening company profile of Wal-Mart, firms going international have many potential entry modes at their disposal, and their selection depends on many factors, including experience in a market, amount of control that managers desire, and potential size of the market. Let's now explore each of the three categories of entry modes that are available to companies:

1. Exporting, importing, and countertrade
2. Contractual entry
3. Investment entry

EXPORTING, IMPORTING, AND COUNTERTRADE

The most common method of buying and selling goods internationally is exporting and importing. Recall from Chapter 1 that *exporting* is the act of sending goods and services from one nation to others and that *importing* is the act of bringing goods and services into a country from other countries. Companies often import products in order to obtain less expensive goods or those that are simply unavailable in the domestic market. Companies export products when the international marketplace offers opportunities to increase sales and, in turn, profits. Companies worldwide often look to the United States as a great export opportunity because of the size of the market and the strong buying power of its citizens (see the World Business Survey titled "Land of Opportunity").

WORLD BUSINESS SURVEY

Land of Opportunity

Non-U.S. exporters often think of U.S. consumers when they consider international business opportunities. Many exporters truly see the U.S. market as a "Land of Opportunity" in which to sell their goods. Below are the top 10 exporters to the United States. As you can see, the list contains both developed and developing countries.

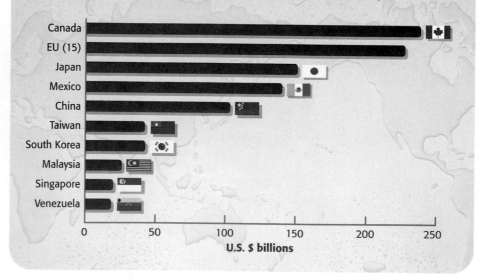

Because this chapter focuses on how companies take their goods and services to the global marketplace, the following discussion concentrates on exporting. The other side of the transaction, importing, is a sourcing decision for most firms and, therefore, is covered in Chapter 15. The subsequent section explains how companies use counter-trade to do business across borders when exporting and importing products in exchange for cash is not an option.

WHY COMPANIES EXPORT

In the global economy, companies increasingly sell goods and services to wholesalers, retailers, industrial buyers, and consumers in other nations. Generally speaking, there are three main reasons why companies begin exporting:

1. *Expand sales.* Most large companies use exporting as a means of expanding total sales when the domestic market has become saturated. Greater sales volume allows them to spread the fixed costs of production over a greater number of manufac-tured products, thereby lowering the cost of producing each unit of output. In short, going international is one way to achieve economies of scale.
2. *Diversify sales.* Exporting permits companies to diversify their sales. In other words, they can offset slow sales in one national market (perhaps due to a recession) with increased sales in another. Diversified sales can level off a company's cash flow—making it easier to coordinate payments to creditors with receipts from customers.
3. *Gain experience.* Companies often use exporting as a low-cost, low-risk way of get-ting started in international business. For example, owners and managers of small companies, which typically have little or no knowledge of how to conduct business in other cultures, use exporting to gain valuable international experience.

DEVELOPING AN EXPORT STRATEGY: A FOUR-STEP MODEL

Companies are often drawn into exporting when customers in other countries solicit their goods. This is a fairly natural way for companies to become aware of their prod-uct's international potential. In the process, companies get their first taste of how inter-national business differs from that in the domestic market. Unfortunately, it is also dur-ing these initial tentative steps outside the domestic market that companies commit their first international blunders.

Firms should not fall into the habit of simply responding to random international requests for their products. A more logical approach is to research and analyze interna-tional opportunities and to develop a coherent export strategy. A firm with such a strat-egy actively pursues export markets rather than sitting back and waiting for interna-tional orders to come in by fax or e-mail. Let's now take a look at each of the four steps in developing a successful export strategy.

Step 1: Identify a Potential Market In order to identify clearly whether demand exists in a particular target market, market research should be performed and the results interpreted (see Chapter 12). Novice exporters should focus on one or only a few markets. For example, a first-time Brazilian exporter might not want to export simultaneously to Argentina, Britain, and Greece. A better strategy would probably be to focus on Argentina because of its cultural similarities with Brazil (despite different, although related, languages). The company could then expand into more diverse markets after it gains some international experience in a nearby country. Also, the would-be exporter should seek the advice of experts on the regula-tions and the process of exporting in general, and exporting to the selected target market in particular.

Step 2: Match Needs to Abilities The next step is to assess carefully whether the company has the ability to satisfy the needs of the market. For instance, suppose a market located in a region with a warm, humid climate for much of the year displays the need for home air-conditioning equipment. If a company recognizes this need but makes only industrial-size air-conditioning equipment, it might not be able to satisfy demand with its current product. However, if the company is able to use its smallest industrial air-conditioning unit to satisfy the needs of several homes, it might have a market opportunity. If there are no other options or if consumers want their own individual units, the company will probably need to rule out entry into the market or design a smaller air-conditioning unit.

Step 3: Initiate Meetings Having meetings early with potential local distributors, buyers, and others is a must. Initial contact should focus on building trust and developing a cooperative climate among all parties. The cultural differences between the parties will come into play already at this stage. Beyond building trust, successive meetings are designed to estimate the potential success of any agreement if interest is shown on both sides. At the most advanced stage, negotiations take place and details of agreements are finalized.

A group of companies from Arizona called the Environmental Technology Industry Cluster was searching for a market for its environmental products in Taiwan. When a delegation from Taiwan arrived in the Arizona desert to survey the group's products, it was not all formal meetings and negotiations. Although the schedule during the day was busy with company visits, evenings were designed to build relationships, which are important to businesspeople from Taiwan. There were outdoor barbecues, hayrides, line dancing, and visits to Mexican restaurants and frontier towns to give the visitors from Taiwan a feel for local culture and history. To create the type of environment in which their counterparts from Taiwan prefer getting to know business associates, nighttime schedules also included visits to karaoke spots and Chinese restaurants, where a good deal of singing took place. Follow-up meetings resulted in several successful deals.[3]

Step 4: Commit Resources After all the meetings, negotiations, and contract signings, it is time to put the company's human, financial, and physical resources to work. First, the objectives of the export program must be clearly stated and should extend out at least 3 to 5 years. For small firms, it may be sufficient to assign one individual the responsibility for drawing up objectives and estimating resources. However, as companies expand their activities to include more products and/or markets, many firms discover the need for an export department or division. The head of this department usually has the responsibility (and authority) to formulate, implement, and evaluate the company's export strategy. See Chapter 11 for a detailed discussion of important organizational design issues to be considered at this stage.

DEGREE OF EXPORT INVOLVEMENT

Entrepreneurs, small and medium-sized companies, and large multinational firms all engage in exporting. However, not all companies get involved in exporting activities to the same extent. Some companies (usually entrepreneurs and small and medium-size firms) perform few or none of the activities necessary to get their products in a market abroad. Instead they use intermediaries that specialize in getting products from one market into another. Other companies (usually only the largest of companies) perform all of their export activities themselves, with an infrastructure that bridges the gap between the two markets. Let's take a closer look at the two basic forms of export involvement—*direct exporting* and *indirect exporting*.

direct exporting
Practice by which a company sells its products directly to buyers in a target market.

Direct Exporting Some companies become deeply involved in the export of their products. **Direct exporting** occurs when a company sells its products directly to buyers in a target market. Direct exporters operate in industries such as aircraft (Boeing) (www.boeing.com), industrial equipment (John Deere) (www.deere.com), apparel (Lands' End)(www.landsend.com), and bottled beverages (Evian) (www.evian.com). Bear in mind that "direct exporters" need not sell directly to *end users*. Rather, they take full responsibility for getting their goods into the target market by selling directly to local buyers and not going through intermediary companies. Typically, they rely on either local *sales representatives or distributors*.

Sales Representatives   A *sales representative* (whether an individual or an organization) represents only its own company's products, not those of other companies. They promote those products in many ways, such as by attending trade fairs and making personal visits to local retailers and wholesalers. They do not take title to the merchandise. Rather, they are hired by a company and normally are compensated with a fixed salary plus commissions based on the value of their sales.

Distributors   Alternatively, a direct exporter can sell in the target market through *distributors*, who take ownership of the merchandise when it enters their country. As owners of the products, they accept all the risks associated with generating local sales. They sell either to retailers and wholesalers or to end users through their own channels of distribution. Typically, they earn a profit equal to the difference between the price they pay and the price they receive for the exporter's goods. Although using a distributor reduces the exporter's risk, it also weakens the exporter's control over the prices actually charged to buyers. A distributor who charges unwarranted prices can stunt the growth of an exporter's market share. Therefore, it is important that exporters select reliable distributors. They should choose distributors who are willing to invest in the promotion of their products and who do not sell directly competing products. Despite the benefits of direct exporting, some companies implement a policy of *indirect exporting*.

Indirect Exporting   Some companies have few resources available to commit to exporting activities. Others simply find exporting a daunting experience because of a lack of contacts and experience. Fortunately, there is an option for such firms. **Indirect exporting** occurs when a company sells its products to intermediaries who then resell to buyers in a target market. The choice of intermediary depends on many factors, including the ratio of the exporter's international sales to its total sales, the company's available resources, and the growth rate of the target market. Let's take a closer look at several different types of intermediaries: *agents, export management companies*, and *export trading companies*.

indirect exporting
Practice by which a company sells its products to intermediaries who resell to buyers in a target market.

Agents   Individuals or organizations that represent one or more indirect exporters in a target market are called **agents**. Agents typically receive compensation in the form of commissions on the value of sales. Because establishing a relationship with an agent is relatively easy and inexpensive, it is a fairly common approach to indirect exporting. However, agents should be chosen very carefully because it can be costly and difficult to terminate an agency relationship if problems arise. Careful selection is also necessary because agents often represent several indirect exporters simultaneously. They might focus their promotional efforts on the products of the company paying the highest commission rather than on the company with the better products.

agents
Individuals or organizations that represent one or more indirect exporters in a target market.

Export Management Companies   A company that exports products on behalf of an indirect exporter is called an **export management company (EMC)**. An EMC operates contractually, either as an agent (being paid through commissions based on the value of sales) or as a distributor (taking ownership of the merchandise and earning a profit from its resale).

An EMC will usually provide additional services on a retainer basis, charging set fees against funds deposited on account. Typical EMC services include gathering market

export management company (EMC)
Company that exports products on behalf of indirect exporters.

information, formulating promotional strategies, performing specific promotional duties (such as attending trade fairs), researching customer credit, making shipping arrangements, and coordinating export documents. It is common for an EMC to exploit contacts predominantly in one industry (say, agricultural goods or consumer products) or in one geographic area (such as Latin America or the Middle East). Indeed, the biggest advantage of an EMC is usually a deep understanding of the cultural, political, legal, and economic conditions of the target market. Its staff works comfortably and effectively in the cultures of both the exporting and the target nation. The average EMC tends to deploy a wide array of commercial and political contacts to facilitate business activities on behalf of its clients.

Perhaps the only disadvantage of hiring an EMC is that the breadth and depth of its service can potentially hinder the development of the exporter's own international expertise. But an exporter and its EMC typically have such a close relationship that an exporter often considers its EMC as a virtual exporting division. When this is the case, exporters learn a great deal about the intricacies of exporting from their EMC. Then, after the EMC contract expires, it is common for a company to go it alone in exporting its products.

Export Trading Companies A company that provides services to indirect exporters in addition to activities directly related to clients' exporting activities is called an **export trading company** (ETC). Whereas an EMC is restricted to export-related activities, an ETC assists its clients by providing import, export, and countertrade services, developing and expanding distribution channels, providing storage facilities, financing trading and investment projects, and even manufacturing products.

European trading nations first developed the ETC concept centuries ago. More recently, the Japanese have refined the concept, which they call *sogo shosha*. The Japanese ETC can range in size from small, family-run businesses to enormous conglomerates such as C. Itoh (www.itochuele.co.jp), Mitsubishi (www.mitsubishi.com), and Mitsui (www.mitsui.com). The ETC in South Korea is called a *chaebol* and includes well-known companies such as Hyundai (www.hyundai.com) and Samsung (www.samsung.com).

Because of their enormous success in gaining market share in global markets, Japanese and South Korean ETCs became formidable competitors. These Asian companies quickly came to rival the dominance of large multinationals based in the United States. The U.S. multinationals lobbied lawmakers in their home country for assistance in challenging the large Asian ETCs in global markets. The result was the Export Trading Company Act, passed in 1982. Despite this effort, the ETC concept never really caught on in the United States. Operations of the typical ETC in the United States remain small and are dwarfed by those of their Asian counterparts. One reason for the lack of interest in the ETC concept in the United States relative to Asia is that governments, financial institutions, and companies have much closer working relationships in Asia. Thus, the formation of huge conglomerates that engage in activities ranging from providing financing to manufacturing to distribution is easier to accomplish. In contrast, the regulatory environment in the United States is wary of such cozy business arrangements, and the lines between companies and industries are more clearly drawn.

AVOIDING EXPORT AND IMPORT BLUNDERS

There are several errors common to companies that are new to exporting. First, many fail to conduct adequate market research before exporting. In fact, many companies begin exporting by responding to unsolicited requests for their products. If a company enters a market in this manner, it should quickly devise an export strategy to manage its export activities effectively and not strain its resources.

Second, many companies fail to obtain adequate export advice. National and regional governments are often willing to assist firms that are new to exporting. Such

---

export trading company (ETC)
Company that provides services to indirect exporters in addition to activities related directly to clients' exporting activities.

sources can help managers and small-business owners understand and cope with the vast amounts of paperwork required by each country's exporting and importing laws. Naturally, more experienced exporters can be extremely helpful as well. They can help novice exporters avoid embarrassing mistakes by guiding them through unfamiliar cultural, political, and economic environments.

To better ensure that it will not make embarrassing blunders, an inexperienced exporter might also wish to engage the services of a **freight forwarder**—a specialist in export-related activities such as customs clearing, tariff schedules, and shipping and insurance fees. Freight forwarders also can pack shipments for export and take responsibility for getting a shipment from the port of export to the port of import.

freight forwarder
Specialist in export-related activities such as customs clearing, tariff schedules, and shipping and insurance fees.

COUNTERTRADE

Companies are sometimes unable to import merchandise in exchange for financial payment. The two common reasons for this are that the government of the importer's nation lacks the hard currency to pay for imports or it restricts the convertibility of its currency. Fortunately, there is a way for firms to trade by using either a small amount of hard currency or even none at all. Selling goods or services that are paid for, in whole or part, with other goods or services is called **countertrade**. Although the effective use of countertrade often requires an extensive network of international contacts, even smaller companies can take advantage of its benefits.

Since the 1960s the formerly communist countries in Eastern and Central Europe have used countertrade extensively. The governments of some nations in Africa, Asia, and the Middle East also use countertrade. A lack of adequate hard currency has often forced those nations to employ countertrade to exchange oil for passenger aircraft and military equipment. Today, because of insufficient hard currency, developing and emerging markets frequently rely on countertrade to import goods. The greater involvement of firms from industrialized nations in those markets is causing the use of countertrade to increase.

countertrade
Practice of selling goods or services that are paid for, in whole or part, with other goods or services.

Types of Countertrade   There are several different types of countertrade: *barter, counterpurchase, offset, switch trading,* and *buyback.* Let's take a brief look at each of these.

With Argentina's economy mired in seemingly endless recession, barter is a way of life. Barter, or *trueque,* is a $400-million-a-year business nationwide. With unemployment on the rise and people strapped for cash, the use of *trueque* could grow further. In this market near Buenos Aires, you can swap audio CDs, clothing, fruit, pizzas, plumbing supplies, soup, and vegetables. Even local newspapers run ads for such things as apartments, cars, and washing machines, all offered on a barter basis.

➡ **Barter** is the exchange of goods or services directly for other goods or services without the use of money. It is the oldest known form of countertrade.

➡ **Counterpurchase** is the sale of goods or services to a country by a company that promises to make a future purchase of a specific product from that country. The purpose of this type of agreement is to allow the country to earn back some of the currency that it paid out for the original imports.

➡ **Offset** is an agreement that a company will offset a hard-currency sale to a nation by making a hard-currency purchase of an unspecified product from that nation in the future. It differs from a counterpurchase in that this type of agreement does not specify the type of product that must be purchased, just the amount that will be spent. Such an arrangement gives a firm greater freedom in fulfilling its end of a counter-trade deal.

➡ **Switch trading** is countertrade whereby one company sells to another its obligation to make a purchase in a given country. For example, in return for market access, a firm that wishes to enter a target market might promise to buy a product for which it has no use. The company then sells this purchase obligation to a large trading company that may make the purchase itself because it has a use for the merchandise. Alternatively, if the trading company has no use for the merchandise, it can arrange for yet another buyer, which has a use for the product, to make the purchase.

➡ **Buyback** is the export of industrial equipment in return for products produced by that equipment. This practice usually typifies long-term relationships between the companies involved.

Thus, countertrade can provide access to markets that are otherwise off-limits because of a lack of hard currency. But it can also cause a company a headache. The root cause is that much countertrade involves commodity and agricultural products such as oil, wheat, or corn—products whose prices on world markets tend to fluctuate a good deal. A problem arises when the price of a bartered product falls on world markets between the time that a deal is arranged and the time at which one party tries to sell the product. Thus, fluctuating prices generate the same type of risk that is encountered in currency markets. Managers might be able to hedge some of this risk on commodity futures markets in much the same way as they hedge against currency fluctuations in currency markets (see Chapter 9).

EXPORT/IMPORT FINANCING

International trade poses risks for both exporters and importers. Exporters run the risk of not receiving payment after their products are delivered. Importers fear that delivery might not occur once payment is made for a shipment. Accordingly, a number of export/import financing methods are designed to reduce the risk to which exporters and importers are exposed. These include *advance payment*, *documentary collection*, *letter of credit*, and *open account*. Let's take a closer look at each of these methods and the risk each holds for exporters and importers.

Advance Payment   Export/import financing in which an importer pays an exporter for merchandise before it is shipped is called **advance payment**. This method of payment is common when two parties are unfamiliar with each other, the transaction is relatively small, or the buyer is unable to obtain credit because of a poor credit rating at banks. Payment normally takes the form of a wire transfer of money from the bank account of the importer directly to that of the exporter. Although prior payment eliminates the risk of nonpayment for exporters, it creates the complementary risk of nonshipment for importers—importers might pay for goods but never receive them. Thus, advance payment is the most favorable method for exporters but the least favorable for importers (see Figure 13.1).

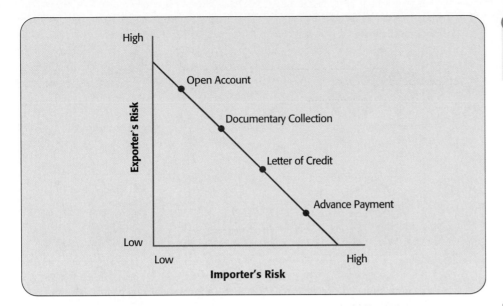

FIGURE 13.1

Risk of Alternative Export/Import Financing Methods

High

Open Account

Documentary Collection

Letter of Credit

Advance Payment

Low

Exporter's Risk

Low   High

Importer's Risk

Documentary Collection   Export/import financing in which a bank acts as an intermediary without accepting financial risk is called **documentary collection**. This payment method is commonly used when there is an ongoing business relationship between two parties. The documentary-collection process can be broken into three main stages and nine smaller steps (see Figure 13.2).

1. Before shipping merchandise, the exporter (with its banker's assistance) draws up a **draft (bill of exchange)**—a document ordering the importer to pay the exporter a specified sum of money at a specified time. A *sight draft* requires the importer to pay when goods are delivered. A *time draft* extends the period of time (typically 30, 60, or 90 days) following delivery by which the importer must pay for the goods. (When inscribed "accepted" by an importer, a time draft becomes a negotiable instrument that can be traded among financial institutions.)

2. Following the creation of the draft, the exporter delivers the merchandise to a transportation company for shipment to the importer. The exporter then delivers to its banker a set of documents that includes the draft, a *packing list* of items shipped, and a **bill of lading**—a contract between the exporter and shipper that specifies destination and shipping costs of the merchandise. The bill of lading is proof that the exporter has shipped the merchandise. An international ocean shipment requires an *inland bill of lading* to get the shipment to the exporter's border, and an *ocean bill of lading* for water transport to the importer nation. An international air shipment requires an *air way bill* that covers the entire international journey.

3. After receiving appropriate documents from the exporter, the exporter's bank sends the documents to the importer's bank. After the importer fulfills the terms stated on the draft and pays its own bank, the bank issues the bill of lading (which becomes title to the merchandise) to the importer.

Documentary collection reduces the importer's risk of nonshipment, because the packing list details the contents of the shipment and the bill of lading is proof that the merchandise was shipped. The exporter's risk of nonpayment is increased because although the exporter retains title to the goods until the merchandise is accepted, the importer does not pay until all necessary documents have been received. Although importers have the option of refusing the draft (and, therefore, the merchandise), this action is unlikely. Refusing the draft—despite all terms of the agreement being fulfilled—would cause the importer's bank to be leery of doing business with the importer in the future.

documentary collection
Export/import financing in which a bank acts as an intermediary without accepting financial risk.

draft (bill of exchange)
Document ordering an importer to pay an exporter a specified sum of money at a specified time.

bill of lading
Contract between an exporter and a shipper that specifies merchandise destination and shipping costs.

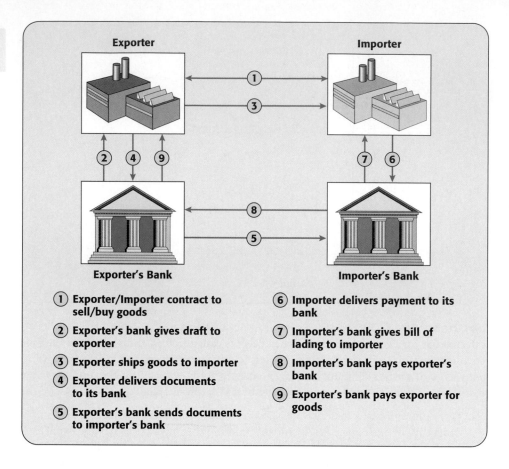

FIGURE 13.2

Documentary Collection Process

Exporter

Importer

Exporter's Bank

Importer's Bank

(1) Exporter/Importer contract to sell/buy goods

(2) Exporter's bank gives draft to exporter

(3) Exporter ships goods to importer

(4) Exporter delivers documents to its bank

(5) Exporter's bank sends documents to importer's bank

(6) Importer delivers payment to its bank

(7) Importer's bank gives bill of lading to importer

(8) Importer's bank pays exporter's bank

(9) Exporter's bank pays exporter for goods

Letter of Credit   Export/import financing in which the importer's bank issues a document stating that the bank will pay the exporter when the exporter fulfills the terms of the document is called **letter of credit**. A letter of credit is typically used when an importer's credit rating is questionable, when the exporter needs a letter of credit to obtain financing, and when a market's regulations require it.

Before a bank issues a letter of credit, it checks on the importer's financial condition. Banks normally issue letters of credit only after an importer has deposited on account a sum equal in value to that of the imported merchandise. The bank is still required to pay the exporter, but the deposit protects the bank if the importer fails to pay for the merchandise. Banks will sometimes waive this requirement for their most reputable clients.

There are several types of letters of credit:

➡ An *irrevocable letter of credit* allows the bank issuing the letter to modify its terms only after obtaining the approval of both exporter and importer.

➡ A *revocable letter of credit* can be modified by the issuing bank without obtaining approval from either the exporter or the importer.

➡ A *confirmed letter of credit* is guaranteed by both the exporter's bank in the country of export and the importer's bank in the country of import.

The letter of credit process for the payment of exports is shown in Figure 13.3. Following the issuance of a letter of credit, the importer's bank informs the exporter (through the exporter's bank) that a letter of credit exists and that it may now ship the merchandise. The exporter then delivers a set of documents (according to the terms of

letter of credit
Export/import financing in which the importer's bank issues a document stating that the bank will pay the exporter when the exporter fulfills the terms of the document.

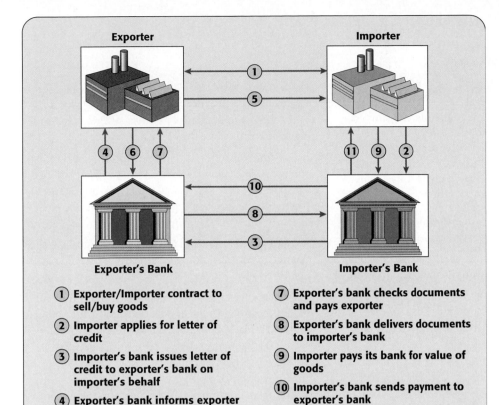

FIGURE 13.3
Letter of Credit Process

Exporter

Importer

Exporter's Bank

Importer's Bank

1. Exporter/Importer contract to sell/buy goods
2. Importer applies for letter of credit
3. Importer's bank issues letter of credit to exporter's bank on importer's behalf
4. Exporter's bank informs exporter of letter of credit
5. Exporter ships goods to importer
6. Exporter delivers documents to its bank

7. Exporter's bank checks documents and pays exporter
8. Exporter's bank delivers documents to importer's bank
9. Importer pays its bank for value of goods
10. Importer's bank sends payment to exporter's bank
11. Importer's bank delivers documents to importer

the letter) to its own bank. These documents typically include an invoice, customs forms, a packing list, and a bill of lading. The exporter's bank ensures that the documents are in order and pays the exporter.

When the importer's bank is satisfied that the terms of the letter have been met, it pays the exporter's bank. At that point, the importer's bank is responsible for collecting payment from the importer. Letters of credit are popular among traders because banks assume most of the risks. The letter of credit reduces the importer's risk of nonshipment (as compared with advance payment) because the importer receives proof of shipment before making payment. Although the exporter's risk of nonpayment is slightly increased, it is a more secure form of payment for exporters because the nonpayment risk is accepted by the importer's bank when it issues payment to the exporter's bank.

Open Account Export/import financing in which an exporter ships merchandise and later bills the importer for its value is called **open account**. Because some receivables may not be collected, exporters should reserve shipping on open account only for their most trusted customers. This payment method is often used when the parties are very familiar with each other or for sales between two subsidiaries within an international company. The exporter simply invoices the importer (as in many domestic transactions), stating the amount and date due. This method reduces the risk of nonshipment faced by the importer under the advance payment method.

open account
Export/import financing in which an exporter ships merchandise and later bills the importer for its value.

By the same token, the open account method increases the risk of nonpayment for the exporter. Thus, open account is the least favorable for exporters but the most favorable for importers. The Entrepreneurial Focus titled "Global Collection Guidelines" provides some insight on how small exporters can increase the probability of getting paid for a shipment.

CONTRACTUAL ENTRY MODES

The products of some companies simply cannot be traded in open markets because they are *intangible*. Thus, a company cannot use importing, exporting, or countertrade to exploit opportunities in a target market. Fortunately, there are other options for this type of company. A company can use a variety of contracts—*licensing, franchising, management contracts*, and *turnkey projects*—to market highly specialized assets and skills in markets beyond its nations' borders. Let's examine each of these entry modes in detail.

LICENSING

licensing
Practice by which one company owning intangible property (the licensor) grants another firm (the licensee) the right to use that property for a specified period of time.

Companies sometimes grant other firms the right to use an asset that is essential to the production of a finished product. **Licensing** is a contractual entry mode in which a company that owns intangible property (the *licensor*) grants another firm (the *licensee*) the right to use that property for a specified period of time. Licensors typically receive royalty payments based on a percentage of the licensee's sales revenue generated by the licensed property. The licensors might also receive a one-time fee to cover the cost of transferring the property to the licensee. Commonly licensed intangible property includes patents, copyrights, special formulas and designs, trademarks, and brand names. Thus, licensing often involves granting companies the right to use *process technologies* inherent to the production of a particular good.

Here are a few examples of successful licensing agreements:

➡ Novell (United States) licensed its software to three Hong Kong universities that installed it as the campuswide standard.

→ Hitachi (Japan) licensed from Duales System Deutschland (Germany) technology to be used in the recycling of plastics in Japan.

→ Hewlett-Packard (United States) licensed from Canon (Japan) a printer engine for use in its monochrome laser printers.

An *exclusive* license grants a company exclusive rights to produce and market a property, or products made from that property, in a specific geographic region. The region can be the licensee's home country or may extend to worldwide markets. A *nonexclusive* license grants a company the right to use a property but does not grant it sole access to a market. Thus, a licensor can grant several or more companies the right to use a property in the same region.

Cross licensing occurs when companies use licensing agreements to swap intangible property with one another. For example, Fujitsu (**www.fujitsu.com**) of Japan signed a 5-year cross-licensing agreement with Texas Instruments (**www.ti.com**) of the United States. The agreement allowed each company to employ the other's technology in the production of its own goods—thus lowering R&D costs. It was a very extensive arrangement, covering all but a few semiconductor patents owned by each company.[4] Because asset values are seldom exactly equal, cross licensing also typically involves royalty payments from one party to the other.

cross licensing
Practice by which companies use licensing agreements to exchange intangible property with one another.

Advantages of Licensing   There are several advantages to using licensing as an entry mode into new markets. First, licensors can use licensing to finance their international expansion. Most licensing agreements require licensees to contribute equipment and investment financing, whether by building special production facilities or by using existing excess capacity. Access to such resources can be a great advantage to a licensor who wants to expand but lacks the capital and managerial resources to do so. Moreover, because it need not spend time constructing and starting up its own new facilities, the licensor earns revenues sooner than it would otherwise.

Second, licensing can be a less risky method of international expansion for a licensor than other entry modes. For instance, whereas some markets are risky because of social or political unrest, others defy accurate market research for a variety of reasons. Licensing helps shield the licensor from the increased risk of operating its own local production facilities in markets that are unstable or hard to assess.

Third, licensing can help reduce the likelihood that a licensor's product will appear on the black market. The side streets of large cities in many emerging markets are dotted with tabletop vendors eager to sell bootleg versions of computer software, Hollywood films, and recordings of internationally popular musicians. Producers can, to some extent, foil bootleggers by licensing local companies to market their products at locally competitive prices. Granted, the royalties will be lower than the profits generated by sales at higher international prices, but lower profits are better than no profits at all—which is what owners get from bootleg versions of their products.

Finally, licensees can benefit from licensing by using it as a method of upgrading existing production technologies. For example, manufacturers of plastics and other synthetic materials in the Philippines are working to meet the high standards demanded by the local subsidiaries of Japanese electronics and office-equipment producers. Thus, D&L Industries of the Philippines upgraded its manufacturing process by licensing materials technology from Nippon Pigment of Japan.[5]

Disadvantages of Licensing   There also are some important disadvantages to using licensing. First, it can restrict a licensor's future activities. For example, suppose that a licensee is granted the exclusive right to use an asset but fails to produce the sort of results that a licensor expected. Because the license agreement is exclusive, the licensor cannot simply begin selling directly in that particular market to meet demand itself or contract with another licensee. Thus, a good product and lucrative market do not, in themselves, guarantee success for a producer trying to enter a market through the use of licensing.

Second, licensing might reduce the global consistency of the quality and marketing of a licensor's product in different national markets. A licensor might find the development of a coherent global brand image an elusive goal if each of its national licensees is allowed to operate in any manner it chooses. Promoting a global image might later require considerable amounts of time and money to change the misconceptions of buyers' in the various licensed markets.

Third, licensing might amount to a company "lending" strategically important property to its future competitors. This is an especially dangerous situation when a company licenses assets on which its competitive advantage is based. Licensing agreements are often made for several years or more (perhaps even a decade or more). During this time, licensees often become highly competent at producing and marketing the licensor's product. When the agreement expires, the licensor might find that its former licensee is capable of producing and marketing a better version of the product. Licensing contracts can (and should) restrict licensees from competing in the future with products based strictly on licensed property. However, enforcement of such provisions works only for identical or nearly identical products, not when substantial improvements are made.

FRANCHISING

Franchising is a contractual entry mode in which one company (the *franchiser*) supplies another (the *franchisee*) with intangible property and other assistance over an extended period. Franchisers typically receive compensation as flat fees, royalty payments, or both. The most popular franchises are those with widely recognized brand names, such as Mercedes (www.mercedes.com), McDonald's (www.mcdonalds.com), and Holiday Inn (www.holiday-inn.com). In fact, the brand name or trademark of a company is normally the single most important item desired by the franchisee. For this reason, smaller companies with lesser known brand names and trademarks have greater difficulty locating interested franchisees.

Franchising differs from licensing in several important ways. First, franchising gives a company greater control over the sale of its product in a target market. Franchisees must often meet strict guidelines on product quality, day-to-day management duties, and marketing promotions. Second, although licensing is fairly common in manufacturing industries, franchising is primarily used in service industries such as auto dealerships, entertainment, lodging, restaurants, and business services. Third, although licensing normally involves a one-time transfer of property, franchising requires ongoing assistance from the franchiser. In addition to the initial transfer of property, franchisers typically offer start-up capital, management training, location advice, and advertising assistance to their franchisees.

Some examples of the kinds of companies involved in international franchising include:

➡ Ozemail (Australia) awarded Magictel (Hong Kong) a franchise to operate its Internet phone and fax service in Hong Kong.
➡ Jean-Louis David (France) awarded franchises to franchisees for more than 200 of its hairdressing salons in Italy.
➡ Brooks Brothers (U.S.) awarded Dickson Concepts (Hong Kong) a franchise to operate Brooks Brothers stores across Southeast Asia.

Companies based in the United States dominate the world of international franchising. While U.S. companies were perfecting the practice of franchising (due to a large, homogeneous domestic market and low barriers to interstate trade and investment),

Like the Hong Kong Hilton shown here, the lodging industry typically relies on franchising to exploit international opportunities. Franchising allows Hilton (**www.hilton.com**) and others to maintain strict control over hotels carrying their names. In this way, they can ensure that guests experience a stay that meets the company's guidelines regarding such things as cleanliness, service, and meal preparation. Do you know of any other industries that employ franchising?

most other markets remained small and dissimilar to one another. However, franchising is growing in the European Union with the advent of a single currency and, since 1999, a unified set of franchise laws. Many European managers with comfortable early-retirement packages have discovered franchising to be an appealing second career. Franchising across much of Europe is expected to grow at between 10 percent and 15 percent per year through 2007.[6]

Despite projections for such robust growth, obstacles remain. For one thing, local European managers often misunderstand the franchising concept. For instance, Holiday Inn's Spanish franchise expansion is going more slowly than expected. According to the company's development director in Spain, Holiday Inn finds that it must convince local managers that the franchiser does not want to "take control" of their hotels.[7] In some eastern European countries, local managers do not understand why they must continue to pay royalties to brand and trademark owners. Franchise expansion in eastern European markets also suffers from a lack of local capital, high interest rates, high taxes, bureaucratic obstacles, restrictive laws, and corruption.[8]

Advantages of Franchising   There are several important advantages of franchising. First, franchisers can use franchising as a low-cost, low-risk entry mode into new markets. In particular, companies following global strategies rely on consistent products and common themes in worldwide markets. Franchising allows them to maintain consistency by replicating the processes for standardized products in each target market. However, many franchisers make small modifications in products and promotional messages when marketing specifically to local buyers. But because franchisers exercise a high degree of control over operations, they do maintain consistency across national markets.

Second, franchising is an entry mode that allows for rapid geographic expansion. Firms often gain a competitive advantage by being first in seizing a market opportunity. For instance, Microtel Inns & Suites (**www.microtelinn.com**) of Atlanta, Georgia, is using franchising to fuel its international expansion. Although it operates only 42 locations in the United States, Microtel is boldly entering Argentina and Uruguay and eyeing opportunities in Brazil and Western Europe. Rooms cost $50 to $60 per night and target business travelers who cannot afford $200 per night.[9]

Finally, franchisers can profit from the cultural knowledge and know-how of local managers. This aspect of franchising is helpful both in lowering the risk of business failure in unfamiliar markets and in creating a competitive advantage.

Disadvantages of Franchising   Franchising can also pose problems for both franchisers and franchisees. First, franchisers may find it cumbersome to manage a large number of franchisees in a variety of national markets. A major concern is that product quality and promotional messages among franchisees will not be consistent from one market to another. One way to ensure greater control is by establishing in each market a so-called *master franchisee* that is responsible for monitoring the operations of individual franchisees.

Second, franchisees can experience a loss of organizational flexibility in franchising agreements. Franchise contracts can restrict their strategic and tactical options, and they may even be forced to promote products owned by the franchiser's other divisions. For example, for years PepsiCo (**www.pepsico.com**) owned the well-known restaurant chains Pizza Hut, Taco Bell, and KFC. As part of their franchise agreements with PepsiCo, restaurant owners were required to sell only PepsiCo beverages to their customers. Many franchisees worldwide were displeased with such restrictions on their product offerings and were relieved when PepsiCo spun off the restaurant chains.[10]

MANAGEMENT CONTRACTS

management contract
Practice by which one company supplies another with managerial expertise for a specific period of time.

Under the stipulations of a **management contract**, one company supplies another with managerial expertise for a specific period of time. The supplier of expertise is normally compensated with either a lump-sum payment or a continuing fee based on sales volume. Such contracts are commonly found in the public utilities sectors of both developed and emerging markets.

Two types of knowledge can be transferred through management contracts—the specialized knowledge of technical managers and the business-management skills of general managers. BAA (**www.baa.co.uk**) of Britain, for example, possesses general airport-management skills. In the United States, BAA operates the Indianapolis Airport under a 10-year management contract and provides retail management at the Air Mall in the Pittsburgh Airport.[11]

Other examples of management contracts include:

➡ DBS Asia (Thailand) awarded a management contract to Favorlangh Communication (Taiwan) to set up and run a company supplying digital television programming in Taiwan.
➡ Lyonnaise de Eaux (France) and RWE Aqua (Germany) agreed to manage drinking-water quality and client billing and to maintain the water infrastructure for the city of Budapest, Hungary, for 25 years.

Advantages of Management Contracts   Management contracts can benefit both organizations and countries. First, a firm can award a management contract to another company and thereby exploit an international business opportunity without having to place a great deal of its own physical assets at risk. Financial capital can then be reserved for other promising investment projects that would otherwise not be funded.

Second, governments can award companies management contracts to operate and upgrade public utilities, particularly when a nation is short of investment financing. That is why the government of Kazakhstan contracted with a group of international companies called ABB Power Grid Consortium to manage its national electricity-grid system for 25 years. Under the terms of the contract, the consortium paid past wages owed to workers by the government and is to invest more than $200 million during the first 3 years of the agreement. The Kazakhstan government had neither the cash flow to pay the workers nor the funds to make badly needed improvements.[12]

Third, governments use management contracts to develop the skills of local workers and managers. For example, ESB International (www.esb.ie) of Ireland signed a 3-year contract not only to manage and operate a power plant in Ghana, Africa, but also to train local personnel in the skills needed to manage it at some point in the future.[13]

Disadvantages of Management Contracts   Unfortunately, management contracts also pose two important disadvantages for suppliers of expertise. For one thing, although management contracts reduce the exposure of physical assets in another country, the same is not true for the supplier's personnel. International management in countries that are undergoing political or social turmoil, can place managers' lives in significant danger.

Secondly, suppliers of expertise may end up nurturing a formidable new competitor in the local market. After learning how to conduct certain operations, the party that had originally needed assistance may be in a position to compete on its own. Obviously, firms must weigh the financial returns from a management contract against the potential future problems caused by a newly launched competitor.

TURNKEY PROJECTS

When one company designs, constructs, and tests a production facility for a client, the agreement is called a **turnkey (build–operate–transfer) project**. The term *turnkey project* derives from the understanding that the client, who normally pays a flat fee for the project, is expected to do nothing more than simply "turn a key" to get the facility operating. The expression conveys the fact that the company awarded a turnkey project leaves absolutely nothing undone when preparing the facility for the client.

Like management contracts, turnkey projects tend to be large-scale and often involve government agencies. However, unlike management contracts, turnkey projects transfer special process technologies or production-facility designs to the client. They typically involve the construction of power plants, airports, seaports, telecommunication systems, and petrochemical facilities that are then turned over to the client. Under a management contract, the supplier of a service retains the asset—the managerial expertise.

turnkey (build–operate–transfer) project
Practice by which one company designs, constructs, and tests a production facility for a client firm.

A turnkey project is a venture in which one organization designs, builds, and tests a facility for another, which then merely "turns the key" to get things underway. This arrangement characterizes the building of four hydroelectric dams on Turkey's Coruh River. The Turkish government benefited from the expertise of two international consortiums it hired for the project. What other types of operations do you think would be appropriate for a turnkey project?

Here are two examples of international turnkey projects:

➡ Telecommunications Consultants India constructed telecom networks in both Madagascar and Ghana—two turnkey projects worth a combined total of $28 million.

➡ Lubei Group (China) agreed with the government of Belarus to join in the construction of a facility for processing a fertilizer by-product into cement.

Advantages of Turnkey Projects   Turnkey projects provide benefits to both providers and recipients. First, turnkey projects permit firms to specialize in their core competencies and to exploit opportunities that they could not undertake alone. Mobil Exploration (now ExxonMobil, www.exxonmobil.com), for example, awarded a turnkey project to PT McDermott Indonesia (www.mcdermott.com) and Toyo Engineering (toyo-eng.co.jp) of Japan to build a liquid natural gas plant on the Indonesian island of Sumatra. The providers are responsible for constructing an offshore production platform, laying a 100-kilometer underwater pipeline, and building an on-land liquid natural gas refinery. The $316 million project is feasible only because each company will contribute unique expertise to the design, construction, and testing of the facilities.[14]

Second, turnkey projects allow governments to obtain designs for infrastructure projects from the world's leading companies. For instance, Turkey's government enlisted two separate consortiums of international firms to build four hydroelectric dams on its Coruh River. The dams combine the design and technological expertise of each company in the two consortiums.[15] The Turkish government also awarded a turnkey project to Ericsson (www.ericsson.com) of Sweden to expand the country's mobile telecommunication system.[16]

Disadvantages of Turnkey Projects   Among the disadvantages of turnkey projects is the fact that a company may be awarded a project for political reasons rather than for technological know-how. Because turnkey projects are often of high monetary value and awarded by government agencies, the process of awarding them can be highly politicized. When the selection process is not entirely open, companies with the best political connections often win contracts, usually at inflated prices—the costs of which are typically passed on to local taxpayers.

Second, like management contracts, turnkey projects can create future competitors. A newly created local competitor could become a major supplier in its own domestic market and perhaps even in other markets in which the supplier operates. Therefore, companies try to avoid projects in which there is danger of transferring their core competencies to others.

INVESTMENT ENTRY MODES

The final category of entry modes is investment entry. Investment entry modes entail direct investment in plant and equipment in a country coupled with ongoing involvement in the local operation. Entry modes in this category take a company's commitment to a market to the next level. Let's now explore three common forms of investment entry: *wholly owned subsidiaries*, *joint ventures*, and *strategic alliances*.

WHOLLY OWNED SUBSIDIARIES

wholly owned subsidiary
Facility entirely owned and controlled by a single parent company.

As the term suggests, a **wholly owned subsidiary** is a facility entirely owned and controlled by a single parent company. Companies can establish a wholly owned subsidiary either by forming a new company from the ground up and constructing entirely new facilities (such as factories, offices, and equipment) or by purchasing an existing company and internalizing its facilities. Whether an international subsidiary is purchased or newly created depends to a large extent on its proposed operations. For example, when a parent company designs a subsidiary to manufacture the latest high-tech products, it typically must build new facilities because state-of-the-art operations are hard to locate. In other words, it is easier to find companies in most target markets that make pots and pans rather than produce the most advanced computer chips. The major drawback of creation from the ground up is the time it takes to construct new facilities, hire and train employees, and launch production.

Conversely, finding an existing local company capable of performing marketing and sales will be easier because special technologies are typically not needed. By purchasing the existing marketing and sales operations of an existing firm in the target market, the parent can have the subsidiary operating relatively quickly. Buying an existing company's operations in the target market is a particularly good strategy when the company to be acquired has a valuable trademark, brand name, or process technology.

Advantages of Wholly Owned Subsidiaries   There are two main advantages to entering a market using a wholly owned subsidiary. First, managers have complete control over day-to-day operations in the target market and over access to valuable technologies, processes, and other intangible properties within the subsidiary. Complete control also decreases the chance that competitors will gain access to a company's competitive advantage, which is particularly important if it is technology-based. Managers also retain complete control over the subsidiary's output and prices. Unlike licensors and franchisers, the parent company also receives all profits generated by the subsidiary.

Second, a wholly owned subsidiary is a good mode of entry when a company wants to coordinate the activities of all its national subsidiaries. Companies employing global strategies (see Chapter 11) view each of their national markets as one part of an interconnected global market. Thus, the ability to exercise complete control over a wholly owned subsidiary makes this entry mode attractive to companies that are pursuing global strategies.

Disadvantages of Wholly Owned Subsidiaries   Wholly owned subsidiaries also present two primary disadvantages. First, they can be expensive undertakings. Companies must finance investments internally or raise funds in financial markets. Therefore, obtaining the needed funding can be difficult for small and medium-size companies. As a rule, only large companies are equipped to establish international wholly owned subsidiaries. However, citizens of one country living abroad in another country can find their unique knowledge and abilities an advantage.

Second, risk exposure is high because a wholly owned subsidiary requires substantial company resources. One source of risk is political or social uncertainty or outright instability in the target market. Such risks can place both physical assets and personnel in serious jeopardy. The sole owner of a wholly owned subsidiary also accepts all the risk that buyers will reject the company's product. Parent companies can reduce this risk by gaining a better understanding of target-market consumers prior to entry into the market.

JOINT VENTURES

Under certain circumstances, companies prefer to share ownership of an operation rather than take complete ownership. A separate company that is created and jointly owned by two or more independent entities to achieve a common business objective is called a **joint venture**. Joint venture partners can be privately owned companies, government agencies, or government-owned companies. Each party may contribute anything valued by its partners, including managerial talent, marketing expertise, market access, production technologies, financial capital, and superior knowledge of or techniques of research and development.

joint venture
Separate company that is created and jointly owned by two or more independent entities to achieve a common business objective.

Examples of joint ventures include:

→ A joint venture between Suzuki Motor Corporation (Japan) and the government of India to manufacture a small-engine car specifically for the Indian market

→ A joint venture between a group of Indian companies and a Russian partner to produce television sets in Russia for the local market

→ Biltrite Corporation (United States) and Shenzhen Petrochemical (China) created a shoe-soling factory as a joint venture in China to supply international shoe manufacturers located in China

Joint Venture Configurations As you can see from Figure 13.4, there are four main joint venture configurations.[17] Although we illustrate each of these as consisting of just two partners, each configuration can also apply to ventures of several or more partners.

Forward Integration Joint Venture Figure 13.4(a) outlines a joint venture characterized by *forward integration*. In this type of joint venture, the parties choose to invest together in *downstream* business activities—activities farther along in the "value system" that are normally performed by others. For instance, Hewlett-Packard (www.hp.com) and Apple Computer (www.apple.com) opening a retail outlet in a developing country would

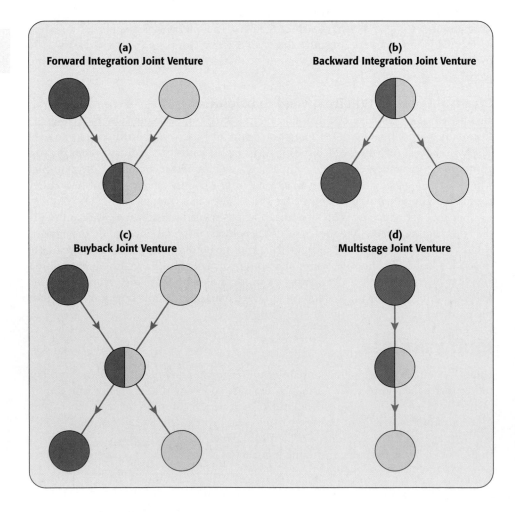

FIGURE 13.4

Alternative Joint Venture Configurations

(a)
Forward Integration Joint Venture

(b)
Backward Integration Joint Venture

(c)
Buyback Joint Venture

(d)
Multistage Joint Venture

be a joint venture characterized by forward integration. The two companies now perform activities normally performed by retailers farther along in the product's journey to buyers.

Backward Integration Joint Venture Figure 13.4(b) outlines a joint venture characterized by *backward integration*. In other words, the joint venture signals a move by each company into *upstream* business activities—activities earlier in the value system that are normally performed by others. Such a configuration would result if two steel manufacturers formed a joint venture to mine iron ore. The companies now engage in an activity that is normally performed by mining companies.

Buyback Joint Venture Figure 13.4(c) outlines a joint venture whose input is provided by, and whose output is absorbed by, each of its partners. A *buyback joint venture* is formed when each partner requires the same component in its production process. It might be formed when a production facility of a certain minimum size is needed to achieve economies of scale, but neither partner alone enjoys enough demand to warrant building it. However, by combining resources the partners can construct a facility that serves their needs while achieving savings from economies of scale production. For instance, this was one reason behind the $500 million joint venture between Chrysler (www.chrysler.com) and BMW (www.bmw.com) to build small-car engines in Latin America. Each party benefited from the economies of scale offered by the plant's annual production capacity of 400,000 engines—a volume that neither company could absorb alone.

Multistage Joint Venture Figure 13.4(d) outlines a joint venture that features downstream integration by one partner and upstream integration by another. A *multistage joint venture* often results when one company produces a good or service required by another. For example, a sporting goods manufacturer might join with a sporting goods retailer to establish a distribution company designed to bypass inefficient local distributors in a developing country.

Advantages of Joint Ventures Joint ventures offer several important advantages to companies going international. Above all, companies rely on joint ventures to reduce risk.[18] Generally, a joint venture exposes fewer of a partner's assets to risk than would a wholly owned subsidiary—each partner risks only its own contribution. That is why a joint venture entry might be a wise choice when market entry requires a large investment or when there is significant political or social instability in the target market. Similarly, a company can use a joint venture to learn about a local business environment prior to launching a wholly owned subsidiary.[19] In fact, many joint ventures are ultimately bought outright by one of the partners after it gains sufficient expertise in the local market.

Second, companies can use joint ventures to penetrate international markets that are otherwise off-limits. For instance, some governments either require nondomestic companies to share ownership with local companies or provide incentives for them to do so. Such requirements are most common among governments of developing countries. The goal is to improve the competitiveness of local companies by having them team up with and learn from international partner(s).

Third, a company can gain access to another company's international distribution network through the use of a joint venture. The joint venture between Caterpillar (www.caterpillar.com) of the United States and Mitsubishi Heavy Industries (www.mitsubishi.com) of Japan was designed to improve the competitiveness of each against a common rival, Komatsu (www.komatsu.com) of Japan. While Caterpillar gained access to Mitsubishi's distribution system in Japan, Mitsubishi got access to Caterpillar's global distribution network—helping it to compete more effectively internationally.[20]

Finally, companies form international joint ventures for defensive reasons. Entering a joint venture with a local government or government-controlled company gives the government a direct stake in the venture's success. In turn, the local government will be less likely to interfere if it means that the venture's performance will suffer. This same strategy can also be used to create a more "local" image when feelings of nationalism are running strong in a target country.

Disadvantages of Joint Ventures   Among its disadvantages, joint venture ownership can result in conflict between partners. Conflict is perhaps most common when management is shared equally—that is, when each partner supplies top managers in what is commonly known as a "50–50 joint venture." Because neither partner's managers have the final say on decisions, managerial paralysis can result, causing problems such as delays in responding to changing market conditions. Conflict can also arise from disagreements over how future investments and profits are to be shared. Parties can reduce the likelihood of conflict and indecision by establishing unequal ownership, whereby one partner maintains 51 percent ownership of the voting stock and has the final say on decisions. A multiparty joint venture (commonly referred to as a *consortium*) can also feature unequal ownership. For example, ownership of a four-party joint venture could be distributed 20–20–20–40, with the 40 percent owner having the final say on decisions.

Second, loss of control over a joint venture's operations can also result when the local government is a partner in the joint venture. This situation occurs most often in industries considered culturally sensitive or important to national security, such as broadcasting, infrastructure, and defense. Thus, the profitability of a joint venture could suffer because the local government would have motives that are based on cultural preservation or security.

STRATEGIC ALLIANCES

Sometimes companies who are willing to cooperate with one another do not wish to go so far as to create a separate jointly owned company. A relationship whereby two or more entities cooperate (but do not form a separate company) to achieve the strategic goals of each is called a **strategic alliance**. Like joint ventures, strategic alliances can be formed for relatively short periods or for many years, depending on the goals of the participants. Strategic alliances can be established between a company and its suppliers, its buyers, and even its competitors. In forming such alliances, sometimes each partner purchases a portion of the other's stock. In this way, each company has a direct stake in its partner's future performance. In turn, this stake decreases the likelihood that one partner will try to take advantage of the other.

Examples of strategic alliances include:

➡ An alliance between Siemens (Germany) and Hewlett-Packard (United States) to create and market devices used to control telecommunications systems
➡ A strategic alliance between Nippon Life Group (Japan) and Putnam Investments (United States) to permit Putnam to develop investment products and manage assets for Nippon

Advantages of Strategic Alliances   Strategic alliances offer several important advantages to companies. First, companies use strategic alliances to share the cost of an international investment project. For example, many firms are developing new products that not only integrate the latest technologies but also shorten the life spans of existing products. In turn, the shorter life span is reducing the number of years during which a company can recoup its investment. Thus, many companies are cooperating to share the costs of developing new products. For example, Toshiba (www.toshiba.com) of Japan, Siemens (www.siemens.com) of Germany, and IBM (www.ibm.com) of the United States shared the $1 billion cost of developing a facility near Nagoya, Japan, to manufacture small, efficient computer memory chips.

strategic alliance
Relationship whereby two or more entities cooperate (but do not form a separate company) to achieve the strategic goals of each.

Second, companies use strategic alliances to tap into competitors' specific strengths. Some alliances formed between Internet portals and technology companies are designed to do just that. For example, an Internet portal provides access to a large, global audience through its Web site, while the technology company supplies its know-how in delivering, say, music over the Internet. Meeting the goal of the alliance—marketing music over the Web—requires the competencies of both partners.

Finally, companies turn to strategic alliances for many of the same reasons that they turn to joint ventures. Some use strategic alliances to gain access to a partner's channels of distribution in a target market. Others use them to reduce exposure to the same kinds of risks from which joint ventures provide protection.

Disadvantages of Strategic Alliances   Perhaps the most important disadvantage of a strategic alliance is that it can create a future local or even global competitor. For example, one partner might be using the alliance to test a market and prepare the launch of a wholly owned subsidiary. By declining to cooperate with others in the area of its core competency, a company can reduce the likelihood of creating a competitor that would threaten its main area of business. Likewise, a company can insist on contractual clauses that constrain partners from competing against it with certain products or in certain geographic regions. Firms are also careful to protect special research programs, production techniques, and marketing practices that are not committed to the alliance. Naturally, managers must weigh the potential for encouraging new competition against the benefits of international cooperation.

As in the case of joint ventures, conflict can arise and eventually undermine cooperation. As a rule, then, alliance contracts are drawn up to cover as many such contingencies as possible. Even so, communication and cultural differences can arise. As Tsuyoski Kawanishi, Toshiba (www.toshiba.com) director and senior executive vice president for partnerships and alliances, explains, "Each pact includes the equivalent of a prenuptial agreement, so both sides know who gets what if the partnership doesn't work out. During the honeymoon time, everything is great. But as you know, divorce is always a possibility, and that's when things can get bitter."[21]

SELECTING PARTNERS FOR COOPERATION

Every company's goals and strategies are influenced by both its competitive strengths and the challenges it faces in the marketplace. Because the goals and strategies of any two companies are never exactly alike, cooperation can be difficult. Moreover, ventures and alliances often last many years, perhaps even indefinitely. Therefore, partner selection is a crucial ingredient for success. The following discussion focuses on partner selection in joint ventures and strategic alliances. However, many of the same points, also apply to contractual entry modes such as licensing and franchising, in which choosing the right partner is also important.

Every partner must be firmly committed to the goals of the cooperative arrangement. Many companies engage in cooperative forms of business, but the reasons behind each party's participation are never identical. Sometimes, a company stops contributing to a cooperative arrangement once it achieves its own objectives. Therefore, detailing the precise duties and contributions of each party to an international cooperative arrangement through prior negotiations can go a long way toward ensuring continued cooperation. See the Global Manager titled "Negotiating the Terms of Market Entry" for some important considerations in negotiating international agreements.

Although the importance of locating a trustworthy partner seems obvious, cooperation should be approached with caution. Companies can have hidden reasons for cooperating. Sometimes they try to acquire more from cooperation than their partners realize. If a hidden agenda is discovered during the course of cooperation, trust can

GLOBAL MANAGER

Negotiating the Terms of Market Entry

The participants in any international business arrangement must negotiate the terms of their deals. A cooperative atmosphere between partners to a deal depends on both parties viewing contract negotiations as a success. Managers should be aware of the negotiation process and influential factors. The process normally occurs in four stages.

Stage 1: Preparation. Negotiators must develop a clear vision of what the company wants to achieve. For instance, is the proposed business arrangement a one-time technology transfer to a local company or the first phase of a long-term relationship?

Stage 2: Launch of Discussions. Discussions begin with each side stating its opening position—the most favorable terms for itself. Parties might state their positions immediately or make them known gradually so as to leave themselves room to modify them.

Stage 3: Bargaining and Persuasion. The bargaining power of each party plays an important role in the final outcome of negotiations. Although this is the stage at which direct conflict is most likely, cultures differ in their attitudes toward conflict. For instance, Chinese negotiators try to avoid conflict more than Canadians do. But if conflict erupts the Chinese are more likely to pursue negative strategies, including calling off talks.

Stage 4: Agreement. Negotiations reaching this stage are a success. Negotiators from Western cultures view the signing of contracts as the end of negotiations. Yet in most Asian cultures it signals the beginning of a long-term working relationship; terms can be modified as the relationship matures and circumstances change.

Two key elements influence international business negotiations:

Cultural Elements. Negotiating styles differ from one culture to another. Negotiating in Asian cultures revolves around protecting the other party from losing face (being embarrassed or shamed). Thus, "victory" normally means that each party gives equal ground and meets the other halfway. In most Western cultures negotiators typically hope to gain as many concessions as possible with little concern for whether the other party appears to have "lost" the negotiations.

Political and Legal Elements. Negotiators must be aware of any political motives underlying their counterparts' strategy. For example, an inflexible public posture might simply be a ploy to show company or government officials back home that they are working first and foremost in the company's or nation's interest. Also, consumer groups, labor unions, and even stockholders can influence the outcome of a firm's negotiations. If consumer groups feel that a proposed arrangement will increase prices or restrict product choice, they might lobby government officials to kill the deal.

---

break down—in which case the cooperative arrangement is virtually destroyed. Because trust is so important, firms naturally prefer partners with whom they have had a favorable working relationship in the past. However, such arrangements are much easier for large multinationals than for small and medium-size companies with little international experience and few international contacts.

Each party's managers must be comfortable working with people of other cultures and traveling to (even perhaps living in) other cultures. As a result, cooperation will go more smoothly and the transition—both in work life and personal life—will be easier for those managers who are sent to work for a joint venture. Each partner's managers should also be comfortable working with, and within, one another's corporate culture. For example, although some companies encourage the participation of subordinates in decision making, others do not. Such differences often reflect differences in national culture, and when managers possess cultural understanding, adjustment and cooperation is likely to run more smoothly.[22]

Above all, a suitable partner must have something valuable to offer. Firms should avoid cooperation simply because they are approached by another company. Rather, managers must be certain that they are getting a fair return on their cooperative efforts. In short, they must evaluate the benefits of a potential international cooperative arrangement just as they would any other investment opportunity.

The choice of entry mode has many important strategic implications for a company's future operations.[23] Because enormous investments in time and money can go into determining an entry mode, the choice must be made carefully. Several key factors that influence a company's international entry mode selection are the *cultural environment*, *political and legal environments*, *market size*, *production and shipping costs*, and *international experience*. Let's now explore each of these factors in-depth.

CULTURAL ENVIRONMENT

As we saw in Chapter 2, the dimensions of culture—values, beliefs, customs, languages, religions—can differ greatly from one nation to another. In such cases, managers can be less confident in their ability to manage operations in the host country. They can be concerned about the potential not only for communication problems but also for inter-personal difficulties. As a result, they may avoid investment entry modes in favor of exporting or a contractual mode. On the other hand, cultural similarity encourages manager confidence and thus the likelihood of investment. Likewise, the importance of cultural differences diminishes when managers are knowledgeable about the culture of the target market.[24]

POLITICAL AND LEGAL ENVIRONMENTS

As mentioned earlier in this chapter, political instability in a target market increases the risk exposure of investments. That is why significant political differences and levels of instability cause companies to avoid large investments and to favor entry modes that shelter assets.

A target market's legal system also influences the choice of entry mode. For example, certain import regulations such as high tariffs or low quota limits can encourage investment: A company that produces locally avoids tariffs that increase product cost and does not have to worry about making it into the market below the quota (if there is one). But low tariffs and high quota limits discourage investment. Also, governments may enact laws that ban outright certain types of investment. For many years (but no longer), China banned wholly owned subsidiaries by non-Chinese companies and required that they form joint ventures with local partners. Finally, because investment entry often gives a company greater control over assets and marketing, firms tend to prefer investment when a market is lax in enforcing copyright and patent laws.

MARKET SIZE

The size of a potential market also influences the choice of entry mode. For example, rising incomes in a market encourage investment entry modes because investment allows a firm to prepare for expanding market demand and to increase its understanding of the target market. Thus, high domestic demand in China is attracting investment in joint ventures, strategic alliances, and wholly owned subsidiaries. On the other hand, if investors believe that a market is likely to remain relatively small, better options might include exporting or contractual entry.

PRODUCTION AND SHIPPING COSTS

By helping to control total costs, low-cost production and shipping can give a company an advantage. Accordingly, setting up production in a market is desirable when the total cost of production there is lower than in the home market. Low-cost local production might also encourage contractual entry through licensing or franchising. If production costs are sufficiently low, the international production site might even begin supplying other markets, including the home country. An additional potential benefit of local production might be that managers observe buyer behavior and modify products to be better suited to the needs of the local market. Lower production costs at home makes it more appealing to export to international markets.

Naturally, companies that turn out products with high shipping costs typically prefer local production. Contractual and investment entry modes are viable options in this case. Alternatively, exporting is feasible when products have relatively lower shipping costs. Finally, because they are subject to less price competition, products for which there are fewer substitutes or those that are discretionary items can more easily absorb higher shipping and production costs. In this case exporting is a likely selection.

INTERNATIONAL EXPERIENCE

By way of summary, Figure 13.5 illustrates the control, risk, and experience relationships of each entry mode. Most companies enter the international marketplace through exporting. As companies gain international experience, they will tend to select entry modes that require deeper involvement. But this means that they must accept greater risk in return for greater control over operations and strategy. Eventually, they may explore the advantages of licensing, franchising, management contracts, and turnkey projects. Once they become comfortable in a particular market, joint ventures, strategic alliances, and wholly owned subsidiaries become viable options.

Bear in mind that this evolutionary path of accepting greater risk and control with experience does not hold for every company. Whereas some firms remain fixed at one point, others skip several entry modes altogether. In particular, advances in technology and transportation are allowing more and more small companies to leapfrog several stages at once. These relationships will also vary for each company depending on its product and the relevant characteristics of the home and target markets.

FIGURE 13.5

Evolution of the Entry Mode Decision

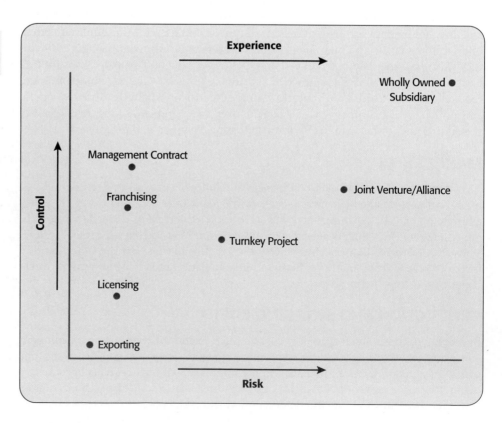

This chapter explained the important factors in selecting entry modes and key aspects in their management. We studied the circumstances under which each entry mode is most appropriate and the advantages and disadvantages that each provides. The choice of which entry mode(s) to use in entering international markets matches a company's international strategy. Some companies will want entry modes that give them tight control over international activities because they are pursuing a global strategy, for example. Meanwhile, another company might not require an entry mode with central control because it is pursuing a multinational strategy. The entry mode must also be chosen to align well with an organization's structure.

There is a variety of additional material available on the Companion Website that accompanies this book. You can access this information by visiting the Website at (www.prenhall.com/wild).

summary

❶ Explain why and how companies use *exporting, importing,* and *countertrade.* Companies begin exporting to *expand sales, diversify sales,* or *gain experience.* Companies often use exporting as a low-cost, low-risk way of getting started in international business. A successful export strategy involves four steps: (1) *Identify a potential market;* (2) *Match needs to abilities;* (3) *Initiate meetings;* and (4) *Commit resources.*

There are two basic forms of export involvement. *Direct exporting* occurs when a company sells its products directly to buyers in a target market. Typically, they rely on either local *sales representatives* (who represent only their own company's products, not those of other companies) or *distributors* (who take ownership of merchandise when it enters their countries). *Indirect exporting* occurs when a company sells its products to intermediaries who then resell to buyers in a target market. There are three general types of intermediaries: *agents* (individuals or organizations that represent one or more indirect exporters in a target market); *export management companies* (firms that export products on behalf of indirect exporters); and *export trading companies* (firms that provide services to indirect exporters in addition to the activities directly related to clients' exporting activities).

Selling goods or services that are paid for, in whole or part, with other goods or services is called *countertrade.* There are several different types of countertrade: (a) *barter;* (b) *counterpurchase;* (c) *offset;* (d) *switch trading;* and (e) *buyback.*

❷ Explain the various *means of financing* export and import activities. With *advance payment,* an importer pays an exporter for merchandise before it is shipped. *Documentary collection* calls for a bank to act as an intermediary without accepting financial risk. A *draft (bill of exchange)* is a document ordering the importer to pay the exporter a specified sum of money at a specified time. A *bill of lading* is a contract between an exporter and a shipper that specifies destination and shipping costs of the merchandise.

Under a *letter of credit,* the importer's bank issues a document stating that the bank will pay the exporter when the exporter fulfills the terms of the document. There are several types of letters of credit. An *irrevocable letter of credit* allows the bank issuing the letter to modify the terms of the letter only after obtaining the approval of both exporter and importer. A *revocable letter of credit* can be modified by the issuing bank without obtaining approval from either the exporter or the importer. A *confirmed letter of credit* is guaranteed by both the exporter's bank in the country of export and the importer's bank in the country of import.

Finally, under *open account,* an exporter ships merchandise and later bills the importer for its value.

❸ Describe the different *contractual entry modes* that are available to companies. The products of some companies simply cannot be traded in open markets because they are *intangible.* *Licensing* is a contractual entry mode in which a company that owns intangible property (the *licensor*) grants another firm (the *licensee*) the right to use that property for a specified period of time. An *exclusive* license grants a company exclusive rights to produce and market a property, or products made from that property, in a specific geographic region. A *nonexclusive* license grants a company the right to use a property but does not grant it sole access to a market. *Cross licensing* occurs when companies employ licensing agreements to swap intangible property with one another.

Franchising is a contractual entry mode in which one company (the *franchiser*) supplies another (the *franchisee*) with intangible property and other assistance over an extended period. Under the stipulations of a *management contract*, one company supplies another with managerial expertise for a specific period of time. Two types of knowledge can be transferred through management contracts—the specialized knowledge of technical managers and the business-management skills of general managers.

When one company designs, constructs, and tests a production facility for a client, the agreement is called a *turnkey (build–operate–transfer) project*. Turnkey projects permit firms to specialize in their core competencies and to exploit opportunities that they could not undertake alone.

4 **Explain the various types of *investment entry modes*.** *Investment entry modes* entail the direct investment in plant and equipment in a country coupled with ongoing involvement in the local operation. A *wholly owned subsidiary* is a facility entirely owned and controlled by a single parent company.

A separate company that is created and jointly owned by two or more independent entities to achieve a common business objective is called a *joint venture*. In a joint venture characterized by *forward integration*, the parties choose to invest together in downstream business activities. A joint venture characterized by *backward integration* signals a move by each company into upstream business activities. A *buyback joint venture* is one whose input is provided by, and whose output is absorbed by, each of its partners. A *multistage*

joint venture features downstream integration by one partner and upstream integration by another.

A relationship in which two or more entities cooperate (but do not form a separate company) to achieve the strategic goals of each is called a *strategic alliance*. Companies use strategic alliances to share the cost of an international investment project, tap into competitors' strengths, and gain access to a distribution channels.

5 **Discuss the important *strategic factors* in selecting an entry mode.** The key factors that influence a company's international entry mode selection are the *cultural, political, and legal environments, market size, production and shipping costs*, and *international experience*.

Managers are typically less confident in their ability to manage operations in unfamiliar cultures and may avoid investment entry modes in favor of exporting or a contractual mode. On the other hand, cultural similarity increases the likelihood of investment. Likewise, political differences and levels of instability cause companies to avoid large investments and favor entry modes that shelter assets.

The size of a potential market also influences the choice of entry mode. For example, rising incomes in a market encourage investment entry modes because investment allows a firm to prepare for expanding market demand and to increase its understanding of the target market.

Setting up production in a market is desirable when the total cost of production in that market is lower than in the home market. Naturally, companies that turn out products with high shipping costs typically prefer local production. Contractual and investment entry modes are viable options in this case. Alternatively, exporting is feasible when products have relatively lower shipping costs.

Finally, most companies make their initial foray into the international marketplace through exporting. As companies gain international experience, they will tend to select entry modes that require deeper involvement.

questions for review

1. What are the three categories of *entry mode* available to companies? Explain how they differ from one another.

2. What are the four steps of building an export strategy? Describe each briefly.

3. How does *direct exporting* differ from *indirect exporting*?

4. Explain how *export management companies (EMCs)* differ from *export trading companies (ETCs)*.

5. What are the four primary methods of *export/import financing*? Discuss the risks each poses for exporters and importers.

6. Why do companies engage in *countertrade*? List the five kinds of countertrade.

7. What is *licensing*? Identify the advantages and disadvantages of licensing.

8. Define *franchising*. How does it differ from *licensing*?

9. What is a *management contract*? Identify the two types of knowledge transferred using management contracts.

10. Explain how *turnkey projects* differ from management contracts.

11. What is a *wholly owned subsidiary*? State its advantages and disadvantages.

12. What is a *joint venture*? Identify the four joint venture configurations.

13. Explain how *strategic alliances* differ from joint ventures.

14. List several points to consider when selecting a partner for cooperation.

15. What *strategic factors* should be considered when selecting an entry mode? Discuss each briefly.

questions for discussion

1. Not all companies "go international" by exporting, then using contracts, and then investing in other markets. How does a company's product influence the process of going international? How (if at all) is technology, like the Internet, affecting the process of going international?

2. "Companies should use investment entry modes whenever possible because they offer the greatest control over business operations." Do you agree or disagree with this statement? Are there times when other types of market entry offer greater control? When is investment entry a poor option?

3. In earlier chapters, we learned how governments get involved in the international flow of trade and foreign direct investment. We also learned how regional economic integration is influencing international business. Identify two market entry modes and describe how each might be affected both by the actions of governments and by increasing regional integration.

in practice

Read the article below and answer the questions that follow.

Kyocera Forms China Joint Venture

TOKYO, Japan—Kyocera said Thursday that it is setting up a joint venture in Dongguan, China, to produce and market laser printers and digital copying machines.

The new company, called Kyocera Mita Office Equipment (Dongguan) Co., will have an initial capitalization of $15 million and a staff of 5,500 people. Kyocera will own 90 percent of the venture, and a local entity will own 10 percent. The joint venture will ship products to the global market and sell them in China.

"The purpose of forming the joint venture with a local entity is to market the products in China," said a Kyocera spokesman. Most of the current production of laser printers and copying machines at its Hong Kong plant will be transferred to the new plant in China, the spokesman said.

1. Locate an article or two in the business press that discusses the economics of the electronics industry today. What do you think are Kyocera's reasons for forming the joint venture with a local partner in China? List as many potential reasons as you can. Did macroeconomics play a role in the move?

2. The article states that the local partner will own just 10 percent of the joint venture. What do you think is the main motivation to form the venture from the perspective of the Chinese partner? Again, list as many possible reasons as you can.

3. Review Chapter 2 and locate several references that discuss Chinese culture and Japanese culture. Because of the cultural differences between the two peoples, what potential problems do you think the venture could face in the future? Do you think differences in organizational culture that are rooted in national culture will also play a role in possible future conflicts?

projects

1. Make a list of five goods or services that you have consumed within the past week (this list might include food products, Internet services, television programs, etc.). For the company that produces each of these, which entry modes are possible options for entering new markets? Provide a one- to two-paragraph explanation of your answer for each good or service.

2. With several of your classmates, interview a manager of a company involved in international business. What method did the company use to go international initially? Which entry mode is the company currently using? Does the company export? If so, is it a direct or an indirect exporter? How does the company receive payment for its goods? Does the company use different entry modes in different markets? What factors influenced its choice of entry mode in each case? How do managers deal with cultural differences when negotiating across cultures? Provide any other information on the company that is relevant to the discussion of market entry.

3. The following project is designed to introduce you to the complexity of negotiations and to help develop your negotiating skills.

    Background: A western European automobile manufacturer is considering entering markets in Southeast Asia. The company wants to construct an assembly plant outside Bangkok, Thailand, to assemble its lower-priced cars. Major components would come in from manufacturing plants in Brazil, Poland, and China. The cars would then be sold in emerging markets throughout Southeast Asia and the Indian subcontinent. Managers are hoping to strike a $100 million joint venture deal with the Thai government. The company would supply technology and management for the venture, and the government would contribute a minority share of financing to the venture. The company considers the government's main contributions to be providing tax breaks (and other financial incentives) and a stable business environment in which to operate.

    Financial capital is flowing into Thailand at a fair pace, although not in the volume it did in the mid-1990s. The currency is strong and inflation remains low. Unlike some other nations in the region, there is general political and social stability. The new auto assembly plant would boost the local economy, reduce unemployment, and increase local wages. Some local politicians fear the company might be interested only in exploiting the country's relatively low cost labor.

    Activity: Break into an equal number of negotiating teams of three or four persons. Half the teams are to represent the company and the other half, the government. As a team, meet for 15 minutes to develop your opening position and negotiating strategy. Meet with a team from the other side and undertake 20 minutes of negotiations. After the negotiating session, spend 15 minutes comparing the progress of your negotiations with that of the other pairs of teams.

business case 13

THE BRAVE NEW WORLD OF TELECOMMUNICATION JOINT VENTURES

The world of telecommunications is changing. The era of the global information superhighway is upon us, driven by new technologies such as cellular telephones, fax machines, and fiber optic cable that make possible video telephone connections and high-speed data transmission. Annual worldwide revenues for telecommunications services total $600 billion, with international companies accounting for 20 percent of the business.

Market opportunities are opening around the world as post, telephone, and telegraph (PTT) monopolies are undergoing privatization. Since 1998 telecom deregulation has been taking place in earnest in Europe. Meanwhile, governments in developing countries are boosting investments in infrastructure improvements to increase the number of available telephone lines. The demand for telephone service is growing at a sharp pace—international telephone call volume more than doubled over a recent 6-year period. The net result of these changes is the globalization of the telecommunications industry. As William Donovan, a vice president at Sea-Land Service, said recently, "I don't want to have to talk to a bunch of different PTTs around the world. I don't want to have to go to one carrier in one country and a second in another just because it doesn't have a presence there."

Several alliances and joint venture partnerships have been formed between companies hoping to capitalize on the changed market and business environment. France Telecom, Deutsche Telekom, and Sprint created Global One to bring international telecommunications services to Multinational companies. As part of the deal, Sprint sold 10 percent of its stock to each of its French and German partners. One hurdle for the company has been to integrate the three partners' communication networks into a unified whole. Start-up costs have been high, and the need to communicate in three different languages has created some friction among personnel. Early on, lengthy negotiations were required to reach agreement about the value each partner brought to the venture. A former Global One executive noted, "There is no trust among the partners." Other problems include equipment and billing incompatibilities resulting from distribution agreements with telephone monopolies in individual countries. And financial losses prompted Sprint chairman William T. Esrey to install Sprint executive Gary Forsee as CEO and president of Global One.

AT&T is also depending on various partnership strategies as entry modes. WorldPartners began in 1993 as an alliance of AT&T, Kokusai Denshin Denwa (KDD) of Japan, and Telecom of Singapore. The goal was to provide improved telecommunications services for companies conducting business globally. Guaranteeing that virtually any call can be completed required better wiring as well as improved network transmissions systems. Today WorldPartners is comprised of 10 companies, including Telecom New Zealand, Telstra (Australia), Hong Kong Telecom, and Unisource.

Unisource is itself a joint venture that originally included Sweden's Telia AB, Swiss Telecom PTT, and PTT Telecom Netherlands. Later, Telefonica de España became an equal equity partner in Unisource. Unisource and AT&T then agreed to form a 60–40 joint venture known as AT&T-Unisource Communications services to offer voice, data, and messaging services to businesses with European operations. AT&T would have preferred to form a joint venture with the French or German telephone companies. However, European regulators, concerned about AT&T's strong brand name and enormous size, refused to approve such a deal.

There was strong logic for the deal. As AT&T–Unisource CEO James Cosgrove explained from headquarters near Amsterdam in Hoofddorp, "You have to be European to play in Europe and yet you have to offer global solutions." Despite the fact that there are five corporate parents, a sense of equality and congeniality has developed. Notes CEO Cosgrove, "Working practices of 2 years have ironed out remarkably well. We have learned that you have to see this thing as a common operation. Otherwise too many bad compromises can be made." The presence of Telefonica de España in the alliance was especially significant for AT&T because the Spanish company has a strong influence in Latin America. Unfortunately, the alliance was weakened when Telefonica decided to ally itself with Concert. To fill the void, AT&T and Italy's Stet announced a new alliance that would expand communication services to Latin America as well as Europe.

The third major telecommunications alliance, Concert Communications, was formed when British Telecommunications PLC bought a 20 percent stake in MCI Communications. Again, the goal of the alliance was to offer global voice and data network services to global corporations.

thinking globally

1. What strengths did AT&T bring to its joint venture with Unisource?

2. Can you think of any potential complications that could arise in the AT&T–Unisource joint venture?

3. Assess the formation of Global One, Unisource, and other partnerships discussed in this case in terms of the strategic factors for selecting entry modes identified in the chapter.

a question of ethics

1. U.S. firms doing business in Russia today must grapple with both differences and similarities between the ways in which U.S. and Russian managers view business ethics. The four categories of business behaviors and principles listed below have been proposed. After studying them tell what you think a U.S. businessperson could do to minimize ethical friction when doing business in Russia.

   - Those considered ethical by both U.S. and Russian managers: keeping one's word, maintaining trust, fair competition, and rewards commensurate with performance.
   - Those considered unethical by both U.S. and Russian managers: gangsterism, racketeering, extortion, black marketeering, price gouging, and failure to honor debts.
   - Those considered ethical by Russian managers but unethical by U.S. managers: personal favoritism, "grease" payments, price-fixing, data manipulation, and ignoring nonsensical laws and regulations.
   - Those considered ethical by U.S. managers but unethical by Russian managers: maximizing profits, exorbitant differentials in salaries, layoffs, and whistle-blowing.[25]

2. A recent study investigated the differences between ethical perceptions of business managers from Australia and Hong Kong. The researchers determined that two factors had an impact on the perception of ethical problems: (a) culture and (b) the particular mode of market entry (e.g., exporting, contractual, investment in subsidiaries, or joint ventures). What ethical issues do you think might arise in conjunction with the market entry modes discussed in this chapter?

3. Special ethical concerns can arise when international companies consider a cooperative form of market entry (such as a joint venture) with local partners. This is especially true when each partner contributes personnel in addition to physical and financial assets. Perhaps the most important ethical concern is how to set the joint venture's ethical guidelines when the venture employs people from widely divergent cultural backgrounds. Cultural perspectives cause people to see ethical decisions differently. Is there anything that two partners from diverse cultures can do to establish ethical principles in such a situation—either before or after formation of the cooperative arrangement? Can you think of a company that succeeded in the face of such difficulties?

14

developing and marketing products

LEARNING OBJECTIVES

After studying this chapter, you should be able to

1 Explain the impact *globalization* is having on international marketing activities.

2 Describe the types of things that managers must consider when developing international *product strategies*.

3 Discuss the factors that influence international *promotional strategies* and the blending of product and promotional strategies.

4 Explain the elements that managers must take into account when designing international *distribution strategies*.

5 Discuss the elements that influence international *pricing strategies*.

BEACONS

A Look Back

CHAPTER 13 explained the pros and cons of international entry modes and when each one is most appropriately used. We also described management issues with regard to each entry mode and the important strategic factors in their selection.

A Look at This Chapter

This chapter explores how globalization and differences in national business environments impact the development and marketing of products internationally. We examine the many variables that must be considered when creating product, promotional, distribution, and pricing strategies.

A Look Ahead

CHAPTER 15 explains how companies launch and manage their international production efforts. Again, an emphasis is placed on how environmental variables affect production strategies.

Learning to Fly

VIENNA, Austria—When Dietrich Mateschitz traveled to Asia on business, he got a taste of some popular energy drinks. Sensing opportunity, he brought a sample of the drinks back to Austria and started Red Bull, GmbH (**www.redbull.com**) in 1987. Red Bull Energy Drink is now sold in more than 45 countries, generating over $1 billion in revenue each year.

Red Bull is identical in every market in which it's sold. The slender red, blue, and silver can packs 8.3 ounces of caffeine, carbohydrates, vitamins, and taurine—an amino acid. That's music to the ears of club-goers who swear by the drink's ability to keep them going till dawn. In fact, sales are soaring partly due to the word-of-mouth advertising the company gets from loyal customers. "We're building a billion-dollar brand . . . . We've been surprised at how powerful word of mouth is," says a company spokesperson.

Red Bull is also racking up double-digit revenue growth with creative TV ads in some markets. The ads display the company's "Red Bull Gives You Wings" tag line after cartoon characters float into the air after downing a can of the sweet stuff. The company also sponsors top athletes and sporting events, including windsurfing, snowboarding, hang-gliding, and skateboarding. Around the world, Red Bull recruits young people to be "brand ambassadors" to hand out free samples at events and hires "student managers" who spread the word and drink on campuses.

And although some people complain about the extreme sweetness of the drink, the company doesn't seem to mind. "It's not meant to be a taste drink, you either love us or you hate us," says the spokesperson. So far, it seems that many are running with the bulls. As you read this chapter, think about the many ways that products are marketed around the world.[1]

In earlier chapters, we continually emphasized the greater complexity of managing an international business as compared with a purely domestic one. Myriad differences in all aspects of a nation's business environment complicate management. Managing marketing activities that span time zones and cultures can test the most seasoned marketing managers.

We first introduced the concept of globalization and how it affects international business activities in Chapter 1 and returned continuously to this theme in subsequent chapters. We have seen that globalization's impact is not uniform. It affects different industries and products in different ways and to varying degrees. Some companies can take advantage of globalization's effects and create a single product that is marketed identically around the world. As we saw in this chapter's opening company profile, Red Bull (www.redbull.com) markets an identical energy drink in the same manner in over 45 countries around the world. Others realize that differences in national business environments are too great to ignore. This group then must create new products, modify promotional campaigns, or adjust their marketing strategies in some other way.

We begin this chapter by taking a brief look at the debate over the extent to which globalization *should* affect marketing strategies. We then describe how marketing internationally differs in terms of how companies create their product strategies, promote and advertise a product, decide on a pricing strategy, and design distribution channels. Throughout the chapter, we examine how globalization on one hand and national differences on the other is impacting international marketing activities.

GLOBALIZATION AND MARKETING

Globalization is transforming the way some products are marketed internationally, but not all. Some companies implement a global strategy that uses similar promotional messages and themes to market the same product around the world. Others find that their products require physical changes so that they suit the tastes of consumers in markets abroad. Yet other products need different marketing campaigns to reflect the unique circumstances of local markets. How do managers decide when their marketing strategies need modifying? In this section, we explain the impact of globalization on the standardization versus adaptation decision.

STANDARDIZATION VERSUS ADAPTATION

In a well-known article, U.S. researcher Theodore Levitt argued that because the world is becoming standardized and homogeneous, companies should market the same products in the same way in all countries.[2] Technology, claimed Levitt, was already causing people's needs and preferences to converge throughout the world. He urged companies to reduce production and marketing costs by standardizing both the physical features of their products and their strategies for marketing them.

Since that article appeared some researchers have countered that standardization is just one of a number of strategies with which firms have successfully entered the international marketplace.[3] Still others argue that standardization is not always the best strategy and advise smaller companies to adapt to local cultures while exploiting their unique international images to gain local market share.[4]

Influence of National Business Environments Consumers in different national markets often demand products that reflect their unique tastes and preferences. Cultural, political, legal, and economic environments have a great deal to do with the

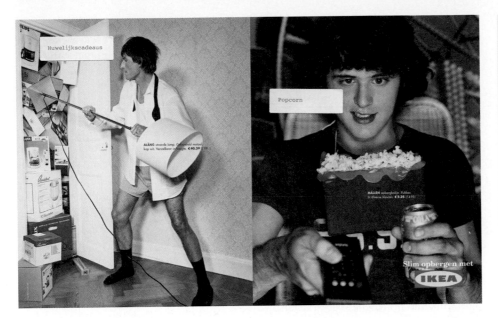

preferences of both consumers and industrial buyers worldwide. Recall from Chapter 2 that a culture's aesthetics involves, among other things, preferences for certain colors. Ohio-based Rubbermaid (www.rubbermaid.com) discovered the role of aesthetics as it attempted to increase its international sales. Consumers in the United States prefer household products in neutral blues or almond; in southern Europe, red is the preferred color. The Dutch want white. In addition, many European cultures perceive plastic products as inferior and want tight lids on metal wastebaskets as opposed to U.S.-style plastic versions with open tops.[5]

But certain products do appeal to practically all cultures. Although it is not a traditional Asian drink, a passion for red wine is currently sweeping Asian markets such as Hong Kong, Singapore, Taiwan, and Thailand. Driving this demand are medical studies reporting the health benefits of red wine (the king of Thailand has publicly proclaimed its healthy properties). But other factors—including the fact that red is considered good luck in many Asian cultures—are also at work. Many Asians choose red wine at restaurants because of its image as the beverage of choice for people who are sophisticated and successful. (The same is not true of white wine because from a distance it may resemble water.) Today in Beijing, fashionable young people often give red wine as a housewarming present instead of the traditional favorites of their parents and grandparents.[6]

Product standardization is more likely when nations share the same level of economic development. In the 1980s, consumers in India faced limited options when it came to purchasing automobiles. Most were made in India, expensive, and not fuel-efficient. Thanks to a fairly good record of economic progress over the past two decades, Indian consumers have a better standard of living and more discretionary income. Affording an imported brand-name automobile with a global reputation, such as Suzuki (www.suzuki.co.jp) or Ford (www.ford.com), is more commonplace in Indian cities than it was years ago.

With this brief introduction to some of the relevant issues to international marketing strategy behind us, let's take an in-depth look at the elements that influence a company's *product*, *promotional*, *distribution*, and *pricing strategies*.

DEVELOPING PRODUCT STRATEGIES

Companies can standardize or adapt their products in many alternative ways when they decide to "go international." Let's take a look at some of the factors that influence the standardize-versus-adapt decision as well as several other international product strategy issues.

LAWS AND REGULATIONS

Companies often must adapt their products to satisfy the laws and regulations in a target market. Consider the dilemma facing chocolate makers in a unified European Union (EU). People's tastes, of course, vary across markets, and taste in chocolate is no exception to the rule. A so-called Chocolate War has erupted in the EU as it tries to standardize member countries' product content regulations. On one side stand the so-called cocoa purists, including Belgium, France, Germany, Spain, Italy, The Netherlands, Luxembourg, and Greece. Opposite stand Britain, Denmark, Portugal, Austria, Finland, and Sweden—nations who permit manufacturers to add vegetable fats to chocolate products. The purists argue not only that European advertising should restrict the word "chocolate" to 100 percent cocoa products, but also that the term "milk chocolate" be outlawed altogether. They want nonpure products labeled something like "chocolate with milk and noncocoa vegetable fats."[7]

The fact that many developing countries have fewer consumer-protection laws creates an ethical issue for some companies. Ironically, lower levels of education and less buying experience mean that consumers in developing countries are more likely to need protection. However, many governments impose fewer regulations in order to hold down production costs and consumer prices. Unfortunately, this can be an invitation for international distributors to withhold full information about products and their potential dangers.

CULTURAL DIFFERENCES

Companies also adapt their products to suit local buyers' product preferences that are rooted in culture. Häagen-Dazs (www.haagendazs.com) is an international company that prides itself in its ability to identify the taste preferences of consumers in target markets. It then modifies its base product with just the right flavor to make a product that satisfies consumers' needs. Following years of trial and error developing secret formulas and conducting taste tests, Häagen-Dazs finally launched its green-tea flavor ice cream throughout Japan. The taste is that of *macha* tea—an elite strain of green tea that's been used in elaborate Japanese ceremonies for centuries. Green-tea ice cream was a hit instantly and one day may even surpass Häagen-Dazs' perennial flavor champion in Japan—vanilla.[8]

Not all companies need to modify their product to the culture; instead they may need to identify a different cultural need that it satisfies. Altoids (www.altoids.com), for example, is a British product that has been used for 200 years to soothe upset stomachs. But the company identified a different use for its product in the United States. Because of its strong flavor, Altoids also acts as a breath mint. Altoids breath mints have pushed aside weaker-flavored candies, including Certs (www.certs.com), to command 17 percent of the $281 million U.S. market.[9]

BRAND AND PRODUCT NAMES

brand name
Name of one or more items in a product line that identifies the source or character of the items.

Several issues related to a company's brand name are important concerns for the day-to-day activities of international managers. A **brand name** is the name of one or more items in a product line that identifies the source or character of the items. When we see a product labeled with a particular brand name, we assign to that product a certain value based on our past experiences with that brand. That is why a brand name is central to a product's personality and the image that it presents to buyers. It informs buyers about a product's source and protects both customer and producer from copycat products. Brand names help consumers to select, recommend, or reject products; they also function as legal property that owners can protect from trespass by competitors.

Indeed, a strong brand can become a company's most valuable asset and primary source of competitive advantage. A consistent worldwide brand image is increasingly important as more consumers and businesspeople travel internationally than ever before. Any inconsistency in brand name can confuse existing and potential customers. Although companies keep their brand names consistent across markets, they often do create new product names or modify existing ones to suit local preferences.

Companies also need to review the image of their brand from time to time and update it if it seems old fashioned. For instance, Lipton (www.lipton.com) is trying to get people to think of Lipton tea as an alternative to colas and other soft drinks. Since the 1890s Lipton had as its mascot Sir Thomas J. Lipton, the tea maker's founder. But in a major overhaul of the brand all references to Mr. Lipton were removed. "The guy had to go," admits vice president John Caron. "The Lipton brand is known all over the world, but people told us, 'My mother drinks that stuff.' In the world of branding, that isn't a good thing." Lipton booted the founder in favor of 'Tom,' a sassy young Briton.[10]

Selecting International Brand and Product Names　Whether they are standardized or adapted locally, products in international markets need carefully selected names. All company and product brand names (like all nouns) are made up of *morphemes*—semantic elements, or language building blocks, such as the *van* in *advantage*. NameLab (www.namelab.com) is an identity-consultant firm that uses over 6,000 morphemes to develop new product names. NameLab points out that because most Western languages stem from the same linguistic source—Indo-European—companies can create brand names having similar meanings in these nations. *Accu*, for example, connotes *accuracy* in both Western and Japanese cultures. Thus, Honda (www.honda.com) created the upscale car division Acura. Other names that are constructed to have similar connotations in many languages or to embody no cultural bias include Compaq (www.compaq.com), Kodak (www.kodak.com), and Sony (www.sony.co.jp).[11] Once a name is chosen, companies can survey local native speakers about their reactions to it.

A brand name is central to a product's personality and to how buyers perceive it. Shown in this photo illustration are some of the most powerful global brands that exist today. As you can see, they span all sorts of industries, including photographic film, delivery services, mobile phones, financial services, computer software, and aerospace. Take a moment to think about some of the brands shown here. What is your perception of each?

These techniques help companies reduce the likelihood of committing potential marketing blunders.

Brand names seldom offend people in international markets, but product names can be highly offensive if they are not carefully researched and selected. Clarks Shoes (www.clarks.com), a British shoe company, once gave a name to a line of shoes that was offensive to the Hindu religious community in Britain. Consequently, the company had to issue the following apology in the British press:[12]

> Clarks Shoes are concerned that the naming of some of their products with the names of Hindu Gods Vishnu and Krishna has caused hurt and offence to the British Hindu Community. The Company apologises for this mistake and is withholding the products before resuming sales with new names. In the future the company will carry out more detailed research before naming products.

Other times, product names must be changed not because they're offensive, but because they mislead consumers. Consider the problem faced by the British beverage and chocolate producer Cadbury Schweppes (www.cadburyschweppes.com). When Swiss chocolate manufacturers sued on the grounds that the public was being misled into thinking that Cadbury's Swiss Chalet bar was genuine Swiss chocolate, the company was forced to withdraw the product from the marketplace. A British court confirmed that the name and packaging of the product—the "Swiss" part of the name and the image of a snow-capped Swiss Alp—were likely to mislead consumers.[13]

NATIONAL IMAGE

The value that customers obtain from a product is heavily influenced by the image of the country in which it is designed, manufactured, or assembled. We consider the influence of a country's name when thinking of Italian shoes, German luxury cars, and Japanese electronics. This image can be positive for some products but negative for others. For example, the best Russian caviar and vodkas have reputations of quality around the world. But what about Russian automobiles or computers? Attaching "Russia" to certain products is beneficial, whereas attaching it to others could be a detriment.

Because it affects buyers' perceptions of quality and reliability, national image is an important element of product policy. However, national image can and does change over time—although slowly. Decades ago, Japanese products were considered to be of poor quality and rather unreliable. But a national effort toward quality improvement and the installation of quality-control procedures by companies earned Japan a national image for precision and quality products.[14] Japanese cars, which were once vehicles for the budget-conscious consumer, now have luxury models that rival the quality and technological advancement of German autos.

Likewise, years ago Taiwan was known for basic, no-frills items such as toys and industrial products of all sorts. But today many of Taiwan's industries possess a reputation for innovation—designing products that reflect decades of investing in people's research and engineering skills. One company that benefited from an intense devotion to R&D is Giant Manufacturing (www.giant-bicycles.com), Taiwan's leading bicycle manufacturer. The company began in Taichung, Taiwan, nearly three decades ago producing bikes under the brand names of other companies. But in 1980 the company began to manufacture under its own brand and today has a solid niche in the mountain bike market. Giant's innovation in using lightweight materials and creating groundbreaking designs even earned it sponsorship of Spain's world-champion racing team. Today, high-tech products, and even those not traditionally thought of as high tech (such as bikes), stamped "Made in Taiwan" command respect in global markets.[15]

COUNTERFEIT GOODS AND BLACK MARKETS

In Chapter 3 we discussed how companies are trying to protect their intellectual property and trademarks from counterfeit goods. Recall that *counterfeit goods* are imitation products passed off as legitimate trademarks, patents, or copyrighted works—products that normally enjoy legal protection. Because developing nations often are weakest in enforcing such legal protections, they normally have the most active counterfeiting markets. Countries that top the list for the portion of their markets comprised of counterfeits include Bulgaria, China, India, Russia, and Turkey. Currently representing between 5 and 10 percent of international trade, counterfeiting is worth as much as $50 billion to $80 billion worldwide.[16]

Counterfeiting is common among highly visible brand-name consumer goods, including watches, perfumes, clothing, movies, music, and computer software. Counterfeit products are typically sold to consumers on what is called the *black market*—a marketplace of underground transactions that typically appears because a product is either illegal (such as counterfeits) or tightly regulated. Tabletop vendors working the back streets of the world's largest cities represent the retail side of the black market. For instance, in Sofia, the capital of Bulgaria, you can buy one CD-ROM that contains 50 software applications for $10; buying all the official versions of these products would cost about $5,000.[17] In Estonia's Kadaka flea market you can find the full Microsoft Office (**www.microsoft.com**) software bundle for around $18—about one fiftieth of its official selling price.[18] Increasingly, engineered industrial components such as aircraft parts, medicines, and other pharmaceutical products are also becoming targets of counterfeiters.

Counterfeit goods can damage buyers' image of a brand when the counterfeits are of inferior quality—which is nearly always the case. Buyers who purchase an item bearing a company's brand name expect a certain level of craftsmanship and, therefore, satisfaction. But when the product fails to deliver on the expectations, the buyer is dissatisfied and the company's reputation is tarnished. Japanese motorcycle manufacturers recently saw their sales in China fall sharply as people are buying near-replicas of their products at discounts of up to 40 percent to the originals. But the counterfeiting problem is more serious today because the Chinese producers are now exporting their cycles to other Asian nations. Yamaha (**www.yamaha.co.jp**), Japan's second-largest motorcycle

Bangkok officials rake over seized pirated videotapes to demonstrate their government's resolve against piracy. The issue has become a major area of dispute in trade between Thailand and the United States. But the effect of such staged demonstrations in combating the flow of stolen and counterfeited goods remains to be seen. What else do you think officials in countries around the world could do to reduce counterfeiting?

producer, is considering legal action against one Chinese company. Yamaha officials say the Chinese firm's products resemble its own models right down to the Yamaha name stamped on the side.[19]

SHORTENED PRODUCT LIFE CYCLES

Companies traditionally managed to extend a product's life by introducing it into different markets consecutively. This was accomplished by introducing products in industrialized countries and only later marketing them in developing and emerging markets. Thus, while a product's sales are declining in one market, they might be growing in another.

However, advances in telecommunications have alerted consumers around the world to the latest product introductions. Consequently, consumers in developing and emerging markets also demand the latest products and are not happy with receiving yesterday's fad in the highly developed nations. Also, the rapid pace with which technological innovation occurs today is shortening the life cycles of products. The actions of international companies themselves actually helped to create this situation. Companies are undertaking new-product development at an increasingly rapid pace and thus shortening the life cycles of their products.

CREATING PROMOTIONAL STRATEGIES

Efforts by a company to reach distribution channels and target customers through communications such as personal selling, advertising, public relations, and direct marketing are called its **promotion mix**. Not surprisingly, promotional activities often receive the greatest attention among marketers because many people, even professionals, tend to equate "marketing" with "promotion." After we examine two general promotional strategies, we discuss the complications that can arise in international advertising and communications.

PUSH AND PULL STRATEGIES

There are two general promotional strategies that companies can use to get their marketing message across to buyers. They can rely completely on just one of these or use them in combination. A promotional strategy designed to create buyer demand that will encourage channel members to stock a company's product is called a **pull strategy**. In other words, buyer demand is generated in order to "pull" products through distribution channels to end users. Creating consumer demand through direct marketing techniques is a common example of a pull strategy. For instance, when Procter & Gamble (**www.pg.com**) encountered distribution difficulties in trying to introduce Rejoice haircare products into Asia, the company opted to generate grassroots consumer demand. The company hired a fleet of trucks to drive through village squares and hand out free trial packages to potential end users.

In contrast, a **push strategy** is a promotional strategy designed to pressure channel members to carry a product and promote it to final users. Manufacturers of products that are commonly sold through department and grocery stores often use a push strategy. For example, manufacturer's sales representatives are constantly calling on Wal-Mart (**www.walmart.com**) to encourage it to stock the manufacturer's product and give it good visibility. Push strategies are also employed for office products, including computers and office furniture. A company's international sales force is the key to successfully implementing a push strategy abroad. See the Global Manager titled "Managing an International Sales Force" for insight into how companies can better manage their salespeople in other cultures.

Whether the push or pull strategy is most appropriate in a given marketing environment depends on several factors:

promotion mix
Efforts by a company to reach distribution channels and target customers through communications such as personal selling, advertising, public relations, and direct marketing.

pull strategy
Promotional strategy designed to create buyer demand that will encourage channel members to stock a company's product.

push strategy
Promotional strategy designed to pressure channel members to carry a product and promote it to final users of the product.

GLOBAL MANAGER

Managing an International Sales Force

Today, companies are reaping a greater portion of their revenues from international sales. How can you become a better global manager of your company's international sales force? Here are some helpful hints on improving the effectiveness of your company's representatives abroad.

➡ **Know the sales scene.** Your company should conduct research before hiring and managing an international sales force. Then formulate a targeted sales strategy and empower your sales force to meet their performance targets. The amount of compensation as well as the way in which it is delivered varies from country to country. For instance, in the United States a greater portion of salary is based on commission than it is in Europe. Know the salary structure and incentive plans that salespeople with similar jobs have at local companies.

➡ **Research the customer.** Do not assume that customers abroad have the same needs and preferences as customers at home. Investigate what potential buyers want and how much they are willing to pay. When ECA International (a market information provider) expanded into Asia it was unsuccessful time and again. The company found out through its sales force that potential customers wanted to buy research piece-by-piece rather than buy a membership in the company. ECA was able to sell its memberships in Asia only after it adapted its methods to suit local buyers. The sales force is a valuable source of information on the local market.

➡ **Work with the culture.** "In order to motivate individuals, you need to set realistic objectives for salespeople, and much of that is culturally bound," says John Wada, sales and marketing director for IOR, a cross-cultural management company. Your company should seek answers to a host of questions. Do people in the local culture feel differently about work teams and competition than your sales force at home? How about schedules and deadlines? Are you moving into a culture where "time is of the essence" or one where time is far less important? Make sure your company and the local sales force fully understand what is expected of one another.

➡ **Learn from your representatives.** If your salespeople believe they are pushing products that bear no relationship to the local market, their performance will suffer. "I'd do a great job," so the story goes, "but the product just won't sell here." Salespeople may begin focusing on critiquing products rather than selling them. Involve your sales reps in the R&D process so that they have a better sense of what's going on with the product. You might also bring your sales force to the home office each year to learn about your business so that they understand their vital link in your company's chain of business activities. Finally, top managers should visit the local office to better comprehend the needs of local customers.

➡ *Distribution system.* Implementing a push strategy can be difficult when channel members (such as distributors) wield a great deal of power relative to that of producers. It can also be ineffective when distribution channels are lengthy: the more levels of intermediaries there are, the more channel members there are who must be convinced to carry a product. In such cases, it might be easier to create buyer demand using a pull strategy than to persuade distributors to stock a particular product.

➡ *Access to mass media.* Developing and emerging markets typically have fewer available forms of mass media for use in implementing a pull strategy. Accordingly, it is difficult to increase consumer awareness of a product and generate product demand. Many consumers in these markets cannot afford cable or satellite television, or perhaps even glossy magazines. In such cases, advertisers might turn to billboards and radio. At other times, gaining wide exposure can be difficult because existing media have only local, as opposed to national, reach. For example, Indonesia did not launch its first nationwide television station until 1994. In yet other situations, advertising certain products on certain media is unlawful. For example, companies that enter Canada or the United States cannot use television or radio to advertise tobacco products.

➡ *Type of product.* A pull strategy is most appropriate when buyers display a great deal of brand loyalty toward one particular brand name. In other words, brand-loyal buyers know what brand of a product they want before they go out to buy it. On the other hand, push strategies tend to be appropriate for inexpensive consumer goods characterized by buyers who are not brand loyal. Low brand loyalty means that a buyer will go shopping for a product, not knowing which brand is best, and simply will buy one of those carried by the retailer or wholesaler. A push strategy is also suited to industrial products because potential buyers usually need to be informed about a product's special features and benefits.

INTERNATIONAL ADVERTISING

International advertising differs a great deal from advertising in domestic markets. Managers must rely on their knowledge of a market to decide whether an ad is suitable for the company's international promotional efforts. For instance, cultural similarities can mean that ads must be only slightly modified for use in different nations. Cultural differences may mean that entirely new ads must be created.

Coca-Cola's (www.cocacola.com) experience in creating an ad to appeal to Chinese people both in China and throughout the world illustrates the problems that can arise when developing highly specialized ads. Coca-Cola's desire to create a Coke ad that looked authentically Chinese drew it to Harbin, a city in northeast China. But along the way, the bus in which the crew that was to shoot the commercial was traveling stalled. When the driver lit a fire under the gas tank to thaw the fuel, the horrified crew scrambled off the bus thinking it might explode. The crew stood in biting, sub-zero temperatures until the bus was once again running—the director's frostbitten nose bears the scars of the adventure. Then when a local older man hired to be in the ad had trouble following the director's instructions, local villagers pointed out why—he was deaf. Finally, the crew had to trudge around in knee-deep snow first to get a field of frozen red pinwheels to spin and then to reorient the whole set so that the wind (which was blowing in an unfavorable direction) could spin the pinwheels. But it appears that Coke's efforts at creating an ad depicting people celebrating Chinese New Year in the traditional manner in a picturesque village paid off—"It made me feel very emotional," said Fang Chuanbao, an office worker in Shanghai who saw the ad. The localized ads exemplify Coke's "think local, act local" mantra, which was pioneered by Chairman Douglas Daft as part of an effort to remake Coke into the nimble marketer it once was.[20]

Let's now explore some of the factors involved in the decision of whether to standardize or adapt advertisements.

Standardizing or Adapting Advertisements   The vast majority of advertising that occurs in any one nation is produced solely for that domestic audience. But companies that advertise in multiple markets must determine the aspects of the advertising campaign that can be standardized across markets and those that cannot. Companies that do market their products across national boundaries try to contain costs by standardizing as many aspects of their campaigns as possible. However, companies seldom standardize all aspects of their international promotions, for a variety of reasons, including differences in culture and laws.[21]

Firms that standardize advertising usually control campaigns from the home office.[22] This policy helps them to project consistent brand images and promotional messages across all markets—the aim of a global strategy (see Chapter 11). Companies can achieve consistency by standardizing their basic promotional message, creative concepts, graphics, and information content.

Once a company decides to pursue a global marketing strategy, it naturally tries to get the most for its advertising expenditure. An increasingly popular method companies are using to reach a global audience is marketing over the World Wide Web. Companies that use direct marketing (such as telemarketing or leaflets through the mail) have had mixed results with their Web ads. See the World Business Survey titled "Web Ads Grab Attention" for some additional information on the success of marketers' online advertising efforts.

Another way in which companies can reach a global audience is to sponsor global sporting events, such as the Olympics, World Cup Soccer, and Formula One automobile racing. These types of events receive heavy media coverage and are often telecast simultaneously in multiple nations. Even posting banners around the venues of such events can boost recognition of a company's brand name by exposing it to perhaps millions of viewers around the world. In fact, viewers in 102 countries see the banners of companies that sponsor Formula One auto racing.[23]

Case: The Elusive Euro-Consumer The continuing integration of nations belonging to the European Union is causing many marketers to dream of a day when they can standardize their advertising to appeal to a so-called Euro-consumer. But the Euro-consumer remains a rare, almost mythical, beast that is eluding even the world's most clever advertisers.

Some well-known international advertising agencies have tried a pan-European advertising approach only to fail due to national differences. Consider the experience of the acclaimed Leo Burnett Company (www.leoburnett.com) when it took on the goal of creating a single European campaign for United Distillers' Johnnie Walker (www.johnniewalker.com) whiskey. It took many painful tests and revisions before the ad could be rolled out. In the original ad, the tag line read "The Water of Life" and showed a man attending "the running of the bulls" in Pamplona, Spain. After narrowly escaping being trampled by the bull, the man celebrates with a glass of Johnnie Walker Red Label. But in many countries, the Pamplona setting raised hackles because people said, "The Spanish don't know anything about making good whiskey." Tests of the ad in Germany showed it would not work because to Germans it seemed simply reckless—not a widely admired trait there. Says Jenny Vaughn, worldwide brand director for Johnnie Walker, "Also, because of the German animal rights campaigners, you can't show a goldfish in a goldfish bowl on German televi-

WORLD BUSINESS SURVEY

Web Ads Grab Attention

Britain is Europe's largest online-advertising market. A recent survey there revealed that 78 percent of Web users actually responded in some way to online ads—and not by clicking them right off their screens. Below are the percent of respondents that performed each act in response to an online ad.

Visited advertiser Web site	45
Clicked on it	38
Researched a potential purchase	38
Bought an item online	34
Registered for a service	24
Entered a competition	21
Bought an item offline	10
None of these	22

Survey shows 78% had responded to online advertising

---

sion, so a bull run was just not [acceptable]." The tag line "The Water of Life" was baffling in many languages. "People thought it meant watered-down whiskey," said Vaughn, so the line was changed to "Taste Life." Then a voice-over in the ad was incorrectly translated in one language as "when your life flashes in front of you, make sure it's worth watching." In every market the words didn't make sense or the meaning was lost. In Italy the line was totally discarded. In Germany attempts at translation proved so maddening that the line was replaced with "Live every day as if it were your last."

Europe's many languages certainly create thorny translation issues for marketers. Thus, the most successful pan-European ads are those that contain a great deal of visuals, have few written or spoken words, and focus on the product and consumer. One such ad is one for TAG Heuer (www.tagheuer.com) watches, which positions the company's product as competitive and a winner. In the ad, a swimmer is shown racing a shark and a hurdler is shown leaping an oversize razor blade. The highly visual ad gets across the company's message that it is a winner.[24]

BLENDING PRODUCT AND PROMOTIONAL STRATEGIES

When companies extend their marketing efforts internationally, they develop communication strategies that blend product and promotional strategies.[25] A company's communication strategy for a particular market takes into account the nature of the product being marketed and the promotion mix to market it. After we discuss the marketing communication process, we examine five product/promotional methods that companies use and the appropriate situation for each.

Communicating Promotional Messages The process of sending promotional messages about products to target markets is called **marketing communication**.[26] Communicating the benefits of a product can be more difficult in international business than in domestic business for several reasons. Marketing internationally usually means translating promotional messages from one language into another. Marketers must also be knowledgeable of the many cultural nuances that can affect how buyers interpret a promotional message. A nation's laws that govern the promotion of products in another country can also force changes in marketing communication.

marketing communication
Process of sending promotional messages about products to target markets.

Marketing communication is typically considered a circular process as shown in Figure 14.1. The company that has an idea it wishes to communicate is the *source* of the communication. The idea is *encoded* (translated into images, words, and symbols) into a *promotional message* that the company is trying to get across. The promotional message is then sent to the *audience* (potential buyers) through various *media*. Media commonly used by companies to communicate their promotional messages include radio, television, newspapers, magazines, billboards, and direct mailings. Once the audience receives the message, they decode the message and interpret its meaning. Information in the form of *feedback* (purchase or nonpurchase) then flows back to the source of the message. The decoding process by the audience can be disrupted by the presence of *noise*—anything that disrupts the audience's ability to receive and interpret the promotional message. By ignoring important cultural nuances, companies can inadvertently increase the potential for noise that can cloud the audience's understanding of their promotional message. For instance, language barriers between the company and potential buyers can create noise if a company' promotional message is incorrectly translated into the local language.

Product/Communications Extension (Dual Extension) This method extends the same home-market product and marketing promotion into target markets. Under certain conditions, it can be the simplest and most profitable strategy. For example, because of a common language and other cultural similarities, companies based in English-speaking Canadian provinces can sell the same product with packaging and advertising identical to that in the U.S. market—provided the product is not required by the U.S. government to carry any special statements or warnings. Thus, the Canadian

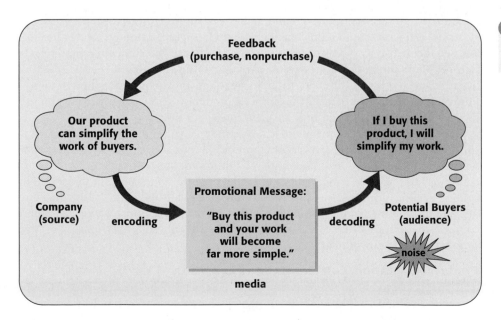

FIGURE 14.1

Marketing Communications Process

companies contain costs by developing a single product and one promotional campaign for both markets. However, it is important for Canadian companies not to ignore any subtle cultural differences that could cause confusion in interpreting the promotional message.

As the information age continues to knit the world more tightly together, this method will probably grow more popular. Today consumers in seemingly remote parts of the world are rapidly becoming aware of the latest worldwide fads and fashions. But it appears that this strategy is better suited for certain groups of buyers, including brand-conscious teenagers, business executives, and wealthy individuals. The strategy also tends to be better suited for companies that use a global strategy with their products, such as upscale personal items with global brand names—examples include Rolex (www.rolex.com) watches, Hermes (www.hermes.com) scarves and ties, and Coco Chanel (www.chanel.com) perfumes. It can also be appropriate for global brands that have mass appeal and cut across all age groups and social classes—such as Canon (www.canon.com), Mars (www.mars.com), and Nokia (www.nokia.com). The strategy also is useful to companies that are the low-cost leaders in their industries. One product and one promotional message keeps costs down.

Product Extension/Communications Adaptation   Under this method, a company extends the same product into target markets but alters its promotion. Communications require adaptation because the product satisfies a different need, serves a different function, or appeals to a different type of buyer. Companies adjust their marketing communication to inform potential buyers that the product either satisfies their needs or serves a distinct function. This approach helps companies contain costs because the good itself does not need to undergo any alteration. However, altering communications can be expensive—especially if there are significant cultural differences among target markets. Filming altered ads with local actors and on location can add significantly to promotional costs.

One company that changes its promotional message for international markets is the Japanese retailer Muji (www.muji.co.jp). Muji offers a wide variety of goods, including writing materials, clothing, and home furnishings. However, everything is inspired by a central theme rooted in centuries of Japanese culture—the simplicity of everyday life. Muji's philosophy is one of selling unbranded quality goods, and company promotions boast the motto "Functional Japanese minimalism for everyone." Its target market in Japan is the average school-aged child and young adult. However, Muji's European stores use a different promotional message. Muji's European customers tend to be older and see themselves as sophisticated and stylish buyers of the company's products. In Europe, Muji's promotional message is "shop at a business that has a very respectable brand name"—clearly different from its message in Japan. Also, the company's European customers are not buying simply a product (as do its Japanese customers); they are buying into the traditional Japanese concept of simplicity.[27]

Low economic development also can demand that communications be adapted to suit local conditions. For instance, companies in Europe, North America, and certain Asian countries can rely on a modern telecommunications system to reach millions of consumers through television, radio, and even the World Wide Web. But in developing countries (such as rural parts of India and China), television and radio coverage are limited and development of the Web is years behind developed nations. Marketers in those countries must use alternative techniques, including door-to-door personal selling and regional product shows or fairs.

Product Adaptation/Communications Extension   Using this method, a company adapts its product to the requirements of the international market while retaining the product's original marketing communication. There are many reasons why companies need to adapt their products; one might be to meet legal requirements in the local market. Moreover, governments can require that firms use a certain amount of local materials, labor, or some other resource in their local production process. If the exact same materials or components are not available locally, the result can be a modified product.

This method can be costly because appropriately modifying a product to suit the needs of local buyers often means that the company must invest in production facilities in the local market. If each national market requires its own production facility, cost savings provided by economies of scale in production can be elusive. However, a company can implement this strategy successfully if it sells a differentiated product for which it can charge a higher price to offset the greater production costs.[28]

Product/Communications Adaptation (Dual Adaptation)   This method adapts both the product and its marketing communication to suit the target market. The product itself is adapted to match the needs or preferences of local buyers. The promotional message is adapted to explain how the product meets those needs and preferences. Because both production and marketing efforts must be altered, this strategy can be expensive; therefore, it is not very common. However, it can be implemented successfully if a sufficiently large and profitable market segment exists.

Product Invention   This method requires that an entirely new product be developed for the target market. Product invention is often necessary when many important differences exist between the home and target markets. One reason for product invention is that local buyers cannot afford a company's current product because of low purchasing power. For example, Honda (www.honda.com) developed a car called the "City" that is designed for budget-conscious buyers in Southeast Asian and European markets.

Product inventions can also arise because of a lack of adequate infrastructure needed to operate certain products. One day, London inventor Trevor Baylis was watching a television documentary on the difficulty of educating Africans about AIDS because much of the continent did not have the electricity infrastructure or batteries to operate radios. Baylis set to work and developed the Freeplay windup radio—30 seconds of cranking keeps it going for 40 minutes. Baylis and several South African businessmen

Companies often extend their product lines to enter new market segments. Essentially, it means creating a new product to fulfill an unmet need. A good example of this is the disposable camera offered by many companies in the photographic imaging industry. The disposable camera by Fuji (**www.fujifilm.co.jp**) takes stop-action photos in which several frames are reproduced in a single image. Can you think of another recent product line extension?

then formed a company called Bay-Gen Power Corporation in Cape Town, South Africa. The radio was first sold only to relief agencies working in developing nations. However, due mostly to word of mouth, it is now popular worldwide among hikers, environmentalists, and even hip shoppers looking for "retro" appliances.[29]

DESIGNING DISTRIBUTION STRATEGIES

distribution
Planning, implementing, and controlling the physical flow of a product from its point of origin to its point of consumption.

Planning, implementing, and controlling the physical flow of a product from its point of origin to its point of consumption is called **distribution**. The physical path that a product follows on its way to customers is called a *distribution channel*. Companies along this channel that work together in delivering products to customers are called *channel members* or *intermediaries*. Bear in mind that manufacturers of goods are not the only producers who need distribution channels. Service providers such as consulting companies, health-care organizations, and news services also need distribution (or delivery) systems to reach their customers. Consider the business of delivering news services over the World Wide Web. Channel members involved in getting news from the newsroom to the Web surfer can include, among others, Internet service providers such as America Online (www.aol.com) and search engine providers such as Excite (www.excite.com).

Companies develop their international distribution strategies based on two related decisions: (1) how to get the goods *into* a country and (2) how to distribute goods *within* a country. We presented the different ways companies get their products into countries in Chapter 13. Thus, here we focus on distribution strategies within countries.

DESIGNING DISTRIBUTION CHANNELS

Managers consider two overriding concerns when establishing channels of distribution: (1) the amount of *market exposure* that a product needs and (2) the *cost* of distributing a product. Let's now take a look at each of these concerns.

Degree of Exposure   In promoting its product to the greatest number of potential customers, a marketer must determine the amount of exposure needed. An **exclusive channel** is one in which a manufacturer grants the right to sell its product to only one or a limited number of resellers. Thus, an exclusive channel gives producers a great deal of control over the sale of their product by channel members such as wholesalers and retailers. It also helps a producer to constrain distributors from selling competing brands. In this way, an exclusive channel creates a barrier that makes it difficult or impossible for outsiders to penetrate the channel. For example, in most countries new car dealerships reflect exclusive distribution—normally, Mitsubishi (www.mitsubishi.com) dealerships cannot sell Toyotas (www.toyota.com) and General Motors (www.gm.com) dealers cannot sell Fords (www.ford.com).

An interesting story comes to us from the Himalayan kingdom nation of Nepal. Although Nepal's per capita gross domestic product is just $150 to $200, people today can more easily afford the personal-care products of companies such as Colgate-Palmolive (www.colgate.com). As a result, competition for shelf space in stores is heating up. In a small spice shop in Katmandu, for example, the shopkeeper says his distributor pays him about $4.20 each month for carrying only Colgate dental-care products. He says this doubles his monthly profit from toothpaste and toothbrush sales.[30]

When a producer wants its product to be made available through as many distribution outlets as possible, it prefers to use an **intensive channel**—one in which a producer grants the right to sell its product to many resellers. An intensive channel provides buyers with location convenience because of the large number of outlets through which a product is sold. However, it does not create strong barriers to channel entry for other producers, nor does it provide much control over reseller decisions such as what competing brands to sell. Large companies whose products are sold through grocery stores

exclusive channel
Distribution channel in which a manufacturer grants the right to sell its product to only one or a limited number of resellers.

intensive channel
Distribution channel in which a producer grants the right to sell its product to many resellers.

and department stores typically take an intensive channel approach to distribution. The obstacle faced by small companies that choose an intensive channel approach is gaining shelf space—especially small companies with lesser-known brands. This problem is exacerbated by the increasing global trend toward retailers developing their own *private-label brands*—brands created by retailers themselves. Manufacturers produce the good for the retailer and label it with the retailer's brand name instead of their own. Thus, retailers give their own products shelf space close to the best brands, and small, lesser-known brands end up getting the poorest shelf location—up high or near the floor.

Channel Length and Cost   *Channel length* refers to the number of intermediaries between the producer and the buyer. In a *zero-level channel*—which is also called *direct marketing*—producers sell directly to final buyers. A *one-level channel* places only one intermediary between the producer and the buyer. Two intermediaries make up a *two-level channel*, and so forth. Generally, the more intermediaries in a channel, the more costly it becomes because each additional player tacks on to the product a charge for its services. This is an important consideration for companies that sell price-sensitive consumer products such as candy, food, and small household items that usually compete on the basis of price. As we saw in Chapter 11, companies that sell highly differentiated products can charge higher prices because of their products' distinctiveness; therefore, they have fewer problems using a channel of several levels.

INFLUENCE OF PRODUCT CHARACTERISTICS

The value of a product relative to its weight and volume is called its **value density**. Value density is an important variable in formulating distribution strategies. As a rule, *the lower a product's value density, the more localized the distribution system*. Most commodities, including cement, iron ore, and crude oil, have low value-density ratios—they're heavy but not particularly "valuable" if gauged in, say, shipping weight per cubic meter. Therefore, relative to their values the cost of transporting them is high. Consequently, such products are processed or integrated into the manufacturing process at points close to their original locations. Products with high value-density ratios include emeralds, semiconductors, and premium perfumes. Because the cost of transporting these products is small relative to their values, they can be processed or manufactured in the optimal location then shipped to market. For instance, because Johnson & Johnson's (**www.johnsonandjohnson.com**) Vistakon contact lenses have high value density, the company produces and inventories its products in one U.S. location and serves the world market from there.

> **value density**
> *Value of a product relative to its weight and volume.*

When products need to be modified for local markets, companies can design their distribution systems accordingly. Caterpillar (**www.caterpillar.com**) redesigned its distribution system so that it doubles as the final component in the company's production system. Each national market carries a range of optional product components for Caterpillar's lift trucks. The company ships partially completed lift trucks, along with optional parts, to distribution warehouses in each target market. After a buyer decides what options it desires, final assembly takes place. Thus, Caterpillar's distribution warehouses now extend the company's assembly line—allowing the company to maintain or improve service at little cost.

SPECIAL DISTRIBUTION PROBLEMS

A nation's distribution system develops over time and reflects its unique cultural, political, legal, and economic traditions. Thus, the distribution system of each nation has its own unique pros and cons. However, it is the negative aspects of distribution that pose the greatest threat to the business activities of international companies. In some countries risks arise mostly from the potential for theft and property damage. In others it is simply the lack of understanding that creates uncertainty and risk. Let's take a look at two special problems that can affect a company's international distribution activities.

Lack of Market Understanding Companies can experience a great deal of frustration and financial loss simply by not fully understanding the local market in which they operate. Amway Asia Pacific Ltd., the Asian arm of U.S.-based Amway (www.amway.com), learned the hard way the pitfalls of overestimating the knowledge of distributors in emerging markets. The company has a worldwide policy of giving distributors a full refund on its soaps and cosmetics if the distributor's customers are dissatisfied—even if the returned containers are empty. But the policy had some bizarre results shortly after Amway entered China. Word of the guarantee spread quickly. Some distributors repackaged the products in other containers, sold them, and took the original containers back to Amway for a refund. Others scoured garbage bins, gathering bags full of discarded bottles. In Shanghai returns were beginning to total $100,000 a day. Amway's Shanghai chief Percy Chin admitted, "Perhaps we were too lenient." Amway changed its refund policy to allow a refund only for bottles at least half full. Amway's distributors were furious. Grumbled one unhappy distributor, "Don't open a company if you can't afford losses."[31]

Theft and Corruption A high incidence of theft and corruption can present obstacles to distribution. For instance, the distribution system in Russia reflects its roughly 75-year experiment with communism. When Acer Computers (www.acer.com) decided to sell its computers in Russia, it built production facilities in Russia's stable neighbor Finland—the company was leery of investing directly in Russia. Acer also considered it too risky to navigate Russia's archaic distribution system on its own. In three years' time, a highway that serves as a main route to get goods overland from Finland to Russia saw 50 Finnish truckers hijacked, two drivers killed, and another two missing. Acer solved its distribution problem by selling its computers to Russian distributors outside its factory in Finland. The Russian distributors, who understood how to negotiate their way through Russia's distribution system, would deal with headaches in Russia.[32]

DEVELOPING PRICING STRATEGIES

The pricing strategy that a company adopts must match its overall international strategy. For instance, the product of a company that is the low-cost leader in its industry usually cannot be sold at a premium price because it likely has few special features and stresses functionality rather than uniqueness. On the other hand, a company that follows a differentiation strategy usually can charge a premium price for its product because buyers value the product's uniqueness. Let's now examine two pricing policies (*worldwide pricing* and *dual pricing*) that companies use in international markets and then explore the important factors that influence managers' pricing decisions.

WORLDWIDE PRICING

> **worldwide pricing**
> Policy in which one selling price is established for all international markets.

A pricing policy in which one selling price is established for all international markets is called **worldwide pricing**. In practice, a worldwide pricing policy is very difficult to achieve. First, production costs differ from one nation to another. Keeping production costs the same is not possible for a company that has production bases within each market it serves. Thus, selling prices often reflect these different costs of production.

Second, a company that produces in just one location (to maintain an equivalent cost of production for every product) cannot guarantee that selling prices will be the same in every target market. The cost of exporting to certain markets will likely be higher than the cost of exporting to other markets. In addition, distribution costs differ across markets. Where distribution is efficient, selling prices might well be lower than in locations where distribution systems are archaic and inefficient. Third, the purchasing power of local buyers must be taken into account. Managers might decide to lower the sales price in a market so that buyers can afford the product and the company can gain market share. Finally, fluctuating currency values also must be taken into account. When the value of the currency in a country where production takes place rises against a target market's currency, the product will become more expensive in the target market.

DUAL PRICING

Because of the problems associated with worldwide pricing, another pricing policy is often used in international markets. A pricing policy in which a product has a different selling price in export markets than it has in the home market is called **dual pricing**. When a product has a higher selling price in the target market than it does in the home market (or the country where production takes place), it is called *price escalation*. It is commonly the result of the reasons just discussed—exporting costs and currency fluctuations.

But sometimes a product's export price is lower than the price in the home market. Under what circumstances does this occur? Some companies determine that domestic market sales are to cover all product costs (such as expenses related to R&D, administration, and overhead). Thus, exports must cover only the *additional* costs associated with exporting and selling in a target market (such as tariffs). In this sense, exports are considered a sort of "bonus."

To apply dual pricing in international marketing successfully, a company must be able to keep its domestic buyers and international buyers separate. Buyers in one market might cancel orders if they discover that they are paying a higher price than are buyers in another market. If a company cannot keep its buyers separate when employing dual pricing, buyers could potentially undermine the policy through *arbitrage*—buying products where they are sold at lower prices and reselling them where they command higher prices. However (as is often the case), the higher selling price of a product in an export market often reflects the additional costs of transportation to the local market and any trade barriers of the target market, such as tariffs. For arbitrageurs to be successful, the profits they earn must be enough to outweigh these additional costs.

dual pricing
Policy in which a product has a different selling price (typically higher) in export markets than it has in the home market.

FACTORS THAT AFFECT PRICING DECISIONS

Many factors have an important influence on managers' pricing decisions. We devote the following discussion to four of the most important—*transfer prices*, *arm's length pricing*, *price controls*, and *dumping*.

Transfer Prices   Prices charged for goods or services transferred among a company and its subsidiaries are called **transfer prices**. It is common for parent companies and their subsidiaries to buy from one another. For example, the parent company often licenses technologies to its subsidiaries in return for royalties or licensing fees. Subsidiaries prefer this route to buying on the open market because they typically enjoy lower prices. Parent companies then buy finished products from subsidiaries at the stated transfer price.

At one time, companies enjoyed a great deal of freedom in setting their transfer prices. Subsidiaries in countries with high corporate tax rates would reduce their tax burdens by charging a low price for their output to other subsidiaries. The subsidiary lowered the taxes that the parent company must pay by reducing its profits in the high-tax country. Likewise, subsidiaries in countries with low tax rates would charge relatively high prices for their output.

Transfer prices followed a similar pattern based on the tariffs of different nations. Subsidiaries in countries that charged relatively high tariffs were charged lower prices to

transfer price
Price charged for a good or service transferred among a company and its subsidiaries.

lower the cost of the goods in the local market. This pattern of transfer prices helped large corporations with many subsidiaries to better manage their global tax burden and become more price-competitive in certain markets.

Arm's Length Pricing

Today, increasing regulation of transfer pricing practices is causing reduced freedom in manipulating transfer prices. In fact, many governments now regulate internal company pricing practices by assigning products approximate transfer prices based on their free-market price. Thus, most international transfers between subsidiaries now occur at a so-called **arm's length price**—the free-market price that unrelated parties charge one another for a specific product.

Another factor that is increasing the use of arm's length pricing is pressure on companies to be good corporate citizens in each of their target markets. Developing and emerging markets are hurt most by lost revenue when international companies manipulate prices to reduce tariffs and corporate taxes. They depend on the revenue for building things such as schools, hospitals, and infrastructure, including telecommunications systems and shipping ports. These items in turn benefit international companies by improving the productivity and efficiency of the local business environment. Indeed, some international companies have even developed codes of conduct specifying that transfer prices will follow the principle of arm's length pricing.

Price Controls

Pricing strategies must also consider the potential for government **price controls**—upper or lower limits placed on the prices of products sold within a country. Upper-limit price controls are designed to provide price stability in an inflationary economy (one in which prices are rising). Companies that want to raise prices in a price-controlled economy must often apply to government authorities to request permission to do so. Companies with good contacts in the government of the target market might be more likely to get a price-control exemption. Those unable to obtain an exemption will typically try to lessen the impact of upper-limit price controls by reducing production costs.

In contrast, lower-limit price controls prohibit the lowering of prices below a certain level. Governments sometimes impose lower-limit prices to help local companies compete against the less expensive imports of international companies. Other times, lower-limit price controls are designed to ward off price wars that could eliminate the competition and thereby give one company a monopoly in the domestic market.

Dumping

We detailed the practice of dumping in Chapter 6 when discussing government involvement in international trade. Recall that *dumping* occurs when the price of a good is lower in export markets than it is in the domestic market. Accusations of dumping are often made against competitors from other countries when inexpensive imports flood a nation's domestic market. Although charges of dumping normally result from deliberate efforts to undercut the prices of competitors in the domestic market, changes in exchange rates can cause unintentional dumping. When a country's government charges another nation's producers of dumping a good on its market, antidumping tariffs are typically imposed. Such tariffs are designed to punish producers in the offending nation by increasing the price of their products to a fairer level.

A FINAL WORD

Despite the academic debate over globalization and the extent to which companies should standardize their international marketing activities, many companies continue to adapt to local conditions. Sometimes this takes the form of only slightly modifying promotional campaigns and at other times it can require the creation of an entirely new product. The causes of alterations in promotional aspects of marketing strategy can be cultural, such as language differences. They can also be legal such as requirements to produce locally so as to help ease local unemployment or to spur local industry around the production facility. Other companies are able to reap the rewards of standardization and centralized production that can result from the ability to sell one product world-wide. In the next chapter, we take an in-depth look at the factors that influence the development of production strategies and the types of decisions managers must make along the way.

There is a variety of additional material available on the Companion Website that accompanies this book. You can access this information by visiting the Website at (www.prenhall.com/wild).

summary

1 **Explain the impact** *globalization* **is having on international marketing activities**. Some experts argue that because the world is becoming standardized and homogeneous, companies should market the same products in the same way in all countries. They claim that technology has already caused people's needs and preferences to converge throughout the world and urge companies to reduce production and marketing costs by standardizing both the physical features of their products and their strategies for marketing them. However, others counter that standardization is just one of a number of strategies or that it is not always the best strategy to use.

Consumers worldwide appear content with a standardized product in *certain* product categories. However, in others they demand products that reflect their unique tastes and preferences. Cultural, political, legal, and economic environments have a great deal to do with the preferences of both consumers and industrial buyers worldwide. Product standardization is more likely when producer and buyer nations share the same level of economic development.

2 **Describe the types of things that managers must consider when developing international** *product strategies*. Many elements influence a company's decision of whether to standardize or adapt its product. First, companies undertake mandatory product adaptation in response to a target market's *laws and regulations*. Companies also adapt their products to suit *cultural differences*. Sometimes companies do not need to modify their product if they can identify a different need that the product serves in the culture.

Although companies keep their *brand names* consistent across markets, they often create new *product names* or modify existing ones to suit local preferences. The *image of a nation* in which a company designs, manufactures, or assembles a product influences buyers' perceptions of quality and reliability. *Counterfeit goods* can damage buyers' image of a brand when the counterfeits are of inferior quality—which is nearly always the case. Buyers expect a certain level of craftsmanship from any given brand but are disappointed with the counterfeited product's performance, which tarnishes the company's reputation. Finally, *shortened product life cycles* are affecting the timing of when to market internationally.

3 **Discuss the factors that influence international** *promotional strategies* **and the blending of product and promotional strategies**. Efforts by a company to reach distribution channels and target customers through communications such as personal selling, advertising, public relations, and direct marketing are called its *promotion mix*. A promotional strategy designed to create buyer demand that will encourage channel members to stock a company's product is called a *pull strategy*. In contrast, a promotional strategy designed to pressure channel members to carry a product and promote it to final users of the product is called a *push strategy*.

Companies blend their international product and promotional policies to create five generic promotional methods. *Product/communications extension (dual extension)* extends the same home-market product and marketing promotion into target markets. *Product extension/communications adaptation* extends the same product into new target markets but alters its promotion. *Product adaptation/communications extension* adapts a product to the requirements of the international market while retaining the product's original marketing communication. *Product/communications adaptation (dual adaptation)* adapts both the product and its marketing communication to suit the target market. *Product invention* requires that an entirely new product be developed for the target market.

4 **Explain the elements that managers must take into account when designing international *distribution strategies*.** Planning, implementing, and controlling the physical flow of a product from its point of origin to its point of consumption is called *distribution*. The physical path that a product follows on its way to customers is called a *distribution channel*. An *exclusive channel* is one in which a manufacturer grants the right to sell its product to only one or a limited number of resellers. An exclusive channel provides a great deal of control over their products' sale by wholesalers and retailers. An *intensive channel* is one in which a producer grants the right to sell its product to many resellers. This type of channel offers less control over reseller decisions.

Channel length refers to the number of intermediaries between the producer and the buyer. In a *zero-level* channel producers sell directly to final buyers. A *one-level channel* places only one intermediary between producer and buyer, two intermediaries make up a *two-level channel*, and so forth. The value of a product relative to its weight and volume is called its *value density*. As a rule, the lower a product's value density, the more localized the distribution system.

A nation's distribution system develops over time and reflects its unique cultural, political, legal, and economic traditions. Special distribution problems that pose the biggest threat for international marketing efforts include a lack of market understanding and theft and corruption.

5 **Discuss the elements that influence international *pricing strategies*.** *Worldwide pricing* is a pricing policy in which one selling price is established for all international markets—a difficult task to achieve in practice. A pricing policy in which a product has a different selling price in export markets than it has in the home market is called *dual pricing*. When a product has a higher selling price in the target market than it does in the home market (or the country where production takes place) it is called *price escalation*.

Several factors have an important influence on managers' pricing decisions. A *transfer price* is the price charged for products sold between a company's divisions or subsidiaries. Today many governments regulate internal company pricing practices by assigning products approximate transfer prices based on a so-called *arm's length price*—the free-market price that unrelated parties charge one another for a specific product.

Price controls are upper or lower limits placed on the prices of products sold within a country. Upper-limit price controls are designed to provide price stability in an inflationary economy. When a country's government charges another nation's producers of *dumping* a good on its market, antidumping tariffs are typically imposed to punish producers in the offending nation.

questions **for review**

1. How is *globalization* affecting international marketing activities? List the elements in national business environments that may affect the decision about *standardization versus adaptation*.

2. Identify at least four factors that influence a company's product strategies in international markets.

3. Define the term *promotion mix*.

4. Briefly describe the difference between a *push strategy* and a *pull strategy*. What are some factors that affect the choice of an appropriate strategy?

5. What are some of the factors that affect the decision about standardizing versus adapting as it pertains to international advertising?

6. What is *marketing communication*? Describe each element in the marketing communications process and how they interact.

7. What are the *five generic methods* for blending product and promotional strategies for international markets? Describe each briefly.

8. What is *distribution*?

9. What is the difference between *exclusive* and *intensive* channels of distribution? Give an example of a product sold through each type of channel.

10. What is *value density*? Explain its importance to distribution strategies.

11. Briefly explain the difference between *worldwide pricing* and *dual pricing*.

12. Explain the influence of *transfer prices*, *arm's length pricing*, *price controls*, and *dumping* on the pricing decisions of international companies.

questions **for discussion**

1. Suppose that the product preferences of cultures and people around the world continue to converge. Identify two products that will likely be affected and two products that will likely not be affected by such a convergence. For each product that is affected, how will the changes influence the marketing manager's job?

2. The Web sites of both Adobe (www.adobe.com) and Amazon (www.amazon.com) have reputations as being excellent for international marketing. Partner with another student and visit the Web site of one of these companies while your partner visits the other firm's Web site. For the site you chose, what features do you think account for the favorable reputation? List the different ads on the site and rate their effectiveness. Compare your findings with those of your partner.

3. Price escalation can present serious problems for companies wishing to export their products to other markets under a worldwide pricing policy. How might companies combat the effects of price escalation? List as many possibilities as you can.

in **practice**

Read the following brief article and answer the questions that follow.

Ad with Hitler Causes Furor in Thailand

The Thai television ad depicts Adolf Hitler eating brand "X" potato chips and then being transformed by a voodoo spell into a good person. The ad closes with Hitler stripping off his Nazi uniform and dancing, a Nazi swastika morphing into the logo for the Thai potato chip brand "X."

This week, after days of outcry from critics including the Israeli Embassy in Bangkok, the agency that created the campaign, Leo Burnett, recalled it. The agency said in a statement that the ad "was never intended to cause ill feelings." The agency also promised to remove print versions of the ad from all tuk-tuks, or three wheeled taxis.

The situation sheds light not only on how far some ad agencies will go to create striking images, but also how a lack of internal controls at agencies can cause problems, some ad-industry insiders say. That's because the local units of international ad agencies aren't typically required to consult with parent companies when creating ads for the domestic audience.

Leo Burnett says the ad was not intended as a publicity stunt for the potato chip brand. "The brand already has 10 percent market share," says spokeswoman Simone Wheeler. Asked if her agency will introduce new review steps to avoid similar problems, Ms. Wheeler says, "We haven't talked about it at this stage, but it's not to say that they will be or they won't be."

1. The international subsidiaries of advertising agencies tend to have a great deal of freedom in developing ads for the local market. Do you think this is a wise decision? Why or why not?

2. If you were the CEO of a large agency based in London, what could you do to tighten controls in your international offices? What impact, if any, would tighter controls have on the creative talent in local offices?

3. The Hitler ad was successfully market-tested with teenagers (who likely knew who Hitler was) before it was aired. Why do you think the ad was tested successfully?

4. Despite any potential cultural influence, do you think the fact that Hitler's reign was more than 50 years ago played a role in the successful testing of the ad? How do you think teens in your own country would react to such an ad? Explain.

projects

1. Choose a company that you are interested in. Consult recent annual reports or other sources to find out what new products that company has brought to market in the past year or two. Are those products truly new innovations, or are they simply extensions of existing products? What considerations guided the company in its product development efforts?

2. Gather several magazines from different parts of the world. Look through each of them for ads from one company or for advertisements featuring a particular product or brand. After you have identified three or four such ads, determine which of the five types of product and promotion policies is being used: dual extension, product extension/communications adaptation, product adaptation/communications extension, dual adaptation, or product invention. What explanation do you have for the particular method being used?

business case 14
FAIR GAME OR OUT-OF-BOUNDS?

It's no secret that marketers employ a good dose of psychology in both designing and implementing their promotional campaigns—or at least it shouldn't be. But some people, including Gary Rushkin of Washington, D.C.–based Commercial Alert (www.commercialalert.org), argue that parents are being duped. "I don't think people understand the extent of psychological tools employed against their kids to whip up their desire to buy products," says Rushkin. "When they find out, they're horrified." Rushkin's organization was behind a recent letter signed by 60 U.S. psychologists that was sent to the American Psychological Association (www.apa.org) that complained of "the use of psychology to exploit and influence children for commercial purposes."

What was the cause of their fury? Apparently, it was an article by Dr. James McNeal appearing in *Marketing Tools* magazine that described what is called a projective completion test. Suppose a children's TV program is a hit and boys are buying the company's toy that is tied to the program but girls aren't. To find out why, a company assembles a group of girls. They are given a picture of a boy and girl watching the program in which the boy is asking the girl, "Why do you like watching this program?" The girls' answers help provide clues to how the company can modify its marketing strategy to appeal to girls. Dr. McNeal refers to the method as "good sense and good science." Rushkin counters, "Psychologists are going to have to decide whether psychology is a tool for healing or for exploitation . . . ." the American Psychological Association admits that there are currently no guidelines for psychologists working in advertising.

Advertising executives are not just busy creating TV ads. Over a 1-year period from 2000 to 2001, the number of children's sites with no advertising dropped from 10 percent down to 2 percent. In what forms do the promotions appear? One tool is *games*. Roughly 55 percent of all children's and teens' Web sites feature games. Ellen Neuborne told her 6-year-old that he could choose a candy at the supermarket checkout. With a pack of Sweet Tarts in hand, he broke into a little song-and-dance about the sweets.

When asked if that was from the TV commercial, he replied, "No. It's from the Sweet Tarts Internet game." With the use of such games, companies get to spend an extended period of time with kids—far more than they get from a TV ad. Another tool is *e-mail*. The U.S. Children's Online Privacy Act forbids companies from using e-mail to sell to kids under 13 without parental permission. But companies get around the problem by having kids e-mail each other. For instance, children can go to the Web site (www.sesameworkshop.org) and e-mail a greeting card to a friend that features a *Sesame Street* character. And then there are the *chat rooms*. Brian Rubash is manager for technical marketing at Tiger electronics (www.tigertoys.com), a division of toy-maker Hasbro (www.hasbro.com). He says he regularly signed on to a newsgroup he found on Yahoo! (www.yahoo.com) to offer product news and answer questions about the i-Cybie robotic dog the company was launching.

European nations have some of the strictest regulations covering marketing to children. However, nations belonging to the European Union (EU) have widely varying rules. For example, Greece bans all TV ads for war toys and bans ads for all other toys between 7 A.M. and 10 P.M. The Dutch-speaking part of Belgium bans TV advertising within 5 minutes of the start and end of children's programs. But Sweden bans all ads aimed at children under age 12. This means that when kids in Sweden watch the Pokemon cartoon series, they don't hear the closing jingle "Gotta catch 'em all" that plays elsewhere. But the problem for the Swedes (and others with more restrictive bans) is that they can only enforce their laws on programs originating from within the country. They have no power of enforcement over programs broadcast from other nations or from satellite transmissions. That is why the Swedes are pushing for a common restrictive policy toward advertising aimed at children. Says Stephan Loerke, a lobbyist for the World Federation of Advertisers (www.wfanet.org) in Brussels, "They're gradually trying to forge a consensus among the member states." Although an outright ban like Sweden's is unlikely, partial bans such as that in place in Belgium could be implemented. To forestall stricter EU-wide legislation, advertisers could initiate "voluntary" limits themselves.

Yet some marketers are defending their actions. Advertising executive Geoffrey Roche of Toronto, Canada, dismissed the influence of psychologists saying that, "They don't have mind-altering powers and kids are a lot smarter than we give them credit for. I don't think there is any way that we, as advertisers, can convince children of anything." But Dr. Allen Kanner asks, "If advertising is so ineffective, then why do they spend billions of dollars on it each year?" Dr. Curtis Haugtvedt, president of the Society for Consumer Psychology, says that although evidence of the negative aspects of advertising does exist, ads can also benefit kids. "Even Barbie has pluses and minuses," says Haugtvedt. "Barbie helps kids imagine and play with one another, but Barbie also portrays the image of a certain body shape." Haugtvedt also stresses the role of guidance in helping kids become responsible consumers, saying, "The child hopefully is not making choices about purchasing things in a vacuum."

thinking globally

1. Put yourself in the position of Stephan Loerke of the World Federation of Advertisers. First, make an argument for why the EU should not enact more strict advertising laws. Second, make a case for why advertisers operating in the EU should initiate "voluntary" limits. Third, make a case for why current laws need no modification whatsoever. Which case do you agree with? Which case do you think is the strongest?

2. Certain organizations regularly attack advertisers for their promotional methods. What do you think the advertising industry could do to make themselves a smaller target for such criticisms? Be specific.

3. Some critics charge advertisers with creating wants among consumers rather than helping them satisfy needs. Select a product and describe how, if it were marketed in a developing economy, it can create wants and not satisfy needs. Explain the ethical issues surrounding the decision of whether to market the product in developing nations.

a question of ethics

1. The International Chamber of Commerce in Paris issued a set of voluntary guidelines on tactics for interactive marketing and advertising on the Internet. It is hoped that the guidelines will both reduce consumer resistance to online ads and quiet calls for restrictive legislation. The document contains, among other things, "users' rights" guidelines stating that advertisers should disclose their reasons for collecting personal information on Web users and not sell such information to others without permission. Do you think that all the companies that sign on to such guidelines actually follow them? Do you think it is more difficult for small companies to resist the temptation to sell data on their users—particularly because such data can fetch a fairly high selling price? Do you think selling such data is ethical?

2. The practices ascribed to global tobacco companies such as Philip Morris put the "standardization versus adaptation" issue in an unusual perspective. Competitors allege that in important developing markets such as Turkey, Philip Morris created special blends containing additives that give brands such as Marlboro an extra "kick." If cigarette companies do, in fact, adapt their products in this way, do you believe such policies are ethical?

15 launching and managing production

LEARNING OBJECTIVES

After studying this chapter, you should be able to

1 Identify the elements that are important to consider when formulating *production strategies*.

2 Identify key considerations when *acquiring physical resources*.

3 Identify several production matters that are of special concern to managers.

4 Describe the three potential *sources of financing* and the main financial instruments of each.

BEACONS

A Look Back

CHAPTER 14 explored the influence of globalization on international marketing activities. We also examined how differences in national business environments have an impact on the development of marketing strategies.

A Look at This Chapter

This chapter examines how companies launch and manage their international production efforts. We analyze how companies acquire the materials and products they need and how aspects of the business environment affect production strategies. We also look briefly at how companies finance their activities.

A Look Ahead

CHAPTER 16 examines how international companies manage their human resources. Topics include international staffing policies, recruitment, training, compensation, labor relations, and culture shock.

Connecting People

HELSINKI, Finland — Is it the end of the line for mobile phones? A maturing market is causing some to say that mobile phones are going the way of the personal computer. But Nokia Corporation (**www.nokia.com**), for one, is not buying it. The firm controls about one third of the total worldwide market for mobile phones and is a leading supplier of the networks that comprise the infrastructure for voice and data communications. Nokia is betting that its market power will help it to extend the life of the mobile handset.

Nokia's activities are spread across the globe. In fact, it has sales in over 130 countries, manufactures in 18 facilities in 10 countries, and conducts research and development in 15 nations. The company employs 54,000 people and has annual sales of more than $28 billion. It is one of the only remaining companies that designs and makes its own chips, software, and phones. Nokia's size makes this strategy economically viable. Smaller players such as Philips (**www.philips.com**) and Alcatel (**www.alcatel.com**) outsource their phone production. Naturally, a firm like Nokia must undertake a great deal of planning for things such as production capacity, where to locate facilities, the technology used in production, and the layout of the facilities.

As you can imagine, building production facilities and a communications infrastructure requires a great deal of money. For part of its funding, Nokia looks to capital markets in Finland and abroad. In order to access the large pool of investors in the U.S. capital market, Nokia does what many non–U.S. companies do and issues what are called *American Depository Receipts (ADRs)*. These ADRs are certificates that trade in the United States and represent a specific number of shares of Nokia's stock.

Nokia also finances its activities with internal funding. For example, the Nokia Research Center is divided into six "strategic focus areas." Each area is profit-driven and obtains about 70 percent of its funding from the business groups it serves within the company. As you read this chapter, consider all the ways that companies structure their global production activities and how they finance their production (and other) activities.[1]

Whether an international company's production activity involves manufacturing a product or providing a service, it must acquire many resources before beginning operations. Where will it get the raw materials or components it needs to perform its production activities? How much production capacity is needed? Will the company construct or buy new facilities? How large must its service centers be? Where will it get the financial capital it needs? The answers to these questions are complex and interrelated.

This chapter begins by examining important considerations when formulating international production strategies. The topics covered include the decision of whether to centralize or decentralize production and whether production will be standardized or adapted to national markets. In the process, we draw linkages to earlier discussions, including overall corporate strategy and marketing strategy. We then describe how companies acquire the resources they need to accomplish their production goals. Specifically, we explain how firms acquire fixed (or tangible) assets such as production facilities, offices, equipment, and materials. We also consider several key production concerns such as international logistics and total quality management. We then explain the important factors influencing managers' decisions of whether to expand or reduce operations abroad. We close by taking a brief look at how companies finance their international production operations and other activities.

PRODUCTION STRATEGY

Production operations are important to achieving a company's strategy. Careful planning of all aspects of production helps companies cut costs (to become low-cost leaders) or design new products and product features necessary for a differentiation strategy. Among the important strategic issues that managers must consider are planning for production capacity, the location of facilities, production processes to be used, and the layout of facilities.

CAPACITY PLANNING

capacity planning
Process of assessing a company's ability to produce enough output to satisfy market demand.

The process of assessing a company's ability to produce enough output to satisfy market demand is called **capacity planning**. Companies must estimate global demand for their products as accurately as possible. If capacity now used is greater than the expected market demand, production must be scaled back. For example, the number of employees or work shifts can be reduced at certain locations. However, countries have different laws regulating the ability of employers to eliminate jobs. Depending on the country, a firm may or may not need to give advance notice of layoffs or plant closings. On the other hand, if market demand is growing, managers must determine in which facilities to expand production or whether additional facilities are needed to expand capacity. In fact, rather than miss out on potential sales, a company might contract with other producers to meet the excess demand until new facilities are up and running.

Capacity planning is also extremely important for service companies. For example, a hotel chain that is moving into a new geographic market must estimate the number of rooms that its facilities should contain. It must also determine whether a facility will be used for conventions and the like and the number of meeting rooms that it must build. Videoconferencing facilities might be added if local firms require them to keep in touch with geographically dispersed operations.

FACILITIES LOCATION PLANNING

Selecting the location for production facilities is called **facilities location planning**. Companies often have many potential locations around the world from which to choose a site for production, research and development, or some other activity. Aspects of the business environment that are important for facilities location planning include the cost and availability of labor and management, raw materials, component parts, and energy. Other key factors include political stability, the extent of regulation and bureaucracy, economic development, and the local culture, including beliefs about work and important traditions.

Reducing production costs by taking advantage of lower wages in another country is often essential to keeping a company's products competitive in terms of pricing. This is especially important when labor accounts for a large portion of total production costs. However, the lower wages of a nation's workforce must be balanced against its potentially lower productivity. Worker productivity tends to be lower in most developing nations and some emerging markets as compared with developed nations. See this chapter's World Business Survey, titled "The Gap in Minimum Wages," to see how nations differ in their statutory minimum wage rates.

Although most service companies must locate near their customers, they must still consider a wide variety of customers' needs when locating facilities. Are convenience and being located in a high-traffic area important to customers? Such a location is

facilities location planning
Selecting the location for production facilities.

WORLD BUSINESS SURVEY

The Gap in Minimum Wages

There is a huge gap in statutory minimum wages between countries. Yet even within the European Union there are wide differences. Spain's minimum wage is about one-fifth as big as Luxembourg's.

Country	Minimum wage, $ per hour
Luxembourg	~8.7
Netherlands	~6.5
France	~6.0
Britain	~6.0
Italy	~5.6
United States	~5.1
Japan	~5.0
New Zealand	~3.2
Taiwan	~3.1
Greece	~2.4
Portugal	~1.9
Spain	~1.6
South Korea	~1.4

Minimum wage, $ per hour

clearly important for some companies, including restaurants, banks, and cinemas. For other service businesses, such as consulting companies or public utilities, a convenient location is less important.

Supply issues are also important in location planning. For any one mode of transportation, the greater the distance between production facilities and target markets, the longer it takes for customers to receive shipments. In turn, companies must compensate for delays by maintaining larger inventories in target markets—adding to storage and insurance costs. Shipping costs themselves are also greater when production is conducted away from target markets. Transportation costs are one of the driving forces behind the globalization of the steel industry. Shipping costs for steel can run $40 to $50 per ton—a significant amount when steel sells for $400 to $500 per ton. By building steel mills in countries where their customers are located, steel producers significantly reduce their transportation costs.

Automobile makers from Japan and Germany invested in production facilities inside the United States for some of the reasons just identified. For example, Toyota (www.global.toyota.com) and other Japanese auto companies manufacture cars in the United States to offset the risks from currency fluctuations, to defuse political concerns about the United States' trade deficit with Japan, and to be closer to their customers. BMW (www.bmw.com) of Germany assembles automobiles in the United States for similar reasons. For one thing, the strength of Germany's currency in the 1990s made German products more expensive on world export markets. Another reason is that Germany is home to the world's highest paid workers—the average hourly income is approximately $32. Finally, German companies are attracted by the lower cost of land along with concessions, such as tax breaks, offered by state governments eager to attract industry.

Location Economies   Selecting highly favorable locations often allows a company to achieve **location economies**—economic benefits derived from locating production activities in optimal locations. Location economies result from the right mix of the kinds of elements just described. To take advantage of location economies, companies either undertake business activities themselves in a particular location or obtain products and services from other companies located there. Location economies can involve practically any business activity that companies in a particular location do very well, including performing research and development or providing financial or advertising services.

The following examples illustrate the extent to which service and manufacturing companies exploit location economies. One company designed its precision ice hockey equipment in Sweden, obtained financing from Canada, assembled it in Cleveland and Denmark, and marketed it in North America and Europe. This equipment incorporated alloys whose molecular structure was researched and patented in Delaware and fabricated in Japan. Airplane manufacturer Boeing (www.boeing.com) designed aircraft in the state of Washington and Japan, which was assembled in Seattle with tail cones made in Canada, special tail sections made in China and Italy, and engines from Britain. Finally, one company's advertising campaign was conceived in Britain, shot in Canada, dubbed in Britain, and edited in New York.[2]

The key fact to remember here is that *each production activity generates more value in a particular location than could be generated elsewhere.* Productivity is a very important (though not the only) factor in determining the value that a location adds to a certain economic activity. The productivity of a location is heavily influenced by two resources—labor and capital.

Granted, in order to take advantage of location economies, managers might need to familiarize themselves with vastly different customs and traditions. For example, political and legal differences, can force firms to retain outside consultants or to train corpo-

location economies
Economic benefits derived
from locating production
activities in optimal locations.

One reason Nissan is locating production near its customers is to minimize shipping costs. Here Nissan CEO, Carlos Ghosn, and governor Ronnie Musgrove look over a model of a new Nissan (**www.nissan.com**) plant being built in Mississippi. The company is moving a large portion of its production from Japan to its U.S. factories. The move also helps the company avoid currency swings that affect the prices of its cars when exported to the United States.

rate lawyers in local traditions. Language differences might mean translating important documents on an ongoing basis. For these reasons, companies sometimes hire other companies in a location to perform an activity for them.

Centralization versus Decentralization   An important consideration for production managers is whether to centralize or decentralize production facilities. *Centralized production* refers to the concentration of production facilities in one location. With *decentralized production*, facilities are spread over several locations and could even mean having one facility for each national business environment in which the company markets its products—a common policy for companies that follow a multinational strategy. Companies often centralize production facilities in pursuit of low-cost strategies and to take advantage of economies of scale—a typical policy for companies that follow a global strategy. By producing large quantities of identical products in one location, the companies cut costs by reducing the per-unit cost of production.

Transportation costs and the physical landscape also affect the centralization versus decentralization decision. For example, because they usually sell undifferentiated products in all their markets, low-cost competitors generally do not need to locate near their markets in order to stay on top of changes in buyer preferences. That is why low-cost producers often choose locations with the lowest combined production and transportation costs. But even these firms must balance the cost of getting inputs into the production process and the cost of getting products to markets. Key factors in the physical environment that affect the transport of goods are the availability of seaports, airports, or other transportation hubs.

Conversely, companies that sell differentiated products may find decentralized production the better option. By locating separate facilities near different markets, they remain in close contact with customers and can respond quickly to changing buyer preferences. Closer contact with customers also helps firms develop a deeper understanding of buyer behavior in local cultures.

When close cooperation between research and development and manufacturing is essential for effective differentiation, both activities are usually conducted in the same place. However, new technologies are giving companies more freedom to separate these activities. The speed with which information travels today allows the rapid relay of information between subsidiaries and the home office.

PROCESS PLANNING

Deciding the process that a company will use to create its product is called **process planning**. The particular process to be used is typically determined by a firm's business-level strategy. For instance, low-cost strategies normally require large-scale production because producers want the cost savings generated by economies of scale. A company that mass-produces snowboards for average skiers will typically employ a highly automated production process that integrates advanced computer technology. However, differentiation strategies demand that producers provide extra value by offering customers something unique, such as superior quality, added features, or special brand images. Companies that handcraft snowboards for professionals will rely not on automated production but on skilled craftspeople. The company will design and produce each snowboard to suit the habits and special needs of each individual snowboarder. For such a company, service is a major component of the production process.

Availability and cost of labor in the local market is crucial to process planning. If labor in the host country is relatively cheap, an international company will likely opt for less technology and more labor-intensive methods in the production process—depending on its particular product and strategy. But again, the availability of labor and the level of wages in the local market must be balanced against the productivity of the local workforce.

Standardization versus Adaptation

Another important issue in production strategy is deciding whether the production process will be standardized for all markets or adapted to manufacture products modified for different markets. For example, low-cost leadership often dictates automated, standardized production in large batches. Large production batches reduce the cost of producing each unit, thus offsetting the higher initial investment in automation. Costs are further reduced as employees improve performance through repetition and a continual learning process that minimizes errors and waste.

But differentiation often demands decentralized facilities designed to improve local responsiveness. Because decentralized production facilities produce for one national market or for a regional market, they tend to be smaller. This tends to eliminate the potential to take advantage of economies of scale and therefore increases per-unit production costs. Similarly, the smaller market share at which a differentiation strategy aims normally calls for relatively smaller-scale production. Differentiating a product by incorporating certain features desired by customers requires more costly manufacturing processes. Research and development costs also tend to be higher for products with special product designs, styles, and features.

FACILITIES LAYOUT PLANNING

Deciding the spatial arrangement of production processes within production facilities is called **facilities layout planning**. Consider the fact that in Japan, Singapore, and Hong Kong, the supply of land is limited and its cost is high. Companies that locate in these markets must use the available space wisely by designing compact facilities. Conversely, in countries such as Canada, China, and the United States, an abundance of space reduces the cost of building facilities in many locations. Because land is cheaper, companies have more flexibility in designing facilities.

More importantly, facility layout depends on the type of production process a company employs, which in turn depends on a company's business-level strategy. For instance, rather than produce mass quantities of computers to be stored in inventory, Compaq (www.compaq.com) competes by manufacturing computers as it receives orders from individual customers. To implement this business strategy, Compaq executives decided to replace mass-assembly lines with three-person work cells. In production trials at a plant in Scotland, output increased 23 percent as compared with the best assembly line. In addition, output per square foot went up 16 percent—a significant increase in the efficiency within the facility.

Before an international company begins operations, it must acquire a number of physical resources. For example, managers must answer questions such as will the company make or buy the components it needs in the production process? What will be the sources of any required raw materials? Will the company acquire facilities and production equipment or build its own? in this section, we present the main elements that managers need to consider when answering these types of questions.

ACQUIRING PHYSICAL RESOURCES

MAKE-OR-BUY DECISION

The typical manufacturing company requires a wide range of inputs into its production process. These inputs typically enter the production line either as raw materials that require processing or as components needing only assembly. Bear in mind, too, that a component may require minor adjustments or other minor processing before it goes into production. Deciding whether to make a component or to buy it from another company is called the **make-or-buy decision**. Each option has its own set of advantages and disadvantages.

Reasons to Make   The process by which a company extends its control over additional stages of production—either inputs or outputs—is called **vertical integration**. When a company decides to make a product rather than buy it, it engages in "upstream" activities: production activities that come before a company's current business operations. For example, a car maker that decides to manufacture its own window glass engages in a new upstream activity.

Lower Costs   Above all, companies make products rather than buy them in order to reduce total costs. Generally speaking, the manufacturer's profit is the difference between the product's selling price and its production cost. When a company buys a product, it rewards the manufacturer by contributing to the latter's profit margin. Therefore, companies often undertake in-house production when they can manufacture a product for less than they must pay someone else to produce it. Thus, in-house production allows a company to reduce its own production costs.

For example, a computer motherboard is the physical foundation of a personal computer to which the microprocessor, memory chips, and other components are attached. This critical component accounts for about 40 percent of a personal computer's total cost. Compaq (www.compaq.com) discovered that it could produce motherboards itself for $25 less than its Asian suppliers and save 2 weeks' shipping time in the process.

Small companies are less likely than large ones to make rather than buy, especially when a product requires a large financial investment in equipment and facilities. However, this rule of thumb might not necessarily hold if the company possesses a proprietary technology or some other competitive advantage that is not easily copied.

Greater Control   Companies that depend on others for key ingredients or components give up a degree of control. Making rather than buying can give managers greater control over raw materials, product design, and the production process itself—all of which are important factors in product quality. In turn, quality control is especially important when customers are highly sensitive to even slight declines in quality. For the same reason, greater quality control also gives a company greater control over its reputation among customers.

> **make-or-buy decision**
> *Deciding whether to make a component or to buy it from another company.*

> **vertical integration**
> *Extension of company activities into stages of production that provide a firm's inputs (backward integration) or absorb its output (forward integration).*

In addition, persuading an outside supplier to make significant modifications to quality or features can be difficult. This is especially true if modifications entail investment in costly equipment or if they promise to be time-consuming. If just one buyer requests costly product adaptations, or if there is reason to suspect that a buyer will eventually take its business elsewhere, a supplier may be reluctant to undertake a costly investment. Unless that buyer purchases in large volumes, the cost of the modifications may be too great for the supplier to absorb. In such a case, the buyer simply may be unable to obtain the product it wants without manufacturing it in-house. Thus, companies maintain greater control over product design and product features if they manufacture components themselves.

Finally, making a product can be a good idea when buying from a supplier means providing the supplier with a firm's key technology. Through licensing agreements (see Chapter 13), companies often provide suppliers in low-wage countries with the technologies needed to make their products. However, if a company's competitive advantage depends on that technology, the licensor could inadvertently be creating a future competitor. When controlling a key technology is paramount, it is often better to manufacture in-house.

Reasons to Buy The practice of buying from another company a good or service that is not central to a company's competitive advantage is called **outsourcing**. Outsourcing results from continuous specialization and technological advancement. For each successive specialization of its operations process, a manufacturer requires greater skill and knowledge than it did before. By outsourcing, a company can reduce the degree to which it is vertically integrated and the overall amount of specialized skills and knowledge that it must possess.

Outsourcing has become extremely popular in the business of computer manufacturing. Component makers, including Intel (www.intel.com) in microprocessors, Seagate (www.seagate.com) in hard drives, U.S. Robotics (www.usr.com) in modems, and Mitsumi (www.mitsumi.com) in CD-ROM drives, supply big and small manufacturers worldwide. Computer companies buy components from these manufacturers, assemble them in their own facilities, and sell completed systems to consumers and

outsourcing
Practice of buying from another company a good or service that is not central to a company's competitive advantage.

Dell Computer Corporation (**www.dell.com**) has perfected the art of outsourcing. The company designs and builds computing systems for both consumers and companies, but it does not build the components themselves. The production strategy has made Dell a model of efficiency in the PC industry. Dell can deliver custom-made PCs in just 3 days while most of its rivals measure their delivery times in weeks. Do you think outsourcing will (will not) gain wider acceptance in the future?

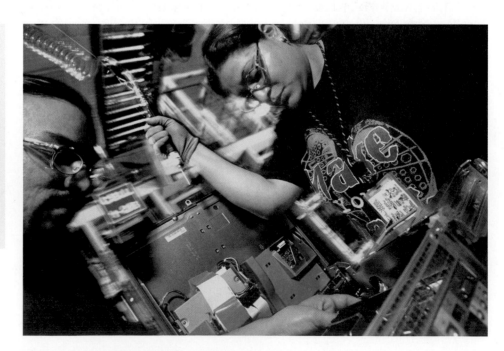

businesses. A related practice in the computer industry is known as "stealth manufacturing," which calls for outsourcing the actual assembly of the computers themselves, plus the job of shipping them to distributors and other intermediaries.[3]

A new and interesting type of outsourcing seems to be catching on in the pharmaceutical industry. Eli Lilly & Company (www.lilly.com) and other drug companies sometimes run into chemistry problems that their internal scientists need help solving. So, Lilly established a subsidiary company called Innocentive (www.innocentive.com). The subsidiary's Web site lists chemistry problems that need solving and the amount that Lilly will pay for the solution. Lilly offers cash awards of as much as $100,000 to the solution finder. In this way, Lilly goes beyond its own 600 scientists and taps a global pool of scientists from countries such as India and China.[4]

Many companies buy when buying is the lower-cost option. When a firm cannot integrate vertically by manufacturing a product for less than a supplier can, it will typically outsource. Let's explore some other reasons why companies prefer to buy rather than make.

Lower Risk   In earlier chapters, we described the many types of risks faced by companies that construct and staff facilities in other countries. For example, recall that political risk is quite high in certain markets. Social unrest or open conflict can threaten physical facilities, equipment, and employee safety.

One way a company can eliminate the exposure of assets to political risk in other countries is simply by refusing to invest in plants and equipment abroad. It can instead purchase products from international suppliers. This policy also eliminates the need to purchase the expensive insurance coverage that is needed when a company undertakes production in an unstable country. However, this policy will not completely shield the buyer from all potential disruptions—political instability can cause delays in the timely receipt of needed parts. Indeed, even under normal circumstances, the longer delivery times involved in international outsourcing can increase the risk that the buyer will not meet its own production schedule.

Greater Flexibility   Maintaining sufficient flexibility to respond to market conditions is increasingly important for companies everywhere. Making an in-house product that requires large investments in equipment and buildings often reduces flexibility. In contrast, companies that buy products from one or more outside suppliers gain flexibility. In fact, added flexibility is the key factor in a fundamental change in attitude toward outsourcing, which many managers now regard as a full-fledged strategy for change rather than a limited tactical tool for solving immediate problems.

Maintaining flexibility is important when the national business environments of suppliers are volatile. By buying from several suppliers, or by establishing production facilities in more than one country, a company can outsource products from one location if instability erupts in another. The same is true during periods of great volatility in exchange rates. Exchange-rate movements can increase or decrease the cost of importing a product from a given country. By buying from multiple suppliers located in several countries, a company can maintain the flexibility needed to change sources and reduce the risk associated with sudden swings in exchange rates.

Companies also maintain operational flexibility simply by not having to invest in production facilities. Unencumbered by investment in costly production equipment and facilities, a firm can alter its product line very quickly. This capability is especially important for products with small production runs or those with highly uncertain potential. Furthermore, a company can obtain financial flexibility if its capital is not locked up in plants and equipment. It can then use excess financial capital to pursue other domestic or international opportunities. Outsourcing can also free a company from having to recoup large investments in research and development.

Market Power   Companies can gain a great deal of power in their relationships with suppliers simply by becoming important customers. In fact, sometimes a supplier can become a sort of hostage to one particular customer. This situation occurs when a supplier becomes heavily dependent on a company that it serves with nearly all of its production capacity. If the main buyer suddenly begins outsourcing elsewhere, the supplier will have few other customers to whom it can turn. This situation gives the buyer significant control in dictating quality improvements, forcing cost reductions, and making special modifications.

Barriers to Buying   For various reasons, companies sometimes face obstacles when buying products from international suppliers. First, the government of the buyer's country may impose import tariffs designed to improve the nation's balance of trade. Tariffs can add anywhere from 15 to 50 percent to the cost of a component that a manufacturer needs from abroad.

Second, the services provided by intermediaries increase the cost of buying abroad. Obtaining letters of credit, arranging physical transportation, and obtaining insurance all add to the final cost that a manufacturer pays for a product supplied from abroad. Although these expenses are currently lower than they have ever been, they can significantly increase total product cost. If high enough, they can negate any advantage of buying from an international supplier.

RAW MATERIALS

Decisions about the selection and acquisition of raw materials are important to many different types of manufacturers. The twin issues of quantity and quality drive many of these decisions. First, some industries and companies rely almost exclusively on the quantity of locally available raw materials. This is most true for companies involved in mining, forestry, and fishing. There must be an adequate supply of iron ore, oil, lumber, or fish to justify the large financial investment required to build processing facilities.

Second, the quality of raw material has a huge influence on the quality of a company's end product. For instance, food-processing companies must examine the quality of the locally grown fruit, vegetables, grains, and any other ingredients. Beverage companies must assess the quality of the local water supply. Some markets may require large financial investments to build water-purifying facilities. Elsewhere (such as much of the Middle East), the only local water source may be seawater, which must be desalinized.

FIXED ASSETS

fixed (tangible) assets
Company assets such as production facilities, inventory warehouses, retail outlets, and production and office equipment.

Most companies must acquire **fixed (tangible) assets**—such as production facilities, inventory warehouses, computer storage capacity, retail outlets, and production and office equipment—in the host country. Many companies have the option of either (1) acquiring or modifying existing factories, or (2) building entirely new facilities—called a *greenfield* investment. Considering either option involves many individuals within the company. For example, production managers must verify that an existing facility (or an empty lot) is large enough and will suit the company's facility layout needs. Site-acquisition experts and legal staff must guarantee that the proposed business activity abides by local laws. Public relations staff must work with community leaders to ensure that the company does not jeopardize the rights, values, and customs of the local population.

Finally, managers must make sure that the local infrastructure can support the firm's proposed on-site business operations. Also, factory and office equipment is likely to be available locally in most newly industrialized and developed markets. However, little, if any, equipment is likely to be available in developing markets. Thus, managers must assess both the cost in tariffs that will be imposed on imported equipment and the cost in time and effort that will be required to import it.

In Chapter 11 we covered the issues surrounding the number and location of manufacturing facilities because of their important influence on company strategy and organizational structure. At this point, there remain just several issues to discuss related to manufacturing operations. In this section, we first examine how companies maximize quality and minimize shipping and inventory costs. Then we take a brief look at the important reinvestment versus divestment decision.

QUALITY-IMPROVEMENT EFFORTS

Companies strive toward quality improvement for two reasons: costs and customer value. First, quality products help keep production costs low because they reduce waste in valuable inputs, reduce the cost of retrieving defective products from buyers, and reduce the disposal costs that result from defective products. Second, some minimum level of acceptable quality is an aspect of nearly every product today. Even companies that produce low-cost products try to maintain or improve quality, as long as it does not erode their position in what is typically a price-competitive market or market segment. A company that succeeds in combining a low-cost position with a high-quality product can gain a tremendous competitive advantage in its market.

Improving quality is also important for a company that provides services—whether as its only product or in conjunction with the goods it manufactures and markets. Managing quality in services is complicated by the fact that a service is created and consumed at the same time. For this reason, the human interaction between an employee who delivers a service and the buyer is important to service quality. However, activities that must be conducted prior to the actual delivery of a service are also important. For example, it is important that a restaurant be clean and have an inventory of the ingredients it needs to prepare the meals on its menu. Likewise, a bank can provide high-quality service only if employees arrive for work on time and interact professionally with customers.

Let's now take a brief look at two movements that inspire the drive toward quality—total quality management and International Standards Organization (ISO) 9000 certification.

Total Quality Management   An emphasis on continuous quality improvement to meet or exceed customer expectations is called **total quality management (TQM)**. TQM stresses a company-wide commitment to quality-enhancing processes. It also places a great deal of responsibility on each individual to be focused on the quality of his or her own output—regardless of whether the employee's activities are based in the factory, in administration, or in management.

By continuously improving the quality of its products, a company can differentiate itself from rivals and attract loyal customers. The TQM philosophy initially took hold in the 1960s and 1970s in Japan, where electronics and automobile firms applied TQM techniques to reduce costs and thereby gain significant market share around the world through price competitiveness and a reputation for quality. It was not until U.S. and European companies lost a great deal of market share to their Japanese rivals that they embraced TQM principles.

ISO 9000   The International Standards Organization (ISO) 9000 is an international certification that companies get when they meet the highest quality standards in their industries. Firms in the European Union are leading the way in quality certification. But

> **total quality management (TQM)**
> Emphasis on continuous quality improvement to meet or exceed customer expectations involving a company-wide commitment to quality-enhancing processes.

both European and non-European companies alike are working toward certification in order to ensure access to the European marketplace. To become certified, companies must demonstrate the reliability and soundness of all business processes that affect the quality of their products. Many companies also seek ISO 9000 certification because of the message of quality that certification sends to prospective customers. To see how companies can blend together TQM principles and the drive toward ISO 9000 certification, see the Global Manager titled "Linking TQM and ISO 9000 Standards."

SHIPPING AND INVENTORY COSTS

Shipping costs can have a dramatic effect on the cost of getting materials and components to the location of production facilities. When the cost of getting inputs into the production process is a large portion of the product's total cost, producers tend to locate close to the source of those inputs. Shipping costs are affected by many elements of a nation's business environment, such as its general level of economic development, including the condition of seaports, airports, roads, and rail networks.

It used to be the practice that producers bought large quantities of materials or components and stored them in large warehouses until they were needed in the production process. However, storing great amounts of inventory for production is costly in terms of insuring them against damage or theft and the rent or purchase price of the warehouse needed to store them.

GLOBAL MANAGER

Linking TQM and ISO 9000 Standards

In today's competitive environment many companies are applying TQM principles. When doing business internationally, ISO 9000 certification is becoming increasingly important. However, the ISO 9000 standards do not specify how a company should develop its quality processes. Rather, ISO requires each company to define and document its own quality processes and show evidence of implementing them. The following is a framework describing how TQM and ISO 9000 principles can be linked to enhance a company's capability for delivering quality products or services.

The main principles of TQM include:

➡ **Delight the customer**. Companies must strive to be the best at what customers consider most important. This can change over time, so business owners must be in close touch with customers.

➡ **Use people-based management**. Systems, standards, and technology cannot, in and of themselves, guarantee quality. The key is to provide employees with the knowledge of what to do and how to do it and to provide feedback on performance.

➡ **Continuous improvement**. TQM is not a short-term quick fix. Major breakthroughs are less important than incremental improvement.

➡ **Management by fact**. Quality management and improvement requires that managers clearly understand how consumers perceive the performance of a company's goods and services. Rather than trusting "gut feelings," obtain factual information and share it with employees.

Companies can link these TQM principles to ISO 9000 standards in three ways:

➡ **Process definition**. The existing business process must be defined. Once defined, it must be satisfying to key stakeholders and it must "delight the customer."

➡ **Process improvement**. Everyone within the organization must use the defined process properly. If this is not the case, then a company must improve the management of its human resources.

➡ **Process management**. Management and employees must possess factual knowledge about process details in order to manage them properly.

Because companies have far better uses for the money tied up in such inventory, they developed better inventory-management techniques. A production technique in which inventory is kept to a minimum and inputs to the production process arrive exactly when they are needed (or *just in time*) is called **just-in-time (JIT) manufacturing**. Although the technique was originally developed in Japan, it quickly spread throughout manufacturing operations worldwide. JIT drastically reduces the costs associated with large inventories. It also helps reduce wasteful expenses because defective materials and components are spotted quickly during production. Under traditional systems, defective materials or components were sometimes discovered only after being built into finished products.

REINVESTMENT VERSUS DIVESTMENT

Companies maintain the current level of operations when no new opportunities are foreseen. Yet, changing conditions in the competitive global marketplace often force managers to choose between *reinvesting* in operations and *divesting* them.

Companies often continue to reinvest profits in markets that require long payback periods so long as the long-term outlook is good. This is often the case in developing countries and large emerging markets. For example, corruption, red tape, distribution problems, and a vague legal system present challenges for non-Chinese companies. Yet, because long-term returns on their investments are expected, Western companies reinvested heavily in China despite uncertain short-term profits.[5] Most of these companies invested in production facilities to take advantage of a low-cost labor pool and low-cost energy.

Companies scale back their international operations when it becomes apparent that making operations profitable will take longer than expected. Again, China serves as a good example. Some companies were lured to China by the possibilities for growth offered by 1.2 billion consumers. However, some had to scale back their ambitions that were based on overly optimistic marketing plans.

Companies usually decide to reinvest when a market is experiencing rapid growth. Reinvestment can mean either expanding in the market itself or expanding in a location that serves the growing market. Investing in expanding markets is often an attractive option because potential new customers usually have not yet become loyal to the products of any one company or brand. It can be easier and less costly to attract customers in such markets than it is to gain market share in markets that are stagnant or contracting.

Yet, problems in the political, social, or economic sphere can force a company either to reduce or eliminate operations altogether. Such problems are usually intertwined with one another. For example, in the late 1990s Western companies pulled their personnel out of Indonesia because of intense social unrest stemming directly from a combination of political problems (discontent with the nation's political leadership) and economic upheaval (the collapse of the Indonesian economy).

Finally, companies invest in the operations that offer the best return on their investments. That policy often means reducing or divesting operations in some markets, even though they may be profitable, in order to invest in more profitable opportunities elsewhere.

Companies need financial resources to pay for a variety of operating expenses and new projects. They must buy raw materials and component products for manufacturing and assembly activities. At certain times, they need large sums of capital, whether for expanding production capacity or entering new geographic markets. But companies also need financing to pay for all sorts of activities in addition to those related to pro-

FINANCING BUSINESS OPERATIONS

duction. They must pay for training and development programs and compensate workers and managers. They must pay advertising agencies for helping the company promote its goods and services. They also must make periodic interest payments to lenders and perhaps reward stockholders with dividends.

But all companies have a limited supply of resources at their disposal to invest in current operations or new endeavors. So, where do companies obtain needed funds? Generally speaking, organizations obtain financial resources through one of three sources:

1. Borrowing (debt)
2. Issuing equity (stock ownership)
3. Internal funding

BORROWING

International companies (like domestic companies) try to get the lowest interest rates possible on borrowed funds. However, this objective is more complex on a global scale. Difficulties include exchange-rate risk, restrictions on currency convertibility, and restrictions on the international flow of capital.

Borrowing locally can be advantageous, especially when the value of the local currency has fallen against that of the home country. Suppose a Japanese company borrows from U.S. banks for investment in the United States. Let's say that one year later, the U.S. dollar has fallen against the Japanese yen; in other words, fewer yen are now needed to buy one dollar. In that case, the Japanese company can repay the loan with fewer yen than would have been required if the value of the dollar had not fallen.

But companies are not always able to borrow funds locally. Often they are forced to seek international sources of capital. This is sometimes the case when a subsidiary is new to the market and has not yet built a reputation with local lenders. In such cases, a parent firm can help a subsidiary acquire financing through a so-called **back-to-back loan**—a loan in which a parent company deposits money with a host-country bank, which then lends the money to a subsidiary located in the host country.

For instance, suppose that a Mexican company forms a new subsidiary in the United States but that this subsidiary cannot obtain a U.S. bank loan. The Mexican parent company can deposit Mexican pesos in the branch of a U.S. bank in Mexico (see Figure 15.1). The U.S. bank's home office then lends dollars to the subsidiary in the United States. The amount of money lent in dollars will be equivalent to the amount of pesos on deposit with the U.S. bank's Mexican branch. When the U.S. subsidiary repays the loan in full, the parent company withdraws its deposit (plus any interest earned) from the U.S. bank's Mexican branch.

ISSUING EQUITY

Recall from Chapter 9 that the *international equity market* consists of all stocks bought and sold outside the home country of the issuing company. Companies issue such stock primarily to access pools of investors with funds that are unavailable domestically. However, getting shares listed on another country's stock exchange can be a complex process. For one thing, complying with all the rules and regulations governing the operation of a particular stock exchange costs a great deal of time and money. Therefore, only large companies tend to list shares on multiple exchanges.

Issuing American Depository Receipts   To maximize international exposure (and access to funds), non–U.S. companies often list themselves on U.S. stock exchanges. Non–U.S. companies can list shares directly in the United States by issuing

back-to-back loan
Loan in which a parent company deposits money with a host-country bank, which then lends the money to a subsidiary located in the host country.

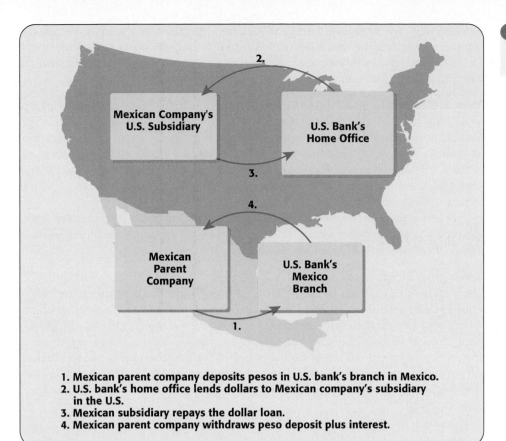

FIGURE 15.1

Mexico–United States Back-to-Back Loan

1. Mexican parent company deposits pesos in U.S. bank's branch in Mexico.
2. U.S. bank's home office lends dollars to Mexican company's subsidiary in the U.S.
3. Mexican subsidiary repays the dollar loan.
4. Mexican parent company withdraws peso deposit plus interest.

American Depository Receipts (ADRs)—certificates that trade in the United States and represent a specific number of shares in a non–U.S. company. Large U.S. banks, such as Citibank (www.citibank.com), issue ADRs that then trade on the New York Stock Exchange (www.nyse.com), the computerized National Association of Securities Dealers Automated Quotation system (www.nasdaq.com), and the over-the-counter (OTC) market. As we saw in the company profile at the start of this chapter, Finland-based Nokia (www.nokia.com) accesses U.S. investors by issuing ADRs.

International companies also make use of Global Depository Receipts (GDRs). These are similar in principle to ADRs but are listed and traded in London and Luxembourg. Companies from India aggressively issue GDRs to circumvent stringent listing requirements in their home market.[6]

Advantages of ADRs Companies gain several important advantages through ADRs. First, investors who buy ADRs pay no currency-conversion fees. In contrast, if a U.S. investor were to purchase the shares of a non–U.S. company on another country's stock exchange, he or she would incur the expense of converting currencies. Avoiding such expenses, plus the added convenience of paying in dollars, encourages U.S. investors to buy ADRs. Second, there are no minimum purchase requirements for ADRs, as there sometimes are for shares of a company's stock.

Third, companies offer ADRs in the United States to appeal to mutual funds. Investment laws in the United States limit the amount of money that a mutual fund can invest in the shares of companies not registered on U.S. exchanges. U.S. mutual fund managers were forced to sell shares of German software producer SAP (www.sap.com) when they appreciated in price. Says Kevin McKay, chief operating officer of SAP America: "Some of these guys were telling us, 'We hate to sell, but we have to. Please get

American Depository Receipt (ADR)
Certificate that trades in the United States and represents a specific number of shares in a non–U.S. company.

some ADRs.'" SAP complied. Listing ADRs in the United States also allowed the company to reward employees with discounted shares of company stock—something that it could not have done otherwise because companies are barred from awarding shares in unregistered companies to employees in the United States.[7]

Venture Capital   Another source of equity financing for entrepreneurial start-ups and small businesses is **venture capital**—financing obtained from investors who believe that the borrower will experience rapid growth and who receive equity (part ownership) in return. Those who supply the venture with the capital it needs are called *venture capitalists*. Although there is often substantial risk associated with new, rapidly expanding enterprises, venture capitalists invest in them because they can also generate very large returns on investment.

In recent years, the venture capital industry has become global. For some key strategies that savvy entrepreneurs use to find international investors, see the Entrepreneurial Focus titled "Get Global Cash: Overseas Investors Await You."

Emerging Stock Markets   Naturally, companies from countries with emerging stock markets face certain problems. First, emerging stock markets commonly experience extreme volatility. An important contributing factor is that investments into emerging stock markets are often so-called *hot money*—money that can be quickly withdrawn in times of crisis. In contrast, *patient money*—foreign direct investment in factories, equipment, and land—cannot be pulled out as readily. Large and sudden sell-offs of equity are signs of market volatility that characterize many emerging stock markets. Such large sell-offs occur because of uncertainty regarding the nation's future economic growth.

ENTREPRENEURIAL FOCUS

Get Global Cash: Overseas Investors Await You

Small-business financing is becoming more global as the economies of different nations become interwoven and technology continually makes it easier to communicate between nations. As we know, the international capital market offers entrepreneurs many advantages. For example, in order to gain a market or technology position in the United States, international investors may accept lower returns than their U.S. counterparts. Here are some tips from entrepreneurs who have succeeded in finding international capital for their companies:

➡ **Contact business schools with strong international programs** to build up contacts. Instructors of international business courses often have contacts in both education and industry abroad. To break into this network, you might visit your local college, take an executive education course there, or perhaps even join a program in which you can work closely with entrepreneurial advisers.

➡ **Consult your country's commerce department** about potential international markets in which your product might be appealing. Developing, newly industrialized,

and highly developed countries all have needs in practically every economic sector. Your nation's commerce department can help in your preliminary scouting of opportunities, as can your country's embassies.

➡ **Leverage your contacts** and tap the professionals with whom you work—especially attorneys and accountants with international ties. Long before you start pursuing overseas investors, consider asking a respected executive with international experience to serve on your board of directors.

➡ **Attend industry events in other countries** to increase your contacts and exposure. Your specific trade association should be able to provide you with a schedule of shows taking place in other countries.

➡ **Consider hiring an intermediary** to help find capital. These types of intermediaries can help locate funding from international venture-capital firms, banks, and other lending institutions. They also can help expanding businesses get capital from Canadian, European, and Asian financial institutions.

Second, companies that issue equity on their countries' emerging stock markets are often plagued by poor market regulation. This can allow large local companies to wield a great deal of influence over their domestic stock markets. As long as powerful domestic shareholders dominate such exchanges, international investors will likely hesitate to enter. The root of the problem often lies in regulation that favors insiders over international investors.

INTERNAL FUNDING

Ongoing international business activities and new investments can also be financed internally, whether with funds supplied by the parent company or by its international subsidiaries.

Internal Equity, Debt, and Fees   Spin-off companies and new subsidiaries typically require a period of time before they become financially independent. During this period, they often obtain internal financing from parent companies.

Many international subsidiaries obtain financial capital by issuing equity, which as a rule is not publicly traded. In fact, equity is often purchased solely by the parent company, which obviously enjoys great influence over the subsidiary's decisions. If the subsidiary performs well, the parent earns a return from the appreciating share price, which reflects the increasing valuation of the company. If the subsidiary decides to pay stock dividends, the parent company can also earn a return in this way. Parent companies commonly lend money to international subsidiaries during the start-up phase and when subsidiaries undertake large new investments. Conversely, subsidiaries with excess cash often lend money to parent or sister companies when they need financial capital.

Revenue from Operations   Money earned from the sale of goods and services is called **revenue**. This source of capital is the lifeblood of international companies and their subsidiaries. If a company is to succeed in the long term, it must at some point generate sufficient internal revenue to sustain day-to-day operations. At that point, outside financing is required only to expand operations or to survive lean periods—say, during seasonal sales fluctuations.

revenue
Monies earned from the sale of goods and services.

As we saw in earlier chapters, international companies and their subsidiaries also generate revenues internally through so-called *transfer prices*—prices charged for goods or services transferred among a company and its subsidiaries. Companies set subsidiaries' transfer prices high or low according to their own goals. For instance, often they pursue transfer pricing aggressively when they wish to minimize taxes in a high-taxation country. Transfer pricing can be used if there are no national restrictions on the use of foreign exchange or on the repatriation of profits to home countries. Figure 15.2 summarizes the internal sources of capital for international companies and their subsidiaries.

CAPITAL STRUCTURE

capital structure
Mix of equity, debt, and internally generated funds used to finance a company's activities.

The **capital structure** of a company is the mix of equity, debt, and internally generated funds that it uses to finance its activities. Firms try to strike the right balance among financing methods in order to minimize risk and the cost of capital.

Debt requires periodic interest payments to creditors such as banks and bondholders. If the company defaults on interest payments, creditors can take the company to court to force it to pay—even forcing it into bankruptcy. On the other hand, in the case of equity only holders of certain types of preferred stock (which companies issue sparingly) can force bankruptcy because of default. As a rule, then, companies do not want to carry so much debt in relation to equity that it increases its risk of insolvency. However, debt appeals to companies in many countries because interest payments can be deducted from taxable earnings—thus lowering the amount of taxes the firm must pay.

The basic principles of capital structure do not vary from domestic to international companies. However, research indicates that multinational firms have lower ratios of debt to equity than domestic firms. Why is this so? Some observers cite increased political risk, exchange-rate risk, and the number of opportunities available to multinationals as possible explanations for the difference.[8] Others suggest that the debt-versus-equity option depends on a company's national culture.[9] However, this suggestion has come under fire because companies from all cultures want to reduce their cost of capital. Moreover, many large international companies generate revenue from a large number of countries. How does one determine the "national culture" of these companies?

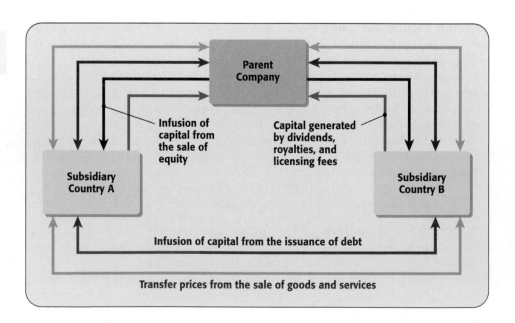

FIGURE 15.2

Internal Sources of Capital for International Companies

National restrictions can influence the choice of capital structure. These restrictions include limits on the international flows of capital, the cost of local financing versus the cost of international financing, access to international financial markets, and controls imposed on the exchange of currencies. The choice of capital structure for each of a company's international subsidiaries—and, therefore, its own capital structure—is a highly complex decision.

Whether an international company's production activity involves manufacturing a product or providing a service, it must acquire many resources before beginning operations. It needs to resolve such issues as where it will get raw materials or components, how much production capacity it needs, whether to construct or buy new facilities, the size of service centers, and where it will get financing. The answers to these questions are complex and interrelated.

This chapter discussed important considerations when formulating international production strategies, including planning for production capacity, the location of facilities, production processes to be used, and the layout of facilities. We also presented the decision of when companies prefer to centralize or decentralize production and whether production will be standardized or adapted to national markets. In the process, we saw how production issues are linked to earlier discussions of overall corporate strategy and marketing strategy. We closed the chapter with a discussion of how companies finance their international production operations and other activities.

There is a variety of additional material available on the Companion Website that accompanies this book. You can access this information by visiting the Website at (**www.prenhall.com/wild**).

summary

❶ Identify the elements that are important to consider when formulating *production strategies.* The process of assessing a company's ability to produce enough output to satisfy market demand is called *capacity planning.* If capacity is greater than the expected market demand, production must be scaled back, and *vice versa.*

Selecting the location for production facilities is called *facilities location planning.* Selecting highly favorable locations often allows a company to achieve *location economies*—economic benefits derived from locating production activities in optimal locations. Another important consideration is whether to centralize or decentralize production facilities. *Centralized production* refers to the concentration of production facilities in one location. With *decentralized production,* facilities are spread over several locations.

Deciding the process that a company will use to create its product is called *process planning.* Another important production issue is deciding whether the production process will be *standardized* for all mar-

kets or *adapted* to manufacture products modified for different markets.

Deciding the spatial arrangement of production processes within production facilities is called *facilities layout planning.* Facility layout depends on the type of production process a company employs.

❷ Identify key considerations when *acquiring physical resources.* In essence, the *make-or-buy* decision represents the decision for or against greater *vertical integration*—the process whereby a company extends control over additional stages of production. A firm that chooses to *make* a particular product or component often does so to take advantage of lower costs or to achieve greater control. On the other hand, *outsourcing*—buying from another company a good or service that is not central to a firm's competitive advantage—can provide greater flexibility while reducing the exposure to exchange-rate fluctuations and other forms of risk.

Decisions about the selection and acquisition of raw materials are also important. First, some companies must rely exclusively on the *quantity* of locally available raw materials such as iron ore, oil, lumber, or fish. Second, the *quality* of raw material has a huge influence on the quality of a company's end product such as fruit, vegetables, grains, and water.

Finally, most companies must acquire *fixed (tangible) assets* in a host country. Many companies have the option of either (1) acquiring or modifying existing factories, or (2) building entirely new facilities. Managers also must make sure that the local infrastructure can support the firm's proposed on-site business operations.

3 **Identify several production matters that are of special concern to managers.** Companies strive toward quality improvement for two reasons: costs and customer value. An emphasis on continuous quality improvement to meet or exceed customer expectations is called *total quality management (TQM)*. TQM stresses a company-wide commitment to quality-enhancing processes. The *International Standards Organization (ISO) 9000* is an international certification that companies get when they meet the highest quality standards in their industries. Many companies seek ISO 9000 certification because of the message of quality that certification sends to prospective customers.

Shipping costs can have a dramatic effect on the cost of getting materials and components to production facilities. A production technique in which *inventory* is kept to a minimum and inputs to the production process arrive exactly when they are needed is called *just-in-time (JIT) manufacturing*. JIT drastically reduces the costs associated with large inventories.

Managers also monitor events and might *reinvest* in operations or *divest* them. Companies often reinvest when (1) managers believe a market will provide a large return over time, and (2) a market is experiencing rapid growth. Companies often divest (reduce investments) when (1) profitability is further off than expected, (2) problems in the political, social, or economic sphere arise; and (3) more profitable opportunities arise in other markets.

4 **Describe the three potential *sources of financing* and the main financial instruments of each.** One source of financing is borrowing. Because interest rates vary around the world, cross-border borrowing can be attractive. In *back-to-back loans*, parent firms loan money to subsidiaries by depositing money in host-country banks.

Another source of funds is *equity financing*, wherein a company sells stock to raise capital. Companies outside the United States can still access its capital market by issuing what are called *American depository receipts (ADRs)*—Certificates that trade in the United States and represent a specific number of shares in a non–U.S. company. *Venture capital* is a source of equity for entrepreneurial start-ups and small businesses.

A third source of financing is *internal funding*. Parent companies and their subsidiaries can obtain internal funding through (1) a swapping of debt or equity, and (2) charging one another royalties and licensing fees. *Revenue* from ongoing operations can be used to finance company growth and expansion. International companies and their subsidiaries can also obtain funds from *transfer prices*—prices charged one another for goods and services purchased internally.

questions **for review**

1. What is *capacity planning*? Explain why it is important when formulating production strategy.

2. Define *facilities location planning*. How is it affected by *location economies* and centralization versus decentralization of production?

3. What is *process planning*? Explain how it is affected by the standardization versus adaptation decision.

4. Define *facilities layout planning*. How is it relevant to the formulation of production strategies?

5. What is meant by the phrase *make-or-buy decision*? List the reasons why a company might decide to make or buy a component.

6. What are the main factors involved in acquiring *raw materials*? *Fixed assets*?

7. How do *total quality management (TQM)* and *ISO 9000* help companies improve quality and control costs?

8. How do *shipping and inventory costs* influence a company's international logistics decision?

9. What is *just-in-time (JIT) manufacturing*? Explain its significance.

10. Compare and contrast the considerations underlying the decision to *reinvest* in business operations with the considerations underlying the decision to *divest* operations.

11. What are the three means by which international companies can acquire *financial resources*?

12. What is a *back-to-back loan*? Explain when it might be useful.

13. Why might a company list its stock in the *international capital market*? Explain the advantages of issuing an *American Depository Receipt (ADR)*.

14. What is *venture capital*? Explain its importance to entrepreneurs and small businesses.

15. What are some of the difficulties facing companies that issue equity on *emerging stock markets*?

16. Why is *revenue* from operations so important to a company's future success?

17. What is meant by a company's *capital structure*? Briefly explain its significance.

questions **for discussion**

1. Companies around the world are increasingly committing themselves to attaining International Standards Organization (ISO) certification in a variety of areas, including quality and pollution minimization. Do you think this is just the beginning of a trend toward worldwide homogenization of product and process standards? Do you think that someday all companies and their products will need certification in order to conduct international business? Explain your answers.

2. Despite the difficulties many technology companies experienced when the dot-com bubble burst, Internet commerce (e-business) is here to stay. What resources does an Internet retailer need other than merely a storefront on the Internet? Does it require fewer physical, financial, and human resources than a traditional retailer or just as many? Explain.

in **practice**

Read the brief article below and answer the questions that follow.

Xerox to Invest in Irish Facilities

DUBLIN, Ireland—The Xerox Corp. has said it will invest $270 million in new production and support facilities in Dublin and Dundalk, Ireland. The company plans to locate a large portion of its European shared services and customer support operations, as well as some of its customer financing and management, in the Dublin suburb of Blanchardstown. In addition, Xerox has acquired more than 100 acres in Dundalk—near the border with Northern Ireland—as the site of several facilities for color toner cartridge manufacturing, logistics, technical support, and other nonmanufacturing activities.

1. Why might Xerox (www.xerox.com) have decided to build a facility in Ireland to produce toner cartridges itself rather than contract with a supplier for their production? List some benefits Xerox might expect to gain by making instead of buying.

2. Why do you think Xerox chose Ireland for expansion? How might relative unrest or instability in Northern Ireland affect the performance of its facilities so near the border between Ireland and Northern Ireland?

3. What sort of fixed assets might Xerox need for each type of activity it is proposing to carry out in Ireland?

projects

1. The United States is home to some of the world's leading computer software companies, most of which commonly outsource software development to other countries, including Egypt, India, Ireland, Israel, Malaysia, Hungary, and the Philippines. Select one of these countries and explain why it has become a supplier to the computer software industry. Do you think that development of the industry in your chosen country is a threat to companies in the United States? Why or why not?

2. With several classmates, contact a manager at a local company that does business internationally. Talk to the manager about total quality management and ISO standards. Find out whether the company has a formal TQM program and whether

it has obtained any type of ISO certification. Compile your findings and present them to the class in a short talk. Compare and contrast the findings obtained for each company the class studied.

3. Suppose that you are the chief financial officer of a consumer-goods company based in Mexico. Your company wishes to expand internationally but lacks the necessary financial capital. Describe all the financing options that you think are available to your company. Explain why you think each option is feasible, taking into account the prevailing situation in the Mexican and international capital markets. Develop a short presentation to be delivered to your board of directors (your classmates).

Toyota Motor Corporation (www.global.toyota.com) commonly appears in most rankings of the world's most respected companies. One reason for Toyota's strong showing in such rankings is that the company seems to always manage to maintain profitability in the face of economic downturns and slack demand. Another reason is that leaders in a wide range of industries have high regard for Toyota's management and production practices.

Toyota first began producing cars in 1937. In the mid-1950s, a machinist named Taiichi Ohno began developing a new concept of automobile production. Today, the approach known as the Toyota Production System (TPS) has been intently studied and widely copied throughout the automobile industry. Ohno, who was addressed by fellow employees as *sensei* ("teacher and master"), followed the lead of the family that founded Toyota (spelled Toyoda) by exhibiting high regard for workers. Ohno also believed that mass production of automobiles was obsolete and that a flexible production system that produced cars according to specific customer requests would be superior.

It was at Toyota that the well-known just-in-time approach to inventory management was developed and perfected. Implementing just-in-time required *kanban*, a simple system of colored paper cards that accompanied the parts as they progressed down the assembly line. *Kanban* eliminates inventory buildup by quickly telling the production personnel which parts are being used and which are not. The third pillar of the Toyota Production System was quality circles, groups of workers that discuss ways of improving the work process and making better cars. Finally, the entire system was based on *jidoka*, which literally means "automation." However, as used at Toyota, the word expresses management's faith in the worker as a human being and a thinker.

A simple example illustrates the benefits of Toyota's system. Toyota dealerships found that customers kept returning their vehicles with leaking radiator hoses. When a team of workers at the U.S. plant where the vehicle was made was asked to help find a solution, they found the problem was the clamp on the radiator hose. In assembly, the clamp is put over the hose, a pin on the side is pulled out, and the hose is secured. But sometimes the operator would forget to pull the pin. The hose would remain loose and would leak. So the team installed a device next to the line that contains a funnel and electric eye. If a pin is not tossed into the funnel (passing the electric eye) every 60 seconds, the device senses that the operator must have forgotten to pull the pin and stops the line. As a result, a warranty problem at the dealerships was eliminated, customer dissatisfaction was reduced, and productivity increased.

Nearly 50 years after the groundwork for the Toyota Production System was first laid, the results speak for themselves. Toyota's superior approach to manufacturing has been estimated to yield a cost advantage of $600 to $700 per car due to more efficient production, plus another $300 savings per car because fewer defects mean less warranty repair work. Ohno's belief in flexible production can also be seen in the fact that Toyota's Sienna minivan is produced on the same assembly line in Georgetown, Kentucky, as the company's Camry models. The Sienna and Camry share the same basic chassis and 50 percent of their parts. Out of 300 different stations on the assembly line, Sienna models require different parts at only 26 stations. Toyota expects to build one Sienna for every three Camrys that come off the assembly line.

thinking globally

1. Chrysler (www.chrysler.com) engineers helped Toyota develop its Sienna minivan. In return, Toyota provided input on automobile production techniques to Chrysler. Why do you think Chrysler was willing to share its minivan know-how with a key competitor?

2. Many companies seek to cut costs and improve quality by introducing techniques such as just-in-time and quality circles. However, the results often fall short of those achieved at Toyota. Why do you think this is the case?

3. What other benefits do you think Toyota obtains from its production system? Think in broader terms than just production, and consider financial, marketing, and human resource management issues.

a question of ethics

1. At some companies, "reengineering" was synonymous with "downsizing"; that is, laying off employees or reducing employment ranks through early retirement or other approaches. Ironically, some companies are hiring back "downsized" employees as contract workers with lower pay and fewer benefits. Is it ethical for companies to behave in this manner?

2. You work in the governor's office was a southeastern U.S. state. Unemployment rates in your state, especially rural areas, is above the national average and the governor was elected on a pledge to attract industry and create jobs. A European automobile maker has put your state on its short list of potential sites for a new manufacturing facility. The facility is expected to employ about 1,500 people. Your boss (the governor) knows that the automobile maker expects a significant package of incentives and concessions. The governor, who is planning to offer some $300 million in tax breaks and subsidies in an effort to bring the new plant to the state, wants your insight and recommendation. Do such outlays represent proper use of taxpayer money? Why or why not?

16

hiring and managing employees

LEARNING OBJECTIVES

After studying this chapter, you should be able to

1 Explain the three different types of *staffing policies* used by international companies.

2 Describe the *recruitment* and *selection* issues facing international companies.

3 Discuss the importance of *training* and *development programs*, especially cultural training.

4 Explain how companies *compensate managers* and *workers* in international markets.

5 Describe the importance of *labor–management relations* and how it differs around the world.

BEACONS

A Look Back

CHAPTER 15 examined how companies launch and manage their international production efforts. We also explored briefly how companies finance their various international business operations.

A Look at This Chapter

This final chapter examines how a company acquires and manages its most important resource—its employees. The topics we explore include international staffing policies, recruitment and selection, training and development, compensation, and labor-management relations. We also learn about culture shock and how employees can deal with its effects.

Culture Inside

SANTA CLARA, California—Intel (**www.intel.com**) created the world's first micro-processor in 1971. Today, annual revenue is $26.5 billion, of which around 60 percent of it is earned outside the United States. Intel is the world's largest maker of computer chips and a leading manufacturer of computer, networking, and communications products.

A global company such as Intel, which has 85,000 employees worldwide, must deal with many issues when managing its employees. Naturally, with offices in 45 countries Intel must select people who will manage each local office by answering several key questions. Can a qualified manager be found locally? What will it pay a manager hired locally? Or, will it send in a manager from the United States or from an office in another nation? If it sends someone in, what will be his or her pay? Because of different practices around the world, Intel's compensation and benefits packages vary greatly from one country to another.

Then there is the issue of culture. A manager hired locally understands the culture, but what if a manager is brought into the local market? Although the depth of knowledge required differs, Intel wants all of its employees to be knowledgeable about other cultures. That is why Intel created culture-specific training courses that teach how business is conducted internationally and how business differs across cultures. The firm says its training is designed "to develop the knowledge, awareness, and skills to ensure effectiveness and productivity and to identify strategies for successfully doing business in other countries and with people from other countries."

So, whether a globetrotting manager or a tech-support rep dealing with customers in other nations by telephone or e-mail, Intel believes all its employees need an ability to communicate across cultures. As you read this final chapter, think of all the human resource issues that arise when international companies manage their employees around the world.[1]

Perhaps the most important resource of any successful business is the people who comprise it. If a company gives its HRM practices the importance they deserve, it can have a profound impact on performance. Highly trained and productive employees who are proficient in their duties allow a company to achieve its business goals both domestically and internationally. **Human resource management (HRM)** is the process of staffing a company and ensuring that employees are as productive as possible. It requires managers to be effective in recruiting, selecting, training, developing, evaluating, and compensating employees and in forming good relations with them.

International HRM differs considerably from HRM in a domestic setting because of differences in national business environments. For one thing, there is the issue of **expatriates**—citizens of one country who are living and working in another. Companies must deal with many issues when they have expatriate employees on job assignments that could last several years. Some of these issues are related to the inconvenience and stress of living in an unfamiliar culture. In the company profile at the start of this chapter, we saw how Intel (www.intel.com) enrolls its employees in culture-specific training courses to prepare them for doing business internationally. We learned in Chapter 1 that many companies today want their employees to have a *global mindset*—part of which involves cultural tolerance. Because culture is so important to international business, we studied culture early (Chapter 2) and returned repeatedly to the topic throughout this book. For these reasons, culture is central to this final chapter's discussion of how international companies manage their employees.

Likewise, training and development programs must often be tailored to local practices. Some countries, such as Germany and Japan, have extensive vocational-training schools that turn out graduates who are quite well prepared to perform their jobs proficiently. Finding well-qualified nonmanagerial workers in those markets is relatively easy. In contrast, developing a production facility in many emerging markets requires far more basic training of workers. For example, workers in China work hard and tend to be well educated. But because China lacks a vocational training system like those in Germany and Japan, Chinese workers tend to require more intensive on-the-job training. Also, recruitment and selection practices must often be adapted to the host nation's hiring laws. Hiring practices regarding nondiscrimination among job candidates must be carefully monitored so that the company does not violate such laws.

Many companies go abroad in the first place to take advantage of a lower pay scale in another country. Then they adjust their pay scales and advancement criteria to suit local customs. Union Bank of Switzerland in Zurich publishes an annual survey of earnings around the world. This survey has an interesting twist: It ranks earnings in terms of how long the average wage earner must work to be able to afford a Big Mac at McDonald's (www.mcdonalds.com). According to the survey of Big Mac buying power (see Table 16.1), employees in Chicago, Houston, Tokyo, Los Angeles, and Hong Kong enjoy the highest take-home pay. Workers in Nairobi, Caracas, Moscow, Jakarta, and Budapest rank at the bottom.

We begin this chapter by discussing the different types of human resource staffing policies that international companies use. We then learn about the important factors that have an effect on recruitment and selection practices internationally. Later, we explore the many different types of training and development programs companies can use to improve the effectiveness of their employees. We also examine the compensation policies of international companies. Finally, we close the chapter with a discussion of the importance of labor–management relations around the world.

TABLE 16.1 *The Amount of Time It Takes to Earn a Big Mac*

Longest Time		Shortest Time	
City	**Minutes**	**City**	**Minutes**
Nairobi	193	Chicago, Houston, Tokyo	9
Caracas	117	Los Angeles	10
Moscow	104	Hong Kong	11
Jakarta	103	Toronto, New York	12
Budapest	91	Luxembourg	13
Bombay	85	Montreal, Sydney, Zurich	14
Manila	77	Athens, Geneva	15
Shanghai	75	Frankfurt	16
Mexico City	71	Vienna	17
Prague	56	Berlin	18

INTERNATIONAL STAFFING POLICY

The customary means by which a company staffs its offices is called its **staffing policy**. Staffing policy is greatly influenced by the extent of a firm's international involvement. There are three main approaches to the staffing of international business operations— *ethnocentric*, *polycentric*, and *geocentric*. Although we discuss each of these approaches as being distinct from one another, companies often blend different aspects of each staffing policy in practice. The result is an almost infinite variety of international staffing policies among international companies.

> **staffing policy**
> The customary means by which a company staffs its offices.

ETHNOCENTRIC STAFFING

In **ethnocentric staffing**, individuals from the *home* country manage operations abroad. This policy tends to appeal to companies that want to maintain tight control over decision making in branch offices abroad. Accordingly, those companies work to formulate policies designed to work in every country in which they operate. However, note that firms generally pursue this policy only for the top managerial posts in their international operations. Implementing it at lower levels is typically impractical.

> **ethnocentric staffing**
> Staffing policy in which individuals from the home country manage operations abroad.

Advantages of Ethnocentric Staffing Firms pursue this policy for several reasons. First, locally qualified people are not always available. In developing and newly industrialized countries, there is often a shortage of qualified personnel—resulting in a highly competitive local labor market.

Second, companies use ethnocentric staffing to re-create local operations in the image of home-country operations. Especially if they have climbed the corporate ladder in the home office, expatriate managers tend to infuse branch offices with the corporate culture. Naturally, this policy is important for companies that need a strong set of shared values among the people in each international office—such as firms implementing global strategies. For example, Mihir Doshi was born in Bombay but his family moved to the United States in 1978. Doshi graduated from New York University and became a naturalized U.S. citizen in 1988. In 1995 he became executive director of Morgan Stanley's (www.ms.com) operations in India. "Mentally," he reports, "I'm very American. Here, I can be Indian. What the firm gets is somebody to indoctrinate Morgan Stanley culture. I provide the link."[2]

By the same token, a system of shared values is important when a company's international units are highly interdependent. For instance, fashioning branch operations in the image of home-office operations can also ease the transfer of special know-how. This advantage is particularly valuable when that know-how is rooted in the expertise and experience of home-country managers.

Finally, some companies feel that managers sent from the home country will look out for the company's interests more earnestly than will host-country natives. Japanese companies are notorious for their reluctance to place non-Japanese managers at the helm of international offices, and when they do, they often place a Japanese manager in the office to monitor important decisions and report back to the home office. Companies that operate in highly nationalistic markets and those worried about industrial espionage also typically find an ethnocentric approach appealing.

Disadvantages of Ethnocentric Staffing   Despite its advantages, ethnocentric staffing has its negative aspects. First, relocating managers from the home country is expensive. The bonuses that managers often receive for relocating, plus relocation expenses for entire families, can increase the cost of a manager several times over. Likewise, the pressure of cultural differences and long periods away from relatives and friends can contribute to the failure of managers on international assignments.

Second, an ethnocentric policy can create barriers for the host-country office. The presence of home-country managers in the host country might encourage a "foreign" image of the business. Lower-level employees might feel that managers do not really understand their needs because they come from another culture. Occasionally they are right: Expatriate managers sometimes fail to integrate themselves into the local culture. As they fail to overcome cultural barriers, they fail to understand the needs not only of their local employees but those of their local customers.

POLYCENTRIC STAFFING

polycentric staffing
Staffing policy in which individuals from the host country manage operations abroad.

In **polycentric staffing**, individuals from the *host* country manage operations abroad. Companies can implement a polycentric approach for top and mid-level managers, for lower-level staff, or for nonmanagerial workers. It is well suited to companies who want to give national units a degree of autonomy in decision making. This policy does not

According to Microsoft (**www.microsoft.com**) CEO Bill Gates, when opening an international office, "it sends the wrong message to have a foreigner come in to run things." So, when Microsoft opened a branch in India, it hired native Indian Rajiv Nair to see that legitimate copies of Microsoft software went into the hundreds of thousands of PCs built in India each year. Five years later, Indian operations were promoted to a full-fledged subsidiary, with Nair as general manager.

mean that host-country managers are left to run operations in any way they see fit. Large international companies usually conduct extensive training programs in which host-country managers visit home offices for extended periods. In this way they are exposed to the company's culture and specific business practices. Small and medium-size companies can find this policy expensive, but being able to depend on local managers who fully understand what is expected of them can far outweigh any costs.

Advantages and Disadvantages of Polycentric Staffing Polycentric staffing places managerial responsibility in the hands of people intimately familiar with the local business environment. Managers with deep cultural understanding of the local market can be an enormous advantage. They are familiar with local business practices and can read the subtle cues of both verbal and nonverbal language. They need not overcome any cultural barriers created by an image of being an outsider, and they tend to have a better feel for the needs of employees, customers, and suppliers.

Another important advantage of polycentric staffing is elimination of the high cost of relocating expatriate managers and families. This advantage can be extremely helpful for small and midsize businesses that cannot afford the expenses associated with expatriate employees. See the Entrepreneurial Focus titled "Growing Global" for additional issues that small companies should consider when staffing internationally.

The major drawback of polycentric staffing is the potential for losing control of the host-country operation. When a company employs natives of each country to manage local operations, it runs the risk of becoming a collection of discrete national businesses. This situation might not be a problem when a firm's strategy calls for treating each national market differently. It is not a good policy, however, for companies that are following global strategies. If these companies lack integration, knowledge sharing, and a common image, performance will surely suffer.

ENTREPRENEURIAL FOCUS

Growing Global

For an entrepreneur or small business, going global can put a strain on resources, including time, money, and people. Here is some advice on important human resource issues to consider when expanding internationally:

➡ **Don't entrust the local operations solely to U.S. expatriates**. "While they understand the company and the product, they don't understand the local practices and culture and don't have the relationships," said Joseph Monti, a partner at Grant Thornton LLP (**www.gt.com**). "The best strategy is to have a local general manager with a support staff that could be seeded with U.S. expatriates."

➡ **Contacts don't guarantee contracts**. "Relationships matter more than mere contacts," said Virginia Kamsky, CEO of Kamsky Associates Inc. (**www.kamsky.com**). "Don't assume that hiring the son of a government official will automatically get you business. It's more important to hire a person with a good attitude and strong relationship-building skills," she added.

➡ **Treat your employees abroad as you want to be treated**. "People are basically the same worldwide; it doesn't matter where you are," notes Jeff Dzuira, director of international sales at Ferris Manufacturing Corp. (**www.ferrispolymem.com**). "Awareness and respect of cultural protocol demonstrates honesty and goodwill, and this leads to trust, which in turn leads to mutually profitable relationships."

➡ **Employ the Web in your search**. One of the largest employment Web sites is Monster, (**www.monster.com**). It has branches in 22 countries and literally millions of resumes. Another popular Web site for international job seekers is at (**www.hotjobs.com**). Employers can also post job announcements on the Web site at (**www.overseasjobs.com**). Of course, there are many more Web sites out there.

GEOCENTRIC STAFFING

geocentric staffing
Staffing policy in which the best-qualified individuals regardless of nationality manage operations abroad.

In **geocentric staffing**, the best-qualified individuals regardless of nationality manage operations abroad. The local operation may choose managers from the host country, from the home country, or from a third country. The choice depends on the operation's specific needs. This policy is typically reserved for top-level managers.

Advantages and Disadvantages of Geocentric Staffing Geocentric staffing helps a company develop global managers who can adjust easily to any business environment—particularly to cultural differences. This advantage is especially useful for global companies trying to break down nationalistic barriers, whether between managers in a single office or between different offices. One hope of companies using this policy is that a global perspective among its managers will help them seize opportunities that may otherwise be overlooked.

The downside of geocentric staffing is the expense. Understandably, top managers who are capable both of fitting into different cultures and being effective at their jobs are highly prized among international companies. The combination of high demand for their skills and their short supply inflates their salaries. Moreover, there is the expense of relocating managers and their families—sometimes every year or 2.

RECRUITING AND SELECTING HUMAN RESOURCES

Naturally, companies try to recruit and select qualified managers and nonmanagerial workers who are well suited to their tasks and responsibilities. But how does a company know the number of managers and workers it needs? How does it recruit the best available individuals? How does it select from the pool of available candidates? In this section, we explore some answers to these and other important questions about recruiting and selecting employees.

HUMAN RESOURCE PLANNING

human resource planning
Process of forecasting both a company's human resource needs and supply.

Recruiting and selecting managers and workers requires **human resource planning**—the process of forecasting both a company's human resource needs and supply. The first phase of HR planning involves taking an inventory of a company's current human resources—that is, collecting data on every employee, including educational background, special job skills, previous jobs, language skills, and experience living abroad.

The second phase of HR planning is estimating the company's future HR needs. For example, consider a firm that plans to sell its products directly to buyers in a new market abroad. Will it create a new operation abroad and staff it with managers from the home office, or will it train local managers? Will it hire its own local sales force, or will it hire a distributor? Likewise, manufacturing or assembling products in an international market requires factory workers. A company must decide whether to hire these people itself or to subcontract production to other producers—thus eliminating the need for it to hire factory workers.

As we have noted in previous chapters, this decision frequently raises ethical questions. The general public is becoming increasingly well informed about the fact that global companies make extensive use of subcontractors in low-wage nations. Of particular concern is the question of whether subcontractors are taking advantage of "sweatshop labor." But publicity generated by allegations of workplace abuse cause many firms to establish codes of conduct and step up efforts to ensure compliance. For example, in the late 1990s Nike (www.nike.com) severed ties with subcontractors in Indonesia that paid wages below the minimum levels set by the government.

In the third phase of HR planning, managers develop a plan for recruiting and selecting people to fill vacant and anticipated new positions, both managerial and nonmanagerial. Sometimes, a firm must also make plans for reducing its workforce—a process called *decruitment*—when current HR levels are greater than anticipated needs. Planning for decruitment normally occurs when a company decides to discontinue manufacturing or selling in a market. Unfortunately, the decision by global companies to shift the location of manufacturing from one country to another can also result in lost jobs. Let's now take a closer look at the recruitment and selection processes.

RECRUITING HUMAN RESOURCES

The process of identifying and attracting a qualified pool of applicants for vacant positions is called **recruitment**. Companies can recruit internally from among their current employees or look to external sources.

Current Employees   Finding an international manager among current employees is easiest for a large company with an abundance of internal managers. Likely candidates within the company are managers who were involved in previous stages of an international project—say, in *identifying* the new production site or potential market. It is likely that these individuals have already made important contacts inside the host country and they have already been exposed to its culture.

Recent College Graduates   Companies also recruit from among recent college graduates who have come from other countries to attend college in the firm's home country. This is a particularly common practice among companies in the United States. Over a 1-year period, these new hires receive general and specialized training and then are given positions in their native countries. As a rule, they learn about the organization's culture and the way in which it conducts business. Most important, perhaps, is their familiarity with the culture of the target market, including its customs, traditions, and language.

recruitment
Process of identifying and attracting a qualified pool of applicants for vacant positions.

"WHEN YOU CAME TO WORK WITH US, WALSH, YOU STRESSED THAT YOU HOPED TO GO FAR WITH THE COMPANY. WELL, WE'VE DECIDED TO OPEN AN OFFICE IN TIBET, AND..."

Local Managerial Talent Companies can also recruit local managerial talent. Hiring local managers is common when cultural understanding is a key job requirement. Hiring local managers with government contacts can speed the process of getting approvals for local operations. In some cases, governments force companies to recruit local managers so that they can develop their own internal pools of managerial talent. Also, governments sometimes restrict the number of international managers that can work in the host country.

Nonmanagerial Workers Companies typically recruit locally for nonmanagerial positions because there is often little need for highly specialized skills or training. However, a specialist from the home country is typically brought in to train people chosen for more demanding positions.

Firms also turn to the local labor market when governments restrict the number of people allowed into the host country for work purposes. Such efforts are usually designed to reduce unemployment among the local population. On the other hand, countries sometimes permit the importation of nonmanagerial workers. Kuwait, a wealthy oil-producing country in the Middle East, has brought in large numbers of nonmanagerial workers for its blue-collar and technical jobs. Many of these workers come from Egypt, India, Lebanon, Pakistan, Palestinian territories, and the Philippines in search of jobs or higher wages.

SELECTING HUMAN RESOURCES

selection
Process of screening and hiring the best-qualified applicants with the greatest performance potential.

The process of screening and hiring the best-qualified applicants with the greatest performance potential is called **selection**. The process for international assignments includes measuring a person's ability to bridge cultural differences. Expatriate managers must be able to adapt to a new way of life in the host country. Conversely, native host-country managers must be able to work effectively with superiors who have different cultural backgrounds.

In the case of expatriate managers, cultural differences between home country and host country are important factors in their potential success. Culturally sensitive managers increase the likelihood that a company will achieve its international business goals. Recruiters can assess cultural sensitivity by asking candidates questions about their receptiveness to new ways of doing things and questions about racial and ethnic issues. They can also employ global aptitude tests such as the one mentioned in the In Practice exercise at the end of this chapter.

It is also important to examine the cultural sensitivity of each family member who will be going to the host country. The inability of a family member (particularly a spouse) to adapt to a new culture is the most common reason for the failure of expatriate managers. In fact, in one recent survey of Canadian and U.S. companies, nearly 20 percent cited "lack of adaptability by the employee's spouse" as the number-one cause of failed relocation.[3]

CULTURE SHOCK

Successful international managers typically do not mind, and often enjoy, living and working outside their native lands. In extreme cases, they might even be required to relocate every year or so. These individuals are capable of adapting quickly to local conditions and business practices. Such managers are becoming increasingly valuable with the emergence of markets in Asia, Central and Eastern Europe, and Latin America. They are also helping to create a global pool of managers who are ready and willing to go practically anywhere on short notice. However, the size of this pool remains limited because of the difficulties that many people experience in relocating to unfamiliar cultures.

Living in another culture can be a stressful experience. Therefore, selecting managers who are comfortable traveling to and living in unfamiliar cultures is an extremely important factor in recruitment for international posts. Set down in the midst of new cultures, many expatriates experience **culture shock**—a psychological process affecting people living abroad that is characterized by homesickness, irritability, confusion, aggravation, and depression. In other words, they have trouble adjusting to the new environment in which they find themselves. *Expatriate failure*—the early return by an employee from an international assignment because of inadequate job performance—often results from cultural stress. The higher cost of expatriate failure is convincing many companies to invest in cultural-training programs for employees sent abroad. For a detailed look at the culture-shock process and how to reduce its effects, see the Global Manager titled "A Shocking Ordeal."

culture shock
Psychological process affecting people living abroad that is characterized by homesickness, irritability, confusion, aggravation, and depression.

REVERSE CULTURE SHOCK

Ironically, expatriates who successfully adapt to new cultures often undergo an experience called **reverse culture shock**—the psychological process of readapting to one's home culture. Because values and behavior that once seemed so natural now seem so strange, reverse culture shock may be even more disturbing than culture shock. In addition, returning managers often find that either no position or merely a "standby" position awaits them in the home office. Often, companies do not know how to take full advantage of the cross-cultural abilities developed by managers who have spent several potentially valuable years abroad. In fact, expatriates commonly leave their companies within a year of returning home because of difficulty blending back into the company culture.

Moreover, spouses and children often have difficulty leaving the adopted culture and returning home. For many Japanese employees and their families, reentry into Japanese culture after a work assignment in the United States can be particularly difficult. The fast pace of business and social life in the United States, plus the relatively high degree of freedom and independence for women, contrasts sharply with conditions in

reverse culture shock
Psychological process of readapting to one's home culture.

GLOBAL MANAGER

A Shocking Ordeal

Culture shock typically occurs during stays of a few months or longer in an unfamiliar culture. It begins on arrival and normally occurs in four stages (although not all people go through every stage):

➡ **Stage 1**, the "honeymoon," typically lasts from a few days to a few weeks. New arrivals are fascinated by local sights, pleasant hospitality, and interesting habits. They are thrilled about their opportunity and optimistic about prospects for success. However, this sense of security is often false because, so far, interactions with locals are similar to those of a tourist.

➡ **Stage 2**, lasts from a few weeks to a few months; in fact, some people never move on to stage 3. Unpredictable quirks of the culture become annoying, even maddening. Visitors begin mocking the locals and regarding the ways of their native cultures as superior. Relationships with spouses and children suffer, and depression, perhaps even despair, sets in.

➡ **Stage 3**, emotions hit bottom—and recovery begins. As visitors begin to learn more about the local culture, interact more with locals, and form friendships, cynical remarks cease.

➡ **Stage 4**, visitors not only better understand local customs and behavior but actually appreciate many of them. They now treat differences as "unique" solutions to familiar problems in different cultural contexts. Reaching Stage 4 is a sign that the expatriate has adapted well and that success in his or her international assignment is likely.

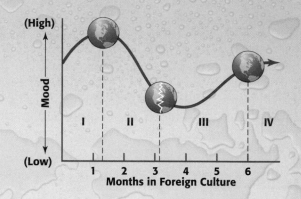

Here are some steps that prospective expatriates can take to reduce the burden of culture shock during an international assignment:

➡ Undergo extensive psychological assessment to ensure that both you and your family members are emotionally able to handle the assignment.

➡ Obtain knowledge of the local culture (especially the language) and critically examine your own culture biases before leaving home.

➡ If possible, visit the assigned country, mingling with local people and getting a feel for your future assignment. Ask about local educational, financial, and health-care services.

➡ Once you are inside a culture, meet with others—both natives and expatriates—to discuss your negative and positive experiences.

➡ Most important: Relax, be adventurous, take a worldly perspective, and keep your sense of humor.

Japan. Returning Japanese expatriates can find it difficult to adjust back to life in Japan after years of living in the United States.

Dealing with Reverse Culture Shock   The effects of reverse culture shock can be reduced. Home-culture reorientation programs and career-counseling sessions for returning managers and their families can be highly effective. For example, the employer might bring the entire family home for a short stay several weeks before the official return. This kind of trip allows returnees to prepare for at least some of the reverse culture shock that may await them.

Likewise, good career development programs can help companies retain valuable managers. Ideally, the career development plan was worked out before the employee went abroad and revised before his or her return. Some companies work with employees before they go abroad to plan career paths of up to 20 years within the company. Mentors who have previously gone abroad and had to adjust upon returning home can also be assigned to returning managers. The mentor becomes a confidant with whom the expatriate manager can discuss particular problems related to work, family, and readjusting to the home culture.

After a company recruits and selects its managers and other employees, it normally identifies the skills and knowledge that employees have and those that they need to perform their duties. Employees who lack the necessary skills or knowledge can then be directed into specific training or development programs.

According to the National Foreign Trade Council (www.nftc.org), 250,000 U.S. citizens live outside the United States on international assignments—in addition to hundreds of thousands more who travel abroad on business for stays of up to several weeks. Some of the many costs of relocating an employee for a long-term international assignment include moving expenses and ongoing costs for things such as housing, education, and cost-of-living adjustments. That is why many companies realize the need for in-depth training and development programs if they are to get the maximum productivity from managers posted abroad.

TRAINING AND DEVELOPMENT

METHODS OF CULTURAL TRAINING

Ideally, everyone involved in business should be culturally literate and prepared to go anywhere in the world at a moment's notice. Realistically, many employees and many companies do not need or cannot afford to be entirely literate in another culture. The extent of a company's international involvement demands a corresponding level of cultural knowledge from its employees. Companies whose activities are highly international need employees with language fluency and in-depth experience in other countries. Meanwhile, small companies or those new to international business can begin with some basic cultural training. As a company increases its international involvement and cross-cultural contact, employees' cultural knowledge must keep pace.

As you can see from Figure 16.1, companies use many methods to prepare managers for an international assignment. These methods tend to reflect a manager's level of

FIGURE 16.1

International Assignment Preparation Methods

Extent of Manager's International Involvement

Field Experience

Language Training

Sensitivity Training

Cultural Assimilation

Cultural Orientations

Environmental Briefings

international involvement. The goal is to create informed, open-minded, flexible managers with a level of cultural training appropriate to the duties required of them.

Environmental Briefings and Cultural Orientations   *Environmental (area) briefings* constitute the most basic level of training—often the starting point for studying other cultures. Briefings include information on local housing, health care, transportation, schools, and climate. Such knowledge is normally obtained from books, films, and lectures. *Cultural orientations* offer insight into social, political, legal, and economic institutions. Their purpose is to add depth and substance to environmental briefings.

Cultural Assimilation and Sensitivity Training   *Cultural assimilation* teaches the culture's values, attitudes, manners, and customs. So-called guerrilla linguistics, which involves learning some phrases in the local language, is often used at this stage. It also typically includes role playing: The trainee responds to a specific situation in order to be evaluated by a team of judges. This method is often used when someone is given little notice of a short stay abroad and wishes to take a crash course in social and business etiquette and communication. *Sensitivity training* teaches people to be considerate and understanding of other people's feelings and emotions; it gets the trainee "under the skin" of the local people.

Language Training   The need for more thorough cultural preparedness brings us to intensive *language training*. This level of training entails more than memorizing phrases for ordering dinner or asking directions. It gets a trainee "into the mind" of local people. The trainee learns more about why local people behave as they do. This is perhaps the most critical part of cultural training for long-term assignments.

A survey of top executives found that foreign-language skills topped the list of skills needed to maintain a competitive edge. According to the survey, 31 percent of male employees and 27 percent of female employees lacked foreign-language skills. To remedy this situation, many companies either employ outside agencies that specialize in language training or develop their own programs. Employees at 3M Corporation (**www.3m.com**) developed a third way. They created an all-volunteer "Language Society" comprised of current and retired employees and family members. About 1,000 people are members, and the group offers classes in 17 languages taught by 70 volunteer employee teachers. The society meets 45 minutes per week and charges a nominal membership fee of $5. Officials at 3M say that the society nicely complements the company's formal language education program.[4]

Field Experience   *Field experience* means visiting the culture, walking the streets of its cities and villages, and becoming absorbed by it for a short time. The trainee gets to enjoy some of the unique cultural traits and feel some of the stresses inherent in living in the culture.

Finally, remember that spouses and children also need cultural training. Training for them is a good investment because the alternatives—an international "commuter marriage" or expatriate failure—are both psychologically and financially expensive options.[5]

COMPILING A CULTURAL PROFILE

Cultural profiles can be quite helpful in deciding whether to accept an international assignment. The following are some excellent sources for constructing a cultural profile:

➡ *Culturgrams.* Published by the David M. Kennedy Center for International Studies at Brigham Young University (**www.kennedy.byu.edu**), this guide can be found in the reference section of many libraries. Frequent updates make *Culturgrams* a timely source of information. Individual sections profile each culture's background and its people, customs and courtesies, lifestyle, and society. A section entitled "For the Traveler" covers details such as required entry visas and vaccinations.

➡ *Country Studies Area Handbooks.* This series explains how politics, economics, society, and national security issues are related to one another and shaped by culture in more than 70 countries. Handbooks tend to be politically oriented because they are designed for U.S. military personnel. The Country Studies Area Handbooks are available on the Web at (**http://lcweb2.loc.gov/frd/cs/cshome.html**).

➡ *Background Notes.* These notes contain much relevant factual information on human rights and related issues in various countries. However, because they are published by the U.S. Department of State (**www.state.gov**), they take a U.S. political perspective.

Information can also be obtained by contacting the embassies of other countries in your home nation. People with firsthand knowledge and specific books and films are also good sources of information. Once you're inside a country, you'll find your home country's embassy a good source of further cultural advice. Embassies maintain networks of home-nation professionals who work in the local culture, some with many years of experience upon which you can draw.

NONMANAGERIAL WORKER TRAINING

Nonmanagerial workers also have training and development needs. This is especially true in some developing and newly industrialized countries where people have not even completed primary school. Even if the workforce is fairly well educated, workers may lack experience working in industry. In such cases, companies that do business abroad can train local workers in how to work on an assembly line or cultivate business leads to make sales. The need for such basic-skills training continues to grow as companies increasingly explore opportunities in emerging markets.

In many countries, national governments cooperate with businesses to train nonmanagerial workers. Japan and Germany lead the world in vocational training and apprenticeship programs for nonmanagerial workers. Students who are unable or unwilling to enter college can enter programs paid for by the government and private industry. They undergo extensive practical training that exposes them to the cutting-edge technologies employed by the country's leading companies. For example, Germany's Mittelstand is a network of 3 million small and midsize companies that account for about two-thirds of the country's jobs. Mittelstand companies provide 80 percent of Germany's apprenticeships. Although they typically employ fewer than 100 people, many Mittelstand companies are export powerhouses.

EMPLOYEE COMPENSATION

Essential to good international HRM is a fair and effective compensation (reward) system. Such a system is designed to attract and retain the best and brightest employees and to reward them for their performance. Because a country's compensation practices are rooted in its culture and legal and economic systems, determining compensation can be complicated. For example, base pay accounts for nearly all employee compensation in some countries. In others, bonuses and fringe benefits account for more than half.

MANAGERIAL EMPLOYEES

Naturally, compensation packages for managers differ from company to company and from country to country. Good packages are fairly complicated to design for several reasons. First, consider the effect of *cost of living*, which includes factors such as the cost of groceries, dining out, clothing, housing, schooling, heath care, transportation, and utilities. Quite simply, it costs more to live in some countries than in others. Moreover, within a given country the cost of living typically varies from large cities to rural towns and villages. Most companies add a certain amount to an expatriate manager's pay to cover greater cost-of-living expenses. On the other hand, managers who are relocating to lower cost-of-living countries are typically paid the same amount that they were receiving at the home office. Otherwise, they would be financially penalized for accepting an international job assignment.

Even when the cost of living abroad is lower than at home, companies must cover other costs incurred by expatriate managers. One important concern for relocating managers is the quality of local education. In many cases, children cannot immediately enter local classes because they do not speak the local language. In such instances, most companies pay for private-school education.

Bonus and Tax Incentives   Companies commonly offer managers inducements to accept international postings. The most common is a financial bonus. This bonus can be in the form of a one-time payment or an add-on to regular pay—generally 15 to 20 percent. Bonuses for managers who are asked to go into a particularly unstable country or one with a very low standard of living often receive *hardship* or *combat pay*.

Managers can also be attracted by another income-related factor. For example, the U.S. government permits citizens working abroad to exclude "foreign-earned income" from their taxable income in the United States—even if it was earned in a country with no income tax.

Cultural and Social Contributors to Cost   Culture also plays an important role in the compensation of expatriate managers. Some nations offer more paid holidays than others. Many offer free medical care to everyone living and working there. Granted, the quality of locally available medical care is not always good. Therefore, many companies have plans for taking seriously ill expatriates and family members home or to nearby countries where medical care is equal to that available in the home country.

Companies that hire managers in the local market might encounter additional costs engendered by social attitudes. For instance, in some countries employers are expected to provide free or subsidized housing. In others, the government obliges employers to provide paid maternity leaves of up to one and one-half years. Table 16.2 shows government-mandated maternity leaves for a sample of European countries. Although companies need not absorb all such costs, they tend to be reflected in a generally higher cost of doing business in a given country.

Managers recruited from within the host country generally receive the same pay as managers who work for local companies. However, they often receive perks not offered by local firms. For example, some are required to visit the home office two or three times per year. If time allows, many managers will make these into short vacations by taking along their families and adding a few extra days onto the length of the trip.

NONMANAGERIAL WORKERS

Two main factors influence the wages of nonmanagerial workers. First, their compensation is strongly influenced by increased cross-border business investment. Employers can relocate fairly easily to nations where wages are lower. Meanwhile, in the home country workers must often accept lower wages when an employer gives them a choice of accepting the reduction or watching their jobs move abroad. One result of this situation is a trend toward greater equality in workers' pay around the world. In turn, this equalizing effect encourages economic development and improvement in workers' lives in some countries at the expense of those in others.

Country	Length of Leave	Pay	Limits
Austria	24 months	Flat rate	Up to fourth birthday
Denmark	10 weeks (plus six months extended leave)	Flat rate	Up to 36 months throughout career
Finland	Until child is 36 months	First six months linked to earnings, then flat rate	Up to third birthday
France	Until child is 36 months	Flat rate, but only for second and subsequent children	Up to third birthday
Germany	Until child is 36 months	Flat rate for 24 months, then means tested	Up to third birthday
Spain	Until child is 36 months	No benefit	Up to third birthday
Sweden	38 weeks per family, per child	80–90 percent of earnings	Up to eighth birthday
The Netherlands	Six months	No benefit	Up to fourth birthday, but only part-time

TABLE 16.2 Parental Leave in Europe

However, the freedom with which an employer can relocate differs from country to country. Although firms in some countries are allowed to move with little notice, in others they are highly restricted. In fact, some countries force companies to compensate workers who lose their jobs because of relocation. This policy is common in European countries that have erected extensive social safety nets for unemployed workers.

Second, the fact that labor is more mobile today than ever before also affects wages. Although labor laws in Europe are still more stringent than in the United States, the countries of the European Union are abolishing the requirement that workers from one EU nation must obtain visas to work in another. If workers in Spain cannot find work at home, or if they feel that their current pay is inadequate, they are free to move to another EU country where unemployment is lower (say, Britain). A problem that plagues some European countries today is that they seem to be creating a group of people who are permanently unemployed. See this chapter's World Business Survey titled "Long Time, No Work," to see how a group of countries compare on this point.

LABOR–MANAGEMENT RELATIONS

The positive or negative condition of relations between a company's management and its workers (labor) is referred to as **labor–management relations**. Cooperative relations between labor and management can give a firm a tremendous competitive advantage. When management and workers realize they depend on one another, the company is often better prepared to meet its goals and surmount unexpected obstacles that may

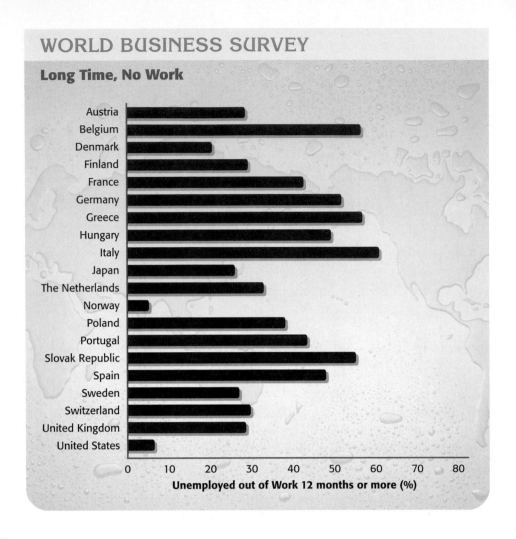

WORLD BUSINESS SURVEY

Long Time, No Work

Unemployed out of Work 12 months or more (%)

Countries (top to bottom): Austria, Belgium, Denmark, Finland, France, Germany, Greece, Hungary, Italy, Japan, The Netherlands, Norway, Poland, Portugal, Slovak Republic, Spain, Sweden, Switzerland, United Kingdom, United States

X-axis: 0, 10, 20, 30, 40, 50, 60, 70, 80

labor–management relations

Positive or negative condition of relations between a company's management and its workers.

crop up. Giving workers a greater stake in the company—say, through profit-sharing plans—is one way to increase morale and generate commitment to improved quality and customer service.

Because relations between laborers and managers are human relations, they are rooted in culture and are often affected by political movements in a market. Large international companies tend to make high-level labor decisions at the home office because it gives them greater control over their network of production operations around the world. However, lower-level decisions are often left to managers in each country. In effect, this policy places decisions that have a direct impact on workers' lives in the hands of experts in the local market. Such decisions might include the number of annual paid holidays, the length of maternity leave, and the provision of day-care facilities. Localizing such management decisions tends to contribute to better labor–management relations because managers familiar with local practices are better equipped to handle matters that affect workers personally.

IMPORTANCE OF LABOR UNIONS

The strength of labor unions in a country where a company has operations is important to its performance and can even affect the selection of a location. Developing and emerging markets in Asia are a popular location for international companies. Some Asian governments appeal to international companies to locate facilities in their nations by promising to keep labor unions in check. But companies also find developed nations attractive if, for whatever reason, a cooperative atmosphere exists between company management and labor unions. In some Asian countries, especially Japan, a cultural emphasis on harmony and balanced interests discourages confrontation between labor and management.

Meanwhile, Britain and Ireland are becoming favorite locations for toeholds in the European Union (EU). The main attractions are productive labor, lower wages, and a reduced likelihood of disruptive strikes. Labor unions are not as strong in these countries as they are on the continent, particularly in France and Germany. Nevertheless, Germany has not been immune to the trend of falling union membership. Union membership has dropped off in Germany over the past decade from about 12 million to about 8 million workers. The main reason for the decline is the lack of interest in union membership in the former East German territories. By contrast, labor unions comprise only about 9 percent of the labor force in the United States today, compared with 36 percent 50 years ago.[6]

Despite declines in union membership, labor in Germany exercises a good deal of power in management decisions. In fact, under a plan called *codetermination*, German workers enjoy a direct say in the strategies and policies of their employers. This plan allows labor representatives to participate in high-level company meetings by actually voting on proposed actions.

International Labor Movements The global activities of unions are making progress in areas such as improving the treatment of workers and reducing incidents involving child labor. However, the efforts of separate national unions to increase their cooperation are somewhat less successful. Although unions in one nation might wish to support their counterparts in another country, generating grassroots support is difficult for two reasons. First, events taking place in another country are difficult for many people to comprehend. Distance and cultural difference make it hard for people to understand others who live and work elsewhere.

Second, whether they realize it or not, workers in different countries sometimes compete against one another. For example, today firms can relocate internationally rather easily. Thus, labor unions in one country might offer concessions in order to attract the jobs

Workers in Germany and France are typically protected by very powerful labor unions. In fact, German workers have a direct influence on company decisions through a plan called *codetermination*. Here German autoworkers take to the streets to demand action on their request for a pay hike. Why do you think countries around the world differ in the amount of influence that they give labor unions?

that will be created by a new production facility. In this way, unions in different nations can wind up competing against one another. Some observers argue that this phenomenon creates downward pressure on both wages and union power worldwide.[7]

A FINAL WORD

This chapter concluded our survey of international business. We did so by studying how firms, ranging from small and medium-size businesses to large global companies, hire and manage their most important resource—their employees. We covered a great deal of territory in our "tour" of international business. We hope we piqued your interest in the goings-on of the global marketplace and in the activities of international companies of all types and sizes. Nevertheless, our learning does not end here. Each of us will continue to be exposed to international business in our daily lives—whether as consumers or as current or future business managers. As a result, we will continue to expand our knowledge of other national cultures, the international business environment, and how companies manage their international operations. We wish you well on your continued journey through this fascinating and dynamic subject.

There is a variety of additional material available on the Companion Website that accompanies this book. You can access this information by visiting the Website at (**www.prenhall.com/wild**).

summary

❶ Explain the three different types of *staffing policies* used by international companies. In a company with an *ethnocentric staffing policy*, operations outside the home country are staffed and managed by home-country nationals. To provide headquarters with tight controls over the decision making of branch offices in other countries, policies are designed to work in each market in which the company operates. A *polycentric staffing policy* accomplishes just the opposite: International operations are staffed and managed by host-country natives who usually have participated in extensive training programs. Such policies are generally designed to give national units a certain level of autonomy in decision making. *Geocentric staffing* means staffing operations outside the home country with the best-qualified individuals regardless of nationality. This policy is typically reserved for top-level managers, who may be chosen from the home country, from the host country, or from a third country.

❷ Describe the *recruitment* and *selection* issues facing international companies. Large companies often recruit international managers from within the ranks of existing employees. Because small and midsize companies may not have qualified managers, managers for international assignments may have to be hired from other companies. Sometimes international students who have graduated from local colleges are hired, trained locally, and then posted in their home countries. Local managerial talent can also be recruited in the host country; such persons bring special capabilities, such as an understanding of the local culture and political system. In addition, local hires are often required when a company sets up manufacturing abroad or engages in extensive marketing activities. When selecting employees for international positions, companies look for an ability to adapt to cultural differences. When hiring in-country personnel, the employer's home-country bias may make it difficult to determine technical competence or leadership ability.

❸ Discuss the importance of *training* and *development programs*, especially cultural training. *Culture shock* refers to the psychological difficulties experienced when living in an unfamiliar culture—it is often characterized by homesickness, irritability, confusion, aggravation, and depression. Ironically, returning managers often experience *reverse culture shock*: the psychological process of readapting to one's home culture. For these reasons, cultural training is becoming increasingly important.

Cultural training is often effective in reducing the effects of both culture shock and reverse culture shock. Training ranges from reading books and seeing films about a culture to visiting it on a field trip, and there are various methods for preparing people for international assignment. *Environmental briefings* and *cultural orientations* provide insight on matters such as local housing and health care and describe political, economic, and social institutions. *Cultural assimilation* and *sensitivity training* explain the local values, attitudes, and customs and stress the importance of understanding local feelings and emotions. *Language training* provides specific, practical skills that allow employees to communicate in the local language. *Field experience* means visiting the culture for a brief period to begin growing accustomed to it.

4 **Explain how companies *compensate managers* and *workers* in international markets.** An effective compensation policy takes into account local cultures, laws, and practices. Issues include base pay as a percentage of total compensation, bonuses, and fringe benefits. Managerial compensation packages may have to be adjusted to reflect the cost of living; the cost of education for family members may also be a consideration. *Bonus payments* or hardship pay may be required as an incentive for managers to accept international assignments. Nonmanagerial compensation levels can be influenced by wage rates in other countries. Investment capital tends to flow to nations with low-cost labor, resulting in increased equality in workers' pay from country to country.

5 **Describe the importance of *labor–management relations* and how it differs around the world.** The positive or negative condition of relations between company management and its workers is referred to as *labor–management relations*. When management and workers realize they depend on one another, the company is often better prepared to meet its goals and to surmount unexpected obstacles that may crop up. Because relations between labor and managers are human relations, they are rooted in culture and are often affected by political movements in the local market. Finally, the strength of labor unions in a country where a company has operations is important to its performance and can even affect the selection of a location.

questions **for review**

1. List some of the ways in which *international HRM* differs from HRM in the domestic environment.

2. What are the three different types of *international staffing policies* that companies can implement? Identify the advantages and disadvantages of each?

3. What is *human resource planning*? Explain its importance to recruitment.

4. What are the main sources from which companies *recruit* their international managers?

5. What is *culture shock*?

6. Explain the importance of culture shock in the *selection* of international managers.

7. What is *reverse culture shock*?

8. Identify the types of *training and development* used for international managers and nonmanagerial workers.

9. What are the main variables involved in decisions regarding employee *compensation* for managers and nonmanagerial workers?

10. What is *hardship* or *combat pay*? Under what circumstances do companies provide such compensation?

11. What does *labor–management relations* mean? Explain how labor–management relations differ around the world.

questions **for discussion**

1. Many Japanese companies utilize *ethnocentric* staffing policies in international operations. Why do you think Japanese companies prefer to have Japanese in top management positions? Would you recommend a change in this policy?

2. Have you ever experienced culture shock? If so, in which country did it occur? What, if anything, did you do to overcome it? Did your methods work? Did you experience reverse culture shock upon returning home?

in practice

Read the article below and answer the questions that follow.

Do You Have the Right Stuff?

LONDON, England—Personality testing is all the rage. Because they provide a quick, efficient way to screen candidates, these tests cut down on screening time and workload for the human resources staff.

In fact, one British company found that the top three reasons people quit or underperform are rooted in personality, rather than skill, knowledge, or qualification. Companies are today taking personality tests one-step further and designing global aptitude tests.

Intercultural Business Center's Global Mentality Test (GMT) measures a person's aptitude of doing business globally. The test evaluates an individual's openness and flexibility in mindset, understanding of global principles and terminology, and strategic implementation abilities. It also identifies areas in which improvement and/or additional training is needed and generates a list of recommended training programs.

1. The article mentions a company that identified the top-three reasons people quit or underperform their jobs are rooted in personality. What do you think are the aspects of a person's personality that cause this to occur? Explain.

2. Personality testing in the workplace is widespread in Australia, Europe, and the United States. However, it is just beginning to catch on in Asia. Why do you think this is? Do you think the reason could be rooted in Asian societies and culture? Explain.

3. In addition to the benefits listed in the article, what other advantages do you think global aptitude tests might offer companies doing business internationally?

4. What personal characteristics do you think make someone better suited to doing business globally? Be specific. Do you think these characteristics are innate or can they be learned?

projects

1. Suppose that you are vice president of operations for a major automobile manufacturer. Among your company's worldwide operations are plants in Spain and Germany. Your company is considering closing these two plants and moving production to Poland in order to take advantage of lower wages. Write a short report explaining how easy (or how difficult) it will be for your company to close the plant and lay off workers in both Spain and Germany.

2. Small and medium-size businesses face some real obstacles when expanding operations abroad. Write a report on the obstacles they face in the area of recruiting and selecting employees when first venturing internationally. Address specific issues such as financial constraints, a lack of contacts, cultural differences, legal issues, geographical distance, and so on.

business case 16
EXPATRIATION OR DISCRIMINATION?

One issue faced by companies with international operations is determining the right time to bring expatriate managers home, or "repatriate" them. Promoting host-country personnel into key managerial positions can boost morale and provide a sense of equal opportunity. Also, local managers often have keen insights into local business conditions and, therefore, a potential advantage when it comes to decision making. Moreover, by bringing expatriate managers home, firms can often save considerable amounts of money. In China, for example, compensation for an expatriate can cost between $200,000 and $300,000 per year; the total package includes both cost-of-living and hardship allowances of 15 to 20 percent each. By comparison, total compensation for a top-notch Chinese manager would be only about $50,000 per year.

Despite the benefits to be gained from turning over control to local managers, some industry experts warn that "localizing" too quickly can be a mistake. For example, as one expatriate manager in China put it, "Doing business the Chinese way is much less well-documented and can be dangerous. There is a serious risk when you give up financial control." Another problem is the fact that many expatriate managers are evaluated according to operating results rather than their efforts to train local managers.

The issue of expatriate assignments is not limited to such emerging markets as China. In developed countries, laying off employees or replacing local managers with persons from the home country can be controversial moves. For example, Japanese-owned Ricoh Corporation (www.ricoh.com) replaced a U.S. manager with a Japanese manager in charge of optical computer-disk sales at its California File Products Division (FPD). After being laid off as a result of the move, Chet Mackentire sued his former employer for discrimination under Title VII of the Civil Rights Act of 1964. But Ricoh argued that Mackentire was laid off for business reasons, not because he was a Caucasian-American.

Mackentire lost his case. The court said that it found "no evidence to support Mackentire's theory that the layoff was discriminatory" and ruled that there was "substantial evidence that it was due to business necessity." Mackentire appealed the ruling, but lost again. The appellate court wrote that Ricoh "offered affidavits stating that FPD was losing money, running into the millions of dollars annually. It also offered evidence that it reorganized the division to de-emphasize the product for which Mackentire was most responsible."

thinking globally

1. What are some key reasons for keeping expatriate managers in top positions?

2. Suppose a company decides that it has made a mistake by hiring local personnel in a key Asian country. What are some potential problems that it will face if it decides to install or reinstate expatriate managers in these positions?

3. In addition to those mentioned in the case, what are some other advantages associated with the hiring of local managers in emerging markets?

4. What steps should a company take to ensure that, if taken to court, it can demonstrate that staffing cuts have not been discriminatory?

a question **of ethics**

1. Imagine yourself on your first assignment abroad as a manager at a manufacturing facility in Asia. You are aware of increasing concern among your employees (mostly young women) about wages that barely permit them to live at subsistence level. The plant is not unionized, and you know that your superiors in your home country are not particularly supportive of efforts to organize workers. You also know that if workers vote to form a union and then demand higher wages, headquarters is likely to shift production elsewhere. If the plant were shut down, your employees would lose their jobs, and you would be transferred. Should you encourage or discourage your workers in their efforts to unionize? Explain your decision.

2. After graduating from college, you were hired by a financial-services company that is expanding operations in Latin America. You got the job and were sent to Mexico City, Mexico, in part because you double-majored in Spanish and finance and spent a semester abroad there. Your company's policy is to provide you and your expatriate colleagues with hardship pay, a generous housing allowance, a company car, and a fund of several thousand dollars to be used at your discretion. You are quite comfortable living abroad, but you have some expatriate friends who have not adjusted so well. Every 2 months or so, they fly back home to visit friends and get a change of scenery. You are not homesick at all, but your friends want you to go with them on an upcoming holiday. What would you do? Would you dip into your discretionary funds and go along? Or, would you remain in the community and do volunteer work with a local charity?

Chapter 1: International Business Today

CHINA: NOW OPEN FOR BUSINESS, BUT HOW DO YOU GET IN?

China's breed of socialism is a radical departure from the system that existed in the past. But economists and China watchers generally agree that the country's leaders are genuinely determined to tackle even the most difficult economic issues. China is, for all intents and purposes, open for business.

Translating policy into action is difficult though. Entrenched ways of doing things are not that easy to change, especially in such a complex environment as China. The country's accession to the World Trade Organization, while extremely important and frequently discussed, is nevertheless just one step in the process of converting China to a truly open, market-based economy. Among numerous obstacles, the government has no intention of abandoning its oversight of the economy. In addition, political reforms have not materialized to any significant degree. Some commentators argue that until there is real political reform, economic reforms will be unbalanced and lack the scope needed to turn China into a true market economy—one with the openness and transparency that come with it. The absence of radical reforms in areas such as property rights is also seen as impeding the country's long-term economic progress.

The same holds true for China's newly reformed financial system. While a banking system loosely along Western lines has replaced the centralized state budget, its lending decisions still strongly favor the state and the its long-term planning goals. The state-controlled industrial sector, for example, takes 70 percent of bank loans but contributes only one-third of the country's total output. At the same time, many state-owned commercial banks have enormous bad debts and by Western standards are technically insolvent. Unless these issues are resolved, they will further add to the fragility of the country's financial system and make it vulnerable to changing world financial conditions.

All this underscores the impact globalization is having on China. To succeed economically, the country must open its doors. However, the country does not want to abandon many aspects of its centuries-old culture. The question remains: Are globalization and national interests compatible?

FOREIGN COMPANIES

Enormous challenges continue to face foreign companies seeking a presence in China. But the rewards can be great, too. The prospect of a burgeoning consumer market and of an increasingly business-friendly environment can be extremely enticing. But ask foreign businesspeople about their experiences in China and you will hear complaints about its entrenched and unwieldy bureaucracy, lack of transparency, and far-from-mature legal framework. The most common response, though, is that the country is undergoing extraordinary change.

The government's commitment to further opening up the economy to foreign direct investment is now assured, and the amount of money coming in has been increasing dramatically. Much of this investment money has been directed toward export industries.

As China's economy becomes more integrated, a huge internal market is developing as well. From Kodak to Procter & Gamble to Coca-Cola, foreign consumer brands are now enjoying substantial success in the Chinese marketplace. However, huge investments are needed in infrastructure development, including in the communications sector.

The energy sector has also attracted a lot of foreign investment in recent years. Enron, BP, and Shell are just a few of the many multinationals that have entered into partnerships with Chinese companies.

PRACTICAL CONSIDERATIONS OF DOING BUSINESS WITH CHINESE COMPANIES

Any foreign-funded business in China is likely to find itself in a web of complicated relationships with Chinese companies. For example, a company might be a partner with several Chinese firms, in various locations throughout the country and with a number of shareholding structures. Another company might market products manufactured in China to both domestic and international markets and also purchase supplies from both sources. Even the foreign company with just a single Chinese operation may find that establishing and maintaining good business relationships with Chinese partners, distributors, and suppliers can be a major challenge.

The most successful alliances are usually those with Chinese companies whose ownership structure is transparent, that operate in deregulated markets, and that have a good record of market performance. In regulated markets, the relationship between the Chinese company and the various levels of the Chinese government is important in shaping the partnership. Companies with close relationships to the various centers of government power and influence are often the best to target when considering strategic alliances.

Market power should be one of the primary determinants when seeking alliances with Chinese companies. Large national companies command larger sales territories and have wide distribution networks. They tend to be competitively driven as well.

On the other hand, smaller firms, state owned or otherwise, tend to be better than large unwieldy companies at accommodating foreign-funded enterprises. These smaller companies are usually better at adapting to foreign ways of doing business and are eager to adopt global standards. A number of these smaller firms have grown into large corporations just by providing multinationals in China with much-needed supplies.

MULTIMEDIA EXPLORATION

(WWW.PRENHALL.COM/WILD)

Giving gifts in China is vital to relationship building. But taking the price tag off before you present them is a big mistake!

READ, SEE, and **HEAR** *more about China and why culture is so important in shaping its people, its economy, and the way business is done.*

TEST YOUR KNOWLEDGE *by answering the questions as well.*

Chapter 2: Culture in Business

LATIN AMERICA: ANCIENT CIVILIZATIONS, ISOLATED FORESTS, IMPENETRABLE MOUNTAINS . . . AND BIG EXPENSE ACCOUNTS?

Home to almost one-tenth of the world's population, Latin America is one of the most diverse, colorful, and vibrant regions on the globe. But, despite its enormous potential, the region is beset by what at times seem insurmountable problems. With both wealth and poverty on a vast scale, awe-inspiring natural splendor, and some of the world's largest and most sophisticated urban areas, Latin America is a feast for the eyes, a challenge to the senses, and, most of all, a place that inspires, confounds, challenges, and frustrates—sometimes all at the same time. Understanding the region's culture is vital for business success.

Geography has helped define culture in Latin America for centuries. Ancient civilizations remained isolated in vast forests and in almost impenetrable mountains. After colonization, geography shaped the cultures of the new countries, giving birth to the development of vibrant cities close to rich mineral deposits and natural harbors and waterways.

If you're doing business in Latin America, there are a few things to bear in mind. The business culture of the region differs depending on where you go. A lot has to do with the size of the country in question, the extent to which it has developed a modern industrial sector, and its openness to outside influences and the global economy.

Visit some of the major industrial and commercial centers and you'll come across a business culture that is highly sophisticated, international in outlook, and on a par with that in Europe or North America. You'll find modern offices and businesspeople with expense accounts and strong business acumen.

Move away from the cities, however, and things will start to change as local conditions and local customs begin to enter the equation. Often in the tropical regions, you'll find things slow down quite a bit to match the intense heat and humidity. Similarly, as you move farther from the big cities, the infrastructure may become less reliable, forcing people to become highly innovative in circumventing the hardships facing them and their businesses.

Generally speaking, though, you'll notice several common themes running throughout Latin America when it comes to business culture: Businesses are hierarchical in their structure, with decisions made from the top down; and developing trust and gaining respect in the business environment is all about forging and maintaining good relationships. This may require quite a bit of socializing.

Another important factor influencing the business culture is the concept of time. In Latin America, "*El tiempo es como el espacio.*" In other words, time is space. More often than not, situations take precedence over schedules. Many people unfamiliar with Latin American customs, especially those from highly time-conscious countries like the U.S., Canada, and those in Northern Europe, can find the lack of punctuality and the more fluid view of time annoying and wasteful. It's more useful to see the unhurried approach as an opportunity to develop good relations and to enjoy what's on offer without always having to glance at your watch. This is a generalization, though, and in the megacities of Latin America, time definitely equals money.

You'll need to mind your manners, too. In most Latin American countries, Old World manners are still the rule, and an air of formality pervades most business interactions and interpersonal relationships, especially when the parties are not well acquainted.

In most of the region's larger cities, it's important to carry yourself with a sense of style: Dress well, be polite, and, most importantly, take social cues from the people you're interacting with.

Also remember that Latin Americans are generally physical people and outgoing in their expressions and body language. They frequently stand close to one another when talking, sometimes touch each other, and even kiss on first meeting. You won't be expected to know all the nuances of social interactions, but at least be prepared for subtle—and not-so-subtle—forms of behavior that may be quite different from what you're used to.

MULTIMEDIA EXPLORATION

(WWW.PRENHALL.COM/WILD)

Three kisses, or two? You'd better get it right. Kissing's a fine art in Latin America.

READ, SEE, and **HEAR** more about Latin America and why culture is so important in shaping its people, its economy, and the way business is done.

TEST YOUR KNOWLEDGE by answering the questions as well.

Chapter 3: Politics and Law in Business

JAPAN: MORE LAWS, FEWER LAWYERS

The Japanese political and legal system presents a complex picture. On the one hand, Japan is a democratic state, with strong civic and legal institutions. On the other hand, the country has characteristics of nondemocratic systems. It is a democracy yet just one party, the Liberal Democratic Party (LDP), has held sway since the end of World War II. Japan is highly bureaucratic as well. Decisions affecting national policy are often made by ministries with substantial power and influence and ties to business and industrial groups. As a result, it is often said that Japan lacks the pragmatic approach to change that is common in Western democracies, and this is seen as contributing to Japan's extended economic malaise.

To most foreigners, Japanese politics may appear somewhat puzzling. Policy does not seem to change regardless of who is leading the country, and, in fact, that's the argument the person in the street gives when asked about his or her lack of interest in politics. "Why bother, nothing changes." Actually, most legislation isn't produced by the members of the Diet but by ministers and bureaucrats.

The policy-making process in Japan is more similar to the parliamentary systems of Europe and contrasts with the American system, in which presidential appointees attempt to exercise control over branches of the bureaucracy on behalf of the president. It's not uncommon in Japan for the influence and power of a Japanese ministry or agency to outlive the reign of a prime minister, as evident in the powerful Ministry of International Trade and Industry, better known as MITI.

Not surprisingly given the culture, the Japanese political system also has a tradition of group rather than personalized leadership. Elderly statesmen and party chiefs, not individual prime ministers, often make political decisions. Cabinet members are usually appointed to head ministries or agencies for very brief periods of time and at most establish only general policy control. Recently, commentators have begun to question this lack of action.

Japan's legal system is very different from what most Westerners are used to. For example, only since 1986 have foreign legal consultants (*Gaigokuho-Jimu-Bengoshi*) been allowed to provide legal services. The requirements were modified in 1994 with the signing of the Amendments to the Foreign Attorney Law. In certain types of practices, licensed legal consultants from other countries can now practice together with Japanese attorneys.

Anyone planning on doing business in Japan should bear in mind that prefectures and municipalities may create laws and regulations independently of each other, so long as they do not contradict national laws. In other words, there are local laws and regulations in addition to laws that are consistent and uniform throughout the country. Each of the 47 prefectures may have a slightly different requirement concerning paperwork, for example.

The Japanese are not very litigious; they generally prefer arbitration and compromise to instituting lawsuits. Lawyers encourage settlement out of court for all disputes, and the amount of money awarded as compensation is a fraction of the amounts awarded in America, for example.

In recent years, more cases have been brought to court, but they have tended to be high-profile suits that had the support of a group. The judge makes the ruling and decides whether and how much to award as compensation; such cases do not go before a jury. Japan had a jury system at one time, but it was discontinued after five years since ordinary citizens were very reluctant to make important decisions about other people's lives. To deter people from filing suits, the plaintiff is required to pay a large filing fee and all legal costs; attorneys may not take cases on contingency.

One of the most significant differences between Japanese law and the law in many other countries has to do with the power of contracts. Japanese contracts are not necessarily meant to be binding. Rather, founded on trust (*shinyô*), they're often more short statements of mutual intent. The assumption is that if a change occurs in the circumstances of the contract, the terms will be renegotiated.

If you enter into a Western-style contract, which more companies are using as they work with overseas businesses, you will want to hire an English-speaking Japanese lawyer or a lawyer very familiar with Japanese law to guide you through the process. If you or your company is drafting the contract, keep the language as simple as legally possible or provide explanations for legal jargon. Especially in smaller companies, the person appointed to translate or interpret the contract may have limited English-language skills. Legalese will make the document incomprehensible. As you would do with any cross-cultural agreement, be sure to define currency exchange rates and legal processes and language especially clearly.

MULTIMEDIA EXPLORATION

(WWW.PRENHALL.COM/WILD)

The Diet is not something Japanese go on to loose weight; it's the name given to the Japanese equivalent of the U.S. House of Representatives.

READ, **SEE**, and **HEAR** more about Japan and its political and legal system and why culture is so important in shaping its people, its economy, and the way business is done.

TEST YOUR KNOWLEDGE by answering the questions as well.

GERMANY: DETAILS, DETAILS, DETAILS . . . AND SIX WEEKS VACATION

The German economic system is best described as "mixed," in that the government retains a substantial say in the running of the economy and there is a strong partnership between the government sector and the private sector. In addition, Germany has an extensive welfare system that seeks to insulate citizens from economic hardship.

Since the end of World War II, successive governments have sought to retain the basic elements of Germany's complex economic system (the *Soziale Marktwirtschaft*). Notably, relationships between employer and employee and between private industry and the government have remained stable. Over the years, the country has had few industrial disputes. Furthermore, active participation by all groups in the economic decision-making process has ensured a level of cooperation unknown in many other Western countries. This relationship has laid the foundation for decades of solid economic growth. All this is changing, though, as Germany is forced to become more competitive in the global environment. Increasingly, demands have arisen for a more flexible and open system, especially as privatization continues.

Businesses in Germany, both large and small, operate under a complex system of rules and regulations, much of which is contained in the Works Constitution Act of 1972 (*Betriebsverfassungsgesetz*). Unlike workers in many other Western countries, employees in Germany play an active role in issues affecting the workplace. The nature of this role is outlined in detail in a "social pact," or Soziale Marktwirtschaft, as it is often called. The ultimate goal is to improve the worker-employer relationship, which is traditionally adversarial in Western countries.

The German workplace is generally harmony-oriented, in part because it is controlled by such an elaborate system of regulations. There is a strong desire to deal with difficult or sensitive issues clearly, logically, and fairly. Conflicts can generally be avoided by relying on a legally based conflict-resolution mechanism.

The Works Constitution Act of 1972 lays down the structural relationship between workers and the employer in any company with five or more employees. It guarantees every employee the right to be heard and to be clearly informed on issues concerning wages, personnel considerations, and other important social and economic matters. The document also sets out guidelines for addressing safety matters in the workplace.

Legally, management must advise the committee of any major investments or financial plans the company is considering. Ultimately, though, management makes all business decisions. While particularly relevant to the industrial and blue-collar sectors of the economy, these committees nevertheless operate across all industries.

Employers and employees usually contribute equally to pension funds and for unemployment and health insurance. Regardless of job level and salary, all employees contribute about 20 percent of their earnings toward their pensions. Deductions for unemployment insurance average about 7 percent of gross earnings and about 13 to 14 percent for healthcare. German workers have heavy burdens indeed, but they also receive substantial benefits.

More than 90 percent of the German population belongs to the healthcare system provided for by the government. Private insurance companies generally appeal to self-employed professionals. German employers must also cover half the benefit contributions for sick leave, maternity leave, parental leave, and holidays. German workers requiring extended sick leave (more than six weeks) are guaranteed 80 percent of their usual wages.

Under federal law, all employees receive a minimum of 20 days paid leave per year. In fact, many receive much more. Because trade unions are so strong in Germany, almost 70 percent of Germans receive six weeks of vacation. The other 30 percent receive between four and six weeks, and this is in addition to public holidays. Anyone younger than 18 is guaranteed between 25 and 30 days of vacation.

Traditionally, German trade unions have exercised considerable power, although this is less true in recent years. They are organized by industry and accept workers within that industry or economic sector regardless of the work they perform. Unlike unions in some parts of the world, German unions are not connected to any political party and do not have religious affiliations.

All the unions are active in collective bargaining on aspects of the work environment: working hours, holidays, benefits, and overtime pay. Wages and compensation issues are usually negotiated annually, while benefits and quality-of-life issues are reconsidered every few years.

The influence of German unions goes far beyond matters directly affecting the work environment. For example, the right of codetermination (*Mitbestimmungsrecht*) gives union representatives voting power on several critical management issues. These include product development, marketing strategies, capital investment, and the hiring of key management personnel. Also, in most large corporations, unions have one or more seats on the board of management.

MULTIMEDIA EXPLORATION

(WWW.PRENHALL.COM/WILD)

Freizeit is not something cooked in oil. It means "free time." And to the Germans this is a very precious thing. Working more than eight hours a day can mean you're not doing your job properly.

READ, **SEE**, and **HEA**R more about Germany and its unique economic system and why culture is so important in shaping its people, its economy, and the way business is done.

TEST YOUR KNOWLEDGE by answering the questions as well.

Chapter 5: International Trade

SINGAPORE: FROM THE SPICE TRAIL TO THE SEAWAYS

Many of today's global economies are historical success stories, highlighting the benefits of international trade. One clear example is Singapore, a tiny island in Asia off the coast of Malaysia. Singapore's location as the geographic center of several key maritime trade routes, including the paramount waterway between India and China, has historically made it an important component of international trade, ensuring its place as the "clearinghouse of the East." Singapore remains a premier maritime center today. Its port and sheltered deep-water harbor are among the busiest in the world, in a class with those in Rotterdam, Hong Kong, and New York.

The first traders came to the island of Singapore in the third century AD, while navigating between India and China. By the sixteenth century, Singapura, as it was originally called, had become a prosperous commercial center controlled by various Asian rulers.

In 1613, the Portuguese burned down the trading post the ruler had left behind, and for about 200 years the island of Singapura was largely abandoned. abandoned. However, with the growth of the international spice trade, the island attracted new attention, and in 1819, Sir Thomas Stamford Raffles, a British official of the East India Company, set up a trading post. Soon traders, merchants, and settlers from Asia, the Middle East, and Europe were frequenting the island, once again named Singapura. This international trade between Chinese, Arab, Indian, Thai, Malay, and Javanese traders resulted in a colorful mix of cultures and languages. It was Raffles's vision of "a great commercial emporium" in the East, founded on trade, not territorial conquest, that spawned the mercantile enterprise in Singapore.

Granted free-trade status by the British, Singapore began its nineteenth-century ascendance as a major trade center in Southeast Asia, with merchants and vessels flocking to its port. The Chinese ships brought silver, while vessels from Cochin-China (Vietnam) carried sugar, rice, and coconut oil. Commerce with Calcutta, India, brought cotton and wheat, in exchange for opium, silver dollars, tin, and pepper. Boats from Borneo brought camphor, rattans, edible bird's nest, gold, and other jungle products. Loaded with spices, Arab *dhows* sailed out of Batavia (Jakarta) under the Dutch flag.

Singapore's global importance as a trade center continued over the centuries. Modern-day Singapore has focused its attention on building an economically secure, strong nation. From its early days of independence in 1965, Singapore set about becoming a major player in the competitive world of international business. From 1968 until 1997, the economic growth rate averaged an enviable 9 percent per year. Even more remarkable, Singapore is among the most competitive nations in the world. Most years, only the United States is considered better able to attract new business. And, among Asian countries, only Japan has a higher per capita income. Shipping and reprocessing formed the foundation for the island's growth as a business leader. Today, other economic strengths include tourism, finance, and the manufacture of high-tech value-added products.

Singapore's manufacturing sector accounts for approximately 30 percent of its GDP. The emphasis has been on the development of high-tech industries, such as aerospace, petrochemicals, healthcare, and information technology. Corporate giants, such as Shell, Thomson, Compaq Computer, Motorola, and Becton Dickinson, all have manufacturing operations on the island. Oil refining is also important. Several offshore refineries are located on the islands in the Johor Straits.

Singapore's tourist industry generates about S$8 billion per year and employs one million people, making tourism a key component of the island's economy. More than five million tourists visit each year—many from Asia—lured in large part by the island's modern yet traditional Asian culture.

The services sector, especially financial services, is an area of considerable growth. Software developers, financial services, consulting businesses, and medical service companies have sprung up, and the island is frequently a site for international conferences and exhibitions.

Singapore also has a comprehensive banking system, offering everything from investment to consumer services. Money is safe and fully protected by confidentiality. These features have been major pluses in the development of Singapore as a global mutual funds management center, foreign exchange trading center, and regional banking center.

Managers of foreign companies generally find Singapore a great place to do business. Among the attractions they cite are the island's political stability, generally unrestrained capitalist economy, seemingly faultless infrastructure, laws and tax incentives that encourage foreign investment, and emphasis on automation and training. The Singapore government manages the island's economy much like a bank manages its holdings, reinvesting revenues into national road construction, education, housing, and other infrastructural improvements. The objective is to use the benefits of international trade to create a standard of wealth equal to—and eventually better than—Europe's.

MULTIMEDIA EXPLORATION

(WWW.PRENHALL.COM/WILD)

Loosing face is not a severe medical condition. But it's something no one in Singapore likes to experience, and it could affect you too if you're not careful.

READ, **SEE**, and **HEAR** *more about Singapore and its place at the crossroads of Asia and why culture is so important in shaping its people, its economy, and the way business is done.*

TEST YOUR KNOWLEDGE *by answering the questions as well.*

Chapter 6: Business-Government Trade Relations

JAPAN: *ZAIBATSU* AND *KEIRETSU* . . . THE SUMO WRESTLERS OF BUSINESS

Governments around the world have routinely intervened in trade and investment policy. Japan's post-war economic rise shows how government intervention was used first to promote Japanese industry and exports and then, as a result of external pressures, to increase domestic demand and consumption.

Much of Japan's post-World War II success was the result of a well-crafted economic policy closely administered by the government in alliance with big businesses. Historically, Japan's economy was controlled by *zaibatsu*, huge conglomerates. The main ones, Mitsubishi, Mitsui, Sumitomo, and Yasuda, were interested primarily in making profits and expanding their heavy industries, banking, and international trade, and their leaders largely ignored the mounting financial crisis. To support its growing

heavy industry, Japan needed a steady supply of oil, iron ore, and coal. Thus began a period of military aggression in Southeast Asia, Korea, and China, which eventually led to the outbreak of war in the Pacific on December 7, 1941. After Japan's defeat in World War II, Allied forces under U.S. general MacArthur occupied Japan, with the purpose of establishing a "stable democracy."

General MacArthur had planned to dismantle the zaibatsu and other monopolistic companies after the war, but concerns about the U.S. involvement in Korea and the growing Cold War with the Soviet Union led the United States to focus instead on strengthening the Japanese economy. In fact, the financial aid the United States pumped into Japan helped the zaibatsu, which reemerged, with the addition of some new groups, as a stronger network of interdependent companies called *keiretsu*. The keiretsu are conglomerates that share resources, customers, and distributors. Unlike the former zaibatsu firms, which were controlled by holding companies, horizontal keiretsu are tied to a bank that may hold shares in other companies; hence, the companies and bank have very strong links financially. The companies may be affiliated, or they may be in completely different industries and of varying sizes. Keiretsu may also take a vertical form. In this case, they usually include a supplier and a distributor, and a large manufacturer is at the center. One of the advantages of keiretsu is that they can take over large projects that smaller companies could not support.

The keiretsu have long enjoyed a very close relationship with the government. Since 1990, the United States has challenged some of their exclusionary practices, and, as a result of changes in their economic influence and roles, it has gradually become easier for foreign companies to do business in Japan.

The outbreak of the Korean War accelerated Japan's opportunity to export its products, and from 1954 until 1972, the gross national product increased at a rate of more than 10 percent annually. Silk textiles were a major export, accounting for about one-third of the total. Production increased by 300 percent in the decade following 1962. Bolstered by its cheap labor force, high-quality products, and government-supported industrial output, Japan became a leader in exporting ships, steel, and electrical goods, followed by automobiles and electronic products. By 1971, Japan was the third-largest exporter in the world.

Faced with two oil crises in the 1970s, Japanese companies started developing more fuel-efficient products and more efficient manufacturing processes. Throughout this period, the value of the yen was as low as 308 to the dollar, making imports very expensive. In 1985, the Plaza Accord (G-5 Plaza Accord), an agreement among the world's major industrialized countries, took steps to reduce this imbalance by low-ering the value of the dollar. Japan also agreed to stimulate consumer desire to buy American. As the rate of the dollar dropped, imports became cheaper and the price of exports became higher. Thousands of import regulations were eliminated, and Japanese business began to feel the competition as profit margins dropped. Many companies adapted by cutting their production costs and moving their manufacturing operations to Europe and America.

Japan's so-called bubble economy grew soon after the signing of the Plaza Accord and of other trade agreements in the mid-1980s that committed Japan to a policy of increasing domestic demand and lowered interest rates. By 1991, though, Japan had plunged into its worst recession in the modern era.

Japan's huge trade surpluses and what many claimed were unfair trading practices damaged its relations with the United States and with major countries in Europe. By 2000, these relationships were strained even further by a perceived lack of understanding and attempts by the Japanese government to reform its economy. Despite the government's efforts, which included spending vast sums from the public coffers on infrastructure projects, prospects for the short term remained bleak.

The government is now actively pursuing more foreign investment by pushing ahead with measures to create a new tax system, better work environments, and improved health and education services for foreign nationals.

MULTIMEDIA EXPLORATION
(WWW.PRENHALL.COM/WILD)

In Japan, Sumo wrestlers are not just big, they're some of the hottest sex symbols around and they capture the hearts—and minds—of many an admirer.

READ, SEE, and HEAR *more about Japan and why culture is so important in shaping its people, its economy, and the way business is done.*

TEST YOUR KNOWLEDGE *by answering the questions as well.*

HONG KONG: FROM JUNKS TO JETS . . .THE RISE OF A GLOBAL POWERHOUSE

Policies of openness to foreign direct investment and international trade have enabled countries around the world to leapfrog economically over their neighbors. The historical rise of Hong Kong is one example. Hong Kong's economic strengths can be traced to a combination of factors, including its business-friendly laws and policies, a local population that is culturally oriented to transacting trade and business, and Hong Kong's geographic proximity to the major economies of China, Japan, and Taiwan.

Hong Kong has always been open to global trade. Many peoples, from the Chinese to the Japanese to the British, have occupied Hong Kong over the centuries, and all of them have contributed to its development as one of the world's great ports and trading centers.

In 1997, Hong Kong reverted back to Chinese control; however, free enterprise will be governed under the agreement of Basic Law, which established Hong Kong as a separate Special Administrative Region (SAR) of China. Under its Basic Law, in force until 2047, Hong Kong will retain its legal, social, economic, and political systems apart from China's. Thus, Hong Kong is guaranteed the right to its own monetary system and financial autonomy. Hong Kong is allowed to work independently with the international community; to control trade in strategic commodities, drugs, and illegal transshipments; and to protect intellectual property rights. Under the Basic Law, the Hong Kong SAR maintains an independent tax system and the right to free trade.

Hong Kong has an open business structure, which freely encourages foreign direct investment. Any company that wishes to do business here is free to do so as long as it complies with local laws. Hong Kong's legal and institutional framework combined with its good banking and financial facilities and business-friendly tax systems have encouraged foreign direct investment as many multinationals located their regional headquarters in Hong Kong.

According to a 2000 government survey, 619 Japanese companies have their regional headquarters or offices in Hong Kong; 570 U.S. companies; and 236 British companies. The late 1980s and early to mid-1990s were especially prosperous times in Hong Kong as many of these international companies set up regional headquarters. Businesses scrambled for office space, and apartment prices skyrocketed. It was not uncommon during this period for brand-new residential buildings suddenly to be demolished and replaced with even taller structures following changes in zoning regulations.

As a base for doing business with China, Hong Kong now accounts for half of all direct investments in the mainland and is China's main conduit for investment and trade. China has also become a major investor in Hong Kong.

Culturally, many foreign firms are attracted to Hong Kong by its skilled workforce and the fact that Hong Kong still conducts business in English, a remnant of its British colonial influence. The imprint of the early British trading firms, known as *hongs*, is particularly strong today in the area of property development. Jardine Matheson and Company, for instance, founded by trader William Jardine, remains one of Hong Kong's preeminent firms. In many of these companies, British management practices remain firmly in place. Every aspect of Hong Kong's business laws—whether pertaining to contracts, taxes, or trusts—bears striking similarities to the laws in Britain. All of these factors contribute to a business culture that is familiar to people in many multinationals.

Chinese cultural influences have always affected business and are increasingly so today. Many pundits claim that Hong Kong already resembles China's free-trade zone. And, indeed, the two economies are becoming increasingly intertwined. Much of this economic commingling began in the 1990s, when Hong Kong companies began relocating production centers to the mainland—especially to Guangdong province.

Because of the shift in production to mainland China and other Asian countries, there is not much manufacturing left in Hong Kong. What remains is light in nature and veers toward high-value-added products. In fact, 80 percent of Hong Kong's gross domestic product now comes from its high value-added service sector: finance, business and legal services, brokerage services, the shipping and cargo industries, and the hotel, food, and beverage industry.

Local Hong Kong companies, as well as foreign businesses based there, are uniquely positioned to play important roles as brokers and intermediaries between the mainland and global corporations. Doing business in China is not only complex and daunting but also requires connections, locally known as *guanxi*, to influential people and an understanding of local laws and protocol. Developing these relationships and this knowledge is almost impossible without the assistance of an insider. It is in this role that the Hong Kong business community stands to contribute enormously. Hong Kong's openness to foreign investment coupled with its proximity to China will ensure its global economic competitiveness for decades to come.

MULTIMEDIA EXPLORATION

(WWW.PRENHALL.COM/WILD)

People in Hong Kong are very sensitive to numbers. Avoid the number 4. When spoken in Cantonese, it sounds the same as the word for "death". Best to choose the number 8 as your lucky number. Better still, 88, which has double the luck potential.

READ, SEE, and HEAR *more about Hong Kong and why culture is so important in shaping its people, its economy, and the way business is done.*

TEST YOUR KNOWLEDGE *by answering the questions as well.*

Chapter 8: Regional Economic Integration

MEXICO: AFTER NAFTA WHERE WOULD YOU RATHER BE, NORTH OR SOUTH?

The Mexican economy has undergone dramatic changes during the last decade as the country has become integrated into the global marketplace. Once highly protected, Mexico is now "open for business." Successive governments have instituted far-reaching economic reforms, which have had a major impact on the way business is conducted. The scale of business has changed as well. Forced to compete with large multinationals and Mexican conglomerates, many traditional family-owned firms have had to close because they were unable to compete in the global marketplace.

The North American Free Trade Agreement (NAFTA) has added to the already-strong U.S. influence on Mexico's corporate and business practices. In particular, competitiveness and efficiency have become higher priorities, although company owners and managers still like to surround themselves with people they know and to groom their sons and sometimes their daughters to be their successors. American influence is also pervasive in the products and services offered throughout Mexico.

Mexico has always had a strong entrepreneurial business culture, but until recently it was protected from the pressures of international finance and the global marketplace. Business and particularly interpersonal business relationships were viewed as something that should be pleasurable, like other important aspects of life.

Long-term relationships are still the foundation on which trust is established and business is built. In Mexico, patience and the willingness to wait are still highly valued—and necessary—in business transactions. This is slowly changing, spurred in part by an aggressive cadre of young professionals who pursued graduate education in the United States.

Since the mid-1960s, production facilities known as *maquiladoras* have been a regular feature of Mexico border towns, especially on the borders of Texas and New Mexico. Of the more than 3,600 maquiladoras in northern Mexico, most are run by U.S. multinational companies. These include such companies as John Deere, Zenith, Mattel, and Xerox. Billions of dollars worth of products—from TVs, to clothes, to auto parts—are assembled in maquiladoras then shipped back, tax free, to the United States for sale to U.S. consumers.

Maquiladoras employ close to a million Mexicans, mostly unskilled women in their twenties and early thirties who work long hours. Wages and benefits are generally poor but much better than in the rest of Mexico. The huge growth in trade between the U.S. and Mexico has greatly expanded the role—and scale—of these assembly operations.

With the benefits of increased trade have also come challenges. A large number of Mexicans are concerned that wealth is distributed more unevenly than ever. For example, many commentators see the political situation in the state of Chiapas as underscoring the alienation large groups have suffered as a result of the opening of the Mexican economy to global forces. A rural region in southern Mexico, Chiapas is home to extremely poor Maya, Chol, Zoque, and Lacandón Indians. Yet, though it is the poorest state in Mexico, Chiapas has the richest natural resources, including oil, minerals, and electrical power.

In January 1994, the day NAFTA officially took effect, a group of Indian peasants, commanded by Subcomandante Marcos, rose up in armed rebellion. This was shocking not only to Mexico's leadership but to the international community. The unrest in Chiapas stems from longstanding economic and social injustice in the region and from the Indians' isolation and exploitation by the local oligarchy of landowners and mestizo bosses (*caciques*).

Since 1994, the group, calling itself the Zapatista National Liberation Army (Ejército Zapatista de Liberación Nacional, or EZLN), has engaged in only a smattering of guerrilla activities in Chiapas, around San Cristobal de las Casas and Ocosingo. However, using a combination of strategies, including effective use of the Internet, Marcos and the Zapatistas have continued to increase awareness about the plight of Mexico's indigenous peoples.

Equally important, the Zapatistas have opened a debate about the national legitimacy of the PRI, particularly its use of fraud, bribes, and other corrupt tactics to control and win elections at national, state, and local levels. Among the concerns are the PRI's authoritarianism, repression of opposition groups, and increasing alliance with and dependence on the U.S. government.

The Mexican government has indicated that improving the social conditions in the region is a high priority. However, only partial accords have been reached between the government and the peasants. At the same time, the army continues to exert tight control over the state, particularly in and around towns where residents are known to support the rebels.

The low standard of living in Chiapas, and of Indians throughout Mexico, remains a significant challenge for the Mexican government. In the years following the Chiapas uprising, poverty in southern Mexico has risen to about 40 percent, while in the north, poverty has decreased thanks to closer economic links with the U.S.

MULTIMEDIA EXPLORATION

(WWW.PRENHALL.COM/WILD)

Cinco de Mayo might be a major Mexican festival in the United States, but it's hardly celebrated at all in Mexico itself.

READ, SEE, and HEAR *more about Mexico and how traditional Mexican culture is coming face-to-face with the new realities of the global marketplace.*

TEST YOUR KNOWLEDGE *by answering the questions as well.*

Chapter 9: International Financial Markets

SINGAPORE: HOW STRONG IS YOUR *KIASU*?

Many analysts argue that a country's culture plays a large part in its degree of openness—or integration—into world financial markets. The United States is often quoted as a place where an ethic of capital accumulation and wealth-creation has led to an open economy with a stock market valued in trillions of dollars. Different countries have different approaches when it comes to financial markets. The most laissez faire economies have tended to foster the development of world financial centers—all closely interlinked. In these centers, managing—and making—money is the order of the day and a highly competitive spirit prevails. What's more, conspicuous consumption is the norm, albeit tempered, by the cultural norms of that country. Here are two examples:

CASE STUDY: THE UNITED STATES

Perhaps because of the way this relatively young country has developed—with the emphasis on the accumulation of personal wealth—material gains are seen as the benchmark measure of success. Not only is it socially acceptable to pursue and display wealth here, but that's also the primary goal of millions of Americans.

Social classes are defined more by income than so-called breeding or status, with the richest people at the top and the poorest at the bottom. This is in stark contrast to some European cultures where class distinctions are based more on education and position in society than on wealth.

The country's stock markets have been cornerstones of the economy for more than a century and hold an ever-more-significant place in the everyday life of everyday Americans, who see investing in stocks as a way of getting rich. There are a huge number of individual investors here, and you'll encounter stock quotes at every turn: on computer Web pages, in public spaces, on the radio and television.

People coming from other cultures where overt materialism is considered less acceptable may find the focus on wealth accumulation somewhat overwhelming. It's particularly obvious in the country's financial nerve center, New York City, where, they say, you can almost hear the money changing hands.

CASE STUDY: SINGAPORE

Unlike many countries, especially in Asia, Singapore has almost no poverty. In fact, its people are relatively rich. Most are either middle class or better. But, while Singapore's financial markets may be unfettered by government control, the government exerts its influence in other ways, including keeping a close eye on the press and media, and the use of campaigns to encourage the population to behave in certain ways.

The country boasts a per capita gross national product that places it in the league of first world countries. Middle and senior managers are generally paid on par with their European and American counterparts. As in other wealthy countries, a small portion of the population makes substantially less money.

The Singapore government urges islanders to be competitive and alert to economic opportunities and to strive to improve themselves financially. This message was summed up several years ago in a government jingle aimed at increasing productivity:

Good, better, best
Never let it rest
Till your good is better
And your better is best

With this competitive spirit has come a focus on acquiring material possessions and keeping up with the neighbors. In the 1990s, wealthier Singaporeans seemed especially obsessed with what were referred to as the five Cs: credit card, cash, car, condominium, and country club. Per capita, there are more Mercedes-Benzes on the road than in any other nation. Middle-class Singaporeans are also very materialistic but somewhat less brand conscious.

Singaporeans are willing to spend money, but they also want their money's worth. They joke that *kiasu* "an obsessive desire to get value for the money," is a national fixation. For example, eighty thousand visitors swarmed the national aviary at Bird Park on Christmas Day—when admission was free—and people routinely gorge at buffets, cheat to get better parking spaces, and remove in-flight utensils from aeroplanes. To some, *kiasu* is simply an example of pushing the idea of survival of the fittest to an extreme.

But at what price *kiasu*? Most Singaporeans appear willing to give up some freedom of speech and to accept a one-party system in order to retain their affluence, low unemployment and crime rates, and business awards.

MULTIMEDIA EXPLORATION

(WWW.PRENHALL.COM/WILD)

Singaporeans might like to show off their material possessions, but when it comes to personal interactions there's a lot of reserve and staring or looking into the eyes of someone is one of the worst things you can do.

READ, SEE, and HEAR more about how people in the U.S. and Singapore view wealth and making money. And, get up to speed on some of the basic cultural underpinnings of these countries.

TEST YOUR KNOWLEDGE by answering the questions as well.

Chapter 10: International Monetary System

BRAZIL: WHAT IS A *REAL* REALLY WORTH?

As with many economies in Latin America, the economy of Brazil has suffered from the combined effects of inflation, low growth rates, and, at times, a confusing and inequitable exchange rate policy. In turn, economic uncertainties have affected the distribution of wealth and how Brazilians view outsiders. In recent years, a more stable exchange rate has led to increased transparency in the economy. But a lot remains to be done to place the country on a more secure economic footing and to make exchange rates more stable.

Industry came to Brazil in the mid-1800s. The Depression of 1929 threw a wrench in development, but the setback was only temporary, and during subsequent decades expansion was steady. Growth was especially healthy between the 1960s and the oil crisis of 1979.

It wasn't until the 1980s, when interest rates busted the charts, that the economy began its descent. The flow of foreign and domestic capital slowed to a trickle, devaluations played havoc with the national currency, and foreign companies initiated debilitating cutbacks or left the country altogether. Severely handicapped in its ability to invest, Brazil plunged into a period of runaway inflation and negative growth rates. To this day, the 1980s are referred to as "the lost decade." On the political front, remarkably, these were years of peaceful transition from military dictatorship to freely elected government.

In the 1990s, the government honed in on three economic goals: trade reform, stabilizing the economy, and building the country's relationship with the world financial community. In 1994, the minister of finance, Fernando Henrique Cardoso (often called FHC), launched the Real Plan, which also gave its name to the currency. The plan, with its accent on the need for a strong currency, high interest rates, and an opening up of the economy, touched off a boom in Brazil. Foreign capital began pouring in. Brazil's economic wizards outwitted the forces that wracked Mexico in the mid-1990s as well as Southeast Asia in 1997 and 1998. Their main abracadabra was a strong (i.e. increasingly overvalued) real and spiraling interest rates. The charm inevitably broke when, in January 1999, the Central Bank stopped defending the grandiose real and let the currency float freely. Within a month, it tumbled from R$1.21 to the dollar to R$2.20 to the dollar before recovering to approximately R$1.66 to the dollar in May of that year.

Economically, the remainder of the 1990s was a qualified success, and the FHC regime was handed a second term in office. The success of this regime suggests that Brazilians will begrudgingly tolerate economic hardship over a return to inflationary policies. As recently as the late 1990s, economists warned that Brazil's rate of inflation would exceed 20 percent. They also predicted a 7 percent depletion of the GDP. In fact, in 1999, the rate of inflation was nearly zero. Despite the calamities suffered by many other emerging economies, Brazil's economic team finessed a traumatic devaluation, took steps to trim government spending, and faced down a rebellion by the opposition (governors led by FHC's predecessor, Itamar Franco, himself the governor of the state of Minas Gerais). This is the same team charged with creating these problems to begin with.

Being forced to deal with uncontrollable circumstances, from poor phone service to economic and exchange rate uncertainty, has been a day-to-day challenge for Brazilians. It has tended to make them an adaptable people. Rather than becoming frustrated by all they cannot control, they have learned to live with these limitations. In recent years, though, improvements in the infrastructure, particularly telecommunications, have enabled Brazilian companies to operate more efficiently and more in line with international norms and practices.

But attitudes can be ingrained, and, because of the constant need to adapt, Brazilian workers may strike you as more content than many people to accept "good enough." Form—the way things are done—often takes precedence over content and quality. As a result, you may be surprised by less-than-perfect, sometimes even mediocre, standards. Workers accept what they consider small problems (*probleminhos*). For example, although a business letter he wrote contained several typos, a Brazilian was about to mail it. When his American boss questioned him about the errors, the Brazilian's response was "So what if I made a few mistakes?" However exasperated you may be by their relaxed standards, you are likely to be impressed by the Brazilians' ability to cope with rapidly changing conditions. Also remember, the situation is improving. Many Brazilians, especially those in the younger generation, are both ambitious and entrepreneurial.

Some newcomers have commented on Brazil's love-hate relationship with foreigners. Insights into its soft underbelly reveal a complicated mix of national pride and shame. Brazilians love their country but are not without embarrassment about its inefficiencies and technological inadequacies compared to the countries they look up to.

They are quick to apologize for the limitations of their emerging economy, yet their sense of national pride can sometimes lead them to resent citizens of more highly developed nations.

MULTIMEDIA EXPLORATION

(WWW.PRENHALL.COM/WILD)

If you have a date with someone in Brazil that's scheduled for 8:00PM never show up at that time. It'll pay to know the correct etiquette when it comes to timelines—or lack of it.

READ, SEE, and HEAR *more about Brazil and how its economy business practices and attitudes to the outside world reflect its unique cultural underpinnings.*

TEST YOUR KNOWLEDGE *by answering the questions as well.*

MEXICO: *CAMARILLAS* . . . BEYOND YOUR POCKET PC

In recent years, Mexico has become an extremely attractive place to do business. To a large extent, this is a result of the opening up of the Mexican economy and the dismantling of government controls. However, as in all countries, local culture still heavily influences the way business is conducted. Setting up shop in Mexico requires a thorough knowledge not just of political, legal, economic, and financial forces but also of the country's culture: management practices, attitudes toward time, social relationships, and so forth.

Already the close relationship of the United States with Mexico is having a strong influence on Mexico's corporate and business practices. In particular, competitiveness and efficiency have become higher priorities, although company owners and managers still like to surround themselves with people they know and groom their sons and sometimes their daughters to be their successors. American influence is also pervasive in the products and services offered throughout Mexico.

In other respects, Mexico's business culture is uniquely Mexican. Especially if you're used to Western or American corporate practices, some business behavior may seem overly traditional and leave you feeling somewhat frustrated. It may be useful to keep in mind that injustice and authoritarianism have been norms throughout Mexico's history. Mexicans are a very proud people, but their past has left many scars. Many are noticeable in the workplace.

Mexico has always had a strong entrepreneurial business culture, but until recently it was protected from the pressures of international finance and the global marketplace. Business and particularly interpersonal business relationships were viewed as something that should be pleasurable, like other important aspects of life.

As in many countries, both Latin American and European, business relationships in Mexico are built on a strong foundation of trust. Patience is extremely important. Before making a commitment, Mexicans want to know whom they're dealing with. Traditionally, first-time business meetings are focused primarily on establishing rapport and getting to know one another. Only then can one decide if business with the person can be pleasurable. First-time meetings are often social occasions—a late lunch (*comida*) or a dinner (*cena*) perhaps, usually at a restaurant. The mood is likely to be relaxed and leisurely—a two-hour get-together is not unusual—and often little or no business is discussed.

Although business practices are changing, nepotism is still the rule in many Mexican companies. Businesses still tend to be hierarchical and paternalistic. Reflecting this makeup, power is at the top—in the hands of the boss, or, as Mexicans call him, the *patrón* or *jefe*.

Traditionally, the boss commands a great deal of authority and respect. The boss's status and the respect his subordinates bestow on him are evident in the size of his office, his appearance, and his role in making decisions that affect company policy. Often, the boss wields his authority autocratically.

Typically, the responsibilities of the boss extend beyond supervision of employees to serving as protector and mentor. The boss is frequently called upon to provide moral and material assistance to an employee's family and may be asked to be godfather (*padrino*) to an employee's child.

Mexicans, especially in the middle and lower classes, have been trained since childhood to defer to their elders and authority figures, to respect power and wealth, and not to question authority. Likewise, the patrón is unlikely to seek subordinates' opinions or to grant them decision-making power. Instead, they are given relatively limited, well-defined tasks that they are expected to carry out under management's close supervision. Outsiders doing business in Mexico need to be aware of these social responsibilities and financial obligations.

In recent years, Mexico's highly patriarchal system has begun eroding, especially in large enterprises in the country's major cities. Here one finds a smattering of managers who are educating their employees in team-based, egalitarian management styles. Decision making is decentralized, and the managers recognize the value of teamwork. Increasingly, the employees recognize its value as well.

In Mexico, *camarillas* (personal networks) or *palancas* (personal connections or influences) are essential to doing business. In contrast to some countries, in Mexico, power and influence often reside with an individual person or family, not with his job title or so-called position. Those who lack such connections are severely restricted from gaining access to Mexico's corporate environment, particularly in dealing with the government. Traditionally, politicians had both extensive camarillas and palancas, leading to broad influence. As the stature of Mexico's top business leaders slowly evolves, some business executives are amassing as much leverage as some politicians.

MULTIMEDIA EXPLORATION

(WWW.PRENHALL.COM/WILD)

Mexicans are a physical people and even touching among strangers is quite common. But don't go hugging everyone you come into contact with. It's not as simple as it seems.

READ, SEE, and HEAR more about Mexico and how its culture affects every aspect of doing business from interpersonal communications to the way companies are structured.

TEST YOUR KNOWLEDGE by answering the questions as well.

Chapter 12: Analyzing International Opportunities

BRAZIL: HOW DO YOU USE *JEITINHO*?

Anyone setting up a business in another country should take into account the culture of that country from the earliest stages of planning. An important aspect of this culture is how uncertainty is dealt with. In some cultures, life is not considered predictable or certain and the business culture tends to reflect this: Some risk is built into planning and decision-making, and pragmatism is the order of the day. In other cultures, uncertainty makes people uncomfortable, and they work hard to avoid it. People in such cultures are likely to err on the side of the caution when making business decisions and sometimes take a long time to make them. Whatever the case, an international corporation needs to be aware of local attitudes and values and meld them into the company's way of doing things.

Tolerance for ambiguity is a very important cultural measuring stick. How does your culture deal with uncertainty? Does it favor risk taking? Value loyalty to superiors? Favor or discourage change?

In all cultures, understanding where the individual stands can be quite an effort. That's where rules and rituals come in. In most Asian cultures, for example, greetings can be highly ritualized and learning these rituals is important to gaining acceptance. It may not suffice to say "hello" without stating your name, title, and occupation.

Similarly, people in Asia may take a long time before disclosing personal details and accepting strangers into their groups. The degree of sincerity and openness they show reflects how much the outsider has been accepted. If you're accustomed to quicker acceptance of others, you might find this a bit of an adjustment.

People who have a low tolerance for uncertainty generally prefer to steer clear of conflict and competition. They tend to appreciate clear instructions. At the office, sharply defined rules and rituals are used to usher tasks to completion. Japan is often considered an example of such a society.

Conversely, Northern Europeans and Americans accept a relatively high threshold of uncertainty. Judging by the degree of dissent and risk they indulge in, they generally log lower stress levels in their relationships. Yet their relationships tend to be more superficial and less committed. Friendships form quickly, but relationships, even between them and their 300 "best friends," are not necessarily binding or enduring. Members of these cultures require less formal rules to interact.

CASE STUDY: BRAZIL

A hallmark of Brazilian business culture is a creative approach known simply as *jeitinho*. *Jeitinho* means "to find a way." For Brazilians, there's always another way to get something done. An individual who needs a document, for example, might take the bureaucratic steps necessary to obtain it. Unfortunately, because of rules and regulations, obtaining it might become impossible. However, by using personal connections, bending the rules, making a "contribution," or simply approaching the problem from a different angle, he or she might be able to find a way. In other words, the individual would use *jeitinho*.

The focus appears to be on the goal—in this case, obtaining the document. Actually, it's on the process of accomplishing it. In the process, the goal may change, or coming close to reaching the goal might become a sufficient achievement.

Jeitinho never involves an aggressive attack on authority. Rather, it's a complex dance that enables individuals to go around a problem, not through it. Another example occurred after the government placed a ceiling on price increases. After being questioned by patrons about price hikes, one restaurateur commented that he hadn't raised prices; he'd stopped giving discounts.

Brazilians are able to get things done in part because they have become so adept at adapting to new circumstances. Few things bother Brazilians. They are accustomed to dealing with the inevitable frustrations that occur in a constantly changing economic and political environment, including the bureaucracy. This philosophy extends to the business arena as well. They make fewer efforts to change things than people might in other cultures. The bureaucracy and lack of efficiency are often trying for foreigners. Bear in mind, though, for Brazilians, they are part of life, and they accept them.

Multinational companies may try to limit the amount of *jeitinho*, but rarely do they totally prohibit it. Most multinationals do not allow employees to take bribes or to "grease" payments. Yet they depend on dispatchers or brokers called *despachantes* to take care of visas and other document-related issues. In addition, when difficult situations arise, they may hire a local consultant to "resolve" problems and expedite business transactions.

You may have the impression that Brazilians break, bend, or otherwise avoid all rules. In reality, Brazilians use *jeitinho* to cope with a vast number of rules and regulations that not only appear to defy logic but change regularly. There is also a propensity in Brazil toward short-term planning in the workplace. This phenomenon is probably a legacy of a history of inflation. The economic uncertainty that has plagued Brazil makes long-term planning difficult.

MULTIMEDIA EXPLORATION

(WWW.PRENHALL.COM/WILD)

Brazilians are masters of sign language. It's an essential element of interpersonal communications. But if you're not well versed in its use, don't do it! It can place you in some very embarrassing situations.

READ, SEE, and HEAR more about Brazil and how its culture affects every aspect of doing business from attitudes towards work, to navigating the complex bureaucracy.

TEST YOUR KNOWLEDGE by answering the questions as well.

Chapter 13: Selecting and Managing Entry Modes

CHINA: HOW TO TELL A WOOFIE FROM A JV

Enormous challenges face foreign companies seeking a presence in China. But the rewards can be great too. The prospect of a burgeoning consumer market and of an increasingly business-friendly environment can be extremely enticing. But ask foreign businesspeople about their experiences in China and you'll hear complaints about its entrenched and unwieldy bureaucracy, lack of transparency, and far-from-mature legal framework. The most common response, though, is that the country is undergoing extraordinary change.

The government's commitment to further opening up the economy to foreign direct investment is now assured, and the amount of money coming in has been increasing dramatically—by more than a third in 2000. Much of this has been directed toward export industries.

In the past, joint ventures (JVs) were the only relationship foreign companies could form with Chinese companies. These ventures suited the Chinese way of doing things, with its emphasis on networking and collaboration under the watchful eye of the government. JVs also suited the government and its agencies, which could channel resources into various sectors by opening them up to foreign investment. For their part, foreign companies tended to regard JVs as a good way to ease themselves into the complex and very unfamiliar Chinese environment and gain access to the centers of power and influence. There are pitfalls, though, including entrenched cultural differences and mistrust that can build up over time. The key to the success of a joint venture seems to be the extent to which both partners can be pragmatic and adaptive.

Wholly owned foreign enterprises (WOFEs— sometimes referred to as "woofies") were started in the mid-1990s as a way to solve some of the problems associated with joint ventures. It was thought that by going it alone in China, companies would be free from the constraints of having to work in partnership with a Chinese company. The reality, though, is that WOFEs haven't been the ideal structure some thought they would be.

For one, WOFEs must still cooperate with Chinese businesses and with the government and its various agencies. For another, entering a complex market like China, with its significant cultural and regulatory differences, can be a real challenge to an uninitiated company without the guiding hand of a Chinese partner. Still, some companies are making it alone and have established China-based operations with a high degree of autonomy from their head offices.

Any foreign-funded enterprise in China is likely to find itself in a web of complicated business relationships with Chinese companies. A company might be a partner with several Chinese firms, in various locations throughout the country and with a number of shareholding structures. Another company might market products manufactured in China to both domestic and international markets, and also purchase supplies from both sources. Even the foreign company with just a single Chinese operation may find that establishing and maintaining good business relationships with Chinese partners, distributors, and suppliers can be a major challenge.

Some Chinese companies possess much greater power in the marketplace than others. In the case of state companies, market influence tends to correlate with the companies' current or earlier status in the government hierarchy. Other factors that determine influence include:

➡ the degree to which the company is free to conduct business in regulated or prohibited areas
➡ whether the company is allowed to form alliances and partnerships with foreign companies
➡ the company's sales and purchasing territory, determined by government agencies
➡ the company's relationship with specific government agencies

➡ the company's access to financial, technical, and human resources.

The most successful alliances are usually those with Chinese companies whose ownership structure is transparent, that operate in deregulated markets, and that have a good record of market performance. In regulated markets, the Chinese company's relationship with the various levels of government is important in shaping the partnership. Companies with close relationships to the various centers of government power and influence are often the best to target when considering strategic alliances.

Market power should be one of the primary determinants when seeking alliances with Chinese companies. Large national companies command larger sales territories and have wide distribution networks. They tend to be competitively driven as well.

On the other hand, smaller firms, state owned or otherwise, tend to be better than large unwieldy companies at accommodating foreign-funded enterprises. These smaller companies are usually better at adapting to foreign ways of doing business and are eager to adopt global standards. A number of these smaller firms have grown into large corporations just by providing multinationals in China with much-needed supplies.

MULTIMEDIA EXPLORATION
(WWW.PRENHALL.COM/WILD)

You won't get much accomplished in China without a fair amount of good quanxi. It's a complex system and takes a lot of getting used to.

READ, SEE, and HEAR more about China and how cultivating business relationships is essential to achieving business success.

TEST YOUR KNOWLEDGE *by answering the questions as well.*

FRANCE: MARKETING IN FRANCE? YES, BUT IS IT FRENCH?

While globalization is having an impact on every economy big and small, companies developing products for sale in foreign markets still need to take into account local conditions and cultural nuances. Even in so-called developed—or Western—countries, culture can exert a powerful influence on how foreigners are perceived and, consequently, on how the locals view imports, whether goods or services, movies or other forms of popular culture. France is a case in point. Anyone attempting to do business here would do well to have a good knowledge of local customs and traditions, social and business structures, and attitudes toward foreigners and foreign products. Marketing a product in France is no easy task.

The French are both fascinated by and suspicious of people and products from other cultures. This ambivalence is perhaps easiest illustrated in their view of the United States. A prevailing French stereotype of Americans is that they are uncultured and lack refined tastes. But if imitation is the highest form of flattery, the French have paid Americans *some* compliment. Hollywood, jeans, and Wall Street have long captured the imagination across the Atlantic. Yet many French are also enraged by the colonization of the dollar, as symbolized by McDonald's, Euro Disney, and generally life in fast forward.

The French lump together other English speakers as Anglo-Saxon. "Hypocrites" is the epithet they hurl most readily at their historical rivals across the channel. Proud to be sensuous Latins, the French can also be dismissive about the stiffness and reserve they perceive in the British. Their food and social habits fare no better.

They see Australians as cowboys who are overly fond of alcohol—overdrinking isn't seemly in French eyes. Anglo-Canadians, like their French-speaking compatriots, score points for being couth and historically linked to the motherland, but the accent of Quebecois is often derided as provincial.

The Japanese garner admiration on account of their delicate aesthetics and reputation as workaholics. Where they fall short is in their tourist-minded obsession with photography and their herd instinct. If in the past the French mocked the Japanese for being overly committed to work, this is changing as the French office is becoming more concerned with efficiency. The French tend to see other Asians as an undifferentiated, if simpatico, mass that shares strong family ties, diligence, and courtesy. Where incompatibilities come in are in the masked emotions and duplicities attributed to Asian people.

Being good Cartesians, the French have a reputation for individualism. While this explains why there are so many excellent chefs, it doesn't always commend them as team players. This is not to say that cooperation and flexibility have no place in the French office. They may voice their dissent, but they'll also pull together for a common project. Employees put great stock in their relationships and value well-rounded personalities. France is not the place to be career-obsessed. The atmosphere is seldom cutthroat based on individual performance. It's relatively rare for an employee to be fired, even if he or she makes a mistake.

Paradoxically, for a nation of individualists, the French are highly conscious of social status. Educational achievement, together with family background and affluence, have traditionally determined status in France. In turn, the schools an individual attended and the resulting network of personal relationships he or she cultivated strictly dictate career opportunities. Three out of four senior executives of France's top 200 firms hail from upper-bracket families.

Numerous official and nonofficial elements exert influence over a company's operations in France. It's wise to understand the laws and associations that sculpt the business environment and impact the bottom line. Chambers of commerce, banks, the media, and educational bodies are examples of institutions that hold sway in the private sector.

➡ Appointed bodies, such as chambers of commerce, have a direct influence on the day-to-day business operations within their purview. So do economic development agencies funded by local elected officials. Their members often serve on the boards of local businesses and professional groups.

➡ Banks and other financial groups are instrumental in shaping the private sector, most obviously by granting or withholding funds. They additionally work with elected officials and professional organizations to prevent bankruptcies or to facilitate land acquisition for expansion.

- Training and research organizations also enter the picture. By cultivating the skills required to meet future business needs, both private and public educational institutions help determine the profile of the workforce.
- The role of the media in crafting public opinion cannot be overstated. Activists and corporations alike regularly mount public-relations campaigns to promote official and private policy affecting business.
- Laws also regulate the private sector. Legislated in 1901, Loi 1901, for example, still determines eligibility for not-for-profit status.

MULTIMEDIA EXPLORATION

(WWW.PRENHALL.COM/WILD)

Smiling is always a good way to break the ice in France, but be extra careful not to overdo it. You may come across as being silly or less than bright.

READ, SEE, and HEAR more about France. Doing business in France relies a lot on knowing the correct rules of etiquette and ways of behaving.

TEST YOUR KNOWLEDGE by answering the questions as well.

Chapter 15: Launching and Managing Production

CHINA AND THE U.S: COWBOY ENTREPRENEURS

Launching and managing production in another country requires a good deal of knowledge about the way management practices and decision making are conducted. These functions in turn are closely related to the cultural underpinnings of a country's business sector. Following are two examples.

CASE STUDY: CHINA

For the best part of the last century, the Chinese government held such a firm grip on industry and commerce that Western-style managers were nonexistent in China. There was no market and therefore no need for an understanding of market forces. Decisions were handed down from Party officials, and managers were only required to make sure those decisions were executed.

After the reforms of 1978, managers were somewhat liberated from the iron grip of the Party and they quickly fell into two categories. On one side were bureaucratic administrators, resisting change despite the introduction of limited market forces. On the other side was a new breed of cowboy entrepreneurs, determined to take full advantage of the latest opportunities. Although some Chinese companies now have Western-style managers, most managers still fall into these two categories.

In China, the group is always more important than the individual, at home or at work, and reaching consensus is a major goal. Because of this emphasis on the collective good, decision making is rarely the responsibility of one person in a company. More often decisions can't be made until there's input from the entire work group, at national, provincial, and local levels.

China's complex decision-making process has serious implications for foreigners trying to do business here. First, you should expect decisions to take a lot longer to be made in China than in Western countries. And, second, tracking down the key decision maker may be extremely difficult, since very often there isn't one. The situation gets even more exasperating when more than one bureaucratic unit's involved. Just be patient, and try not to let your Chinese colleagues know you're frustrated. They may try to use your impatience to extract more concessions from you.

Perhaps because so many people are involved in the decision-making process, the Chinese tend to pay a lot of attention to details, even those that may seem trivial to outsiders. This slows down decision making even more, but, on the positive side, it generally leads to carefully thought out decisions and well-informed colleagues. In China, a certain amount of face is at stake with every decision. The Chinese lose face when they go back on a decision since they don't like to give the impression that they've made a mistake. Furthermore, subordinates never question bad decisions made by their superiors, so some policies get left in place even though they're known to be destructive to business.

CASE STUDY: U.S.

Because most U.S. companies embrace democratic principles, at least in theory, rank-and-file employees are sometimes consulted on decisions that will affect them. More often, though, time pressures get in the way, leaving the opinions of nonmanagement workers out of the equation.

There are no formal decision-making systems in the United States, as there are in some countries like Japan. Rather, decision-making processes are modified to suit the culture of a company. For example, some organizations set financial limits on certain decision making. So a middle manager might be allowed to authorize a purchase as long as it involves an outlay of no more than $50,000 but need to get approval from higher management for larger expenditures.

In regions that operate at a fast pace—New York, for instance—decision making is often spread across many levels of management. And in some companies, even junior executives have the authority to make or influence decisions in which major business partnerships and large sums of money are at stake.

While managers in U.S. companies don't usually take long to make decisions, getting to the implementation stage is often a long, drawn-out process. Feedback needs to be gathered and paperwork prepared—often reams of it. And even when a deal has been reached and you've seen preliminary contracts, remember, lawyers are about to be let loose on the documents. The United States is a litigious place, and lawyers will scour the fine print of every page for any details they can change to benefit their client.

Lawyers also provide conditions and suggested steps for a wide range of "what-if" scenarios. Don't be surprised—or offended—if you're dealing with a Fortune 100 company and see an "Event of Bankruptcy" clause, outlining the course of action in a worst-case scenario. American firms are very focused on accounting for all types of worst- and best-case situations.

You may hear the phrase "hands off" in discussions about management. It's a management style that's becoming more popular in the United States, particularly in California. While traditional practices dictate that a manager constantly follow up on projects to see that they're being done on time and to required standards, the hands-off manager waits for employees to bring problems to him or her. A successful hands-off manager is therefore one who employees find helpful and available when necessary but rarely feel the need to access.

MULTIMEDIA EXPLORATION
(WWW.PRENHALL.COM/WILD)

A lot of business in China is conducted around the dining table and slurping your noodles is an absolute necessity. But, if you're using chopsticks, never place them upright in the rice. You may regret the consequences.

READ, SEE, and HEAR more about China and the United States. Both countries exhibit very different characteristics—not only when it comes to table manners, but also when it comes to approaching business opportunities and risk taking.

TEST YOUR KNOWLEDGE by answering the questions as well.

Chapter 16: Hiring and Managing Employees

SOUTH AFRICA: FROM THE *BRAAI* TO THE BOARDROOM . . . CASUAL DINING, FORMAL BUSINESS

If you'll be working in South Africa as a manager, you'll undoubtedly come up against a complex range of issues that need addressing. The importance of each will differ, of course, depending on whether you're replacing a manager of a major multinational corporation or launching a business from the ground up.

You should probably prepare yourself for some hostility from the locals. Expatriates and short-term assignees also report that some South Africans seem withdrawn. Others say that they harbor feelings of superiority in the workplace. In light of the dramatic changes that have occurred in the country in recent years, this is probably not surprising.

These feelings emanate from two basic sources. First, jobs are precious in South Africa, and foreigners are often perceived as "taking" jobs from locals. The reality is that there's a shortage of skilled managers. Nonetheless, assumptions are often made, sometimes bolstered by the popular press. Second, South Africans tend to be protective of all things South African and feel threatened by outsiders with different opinions. Even if old ways of doing things are clearly not working, South Africans are often reluctant to adopt new systems brought in from overseas. There's a growing perception that the people must find their own path if they hope to solve their problems. Attempts at Westernization are sometimes seen as an imposition of an inappropriate approach.

One effect of the prevalence of expatriates in high-level management positions is a slow Westernization of South African business culture. As one local expatriate commented, the global problems he believed he was leaving behind in Europe are slowly finding their way into South Africa.

Attracting and retaining qualified and experienced top-level staff is both a priority and a challenge for South African businesses. The country has a high unemployment rate, but it also has an acute shortage of skilled employees. This is particularly true in the technical and professional disciplines of computing and medicine. Two causes are blamed for the problem: a brain drain, as workers head for perceived better markets, and the undereducation of the majority during the years of apartheid. While there are government programs and incentives to give workers training, this is not always a practical solution.

To find new recruits, begin by consulting the local newspaper, trade press, or perhaps an employment agency. You may also want to contact the local economic development agency or similar organizations. Typically, you'll be referred to someone who knows of sources of skilled people to fit your needs.

For anyone not used to working in a unionized environment, it's important to remember that every employee in South Africa has the right to belong to a union. The labor movement has a history of militancy, and while the number of days lost to strikes is falling, it's still high by international standards. If you're from a culture that is relatively anti-union, remember that the union movement in South Africa is closely associated with the struggle against apartheid. Many people hold unions close to their hearts.

One of your first priorities upon arriving should be getting to know the people you'll be working with and letting them get to know you. Be sure to make your priorities and expectations clear. Once you have your employees' trust, you may be able to cautiously make changes.

Bear in mind that your decisions may be interpreted from a racial perspective. Managers and staff may assume, for instance, that you disciplined an employee because he or she belonged to a certain racial group. You'll need to be equally careful when promoting employees and hiring staff. The best advice is to try to avoid conflict and to be as open and honest as possible.

Issues requiring sensitivity may also come up as you deal with employees on a day-to-day basis. Some may have low literacy rates, for example, or consistently arrive late for work. You may well find this frustrating. On the other hand, you may have unrealistically high expectations. Many lower-paid workers were unable to get an education under apartheid. Many cannot afford to own a car and have to commute long distances on unreliable public transportation. Being flexible is critical.

You may also find that your colleagues seem to have little understanding of business or how to make a profit. Try not to lose your patience.

Finally, given the high incidence of AIDS in South Africa, you may want to learn about the disease and its effect on the country. Many companies have employee-education and AIDS-prevention programs. It's a good idea to become actively involved in these initiatives, or at least familiar with them.

MULTIMEDIA EXPLORATION

(WWW.PRENHALL.COM/WILD)

The Springboks—not to be confused with the national anima—is the national rugby team. Rugby's the major sport in South Africa so you'd better know the difference between a scrum and a try.

READ, SEE, and HEAR more about South Africa and how its complex culture places many challenges on companies doing business there.

TEST YOUR KNOWLEDGE by answering the questions as well.

NOTES, SOURCES, AND CREDITS

NOTES

Chapter 1

1. " 'The Simpsons' Goes Global," *Associated Press*, (**www.cartoons.com**), August 5, 2001; Film Roman Company Profile. Available at (**www.filmroman.com**); Fox's Simpsons Web site, (**www.thesimpsons.com**); The Simpsons Folder Web site, (**www.irsburger.com/special**).
2. Kevin Maney, "Companies Cast Worldwide Net: Technology Is 'Demolishing' Time, Distance," *USA Today*, April 24, 1997, p. B1.
3. Brendan J. Gray, "Profiling Managers to Improve Export Promotion Targeting," *Journal of International Business Studies*, Second Quarter, 1997, pp. 387–420.
4. Suh-kyung Yoon, "The Right Person for the Right Job," *Far Eastern Economic Review*, (**www.feer.com**), March 22, 2001; Intercultural Business Center Web site, (**www.ib-c.com**).
5. Samuel P. Huntington, *The Clash of Civilizations and the Remaking of World Order* (New York: Simon & Schuster, 1996).
6. "Survey Finds American Distrust of Muslim World," *CNN* Web site, (**www.cnn.com**), March 5, 2002.
7. Charles Wesley Orton, "A Fine Kettle of Fish," *World Trade*, (**www.worldtrademag.com**), September 26, 2001.
8. Tom Phillips, "Law & Disorder," *Business 2.0, U.K. edition*, May 2001, pp. 90–95.
9. Neil King, Jr., and Geoff Winestock, "Plan to Rescue U.S. Steel Industry Draws the Ire of Critics Abroad," *Wall Street Journal Online*, (**www.wsj.com**), March 7, 2002.
10. "India Courts Investors," *Wall Street Journal Online*, (**www.wsj.com**), February 26, 2002.
11. Geri Smith et al., "Betting on Free Trade," *Business Week, European edition*, April 23, 2001, pp. 32–35.
12. "A Decline Without Parallel," *The Economist*, March 2, 2002, pp. 27–29.
13. Joanna Parfitt, "A Rewarding Experience," *Financial Times*, (**www.ft.com**).
14. "Abuse in Nike Factories in Vietnam," *Reuters*, (**www.reuters.com**), March 28, 1997.
15. John R. Emshwiller and Rebecca Smith, "Minutes from a 1997 Meeting Reveal Enron Brass Were in Partnership Loop," *Wall Street Journal Online*, (**www.wsj.com**), February 1, 2002.
16. David Fairlamb, "Aftershocks in Europe," *Business Week, European edition*, December 17, 2001, pp. 38–39.
17. Levi-Strauss Web site at (**www.levistrauss.com**).
18. Starbucks Web site at (**www.starbucks.com**); TransFair USA Web site, (**www.transfair.org**).
19. Gordon R. Walker and Mark A. Fox, "Globalization: An Analytical Framework," *Indiana Journal of Global Legal Studies*, Spring 1996, (**ijgls.indiana.edu**).
20. William Greider, *One World, Ready or Not: The Manic Logic of Global Capitalism* (New York: Simon & Schuster, 1997), p. 14.
21. Two Dogs Web site, (**www.twodogs.com**).
22. Catherine Taylor, "U.K. Insur Industry to Cut 70,000 Jobs by 2010–Accenture," *Wall Street Journal Online*, (**www.wsj.com**), February 18, 2002.
23. Kara Swisher, "Silicon Valley Veteran Starts U.S.-Style Tech Town in India," *Wall Street Journal Online*, (**www.wsj.com**), January 7, 2002.
24. "Globalization: Is It at Risk?" *The Economist*, February 2, 2002, pp. 61–63.
25. Ann Keeton, "Genesys CEO Sees Consol, Growth in Corporate Conferencing," *Wall Street Journal Online*, (**www.wsj.com**), March 1, 2002.
26. "The Case for International Videoconferencing," *World Trade Magazine*, Global Online Supplement, (**www.worldtrademag.com**), June 14, 2001.
27. Author conversation with Morten J. Esp, Marketing Planning Manager, Volvo Car Corporation.
28. Fred Hapgood, "Foreign Exchange," *Inc. Technology* 1997, no. 2, pp. 85–86, 88.
29. Lori A. Phlamm, "Business on the Internet," *Checkers Simon & Rosner Newsletter*, Summer 1996.
30. William Gurley, "The Soaring Cost of E-Commerce," *Fortune*, August 3, 1998, pp. 226–228.
31. Don Phillips, "Globalization Helps to Keep Old Economy's Shippers Afloat," *International Herald Tribune*, August 28, 2001, p. 11.
32. Alexander Stille, "Globalization Now, a Sequel of Sorts," *New York Times*, August 11, 2001, p. B7.
33. *Globalization and Human Rights*, PBS Program transcripts, (**www.pbs.org**).
34. Louis Uchitelle, "Globalization Marches on, As U.S. Eases Up on the Reins," *New York Times*, December 17, 2001, p. C12.
35. Michael Elliott, "A Not-So-New World Order," *Time Europe*, April 2, 2001, p. 69.
36. Tyler Cowen and Eric Crampton, "Uncommon Culture," *Foreign Policy*, July/August, 2001, p. 28.
37. "Cross-Border M&As," *The Economist*, July 7, 2001, p. 107.
38. Leslie Wayne, "Wave of Mergers Is Recasting Face of Business in U.S.," *New York Times*, January 19, 1998, p. A1.
39. "The Fortune Global 500: The World's Largest Corporations," *Fortune, European edition*, July 23, 2001, pp. F1–F44.
40. "The Fortune Global 500: The World's Largest Corporations."
41. Richard Cross, "Weekend in Florence Web Site: Is It Better Than the Real Thing?" *Direct Marketing*, August 1996, pp. 14–17.

Chapter 2

1. Hans Greimel, "Gummi Bears Solve a Sticky Problem," *International Herald Tribune*, April 17, 2001, p. 14; Haribo Web site (**www.haribo.com**).
2. For a more detailed definition of culture, see Geert Hofstede, *Culture and Organizations: Software of the Mind* (New York: McGraw-Hill, 1997), pp. 3–19.
3. Suzanne Daley, "In Europe Many Try to Protect Local Languages," *International Herald Tribune*, April 17, 2001, p. 1.
4. Jeffrey E. Garten, "Cities: Investing in Culture Is Simply Good Business," *Business Week, European edition*, March 5, 2001, p. 13.
5. Manjeet Kripalani, "A Corporate Pilgrimage to the Taj," *Business Week, European edition*, June 11, 2001, p. 62.
6. Gerry Khermouch, "An Almost-Invisible $1 Trillion Market," *Business Week, European edition*, June 18, 2001, p. 80.
7. Information obtained from the Web of Culture Web site at (**www.webofculture.com**).
8. Alessandra Galloni, "European Attitudes Toward Technology Vary Widely, Ad Agency's Survey Finds," *Wall Street Journal Online*, (**www.wsj.com**), July 9, 2001.

9. For a more in-depth discussion of cultural effects on the perception of time, see Lalita A. Manrai and Ajay K. Manrai, "Effects of Cultural-Context, Gender, and Acculturation on Perceptions of Work versus Social/Leisure Time Usage," *Journal of Business Research*, 32 (1995): 115–128.

10. Jane Black, "In Britain, "Entrepreneur" Is No Longer an Insult," *Business Week*, (**www.businessweek.com**), February 6, 2001.

11. Larry Levy, "Second Chances," *Business 2.0, U.K. edition*, May 2001, p. 121.

12. As reported in "Why Americans Work So Hard," *Business Week, European edition*, June 11, 2001, p. 14.

13. Beth Rasmussen, "Despite Gains, Female Workers Struggle in Spain," *Wall Street Journal Europe*, June 12, 2001, p. 2.

14. Kerry Capell with Carlos Tromben, William Echikson, and Wendy Zellner, "Renegade Ryanair," *Business Week, European edition*, May 14, 2001, pp. 38–43.

15. Marlise Simons, "Did VW Mock the Gospel? French Bishops Sue," *New York Times*, February 7, 1998, p. A4.

16. Elaine Sciolino, "Explain It Again, Please: Who Says I Can't Wear a Hat?," *New York Times*, February 8, 1998, p. WK7.

17. "McAtlas Shrugged," *Foreign Policy*, May/June 2001, pp. 26–37.

18. Serge Schmemann, "If It's a Hard Sell, Let's Try Beards and Yarmulkes," *New York Times*, February 4, 1998, p. A4.

19. "Beyond Multilingualism," *World Trade Magazine*, (**www.worldtrademag.com**), June 14, 2001; Jennifer L. Schenker, "The Gist of Translation," *Time Europe*, July 16, 2001, p. 42.

20. "Avoid My Party," *Business 2.0*, (**www.business2.com**), February 2000; James Daly, "Going Global Gets More Complicated," *Business 2.0*, (**www.business2.com**), November 27, 2000.

21. Caixia Lu, "Chinese, or Just Chinglish?" *Far Eastern Economic Review*, (**www.feer.com**), April 19, 2001, p. 39.

22. Kitty McKinsey, "The Mother of All Tongues," *Far Eastern Economic Review*, (**www.feer.com**), April 19, 2001, p. 38.

23. Suzanne Daley, "In Europe Many Try to Protect Local Languages," *International Herald Tribune*, April 17, 2001, p. 1.

24. Tatiana D. Helenius, "Body Language Savvy," *CNN Web site*, (**www.cnnfn.com**), May 3, 2000.

25. For a detailed discussion of the connection between education and "brainpower" industries, see Paul Krugman, *Pop Internationalism* (Cambridge, MA: MIT Press, 1996); Michael E. Porter, *The Competitive Advantage of Nations* (New York: Free Press, 1990); Robert B. Reich, *The Work of Nations* (New York: Vintage Books, 1992); and Lester Thurow, *The Future of Capitalism* (New York: William Morrow, 1996).

26. John McBeth, "Indonesians Elect to Line Up for Visas, Not Polls," *Wall Street Journal Online*, (**www.wsj.com**), July 4, 2001.

27. Iain McDonald, "Australian Study Finds Worker Brain Gain, Not Drain," *Wall Street Journal Online*, (**www.wsj.com**), July 17, 2001.

28. "Serbian Government Officials See Inflation at 40% in 2001," *Wall Street Journal Online*, (**www.wsj.com**), July 2, 2001.

29. Elizabeth Pond, "Royal Bequest: A Bright Spot in the Balkans," *Wall Street Journal Online*, (**www.wsj.com**), July 31, 2001.

30. Raymond Scupin, *Cultural Anthropology: A Global Perspective*, 3rd ed. (Upper Saddle River, NJ: Prentice Hall, 1998), p. 47.

31. Delyth Hughes and Andrew McLaughlin, "East Side Story," *Business 2.0, U.K. edition*, May 2001, pp. 122, 124.

32. Florence Kluckhohn and F. L. Strodtbeck, *Variations in Value Orientations* (Evanston, IL: Harper & Row, 1961).

33. David Kruger, "Job Flexibility in Japan," *Far Eastern Economic Review*, (**www.feer.com**), February 8, 2001, p. 66.

34. Geert Hofstede, "The Cultural Relativity of Organizational Practices and Theories," *Journal of International Business Studies*, Fall 1983, pp. 75–89.

35. Hofstede's study, from which his four dimensions were developed, has been criticized on a number of grounds. First, it suffers from a "Western" bias in design and analysis, querying employees in just one firm in one industry. Second, it treats culture as "national" only and, therefore, ignores subcultures. Finally, it now appears old—it was conducted in the 1960s and 1970s. See R. Mead, *International Management: Cross-Cultural Dimensions* (Oxford: Basil Blackwell, 1994), pp. 73–75.

Chapter 3

1. "Geography and the Net," *The Economist*, August 11, 2001, pp. 18–20; Chen May Yee, "Big Internet Companies Often Censor Their Asian Sites to Please Local Officials," *Wall Street Journal Online*, (**www.wsj.com**), July 9, 2001; Tim Phillips, "Law & Disorder," *Business 2.0, U.K. edition*, May 2001, pp. 90–95; Yahoo!, Inc. Web site, (**www.yahoo.com**), various reports.

2. Chen May Yee, "Big Internet Companies Often Censor Their Asian Sites to Please Local Officials," *Wall Street Journal Online*, (**www.wsj.com**), July 9, 2001.

3. Tim Phillips, "Law & Disorder," *Business 2.0, U.K. edition*, May 2001, pp. 90–95.

4. Jeff Fischer, "The Global Ballot Box," *Foreign Policy*, May–June, 2001, p. 24.

5. "An Alarm Call for Latin America's Democrats," *The Economist*, July 28, 2001, pp. 49–50.

6. John Pomfret, "Rewriting Marx: China Allows Capitalists in on the Party," *International Herald Tribune*, July 2, 2001, p. 1.

7. Dexter Roberts, "In Rural China, Baby Steps toward Democracy," *Business Week, European edition*, March 19, 2001, p. 32.

8. "Japan-China Tariff Dispute," *International Herald Tribune*, July 2, 2001, p. 11.

9. Anthony Bianco, "Exxon Unleashed," *Business Week, European edition*, April 9, 2001, pp. 86–94.

10. "Indonesia's Island Fever," *Newsweek, International edition*, March 12, 2001, pp. 20–22.

11. Pete Engardio, "A New World," *Business Week, European edition*, October 8, 2001, pp. 18–19.

12. Suzanne Timmons, "Doing Business among the Body Snatchers," *Business Week*, (**www.businessweek.com**), July 31, 2000.

13. "Taiwan Business Welcomes China Shift," *International Herald Tribune*, August 28, 2001, p. 13; Dexter Roberts, Bruce Einhorn, and Alysha Webb, "Taiwan & China," *Business Week, European edition*, June 11, 2001, pp. 46–50.

14. Shell company Web site, (**www.shell.com**).

15. Ray August, *International Business Law: Text, Cases, and Readings* (Upper Saddle River, NJ: Prentice Hall, 1993), p. 51.

16. *Sixth Annual BSA Global Software Piracy Study* (International Planning and Research Corporation, May 2001), Business Software Alliance Web site, (**www.bsa.org**).

17. "BSA Initiates Legal Proceedings against 7 Irish Companies," Business Software Alliance Web site, (**www.bsa.org**), August 2, 2001.

18. "Recording Companies Urge Vietnam Government to Fight Piracy," *Wall Street Journal Online*, (**www.wsj.com**), July 18, 2001.

19. Thomas Fuller, "Malaysia Fights the Fake-CD War," *International Herald Tribune*, May 19–20, p. 11.

20. "The Patent Debate," *Business 2.0, U.K. edition*, May 2001, pp. 96–99.

21. Theodore Hong, "Birthday Song Blues," International Commentary, *Wall Street Journal Online*, (**www.wsj.com**), August 21, 2001.

22. Tom Spring "Napster Fans Find Lively Alternative," *CNN Web site*, (**www.cnn.com**), July 16, 2001; "Report: Napster Users Lose That Sharing Feeling," *CNN Web site*, (**www.cnn.com**), June 28, 2001.

23. "Canada Bans Sale of Cigarettes Labeled 'Light,' 'Mild,'" *CNN* Web site, (www.cnn.com), August 14, 2001.

24. Michael Elliott, "How Jack Fell Down," *Time, International edition*, July 16, 2001, pp. 16–20.

25. "Rockin' All Over the World: Economic Potential of Music for LDCs," United Nations Conference on Trade and Development Web site, (www.unctad.org), May 16, 2001.

Chapter 4

1. Royal Dutch/Shell Group Web site, (www.shell.com), various reports.

2. Amabelle Layug, "N. Korean Harvest Cannot Avert Food Crisis: UN," *CNN* Web site, (www.cnn.com), October 29, 2001.

3. "Taiwan Drops China Trade Ban," *CNN* Web site, (www.cnn.com), November 7, 2001.

4. "Taiwan Joins China in WTO," *CNN* Web site, (www.cnn.com), November 11, 2001.

5. Robert Kuttner, "Everything for Sale," *Business Week*, March 17, 1997, pp. 92–96.

6. "Economic and Financial Indicators," *The Economist*, November 3, 2001, p. 104.

7. Gail Edmondson, "A Continent at the Breaking Point," *Business Week*, February 24, 1997, pp. 50–51; Craig R. Whitney, "French Jobless Find the World Is Harsher," *New York Times*, March 19, 1998, pp. A1, A6.

8. Carol Matlack and Jack Ewing, "Why Germany and France Are Veering Left," *Business Week, European edition*, May 14, 2001, pp. 22–23.

9. "FTC Settlement Preserves Competition in Global Markets for Rock Processing Equipment," Press Release, *Federal Trade Commission*, (www.ftc.gov), September 7, 2001.

10. Gerald P. O'Driscoll, Kim R. Holmes, and Melanie Kirkpatrick, "Executive Summary," *2001 Index of Economic Freedom* (Washington, DC: The Heritage Foundation, 2001), (www.heritage.org).

11. Maria Atanasov, "Nike's Lead: Just Follow It?" *Fortune*, September 8, 1997, p. 188.

12. *World Development Indicators 2001* (Washington, DC: World Bank, 2001), (www.worldbank.org).

13. Matthew Brzezinski, "For Ukraine, the Economic Statistics Lie," *Wall Street Journal*, May 13, 1996, p. A16.

14. Daniel S. Levine, "Got a Spare Destroyer Lying Around? Make a Trade: Embracing Countertrade as a Viable Option," *World Trade*, June 1997, pp. 34–35.

15. "Central Russian Teachers to Get Paid in Vodka." *CNN* Web site, (www.cnn.com).

16. Tarun Khanna and Krishna Palepu, "Why Focused Strategies May Be Wrong for Emerging Markets," *Harvard Business Review*, July–August 1997, pp. 41–51.

17. Stephen Parker, Gavin Tritt, and Wing Thye Woo, "Some Lessons Learned from the Comparison of Transitions in Asia and Eastern Europe," In: Wing Thye Woo, Stephen Parker, and Jeffrey D. Sachs, eds., *Economies in Transition: Comparing Asia and Europe* (Cambridge, MA: MIT Press, 1997), pp. 3–5; *World Development Report 1996*, "From Plan to Market: Executive Summary" (Washington, DC: World Bank, 1996), p. 2.

18. "Statistics: Monthly Update," *The Economist*, July/August 2001, p. 57.

19. Monika Mudranincová, and Klára Smolová, "Czech Managers Go Global," *The Prague Tribune*, (www.prague-tribune.cz), November 2001.

20. Monika Mudranincová, and Klára Smolová, "Vanda Wolfová: Right Place, Right Time," *The Prague Tribune*, (www.prague-tribune.cz), November 2001.

21. Joe Cook, "Worlds Apart?" *Business Central Europe*, May 1997, p. 48.

22. Jason Bush, Ben Aris, and Vitaly Sych, "Resurrection," A Survey of Russia and the CIS, *Business Central Europe*, April 2001, pp. 53–61.

Chapter 5

1. Henri E. Cauvin, "Coca-Cola Braves Risk in Africa," *International Herald Tribune*, April 23, 2001, p. 13; Drew Robb, "Out of Africa: Rediscovering a Misplaced Market," *World Trade*, November 1998, pp. 32–36; Constance L. Hays and Donald G. McNeil, Jr., "Putting Africa on Coke's Map," *New York Times*, May 26, 1998, pp. C1, C4.

2. "Getting on the Fast Track: Small Business and International Trade," Small Business Survival Committee Web site, (www.sbsc.org).

3. Karen Kerrigan, "Presidential 'Trade Promotion Authority' Good for Small Business," Small Business Survival Committee Web site, (www.sbsc.org), June 11, 2001.

4. "Merchant Fleets," *The Economist*, February 10, 2001 p. 120.

5. *World Development Indicators 1998* (Washington, DC: World Bank, 1998), p. 318.

6. Karen Lowry Miller and John Templeman, "Germany's New East Bloc," *Business Week*, February 3, 1997 pp. 50–52.

7. Geri Smith, "Is the Magic Fading?," *Business Week*, August 6, 2001 pp. 30–32.

8. Adam Smith, *The Wealth of Nations* (Chicago: University of Chicago Press, 1976).

9. David Ricardo, *The Principles of Political Economy and Taxation*, first published in 1817.

10. Paul R. Krugman and Maurice Obstfeld, *International Economics: Theory and Policy* (Reading, MA: Addison-Wesley, 1997), pp. 32–34.

11. Bertil Ohlin, *Interregional and International Trade* (Cambridge, MA: Harvard University Press, 1933).

12. Wassily Leontief, "Domestic Production and Foreign Trade: The American Capital Position Re-Examined," *Economia Internationale*, February, 1954, pp. 3–32.

13. Raymond Vernon and Louis T. Wells, Jr., *Economic Environment of International Business*, 7th ed. (Upper Saddle River, NJ: Prentice Hall, 1991).

14. William Greider, *One World, Ready or Not: The Manic Logic of Global Capitalism* (New York: Simon & Schuster, 1997), p. 15.

15. Gary A. Knight and S. Tamer Cavusgil, "The Global Firm: A Challenge to Traditional Internationalization Theory." *Advances in International Marketing* 8 (1996):11–26.

16. "Ingenico and Palm Plan to Develop Secure Infrastructure for Virtual Card Payment," Palm Press Release at Palm Web site (www.palmos.com), January 6, 2001; David Carnoy, "Teaming Up: Prospering from Alliances with Other Entrepreneurs," *Success*, April 1997, p. 20.

17. Elhanan Helpman and Paul Krugman, *Market Structure and Foreign Trade* (Cambridge, MA: MIT Press, 1985).

18. For a detailed discussion of the first-mover advantage and its process, see Alfred D. Chandler, *Scale and Scope* (New York: Free Press, 1990).

19. Michael E. Porter, *The Competitive Advantage of Nations* (New York: Free Press, 1990).

20. Michael E. Porter, "Clusters and the New Economics of Competition," *Harvard Business Review* (November–December 1998), pp. 77–90.

21. As reported in "India's Sluggish Privatization: Unproductive," *The Economist*, September 8, 2001, pp. 73–74.

Chapter 6

1. Ashok Bhattacharjee, "India's Saregama In Mktg Pact with AOL Time Warner Unit," *Wall Street Journal Online*, (www.wsj.com), March 11, 2002; "Who's Afraid of AOL Time Warner?," *The Economist*, January 26, 2002, pp. 57–58; Tom Lowry, Catherine Yang, and Ronald Grover, "What the Shocker Means," *Business Week*, December 17, 2001, pp. 40–41; Ronald Grover, "Harry Potter and the Marketer's Millstone," *Business Week*, (www.businessweek.com), October 15, 2001.

2. "Guyanans Urged to Be 'Patriotic' and Spurn Imports," *World Trade*, January 1999, p. 20.

3. Dexter Roberts, "Will Kodak Get Lucky in Japan?" *Business Week*, July 28, 1997, p. 48.

4. Stephen Blakely, "Seeds of Change for Farmers," *Nation's Business*, December 1996, pp. 42–44.

5. "Technology Deals with China Harmed U.S. Security, House Committee Says," *CNN* Web site, (**www.cnn.com**), December 30, 1998.

6. Brian Bremner, "Two Japans," *Business Week*, January 27, 1997, pp. 24–28.

7. "U.S. Congress Considers Stiff Restraints against Korea's Firms," *Business Korea*, December 1995–January 1996, p. 79.

8. Steven V. Brull and Catherine Keumhyun Lee, "Why Seoul Is Seething," *Business Week*, January 27, 1997, pp. 44–46.

9. Deborah Baldwin, "The Proof Will Be in the 'Europudding,'" *Los Angeles Times*, April 24, 1997, p. D4.

10. Gareth Porter, "Natural Resource Substitutes and International Policy: A Role for APEC," *Journal of Environment and Development*, September 1997, pp. 276–291.

11. Daniel S. Levine, "Ex-Im Bank Year in Review," *World Trade*, January 1999, p. 30.

12. Ellie Winninghof, "Derailing Critics," *International Business*, May 1996, pp. 20–25; Daniel S. Levine, "Little Big Shots," *World Trade*, December–January 1997, pp. 42–47.

13. Winninghof, "Derailing Critics," pp. 20–25.

14. Anne Stevenson-Yang, "Quiet Incursions," *The China Business Review*, September–October 1996, pp. 36–42.

15. Kenneth E. Grubbs, Jr., "The Opening of Japan," *World Trade*, June 1997, pp. 28–32.

16. Lily Tung, "Behind-the-Scenes Obstacles for Film-Makers," *Asian Business*, February 1996, p. 11.

17. Emily Thornton, "The Japan That Can Say No to Cold Pills," *Business Week*, May 19, 1997, p. 54.

18. "Saudi Arabia Simplifies Import Clearance," *World Trade*, January 1999, p. 24.

19. The facts in this discussion of the GATT and the WTO are drawn from the WTO Web site, (**www.wto.org**).

20. "Unfair Protection," *The Economist*, November 7, 1998, p. 75–76.

21. "Globalization: Is It at Risk?," *The Economist*, February 2, 2002, pp. 61–63.

Chapter 7

1. William Boston and Paul Hofheinz, "Germany's Protection of VW May Hinder EU Takeover Law," *Wall Street Journal Online*, (**www.wsj.com**), February 27, 2002;
Volkswagen Web site, (**www.vw.com**), various reports.

2. United Nations Conference on Trade and Development, *World Investment Report 2001* (New York: United Nations, 2001).

3. United Nations Conference on Trade and Development, *World Investment Report 2000* (New York: United Nations, 2000).

4. "How to Merge: After the Deal," *The Economist*, January 9, 1999, pp. 21–23.

5. Janet Guyon, "Cellular Start-Up: Some Good Old Boys Make Lots of Money Phoning Up Tashkent," *Wall Street Journal*, June 21, 1996, p. A1.

6. This section draws heavily upon the data and analysis contained in: United Nations Conference on Trade and Development, *World Investment Report 2001* (New York: United Nations, 2001).

7. Raymond Vernon and Louis T. Wells, Jr., *Economic Environment of International Business,* 7th ed. (Upper Saddle River, NJ: Prentice Hall, 1991).

8. John H. Dunning, "Toward an Eclectic Theory of International Production," *Journal of International Business Studies,* Spring–Summer, 1980, pp. 9–31.

9. For an excellent discussion of the economic benefits particular geographic locations can provide, see Paul Krugman, "Increasing Returns and Economic Geography," *Journal of Political Economy,* June 1991, pp. 483–499.

10. Naomi Freundlich, "Finding a Cure in DNA?" *Business Week,* March 10, 1997, pp. 90–91.

11. Richard Florida, "The Globalization of R&D: Results of a Survey of Foreign-Affiliated R&D Laboratories in the USA," *Research Policy,* March 1997, pp. 85–103.

Chapter 8

1. "The Taskmaster of Nestle," *Business Week, European edition,* June 11, 2001, p. 32EU28; Julie Forster and Becky Gaylord, "Can Kraft Be a Big Cheese Abroad?" *Business Week, European edition,* June 4, 2001, pp. 54–55; Nestle Web site (**www.nestle.com**), various reports.

2. Geri Smith et al., "Betting on Free Trade," *Business Week, European edition*, April 23, 2001, pp. 32–35.

3. Judith Warner, John Parry, and Stefan Theil, "A Race Won by the Swift and the Strong," *Newsweek*, Euroland Special Issue, Winter 1998, pp. 42–46.

4. Emeric Lepoutre, "Europe's Challenge to the U.S. in South America's Biggest Market," *Christian Science Monitor*, April 8, 1997, p. 19.

5. "NAFTA after Five: The Impact of The North American Free Trade Agreement on
Australia's Trade and Investment," Australian Department of Foreign Affairs and Trade, (**www.dfat.gov.au/geo/americas/nafta**), March 2000.

6. "USTR Documents Benefits of Trade for American Families," Office of the United States Trade Representative, (**www.ustr.gov**), September 19, 2001.

7. "Doing Business in NAFTA Country," *Industrial Distribution* (Supplement), May 1995, pp. S10–S12.

8. Data obtained from United States–Mexico Chamber of Commerce Web site, (**www.usmcoc.org**).

9. Data obtained from Industry of Canada Strategis Web site, (**www.strategis.ic.gc.ca**).

10. "USTR Documents Benefits of Trade for American Families," Office of the United States Trade Representative, (**www.ustr.gov**), September 19, 2001.

11. NAFTA's Seven-Year Itch," Published by the AFL-CIO, (**www.aflcio.org**).

12. Richard Bruner, "Delphi Gets into Gear Now for the Year 2000," *El Financiero International Edition*, June 30–July 6, 1997, p. 16.

13. Geri Smith et al., "Betting on Free Trade."

14. Amy Guthrie, "IMF Advisor Fischer Sees One NAFTA Currency Eventually," *Wall Street Journal Online*, (**www.wsj.com**), October 18, 2001.

15. Stephen Wisnefski, "Free Trade Push Offers Latin America a Glimmer of Hope," *Wall Street Journal Online*, (**www.wsj.com**), October 9, 2001.

16. Ian Katz, "Is Europe Elbowing the U.S. Out of South America?" *Business Week*, August 4, 1997, p. 56.

17. "CARICOM Braves the New World," *Business Week*, Advertising Supplement, March 5, 2001.

18. "Small, Vulnerable—and Disunited," *Economist*, August 11, 2001, pp. 44–45.

19. "Leaders Sign All-Americas Free Trade Agreement," *International Herald Tribune*, April 23, 2001, p. 3.

20. Campion Walsh, "USTR Zoellick: Free Trade More Important Than Ever," *Wall Street Journal Online*, (**www.wsj.com**), September 24, 2001.

21. Geri Smith et al., "Betting on Free Trade."

22. "The Roots of Music Piracy," *World Trade*, December 1998, p. 12.

23. *The European Union and the World* (Brussels, Belgium: European Commission, December 2000), p. 7.

24. "Burma and Laos Admitted to ASEAN," *Wall Street Journal*, July 24, 1997, p. A1.

25. Don Kirk, "Next WTO Chief Sees Speedup on Asia Free-Trade Zone," *International Herald Tribune*, October 19, 2001, p. 15.

26. Julius Caesar Parrenas, "Theme for Shanghai: Stay on Track to Free and Open Trade," *International Herald Tribune*, October 19, 2001, p. 8.

27. Susan Porjes, "Strengthening Diversity," *International Business*, November 1996, pp. 22–23.

Chapter 9

1. Leslie P. Norton, "Playing Games," *Wall Street Journal Online*, (**www.wsj.com**), February 25, 2002; Nintendo Co., Ltd. 2001 Annual Report, Nintendo Web site, (**www.nintendo.com**); Nintendo Web site, (**www.nintendo.com**), various press releases.

2. See Frank J. Fabozzi, Franco Modigliani, and Michael G. Ferri, *Foundations of Financial Markets and Institutions*, 2nd ed. (Upper Saddle River, NJ: Prentice Hall, 1998), p. 18.

3. See Alan C. Shapiro, *Foundations of Multinational Financial Management*, 3rd ed. (Upper Saddle River, NJ: Prentice Hall, 1998), pp. 424–425.

4. Paula Dwyer, Andrew Osterland, Kerry Capell, and Sharon Reier, "The 21st Century Stock Market," *Business Week*, August 10, 1998, pp. 66–72.

5. "Assessing the Damage," *Euromoney*, (**www.euromoney.com**).

6. *Central Bank Survey of Foreign Exchange and Derivatives Market Activity, 2001* (Basel, Switzerland: Bank for International Settlements, March 2002).

7. Chicago Board of Trade Web site, (**www.cbt.com**).

8. Chicago Mercantile Exchange Web site, (**www.cme.com**).

9. Philadelphia Stock Exchange Web site, (**www.phlx.com**).

Chapter 10

1. "Saying Goodbye to the National Currencies," European Union Web site, (**www.europa.eu.int**), February 28, 2002; "Europe's Big Idea," *The Economist*, January 5, 2002, p. 11; "Ring In the New," *The Economist*, January 5, 2002, pp. 22–24; David Fairlamb, "Ready, Set, Euros!," *Business Week*, July 2, 2001, pp. 48–50; Christopher Rhoads and Geoff Winestock, "The Euro: Cash in Hand," *Wall Street Journal Online*, (**www.wsj.com**), September 10, 2001.

2. "Exporters in Germany: The Subtle Curse of a Cheap Mark," *The Economist*, August 16, 1997, pp. 50–51.

3. Keith Naughton, "Who's Afraid of the Dollar?" *Business Week*, February 24, 1997, pp. 34–36.

4. Joshua Levine and Graham Button, "'A' Is for Arbitrage," *Forbes*, July 15, 1996, pp. 116–121.

5. "Big Mac Currencies," *The Economist*, April 21, 2001, p. 82.

6. Stanley Fischer, "The Asian Crisis and the Changing Role of the IMF," *Finance & Development*, June 1998, pp. 2–5.

7. Elizabeth Price, "IMF Says Bosnia Must Foster Private Sector as Aid Falls," *Wall Street Journal Online*, (**www.wsj.com**), March 22, 2002.

8. "Ring In the New," *The Economist*, January 5, 2002, pp. 22–24.

9. "The Asian Crisis: Causes and Cures," *Finance & Development*, June 1998, pp. 18–21; "The Perils of Global Capital," *The Economist*, April 11, 1998, pp. 52–54.

10. Ariel Cohen, "Russia's Meltdown: An Anatomy of the IMF Failure," *The Heritage Foundation*, (**www.heritage.org**), October 23, 1998.

11. Pamela Druckerman, "IMF Returns to an Argentina with Economy Under Pressure," *Wall Street Journal Online*, (**www.wsj.com**), April 2, 2002.

12. Pete Engardio, "Crisis of Faith for the Free Market," *Business Week*, October 19, 1998, pp. 38–39.

13. Steve Barth, "The New Asia?" *World Trade*, November, 1998, pp. 38–42.

Chapter 11

1. "The Ryanair Story," Ryanair Web site at (**www.ryanair.com**); Kerry Capell, et al., "Renegade Ryanair," *Business Week, European edition*, May 14, 2001, pp. 38–43; "Ryanair Takes on Lufthansa," *CNN* Web site, (**www.cnn.com**), November 22, 2001. Kerry Capell, Carol Matlack, and Christine Tierney, "Day of the Discount Airlines," *Business Week*, (**www.businessweek.com**), February 11, 2002.

2. Bausch & Lomb Web site, (**www.bausch.com**).

3. *Cadbury Schweppes 1996 Annual Report*, London, England, p. 1.

4. Gary Hamel and C. K. Prahalad, *Competing for the Future* (Boston: Harvard Business School Press, 1994).

5. Helen Deresky, *International Management: Managing across Borders and Cultures* (New York: HarperCollins, 1997), p. 156.

6. Michael E. Porter, *On Competition* (Boston: Harvard Business School Press, 1998).

7. See Gene Bylinsky, "Five Heroes of U.S. Manufacturing," *Fortune*, May 26, 1997, pp. 104B–104C.

8. Richard Halloran, "Parallel Lives," *World Business*, November–December 1996, p. 25.

9. Sherrie E. Zhan, "Marketing across Cultures: To Minimize Faux Pas, Don't Assume Anything," *World Trade*, February 1999, pp. 80–81.

10. Michael A. Cusumano, "How Microsoft Makes Large Teams Work Like Small

Teams," *Sloan Management Review*, Fall 1997, pp. 9–20; Randall E. Stross, "Mr. Gates Builds His Brain Trust," *Fortune*, December 8, 1997, pp. 84–88.

11. Intel Web site, (**www.intel.com**); Alicia Hills Moore, "Killer Chip," *Fortune*, November 10, 1997, pp. 70–72.

12. *Cadbury Schweppes 1996 Annual Report*, pp. 11, 19.

13. The discussion of these strategies is based on Michael E. Porter, *Competitive Strategy* (New York: Free Press, 1980), pp. 34–46.

14. Dave Barry, "Poopacino Pick-Me-Up Not So Swell after All," *Wisconsin State Journal*, November 9, 1997, p. 3G.

15. Bradley L. Kirkman and Debra L. Shapiro, "The Impact of Cultural Values on Employee Resistance to Teams," *Academy of Management Review*, 22, no. 3 (1997): 730–757.

16. Kirkman and Shapiro, "The Impact of Cultural Values on Employee Resistance to Teams."

17. Helen Axel, "Company Experiences with Global Teams," *HR Executive Review*, 4, no. 2 (1996): 3–18.

Chapter 12

1. Cristine Whitehouse, "Whole Latte Skakin'," *Time Europe*, April 9, 2001, p. 47; "Starbucks Sets Sights on Converting China to Coffee," *CNN* Web site, (**www.cnn.com**), January 11, 1999; Starbucks Web site, (**www.starbucks.com**), various reports.

2. Wendy Zellner, Louisa Shepard, Ian Katz, and David Lindorff, "Wal-Mart Spoken Here," *Business Week*, (**www.businessweek.com**), June 23, 1997.

3. Tim Jackson, *Virgin King: Inside Richard Branson's Business Empire* (Rocklin, CA: Putnam, 1996), p. 316.

4. Jack Lyne, "Nokia Wirelessly Takes On the World," *Site Selection*, December 1997–January 1998, pp. 1124–1128.

5. Robert S. Greenberger, "Africa Ascendant: New Leaders Replace Yesteryears' 'Big Men,' and Tanzania Benefits," *Wall Street Journal*, December 10, 1996, pp. A1, A6.

6. Laurie Joan Aron, "Global Logistics Boosts Competitive Advantage," *Site Selection*, August 1997.

7. Johny K. Johansson, Ilkka A. Ronkainen, and Michael R. Czinkota, "Negative Country-of-Origin Effects: The Case of the New Russia," *Journal of International Business Studies*, 25, no. 1 (1994): 157–176.

8. Samantha Marshall, "Soap Smugglers Cleaning Up in Vietnam," *Wall Street Journal*, April 1, 1998, pp. B1, B15.

9. This discussion is based on S. Tamer Cavusgil, "Measuring the Potential of Emerging Markets: An Indexing

Approach," *Business Horizons*, January–February 1997, pp. 87–91; "Market Potential Indicators for Emerging Markets," Michigan State University CIBER, (**www.ciber.bus.msu.edu**).

10. *World Development Indicators 2001* (Washington, D.C.: World Bank, April 2001), (**www.worldbank.org**).

11. Information obtained from the ProChile Web site, (**www.chileinfo.com**).

12. Tim Venable, "Searching the World for Facility Investments: U.S. States' Global Development Offices," *Site Selection*, December 1997–January 1998, p. 1122.

13. Jennifer Cody, "They Hired Someone to Find Out if People Really Like Chocolate?" *Wall Street Journal*, November 26, 1993, p. B1.

14. Perry A. Trunick, "Trade Shows: Where Culture Meets Commerce," *Transportation & Distribution*, December 1996, pp. 66–67.

Chapter 13

1. "Wal around the World," *The Economist*, December 8, 2001, pp. 59–63; Wal-Mart Web site, (**www.walmart.com**), various reports.

2. Franklin R. Root, *Entry Strategies for International Markets* (Lexington, MA: Lexington Books, 1987), p. 5.

3. Arthur Jones, "The 10 Steps of Global Trade," *World Trade*, Supplement, 1997.

4. Martyn Williams, "Fujitsu Wins Texas Instruments Japan Lawsuit," *Newsbytes News Network*, September 10, 1997.

5. "Philippines: Nippon Pigment Provides Compounding Technology," *Japan Chemical Week*, September 11, 1997.

6. Julie Bennett, "Europe Finally Right for U.S. Franchises," *Franchise Times*, 3, no. 9, p. 13.

7. David Ing, "Spain Proves Tough to Crack," *Hotel & Motel Management*, 212, no. 15, p. 8.

8. Laura Gatland, "Eastern Europe Eagerly Accepts U.S. Franchisors," *Franchise Times*, 3, no. 9, p. 17.

9. Frank H. Andorka, Jr., "Microtel Introduces New-Construction Plan," *Hotel & Motel Management*, 212, no. 13, p. 1.

10. Ian Jones, "She's Leaving Home&eBye-Bye," *World Trade*, May 1997, pp. 90–92.

11. "BAA Takes Majority Stake in Naples," *Airports International*, March 1997, p. 3.

12. "ABB Snatches Grid Management Contract from National Grid," *Modern Power Systems*, June 1997, p. 7.

13. "Power Plant Management Contract," *Power in Europe*, June 6, 1997, p. 30.

14. "$316m LNG Refining Deal," *Power in Asia*, April 7, 1997, p. 21.

15. "Projects," *Power in Europe*, August 29, 1997, pp. 25–26.

16. "Telecom Roundup—Ericsson Inks Turkish Contract," *Newsbytes News Network*, July 28, 1997.

17. This classification is made in Peter Buckley and Mark Casson, "A Theory of Cooperation in International Business," in Farok J. Contractor and Peter Lorange (eds.), *Cooperative Strategies in International Business* (Lexington, MA: Lexington Books, 1988) pp. 31–53.

18. Kathryn R. Harrigan, "Joint Ventures and Competitive Strategy," *Strategic Management Journal*, 9 (1988), pp. 141–158.

19. See, for example, Sanjeev Agarwal, "Socio-Cultural Distance and the Choice of Joint Ventures: A Contingency Perspective," *Journal of International Marketing*, 2, no. 2, 1994, pp. 63–80.

20. Brian Bremner et al., "Cozying Up to Keiretsu," *Business Week*, (**www.businessweek.com**), July 22, 1996.

21. Brenton R. Schlender, "How Toshiba Makes Alliances Work," *Fortune*, October 4, 1993, pp. 116–118.

22. Geert Hofstede, *Cultures and Organizations: Software of the Mind* (New York: McGraw-Hill, 1997), p. 228.

23. This section is based in part on Franklin R. Root, *Entry Strategies for International Markets* (Lexington, MA: Lexington Books, 1987), pp. 8–21.

24. See, for example, Sanjit Sengupta and Monica Perry, "Some Antecedents of Global Strategic Alliances," *Journal of International Marketing*, 5, no. 1, 1997, pp. 31–50.

25. Sheila M. Puffer and Daniel J. McCarthy, "Finding the Common Ground in Russian and American Business Ethics," *California Management Review*, Winter 1995, pp. 29–46.

Chapter 14

1. Darek Klimczak, "As Ski Jumper Leaps to Stardom, Sponsors Win, Too," *Wall Street Journal Europe*, February 23–24, 2001, p. 23; Nicole St. Pierre, "Red Bulls' Energy Drink Claims May Be Hype—But Not Its Sales," *Business Week*, (**www.businessweek.com**), June 30, 2000; Red Bull Web site, (**www.redbull.com**), various reports.

2. Theodore Levitt, "The Globalization of Markets," *Harvard Business Review*, May–June 1983, pp. 92–102.

3. Susan Douglas and Yoram Wind, "The Myth of Globalization," *Columbia Journal of World Business*, Winter 1987, pp. 19–29.

4. Vern Terpstra, *International Dimensions of Marketing*, 3rd ed. (Belmont, CA: Wadsworth, 1993), p. 9.

5. Raju Narisetti, "Can Rubbermaid Crack

Foreign Markets?," *Wall Street Journal*, June 20, 1996, p. B1.

6. Antony Thorncroft, "Do You Drink Lots?," *Financial Times* ('How To Spend It' Magazine Issue), October 18, 1997, pp. 24–32; Janis Robinson, *Financial Times*, September 27–28, 1997, p. 1.

7. Charles Bremner, "All Because the Belgians Do Not Like Milk Tray," *London Times*, October 24, 1997, p. 5.

8. Bill Spindle, "Are Sushi Sundaes Next? Tokyo Screams for Green-Tea Ice Cream," *Wall Street Journal*, August 27, 1997, p. B1.

9. David Leonhardt, "It Was a Hit in Buenos Aires—So Why Not Boise?" *Business Week*, September 7, 1998, pp. 56, 58.

10. Vanessa O'Connell, "Sir Thomas Takes His Leave as Lipton's Marketing Icon," *Wall Street Journal Europe*, May 22, 2001, p. 31.

11. NameLab, Inc. Web site, (**www.namelab.com**).

12. This one-quarter-page apology appeared in *The Independent* (London), November 8, 1997.

13. Robin Young, "Cadbury Loses Swiss Chocolate Bar Wars," *Time*, October 30, 1997, p. 11.

14. Johny K. Johansson, Ilkka A. Ronkainen, and Michael R. Czinkota, "Negative Country-of-Origin Effects: The Case of the New Russia," *Journal of International Business Studies* 25, no. 1 (1994): 157–176.

15. Julian Baum, "Riding High: A Taiwanese Bicycle Maker Races to Success in the West," *Far Eastern Economic Review*, (**www.feer.com**), May 7, 1998.

16. Dan Atkinson, "Fakes the Real Thing on Hooky Street," *The Guardian (London), Jobs and Money Supplement*, October 25, 1997, p. 2.

17. Harry Maurer and Justin Keay, " . . . . 'We Have Nowhere to Go but Up' . . . . but CD Pirates Are Raking It In," *Business Week*, (**www.businessweek.com**), April 28, 1997.

18. William Echikson, "Finnish Cash Helps a Baltic Tiger&eand Buys Some Useful Lessons, Too," *Business Week*, (**www.businessweek.com**), March 23, 1998.

19. Todd Zaun and Peter Wonacott, "Japan Motorcycle Firms Ask China to Stop Fakes," *Wall Street Journal Europe*, February 22, 2001, p. 28.

20. Pamela Yatsko, "Coke on Ice," *Far Eastern Economic Review*, February 27, 1997, p. 54; Alessandra Galloni, "Coca-Cola Tests the Waters with Localized Ads in Europe," *Wall Street Journal*, (**www.wsj.com**), July 18, 2001.

21. See for example, Robert Hite and Cynthia Fraser, "International Advertising Strategies of Multinational Corporations," in Michael Czinkota and Ilkka Ronkainen, eds.,

Readings in Global Marketing (Fort Worth, TX: Dryden Press, 1995), pp. 206–218.

22. Ursula Gruber, "The Role of Multilingual Copy Adaptation in International Advertising," in Stanley Paliwoda and John Ryans, eds., *International Marketing Reader* (London: Routledge, 1995), pp. 202–213.

23. Alan Henry and Ewen MacAskill, "Analysis: Tobacco Sponsorship," *The Guardian* (London), November 6, 1997, p. 21.

24. John Helemann, "All Europeans Are Not Alike," *The New Yorker*, April 28–May 5, 1997, pp. 174–181.

25. This section draws on Warren J. Keegan, *Global Marketing Management*, 5th ed. (Upper Saddle River, NJ: Prentice Hall, 1995), pp. 489–494.

26. John Burnett and Sandra Moriarty, *Introduction to Marketing Communication: An Integrated Approach* (Upper Saddle River, NJ: Prentice Hall, 1998), p. 3.

27. Michael Horsham, "Is High Tech Making Way for an Earthy Orientalism in Japan? Or Is It Just a Case of Smart Marketing?" *The Guardian* (London), October 21, 1994, pp. 4–5.

28. This comparison is made in Tatsuo Ohbora, Andrew Parsons, and Hajo Riesenbeck, "Alternative Routes to Global Marketing," *McKinsey Quarterly,* 3 (1992): 52–74.

29. Kimberely A. Strassel, "Low-Tech, Windup Radio Makes Waves," *Wall Street Journal*, July 15, 1997, p. B1.

30. Jesse Pesta, "Soap Makers Battle It Out for Market Share in Nepal," *Wall Street Journal*, (www.wsj.com), June 28, 2001.

31. Craig S. Smith, "In China, Some Distributors Have Really Cleaned Up with Amway," *Wall Street Journal*, August 4, 1997, p. B1.

32. "Laptops from Lapland," *The Economist*, September 6, 1997, pp. 67–68.

Chapter 15

1. Andy Reinhardt, "Eavesdropping at Europe's Wireless Bash," *Business Week*, (www.businessweek.com), March 6, 2002; Jane Black, "Here Come the Souped-Up Cell Phones," *Business Week*, (www.businessweek.com), February 15, 2002; Nokia Web site, (www.nokia.com), various reports.

2. Robert B. Reich, *The Work of Nations* (New York: Vintage Books, 1992), p. 112.

3. Saul Hansell, "Is This the Factory of the Future?," *New York Times*, July 26, 1998, Sec. 3, pp. 1, 12. See also, Scott Thurm, "Solectron Becomes a Force in 'Stealth Manufacturing,'" *Wall Street Journal*, August 18, 1998, p. B4.

4. "Eli Lilly Prescribes the Cure for Its Chemical Imbalances," *Wall Street Journal Europe*, December 28–29, 2001, p. 23.

5. Richard Tomlinson, "Why So Many Western Companies Are Coming Down with China Fatigue," *Fortune*, May 25, 1998, pp. 60–64.

6. Kenneth M. Morris, Alan M. Siegel, and Beverly Larson, *Guide to Understanding Money and Investing in Asia* (New York: Lightbulb Press, 1998), p. 37.

7. Sandy Serwer, "It's Big. It's German. It's…SAP," *Fortune*, September 7, 1998, p. 191.

8. Charles J.P. Chen et al. "An Investigation of the Relationship between International Activities and Capital Structure," *Journal of International Business Studies* 28, no. 3 (1997): 563–577; Todd A. Burgman, "An Empirical Examination of Multinational Corporate Capital Structure," *Journal of International Business Studies* 27, no. 3 (1996): 553–570.

9. Williams S. Sekely and J. Markham Collins, "Cultural Influences on International Capital Structure," *Journal of International Business Studies* 19, no. 1 (1988): 87–100.

Chapter 16

1. Intel Web site, (www.intel.com), various reports.

2. Barry Newman, "Expat Archipelago: The New Yank Abroad Is the 'Can-Do' Player in the Global Village," *Wall Street Journal*, December 12, 1995, p. A12.

3. Valeria Frazee, "An Unhappy Spouse Is the #1 Deal Breaker," *Global Workforce*, July 1998, p. 8.

4. Stephen Dolainski, "Are Expats Getting Lost in the Translation?" *Workforce*, February 1997, pp. 32–39.

5. Valeria Frazee, "Special Preparation When Relocating with Children," *Global Workforce*, January 1997, p. 10.

6. "Unhappy German Peace," *The Economist*, February 20, 1999, p. 62.

7. William Greider, *One World, Ready or Not: The Manic Logic of Global Capitalism* (New York: Simon & Schuster, 1997).

SOURCE NOTES

Chapter 1

Map 1.1 *International Trade Statistics 2001* (Geneva, Switzerland: World Trade Organization, November 2000), (www.wto.org), Tables A5–A8. **Global Manager: *The Keys to Success*** "The LRMing Curve," *World Trade*, (www.worldtrademag.com), June 28, 2001; John Davies, "That Elusive Success," *International Business*, October 1996, p. 35. **World Business Survey: *The Global Market for Culture*** "The Overall Picture," *Foreign Policy*, July/August 2001, p. 28. **Figure 1.2** "Cross-Border Mergers and Acquisitions," *The Economist*, July 7, 2001, p. 107. **Figure 1.3 and Table 1.1** Data obtained from "The Fortune Global 500: The World's Largest Corporations," *Fortune, European edition*, July 23, 2001, pp. F1–F44. **Entrepreneurial Focus: *Untapped Potential: Four Myths That Keep Small Businesses from Export Success*** "Is Business

Really Going International?," *Inc.*, The State of Small Business, 1997, p. 121. **In Practice** "Lumenis to Buy HGM Medical Laser Systems," *Wall Street Journal Online*, (www.wsj.com), November 8, 2001; "Lumenis to Purchase HGM Medical Laser Systems," November 8, 2001, *Financial Times*, (www.ft.com); M&A Databank, *CNN*, (www.cnn.com). **Business Case 1: *MTV: Going Global with a Local Beat*** "MTV: 20 Years of Entertainment Innovation," *CNN*, (www.cnn.com), August 2, 2001; "Doug Herzog, Dan Cortese on MTV's 20th," *CNN*, (www.cnn.com), August 2, 2001; "MTV: Rewinding 20 Years of Music Revolution," *CNN*, (www.cnn.com), August 2, 2001; "Pan-European Idea Is Dead, Says Three-Way MTV," *New Media Markets*, April 4, 1996, pp. 6–7; Horst Stipp, "MTV German-Style," *American Demographics*, May 1996, p. 49; and Peter Hund, "High Tech Helps MTV Evolve," *World*

Trade, June 1996, p. 10.

Chapter 2

Entrepreneurial Focus: *Give Your Web Site A Local Feel* Theresa Forsman, "Patience Is an e-Virtue," *Business Week*, (www.businessweek.com), July 31, 2001; "Adapting Products and Services for Global e-Commerce," *World Trade*, (www.worldtrademag.com), December 20, 2000; Moira Allen, "Net the World," *Entrepreneur Magazine*, (www.entrepreneur.com), June 2000. **World Business Survey: *Generation Gap*** Romesh Ratnesar, "Generation Europe," *Time Europe*, April 2, 2001, p. 41. **Global Manager: *A Globetrotter's Guide to Manners*** Moira Allen "Talking Heads," *Entrepreneur Magazine*, (www.entrepreneur.com), January 2001; Moira Allen "Touchy-Feely," *Entrepreneur Magazine*, (www.entrepreneur.com), September 2000;

Moira Allen "Czech List," *Entrepreneur Magazine*, (**www.entrepreneur.com**), July 2000; Tatiana D. Helenius, "Body Language Savvy," *CNN Web site*, (**www.cnnfn.com**), May 3, 2000. **Map 2.1** Mapping © Bartholomew, 1990. Extract taken from Plate 5 of *The Comprehensive Atlas of the World*, 8th ed. Reprinted with permission. **Table 2.1** "Web Pages by Language," *Business 2.0, U.K. edition*, May 2001, p. 123. **Figure 2.2** Louis E. Boone, David L. Kurtz, and Judy R. Block, *Contemporary Business Communication*, 2nd ed. (Upper Saddle River, NJ: Prentice Hall, 1997), p. 71. **Table 2.2** Adapted from *World Development Indicators 2001* (Washington, D.C.: World Bank, April 2001), (**www.worldbank.org**). **Figure 2.3** Delyth Hughes and Andrew McLaughlin, "East Side Story," *Business 2.0, U.K. edition*, May 2001, pp. 122, 124. **Figures 2.4 and 2.5** Geert Hofstede, "The Cultural Relativity of Organizational Practices and Theories," *Journal of International Business Studies*, Fall 1983, p. 82, 84. **In Practice** Adapted from Steve Connor, "Speaking in Fewer Tongues," *The World in 2001* (London, The Economist Newspaper Limited, 2000), pp. 142–143. **Business Case 2: Asian Values under Fire** Lara Sowinski, "Southeast Asia Reeling from a One-Two Punch," *World Trade*, (**www.worldtrademag.com**), July 3, 2001; Steve Barth, "The New Asia?," *World Trade*, November 1998, pp. 38–42; Bruce Einhorn and Ron Corben, "Asia's Social Backlash," *Business Week*, August 17, 1998, pp. 46–51; "What Would Confucius Say Now?," *The Economist*, July 25, 1998, pp. 23–28.

Chapter 3

Figure 3.1 Adapted from Jeff Fischer, "The Global Ballot Box," *Foreign Policy*, May–June 2001, p. 24. **Map 3.1** Data obtained from *Freedom in The World, 2000-2001* (New York: Freedom House, 2001), (**www.freedomhouse.org**). **World Business Survey: Doubting Democrats** Adapted from "An Alarm Call for Latin America's Democrats," *The Economist*, July 28, 2001, pp. 49–50. **Map 3.2** Data obtained from *International Country Risk Guide* (East Syracuse, NY: PRS Group, 2001), (**www.countrydata.com**), September 2001, Table 2B. **Table 3.1** Adapted from *The 2001 Corruption Perceptions Index* (Paris: Transparency International, June 2001), Transparency International Web site, (**www.transparency.org**). **Figure 3.2** Adapted from: *Sixth Annual BSA Global Software Piracy Study* (International Planning and Research Corporation, May 2001), pp. 5–6, Business Software Alliance Web site, (**www.bsa.org**). **Entrepreneurial Focus: The Long Arm of The Law** Federal Trade Commission Web site, (**www.ftc.gov**); U.S. Consumer Product Safety Commission Web site, (**www.cpsc.gov**); U.S.

Patent and Trademark Office Web site, (**www.uspto.gov**); U.S. International Trade Commission Web site, (**www.usitc.gov**). **Figure 3.3** United Nations Department of Public Information, (**www.un.org**). **In Practice** Adapted from Mark Landler, "China's High-Tech Role Worries Some U.S. Firms," *International Herald Tribune*, May 30, 2001, p. 13. **Business Case 3: Intellectual Property Rights In Asia** *Sixth Annual BSA Global Software Piracy Study* (International Planning and Research Corporation, May 2001), Business Software Alliance Web site, (**www.bsa.org**); "Now These Copycats Have to Discover New Drugs," *The Economist*, March 24, 1997; "Second Thoughts on Going Global," *The Economist*, March 13, 1995.

Chapter 4

Global Manager: Guidelines for Good Guanxi Steve Barth, "Bridge over Troubled (Cultural) Water," *World Trade*, August 1997, pp. 32–33; Michele Marchetti, "Selling in China? Go Slowly," *Sales & Marketing Management*, January 1997, pp. 35–36; Charlene Marmer Solomon, "The Big Question," *Global Workforce*, July 1997, pp. 10–16. **Map 4.1** Data obtained from *2001 Index of Economic Freedom*, The Heritage Foundation Web site at (**www.heritage.org**). **Figure 4.2** Gerald P. O'Driscoll, Kim R. Holmes, and Melanie Kirkpatrick, "Executive Summary," *2001 Index of Economic Freedom*, (Washington, DC: The Heritage Foundation, 2001), The Heritage Foundation Web site at (**www.heritage.org**). **Map 4.2** Data obtained from World Bank, "2000 Country Classification" section, (**www.worldbank.org**). **Table 4.1** Data obtained from Organisation for Cooperation and Development (OECD), "Statistics" section, (**www.oecd.org**). **Table 4.2** *Human Development Report 2001*, (New Nork, NY: United Nations Development Programme, 2001), (**www.undp.org/hdr2001**), Table 1, pp. 141–144. **World Business Survey: Young Voices** "Young Voices," *Business Central Europe*, June 2001, p. 59. **Figure 4.3** "Resurrection: A Survey of Russia & The CIS," *Business Central Europe*, April 2001, pp. 53–61. **In Practice** "Bone-Crunching: Belarus Is As Gloomy As Ever," *The Economist*, November 17, 2001, p. 46; Daniel Schwammenthal, "EU Commission: 10 Countries on Track for Accession by '04," *Wall Street Journal Online*, (**www.wsj.com**), November 13, 2001; Philip Birzulis, "Tallinn: Estonia's Capital Continues to Thrive off The Back of Its Nordic Neighbors," *Business Central Europe*, May 2001, p. 62. **Business Case 4: Business Administration, Havana Style** Sheridan Prasso, "Think Twice About Havana Holidays," *Business Week*, September 10, 2001; *Wall Street Journal Report* #701; Gail DeGeorge, "A Touch of Capitalism," *Business Week*, March

17, 1997, pp. 50, 52; William C. Symonds and Gail DeGeorge, "Castro's Capitalist," *Business Week*, March 17, 1997, pp. 48–49; Deroy Murdock, "Cuba: This Island of Lost Potential," *World Trade*, August 1997, pp. 28–31.

Chapter 5

Map 5.1 *World Development Indicators 2001* (Washington, D.C.: World Bank, April 2001), (**www.worldbank.org**). **Table 5.1** *International Trade Statistics 2001* (Geneva: World Trade Organization, November 2000), Tables I.5 & I.7, (**www.wto.org**). **Figure 5.1** *International Trade Statistics 2001*, (Geneva, Switzerland: World Trade Organization, November 2000), (**www.wto.org**), Chart II.2. **Figure 5.2** Data obtained from *International Trade Statistics 2000*, (Geneva, Switzerland: World Trade Organization, November 2000), (**www.wto.org**), various tables. **World Business Survey: Who Owns The High Seas?** Adapted from "Merchant Fleets," *The Economist*, February 10, 2001, p. 120. **Table 5.2** *International Trade Statistics 2000*, (Geneva, Switzerland: World Trade Organization, November 2000), (**www.wto.org**), Table III.3. **Global Manager: Building Good Relations in the Pacific Rim** Bradford W. Ketchum, Jr., "Five Rules for Building Good Relations in the 'Rim' and Beyond," *Inc.*, [Advertising Supplement], May 20, 1997. **Figure 5.6** Raymond Vernon and Louis T. Wells, Jr., *The Economic Environment of International Business*, 5e (Upper Saddle River, NJ: Prentice Hall, 1991), p. 85. **Entrepreneurial Focus: Five Common Fulfillment Mistakes** Adapted from "Five Common Fulfillment Mistakes," *World Trade*, Global Online supplement, (**www.worldtrademag.com**), February 27, 2001. **Figure 5.7** Michael E. Porter, "The Competitive Advantage of Nations," *Harvard Business Review* (March-April 1990), p. 77. **Map 5.2** *Harvard Business Review* (November-December 1998), p. 82. **Business Case 5: DHL Worldwide Express: First in Asia and the World** "DHL Earns Gold Medal As Third Party Logistics Provider for Second Year in Quest for Quality Survey," DHL Web site, (**www.dhl.com**), Press release, October 2, 2001; Josephine Bow, "The Fast-Paced World of Asian Express," *Distribution* (February 1996), pp. 44–47; Nagami Kishi and David Russell, *Successful Gaijin in Japan: How Foreign Companies Are Making It in Japan* (Lincolnwood, IL: NTC Business Books, 1996), pp. 315–335.

Chapter 6

Entrepreneurial Focus: Ex-Im Bank: Experts in Export Financing Export-Import Bank of the United States Web site, (**www.exim.gov**). **Global Manager: Surfing the Regulatory Seas** Eric J. Adams, "More Web Galore: There's No End to Trade-Dedicated Web Sites," *World*

Trade, August 1997, pp. 40–42; Adams, "Navigating the Regulatory Seas," *World Trade*, September 1996, pp. 44–46. **Figure 6.3** World Trade Organization Web site, (**www.wto.org**). **Table 6.2** "About the WTO," World Trade Organization Web site, (**www.wto.org**). **World Business Survey:** *Striking Back* "Unfair Trade," *The Economist*, May 5, 2001, p. 105. **In Practice** Adapted from Geoff Winestock and Neil King Jr., "WTO Rules Against U.S. Tax Breaks, Opening the Way for EU Retaliation," *Wall Street Journal Online*, (**www.wsj.com**), January 15, 2002. **Business Case 6:** *Unfair Protection or Valid Defense?* "China to Begin Probe of Synthetic Rubber Imports," *Wall Street Journal Online*, (**www.wsj.com**), March 19, 2002; Neil King, Jr. and Geoff Winestock, "Plan to Rescue U.S. Steel Industry Draws the Ire of Critics Abroad," *Wall Street Journal Online*, (**www.wsj.com**), March 7, 2002; "Mexico Widens Antidumping Measure," *World Trade*, February 1999; "Against Antidumping," *The Economist*, November 7, 1998, p. 18.

Chapter 7

Figure 7.1 *World Investment Report 2000: Cross-Border Mergers and Acquisitions and Development* (Geneva, Switzerland: UNCTAD, 2000), figure I4, p. 13. **Entrepreneurial Focus:** *Cowboy Candy Rides into Manchuria* Adapted from Marcus W. Brauchli, "Global Investing: Pick An Instrument: Sweet Dreams," *Wall Street Journal*, June 27, 1996, R, 10:1. **Global Manager:** *Investing Abroad? Be Prepared for Surprises* Adapted from Jim Schriner, "Be Prepared for Surprises," *Industry Week*, December 2, 1996, p. 22. **Table 7.1** *Survey of Current Business, July 2001*, (Washington, D.C.: U.S. Department of Commerce, 2001), p. 47. **World Business Survey:** *Ups and Downs of Current Accounts* Adapted from "Current Accounts," *The Economist*, April 7, 2001, p. 134. **In Practice** Adapted from Terho Uimonen, "Intel Clears $100 Million to Upgrade Its Philippine Chip-Making Facilities," *Wall Street Journal Online*, (**www.wsj.com**), January 23, 2002. **Business Case 7:** *Mercedes-Benz: Footloose in Tuscaloosa* Based in part on "Real People, Real Choices," #2, *Custom Videos for Marketing*, Part II. Robert Baxter, Mercedes-Benz of North America; Justin Martin, "Mercedes: Made in Alabama," *Fortune*, July 7, 1997, pp. 150–158; Bill Vlasic, "In Alabama, the Soul of a New Mercedes?," *Business Week*, March 31, 1997, pp. 70–71.

Chapter 8

Entrepreneurial Focus: *Czech List* Adapted from Moira Allen, "Czech List: Doing Business with Eastern Europe," *Entrepreneur Magazine*, (**www.entrepreneur.com**), July 2000. **World Business Survey:** *Corruption Perceptions in the FTAA* Adapted from *The 2001 Corruption Perceptions Index* (Paris: Transparency International, June 2001), Transparency International Web site, (**www.transparency.org**). **In Practice** Stephen Wisnefski, "Free Trade Push Offers Latin America A Glimmer of Hope," *Wall Street Journal Online*, (**www.wsj.com**), October 9, 2001; Geri Smith et al., "Betting on Free Trade," *Business Week, European edition*, April 23, 2001, pp. 32–35; and Douglas Stinson, "Building Blocks," *Latin Trade*, January 1999, pp. 44–45. **Business Case 8:** *Tainted Trade: Increasing Imports Brings Increase in Illness* Janet Ginsburg, "Bio Invasion," *Business Week*, September 11, 2000, 70–78; Jeff Gerth and Tom Weiner, "Imports Swamp U.S. Food-Safety Efforts," *New York Times*, September 29, 1997, p. A1; Richard A. Ryan, "Mom Says NAFTA Is A Safety Issue," *Detroit News*, September 10, 1997, p. B3; Lawrence K. Altman, "153 Hepatitis Cases Are Traced to Frozen Imported Strawberries," *New York Times*, April 3, 1997, p. A1.

Chapter 9

Entrepreneurial Focus: *Where Microcredit Is Due* Adapted from Skip Kaltenheuser, "Spearing Loan Sharks," *World Trade*, May 1997, pp. 32–34. **World Business Survey:** *Ranking the Top Investment Banks* "Issuers Shift from Equity to Debt," *Euromoney* Web site, (**www.euromoney.com**), September 2001. **Tables 9.1 and 9.2** *Wall Street Journal Online*, (**www.wsj.com**), February 8, 2002. **Global Manager:** *Five Strategies for More Effective Foreign Exchange Management* Adapted from David Spiselman, *Five Strategies for Saving Money and Improving Control over Foreign Exchange* (San Mateo, CA: Sonnet Financial Inc., 1995), pp. 8–10. **In Practice** Excerpted from Marianne Sullivan, "Further Weakness in Dollar Is Forecast amid Volatility in Currency Markets," *Wall Street Journal*, October 12, 1998, p. C18. **Business Case 9:** *Argentina Stares Into The Abyss* Sonja Ryst, "Argentine Utilities Squeezed Amid Rate Fix, Peso Slide," *Wall Street Journal Online*, (**www.wsj.com**), March 26, 2002; Pamela Druckerman, "Argentine Crisis Deepens As Peso Falls to New Lows," *Wall Street Journal Online*, (**www.wsj.com**), March 26, 2002; Pamela Druckerman and Matt Moffett, "With IMF in Mind, Argentina Switches Dollar Debt to Pesos," *Wall Street Journal Online*, (**www.wsj.com**), March 15, 2002; Bernard Wysocki Jr., "Like a Virus, Contagion Comes in Many Forms," *Wall Street Journal Online*, (**www.wsj.com**), March 4, 2002; "A Decline without Parallel," *The Economist*, March 2, 2002, pp. 27–29; "Between the Creditors and the Streets," *The Economist*, January 5, 2002, pp. 39–40.

Chapter 10

Figures 10.1 and 10.2 "Exchange Rates of Major World Currencies," Economic Report of the President, various years. **Global Manager:** *Exporting Against the Odds: Key Strategies for Success* Louis Uchitelle, "Reconsidering a Trade Equation," *New York Times*, October 31, 1997, pp. D1, D2. **Table 10.1** "Big Mac Currencies," *The Economist*, April 21, 2001, p. 82. **Figures 10.3 and 10.4** *World Economic Outlook* (Washington, DC: International Monetary Fund, various years). **Figure 10.5** Data obtained from *IMF Annual Report, 2001*, (Washington, DC: International Monetary Fund, 2001), Table 6.5, p. 68. **World Business Survey:** *Euro Attitudes* Data obtained from *Flash Eurobarometer 115: Euro Attitudes (wave 6) Euro Zone*, (Brussels, Belgium: EOS Gallup Europe, December 2001), European Union Web site, (**www.europa.eu.int**). **In Practice** Adapted from Jonathan Karp and Michelle Wallin, "Argentina Presents Austere Budget in Hopes of Winning More IMF Aid," *Wall Street Journal Online*, (**www.wsj.com**), February 6, 2002. **Business Case 10:** *Banking On Forgiveness* "US, Europe Debating Grants Vs. Loans For Debt Relief," *Wall Street Journal Online*, (**www.wsj.com**), March 19, 2002; Richard W. Stevenson, "Global Banks Offer a First: Forgiveness on Some Debt," *New York Times*, March 12, 1997, p A5; "Debt Relief for Model Countries," *New York Times*, May 1, 1997, p. A26; World Bank Web site, (**www.worldbank.org**), various reports on the HIPC Debt Initiative.

Chapter 11

Figure 11.2 Michael E. Porter, *On Competition* (Boston: Harvard Business School Press, 1998), p. 77. **Entrepreneurial Focus:** *Know Yourself, Know Your Product* Adapted from Davis P. Goodman, "The First Pillar: Assess Your Capabilities," *World Trade*, March 1999, pp. 48–53. **World Business Survey:** *Invest and Prosper* Adapted from Edward Taylor, "Innovation Snapshots," *Wall Street Journal Europe*, November 26, 2001, p. 32. **Figure 11.4** Michael E. Porter, *Competitive Strategy* (New York: Free Press, 1980), p. 39. **Global Manager:** *Competing with Giants* Adapted from Niraj Dawar and Tony Frost, "Competing with Giants: Survival Strategies for Local Companies in Emerging Markets," *Harvard Business Review*, March–April 1999, pp. 119–129. **In Practice** Cressida Connolly, "Kraft to Close Two Latin Amer. Mfg. Plants," *Wall Street Journal Online*, (**www.wsj.com**), November 30, 2001; Julie Forster and Becky Gaylord, "Can Kraft Be a Big Cheese Abroad?," *Business Week, European edition*, June 4, 2001, pp. 54–55; Kraft Web site, (**www.kraft.com**), various reports. **Business Case 11:** *The IKEA Key to Pricing* "IKEA to Spend GBP50M Extending UK Stores," *Wall Street Journal Online*, (**www.wsj.com**), January 11, 2002; "IKEA to Expand in Southern

Europe," *Wall Street Journal Online*, (**www.wsj.com**), December 18, 2001; Julia Flynn and Lori Bongiorno, "IKEA's New Game Plan," *Business Week*, October 6, 1997, pp. 99, 102; "Furnishing the World," *The Economist*, November 19, 1994, pp. 79–80; "The 1992 Client Media All-Stars: John Sitnik, IKEA," *Mediaweek*, December 12, 1992, pp. 25+; IKEA Web site, (**www.ikea.com**), various reports.

Chapter 12

World Business Survey: *Global Business Climates* "Business Environment," *The Economist*, August 8, 2001, p. 82. **Table 12.1** Adapted from C.K. Prahalad and Kenneth Lieberthal, "The End of Corporate Imperialism," *Harvard Business Review*, July-August 1998, p. 70. **Map 12.1** *World Development Indicators 2001* (Washington, DC: World Bank, April 2001), (**www.worldbank.org**). **Figure 12.2** *Site Selection*, December 1997/January 1998, p. 1122. **In Practice** "Baby Steps toward Change," *The Economist*, December 1, 2001, pp. 50–51; "Mexico's Wagon Is Hitched to a Falling Star," *Business Week, European edition*, October 1, 2001, p. 25; "Mexican Production Offers More Bonuses" *World Trade Magazine* Web site, (**www.worldtrademag.com**), September 1, 2001. **Business Case 12: *Researching Vietnam's Potential*** "Vietnam Buys Boeing As It Inks U.S. Trade Deal," *CNN*, (**www.cnn.com**), December 11, 2001; Samantha Marshall, "Vietnam Pullout: This Time, Investors Pack Up Gear, Stymied by Bureaucracy, Lack of Reforms," *The Wall Street Journal*, June 30, 1998, p. A18; Marshall, "P&G Squabbles with Vietnamese Partner," *The Wall Street Journal*, February 27, 1998, p. A10; Reginald Chua, "Vietnam Frustrate Foreign Investors As Leaders Waffle on Market Economy," *The Wall Street Journal*, November 25, 1996, p. A10.

Chapter 13

World Business Survey: *Land of Opportunity* *International Trade Statistics 2001* (Geneva, Switzerland: World Trade Organization, November 2000), Table III.17, p. 49; Martha L. Celestino, "Imports: Selling in the U.S.," *World Trade*, February 1999, pp. 30–32. **Entrepreneurial Focus: *Global Collection Guidelines*** Adapted from James Welsh, "Covering Your Bets on Credit and Collections," *World Trade*, February 1999, pp. 28–29. **Figure 13.4** Peter Buckley and Mark Casson, "A Theory of Cooperation in International Business," in Farok J. Contractor and Peter Lorange (eds.), *Cooperative Strategies in International Business* (Lexington, MA: Lexington Books, 1988) pp. 31–53. **Global Manager: *Negotiating the Terms of Market Entry*** Andrew C. Inkpen and Paul W. Beamish, "Knowledge, Bargaining Power, and the Instability of International Joint Ventures,"

Academy of Management Review, vol. 22, no. 1, pp. 177–202; Arvind V. Phatak and Mohammed M. Habib, "The Dynamics of International Business Negotiations," *Business Horizons*, May–June 1996, pp. 30–38; David K. Tse, June Francis, and Jan Walls, "Cultural Differences in Conducting Intra- and Inter-Cultural Negotiations: A Sino-Canadian Comparison," *Journal of International Business Studies*, vol. 25, no. 3, pp. 537–555. **Figure 13.5** Franklin R. Root, *Entry Strategies for International Markets* (Lexington, MA: Lexington Books, 1987), pp. 8–21. **In Practice** Adapted from Kanji Ishibashi, "Kyocera Builds New Electronic Equipment Plant in China, To Form JV," *Wall Street Journal Online*, (**www.wsj.com**), December 6, 2001. **Business Case 13: *The Brave New World of Telecommunication Joint Ventures*** Barbara Martinez, "Sprint Names Its Long-distance Chief to Run Loss-Beset Global One Venture," *Wall Street Journal*, February 17, 1998, p. B20; Jennifer L. Schenker and James Pressley, "European Telecom Venture with Sprint Hasn't Become the Bully Some Feared," *Wall Street Journal*, December 23, 1997, p. A11; Alan Cane, "Unisource Partners to Strengthen Ties," *Financial Times*, June 4, 1997, p. 13; Gautam Naik, "Unisource Expected to Merge Operations," *Wall Street Journal*, June 4, 1997, p. B6; Clay Harris, "Complexity Starts at Home," *Financial Times*, Survey, October 29, 1996, p. VI.

Chapter 14

Global Manager: *Managing an International Sales Force* Adapted from Charlene Marmer Solomon, "Managing an Overseas Sales Force," *World Trade*, Global Sales and Technology Special Section, pp. S4–S6. **World Business Survey: *Web Ads Grab Attention*** Adapted from Alessandra Galloni, "Web Ads Vindicated," *Wall Street Journal Europe*, July 16, 2001, p. 25. **Figure 14.1** Adapted from Courtland L. Bovee, John V. Thill, George P. Dovel, and Marian Burk Wood, *Advertising Excellence* (New York, NY: McGraw-Hill, 1995), p. 14. **In Practice** Adapted from Pichayaporn Utumporn, "Ad with Hitler Causes Furor in Thailand," *Wall Street Journal*, June 5, 1998, p. B8. **Business Case 14: *Fair Game or Out-of-Bounds?*** Ellen Neuborne, "For Kids on the Web, It's an Ad, Ad, Ad, Ad World," *Business Week*, (**www.businessweek.com**), August 13, 2001; Brandon Mitchener, "Banning Ads on Kids' TV," *Wall Street Journal Europe*, May 22, 2001, p. 25; James MacKinnon, "Psychologists Act against Ad Doctors," Adbusters Web site, (**www.adbusters.org**).

Chapter 15

World Business Survey: *The Gap in Minimum Wages* Adapted from "Wages," *The Economist*, December 8, 2001, p. 106. **Global Manager: *Linking TQM and ISO 9000 Standards*** Adapted from G.K. Kanji, An Innovative

Approach to Make ISO 9000 Standards More Effective." *Total Quality Management*, February 1998, pp. 67–79. **Entrepreneurial Focus: *Get Global Cash: Overseas Investors Await You*** Adapted from Jenny C. McCune, "Get Global Cash," *Success*, December 1995, p. 16. **In Practice** Adapted from "Xerox to Invest in Irish Facilities," *World Trade*, November 1998, p. 24. **Business Case 15: *TPS: The Benchmark in Production Efficiency*** "Q&A: Pushing Carmakers to Rev Up Factories," *Business Week*, (**www.businessweek.com**), February 18, 2002; William Greider, *One World, Ready or Not: The Manic Logic of Global Capitalism*, (New York, NY: Simon & Schuster, 1997), Chapter 6 "*Jikoda*"; Micheline Maynard, "Camry Assembly Line Delivers New Minivan," *USA Today*, August 11, 1997, p. 3B.

Chapter 16

Table 16.1 Union Bank of Switzerland. **Entrepreneurial Focus: *Growing Global*** Laurel Delaney, "Is It Time to Go Global?," *Entrepreneur Magazine*, (**www.entrepreneur.com**), April 04, 2001; Ysabel de la Rosa, "In Country," *Entrepreneur Magazine*, (**www.entrepreneur.com**), March 2001; Charlotte Mulhern, "Going the Distance," *Entrepreneur Magazine*, (**www.entrepreneur.com**), May 1998. **Global Manager: *A Shocking Ordeal*** Adrian Furnham and Stephen Bochner, *Culture Shock* (London: Methuen, 1986); Kalvero Oberg, "Culture Shock: Adjustments to New Cultural Environments," *Practical Anthropology*, July–August 1960, pp. 177–182; J.T. Gullahorn and J.E. Gullahorn, "An Extension of the U-Curve Hypothesis," *Journal of Social Sciences*, January 1963, pp. 34–47; David Stamps, "Welcome to America: Watch out for Culture Shock," *Training*, November 1996, pp. 22–30; John R. Engen, "Coming Home," *Training*, March 1995, pp. 37–40; Gary P. Ferraro, *The Cultural Dimensions of International Business* (Upper Saddle River, NJ: Prentice Hall, 1994), pp. 145–156. Box Figure from Stephen P. Robbins, *Organizational Behavior: Concept, Controversies, Applications*, 7th ed. (Upper Saddle River, NJ: Prentice Hall, 1996), p. 60. **Table 16.2** *Global Workforce*, July 1998, p. 26. **World Business Survey: *Long Time, No Work*** "Long Time No Work," *Wall Street Journal Europe*, August 28, 2001, p. 15. **In Practice** Adapted from Suh-kyung Yoon, "The Right Person for the Right Job," *Far Eastern Economic Review*, (**www.feer.com**), March 22, 2001; Intercultural Business Center Web site, (**www.ib-c.com**). **Business Case 16: *Expatriation or Discrimination?*** James Harding, "When Expats Should Pack Their Bags," *Financial Times*, September 1, 1998, p. 10; C.K. Prahalad and Kenneth Lieberthal, "The End of Corporate Imperialism," *Harvard Business Review*, July–August 1998 pp. 68–79.

PHOTO CREDITS

Chapter 1
Page 3 Douglas Kirkland/Corbis
Page 13 © Paul Fridman
Page 15 James Leynse/ Corbis/SABA Press
Photos, Inc.
Page 18 Harry Sieplinga, HMS Images/The
Image Bank/Getty Images, Inc.
Page 20 Luca Zennaro/ Agence France-Presse
AFP

Chapter 2
Page 39 AP/Wide World Photos
Page 42 AP/Wide World Photos
Page 47 Strphen Shaver/ Agence France-Presse
AFP
Page 56 Emmanuel Dunand/AFP/ Agence
France-Presse AFP
Page 60 The Far Side by Gary Larson © 1983
Farworks, Inc.

Chapter 3
Page 75 Tom Wagner/Corbis/SABA Press
Photos, Inc.
Page 82 Kaveh Kazemi
Page 91 Radhika Chalasani/ SIPA Press
Page 98 Pepper... and Salt, August 21, 2000.
From the *Wall Street Journal.*Used with per-
mission of Cartoon Features Syndicate.

Chapter 4
Page 109 Jeremy Homer/Corbis
Page 112 Yann Layma/Stone/ Getty Images,
Inc.
Page 115 Suzanne & Nick Geary/Stone/Getty
Images, Inc.

Chapter 5
Page 137 Ron Haviv/ Corbis/SABA Press
Photos, Inc.
Page 145 Keith Dannemiller/ Corbis/SABA
Press Photos, Inc.

Page 156 Tablet PC prototype. Reprinted with
permission from Microsoft Corporation

Chapter 6
Page 165 AP/Wide World Photos
Page 167 AP/Wide World Photos Page169
AP/Wide World Photos
Page 174 Aegean Free Zone Development &
Operating Company
Page 175 ProChile New York
Page 178 Jeffrey Aaronson/ Network Aspen

Chapter 7
Page 193 Susana Gonzalez/ Getty Images, Inc.
Page 195 Museum of Flight/Corbis
Page 201 Selwyn Tait/ TimePix
Page 205 Inge Yspeert/Corbis

Chapter 8
Page 219 Nestle S.A.
Page 228 Chamussy/SIPA Press
Page 232 AP/Wide World Photos

Chapter 9
Page 249 AP/Wide World Photos
Page 251 Tom Wagner/Corbis/SABA Press
Photos, Inc.
Page 254 Tom Wagner/Corbis/SABA Press
Photos, Inc.
Page 261 AP/Wide World Photos

Chapter 10
Page 279 Olivier Matthys/AFP/Corbis
Page 287 Tarik Tinazay/AFP Photo
Page 294 AP/Wide World Photos
Page 301 Youn-Kong/Agence France-Presse
AFP

Chapter 11
Page 311 © Steve Pyke
Page 321 AP/Wide World Photos

Page 323 Larry Davis/ New York Times
Pictures

Chapter 12
Page 339 AP/Wide World Photos
Page 344 Earl Kowall/Corbis
Page 346 AP/Wide World Photos

Chapter 13
Page 369 Greg Girard/ Contact Press Images
Inc.
Page 375 AP/Wide World Photos
Page 383 Carl & Ann Purcell/Corbis
Page 385 Aral/ SIPA Press

Chapter 14
Page 401 Courtesy Red Bull North America,
Inc.
Page 405 Aaron Goodman
Page 407 REUTERS/Will Burgess/Getty
Images Inc.
Page 411 AP/Wide World Photos
Page 415 AP/Wide World Photos

Chapter 15
Page 427 Sean Gallup/Getty Images, Inc.
Page 431 AP/Wide World Photos
Page 434 © Dan Cohen
Page 443 Dilip Mehta/ Contact Press Images
Inc.

Chapter 16
Page 451 AP/Wide World Photos
Page 454 Dilip Mehta/ Contact Press Images
Inc.
Page 457 Pablo Bartholomew/ Getty Images,
Inc.
Page 467 AP/Wide World Photos

Cover
KAN Photography, Inc.

absolute advantage Ability of a nation to produce a good more efficiently than any other nation.

administrative delays Regulatory controls or bureaucratic rules designed to impair the rapid flow of imports into a country.

ad valorem tariff Tariff levied as a percentage of the stated price of an imported product.

advance payment Export/import financing in which an importer pays an exporter for merchandise before it is shipped.

aesthetics What a culture considers to be in "good taste" in the arts, the imagery evoked by certain expressions, and the symbolism of certain colors.

agents Individuals or organizations that represent one or more indirect exporters in a target market.

American Depository Receipt (ADR) Certificate that trades in the United States and represents a specific number of shares in a non–U.S. company.

antidumping duty Additional tariff placed on an imported product that a nation believes is being dumped on its market.

antitrust (antimonopoly) laws Laws designed to prevent companies from fixing prices, sharing markets, and gaining unfair monopoly advantages.

arm's length price Free-market price that unrelated parties charge one another for a specific product.

attitudes Positive or negative evaluations, feelings, and tendencies that individuals harbor toward objects or concepts.

back-to-back loan Loan in which a parent company deposits money with a host-country bank, which then lends the money to a subsidiary located in the host country.

balance of payments A national accounting system that records all payments to entities in other countries and all receipts coming into the nation.

barter Exchange of goods or services directly for other goods or services without the use of money.

base currency In a quoted exchange rate, the currency that is to be purchased with another currency.

Berne Convention International treaty that protects copyrights.

bill of lading Contract between an exporter and a shipper that specifies merchandise destination and shipping costs.

body language Language communicated through unspoken cues, including hand gestures, facial expressions, physical greetings, eye contact, and the manipulation of personal space.

bond Debt instrument that specifies the timing of principal and interest payments.

brain drain Departure of highly educated people from one profession, geographic region, or nation to another.

brand name Name of one or more items in a product line that identifies the source or character of the items.

Bretton Woods Agreement Agreement (1944) among nations to create a new international monetary system based on the value of the U.S. dollar.

buyback Export of industrial equipment in return for products produced by that equipment.

capacity planning Process of assessing a company's ability to produce enough output to satisfy market demand.

capitalism The belief that ownership of the means of production belongs in the hands of individuals and private businesses.

capital market System that allocates financial resources in the form of debt and equity according to their most efficient uses.

caste system System of social stratification in which people are born into a social ranking, or *caste*, with no opportunity for social mobility.

centrally planned economy Economic system in which a nation's land, factories, and other economic resources are owned by the government, which plans nearly all economic activity.

chains of command Lines of authority that run from top management to individual employees and specify internal reporting relationships.

civil law Legal system based on a detailed set of written rules and statutes that constitute a legal code.

class system System of social stratification in which personal ability and actions decide social status and mobility.

clearing Process of aggregating the currencies that one bank owes another and then carrying out the transaction.

climate Weather conditions of a geographic region.

combination strategy Strategy designed to mix growth, retrenchment, and stability strategies across a corporation's business units.

common law Legal system based on a country's legal history (tradition), past cases that have come before its courts (precedent), and the ways in which laws are applied in specific situations (usage).

common market Economic integration whereby countries remove all barriers to trade and the movement of labor and capital between themselves but erect a common trade policy against nonmembers.

communication System of conveying thoughts, feelings, knowledge, and information through speech, actions, and writing.

communism The belief that social and economic equality can be obtained only by establishing an all-powerful Communist Party and by granting the government ownership and control over all types of economic activity.

comparative advantage Inability of a nation to produce a good more efficiently than other nations, but an ability to produce that good more efficiently than it does any other good.

compound tariff Tariff levied on an imported product and calculated partly as a percentage of its stated price and partly as a specific fee for each unit.

confiscation Forced transfer of assets from a company to the government without compensation.

consumer panel Research in which people record in personal diaries, information on their attitudes, behaviors, or purchasing habits.

convertible currency (hard currency) Currency that trades freely in the foreign exchange market, with its price determined by the forces of supply and demand.

copyright Property right giving creators of original works the freedom to publish or dispose of them as they choose.

core competency Special ability of a company that competitors find extremely difficult or impossible to equal.

counterpurchase Sale of goods or services to a country by a company that promises to make a future purchase of a specific product from the country.

countertrade Practice of selling goods or services that are paid for, in whole or part, with other goods or services.

cross licensing Practice by which companies use licensing agreements to exchange intangible property with one another.

cross rate Exchange rate calculated using two other exchange rates.

cross-functional team Team that is composed of employees who work at similar levels in different functional departments.

cultural diffusion Process whereby cultural traits spread from one culture to another.

cultural imperialism Replacement of one culture's traditions, folk heroes, and artifacts with substitutes from another.

cultural literacy Detailed knowledge about a culture that enables a person to function effectively within it.

cultural trait Anything that represents a culture's way of life, including gestures, material objects, traditions, and concepts.

culture Set of values, beliefs, rules, and institutions held by a specific group of people.

culture shock Psychological process affecting people living abroad that is characterized by homesickness, irritability, confusion, aggravation, and depression.

currency arbitrage Instantaneous purchase and sale of a currency in different markets for profit.

currency board Monetary regime that is based on an explicit commitment to exchange domestic currency for a specified foreign currency at a fixed exchange rate.

currency controls Restrictions on the convertibility of a currency into other currencies.

currency futures contract Contract requiring the exchange of a specific amount of currency on a specific date at a specific exchange rate, with all conditions fixed and not adjustable.

currency hedging Practice of insuring against potential losses that result from adverse changes in exchange rates.

currency option Right, or option, to exchange a specific amount of a currency on a specific date at a specific rate.

currency speculation Purchase or sale of a currency with the expectation that its value will change and generate a profit.

currency swap Simultaneous purchase and sale of foreign exchange for two different dates.

current account A national account that records transactions involving the import and export of goods and services, income receipts on assets abroad, and income payments on foreign assets inside the country.

current account deficit When a country imports more goods and services and pays more abroad than it exports and receives from abroad.

current account surplus When a country exports more goods and services and receives more income from abroad than it imports and pays abroad.

customs Habits or ways of behaving in specific circumstances that are passed down through generations in a culture.

customs union Economic integration whereby countries remove all barriers to trade between themselves but erect a common trade policy against nonmembers.

debt Loans in which the borrower promises to repay the borrowed amount (the principal) plus a predetermined rate of interest.

demand Quantity of a good or service that buyers are willing to purchase at a specific selling price.

democracy Political system in which government leaders are elected directly by the wide participation of the people or by their representatives.

derivative Financial instrument whose value derives from other commodities or financial instruments.

devaluation Intentional lowering of the value of a nation's currency.

developed country Country that is highly industrialized, highly efficient, and whose people enjoy a high quality of life.

developing country (less-developed country) Nation that has a poor infrastructure and extremely low personal incomes.

differentiation strategy Strategy in which a company designs its products to be perceived as unique by buyers throughout its industry.

direct exporting Practice by which a company sells its products directly to buyers in a target market.

distribution Planning, implementing, and controlling the physical flow of a product from its point of origin to its point of consumption.

documentary collection Export/import financing in which a bank acts as an intermediary without accepting financial risk.

draft (bill of exchange) Document ordering an importer to pay an exporter a specified sum of money at a specified time.

dual pricing Policy in which a product has a different selling price (typically higher) in export markets than it has in the home market.

dumping Practice of exporting a product at a price either lower than the price that the product normally commands in its domestic market or lower than the cost of production.

eclectic theory Theory stating that firms undertake foreign direct investment when the features of a particular location combine with ownership and internalization advantages to make a location appealing for investment.

economic development Measure for gauging the economic well-being of one nation's people as compared with that of another nation's people.

economic system Structure and processes that a country uses to allocate its resources and conduct its commercial activities.

economic union Economic integration whereby countries remove barriers to trade and the movement of labor and capital, erect a common trade policy against nonmembers, and coordinate their economic policies.

efficient market view View that prices of financial instruments reflect all publicly available information at any given time.

embargo Complete ban on trade (imports and exports) in one or more products with a particular country.

emerging markets Newly industrialized countries plus those with the potential to become newly industrialized.

entry mode Institutional arrangement by which a firm gets its products, technologies, human skills, or other resources into a market.

environmental scanning Ongoing process of gathering, analyzing, and dispensing information for tactical or strategic purposes.

equity Part ownership of a company in which the equity holder participates with other part owners in the company's financial gains and losses.

ethical behavior Personal behavior that is in accordance with rules or standards for right conduct or morality.

ethnocentric staffing Staffing policy in which individuals from the home country manage operations abroad.

ethnocentricity Belief that one's own ethnic group or culture is superior to that of others.

Eurobond Bond issued outside the country in whose currency it is denominated.

Eurocurrency market Market consisting of all the world's currencies (referred to as Eurocurrency) that are banked outside their countries of origin.

exchange rate Rate at which one currency is exchanged for another.

exchange-rate risk (foreign exchange risk) Risk of adverse changes in exchange rates.

exclusive channel Distribution channel in which a manufacturer grants the right to sell its product to only one or a limited number of resellers.

expatriates Citizens of one country who are living and working in another.

export management company (EMC) Company that exports products on behalf of indirect exporters.

exports All goods and services sent from one country to other nations.

export trading company (ETC) Company that provides services to indirect exporters in addition to activities related directly to clients' exporting activities.

expropriation Forced transfer of assets from a company to the government with compensation.

facilities layout planning Deciding the spatial arrangement of production processes within production facilities.

facilities location planning Selecting the location for production facilities.

factor proportions theory Trade theory holding that countries produce and export goods that require resources (factors) that are abundant and import goods that require resources in short supply.

first-mover advantage Economic and strategic advantage gained by being the first company to enter an industry.

Fisher effect Principle that the nominal interest rate is the sum of the real interest rate and the expected rate of inflation over a specific period.

fixed (tangible) assets Company assets such as production facilities, inventory warehouses, retail outlets, and production and office equipment.

fixed exchange-rate system System in which the exchange rate for converting one currency into another is fixed by international agreement.

focus group Unstructured but in-depth interview of a small group of individuals (8 to 12 people) by a moderator to learn the group's attitudes about a company or its product.

focus strategy Strategy in which a company focuses on serving the needs of a narrowly defined market segment by being the low-cost leader, by differentiating its product, or both.

folk custom Behavior, often dating back several generations, that is practiced within a homogeneous group of people.

foreign bond Bond sold outside the borrower's country and denominated in the currency of the country in which it is sold.

Foreign Corrupt Practices Act 1977 statute forbidding U.S. companies from bribing government officials or political candidates in other nations.

foreign direct investment The purchase of physical assets or a significant amount of the ownership (stock) of a company in another country to gain a measure of management control.

foreign exchange market Market in which currencies are bought and sold and their prices determined.

foreign trade zone (FTZ) Designated geographic region in which merchandise is allowed to pass through with lower customs duties (taxes) and/or fewer customs procedures.

forward contract Contract that requires the exchange of an agreed-upon amount of a currency on an agreed-upon date at a specific exchange rate.

forward market Market for currency transactions at forward rates.

forward rate Exchange rate at which two parties agree to exchange currencies on a specified future date.

franchising Practice by which one company (the franchiser) supplies another (the franchisee) with intangible property and other assistance over an extended period.

free float system Exchange-rate system in which currencies float freely against one another, without governments intervening in currency markets.

free trade Pattern of imports and exports that would result in the absence of trade barriers.

free-trade area Economic integration whereby countries seek to remove all barriers to trade between themselves, but each country determines its own barriers against nonmembers.

freight forwarder Specialist in export-related activities such as customs clearing, tariff schedules, and shipping and insurance fees.

fundamental analysis Technique using statistical models based on fundamental economic indicators to forecast exchange rates.

fundamental disequilibrium Economic condition in which a trade deficit causes a permanent negative shift in a country's balance of payments.

GDP or GNP per capita Nation's GDP or GNP divided by its population.

General Agreement on Tariffs and Trade (GATT) Treaty that was designed to promote free trade by reducing both tariff and nontariff barriers to international trade.

geocentric staffing Staffing policy in which the best-qualified individuals regardless of nationality manage operations abroad.

globalization Trend toward greater interdependence among national institutions and economies.

global matrix structure Organizational structure that splits the chain of command between product and area divisions.

global product structure Organizational structure that divides worldwide operations according to a company's product areas.

global strategy Offering the same products using the same marketing strategy in all national markets.

global team Team of top managers from both headquarters and international subsidiaries who meet to develop solutions to company-wide problems.

gold standard International monetary system in which nations linked the value of their paper currencies to specific values of gold.

gross domestic product (GDP) Value of all goods and services produced by a country's domestic economy over a 1-year period.

gross national product (GNP) Value of all goods and services produced by a country during a 1-year period, including income generated by both domestic and international activities.

growth strategy Strategy designed to increase the scale (size of activities) or scope (kinds of activities) of a corporation's operations.

Hofstede framework Framework for studying cultural differences along four dimensions, such as individualism versus collectivism and equality versus inequality.

human development index (HDI) Measure of the extent to which a people's needs are satisfied and the extent to which these needs are addressed equally across a nation's entire population.

human resource management (HRM) Process of staffing a company and ensuring that employees are as productive as possible.

human resource planning Process of forecasting both a company's human resource needs and supply.

imports All goods and services brought into a country that were purchased from organizations located in other countries.

income elasticity Sensitivity of demand for a product relative to changes in income.

indirect exporting Practice by which a company sells its products to intermediaries who resell to buyers in a target market.

industrial property Patents and trademarks.

inefficient market view View that prices of financial instruments do not reflect all publicly available information.

intellectual property Property that results from people's intellectual talent and abilities.

intensive channel Distribution channel in which a producer grants the right to sell its product to many resellers.

interbank interest rates Interest rates that the world's largest banks charge one another for loans.

interbank market Market in which the world's largest banks exchange currencies at spot and forward rates.

interest arbitrage Profit-motivated purchase and sale of interest-paying securities denominated in different currencies.

international area structure Organizational structure that organizes a company's entire global operations into countries or geographic regions.

international bond market Market consisting of all bonds sold by issuing companies, governments, or other organizations outside their own countries.

international business Sum of all business transactions that cross the borders of two or more nations.

international capital market Network of individuals, companies, financial institutions, and governments that invest and borrow across national boundaries.

international division structure Organizational structure that separates domestic from international business activities by creating a separate international division with its own manager.

international equity market Market consisting of all stocks bought and sold outside the issuer's home country.

international Fisher effect Principle that a difference in nominal interest rates supported by two countries' currencies will cause an equal but opposite change in their spot exchange rates.

International Monetary Fund (IMF) Agency created by the Bretton Woods Agreement to regulate fixed exchange rates and enforce the rules of the international monetary system.

international monetary system Collection of agreements and institutions governing exchange rates.

international product life cycle theory Theory holding that a company will begin by exporting its product and later undertake foreign direct investment as a product moves through its life cycle.

international trade Purchase, sale, or exchange of goods and services across national borders.

Jamaica Agreement Agreement (1976) among IMF members to formalize the existing system of floating exchange rates as the new international monetary system.

joint venture Separate company that is created and jointly owned by two or more independent entities to achieve a common business objective.

just-in-time (JIT) manufacturing Production technique in which inventory is kept to a minimum and inputs to the production process arrive exactly when they are needed (or just in time).

Kluckhohn–Strodtbeck framework Framework for studying cultural differences along six dimensions, such as focus on past or future events and belief in individual or group responsibility for personal well-being.

labor–management relations Positive or negative condition of relations between a company's management and its workers.

law of one price Principle that an identical item must have an identical price in all countries when the price is expressed in the same currency.

legal system Set of laws and regulations, including the processes by which a country's laws are enacted and enforced and the ways in which its courts hold parties accountable for their actions.

letter of credit Export/import financing in which the importer's bank issues a document stating that the bank will pay the exporter when the exporter fulfills the terms of the document.

licensing Practice by which one company owning intangible property (the licenser) grants another firm (the licensee) the right to use that property for a specified period of time.

lingua franca Third or "link" language that is understood by two parties who speak different native languages.

liquidity Ease with which bondholders and shareholders may convert their investments into cash.

lobbying Policy of hiring people to represent a company's views on political matters.

local content requirements Laws stipulating that a specified amount of a good or service be supplied by producers in the domestic market.

location economies Economic benefits derived from locating production activities in optimal locations.

logistics Management of the physical flow of products from the point of origin as raw materials to end users as finished products.

low-cost leadership strategy Strategy in which a company exploits economies of scale to have the lowest cost structure of any competitor in its industry.

make-or-buy decision Deciding whether to make a component or to buy it from another company.

managed float system Exchange-rate system in which currencies float against one another, with governments intervening to stabilize their currencies at particular target exchange rates.

management contract Practice by which one company supplies another with managerial expertise for a specific period of time.

manners Appropriate ways of behaving, speaking, and dressing in a culture.

market economy Economic system in which the majority of a nation's land, factories, and other economic resources are privately owned, either by individuals or businesses.

market imperfections Theory stating that when an imperfection in the market makes a transaction less efficient than it could be, a company will undertake foreign direct investment to internalize the transaction and thereby remove the imperfection.

market power Theory stating that a firm tries to establish a dominant market presence in an industry by undertaking foreign direct investment.

market research Collection and analysis of information in order to assist managers in making informed decisions.

marketing communication Process of sending promotional messages about products to target markets.

material culture All the technology employed in a culture to manufacture goods and provide services.

mercantilism Trade theory that holds that nations should accumulate financial wealth, usually in the form of gold, by encouraging exports and discouraging imports.

mission statement Written statement of why a company exists and what it plans to accomplish.

mixed economy Economic system in which land, factories, and other economic resources are more equally split between private and government ownership.

multinational corporation (MNC) Business that has direct investments abroad in multiple countries.

multinational (multidomestic) strategy Adapting products and their marketing strategies in each national market to suit local preferences.

national competitive advantage theory Trade theory holding that a nation's competitiveness in an industry depends on the capacity of the industry to innovate and upgrade.

nationalism Devotion of a people to their nation's interests and advancement.

nationalization Government takeover of an entire industry.

new trade theory Trade theory holding that (1) there are gains to be made from specialization and increasing economies of scale, (2) the companies first to market can create barriers to entry, and (3) government may play a role in assisting its home companies.

newly industrialized country (NIC) Country that has recently increased the portion of its national production and exports derived from industrial operations.

normal trade relations (formerly "most favored nation status") Requirement that WTO members extend the same favorable terms of trade to all members that they extend to any single member.

offset Agreement that a company will offset a hard-currency sale to a nation by making a hard-currency purchase of an unspecified product from that nation in the future.

offshore financial center Country or territory whose financial sector features very few regulations and few, if any, taxes.

open account Export/import financing in which an exporter ships merchandise and later bills the importer for its value.

organizational structure Way in which a company divides its activities among separate units and coordinates activities between those units.

outsourcing Practice of buying from another company a good or service that is not central to a company's competitive advantage.

over-the-counter (OTC) market Exchange consisting of a global computer network of foreign exchange traders and other market participants.

patent Property right granted to the inventor of a product or process that excludes others from making, using, or selling the invention.

planning Process of identifying and selecting an organization's objectives and deciding how the organization will achieve those objectives.

political risk Likelihood that a government or society will undergo political changes that negatively affect local business activity.

political system Structures, processes, and activities by which a nation governs itself.

political union Economic and political integration whereby countries coordinate aspects of their economic and political systems.

polycentric staffing Staffing policy in which individuals from the host country manage operations abroad.

popular custom Behavior shared by a heterogeneous group or by several groups.

portfolio investment Investment that does not involve obtaining a degree of control in a company.

primary market research Process of collecting and analyzing original data and applying the results to current research needs.

private sector Segment of the economic environment comprised of independently owned firms that exist to make a profit.

privatization Policy of selling government-owned economic resources to private companies and individuals.

process planning Deciding the process that a company will use to create its product.

product liability Responsibility of manufacturers, sellers, and others for damage, injury, or death caused by defective products.

promotion mix Efforts by a company to reach distribution channels and target customers through communications such as personal selling, advertising, public relations, and direct marketing.

property rights Legal rights to resources and any income they generate.

pull strategy Promotional strategy designed to create buyer demand that will encourage channel members to stock a company's product.

purchasing power Value of goods and services that can be purchased with one unit of a country's currency.

purchasing power parity (PPP) Relative ability of two countries' currencies to buy the same "basket" of goods in those two countries.

push strategy Promotional strategy designed to pressure channel members to carry a product and promote it to final users of the product.

quota Restriction on the amount (measured in units or weight) of a good that can enter or leave a country during a certain period of time.

quoted currency In a quoted exchange rate, the currency with which another currency is to be purchased.

rationalized production System of production in which each of a product's components are produced where the cost of producing that component is lowest.

recruitment Process of identifying and attracting a qualified pool of applicants for vacant positions.

regional economic integration (Regionalism) Process whereby countries in a geographic region cooperate with one another to reduce or eliminate barriers to the international flow of products, people, or capital.

representative democracy Democracy in which citizens nominate individuals from their groups to represent their political needs and views.

retrenchment strategy Strategy designed to reduce the scale or scope of a corporation's businesses.

revaluation Intentional raising of the value of a nation's currency.

revenue Monies earned from the sale of goods and services.

reverse culture shock Psychological process of readapting to one's home culture.

secondary market research Process of obtaining information that already exists within the company or that can be obtained from outside sources.

secular totalitarianism Political system in which leaders rely on military and bureaucratic power.

securities exchange Exchange specializing in currency futures and options transactions.

securitization Unbundling and repackaging of hard-to-trade financial assets into more liquid, negotiable, and marketable financial instruments (or securities).

selection Process of screening and hiring the best-qualified applicants with the greatest performance potential.

self-managed team Team in which the employees from a single department take on the responsibilities of their former supervisors.

Smithsonian Agreement Agreement (1971) among IMF members to restructure and strengthen the international monetary system created at Bretton Woods.

social group Collection of two or more people who identify and interact with one another.

socialism The belief that social and economic equality is obtained through government ownership and regulation of the means of production.

social mobility Ease with which individuals can move up or down a culture's "social ladder".

social responsibility Practice of companies going beyond legal obligations to actively balance commitments to investors, customers, other companies, and communities.

social stratification Process of ranking people into social layers or classes.

social structure A culture's fundamental organization, including its groups and institutions, its system of social positions and their relationships, and the process by which its resources are distributed.

special drawing right (SDR) IMF asset whose value is based on a "weighted basket" of the currencies of five industrialized countries.

specific tariff Tariff levied as a specific fee for each unit (measured by number, weight, etc.) of an imported product.

spot market Market for currency transactions at spot rates.

spot rate Exchange rate requiring delivery of the traded currency within 2 business days.

stability strategy Strategy designed to guard against change and used by corporations to avoid either growth or retrenchment.

staffing policy The customary means by which a company staffs its offices.

stakeholders All parties, ranging from suppliers and employees to stockholders and consumers, who are affected by a company's activities.

stock Shares of ownership in a company's assets that give shareholders a claim on the company's future cash flows.

strategic alliance Relationship whereby two or more entities cooperate (but do not form a separate company) to achieve the strategic goals of each.

strategy Set of planned actions taken by managers to help a company meet its objectives.

subculture Group of people who share a unique way of life within a larger, dominant culture.

subsidy Financial assistance to domestic producers in the form of cash payments, low-interest loans, tax breaks, product price supports, or some other form.

supply Quantity of a good or service that producers are willing to provide at a specific selling price.

survey Research in which an interviewer asks current or potential buyers to answer written or verbal questions to obtain facts, opinions, or attitudes.

switch trading Practice in which one company sells to another its obligation to make a purchase in a given country.

tariff Government tax levied on a product as it enters or leaves a country.

tariff-quota Lower tariff rate for a certain quantity of imports and a higher rate for quantities that exceed the quota.

technical analysis Technique using charts of past trends in currency prices and other factors to forecast exchange rates.

technological dualism Use of the latest technologies in some sectors of the economy coupled with the use of outdated technologies in other sectors.

theocracy Political system in which a country's political leaders are religious leaders who enforce laws and regulations based on religious beliefs.

theocratic law Legal system based on religious teachings.

theocratic totalitarianism Political system in which religious leaders govern without the support of the people and do not tolerate opposing viewpoints.

topography All the physical features that characterize the surface of a geographic region.

total quality management (TQM) Emphasis on continuous quality improvement to meet or exceed customer expectations involving a company-wide commitment to quality-enhancing processes.

totalitarian system Political system in which individuals govern without the support of the people, government maintains control over many aspects of people's lives, and leaders do not tolerate opposing viewpoints.

trade creation Increase in the level of trade between nations that results from regional economic integration.

trade deficit Condition that results when the value of a country's imports is greater than the value of its exports.

trade mission International trip by government officials and businesspeople that is organized by agencies of national or provincial governments for the purpose of exploring international business opportunities.

trademark Property right in the form of words or symbols that distinguish a product and its manufacturer.

transfer price Price charged for a good or service transferred among a company and its subsidiaries.

turnkey (build–operate–transfer) project Practice by which one company designs, constructs, and tests a production facility for a client firm.

United Nations (UN) International organization formed after World War II to provide leadership in fostering peace and stability around the world.

value added tax (VAT) Tax levied on each party that adds value to a product throughout its production and distribution.

value density Value of a product relative to its weight and volume.

vehicle currency Currency used as an intermediary to convert funds between two other currencies.

venture capital Financing obtained from investors who believe that the borrower will experience rapid growth and who receive equity (part ownership) in return.

vertical integration Extension of company activities into stages of production that provide a firm's inputs (backward integration) or absorb its output (forward integration).

voluntary export restraint (VER) Unique version of export quota that a nation imposes on its exports, usually at the request of an importing nation.

World Bank (International Bank for Reconstruction and Development) Agency created by the Bretton Woods Agreement to provide funding for national economic development efforts.

worldwide pricing Policy in which one selling price is established for all international markets.

NAME/COMPANY INDEX

SUBJECT INDEX

M&A (mergers and acquisitions) and foreign direct investment (FDI), 195-96
Maastricht Treaty, 226, 299
Macao and China, 114
Macro risk, 85
Maintenance of global mindset, 7
Make-or-buy decisions, physical resources, 433-36
Malaysia, spoken language in, 58
Manadated benefits, global management, 203
Management by fact, 438
Management issues
  and ASEAN (Association of Southeast Asian nations), 240
  centralization in international operation organization, 326-27
  Chinese relationships (*guanxi*), 112, 113
  competition with multinational corporations, 325
  contracts as contractual entry modes, 384-85, 394
  e-commerce, 349
  employees (*See* Employees, hiring and management of)
  expatriates and culture shock, 460
  exports and currency strength, 282
  and foreign direct investment (FDI), 200-201
  foreign exchange management effectiveness, 258-71
  global security checklist, 89
  international business, 8, 11-14
  international sales force, 409
  international trade agencies, 176
  investment abroad, 203
  keys to success, 12
  linking TQM and ISO 9000 standards of production, 438
  manners, 49
  market entry negotiation, 392
  as obstacles to economic transition, 126-28
  Pacific Rim contacts, 144
  of production (*See* Production, launch and management of)
  situational, 48
  skills and host country intervention, 208
Managerial talent for recruitment of human resources, 457
Manchuria, 197
Manners, cultural, 49-50
Manufacturing. *See* Production, launch and management of
Maquiladoras in Mexico, 175, 203-4
Market economy, 116-18
  defined, 116
  economic freedom, 117-18
  in economic system continuum, 110
  features of, 116-17
  government's role in, 117
  origins, 116

Market exposure, 416-17
Market imperfections (internalization) theory, 199
MARKET newsletter, 359
Market power theory, 200, 436
Market research, defined, 354. *See also* Research, conducting international
Market-screening process. *See* Screening process, potential markets and sites
Market segment, mission statement, 312
Market sharing, antitrust regulations, 101
Marketing
  communication in, 413-16
  effective and global management, 12
  as fulfillment mistakes by entrepreneurs, 155
  technological innovation in, 19
Marketing Tools (magazine), 424
Markets
  access and e-commerce, 349
  consumption capacity of, 351
  globalization of markets, 14-15
  growth rate of, 351
  potential, 341, 348-51, 371
  receptivity of, **138-39**, 351
  selection of, 353-54
  size and entry mode selection, 393
Mass media access and promotional strategies, 409
Master franchise, 384
Material culture, 63, 64-65
Maturing product stage, international product life cycle theory, 198
Media
  advertising as promotional strategy, 410-12, 423, 424-25
  for marketing communication, 413
  mass media access, 409
Mediterranean culture, attitude toward time, 46
Meeting initiation in export strategy, 372
Mein Kampf (Hitler), 9
Mercantilism in international trade, 145-47
Merchandise current account, 207-8
Merchant ships and shipping, 142
MERCOSUR (Southern Common Market), 224, 233, **234**, 234-35, 243
Mergers and acquisitions (M&A), 22, **23**, 195-96
Message, promotional, in marketing communication, 413
Mexico
  debt and peso crisis, 300-301
  maquiladoras, 175, 203-4
  and NAFTA, 144, 224, 229-33
  North America, map of, **32**
  parliamentary democracy in, 79
Micro risk, 85
Microcredit, 253

Middle East, regional economic integration, 241-42
Mindset, global. *See* Global mindset
Minimum wage comparison, 429
Minority rights, in representative democracies, 78
Mission statements, 312-14
Mixed economy, 114-15
MNCs. *See* Multinational corporations (MNCs)
Mobile phones, 427, 428
Mobility, social, 52
Modifications and make-or-buy decisions, 434
Monetary policy, 286, 293-94
Monetary system, international. *See* International monetary system
Monetary value, international data, 355
Money. *See* Capital markets; Currency
Monopoly, 117
Montreal Protocol, 186
Morphemes, 405-6
"Most favored nation status," 183
Multi-Fiber Arrangement, 179
Multidomestic strategy, 317, 318-19
Multinational corporations (MNCs). *See also* Foreign direct investment (FDI)
  competition with, 325
  and currency strength, 281-82
  defined, 21
  and foreign direct investment (FDI), 197-98
  as key players, 21-24
Multinational strategy, international operation planning, 317, 318-19
Multiple exchange rates, 272
Multistage joint ventures/alliance, 388, 389
Music and culture, 43-44
Music copyrights, 98-99
Muslims, 53, **54-55**. *See also* Islam

NAFTA. *See* North American Free Trade Agreement (NAFTA)
Names and product strategies, 404-6
Narrow participation, politics, 77
Nation-states, 41-42, 146
National business environment, 8-9
National capital markets, purposes of, 250-52
National competitive advantage theory of international trade, 155-59
  defined, 155-56
  demand conditions, 156-57
  factor conditions, 156
  related and supporting industries, 157-58
National culture, 41-42
National image, 406
National income per capita, 120, **122-23**
National security, 167-68

National sovereignty loss and regional integration, 224
Nationalism, 93-94
Nationalization of property and political risk, 89-90
Natural persons presence, GATS, 183
Neo-mercantilism, 146
Nepal, 416
Nepotism, 51
New Guinea, loss of language, 72
New product stage, international product life cycle theory, 198
New trade theory of international trade, 154-55
Newly industrialized countries (NICs), 125-26
NICs (newly industrialized countries), 125-26
Noise in marketing communication, 413
Nominal interest rates, 289
Nonexclusive license, 381
Nongovernmental organizations (NGOs), 308
Nonmanagerial workers, 457, 458, 463, 464-65
Nonpolitical bureaucracies, in representative democracies, 78
Nontariff barriers, 176
Normal trade relations, 183-84
North America, 32. *See also* Canada; Mexico; United States
North American Free Trade Agreement (NAFTA)
  effects of, 231-32
  expansion, 232-33
  food contamination, 246-47
  and globalization, 17
  impact on Australia, 224
  as main regional trading bloc, 243
  market imperfections (internalization) theory, 199
  origins, 229-31, **231**
  as regional integration, 229-33
  spoken language, 58
  trade dependency, 144
Nuclear family in social structure, 51

Ocean bill of lading, export/import financing, 377
Oceania, **37**
Offset, 376
Offshore financial centers, 254-55
One-level channel, 417
Online. *See* World Wide Web (WWW) and Internet
Open account, export/import financing, 379-80
Operation centers, as offshore financial centers, 254
Opportunity analysis. *See* Analysis of international opportunities
Organic growth, 319
Organization of international operations, 310-37
  case studies, 310, 312, 337

U.S. *See* United States (U.S)
U.S.-Canada Free Trade Agreement, 230, **231**
Usage in common law, 94
Uzbekistan cellular phones, 196-97

Value-added taxes (VAT), 99, 100
Value chain analysis, 314-17
Value density, 417
Values
   Asian, and identity crisis in, 72-73
   in culture, 44-48
   and religion, 52-53
VAT (value-added taxes), 99, 100
Vehicle currency, 268-69
Venture capital, 442
VER (voluntary export restraint), 179
Vertical integration, 200, 433
Video conferencing as technological innovation, 18
Vietnam
   Asia, map of, **35**
   attitude toward time, 48
   ethical management behavior, 12
   intellectual property issues, 96
   product country image, 347-48
Violence. *See also* Political risk
   globalization backlash, 20-21
   kidnapping and political risk, 88

Volume
   of international trade, **4-5**, 140, 141
   mergers and acquisitions (M&A), cross border, 195-96
   trade volume in gross domestic product (GDP), **138-39**
Voluntary export restraint (VER), 179
Voter turnout, 77

Wage comparison, minimum, 429
Wall Street Journal, 261
Weak currency, 280
Wealth and economic freedom, 120
Web. *See* World Wide Web (WWW) and Internet
Wholly owned subsidiaries, 386-87, 394
Wide participation, politics, 77
Wine, 403
Women
   microcredit, 253
   and social structure, 51
Work, attitude towards, 46-47
Work teams in organization of international operations, 331-32
Working Capital Guarantee Program export financing programs, Ex-Im Bank, 173

World Atlas, 29, **33-37**
World Bank, 120, 128, 295, 308, 357
World-class product development and global management, 12
World Economic Forum meeting in Davos, Switzerland (2000), 20
World Factbook, 357
World financial centers in capital markets, 254-55
World map (2002), **31**
World Trade Center terrorism, September 11 (2001), 88
World Trade Organization (WTO)
   China's entry, 114, 198
   creation at Uruguay Round of GATT, 183
   dispute settlement, 184
   Doha, Qatar, round of negotiations, 185
   dumping, 184
   and environment, 185-86
   free trade case study, 190
   global trading system and governments, 183-86
   goals of, 17
   meeting in Doha, Qatar (2001), 17, 21
   meeting in Seattle, WA (1999), 20
   patents, 97
   regional integration, 223

subsidies, 185
   trade barriers, 166
World Wide Web (WWW) and Internet
   access in Eastern Europe, 64-65
   advertising in, 411-12
   chat room, 424
   cybermarkets international equity market, 257
   e-commerce, 349
   e-mail, 18, 424
   international, 44
   intranets and extranets as technological innovation, 19
   news over, 416
   portals as technological innovation, 19
   secondary international research, 359-60
   as technological innovation, 18-19
Worldwide pricing, 418-19
WTO. *See* World Trade Organization (WTO)
WWW. *See* World Wide Web (WWW) and Internet

Yankee foreign bonds, 255

Zero-level channel, 417
Zero-sum game, in mercantilism, 147